Object-Oriented Interfacing to 16-BIT Microcontrollers

G. J. Lipovski

University of Texas

P T R Prentice Hall
Englewood Cliffs, New Jersey 07632

Library of Congress Cataloging-in-Publication Data

Lipovski, G. J. (G. Jack)
 Object-oriented interfacing to 16-bit microcontrollers / G.J.
 Lipovski.
     p.   cm.
 Includes bibliographical references and index.
 ISBN 0-13-629221-6
 1. Object-orientd programming. 2. Microcomputers—Programming.
 3. Computer interfaces. I. Title.
 QA76.64.L56 1993   92-15063
 004.6'165—dc20   CIP

Editorial/production supervision: *Ann Sullivan*
Cover design: *Lundgren Graphics*
Prepress buyer: *Mary McCartney*
Manufacturing buyer: *Susan Brunke*
Acquisitions editor: *Karen Gettman*
Editorial assistant: *Barbara Alfieri*

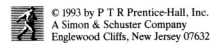
The publisher offers discounts on this book when ordered
in bulk quantities. For more information, write:

Special Sales/Professional Marketing,
Prentice-Hall, Inc.
Professional Technical Reference Division,
Englewood Cliffs, New Jersey 07632

Printed in the United States of America

10 9 8 7 6 5 4 3 2 1

ISBN 0-13-629221-6

Prentice-Hall International (UK) Limited, *London*
Prentice-Hall of Australia Pty. Limited, *Sydney*
Prentice-Hall Canada Inc., *Toronto*
Prentice-Hall Hispanoamericana, S.A., *Mexico*
Prentice-Hall of India Private Limited, *New Delhi*
Prentice-Hall of Japan, Inc., *Tokyo*
Simon & Schuster Asia Pte. Ltd., *Singapore*
Editora Prentice-Hall do Brasil, Ltda., *Rio de Janeiro*

Dedicated to my children

Tom, Kathy, Debbie and Angela Lipovski

Contents

List of Figures

List of Tables

Preface

Microcomputer interfacing is a significant part of computer scientists' and computer engineers' backgrounds. They should understand the fundamental and pervasive notion of the hardware-software tradeoff. They should be familiar with operating systems and their handling of input/output. Finally, because they might have to interface a microcomputer to external equipment, to monitor or control external processes, some computer scientists or computer engineers should be capable of designing and implementing this interface. Microcomputer interfacing – this book's subject – covers these concepts.

Of fundamental importance, any computer scientist or computer engineer should understand what can be done effectively in hardware, what is easily done in software, and what alternative approaches in both are worth considering in a design. This understanding of the hardware-software tradeoff is missing in purely hardware electrical engineering courses or purely software computer science courses, but is necessary for the intelligent design of either hardware or software systems. While an understanding of the hardware-software tradeoff pervades many aspects of computer science and engineering, and appears in many courses therein, nowhere is it so clearly seen as it is in interfacing. A course on interfacing is fundamentally a course on hardware-software tradeoffs.

Of secondary but still major importance, most computer scientists and computer engineers must understand operating systems. Many operating systems courses cover time-sharing and performance modeling, which are important in operating systems used in large mainframe computers. However, personal computers are becoming more important than mainframe computers as time goes on. Operating systems in personal computers mainly support high-level languages. Their input/output infrastructure is one of the most important support functions they provide for high-level languages. A course on interfacing is a course on the infrastructure for high-level language input/output.

A third rationale for this book is that some computer scientists or computer engineers have to interface a microcomputer to external equipment. They provide a basic service and command a premium salary. They need to have a thorough knowledge of the principles of interfacing. A comprehensive course should be provided for them.

However, one of the least important aspects of microcomputer interfacing is the detailed understanding of a particular machine. While details are important for you to get hands-on interfacing experience, these details can easily swamp you. Even though we cover the popular 683xx systems, you are likely to interface some other microcomputer. You must keep details in perspective; they are only a means to an end. Another common but unimportant aspect of interfacing is the use of assembler language. High-level languages like C are more efficient and are being more frequently used in industry.

While some books on interfacing put great emphasis on a particular machine, on special techniques used in it, and on assembler language programming, this book puts greater emphasis on hardware-software tradeoffs, operating system and high-level language interfacing, and the principles of interfacing. Because of this, we believe this book offers a better perspective than other interfacing textbooks. Its approach to interfacing provides a significant background for computer scientists and computer engineers.

This book is oriented to a practical understanding of the use of object-oriented C with the 683xx family. In order to really understand the use of a high-level language with this powerful computer, though, a solid theoretical foundation is needed. The goal of this book is to use the 683xx as a means to understand theory, and to use the 683xx well. Further books, referenced at the end of each chapter, are recommended as a means to further develop a full theory of microcomputer systems design.

This book uses a Macintosh C compiler, Symantec's THINK C ™ version 4.0, to generate code in Macintosh for the upward compatible 683xx microcontroller, which is downloaded from the Macintosh's memory to the microcontroller. While the reader may well use a different compiler, or even a different microcontroller, the book's concrete and debugged examples should stimulate the development of analogous techniques for the reader's own compiler and microcontroller.

This book develops the generally held philosophy that high-level languages should be used in 16-bit microcontrollers such as Motorola's 68332 and 68340, and more powerful microcontrollers that will be developed in the future. In our opinion, assembly language is still useful in smaller 8-bit microcontrollers, but a high-level language like C is demonstrably more efficient for larger computers. This book further develops object-oriented high-level languages. While the reader may be suspicious of "hot topics" such as object-oriented programming, and the author generally is too, object-oriented high-level language interfacing to 16-bit microcontrollers is shown to be a synergetic combination in this book. Writing I/O procedures in object-oriented high-level languages requires some understanding of fundamental concepts like interrupts, and some development of skills, like how to insert and interrupt handler into a C procedure or an object's method. The 68332 and 68340 microcontrollers provide many and varied opportunities to exercise these concepts and skills. By being able to handle all the I/O devices in the 68332 and 68340 microcontrollers, we prove the feasibility, and provide examples of the advantages of object-oriented high-level language interfacing to 16-bit microcontrollers. I think we will be able to convince you of these advantages after you have read this book.

Finally, this book develops operating systems concepts from time-sharing to device drivers. We use Microware's OS9 operating system, because it is a variant of UNIX and is in wide use in embedded systems, for instance in the compact disk system CD-I. It is an excellent operating system for the 683xx microcontroller. Moreover the concepts generalize to other operating systems, and most UNIX and UNIX-based systems in particular. We will discuss how these operating systems execute multiple tasks and threads, using objects and methods for the task and thread, and we will show how to write OS9 device drivers. In addition to providing concrete examples, we contrast the alternatives, using objects and using device drivers to provide I/O interfacing for high-level languages, and develop some insight into the advantages of each, and study some design strategies regarding which to use where.

While this book covers a lot of ground, from 68332 and 68340 microcontrollers and their fairly complex I/O devices, to object-oriented C, to operating systems, these topics are needed to design well the microcontroller interfaces. In addition, they provide an interesting, challenging, and exciting environment to develop an understanding of operating systems of all kinds, and an understanding of the fundamental and pervasive notion of the hardware-software tradeoff.

About the Author

   G. Jack Lipovski has taught electrical engineering and computer science at the University of Texas since 1976, and in 1988, occupied the Grace Hopper Chair of Computer Science at the Naval Postgraduate School. He is a computer architect internationally recognized for his design of the pioneering database computer, CASSM, and the parallel computer, TRAC. His expertise in microcomputers is also internationally recognized by his being a past director of Euromicro and an editor of IEEE Micro and an area editor of the Journal of Parallel and Distributed Computing. Dr. Lipovski has published more than 70 papers, largely in the proceedings of the Annual Symposium on Computer Architecture, the IEEE transactions on computers, and the National Computer Conference. He has authored six books and edited three. He has served as chairman of the IEEE Computer Society Technical Committee on Computer Architecture, member of the Computer Society Governing Board, and chairman of the Special Interest Group on Computer Architecture of the Association for Computer Machinery. He received his Ph.D. from the University of Illinois, 1969, and has taught at the University of Florida. He has consulted for Harris Semiconductor, designing a microcomputer, and for the Microelectronics and Computer Corporation, studying parallel computers. His current interests include database computer architectures, parallel computing, artificial intelligence computer architectures, and microcomputers.

Acknowledgments

The author would like to express his deepest gratitude to everyone who contributed to the development of this book. This text was prepared and printed using a Macintosh and LaserWriter, running WriteNow. Portions of this book have previously appeared in *16 and 32 Bit Microcomputer Interfacing: Programming Examples in C and M68000 Assembly Language,* G.J. Lipovski, © 1990. Reprinted by permission of Prentice Hall Inc., Englewood Cliffs, New Jersey. The cooperation of Motorola in providing chips and information made this book's development a real pleasure. I am pleased to observe that the Motorola 683xx family are incredibly powerful components and vehicles for teaching a considerable range of concepts.

—————————— 1 ——————————

Microcomputer Architecture

Microcomputers, microprocessors, and the subject of microprocessing are at once quite familiar and a bit fuzzy to most engineers and computer scientists. When we teach a course on microcomputer interfacing, we start by asking this simple question, "What is a microcomputer?", and we find a wide range of answers. We need to share some common terms in order to discuss issues in interfacing. In this book, we will use object-oriented C to program I/O devices at a high level. Even so, C will be used in a way that the compiler writer may not have anticipated and the compiler may not generate the best, or even a correct, code. The interface designer must have a reading knowledge of assembler language to understand what code is generated by a C program, and must be able to insert some assembler language into a C program. To do that he or she has to understand the instruction set of the microcomputer. This chapter gives some background in architecture and 683xx assembler language. It contains essential material on microcomputers, microprocessors and their instruction sets needed as a basis for understanding the discussion of interfacing in the rest of the book.

We recognize that the designer must know a lot about basic computer architecture and organization. But the goal of this book is to impart enough knowledge so the reader, on completing it should be ready to design good hardware and software written in C for microcomputer interfaces. We have to trade material devoted to basics for material needed to design interface systems. There is so much to cover and so little space, that we will simply offer a summary of the main ideas. If you have had this material in other courses or absorbed it from your work or from reading those fine trade journals and hobby magazines devoted to microcomputers, this chapter should bring it all together. Some of you can pick up the material just by reading this condensed version. Others should get an idea of the amount of background needed to read the rest of the book. (See the bibliography at the end of this chapter for recommended additional reading.)

For this chapter, we assume the reader has written programs on a large or small computer. Though not necessary, some experience in assembler language programming would help the reader too. However, this chapter itself provides background for the main part of the book. In the chapter, the reader should learn about the software view of microcomputers in general and microcomputers using M68330, M68331, M68332, and M68340 microprocessors in particular.

Portions of Section 1-1 were adopted with permission from "Digital Computer Architecture" pp 298-327 by G.J. Lipovski and "Microcomputers", pp 397-480 by G.J. Lipovski and T. K. Agerwala in the *Encyclopedia of Computer Science and Technology*, 1978, Belzer et. al., Courtesy of Marcel Dekker, Inc.

1-1 An Introduction to the Microcomputer

Just what is a microcomputer and a microprocessor, and what is the meaning of microprogramming – which is often confused with microcomputers? This section will survey these concepts and other commonly misunderstood terms in digital systems design. It describes the architecture of digital computers and gives a definition of architecture. Unfortunately, the study of computers is rather heavy with concepts and, therefore, with terminology. But it is rather light on theorems and formulas. We will offer a lot of concepts and their definitions to help clarify later discussions; but we've got a typical "chicken-and-egg" problem when we try to define these ideas without using terms we haven't defined. This section simply opts to get the flavor of a few important concepts, so using some terms that will be properly defined later shouldn't matter. It can be reread when undefined terms are explained, to get a solid foundation in microcomputing. (Also note that all *italicized* words are in the Index, which serves as a glossary to help you find terms that are defined later.)

Because the microcomputer is just a smaller and less expensive computer, these concepts apply to large computers as well as microcomputers. The concept of the computer is presented first, and the idea of an instruction is scrutinized next. The special characteristics of microcomputers will be delineated. In the next section, the 683xx will be shown as an example of the von Neumann architecture.

1-1.1 Computer Architecture

Actually, the first and perhaps the best paper in computer architecture – "Preliminary Discussion of the Logical Design of an Electronic Computing Instrument," by A. W. Burks, H. H. Goldstein, and J. von Neumann – was written 15 years before the term was coined. We find it fascinating to compare the design therein with all computers produced to date. It is a tribute to von Neumann's genius that this design, originally intended to solve nonlinear differential equations, has been successfully used in business data processing, information handling, and industrial control, as well as in numeric problems. His design is so well defined that most computers – from large computers to microcomputers – are based on it, and they are called *von Neumann computers.*

In the early 1960s a group of computer designers at IBM – including Fred Brooks – coined the term "architecture" to describe the "blueprint" of the IBM 360 family of computers, from which several computers with different costs and speeds (for example, the IBM 360/50) would be designed. The *architecture* of a computer is its instruction set and the input/output (I/O) connection capabilities. Computers with the same architecture can execute the same programs and have the same I/O devices connected to them. Designing a collection of computers with the same "blueprint" is an approach that has been successfully copied by several manufacturers. Motorola has used this idea in developing the computers discussed in this book; computers built from the M68330, M68331, M68332, and M68340 have the same architecture. This strict definition of the term "computer architecture" applies to this fundamental level of design.

However, the term "computer architecture" has popularly been used to describe the computer system in general, including the implementation techniques and organization discussed next. In fact, it is difficult to get two computer architects to agree on a precise definition of computer architecture. While we are frustrated by such vagueness, it is probably due to the rapid evolution of this dynamic and exciting discipline.

The *organization* of a digital system like a computer is usually shown by a block diagram which shows the registers, buses, and data operators in the computer. For example, the M68330/M68331/M68332/M68340 have the same architecture because they have the same instruction set and can use the same I/O devices, but because each has different I/O modules, they have different organizations. These different organizations are described at this chapter's end. Incidentally, the organization of a computer is also called its *implementation*. Finally, the *realization* of the computer is its actual hardware interconnection and construction. For example, the MC68000L4 and the MC68000L8 have the same block diagrams and instruction sets, but the latter may be made with faster transistors, which enable it to run twice as fast as the former. (Actually, the MC68000L4, MC68000L8, and MC68000L12 are made the same way at the same time. They are then tested. One with the fastest transistors is sold as an MC68000L12, the next fastest as an MC68000L8, and the slowest as an MC68000L4.) We say the MC68000L4 has a different realization than the MC68000L8. It is entirely reasonable for a company to change the realization of one of its computers by replacing the hardware in a block of its block diagram with a newer, or faster more costly, type of hardware. The implementation or organization remains the same, while the realization is different. In this book, when we want to discuss an actual realization, we will name the component by its full part number, like MC68000L4 or MC68000L8. But we are usually interested in the architecture or the organization only; then we will refer to the 68000 architecture with no leading letters, and to the organization with a leading M (M68000). This should help clear up any ambiguity, while also being a natural, easy-to-read shorthand.

As better technology becomes available, and as experience with an architecture reveals its weaknesses, a new architecture may be crafted that includes most of the old instruction set and some new instructions. Programs written for the old computer should also run, with little or no change, on the new one, and more efficient programs can perhaps be written using the new features of the new architecture. Such a new architecture is *upward compatible* from the old one if this property is preserved. In this book, we will also focus on the 683xx, which is upward compatible from the 68010, which is upward compatible from its parent, the 68000.

The architecture of von Neumann computers is disarmingly simple, and the following analogy shows just how simple. (For an illustration of the following terms, see Figure 1-1.) Imagine a person in front of a mailbox, with an adding machine and window to the outside world. The mailbox, with numbered boxes or slots, is analogous to the *primary memory;* the adding machine, to the *data operator* (arithmetic-logic unit); the person, to the *controller;* and the window, to *input/output* (I/O). The person's hands *access* the memory. The primary memory is called a *random access memory* (RAM) because the person is free to access words in any order (at random) without having to wait any longer for a word because it is in a different location. Each slot in the mailbox has a paper which has a string of, say, sixteen 1s and 0s (*bits*) on it. A string of eight bits is a *byte*. A string of bits – whether or not it is a byte – in a slot of the memory box is called a *word*. In the 683xx, a word is two bytes long. Each byte in memory has its unique address. Addresses for consecutive words in memory are consecutive even numbers. If an even address is sent to memory with a command to read, the word at that address is read from the memory. (Later, we discuss the reading or writing of individual bytes in a word or pairs of words). Essentially, the M68332's 24 bit address can specify up to 2^{24} bytes, and the M68340's 32 bit address, 2^{32} bytes, in primary memory.

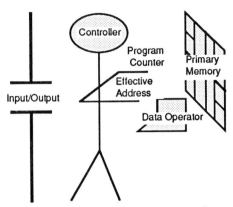

Figure 1-1. Analogy to the von Neumann Computer.

The person's left hand takes out a word from slot or box *n*, reads it as an instruction, and replaces it. Bringing a word from the mailbox (primary memory) to the person (controller) is called *fetching*. The hand that fetches the word is analogous to the *program counter*. It is ready to take the word from the next box, box *n* + 2, when the next instruction is to be fetched. Remember that consecutive words occupy consecutive even-numbered addresses. Although addresses are 24 bits long and the least significant bit of an instruction address must be even, the program counter is 32 bits long.

The program counter is just one of the 32-bit registers in the controller. *Registers* are like (double-width) memory words inside the controller and data operator, but are faster than memory words in primary memory. Other registers in the controller are *address registers* A0 to A7 (A7 is called the *stack pointer*). The data operator has *data registers* D0 to D7. These 32-bit registers can also be used as 16-bit and 8-bit registers. Figure 1-2 shows that there are actually two stack pointers and a vector base register, a 16-bit status, and 3-bit source function code and destination function code registers. 16-bit and 8-bit registers and other registers will be discussed in Section 1-2.1.

An instruction in the 683xx is a *binary code* like 0101001001000000. (We will identify binary numbers in the text, to distinguish them from decimal numbers). Because all those 1s and 0s are hard to remember, a convenient format is often used, called *hexadecimal notation*. Because we will be using C and assembly language embedded in C in this book, we will follow C's convention for hexadecimal notation. In C notation, a 0x (zero ex) is written (to designate that the number is in hexadecimal notation, rather than decimal or binary), and the bits, in groups of four are represented as if they were "binary-coded" digits 0 to 9, or letters A, B, C, D, E, F to represent values 10, 11, 12, 13, 14, and 15, respectively. For example, 0101 is the binary code for 5, and 0010 is the binary code for 2. The binary code 0101001001000000, mentioned previously, is represented as 0x5240 in hexadecimal notation. Whether binary code or the simplified hexadecimal code is used, instructions written this way are called *machine-coded* instructions because that is the actual code fetched from the primary memory of the machine, or computer. However, this notation is too cumbersome. So a *mnemonic* (which means a memory aid) represents the instruction. The instruction 0x5240 in the 683xx adds 1 to data register D0, so it can be written as

ADD #1,D0

Chapter 1 – Microcomputer Architecture

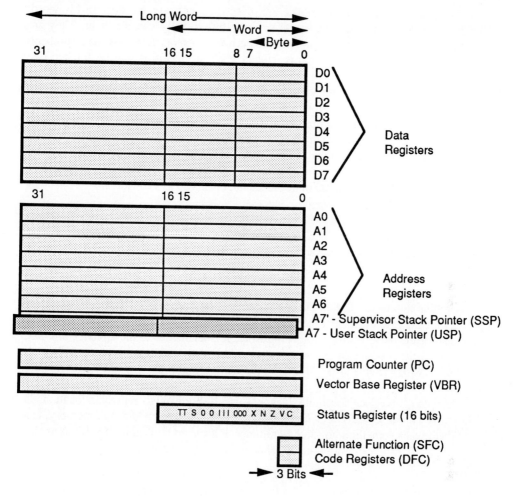

Figure 1-2. Registers and Memory in a 683xx.

An *assembler* is a program that converts mnemonics into machine code so the programmer can write in convenient mnemonics and the output machine code can be put in primary memory to be fetched as an instruction. The mnemonics are therefore called *assembler language* instructions. In a high-level language like C, one line of source code generates many machine code instructions; a program that converts source code written in a high-level language to machine code or assembler language is a *compiler*.

While a lot of interface software is written in C or assembler language and most examples in this book are discussed using C, a portion of the software to interface I/O devices may have to be written in machine code. If a compiler for a 68020 is used to generate code for a 683xx, some instructions for the 683xx that are not in the 68020 will be generated by inserting machine code into the C program. Moreover, an interface designer should want to know exactly how an instruction is stored and how it is understood. Therefore, we will now show machine code for some assembler language instructions to illustrate how you can encode your own machine coded instructions.

Many instructions in the 683xx are described entirely by one 16-bit word. However, some instructions require 32 or more bits to fully specify them. They are stored in words in consecutive even-numbered primary memory locations (box numbers) so that when an instruction like that is fetched, each of the words can be fetched one after another.

Now that we have some ideas about instructions, we resume the analogy to illustrate some things an instruction might do. For example, an instruction may direct the controller to take a word from a box, *m*, in the mailbox, with the right hand, copy it into the adding machine, thus destroying the old word, and put the word back in the box. This is an example of an instruction called the *move* instruction. We say we *load* a register from memory. In the 683xx an instruction to load data register D0 with the word at location 256 in decimal, or 0x100 in hexadecimal, is fetched as two words:

0x3038
0x0100

and is represented by mnemonics as

MOVE 0x100,D0

in assembler language. The main operation – bringing a word from the mailbox (primary memory) to the adding machine (data operator) – is called *recalling* data. The right hand of the person is used to get the word; it is analogous to the *effective address*. If a word in the instruction *is* the effective address, the addressing mode is *(word) direct* addressing. This is also called *absolute* addressing in the documentation for the 683xx.

As with instructions, assembler language uses a shorthand to represent locations in memory. A *symbolic address* or *label,* which is actually some address in memory, is a name that means something to the programmer. For example, location 0x100 might be called ALPHA. Then the previous assembler language instruction can be written as follows:

MOVE ALPHA,D0

(We will be using the symbolic address ALPHA in most of our examples in this chapter, and it will represent location 0x100. Other symbolic addresses and other locations can be substituted, of course. The way a symbolic address is written as a label, and the way the assembler assigns locations to them, will be discussed when we consider assembler language in C programs, Section 2-3.5.) Remember here that a symbolic address is just a representation of a number, which usually happens to be the numerical address of the word in primary memory to which the symbolic address refers. As a number, it can be added to other numbers, doubled, and so on. In particular, the instruction

MOVE ALPHA+2,D0

will load the contents of the word at location 0x102 (ALHPA + 2 is 0x100 + 2) into D0.

Generally, after such an instruction has been executed, the left hand (program counter) is in position to fetch the next instruction in box *n* + 2. For example, the next instruction may give the controller directions to copy the number in the adding machine into a box in the mailbox, causing the word in that box to be destroyed. This is another

Chapter 1 – Microcomputer Architecture

example of a move instruction. We say the register word is *stored* in memory. In the 683xx, the instruction to store data register D0 into location 0x100 can be written as follows:

MOVE D0,ALPHA

The main operation in this store instruction – putting a word from the adding machine (data operator) into a box in the mailbox (primary memory) – is called *memorizing* data. The right hand (*effective address*) is used to put the word into the box.

Before going on, we point out a feature of the von Neumann computer that is easy to overlook, but is at once von Neumann's greatest contribution to computer architecture and yet a major problem in computing. Because instructions *and* data are stored in the primary memory, there is no way to distinguish one from the other except by which hand (program counter or effective address) is used to get the data. We can conveniently use memory not needed to store instructions – if few are to be stored – to store more data, and vice versa. It is possible to modify an instruction as if it were data, just before it is fetched, although a good computer scientist would shudder at the thought. However, through an error (*bug*) in the program, it is possible to start fetching data words as if they were instructions, which produces strange results fast.

A *program sequence* is a sequence of instructions fetched from consecutive locations one after another. To increment the word at location 0x100, we can load it into the data register using the MOVE ALPHA,D0 instruction, increment it there using the ADD #1,D0 instruction, and then put it back using the MOVE D0,ALPHA instruction. (A better way will be shown later, but we do it in three instructions here to illustrate a point.) This program sequence is written in consecutive lines as follows:

MOVE ALPHA,D0
ADD #1,D0
MOVE D0,ALPHA

Unless something is done to change the left hand (program counter), a sequence of words in contiguous boxes will be fetched and executed as instructions. For example, a sequence of load and store instructions can be fetched and executed to copy a collection of words from one place in the mailbox into another place.

However, when the controller reads the instruction, it may direct the left hand to move to a new location (load a new number in the program counter). Such an instruction is called a *jump* or *branch*. A similar instruction is used to execute a program called a *subroutine*, which is located in a different part of memory, and then return to the instruction right below this instruction. Such an instruction – a *jump to subroutine* – not only changes the program counter like a jump, but also saves the old value of the program counter so that when the subroutine is finished, the old value of the program counter is restored (to return to the routine right after the jump to subroutine instruction). The last instruction of the subroutine – a *return from subroutine* instruction – causes the program counter to be restored. Subroutines are especially useful in small computers, so common operations that are not instructions can be made into subroutines, because instructions in a small computer are rather primitive. Moreover, a jump instruction may direct the person in the analogy to jump, for instance, only if the number in the adder is positive. If that number is not positive, the next instruction is fetched and executed because the left hand is not moved. This is a *conditional jump*. Jumps and conditional jumps permit some instructions to be fetched and executed over and over again. In this way, one can write a program consisting of a few hundred instruction words, which can move and change thousands of data words. Jumps and conditional jumps are essential for repeatedly executing the same program sequences. The computer's forte is its ability to "massage" large quantities of data under the control of a program stored in memory.

The *(hardware or I/O) interrupt* is an architectural feature that is very important to I/O interfacing. Basically, it is evoked when an I/O device needs service, either to move some more data into or out of the device, or to detect an error condition. *Handling* an interrupt stops the program that is running, causes another program to be executed to service the interrupt, and then resumes the main program exactly where it left off. The program that services the interrupt (called an *interrupt handler* or *device handler*) is very much like a subroutine, and an interrupt can be thought of as an I/O device tricking the computer into executing a subroutine. However, an interrupt service program should not disturb the current program in any way. The interrupted program should get the same result no matter when the interrupt occurs. One of the problems in satisfying this requirement is that the interrupt service routine may call up subroutines also used by the program that was running. If the subroutine is currently being executed, data from the program that was running could get mixed up with data used in the interrupt service routine, producing errors. If this is avoided, then the subroutine is said to be *reentrant* because it can be entered again, even when it is entered and not finished. Reentrancy is also important in multitasking operating systems, discussed in Section 11-1.2, so that two processes can execute the same program without mixing up their data. Reentrancy is important in designing software for interfaces. Related to it is *recursion* – a property whereby a subroutine can call itself as many times as it wants. While recursion is a nice abstract property and useful in working with some data structures discussed in Chapter 2, it is not generally useful in interfacing; however, recursive subroutines are usually reentrant, and that is important.

Most modern computers have condition code bits which are set by some instruction and tested by a conditional branch instruction. The *status register* containing these bit values also contains bits that control interrupts. The status register, accumulators, program counter, and other registers in the controller and data operator are collectively called the *machine state* and are saved and restored whenever an interrupt occurs.

To facilitate memory access, the effective address can be computed in several ways, called *addressing modes*. These are discussed next.

1-1.2 The Instruction

In this section the concept of an instruction is described from different points of view. The instruction is discussed first with respect to the cycle of fetching, decoding, and sequencing of microinstructions. Then the instruction is discussed in relation to hardware-software tradeoffs. Some concepts used in choosing the best instruction set are also discussed.

The controller fetches a word or a couple of words from primary memory and sends commands to all the modules to execute the instruction. An instruction, then, is essentially a complex command carried out under the direction of a single word or a couple of words fetched as an inseparable group from memory.

The bits in the instruction are broken into several fields. These fields may be the bit code for the instruction or for options in the instruction, for an address in primary memory, or for an address for some registers in the data operator. For example, the instruction MOVE ALPHA,D0 may look like the bit pattern 0011000000111000 0000000100000000 when it is completely fetched into the controller. The left-most two bits – 00 – tell the computer that this is a move instruction. Each instruction must have a different code word, like 00, so the controller knows exactly which instruction to execute just by looking at the instruction word. The next two bits from the left may identify the size of the data moved: 11 indicates a 16-bit word is to be moved. Bits 7 to 9 from the left, 000, indicate the destination addressing mode; 000 indicates a data register. Bits 4 to 6 from the left, 000, indicate the word is to be loaded into data register 0. Bits 10 to 15 from the left, 111000, indicate the source addressing mode (word direct). Finally, the last 16 bits may be a binary number address: 0000000100000000 indicates that the word to be loaded is to come from word 0x100 (ALPHA). Generally, options, registers, addressing modes, and primary memory addresses differ for different instructions. The controller must decode the instruction code word, 00, in this example, before it can be known that the next two bits from the left, 11, are a size indicator, and so on.   The instruction is executed by the controller as a sequence of small steps, called *microinstructions*. As opposed to instructions, which are stored in primary memory, microinstructions are usually stored in a small fast memory called *control memory*. A microinstruction is a collection of data transfer *orders* that are simultaneously executed; the *data transfers* that result from these orders are movements of, and operations on, words of data as these words are moved about the machine. While the control memory that stores the microinstructions is normally written at the factory, never to be rewritten by the user (*read-only memory* – ROM), in some computers it can be rewritten by the user. Writing programs for the control memory is called *microprogramming*. It is the translation of an instruction's required behavior into the control of data transfers that carry out the instruction.

The entire execution of an instruction is called the *fetch-execute cycle* and is composed of a sequence of microinstructions. A *clock* beats out even-spaced time signals and each microinstruction essentially takes one clock time period, a *microcycle*. Because access to primary memory is rather slow, an instruction is fetched, or a data word is memorized or recalled in several microinstructions. That time period is a *memory cycle*. The fetch-execute cycle is thus a sequence of microcycles or of memory cycles. The first memory cycle is the *fetch* cycle when the instruction code is fetched. If the instruction is *n* words long, the first *n* memory cycles are usually fetch cycles. In some computers, the next microcycles *decode* the instruction code to determine what to do next. The 6800 and 68000 generally don't need separate cycles for this. The next microcycles may be for *address calculations*. Data may be read from memory in one or more *recall* memory cycles. Then the instruction's main function is done in *execute* microcycles. Finally, the data may be memorized in a memory cycle, the *memorize* cycle. This sequence is repeated indefinitely as each instruction is fetched and executed.

I/O devices may request an interrupt in any memory cycle. However, the data operator usually has bits and pieces of information scattered around and is not prepared to stop the current instruction. Therefore, interrupts are generally recognized at the end of the current instruction, when all the data are organized into accumulators and other registers (the machine state) that can be safely saved and restored. The time from when an I/O device requests an interrupt until data that it wants moved are moved, or the error condition is reported or fixed, is called the *latency time*. Fast I/O devices require low latency interrupt service. The lowest latency that can be guaranteed is limited to the duration of the longest instruction (and the time to save the machine state) because the I/O device could request an interrupt at the beginning of such an instruction's execution.

It is conceivable to design an instruction to execute a very complicated operation in just one instruction. Also, certain operations can be performed on execution of some address modes in an instruction that uses the address rather than additional instructions. It is also generally possible to fetch and execute a sequence of simple instructions to carry out the same net operation. The program sequence we discussed earlier can actually be done by a single instruction in the 683xx:

ADD #1,ALPHA

It recalls word 0x100, increments it, and memorizes the result in location 0x100 without changing the data register. If a useful operation is not performed in a single instruction like ADD #1,ALPHA, but in a sequence of simpler instructions like the program sequence already described, such a sequence is either a macroinstruction or a subroutine.

It is *macro* if, every time in a program that the operation is required, the complete sequence of instructions is written. It is a subroutine if the instruction sequence is written just once, and a jump to the beginning of this sequence is written each time the operation is required. In many ways macroinstructions and subroutines are similar techniques to get an operation done by executing a sequence of instructions. Perhaps one of the central issues in computer architecture design is this: What should be created as instructions or included as addressing modes, and what should be left out, to be carried out by macros or subroutines? On one extreme, it has been proven that a computer with just one instruction can do anything any existing computer can. It may take a long time to carry out an operation, and the program may be ridiculously long and complicated, but it can be done. On the other extreme, most programmers might find complex machine instructions that enable one to execute a high-level (for example, C) language statement desirable. Such complex instructions create undesirable side effects, however, such as long latency time for handling interrupts. However, the issue is overall efficiency. Instructions, which enable selected operations to be performed by a computer to be translated into programs, are selected on the basis of which can be executed most quickly (speed) and which enable the programs to be stored in the smallest room possible (the inverse of program density) without sacrificing low latency. (The related issue of storing data as efficiently as possible is discussed in the next chapter.) The currently popular RISC (*Reduced Instruction Set Computer*) computer architecture philosophy exploits this concept.

The choice of instructions is complicated in two ways by the range of requirements. Some applications need a computer to optimize speed while others need their computer to optimize program density. For instance, if a computer is used like a desk calculator and the time to do an operation is only 0.1 sec, there may be no advantage to doubling the speed because the user will not be able to take advantage of it, while there may be considerable advantage to doubling the program density because the cost of memory may be halved and the cost of the machine may drop substantially. But, for another instance, if a computer is used in a computing center with plenty of memory, doubling the speed may permit twice as many jobs to be done, so that the computer center income is doubled, while doubling the program density is not significant because there is plenty of memory available. Moreover, the different applications computers are put to require different proportions of speed and density.

No known computer is best suited to every application. Therefore, there is a wide variety of computers with different features, and there is a problem picking the computer that best suits the operations it will be used for. Generally, to choose the right computer from among many, a collection of simple well-defined programs pertaining to the computer's expected use, called *benchmarks*, are available. The following are some benchmarks: multiply two unsigned 16-bit numbers, move some words from one location in memory to another, and search for a word in a sequence of words. Programs are written for each computer to effect these benchmarks, and the speed and program density are recorded for each computer. A weighted sum of these values is used to derive a figure of merit for each machine. If storage density is studied, the weights are proportional to the number of times the benchmark (or programs similar to the benchmark) is expected to be stored in memory, and the figure of merit is called the *static efficiency*. If speed is studied, the weights are proportional to the number of times the benchmark (or similar routines) is expected to be executed, and the figure of merit is called the *dynamic efficiency*. These figures of merit, together with computer rental or purchase cost, available software, reputation for serviceability, and other factors, are used to select the machine.

1-1.3 Microcomputers

One can regard microcomputers as similar to the computers already discussed, but created with inexpensive technology. Small computers have been classified according to the number of bits in a word, the number of words in memory, and the combined price of the data operator, controller, and memory. The original classification of micro-, mini-, and mainframe computers by Bell in 1970 is outdated, so we offer a classification for today. We first offer an informal definition of these terms in Table 1-1.

Table 1-1. Classification of Computers

Class	# Memory Words	Cost ($)	#Bits/Word
Single-Chip Microcomputer	8000	2 - 5	8
Personal Computer	512K	100 - 2000	8 to 32
Minicomputer	2M	10,000	32 to 64
Large (Mainframe) Computer	>2M	1,000,000	~64

Rapid technological improvements have blurred the distinction between these classes and dropped their costs. We offer a more precise delineation than that in Table 1-1. An *integrated circuit die*, or *chip*, is a thin sheet of silicon, about 0.04 by 0.04 inches, on which transistors and other components are constructed, to make part of a system. (See Figure 1-3a.) It is an *LSI* or large-scale integrated circuit chip if it has about 1000 transistors. Such a die is usually put in a ceramic or plastic container, called a *dual in-line package*, about 0.3 by 0.8 inches. (See Figure 1-3b.) The chip can also be put in a *surface mount carrier*, as shown in Figure 1-3c. These are much more compact than dual in-line packages, but are hard to service. It is now possible to put the controller and data operator on a single LSI integrated circuit or a small number of LSI integrated circuits. Such a combination of data operator and controller is called a *microprocessor*. If a memory and I/O module are added, the result is called a *microcomputer*. The integrated circuits are normally put on a *printed circuit card* like the one diagramed in Figure 1-3d, and several cards may be mounted like pages in a book on a *motherboard* (shown on Figure 1-3e) that acts like a book's binder to connect the boards together. If the entire microcomputer (except the power supply and some of the hardware used for I/O) is put in a single chip, we have a *single-chip microcomputer*. The microprocessors: M68330/M68331/M68332/M68340 are almost single-chip computers, having many I/O devices on the same chip as the controller and data operator, but requiring external RAM and ROM, like older multiple-chip microcomputers. The M68331, M68332, and M68340 are each available on a small printed-circuit board (Figure 1-3d) that is the size of a business card; these microcomputers, the business-card computers (BCC) appear to be very similar to a single-chip microcomputer.

Single-chip microcomputers are characterized by very low cost and by the absence of software programs available to use on them. For example, single-chip microcomputers cost around $2 in 1990. A *microcontroller* is a microcomputer intended for control applications. The BCC microcontroller will cost a few hundred dollars. More powerful single-board microcomputers often used in personal computers cost from $100 to $1000. Actually, a *personal computer*, whether small or large, is any computer used by one person at a time. However, single-board microcomputers are quite adequate for the text editing and game playing needs of one person, so personal computers are usually single-board computers. These moderately priced single-board microcomputers and microcontrollers may use operating systems and high-level languages, discussed in Chapter 2, to make it easier and cheaper to write software.

Minicomputers are characterized by the abundance of software (such as loaders, debuggers, assemblers, and compilers) available for them and the ability to run several users' programs "simultaneously" using time-sharing. The distinction between minicomputers and personal computer microcomputers is blurred because some architectures are available either as minicomputers (PDP-ll/45) or as microprocessors (PDP-ll/LSI). The distinction is further blurred by the availability of 32-bit microprocessors and the capability of putting up to 1 gigabyte of memory on a microcomputer. Moreover, more software is becoming available for microcomputers. Nevertheless although the terms are imprecise, the terms microcomputer and minicomputer are commonly used to describe small computers.

Ironically, this superstar of the '70s, the microcomputer, was born of a broken marriage. At the dawn of the decade, we were already putting pretty complicated calculators on LSI chips. So why not a computer? Fairchild and Intel made the PPS-25 and 4004, which were almost computers but were not von Neumann architectures. Datapoint Corporation, a leading and innovative terminal manufacturer and one of the larger users of semiconductor memories, talked both Intel and Texas Instruments into building a microcomputer they had designed. Neither Intel nor Texas Instruments were excited about such an ambitious task, but Datapoint threatened to stop buying memories from them, so they went ahead. The resulting devices were disappointing – both too expensive and an order of magnitude too slow. As a recession developed, Texas Instruments dropped the project, but did get the patent on the microcomputer. Datapoint decided they wouldn't buy it after all, because it didn't meet specs. For some time,

Datapoint was unwilling to use microcomputers. Once burned, twice cautious. It is ironic that two of the three parents of the microcomputer disowned the infant. Intel was a new company and could not afford to drop the project altogether. So they marketed it as the 8008, and it sold. It is also ironic that Texas Instruments has the patent on the Intel 8008. The 8008 was incredibly clumsy to program and took so many additional support integrated circuits that it was about as large as a computer of the same power that didn't use microprocessors. Some claim it set back computer architecture at least ten years. But it was successfully manufactured and sold. It was in its way a triumph of integrated circuit technology because it proved a microcomputer was a viable product by creating a market where none had existed, and because the 8080, which was designed to be upward compatible to the 8008, and its upward compatible derivatives, are the most popular microcomputers in the world.

We will study the 68332 in this book. However, the 80186, 80286, and 80386, descendants of the 8080 just discussed, are at least as popular. These other microcomputers have demonstrably better static and dynamic efficiency for certain benchmarks. Even if they have comparable (or even inferior) performance, they may be chosen because they cost less, have a better reputation for service and documentation, or are available, while the "best" chip is more costly, poorly serviced or documented, or unavailable. The reader is also encouraged to study other microcomputers and to be prepared to use them if warranted by the application.

The microcomputer has unleashed a revolution in computer science and engineering. As the cost of microcomputers approaches ten dollars, computers become mere components. They are appearing as components in automobiles, kitchen appliances, toys, instruments, process controllers, communication systems, and computer systems. They should replace larger computers in process controllers much as fractional horsepower motors replaced the large motor and belt shaft. They are "fractional horsepower" computers. This aspect of microcomputers will be our main concern through the rest of the book, because we will focus on how they can be interfaced to appliances and controllers. However, there is another aspect we will hardly have time to study, which will become equally important: their use in conventional computer systems. We are only beginning to appreciate their significance in computer systems. Consider the following (slightly overstated) conjectures:

1. The problem of software portability - getting a program moved from one computer to another - will be solved! Just buy a software package for $30,000, then that software can be written for a microcomputer, and the firm that wrote the software will give you a *free* microcomputer.
2. The solution of large problems will depend only on the patience of programmers. They could spend a lot of money solving these problems on a large computer. Instead, they buy cheap microcomputers, load a program one night, and return a week later to get the answer. They could even throw away the microcomputers and the cost of solving the problem could still be less than on a large computer.
3. Future computers will be aggregates of microcomputers. A "mess o' micros" will be more economical than a larger processor.

Microcomputers continue to spark startling innovations; however, the features of microcomputers, minicomputers, and large computers are generally very similar. In the following subsections the main features of the 68332, a von Neumann architecture, are examined in greater detail.

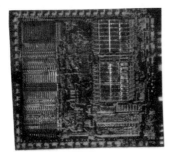

a. Chip

b. Dual In-line Package

c. Surface Mount Carrier

d. Printed Circuit Card

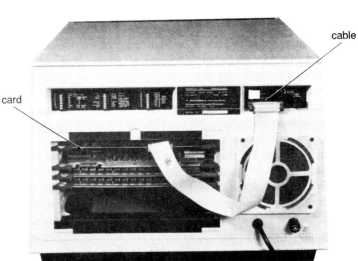

e. System with a Mother Board

Figure 1-3. Microprocessor, Microcomputer, and System.
(Photos © 1992 by Motorola Inc., used with permission.)

Chapter 1 – Microcomputer Architecture

1-2 The 683xx Instruction Set and Addressing Modes

This section talks about the 683xx's instruction set and addressing modes. The only way to really learn an instruction set and addressing modes is to write a lot of programs. It can't be learned just by reading a book (even one as fine as this!). However, as high-level languages become more prominent in interfacing, assembler language becomes less important, and the designer of interface systems really needs only to be acquainted with assembler language rather than be expert in it. He or she needs a reading knowledge of assembler language. In Chapter 2 we will introduce C and use it in our examples. As we emphasize C, we deemphasize assembler language. Sufficient insight can be offered in this chapter by discussing some useful aspects of the instruction set and showing assembler language equivalents to C programs in later chapters.

A typical machine has six types of instructions and several addressing modes. There is no absolute classification of instructions into types. There is no fundamental reason why there should be six classes. There are plenty of instructions that border two or more classes, and could be put in either class. Nevertheless, classification helps the programmer see alternatives. He or she would want to do something; first, determine which class of instruction is needed and then pick the most suitable one from the class. The success or failure of such a classification scheme is based on how well it helps the programmer understand the instruction; we've found Gordon Bell.'s most suitable. Tables 1-3 to 1-7, which we examine in turn throughout the next section, list five of the six types of instructions (move, arithmetic, logical, edit, control, and I/O) these give the instructions of each type in the 683xx that we need for the rest of this book. To describe their operation, we first must discuss the operand sizes and addressing modes used by them (see Table 1-2). Later, we resume the discussion of the 683xx instruction set.

1-2.1 683xx Register and Memory Operands

The instructions discussed in Section 1-1 are those which take a 16-bit word from memory or write a 16-bit word into memory. This section discusses alternative sizes for registers and operands, and differentiated memory spaces available in the 683xx. We also refine our description of the other registers used in the 683xx to prepare for the definition of 683xx instructions.

Figure 1-2 introduced the 683xx registers. Actually, they can be considered as either 8-bit byte wide, 16-bit word wide, or 32-bit long word wide. The 24-bit memory address can handle memories as large as 16 megabytes. (See Figure 1-4.) Each byte has its own address, each word is two bytes that has an even address, and the word address is the same as the byte address of the high-order byte. Any pair of consecutive words can be considered a (32-bit) long word. In a long word, the most significant byte has the lowest address, and the long word address is the same as the address of this byte.

The programmer generally indicates in assembler language the memory or register size by a .B (byte) or .S (short) if it is considered 8 bits, by a .W (word) if 16 bits, and by .L (long) if 32 bits. If no .B .W or .L is written, the instruction is assumed to be word sized, as we used it in the first section of this chapter. For instance, if the programmer writes MOVE.B D0,D1 then the low byte of data register D0 is moved to the low byte of data register D1, the other three bytes of D1 not being changed. Such an instruction is machine coded as 0x3100. MOVE D0,D1 or MOVE.W D0,D1 will move the low word of D0 into the low word of D1, leaving the high word of D1 unchanged. It is machine coded as 0x3200. MOVE.L D0,D1 will move the long word of D0 into D1. It is machine coded as 0x2200. The .B .W or .L mnemonics in assembler language merely change a 2-bit field of the move instruction codeword. We will dissect this codeword in Section 1-2.2. Most 683xx instructions permit all three sizes, but some do not allow one or two of the sizes. Some 683xx addressing modes also use 16-bit or 32-bit displacements or address or data register sizes. These different sizes are indicated by the .W or .L notation on the displacement or register name, as we will discuss in the next subsection.

When a data register is loaded with an 8-bit data or when an 8-bit result is put in the data register, it is always put in the low-order 8-bit part of the register and the upper three-quarters of the register is unchanged. When a 16-bit data or address is loaded into a data or address register or when a 16-bit result is put in the data or address register, it is always put in the low-order 16-bit part of the register, and the upper half of the register is unchanged. Although it is possible to perform some cute tricks by, for instance, loading a 32-bit register and then reloading the low word of the same register, leaving the upper half unchanged, these maneuvers are not done often. If the programmer intends to use the register as a 16-bit register, he or she should generally load it as a 16-bit register (not modifying the upper half) and use it as a 16-bit register (not using the upper half).

The registers in the 683xx were shown in Figure 1-2. Before we can describe the stack registers, we have to discuss the supervisor state, and to do that, we have to start with the description of the status register. The low byte of status register of Figure 1-2 that register contains *condition code bits*, which will be further discussed when we look into conditional branching. The high byte of that register contains some additional *status bits*. The most significant 2 bits, shown as TT, are used to enable debug tracing; the bit shown as S indicates the supervisor mode; the three bits shown as III indicate the interrupt level; and the other bits are zeros. If TT is 10, then the monitor is entered after each instruction is executed, so the programmer can *trace* the execution of his or her program in order to debug it. It is like having a breakpoint after every instruction. If TT is 01, then the monitor is entered after each control instruction reloads the program counter to change the in-line execution sequence. It is like having a breakpoint after every jump instruction. If S is 0, the machine is said to be in the *user state;* and if 1, in the *supervisor state*. The user state is intended to run most programs while the supervisor state is intended to run an operating system, which controls the machine so many users can run their programs without interfering with each other. Each state has its own stack pointer – A7 for the user and A7' for the supervisor. When in the user state (S=0), an instruction using address register A7 uses the user stack pointer, and when in the system state (S=1), it uses the supervisor stack pointer. Some instructions can only be executed when the machine is in the supervisor state; an attempt to execute these in the user state will cause an interrupt called a privilege violation exception. Finally, the three interrupt level status bits III will be explained in Chapter 5.

The 683xx can read a byte from the word-wide memory by simply reading the whole word and, using the least significant bit of the address, routing the high or the low byte of the word into the data operator. If necessary, the memory can be told which byte(s) were requested by some control signals (SIZ[1,0] and address A[0]) discussed in Chapter 3. The 683xx can write a byte into a word by sending these control signals, so the memory will leave the other byte alone and only write the desired byte. The 683xx can read or write a long word by reading or writing two consecutive words in successive memory cycles.

Words or long words must usually be *aligned*. To be word aligned, the address must be even. In the 683xx, reads or writes of words or long words must be word aligned so the memory will not have to read or write parts of consecutive words to read or write non-aligned words or long words. Reading or writing nonaligned words or long words causes an interrupt called an address error exception.

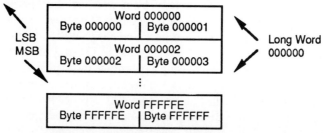

Figure 1-4. Memory in the 683xx.

The 683xx and can have differentiated or common *memory spaces*. A memory space is associated with different access groups such as user data, user program, system data, and system program. If they are differentiated in a 683xx, then word 0x000000 in user data space is not the same as word 0x000000 in user program space, 0x000000 in supervisor data space, or 0x000000 in supervisor program space. If a word is written in user data space address 0x000000, it does not appear when supervisor space word 0x000000 is read. This is illustrated in Figure 1-5a. If they are common in a 683xx, then word 0x000000 in user data space is the same as word 0x000000 in user program space, 0x000000 in supervisor data space, and 0x000000 in supervisor program space. This is illustrated in Figure 1-5b. If the spaces are differentiated, the user spaces are read or written if the status register bit S is 0, otherwise the supervisor spaces are read or written in. If the spaces are differentiated, the program spaces are read if an op code is being fetched or relative addressing is used to read a word, otherwise the data spaces are read or written. Program space is read-only; presumably the program is written before the memory is made program space. Differentiated spaces are useful to prevent the user from accidentally writing over the program, to make the program easier to debug, or with the supervisor, to make it impossible for the user to "break" the operating system.

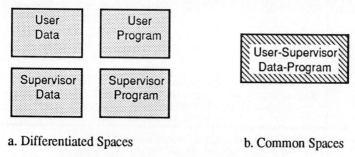

a. Differentiated Spaces   b. Common Spaces

Figure 1-5. Memory Spaces in the 683xx.

The 683xx provides *function code bits* that indicate which space is to be used when memory is read or written. If the memory is designed to decode these bits, it can distinguish between 0x000000 in user data space and 0x000000 in user program space, and so on. This hardware would then have differentiated spaces. If the hardware ignores these bits (they are then called *don't cares*), the machine will have common spaces.

1-2.2 Addressing Modes for the 683xx

The instructions discussed in Section 1-1 involve taking a word from memory where the address of the word is given directly by a word in the instruction (word direct addressing). By the most commonly accepted definition, direct addressing must be able to effectively address any word in primary memory. Within this model, *(long) direct addressing* will mean that all 2^{24} bytes in the 68331 and 68332, or 2^{32} bytes in the 68330 and 68340 can be accessed using a part of the instruction as the effective address.

(Long) direct addressing always requires at least three words per instruction. This hurts static efficiency, because a lot more bits are needed than with other modes introduced in this section. It also hurts dynamic efficiency, because a lot of time is needed to pick up all those words. Then more efficient addressing modes are used to access most often needed words faster and to get to any word in memory by some means, without using as many bits as are needed to directly address each word of memory. This problem leads to the addressing modes that are especially important in small computers. In the remainder of this section, we discuss addressing modes to show what might be generally expected in a computer. The notation used in Motorola's literature differs from that used in other manufacturers' literature and in textbooks. We'll use the general terminology, rather than Motorola's, throughout the book, to relate the principles used in this machine with similar principles used in other machines.

Table 1-2. 683xx Addressing Modes.

Mode (General)	Mode (Motorola)	Example	Use
Long Direct	Absolute Long	MOVE 0x123456,D1	General
Word Direct	Absolute Short	MOVE0x1234,D1	Efficiency
Implied	Inherent	RTS	Efficiency
Register	Address, Data Register	MOVE D0,D1	Efficiency
Immediate	Immediate	MOVE # 0x1234,D1	Provide Constants
Pointer	ARI	MOVE (A0),D1	Efficiency
Autoincrement	ARI with Postincrement	MOVE (A0)+,D1	String, Stack, Queue
Autodecrement	ARI with Predecrement	MOVE -(A0),D1	Stack
Index	ARI with Displacement	MOVE (0x1234,A0),D1	Vector, Linked List
Double Indexed	ARI with Index (8-bit)	MOVE (0x12,A0,D0.W*2),D1	Arrays
"	ARI with Index (Base)	MOVE (0x1234,A0,D0.L*8),D1	
"	"	MOVE (0x12345678,A0,D0.L*8),D1	
Short Relative	Short Relative	BRA.S ALPHA	Position Ind., Effic.
Word Relative	Word Relative	BRA.W ALPHA	"
Long Relative	Long Relative	BRA.L ALPHA	Position Independ.
Rel. Indexed	PCI with Displacement	MOVE 0x1234(PC),D1	"
	PCI with Index (8-bit)	MOVE (0x12,PC,D0.L*8),D1	Program Pointers
	PCI with Index (Base)	MOVE (0x1234,PC,D0.L*8),D1	"
	"	MOVE (0x12345678,PC,D0.L*8),D1	

ARI is Address Register Indirect, PCI is Program Counter Indirect
Rel. is Relative, Ind. is Indirect, PCM Ind. is Program Counter Indirect

In the following discussion of addressing modes, the instruction bits used as an address, or added to get the effective address, are called the *displacement*. Also, in the following discussion an address is calculated the same way – in jump instructions – for the program counter, as for the effective address, in such instructions as MOVE

ALPHA,D0 or MOVE D0,ALPHA. Some people get confused about the addressing modes used in jump instructions because they think that JMP ALPHA should take a word from location ALPHA to put it into the program counter using direct addressing in the same way as in the instruction MOVE ALPHA,D0. No. JMP ALPHA loads the address of ALPHA into the program counter. The simple analogy we used earlier makes it clear that the program counter is, like the effective address, a "hand" to address memory and is treated the same way by the addressing modes.

The simplest addressing mode, used to improve efficiency, is the *word direct* addressing mode (called the absolute short mode). Here, rather than a 32-bit displacement, a signed 16-bit displacement is used to access memory locations 0 to 0x7fff and 32K bytes of high memory. Global data can be put in low memory, and I/O devices can be put in high memory to use this addressing mode. Then two-word can be used in place of three-word instructions to improve static and dynamic efficiency.

Some techniques improve addressing efficiency by avoiding the calculation of an address to memory. *Implied addressing* is a technique whereby the instruction always deals with the same register or a fixed word in memory so that no bits are required within the instruction to specify it. An example is the return from subroutine instruction RTS which is described soon in this subsection. The instruction itself does not contain the usual bits indicating the address of the data: the address is implied. Motorola and others also call this mode "inherent".

A similar mode uses registers as the source and destination of data for instructions. This is called *register addressing*. Data registers D0 or D1 or address registers A0, A1, or A7 can hold the most commonly used data or addresses. In some instructions, such as ADD, one can add one to a word in memory using long direct addressing, as in ADD #1,0x123456, or one can increment a register, such as ADD #1,D0. The former is three words long, while the latter is one word long. Thus, register addressing can be used instead of memory addressing to get data for instructions. This mode substantially improves both static and dynamic efficiency because fewer bits are needed to specify the register than a memory word and a register can be accessed without taking up a memory cycle. In Table 1-2, we use a move instruction where the destination is D1, using register addressing. The instruction MOVE D0,D1 uses register addressing for the source, D0, as well as the destination. It copies the word in D0 into D1 and is coded as

0x3200

Another nonaddressing technique is called *immediate addressing*. Herein, part of the instruction is the actual data, not the address of data. In a sense, the displacement is the data itself. We already saw this mode in the instruction ADD #1,D0. For another example, a type of load instruction,

MOVE #0x1234,D1

puts the number 0x1234 into D1. Using Motorola's notation, an immediate address is denoted by the # symbol. The MOVE instruction, with addressing mode bits for immediate addressing, is 0x323C, so this instruction is stored in machine code like this:

0x323C
0x1234

The number 0x1234 is actually the second word (displacement) of the two-word instruction. This form of addressing has also been called literal addressing.

We may want to execute a loop, in which one instruction picks out a word at a different address each time the loop is executed. Although it is possible to get to different words by rewriting the second word of an instruction using direct addressing, that can lead to difficulties in debugging and is disdainfully referred to as *impure coding* by computer scientists. In the 683xx, rewriting the program can be made even more difficult because the memory that the program is in can be logically separated from the memory that data is in and can be effectively read-only memory. To get different addresses, we put the address in an address register, like A0, A1, or A7, and use an addressing mode called *pointer addressing* to get the data. Motorola calls this mode address register indirect. However, a "small company" called INTEL calls it pointer addressing and our opinion is that most books refer to the mode as pointer addressing, so we do so in this book. Pointer addressing is denoted by putting parentheses around an address register. For example, the instruction MOVE (A0),D1 will move the word pointed to by A0 into D1. It is coded as

0x3210

Rather than a three- or two-word instruction, a one-word instruction is used to get the data. The word in A0 is unchanged by this operation. Note that the address register can be loaded with the address of any word in memory – say with immediate addressing as in MOVE #ALPHA,A0 – so any word can be recalled by means of index addressing. Note that parentheses are needed to denote pointer addressing; MOVE A0,D1 will move the contents of A0 to D1 rather than the word pointed to by A0 into D1.

Sometimes, we need a word from an address close to that address in an address register, and we do not want to change the contents of the address register to get it. A variation of pointer addressing, called *index addressing*, allows a displacement, part of the instruction, to be added to the contents of an index register (without changing the contents of the index register) to get the effective address. For example, if A0 contains 0x2000, MOVE 0x1234(A0),D1 will move the word at 0x3234 into D1. (Some assemblers use the format MOVE (0x1234,A0),D1 for this mode.) It is coded as

0x3208
0x1234

Without changing the address register contents, any word above or below the one the address register points to can be recalled by using different signed number values for the displacement that is added to the address register. This makes index addressing quite versatile for handling arrays. However, pointer addressing is shorter and faster than index addressing. While pointer addressing can be used to recall any word in memory, it is more difficult to use than index addressing because the register must be reloaded each time to recall or memorize a word at a different location.

A different variation of pointer addressing modifies the value of the address register as it is used in an address calculation in the instruction. Two forms, called autoincrementing and autodecrementing, are available in the 683xx and are denoted by a plus sign after, or a minus sign before, an address register in parentheses. *Autoincrement addressing* such as MOVE (A0)+,D1 moves the word pointed to by A0 into D1 and then adds the byte size of the operand (2), to the address register. For example, if A0 was 0x2000, then the word at address 0x2000 is moved to D1 and A0 becomes 0x2002. Note that the operand size (2 bytes) is added to the address register so that the next word is ready to be loaded in a similar instruction. This instruction is coded

Chapter 1 – Microcomputer Architecture

0x3218

Conversely, *autodecrement addressing* – such as MOVE -(A0),D1 – first decrements A0 by the operand size and then reads the word pointed to by the new value of the address register. For example, if A0 were 0x2000, A0 would become 0x1FFE and the word at location 0x1FFE would be loaded into D1. This instruction is coded as

0x3220

The A7 register is the *stack pointer*. It has special meaning and in our experience must be treated with respect. A part of memory, called the *stack buffer*, is set aside for a *stack*. In a microcomputer, the stack is in the random access memory along with the data. The stack pointer, A7, initially contains the address of the word above (at higher address than) any word in the stack buffer. The instruction MOVE D1,-(A7) decrements the stack pointer by 2, and then writes the contents of D1 into the word pointed to by the new value of A7. This is called *pushing* a word in D1 onto this stack. MOVE (A7)+,D1 reads the word pointed to by A7 into D1 and increments the stack pointer A7. This is called *pulling* (or popping) a word from this stack into D1. Special instructions described soon also push or pull words from this stack.

The stack fills out, starting at high addresses and building toward lower addresses, in the stack buffer. If it builds into addresses lower than the stack buffer, a *stack overflow* error occurs, and if it is pulled too many times, a *stack underflow* occurs. If no such errors occur, then the last word pushed onto the stack is the first word pulled from it, a property that sometimes labels a stack a LIFO (last in, first out) stack. Stack overflow or underflow often cause data stored outside of the stack buffer to be modified.

The jump to subroutine instruction (JSR) pushes a two-word return address, and supplies a new value for the program counter using addressing modes available for the instruction, as in a jump instruction. The corresponding return from subroutine instruction RTS pulls two words from the stack into the program counter. (Note that this instruction was used as an example of implied addressing; neither the source of the data, the stack, nor the destination, the program counter, are specified. Both are implied by the instruction.) If nobody changes the stack pointer A7, or if the net number of pushes equals the net number of pulls (the stack is *balanced*) between the jump to subroutine and the corresponding return from subroutine, then the last instruction causes the calling routine to resume exactly where it left off when it called the subroutine.

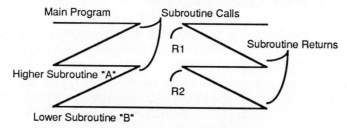

Figure 1-6. Coathanger Diagrams.

Subroutines can be *nested;* that is, one subroutine can call a second. These are nicely described by *coathanger diagrams*. (See Figure 1-6.) The top line represents the main program, with execution flowing from left to right on that line. In the middle, a subroutine "A" is called by an instruction like JSR A. This pushes the return address, R1 on the stack. After some instructions are executed, subroutine "B" is called by an instruction like JSR B. This pushes the return address R2 on the stack. Subroutine "B" ends in an RTS instruction, which pulls the return address R2 from the stack. Subroutine "A" ends in an RTS instruction, which pulls the return address R1 from the stack. This makes the main program resume. Hardware interrupts save return addresses as well as the contents of the status register, by pushing them onto the stack, and a *return from interrupt* instruction pulls them from the stack in reverse order.

The stack in the 683xx is a good place to store local data. It can also be used to supply arguments for a subroutine and return results from it, as discussed later. To save local data, one can push it on the stack and pull it from the stack as in the program segments just mentioned. A reasonable number of words can be stored this way. Moreover, if the subroutine is reentered (see Section 1-1.1 near the end), the local data for the subroutine's first execution are saved on the stack as new local data are pushed on top of them and the new data are used by the subroutine's second execution. When the first execution is resumed, it uses the old data. Keeping all local data on the stack this way ensures reentrancy. (This will be discussed in the next chapter.) Note that the subroutine must pull as many words from the stack as it pushed, before the return from subroutine instruction is executed, or some data will be pulled by that instruction into the program counter, which is a particularly troublesome program bug.

The stack pointer A7 must be treated with respect. It should be initialized to point to the high address end of the stack buffer as soon as possible, right after power is turned on, and should not be changed except by incrementing or decrementing it to effectively push or pull words from it. Some programmers like to reuse data already pulled from the stack, using an instruction sequence like MOVE -2(A7),D1. This is not safe. If an interrupt occurs, or if subroutines store return addresses or local variables on the stack, such words above the stack pointer will be written over. Words above the stack pointer must be considered garbage and may not be read after they are pulled. Some programmers like to set A7 to an address in the middle of good data rather than at the end of a stack buffer, to read the data by pulling them. Woe to those programmers. The stack pointer will generally overwrite good data with return addresses each time a subroutine is called or an interrupt is serviced. Moreover, because the tools used to analyze a faulty program (such as breakpoints and trace steps) use interrupts to store return addresses and condition code register, these tools may be useless for diagnosing faults in a program that mishandles the A7 register.

The 683xx also has a double indexed mode as in MOVE 0x12(A0,D0.W*2),D1 (address register indirect with index and 8-bit displacement) and additional double indexed modes (address register indirect with index and base displacement): MOVE (0x1234,A0,D0.L*8),D1 and MOVE (0x12345678,A0,D0.L*8),D1. These three modes permit the effective address to be the sum of an address register, a data register, and an 8-bit, 16-bit, or 32-bit offset, or the sum of two address registers and an 8-bit, 16-bit, or 32-bit offset. The second address register or the data register can be used as a 16-bit, or 32-bit register; its value can be multiplied by 1, 2, 4 or 8, as noted after the asterisk, before adding it in to get the effective address. This is especially useful if a data register used in a DBRA instruction, discussed later, counts down the data register value used in the double index address. Usually, we use a multiplier of 1 if bytes are being read or written, 2 if words and 4 if long words are read or written. All parts of the address are sign-extended to 32 bits before being combined to get the effective address. Double indexing is primarily useful when we add two variable numbers and a fixed number to get the effective address. This occurs when a two-dimensional array is accessed, but it also occurs when a vector is indexed, and the beginning address of the vector is variable or is in an address register. This mode is also useful when the variable part of an effective address is in a data register because we do arithmetic to get it or we wish to test it for zero upon loading it. A good assembler for the 683xx will automatically select the shortest displacement of the three possible displacements for the displacement value being used.

In double indexed mode, any or all of the registers and displacements can be omitted from the instruction and a value of zero substituted for them. An omitted register is said to be *zero-suppressed*. A zero-suppressed register is not actually modified, but appears as if its value were zero in the effective address calculation. For instance, the instruction MOVE 0x12(D0),D1 suppresses the index register A0 so that the data register D0 can be used like an address register. However, a good assembler for the 683xx will automatically select shorter faster addressing modes if the displacement or second address register is omitted.

A variation of index addressing uses the program counter in place of the address register, but the displacement is treated differently and the (possibly read-only) memory around the program is accessed rather than the (read-write) data area. This will be discussed after a special but simpler case, used only for branch instructions, is discussed.

Short relative addressing calculates the effective address by adding an 8-bit 2's complement displacement to the program counter to get the address for a jump instruction (a *branch*) because one often jumps to a location which is fairly close to where the jump instruction is stored. The displacement is added to the program counter when it actually points to the beginning of the next instruction. This addressing mode only works if the jump address is within -127 to +127 locations of the next instruction's address after the branch instruction. For example, the place we want to branch to may contain the instruction code for MOVE ALPHA,D1. To identify the place we want to jump or branch to, we put a label to the left of the OP code so that the label begins flush against the left margin. (Following THINK C's assembler convention, we denote labels with '@' and a number.) Unlabeled instructions must begin, then, with a space so the assembler will not mistake an instruction mnemonic for a label. If the preceding instruction is at locations 0x200 and 0x202, it is written

@1 MOVE ALPHA,D1

and the label @1 will be the symbolic address of the instruction, to be used in jump or branch statements. For example, a branch to location 0x200 (@1) is denoted like this:

BRA @1

If @1 is at location 0x200 and the instruction is at location 0x1F0, then the program counter is at location 0x1F2 when the address is calculated, and the BRA instruction (whose instruction code is 0x60 plus the 1-byte displacement) will be assembled and stored as

0x600E

Note that the assembler language instruction uses the symbolic address @1 rather than the difference between the addresses, as in BRA @1-0x1F2, and the assembler automatically determines the difference between the current program counter address and the effective address and puts this difference into the second byte (displacement) of the instruction.

If we move the program intact from one place in memory to another (the branch instruction and the place it jumps to move together), their relative address remains unchanged. You may use short relative addressing instead of the direct addressing used in a jump instruction. But the instruction and the data may be more than -127 or +127 locations apart. Therefore, branch instructions can only be used in place of jump instructions for short programs. Other relative addressing modes are also available with 16-bit and 32-bit offsets. To distinguish between them, the assembler language notation uses BRA.S ALPHA to denote short relative, BRA.W ALPHA to denote word relative, and BRA.L ALPHA to denote long relative. In machine code, the displacement for short relative addressing is within the first word of the instruction. However, if it is zero (a useless displacement - use NOP instead of BRA), the machine picks up a second word following the op code and adds this 16-bit word displacement to the program counter to get the branch address. The short displacement 0xFF (rarely used) signals the microprocessor to pick up two words following the op code, and treat these as a long word to be added to the program counter. If .S .W or .L are not used, the assembler can be directed to always use one of these by default, as discussed in the next chapter. The displacement is the second word of the instruction and is added to the program counter, which is the address of the displacement. If a program can be loaded anywhere in memory and it will run without change - thus simplifying program loading - it has a characteristic called *position independence*. Relative addressing plays an important part in making a program position independent. Chapter 10 illustrates how an operating system can take advantage of position independence. Position independence also means that a read-only memory can be loaded with the program and will work wherever it is addressed. They are usable in more systems, so more can be sold at lower cost.

The general case of relative addressing used in non-branch instructions also requires the destination address to be written in the assembler language instruction but puts the difference between the current address and the destination address in the machine coded instruction, just like the BRA instruction. For example, if some data word at address 0x200 has a label @1 (as discussed in the next chapter) and the instruction MOVE @1(PC),D1 is at 0x1F0 so the program counter is at 0x1F2 when it is executed, the machine code would be

0x323A
0x000E

Although this form of relative addressing can be used with JMP and JSR instructions, the specialized BRA and BSR instructions should be used instead.

The 683xx has relative indexed mode (program counter indirect with index and 8-bit displacement, as in MOVE 0x12(PC,D0.W*4),D1, and address register indirect with index and 16-bit or 32-bit base displacement as in MOVE (0x1234,PC,D0.L*8),D1 or MOVE (0x12345678,PC,D0.L*8),D1. These modes are analogous to the double indexed mode except that the program counter replaces the address register and program space is accessed. These modes are very powerful where a data structure such as a character string or vector in user program or supervisor program space is accessed. Because they use the program counter, they access program spaces in a differentiated space memory. The index register can be used to get consecutive bytes from the string as its value is incremented. The index register can be loaded with an index to get an element from the vector.

1-2.3 The 683xx Instruction Set

We now resume our discussion of 683xx instructions. We will proceed with a discussion of each class, beginning with the *move* class.

The simplest type of instruction is a *move,* such as the MOVE instruction that loads or stores a register. This instruction moves a word to or from a register, in the controller or data operator, from or to memory. Typically, a third of program instructions are moves. If an architecture has good move instructions, it will have good efficiency for many benchmarks. The MOVE instruction is the most useful and common instruction in the move class, but it is not the only instruction in the class. We will show how the MOVE instruction is coded in machine code to illustrate how you can read a manual's description of an instruction and write machine code into a C program. We also study the MOVE, MOVEM, LEA, CLR, and TST instructions in the move class of instructions.

The general MOVE instruction is able to move a word from any register (D0 - D7, A0 - A7) or memory location using any addressing mode including immediate or relative, to any register or memory location not using immediate or relative addressing. (see Figure 1-7). Figure 1-7a shows the bit fields in a MOVE instruction, Figure 1-7b shows the coding of the mode fields in the source and in the destination, and Figure 1-7c shows the coding of "special" modes that do not need a register, which are coded in the register field (otherwise the register number is put in that field). Figure 1-7d shows the permissible selection of sources and destinations. Note that because immediate operands and data accessed by relative addressing are supposed to be constants, you should not be able to store into them.

An example of a more complex coding, which is needed when C programs written for the 68000 are copied into the 683xx and the power of double-indexed addressing is needed, is shown in Figure 1-7e, which is double indexed in the source address of a MOVE instruction. Consider the encoding of the index register denoted Xn.size*scale in an 8-bit offset index address, shown in the top part of Figure 1-7e. The index register Xn may be D0 to D7, coded as 0 to 7 respectively, or A0 to A7, coded 8 to 0xf, in the most significant byte of the second word of the instruction. The size .W or .L is coded as a 0 or 1 in the next bit, and the scale *1, *2, *4 or *8 is coded as 0,1,2 or 3 in the next two bits. The next bit is a 0 to indicate that the addressing mode uses an 8 bit offset rather than the 32 bit offset, which shown in the lower part of Figure 1-7e. In the 32-bit offset double indexed address shown there, the base and index register will each be suppressed if the next two bits are 1. Double indexing in the destination address of a MOVE instruction, or in other instructions, can be deduced from this example.

In the discussion of instructions that follow, we do not show the machine code for them. The reader should study the *CPU32 Central Processor Reference Manual (CPU32RM/AD)* Motorola Inc., 1989 to encode any instruction. Compare the MOVE instruction, the manual's page 4-94, to Figure 1-7 above. Then study other instruction codings. You should be able to insert machine coded instructions into C programs, as will be illustrated in Chapter 2. It should also become clear that the microprocessor is really a simple interpreter that reads all the information it needs from the first word of the instruction; then, depending on the addressing mode, it then reads one or more words following it to get immediate addressed or other displacements as required by the addressing modes. Incidentally if both source and destination displacements are needed, because the source address is calculated first, the displacement needed by the source address calculation will be before that needed by the destination address calculation.

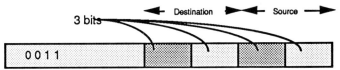

Op Code = MOVE WORD Register   Mode   Mode Register

a. The Fields in a MOVE Instruction

Codes	Modes
000	Data Register
001	Address Register
010	Pointer
011	Autoincrement
100	Autodecrement
101	Indexed
110	Double Indexed
111	(Special)

b. Coding of the Mode Field

"Register"	Special Modes
000	(Word) Direct
010	Relative
100	Immediate

c. Coding of the Register Field
for Mode 111

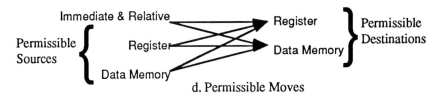

d. Permissible Moves

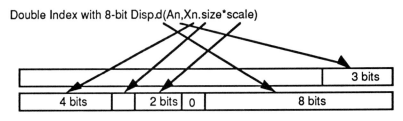

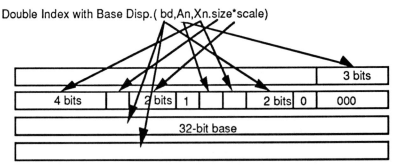

e. Index Addressing

Figure 1-7. Coding of MOVE Instructions.

Table 1-3 shows some instructions indented in the left-most column. Most are special cases of the nonindented general case instruction above them; if a general case mnemonic is written, a full-featured assembler will use the special case when it can, unless the user writes the special case. The middle column lists some classes of registers. SR is the status register, CCR is the status register, and USP is the user stack pointer A7. Rc is any special control register in the 683xx and the source function code register, destination function code register, user stack pointer, vector base register, and supervisor pointer. <ea1> denotes an effective address of type 1, shown in the footnote of the table. Finally, in the right-most column, L, W, B, and 1-32 bits indicate the width of operand fields, long, word, byte, and variable width. A '>' sign indicates the source width(s) to its left and destination width(s) to its right.

Table 1-3. Move Instructions.

MOVE	<ea>,<ea> (see figure 1-7d)	LWB
	<ea>,SR/CCR or SR/CCR,<ea>	W
MOVEA	<ea>,An	LW > L
MOVE	USP,An or An,USP	L
MOVEQ	#<data>,Dn -128≤ data ≤ 127	B > L
MOVEC	Rc,Rn or Rn,Rc	L
MOVES	Rn,<ea> or <ea>,Rn	LWB
EXG	Rn,Rn	L
MOVEP	Dn,(d16,An)	LW
	(d16,An),Dn	LW
MOVEM	list,<ea. or <ea>,list	LW
LEA	<ea>,An	L
PEA	<ea>	L
CLR	<ea>	LWB
TST	<ea>	LWB
BTST	Dn,<ea> or #<data>,<ea>	LB
Scc	<ea>	B

Notes:

Dn	Any data register
An or Am	Any address register
Rn	Any address or data register
Rc	SFC,DFC,VBR, or USP
list	A list of data and/or address registers
#<data>	An immediate operand
<ea>	An addressing mode
<label>	A label on a program statement
cc	A conditon code and value

Condition code bits in the status register hold results from a move or similar instruction to be tested in a later conditional branch instruction. All instructions can set or clear them or leave them alone. The MOVE instruction sets the *zero* bit Z bit if the word that was moved was zero, otherwise it clears Z; and it sets the *negative* bit N bit if the number moved was negative, otherwise it clears the N bit. The other condition code bits, *carry* C and *overflow* V, are cleared, and *extend carry* X is unmodified. However, if the destination is an address register, the condition code bits are unaltered because address modifications are sometimes necessary between the instruction that sets condition code bits and the conditional branch instruction that uses them. For this reason, Motorola uses a different mnemonic, MOVEA, rather than MOVE, when the destination is an address register. One of the most troublesome bugs we have seen results when the programmer incorrectly sets or tests, or inadvertently alters, the condition codes. However, in this book we use the generic MOVE instruction whether or not the destination is an address register. Remember, however, that if the destination is an address register, condition codes are unmodified.

For moving an immediate operand between -128 and 127 into a data register, a special short one-word instruction MOVEQ (move quick), is used. MOVE #2,D0 is coded

303C

0002

While MOVEQ #2,D0 is coded

7002

Use MOVEQ wherever you can to shorten the code.

Special MOVE instructions are used by supervisor mode programs to control user mode programs, and their use in user mode is prohibited. The MOVE instruction with source or destination SR can modify the status register (and the user mode instruction with source or destination CCR can access only the low byte of it). MOVE with source or destination USP can access the user stack pointer. MOVEC can access control registers SFC, DFC, VBR, or the user stack pointer. The MOVES instruction can move data to or from a different space. (See Figure 1-5.) The source function code register is loaded with the space code if a different space is used for the source, and the destination function code register is loaded with the space code if a different space is used for the destination.

EXG can be used to exchange the data in any two registers. These registers can be data or address registers. MOVEP can move a word or long word to or from a data register from or to bytes that are either consecutive even addresses or consecutive odd addresses. These could be eight-bit registers in an I/O device that is connected to eight of the sixteen data bus lines in a 683xx memory, and thus are addressed in consecutive even addresses or consecutive odd addresses.

While it is possible to push or pull registers onto the stack one by one, as just discussed, a more efficient instruction, MOVEM, is provided that can push or pull more than one register on the stack. It can also be used to save registers elsewhere in memory or (re)load them, but we do not discuss the general case in our 683xx, except that the stack register A7 can be replaced by any address register. The second word of this two-word instruction is a *register mask*, which has one bit for each address and data register. If the bit is 1, that register is moved, otherwise it is not. The assembler language expresses this mask as a *register list*, where dash (-) means a range of registers from-to and slash (/) means a list of registers or ranges that are moved. For instance, MOVEM D0/D1/A0-A1, -(A7) will push D0, D1, and A0 to A1 on the stack. MOVEM (A7)+,D0/A0-A1 will pull D0 and A0 to A1 from the stack. Regardless of the order in which the registers are listed, they are pushed in this order: high register numbers first, and all address registers before data registers; they are pulled in the reverse order. Thus they appear on the stack with lower register numbers at lower addresses and data registers at lower addresses than address registers; and when they are pulled with the same register list, the values saved on the stack are put where they came from. For instance, if the instruction MOVEM D0/D1/A0-A1, -(A7) is executed, then the value of D1 that was saved on the stack can be loaded into D0 using the instruction MOVE 2(A7),D0. MOVE (A7)+,D0/D1/A0-A1 restores the registers that were saved on the stack. Using another address register such as A0, we can save the registers D0, D1, A1, and A7 in memory words APLHA to ALPHA+6, if A0 has ALPHA+8 and MOVEM D0/D1/A1/A7, -(A0) is executed. MOVEM does not affect the condition code bits.

Load effective address (LEA) is important for moving data to address registers. It proceeds like a MOVE, getting an effective address, and then, rather than getting the data at this address, the effective address is put into the destination, which must be an address register. The effective address may only be direct, pointer, index, or relative. For example, while MOVE ALPHA,D0 puts the word at location ALPHA into D0; LEA ALPHA,A0 puts the address of APLHA into A0. In a sense, the execution of the MOVE instruction is short-circuited and the effective address is used in place of the data. PEA pushes an effective address that is computed in the manner of the LEA instruction. It is useful to set up addresses of subroutine arguments on the stack.

Two simple alternatives to MOVE are CLR and TST. CLR D0 is equivalent to MOVE #0,D0. Any data memory word or data register can be cleared by this instruction, which is just one word long. Of course, you cannot clear an immediate operand or a relatively addressed word, both of which are supposedly in the nonmodifiable program area. Curiously, you cannot clear an address register using CLR, but you can subtract it from itself to clear it. The TST instruction is like the first half of a MOVE instruction, getting the data from a source and setting the condition codes, but the data are not put in a destination. It can be used to test a data register or a data word in memory to set the condition codes for a later conditional branch. Address register values and immediate or relatively addressed words cannot be a source in TST. You can test address values using a CMP instruction or by moving them to a data register.

The BTST instruction can test any single bit in a register or in memory, but not an address register or immediate operand. The bit to be tested is specified by an immediate operand or the value in a data register. When testing a data register, the bit number must be between 31 (left-most) and 0 (right-most bit). BTST #0,D0 tests the rightmost bit of D0, setting Z if the bit is zero, otherwise clearing Z. (Note that in effect the complement of the bit tested goes to Z.) Other condition code bits are not affected. BTST D0,D1 will test a bit in D1 whose bit number is specified in D0. The selected bit for a BTST instruction may not be in an address register. When testing memory, the byte number is specified by the effective address, rather than the word number and the bit number must be between 7 (left-most) and 0 (right-most bit). The address of a word in memory is the same as the address of the high-order byte in it, and the address of the low-order byte is one greater than the word address. The memory byte tested may be selected by any addressing mode except immediate and relative addressing. BTST #7,ALPHA tests the sign bit of byte ALPHA in memory and BTST D0,ALPHA+1 tests the bit specified by D0 of byte ALPHA+1 in memory (the low-order byte of word ALPHA). The set instruction Scc will be discussed later with conditional branches.

You may find, upon writing your program, that you need to move a word without altering it, or you may have to save a word to restore it later. You should carefully consider where you are moving it to or from and what instructions you will use to move it. Consider using another register to save a word to restore it later, as in MOVE D0,A0, or consider pushing it on the stack, as in MOVE D0,-(A7), or storing it in memory, as in MOVE D0,ALPHA. You may use the special CLR ALPHA instruction in place of MOVE #0,ALPHA. You may want to set the condition codes when you move the data so they can be tested by a conditional branch statement, or you may wish to set the condition codes without actually moving data to the destination. The TST instruction is a useful alternative to the MOVE instruction.

The TBL instruction can be used for table lookup. Piece-wise-linear interpolation is quickly performed by this instruction, which is useful for some control algorithms.

Table 1-4 shows the 683xx arithmetic instructions using a format similar to that of Table 1-3. We consider the ADD, SUB, CMP, NEG, and MULU instructions and the LEA instruction that is an alternative to ADD. We expect that you are familiar with binary addition, subtraction, multiplication, and the negation of 2's complement numbers. We focus on the addressing modes and condition codes of these instructions.

ADD has two operands; the first is added to the second, and the result is put in the second. ADD D0,D1 adds the word in D0 to the word in D1, putting the result in D1. One can add any immediate operand, address or data register word, or word from memory to an address or data register, or one can add an immediate operand or a word from a data register to any word in memory (except using immediate or relative addressing). Some other examples are ADD #1,A0 ADD D0,BETA ADD #1,ALPHA. The last two are quite useful in I/O programs. When the destination is an address register, the condition codes are not affected (see the previous discussion of MOVE-MOVEA). In all other cases, the condition code bits are affected as follows. Usually, the result is 1 bit wider than the operands, and the extra left-most bit is put into the carry flip-flop. For unsigned numbers, the carry is often considered an overflow indicator; if the carry is 1, if the operand size is 16 bits, the result in the data register is incorrect because when the word is put back into the (16-bit-wide) memory, the seventeenth bit in the carry won't fit, and so the result in memory will also be incorrect. The N and Z condition codes are set, just as in the MOVE instructions, to reflect that the result of the addition is negative or zero. An overflow bit V is set to 1 if the result is erroneous as a 2's complement number. A 2's complement overflow will occur if the two numbers being added have the same sign and the result has a different sign. Have you ever added two positive numbers and got a negative number? That's an overflow. Or if you add two negative numbers and get a positive number, that too is an overflow. But if you add two numbers of different signs, an overflow cannot occur. In using these condition codes in branch instructions, we must be careful to test the carry bit, not the overflow bit, after an unsigned binary add, because the carry bit is set if an unsigned overflow occurs; and we must remember to test the overflow bit V after a 2's complement add, because it is set if the result is erroneous as a 2's complement number. The ADD instruction puts the carry out of the adder into both the X and C condition code bits. X is a "carry bit" used for multiple precision addition, which we will not discuss here, and C is a "carry bit" used for conditional branching. X is unaltered by most other instructions, while C is changed by many.

Table 1-4. Arithmetic Instructions.

ADD	<ea>,Dn or <ea>,An or Dn,<ea> or #data,<ea>	LWB
ADDA	<ea>,An	LW
ADDI	#<data>,<ea>	LWB
ADDQ	#data,<ea> 1 ≤ data ≤ 8	LWB
ADDX	Dn,Dn or -(An),-(An)	LWB
ABCD	Dn,Dn or -(An),-(An)	B
LEA	d(An),Am or d(PC),Am	L
SUB	<ea>,Dn or <ea>,An or Dn,<ea> or #data,<ea>	LWB
SUBA	<ea>,An	LW
SUBI	#<data>,<ea>	LWB
SUBQ	#data,<ea> 1 ≤ data ≤ 8	LWB
SUBX	Dn,Dn or -(An),-(An)	LWB
SBCD	Dn,Dn or -(An),-(An)	B
CMP	<ea1>,Dn or <ea>,An or #<data>,<ea>	LWB
CMPA	<ea>,An	LW
CMPI	#<data>,<ea>	LWB
CMPM	(An)+,(An)+	LWB
CHK	<ea>,Dn	LW
CHK2	<ea>,Rn	LWB
CMP2	<ea>,Rn	LWB
NEG	<ea>	LWB
NEGX	<ea>	LWB
NBCD	<ea>	B
DIVU/DIVS	<ea>,Dn	L/W > W:W
	<ea>,Dn	L/L > L
	<ea>,Dn	D/L > L:L
DIVSL	<ea>,Dr:Dq	L/L > L:L
MULU/MULS	<ea>,Dn	WxW > L
	<ea>,Dr:Dq	LxL >L
	<ea>,Dh:Dl	LxL > D

LEA, which has been discussed as a MOVE instruction, can be used as an arithmetic instruction when the effective address uses addition. It is quite useful for setting up an address register, especially from a relative address as in LEA ALPHA(PC),A0, so that pointer, autoincrement, autodecrement, or index addressing may be used with the address register in later instructions. Used with index addressing, LEA adds a constant displacement to the word in an address register. LEA 2(A0),A0 puts the word in A0 plus 2 into A0. This is equivalent to ADD #2,A0. The ADD instruction always puts the result in one of the inputs to the ADD, but LEA can add a constant to one register and put the sum in a different register, as in LEA 2(A0),A1. LEA does not change any condition codes.

SUB works analogously to ADD; it can subtract its first argument from its second, putting the result in the second, and setting the condition codes as follows. N, Z, and V are set to indicate a negative result, 0 result, or 2's complement overflow, as in the ADD instruction. The carry flip-flop is actually the borrow indicator; it is set if subtraction requires a borrow from the next higher byte or if an unsigned underflow error exists because the result, a negative number, can't be represented as an unsigned number. The first argument can be an immediate or register operand, or a memory word selected by any addressing mode, and the second argument can be a data or address register. Alternatively, the first argument can be a data register and the second can be any register or memory word selected by any addressing mode except immediate or relative.

NEG negates any word in a data register or word addressed by any mode except immediate or relative. It inverts each bit and adds one to the result. The condition codes are set in the same manner as in the SUB instruction.

Subtraction is often used to compare two numbers, sometimes just to see if they are equal. The results are tested in conditional branch instructions. However, if we are comparing a given number against several numbers to avoid reloading the given number, it can be left in an data register, and a *compare* instruction, such as CMP, can be used. The first operand may be immediate, in which case the second operand can be any data register or memory word except using the immediate or relative addressing modes, or else the first operand may be any register, in which case the second operand may be any register word or any memory word chosen by any addressing mode. CMP is just like the subtract instruction, but it does not change the destination word, so the number in it can be compared to others in later instructions. The N, Z, V and C condition codes are changed (X is not altered) and can be tested by conditional branch instructions. For instance, the instruction CMP ALPHA,D0 will set the Z bit if D0 is equal to ALPHA because the result after subtraction would be zero. CMP #4,D0 will set the carry bit C if, upon subtracting 4 from D0 there is a borrow, which is when D0 is less than 4, considered as an unsigned number. CMP #-2,ALPHA sets V when subtraction of -2 from the word at ALPHA produces an overflow, and sets N when the result ALPHA-(-2) is negative, which is when the word at ALPHA is less than -2, considered as a 2's complement number.

The ADD, SUB, and CMP have special cases like the MOVE instruction. ADDX propagates the condition code bits, including the X carry and Z zero bits, to effect multiple precision addition. SUBX, CMPM, and NEGX effect multiple precision subtraction, comparison, and negation in similar fashion. In order to perform addition, subtraction, and negation on packed binary coded decimal numbers, which have two BCD digits per byte, the instructions ABCD, SBCD, and NBCD are provided. They work similarly to the ADDX type instructions. There are special, short, one-word forms for the ADD and SUB instructions, used when an immediate operand between 1 and 8 is added to or subtracted from a register or memory word addressed by any mode except immediate or relative addressing. This instruction, add quick (ADDQ), is used by a good assembler whenever the conditions apply and the instruction ADD is used. Similarly SUBQ is used in place of SUB. (There is a subtle reason why MOVEQ is not used in place of MOVE when the immediate operand is between -128 and 127 and the destination is a data register.) Also, when the destination is an address register, the instruction ADD is changed to ADDA and SUB is changed to SUBA in Motorola's documentation because the condition codes are not affected. In this text, we use the generic forms ADD and SUB, and assume the assembler will convert these when it generates machine code. The only effect will be that such converted instructions are shorter than those not able to be converted or they do not affect the condition codes.

The CHK instruction is designed for checking an index in an array. The index, in a data register, is compared to the word or long word value at the effective address; if it is above that value or it is below zero, an exception occurs. CHK2 checks a register to see if it is within an upper and lower bound, trapping if it is not. The bounds are found at the effective address. CMP2 is similar, setting the carry bit if the register is out of bounds.

MULU does an unsigned integer multiplication of any data register word or word from memory with a data register word. MULU ALPHA,D0 multiplies the word in ALPHA by the word in D0, putting the result in D0. Note that one of the operands, which is also the result, must be a data register, and the source may not be an address register. MULU includes versions to multiply 32-bit by 32-bit numbers to give either a 32-bit or 64-bit result. Unsigned or signed division (DIVU or DIVS) divides a word at the effective address into a long word in a data register, leaving the quotient in the high-order word and the remainder in the low-order word of the data register. The corresponding multiply instructions (MULU and MULS) multiply a 16-bit number at the effective address by the 16-bit number in a data register, leaving a 32-bit result in the data register. The divide instructions DIVU, DIVS, DIVUL, and DIVSL, divide 32-bit numbers to give a 32-bit quotient (the remainder is discarded) or a 32-bit quotient and 32-bit remainder, and divide a 64-bit number by a 32-bit number to give a 32-bit remainder and quotient.

Table 1-5. Logical Instructions.

AND	\<ea>,Dn or Dn,\<ea>	LWB
ANDI	#\<data>,\<ea> or #\<data>,CCR/SR	LWB
BCLR	Dn,\<ea> or #\<data>,\<ea>	LB
OR	\<ea>,Dn or Dn,\<ea>	LWB
ORI	#\<data>,\<ea> or #\<data>,CCR/SR	LWB
BSET	Dn,\<ea> or #\<data>,\<ea>	LB
TAS	\<ea>	B
EOR	\<ea>,Dn or Dn,\<ea>	LWB
EORI	#\<data>,\<ea> or #\<data>,CCR/SR	LWB
BCHG	Dn,\<ea> or #\<data>,\<ea>	LB
NOT	\<ea>	LWB

A third group of instructions is the *logical* group. See Table 1-5. These are very useful in the programming of I/O devices. The instruction

AND ALPHA,D0

will logically "and," bit by bit, the word at 0x100 in memory to the word in the data register D0. The destination, which is also one of the operands, must be a data register. For example, if the word at location 0x100 were 0000000001101010 and at data register D0 were 0000000011110000, then after such an instruction is executed the result in data register D0 would be 0000000001100000. The AND instruction can also AND a word in a data register or immediate operand and a memory word, putting the result in the memory word, where the memory word is selected by any addressing mode except immediate or relative. This is quite useful in programming I/O devices. Neither the source nor the destination of an AND instruction may be an address register.

Analogous to the preceding instructions, the OR instruction ORs into a data register any word from memory, or ORs an immediate operand or the word in a data register into a word in memory selected by any mode except immediate or relative.

The complement instruction NOT will complement each bit in the data register or any word in memory. Also analogous to the preceding AND and OR instructions, the EOR instruction exclusive-ORs an immediate operand or the word in a data register into a word in a data register or a word in memory selected by any mode except immediate or relative. There is, however, no way to Exclusive-OR from a word in memory to a data register. That useful operation cannot be done. Note that EOR is a selective complement instruction; wherever the first operand has a 1, the corresponding bit in the second operand is inverted and elsewhere the second operand is unchanged.

The BCLR instruction, with the same format as BTST described earlier, can clear any single bit in a data register or word selected in memory, using any mode except immediate or relative. The selected bit is first inverted and put in the Z condition code as in BTST and is then cleared. For example, BCLR #1,D0 puts the inverse of bit 1 of data register D0 into Z and then clears that bit in D0. If D0 is 3, BCLR D0,ALPHA puts the inverse of bit 3 in the byte at address ALPHA into Z and then clears the bit in ALPHA. Note that the effective address chooses the byte, not the word, in memory. The selected bit for a BCLR instruction may not be in an address register. BSET first tests and then sets any bit in a data register or a memory byte, the bit number specified by an immediate operand or a data register. The bit is tested as in the BTST instruction. BCHG first tests and then complements any bit in a data register or a memory byte, the bit number being specified by an immediate operand or a data register. The bit is tested as in the BTST instruction.

Table 1-6. Edit Instructions.

ASL Dn,Dn or #data>,Dn	LWB
<ea>	W
ASR Dn,Dn or #data>,Dn	LWB
<ea>	W
LSL Dn,Dn or #data>,Dn	LWB
<ea>	W
LSR Dn,Dn or #data>,Dn	LWB
<ea>	W
ROL Dn,Dn or #data>,Dn	LWB
<ea>	W
ROR Dn,Dn or #data>,Dn	LWB
<ea>	W
ROXL Dn,Dn or #data>,Dn	LWB
<ea>	W
ROXR Dn,Dn or #data>,Dn	LWB
<ea>	W
SWAP Dn	L
EXT Dn	B > W or W > L
EXTB Dn	B > L

The fourth group of instructions – the *edit* instructions – rearrange the data bits without changing their meaning. The edit instructions in the 683xx, shown in Table 1-6, can be used to shift either the word in a data register or a word in memory that is selected by any of the addressing modes except immediate and relative. We consider the memory word shift instructions first. The word shifted may be selected by any addressing mode except immediate or relative. A right logical shift LSR ALPHA will shift the bits in the word ALPHA one position to the right, filling a 0 bit into the left-most bit and putting the old right-most bit into the C and X condition code bits. Similarly, a logical left shift LSL ALPHA will shift the bits in the word ALPHA left one position, filling a 0 bit into the right-most bit and putting the old left-most bit into the C and X condition code bits. For both instructions, Z is cleared and N and Z are set as in the MOVE instructions. When shifting the word in a data register, a shift count must be provided by an immediate operand or another data register. LSR #3,D0 shifts the word in D0 right three bit positions, filling with 0s. LSL D0,D1 shifts the word in D1 a number of places which is the number in D0. Data in an address register may not be shifted.

The 683xx has arithmetic left and right shift instructions ASL and ASR, which extend the sign bit on right shift for 2's complement number operations. The ROL and ROR instructions circularly shift left or right a byte, word, or long word. The ROXL and ROXR instructions similarly circularly shift a byte and the X condition code bit as a nine-bit unit, and a word and the X bit as a 17-bit unit, and a long word and the X bit as a 33-bit unit. Shifting though the X bit is useful in multiple byte, word, or long word shifts.

The 683xx has the SWAP instruction to exchange the high and low words in a data register, EXT extends a two's complement byte into a word, or a word into a long word by extending the sign, and an EXTB instruction that extends a byte into a long word.

Table 1-7. Control Instructions.

Unconditional & Subroutine	Conditionals (General)	Conditional 2'S Complement
JMP <ea>	Bcc <label>	BGT <label>
BRA <label>	DBcc Dn,<label>	BGE <label>
BRN <label>	TRAPV	BEQ <label>
NOP	TRAPcc	BLE <label>
JSR <ea>	TRAPcc #<data>	BLT <label>
BSR <label>		
RTS	Conditional	Conditional
RTR	Simple	Unsigned
RTD #<d>		
	BEQ <label>	BHI <label>
LINK An,<d>	BNE <label>	BHS <label>
UNLK An	BMI <label>	BEQ <label>
	BPL <label>	BLS <label>
	BCS <label>	BLO <label>
Interrupt	BCC <label>	
	BVS <label>	
BGND	BVC <label>	
BKPT #<data>		
TRAP #<data>		
RTE		
LPSTOP #<data>		
RESET		

The *control* group of instructions affect the program counter. (See Table 1-7 again.) Next to move instructions, conditional branches are most common, so their performance has a strong impact on a computer's performance. Also, microcomputers with an instruction set missing such operations as floating point arithmetic, multiple word shifts, and high-level language (C) operations, implement these "instructions" as subroutines rather than macros, to save memory space. The machine code produced by a FORTRAN compiler in particular is full of very little else but subroutine calls. Unconditional jumps and related instructions and no-operations are considered here. The conditional branches and subroutine calls are considered in the next section.

The 683xx control instructions are shown in Table 1-7. As noted earlier, the JMP instruction can use word direct (16-bit), pointer, index, or relative addressing mode, but the effective address is put in the program counter. BRA is preferred because it is shorter and uses short relative addressing, which may be preferred for position independent code and thus allows the program to execute properly anywhere in memory. BRA.W and BRA.@1 use 16- and 32-bit offsets, longer than the 8-bit offset used in BRA.S. Conditional branches will be further discussed in the next section. Use the JSR with word direct (16-bit), pointer, index, or relative addressing, or BSR, which allows position independent code. These instructions not only reload the program counter, they also save on the stack its former value, which points to the instruction right below the JSR or BSR and to which one returns at the end of a subroutine using an RTS instruction.

The BGND instruction halts the 683xx and turns over control to an external processor that can examine or change the 683xx registers or memory. BGND is very useful for testing programs as a (software) *breakpoint*. A breakpoint is used to stop a program that is being tested so one can execute a *monitor* program that examines or changes the contents of registers or memory words. The monitor is executed in the external processor rather than the 683xx to reduce side-effects of the monitor on the program being debugged. Being one word long, BGND can be inserted in place of any instruction. Suppose we tried to use a JSR instruction to jump to the monitor running in the 683xx, so we could replace a single-length instruction like MOVE D0,D1, and we also jumped to the instruction just below it from somewhere else. Because the instruction just below must be replaced by the second word of the JMP instruction, and because it also was jumped to from somewhere else, it would jump into the middle of the JMP instruction and do some damage. This is a difficult problem to resolve, especially because a breakpoint is often used in a program that doesn't work right in the first place. So a BGND instruction can be used without fear that some jump instruction might jump into the second word, which might happen with a longer instruction. However, this marvelous trick does not work if the program is in read-only memory, because an instruction in ROM can't be replaced by the BGND instruction.

The 683xx has additional control instructions. BKPT is a special trap instruction used to implement a breakpoint in a debugging monitor running in a 68020 or 683xx, which is designed to work correctly with a memory management chip like the MC68851. The 683xx has a NOP instruction. It does nothing, but it consumes a word in the program and some time in execution. It is useful in real-time programming to insert delays in a program and in debugging machine coded programs to hold a place for an instruction that can be inserted later. The LPSTOP instruction stops execution of the 683xx until an interrupt arrives. It reduces the power needed to run the processor from an already low 300 ma. to a few microamps. A RESET instruction resets all the I/O peripherals attached to the RESET line of the 683xx. Additional instructions for returning from subroutines include RTR, and RTD. The RTR instruction restores the program counter and condition codes (whereas RTS restores only the program counter, and RTE restores the program counter and full status register including condition codes). The RTD instruction restores the program counter and then moves the stack pointer in order to deallocate subroutine parameters passed on the stack. LINK and UNLK are a pair of instructions suited to allocating and deallocating local storage on the stack for subroutines. LINK saves the stack pointer in an address register, where it can be used to get data that had been on the stack, and then adds a displacement (which should be negative) to the stack pointer. UNLK reverses this operation, putting the address register into the stack pointer.

An alternative to the BSR-JSR instruction is the TRAP #*n* instruction, where the immediate operand *n* is 0 to 15. Like a subroutine call, TRAP saves the return address on the stack, but it also pushes the status register in a word on top of it. Then, it loads the program counter from two words stored at memory locations 0x80+n*4 and 0x82+n*4. Note that such an instruction is one word long, but can call up a "subroutine" called a *trap handler,* which may be located anywhere in memory. Up to 16 of the most commonly used "subroutines" can be written as trap handlers, so their calling instructions can be shorter. Hardware interrupts are also serviced by handlers. A handler must end in a return from exception instruction (RTE), which pulls the status register and then the program counter from the stack, rather than the RTS instruction that only pulls the program counter from the stack. This is a common error, in our opinion, and should always be checked when interrupts and TRAPs don't seem to work. TRAP is useful as a convenient subroutine call to execute I/O operations and other complex "instructions," like floating point add. OS-9, discussed in Chapter 10, uses TRAP #0 as an operating system call. The operating system can be modified and moved as long as the words in locations 0x80-0xBF point to its entry addresses. The routines that call the operating system do not have to be modified when it is changed and moved. Conditional traps permit the program to execute a handler handler only if a condition code is tested to be true. These will be discussed in the next section.

The last type of instruction – the *I/O instruction* – is not separately implemented in the Motorola microcomputer instruction sets. Rather, registers in I/O devices are considered to be words in memory. This is called *memory-mapped I/O*. Any instruction that writes a word in memory can therefore be an output instruction, and any that read memory can be an input instruction. Specifically, if an output register is at location 0x1000, an instruction like MOVE D0,0x1000, or MOVE ALPHA,0x1000, or MOVE #0x1234,0x1000 can be used to move data to it from a register, another memory word, or an immediate operand. Moreover, the ADD, SUB, AND, OR, and EOR instructions can have memory locations like an I/O register as the second operand and the result, where the first operand is an immediate operand or a data register. Finally, instructions like LSR 0x1000 and LSL 0x1000 can shift data in an output register. Also, if an input register is at location 0x1000, an instruction like MOVE 0x1000,D0 or MOVE 0x1000,ALPHA can move data from the input register to a data register or memory. CMP 0x1000,D0 or CMP #0x1234,0x1000 can be used to sense the value of an input register word. LSR 0x1000 and LSL 0x1000 can shift bit 0 or bit 15 into the carry bit C. These instructions provide a lot of power to the 683xx for programming I/O devices.

1-2.4 Assembler Language Conditional Branching Techniques

The 683xx conditional branch instructions test one or more condition codes, then branch to another location specified by the displacement if the condition is true, using relative addressing. A set of simple branches can test any one of the condition codes, branching if the bit is set or clear. (See the middle column of Table 1-7.) For example, BCC @1 will branch to location @1 if the carry bit is clear, while BCS @1 will branch there if the carry bit is set. Other branches, in the top right column, test combinations of condition codes (the Z, N, and V bits) that indicate 2's complement inequalities. The branch instructions at the bottom right of Table 1-7 test combinations of the Z and C bits that indicate unsigned inequalities. We will examine these in turn, paying attention to when they should be used in programs.

The middle column of Table 1-7 tests each condition code separately. The BMI and BPL instructions check the sign bit and should be used after MOVE and TST (or equivalent) to check the sign of a 2's complement number that was moved. The BCC and BCS instructions test the carry bit, which indicates an overflow after adding unsigned numbers or the bit shifted out after a shift instruction. The BVS and BVC instruction set tests the V condition code, set if an overflow occurs on adding 2's complement numbers. The Z bit is also tested easily, but because we often compare two numbers to set the Z bit if the two numbers are equal, the instruction is called BEQ and the complementary instruction is BNE. These last two instructions are also used in the 2's complement and unsigned number branches discussed next.

The branches listed in the top right column of Table 1-7 are used after a compare (or subtract) instruction to sense the inequalities of the two numbers being compared as 2's complement numbers. The following program sequence shows an example of the "branch on greater than" instruction (note the comments in lower case on each line):

```
        CMP      ALPHA,D0     compare d0 to alpha
        BGT      @1           branch to 11 if d0 > alpha
        MOVEQ    #0x10,D1     otherwise put 0x10 in d1
        BRA      @2           skip next word
@1      MOVEQ    #0x20,D1     if branched, put 0x20 in d1
@2      ... next instruction
```

If the 2's complement number in data register D0 is greater than the number at location ALPHA, then the branch is taken, putting 0x20 in D1 and going onward. If the 2's complement number in D0 is less than or equal to the number in location ALPHA, the branch instruction does nothing and the next instruction is executed, which puts 0x10 into D1. The next instruction, shown here as BRA @2 effectively skips over the instruction MOVE #0x20,D1. After this instruction is executed, the program following this portion is executed exactly as if the conditional branch had been taken.

The bottom right column of Table 1-7 shows an equivalent set of branches that sense inequalities between unsigned numbers. The program segment just presented could, by putting the instruction BHI in place of BGT, compare the unsigned numbers in D0 against the number at location ALPHA, putting 0x20 in D1 if the register was higher than the word, otherwise putting 0x10 in D1. These instructions test combinations of the C and Z bits and should only be used after a compare or subtract instruction to sense the inequalities of unsigned numbers. To test 2's complement numbers after a compare, use the branches in the top right column of Table 1-7; and to test the sign of numbers after a MOVE or TST, use the BPL or BMI instructions.

As a memory aid in using these conditional branch instructions, remember that signed numbers are greater than or less than and unsigned numbers are higher than or lower than (SGUH). Also, when comparing any register with a word from memory a branch like BGT branches if the register is (greater than) the memory word.

To show the flow of control, *flow charts* are often used. A diamond shows a two-way or a three-way branch on some comparison. Rectangles show program segments. Lines into the top of either show which program segments can precede this one, and lines on the bottom of a rectangle show program segments that follow this segment. If a segment is on another page, its label can be shown in a circle. (See Figure 1-8.)

Flow charts are especially important when complex decision trees are used to analyze data. Because they are also useful in all programs, some believe one must write a flow chart before beginning any part of the program. We believe one should do so when writing more than about a hundred lines of code. In many programs used in interfacing, however, comments on each assembler line of code are more useful than flow charts to document the program well. We will use comments in this book more than flow charts, because most segments we write are rather short. Nevertheless, we encourage the reader to write flow charts for longer programs and for short programs that implement complex decision trees.

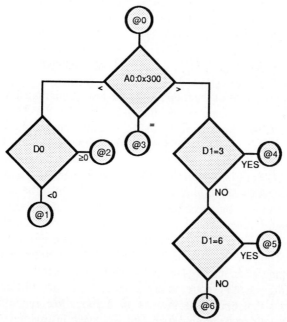

Figure 1-8. Flow Chart of a Decision Tree.

An important use of conditional branches is the *decision tree*. We may need a rather complex set of tests to determine what to do next. For example, consider a decision tree described in Figure 1-8. If we want to go to location @1 when address register A0 is less than 0x300 and data register D0 is negative, to @2 when A0 is less than 0x300 and A is positive, to @3 when A0 is 0x300, to @4 when A0 is greater than

0x300 and data register D1 is 3, to @5 when A0 is greater than 0x300 and B is 6, and to @6 when A0 is greater than 0x300 and B is neither 3 nor 6, use the following:

@0	CMP	#0x300,A0	check a0 against 0x300
	BEQ	@3	if equal, go to @3
	BMI	@7	if less, test d1
	CMP	#3,D1	it is positive; if d1 is 3
	BEQ	@4	go to @4
	CMP	#6,D1	see if it is 6
	BEQ	@5	if so, go to @5
	BRA	@6	otherwise go to @6
@7	CMP	#0,D0	a0 is negative; test d0
	BMI	@1	if a negative, go to @1
	BRA	@2	otherwise, a0 is more, go to @2

Conditional branches are also used in *DO-loops*. A DO-loop repeats a given program segment a given number, say *n*, times. Suppose you want to move 128 words from one memory area to another, and that address register A0 points to the lowest address of the area the words are moved from, while A1 points to the lowest address of the area the words are moved to.

	MOVE	#128,D0	d0 is used as a counter
@0	MOVE	(A0)+,(A1)+	get a word from first to second area
	SUB	#1,D0	count down
	BNE	@0	loop 128 times

Note that the first execution of the loop moves the lowest-addressed word from the first to the second area and increments both pointer registers. The SUB #1,D0 instruction will change data register D0 from 0x80 to 0x7F. Because the result is not 0, the BNE instruction will effect a branch to location @1, which repeats the loop. Note that the loop is executed 0x80 times if 0x80 is put into the data register used as a counter. Instructions like MOVE #128,D0 are *loop initialization* program segments, and instructions like SUB #1,D0 and BNE @1 are *loop control* program segments. The pair of initialization and control instructions in the preceding example are used often, because a data register is useful as a counter. Alternatively, an address register, because it is a 16-bit register, can be used as a word in memory, if the data registers are in heavy use. Further, the loop control can use a compare instruction, like CMP #END,A0, to test whether the address register stops looping when the register points to a final address.

When writing machine code, many programmers have difficulty with relative branch instructions that branch backwards in a loop. We recommend using 16's complement arithmetic to determine the negative branch instruction displacement. The 16's complement is to hexadecimal numbers as the 2's complement is to binary numbers. To illustrate this technique, the preceding program is next listed in machine code. The program begins at location 0x200, and the addresses of each word are shown on the left with the value shown on the right in each line. All numbers are in hexadecimal.

200	303C
202	0080
204	32D8
206	5340
208	66xx

The displacement used in the branch instruction, the last instruction in the program – shown as xx – can be determined as follows. When the branch is executed, the program counter has the value 0x20A, and we want to jump back to location 0x204. The difference, 0x20A - 0x204, is 0x06, so the displacement should be -0x06. A safe way to calculate the displacement is to convert to binary, negate, then convert to hexadecimal. 0x06 is 00000110, so the 2's complement negative is 11111010. In hexadecimal, this is 0xFA. That is not hard to see, but binary arithmetic gets rather tedious. A faster way takes the *sixteen's complement* of the hexadecimal number. Just subtract each digit from 0xF (15), digit by digit, then add 1 to the whole thing. -0x06 is then (0xF-0),(0xF-6) + 1 or 0xF9 + 1, which is 0xFA. That's pretty easy, isn't it!

Loop control is sufficiently important that a special instruction, DBcc, is included specially for that purpose. The DBRA instruction, a special case, is described first. The best way to execute a loop, accounting for the possibility that the loop count which specified the number of times the loop is to be executed may be 0, is shown in Figure 1-9. This "Do-While" construct tests the loop count before the loop is executed even once, and if it is zero, the loop is not executed. It is necessary to branch to the end of the loop to the loop control instruction, which may re-execute the loop if the count was not zero before it was executed. The loop count kept in a data register such as D0 is identified along with the 16-bit relative branch address like @1 in an instruction such as DBRA D0,@1. The instruction tests the count first; if zero, execution falls through to the instruction below it, otherwise it decrements the count and branches to the labeled instruction.

The use of the DBRA instruction is illustrated by rewriting the last example using it. Observe that the loop itself has fewer instructions and executes faster than the last example.

```
        MOVE    #128,D0      d0 is used as a counter
        BRA     @2           go to loop test
@1      MOVE    (A0)+,(A1)+   get a word from first to second area
@2      DBRA    D0,@1        loop 128 times
```

If the loop count may never be zero upon entering the loop, the count can be reduced by one before entering the loop and the loop can be entered at the top, as in

```
        MOVEQ   #127,D0      note that moveq can be used
@1      MOVE    (A0)+,(A1)+   get a word from first to second area
        DBRA    D0,@1        loop 128 times
```

In the 683xx, a tight loop involving a DBRA instruction and one single word instruction like MOVE (A0)+,(A1)+ will be stored inside the controller and not fetched from memory after first being read. Therefore it executes substantially faster than any other loop. This mechanism can be used to clear or move memory or search for a word in memory.

Section 1-2   The 68332 Instruction Set

41

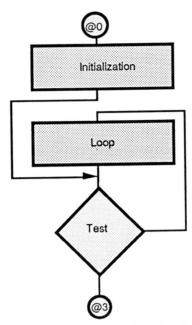

Figure 1-9. Flow Chart of the DBcc Loop.

The DBRA instruction is actually a special case of the more general DBcc instruction in which the condition is never true. In the general case of the instruction, any condition that can be tested by the Bcc instruction can be tested by DBcc. If that condition is true, the looping stops before the loop counter reaches zero at the beginning of the DBcc instruction, and the instruction below DBcc is executed. A NOP is put there just to put the label on something; you should put the next useful instruction below the loop in place of it. For instance, DBCC D0,@1 is equivalent to

```
          BCC       @2
          DBRA      D0,@1
@2        NOP
```

Two other instructions use the condition codes in a manner similar to the conditional branch. TRAPcc traps to an address at location 0x1c if the condition cc is true; it permits an exception trap to occur on any condition code test used in Bcc instructions. For example TRAPEQ will trap if Z is set. TRAPV is a special case inherited to maintain upward compatibility from the 68000, which did not have TRAPcc. Scc, introduced with the MOVE class instructions, puts all 1s into a byte if the condition is true, or else, it clears the byte. It is used to save a condition code result in memory.

1-2.5 Assembler Language Subroutine Techniques

We now consider the programming of subroutines and the methods of handling variables and parameters in them. These assembler language programming issues will be useful in understanding the techniques used by the C compiler and also will better enable you to write short assembly language programs that call C procedures or are called by C procedures.

Chapter 1 – Microcomputer Architecture

Program segments may have multiple entry points and multiple exit points. (See Figure 1-10.) Such a program segment occurs anywhere in a program, usually a part written on consecutive lines. An *entry point* is any instruction that may be executed after an instruction not in the program segment, and an *exit point* is any instruction that may be followed by an instruction not in the program segment. A program segment may or may not be a subroutine; if so, this discussion also applies to subroutines.

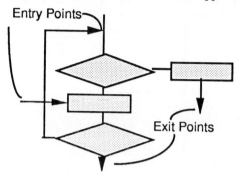

Figure 1-10. A Program Segment.

One problem in writing good programs is the handling of variables. Variables used in programs are local or global. *Global variables* are variables shared by two or more program segments. For example, several program segments may be written to handle a floppy disk, and global variables may be used to keep track of the floppy disk's status, so all program segments can access those variables. Only variables shared by several routines, which are to be located independent of the order of calling subroutines, are global variables. *Local variables* are temporary variables used only by one program segment. A local variable is dynamic if, each time the subroutine is called, the variable is allocated but not initialized. In the 683xx, dynamic local variables should be stored on the stack, for reasons which will be given at the end of this discussion.

A convention that greatly aids an assembly language program's clarity is this:

1. Determine what a program segment will be. Usually it is a subroutine.

2. Determine what variables in the program segment are local. These are temporary variables used in the program segment and not anywhere else.

3. On *each* entry point to the program segment, allocate *all* the local variables at once and in the same way on each entry point; and on *each* exit point, deallocate *all* the local variables in the same way, as shown next. Do *not* push or pull anything on the stack in the rest of the program segment (only nesting is permitted, as discussed later).

In some block-structured languages like ALGOL and PASCAL the program blocks are written so the inner, lower-level blocks can access local variables of outer blocks, using the dynamic (run-time) calling sequence. This can also be done in assembler language programs. Within inner program segments, you can access dynamic local variables of outer program segments, if you know where they are located. You can locate them by knowing how many additional bytes have been allocated on the stack because the outer segment allocated the variable you access in the inner segment, and then adding this number to the offset you used, thus getting the variable in the outer program segment. Figure 1-11 shows the main idea. The local variable of an outer segment is accessed in an inner segment by using an offset equal to the offset used in the outer segment plus the number of bytes that have been allocated since the outer segment. (We assume the inner segment is not a subroutine, so there is no return address on the stack.)

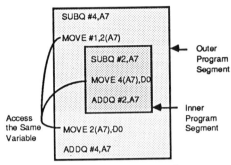

Figure 1-11. Nested Program Segments.

An alternative to adding offsets of variables to sizes of local storage allocated in an inner program segment is to save a copy of the stack pointer in another register just before the inner segment is entered, and use the saved register (called a *link register*) in addresses in place of the stack register. For example, before the dark gray area in Figure 1-11, put MOVE A7,A0. Then inside the segment, the variable can be accessed using MOVE 2(A0),D0 rather than MOVE 4(A7),D0. The LINK instruction not only sets up a link register but saves the former value, and UNLK restores the saved value. Thus, a segment can have an inner segment, and that can have an inner segment, and the LINK instruction at the beginning of each segment and UNLK at the end of each segment will establish a link register to the next outer segment; it is useful for nesting of subroutines.

In the 683xx, the use of the stack to store local variables is usually recommended. Also, the programs become reentrant, so they can – as all such programs can – be used in interrupt handlers. You may never know when a routine may have to be used in a handler, so if it is already reentrant, you won't need to rewrite it. For example, we once wrote a text editor in which all the code was in some interrupt handler or another and the code in the main program did nothing. Also, you may use a routine that is not reentrant in a handler and find out that the resulting program works most of the time but fails sometime for no apparent reason – because an interrupt happened to occur while a non-reentrant program segment, being used by the handler, was being executed.

We now consider implementation details of the 683xx's subroutine call arguments. The passing of arguments is implemented by means of registers, global variables, a stack, an argument list, or a table. In discussing these techniques, we'll be concerned with 683xx features useful in carrying them out.

We first illustrate passing arguments in registers. A call to subroutine POWER is coded in assembler – first the calling routine, then the subroutine – as follows:

```
MOVE      H,D0
MOVE      #3,D1
BSR   POWER
MOVE      D0,M
```

Chapter 1 – Microcomputer Architecture

```
POWER: MOVEM  D0-D1,-(A7)
        MOVE      #1,D0        use D0 to hold power; init to 1
@1      SUBQ#1,2(A7)           decrement saved D1
        BLT  @2
        MULU      0(A7),D0     multiply saved D0
        BRA  @1
@2      ADDQ      #4,A7        balance the stack
        RTS
```

An alphanumeric label followed by a colon is used as a label for a subroutine. A0 to A6, and D0 to D7 registers can serve to hold a subroutine's arguments or results. While the address registers naturally lend themselves to passing addresses, these can be transferred to or exchanged with a data register using MOVE instructions, so they can also be used to pass parameters by value. Similarly, data registers can be used to pass parameters by name. However, it is clearly easier to use data registers for call by value and address registers for call by name parameters. Also, the carry bit in the condition code register can be used to pass a 1-bit result that can be used in instructions like BCC and BCS. If a subroutine does not have many arguments, this is usually the way to pass them that is easy to understand and use.

An argument can be put in a global variable, and then the subroutine can find the argument there. Results can be passed in the other direction through global variables. This is like supplying arguments through FORTRAN COMMON. It is too easy to forget to supply one of the critical arguments, and it is easy to use the same location inadvertently to supply an argument to a subroutine that calls another, and for that subroutine to supply an argument to the subroutine that it calls. Also, arguments for one subroutine can accidentally get mixed up with arguments in another subroutine. To diagram such a situation, we use coathanger diagrams. (See Figure 1-12.) Each horizontal row represents the execution of a routine or subroutine, and the calling and returning points are shown as breaks in the line. If we use a global variable like ARG1 in the first subroutine after another subroutine (perhaps several levels down) that also uses the variable ARG1 is called, then the first subroutine will have the wrong value in ARG1 when it uses ARG1. Finally, such a technique is not reentrant. Global variables have to be used to pass arguments in very small computers like the 6805. There is no way to get to the stack or the return address to use the techniques described next. However, if either of these paths is available in the architecture, global variables should be avoided. We recommend against passing arguments in global variables.

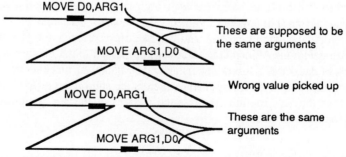

Figure 1-12. Coathanger Diagram Showing a Bug Using Global Variables.

The stack provides a completely general mechanism for passing arguments. Suppose the argument X for the subroutine SIN(X) is in D0. To call the subroutine SIN, execute the following program segment:

```
MOVE D0,-(A7)
BSR SIN
```

Inside the subroutine, we can get the value of the argument, but the obvious way will not work. Do *not* execute the instruction

```
MOVE (A7)+,D0
```

This will pull the high word of the return address into D0, rather than the argument you want. However, because the argument is the third word from the top of the stack, it can be picked up as follows:

```
MOVE 4(A7),D0
```

When the subroutine is finished, the RTS instruction is used to pull the two-word return address from the stack. But we are not through. The argument is still on top of the stack. If the calling routine is itself a subroutine, when it executes its RTS instruction, it will pull the argument from the stack into the program counter and jump to some dangerous place. After the subroutine has returned to the calling routine, the calling routine must remove the argument (balance the stack). To delete it, you could use a MOVE (A7)+,D0 instruction, or, if the argument is no longer needed, an ADDQ #2,A7 instruction. You should recognize this as the special nested program segment case discussed in the last section, whereby the subroutine is (dynamically) executed within the small program segment that puts the arguments on the stack for the subroutine, using the same rules to find variables on the stack for subroutines as were used in inner and outer program segments. You can also think of this as providing "holes on the stack" through which to pass the arguments.

The main disadvantage of passing arguments in registers is that that technique is not completely general. Most high-level languages need a completely general technique because compilers are usually not smart enough to pass parameters some ways to some subroutines and other ways to other subroutines. C uses the stack to pass all arguments except a result of a function. Therefore, if you want to *use* a subroutine that was *written* to be called by a high-level language routine such as a C procedure or you want to *write* a subroutine that can be *called* by a high-level language routine such as a C procedure, you may have to pass the arguments on the stack. Any number of arguments can be pushed onto the stack this way, and can be accessed inside the subroutine using index addressing with the A7 register. Values can be passed in the manner described, as can addresses of data or of a subroutine using call by name. As an example of the latter, the *plot* subroutine may need an argument which is the subroutine of the function to be plotted, such as the SIN routine. To pass the address of the *sin* subroutine, we can execute this routine:

```
LEA       SIN(PC),A0
MOVE      A0,-(A7)
BSR  PLOT
```

Inside the *plot* subroutine, to call the *sin* subroutine, the instruction

```
MOVE      4(A7),A0
JSR   0(A0)
```

can be used. Note that after the *plot* subroutine returns to the calling routine, the argument must be deleted from the stack; an ADDQ #2,A7 instruction can be used.

Results can also be returned on the stack, but again the obvious way doesn't work. If, inside the subroutine, you push a result on the stack, then return and expect to pull it from the stack, the return instruction RTS will pull the result before you can, which will effect a jump to some unknown place. Rather, a "hole" for the result is inserted on the stack before the subroutine is called; the result can be put in the hole with a technique that is the reverse of the one used to pass arguments to the subroutine. Again, this is just a special case of the inner and outer program segment access mechanism described in the last section. The calling routine can be written

```
SUBQ#2,A7
BSR   SIN
MOVE (A7)+,D0
```

And the subroutine can put the result in the "hole" by executing the instructions

```
MOVE D0,4(A7)
```

Note that any number of results can be passed this way. Before the subroutine is called, a "hole" must be created for each result, and, to balance the stack after the subroutine has returned to the calling routine, each result must be pulled from the stack (or deleted). Thus, the stack is a completely general technique for passing arguments and results.

If a second stack is used, not the one used to save the return address, then arguments can be pushed on that stack by the calling routine and pulled by the subroutine, without fear of messing up the return addresses or having them in the way.

For the following mechanism we introduce the assembler directive *DC (define constant)*. DC 0x1234 simply puts the value 1234 into the program storage area. DC.B will insert an 8-bit constant, DC.W will insert a 16-bit constant, and DC.L will insert a 32-bit constant into memory. If A is a label, DC.L A will put the 32-bit address of A into memory. Whereas in assemblers it is used to supply constant or pre-initialized data, compilers and compiler-embedded assemblers do not use this mechanism for data. However, it is used to insert special instruction code words and in-line arguments as shown below.

The next technique for passing arguments is the *argument list*. It is almost as general as the stack technique, and is the most commonly used for some high-level language subroutines. A high-level language subroutine call, like the FORTRAN statement

```
CALL SUB (A,B,C)
```

is most efficiently implemented in assembler language as the following code:

```
            BSR   SUB
            DC.L A
            DC.L B
            DC.L C
```

Note that the microprocessor, when it executes the BSR instruction, saves what it thinks is the return address, which is actually the 32-bit address of the word below the BSR instruction. That turns out to be fortuitous. It helps us get to the argument list, which is the list of addresses stored below the BSR. To put the value of the word at address C into D1 inside the subroutine, execute the following program segment:

```
     MOVE.L    0(A7),A0 get the address of the argument list in a0
     MOVE.L    8(A0),A1 get the third argument into a1
     MOVE      0(A1),D1 get the value of C into d1
```

Note that once one of the address registers, like A0, points to the argument list, any argument can easily be obtained by repeated use of index addressing. Constant arguments can be passed in an in-line argument list, even if it is in ROM. Also variable arguments can be passed this way in ROM, if their addresses are constants and are put in the list. Note that simple execution of RTS will not work if an argument list is used, because the first argument will be executed as an instruction. Rather, if the argument list is 12 bytes long, we can execute the following program segment rather than the RTS:

```
     MOVE   (A7)+,A0   pop the "return address"
     JMP    12(A1)     add 12 to it, then put it into the program counter
```

We reiterate the limitations of passing arguments by value in an in-line argument list. What makes an in-line argument list only *almost* completely general is that, especially in single-chip and small microcomputers, the program may be stored in read-only memory so it doesn't have to be loaded each time power is turned on. This means that the argument list, in read-only memory, cannot be changed. So if arguments are to be called by value, they cannot be placed in the argument list unless they are the same each time the subroutine is called from that place. That condition sometimes occurs with the TRAP #n "subroutine" call. Although not completely general, it is faster than the stack approach because the calling routine does not have to set up and delete the arguments. It can also be used by subroutines called by high-level language programs. Moreover, it can pass the relative address of a local variable on the stack, as long as this address is added to the stack pointer value when it is used, thus giving a reentrant capability to the calling program that is absent if the address is a global address.

A final technique is to pass, using an address register, the address of a list of addresses or data into the subroutine. The contents of the list can be essentially the same as the argument list just described, but because the list need not be in ROM, its elements can be modified and replaced with the results before the subroutine is called. The code to do this is essentially the same as for in-line argument lists, except the address of the table must be loaded into the address register before the call is made to the subroutine, and the subroutine need not extract the return address from the stack, nor need it branch around the argument list. Passing the address of a list is often used in subroutines that handle disks, because the same list can be used as an argument for different disk handling subroutines that access the same disk and different lists can be passed through those subroutines to handle different disks. This technique is often used in operating systems for "low-level access" to disks and other similar complex I/O devices.

The 683xx is a sophisticated computer with rich instruction and addressing modes. We believe these instruction sets and addressing modes are not all that difficult to learn, but learning them well takes time, and that time is needed to study interfacing. A different course on assembler language, Area 3 in the IEEE Curriculum Committee Guidelines, should teach assembler language principles and practices. If that course is a prerequisite for one that uses this book, then the student is well prepared to use better assembler language in the problems at the end of the chapter and the experiments in the laboratory accompanying this course. If not, however, the description of the instruction set in this chapter is adequate preparation for the programming of I/O devices using C. You should be able to read the disassembled code put by the C compiler into memory to verify its correct implementation of what was intended, and to insert some assembler language code into a C program when C is unable to do that for you.

1-3 The 68330/331/332/340 Organizations

In this section, we introduce the organization (block diagram) of Motorola's business card computers (BCCs). One reason for this introduction is to provide a background of definitions and concepts for later chapters. A second reason is that, if a laboratory is used with a class that uses this book, sufficient information is provided to begin the laboratory at this point. The M68332, designed first, is shown first.

1-3.1 The M68332 BCC

The organization of the M68332 Business Card Computer (BCC) is shown in Figure 1-13. The BCC board contains the MC68332 chip and RAM and ROM on a 16-bit data and 24-bit address bus, along with a chip that converts serial signals to those needed by the RS232 interface, to connect a terminal or microcomputer to the board. The MC68332 chip contains within it a small RAM, a *System Integration Module* (SIM), a *Time Processing Unit* (TPU), a *Queued Serial Module* (QSM), and a *Background Debug Module* (BDM). The SIM has in it address decoders, discussed in Chapter 3, and parallel ports, discussed in Chapter 4. The QSM has in it a serial I/O interface called the *Queued Serial Peripheral Interface* (QSPI) discussed in Chapter 4 and an RS232-style *Serial Communication Interface* (SCI) discussed in Chapter 9. The TPU is used to generate and measure pulses and square waves. It will be discussed in Chapter 7. In addition, the M68332 has a Background Debug Module (BDM) that can be connected to a Debug Interface (Di) board. The 6811 single-chip microcomputer on the Di board can be connected to a microcomputer like the Macintosh, and has a comparator module that can observe the M68332 address bus.

The debug system uses the BDM, Di board, and Macintosh or equivalent. We use the Macintosh, running the THINK C ™ compiler, to download and debug programs in the M68332 board. Because the M68332 and Macintosh have nearly identical architectures, it is easy to write C and assembler language programs on the Macintosh, debug them there, and then copy an exact bit-image of the program in the Macintosh into the M68332 memory. The M68332 enters the background mode essentially when the M68332 executes a BGND instruction, or when the Di board asserts a signal to put the M68332 into background mode. The BGND instruction has been described as a *software breakpoint* in this chapter. In background mode, the Di board then can shift commands and data into and out of the M68332 in a manner similar to "scan design" used to trouble-shoot large computers. The Di board can read or modify registers or memory, and start the M68332. The Di board also has a comparator that can check the M68332 address bus for up to four addresses. When an address matches an address stored in the comparator, the Di board asserts a signal to put the M68332 into background mode. Because this matching address can be the address of an instruction or of data, this *hardware breakpoint* can monitor either the program or the data it uses. The 6811 processor, upon a request (*abort* command) from the Macintosh, can also assert this signal. Because the debugging program resides in the 6811 and the Macintosh and not in the M68332, we say the debugger is non-intrusive.

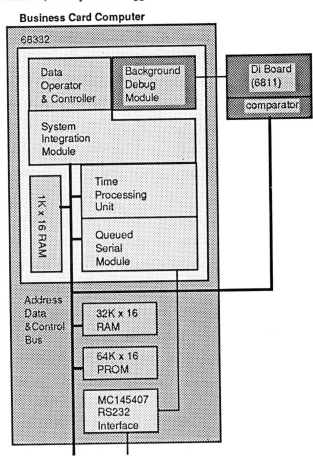

Figure 1-13. The Organization of the M68332 BCC.

The BCC modules that are visible to the programmer are shown in the memory map, Figure 1-14a. The RAM is located at low memory and the I/O devices are located at high memory (although I/O can be put in another place as an alternative). The PROM is put at the top 128 Kbyte block of the bottom 1 Mbyte block of memory (at 0x60000 to 0x7ffff) to make it correctly respond to a decoder in the SIM after reset. The 1K x 16 RAM inside the M68332 can be put anywhere in memory that does not conflict with other devices.

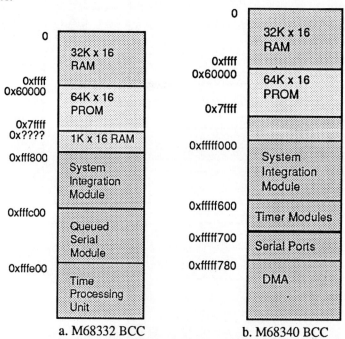

a. M68332 BCC   b. M68340 BCC

Figure 1-14. BCC Memory maps.

1-3.2 The M68340 BCC

The organization of the M68340 Business Card Computer (BCC) is shown in Figure 1-15. The BCC board contains the MC68340 chip and RAM and ROM on a 16-bit data and 32-bit address bus, a chip that converts serial signals to those needed by the RS232 interface, along with a PAL and a NAND gate chip for decoding addresses. The MC68340 chip contains within it a *System Integration Module* (SIM), a *Timer module* (TM), two *UART Serial I/O channels* (DUART), two *Direct Memory Access modules* (DMA), and a *Background Debug Module* (BDM). The M68340 SIM has in it address decoders, discussed in Chapter 3, and parallel ports, discussed in Chapter 4, which are similar to but different from the M68332 address decoders and parallel ports. The M68340 DMA is discussed in Chapter 5. The timer module, TM, is used to generate and measure pulses and square waves. It will be discussed in Chapter 8. The DUART has in it two serial RS232-style interfaces discussed in Chapter 9. In addition, the M68340 has a Background Debug Module (BDM) identical to the 68332's BDM. The debug system uses the BDM, Di board, and Macintosh or equivalent are used in the same way as they are used in the 68332 BCC.

The programmer visible BCC modules are shown in the memory map, Figure 1-14b. The RAM is located at low memory and the I/O devices are located at high memory (although I/O can be put in another place as an alternative). The PROM is put at the same location as it is in the 68332 BCC (at 0x60000 to 0x7ffff) for compatibility.

Business Card Computer

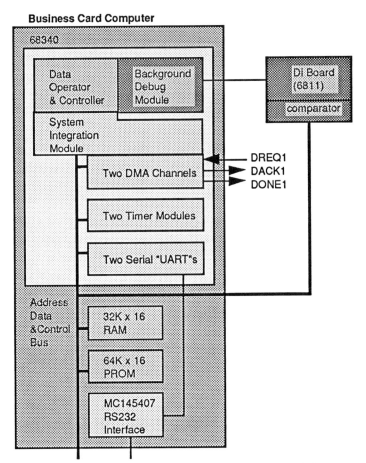

Figure 1-15. The Organization of the M68340 BCC.

1-3.3 The M68330 and M68331

The M68330 is the simplest implementation of the 683xx. It has only the 683xx processor, with a 16-bit data and 32-bit address bus, and the 68340 SIM and BDM. The M68331 is another simple implementation of the 683xx. It has the 683xx processor, with a 16-bit data and 24-bit address bus, and the 68332 SIM, QSM and BDM, but has a simple 6811-style timer in place of the 68332 TPU. Motorola produces a BCC with the 68331 on it, but it is sufficiently similar to that of the 68332 that we do not explicitly cover it in this book, and as of this printing, Motorola has no BCC for the 68330, because it is a strict subset of the 68340. Other implementations of the 683xx can be expected in the future, and a well-heeled user can have special I/O devices integrated into the chip with the 683xx processor and peripherals in the M68331/M68332/M68340.

We will be examining the 68332 and 68340 BCC modules in later chapters. With this brief introduction, we can discuss relationships between them as we study them.

1-4 Conclusions

In this chapter, we have surveyed the background in architecture needed for microcomputer interfacing. The first section covered bare essentials about von Neumann computers, instructions and what they do, and microcomputers. You will find this background helpful as you begin to learn precisely what happens in an interface.

The middle section covered addressing modes and instructions that you may expect in any microcomputer, discussing those in a 683xx in more detail. The general comments there should help if you want to learn about another machine. And the 683xx comments should help you read the examples and do some of the experiments suggested in the book. Some elementary programming techniques, such as decision trees and DO-loops, were also presented. While you probably know these techniques, it is essential to ensure that all readers have the basic information for understanding what follows.

The last section discussed the full 683xx instruction sets. The reader may skip these sections without losing any background for the rest of this book. These sections are written for the advanced reader who wishes to utilize the full capabilities of the 683xx.

If you found any section difficult, we can recommend additional readings. There are plenty of fine books on computer architecture. You may have one already. We encourage you to reread it to reinforce the ideas it presents, rather than read several new ones superficially. But if you haven't read one yet, we recommend *Introduction to Computer Organization and Data Structures,* by H. Stone, McGraw-Hill Inc, 1972 or any of Stone's later books, because he covers architecture and data structures together. Wakerly's *Microcomputer Architecture and Programming - the 68000 Family,* Wiley, 1989, is an excellent coverage of assembler language programming, and also covers some I/O interfacing and operating systems topics that we cover later. Instruction formats, timing and setting of condition codes can be obtained from the *CPU32 Reference Manual (CPU32RM/AD)* Motorola Inc., 1989.

The Business card Computer (BCC) Board is quite suitable for experiments on the 683xx. Motorola supplies a debugger DEBUG332 for this board. However, we prefer to use a more convenient text editor and downloader with the board. A Macintosh running the *THINK C* program can be augmented with a down-loader, so that files created by its assembler or C compiler can be sent to the board. Appendix A gives a program that can be used to download assembler language and C programs written on the Macintosh into the BCC Board.

Because we are using the 683xx architecture and M68330/M68331/M68332/M68340 realizations solely as tools for teaching interfacing principles, we do not attempt to show you every feature of the 683xx. Consult Motorola Data Sheets for information about alternative uses of this chip.

Do You Know These Terms?

At chapter's end, you should be able to use these terms defined in this chapter.
If you do not recognize them, we suggest that you look them up in the index.

von Neumann computer, architecture, organization, implementation, realization, upward compatible, primary memory, data operator, controller, input/output, access, random access memory, bit, byte, word, fetch, program counter, register, address register, stack pointer, data register, binary code, hexadecimal notation, machine-coded instruction, mnemonic, assembler, assembler language, move instruction, load a register, recall data, effective address, (word) direct, absolute addressing, symbolic address, label, store, memorize, bug, program sequence, jump, branch, subroutine, jump to subroutine, (hardware or I/O) interrupt, handle an interrupt, interrupt handler or device handler, reentrant, recursion, status register, machine state, addressing mode, microinstruction, control memory, order, data transfer, read-only memory, microprogramming, fetch-execute cycle, microcycle, memory cycle, memory clock, fetch cycle, decode cycle, address calculation, recall cycle, execute cycle, memorize cycle, latency time, macro, reduced instruction set computer, benchmark, static efficiency, dynamic efficiency, integrated circuit die, chip, LSI, dual in-line package, surface mount carrier, microprocessor, microcomputer, printed circuit card, motherboard, single-chip microcomputer, personal computer, aligned, memory space, function code, bit, don't care, (long) direct addressing, displacement, word, direct, implied addressing, register addressing, immediate addressing, impure coding, pointer addressing, index addressing, autoincrement addressing, autodecrement addressing, stack pointer, stack buffer, stack, push, pull, stack overflow, stack underflow, balanced stack, nested subroutine, coathanger diagram, return from interrupt, zero-suppressed register, short relative addressing, branch, position independence, move, condition code, zero, negative, carry, overflow, extend carry, register mask, register list, compare instruction, logical instruction, edit instruction, control instruction, software breakpoint, monitor, trap handler, I/O instruction, memory-mapped I/O, flow chart, decision tree, do-loop, loop initialization, loop control, 16's complement, entry point, exit point, global variable, local variable, link register, dc (define constant), argument list, system integration module, time processing unit, queued serial module, background debug module, queued serial peripheral interface, serial communication interface, software breakpoint, hardware breakpoint, abort.

2

Programming Microcomputers

We now consider programming techniques used in I/O interfacing. The interface designer must know a lot about them. As the industry matures, the problems of matching voltage levels and timing requirements, discussed in the next chapter, are being solved by better-designed chips, but the chips are getting more complex, requiring interface designers to write more software to control them.

The state-of-the-art M68330/M68331/M68332/M68340 clearly illustrate the need for programming I/O devices in a high-level language, and for programming them in object-oriented languages. The fifty-odd I/O ports in the 68332 SIM and its two dozen QSM and TPU ports will overload many assembler language programmers. But the 64K byte RAM memory in the BCC is large enough to support high-level language programs. Also, object-oriented features like modularity, information hiding, and inheritance will further simplify the task of controlling 683xx systems.

This book develops object-oriented C interfacing techniques. Chapter 1, describing the architecture of a microcomputer, has served well to introduce assembler language, although a bit more will be done in this chapter. We introduce C in this chapter. The simplest C programming constructs are introduced in the first section. Data structure handling is briefly covered in the next section. Programming styles including the writing of structured, modular, and object-oriented programming will be introduced in the last section. Subroutines will be further studied as an introduction to programming style. While this introduction is very elementary and rather incomplete, it is adequate for the discussion of interfacing in this text. Clearly, these concepts must be well understood before we discuss and design those interfaces.

For this chapter, the reader should have programmed in some high-level language. From it, he or she should learn general fundamentals of object-oriented programming in C to become capable of writing and debugging tens of statements with little difficulty, and should learn practices specifically applicable to the M68330/M68331/M68332/M68340 microprocessor. If you have covered this material in other courses or absorbed it from experience this chapter should bring it all together. You may pick up the material just by reading this condensed version. Others should get an idea of the amount of background needed to read the rest of the book. See the bibliography in Section 2.4 for additional reading.

2-1 Introduction to C

I/O interfacing has long been done in assembler language. A slightly different mode of programming is to write the original program in a high-level language like C. Experience has shown that the average programmer can write something like ten lines of (debugged and documented) code per day, whether the language is assembler or higher level. But a line of high-level language code produces about six to 20 useful lines of assembler language code, so if the program is originally written in a high-level language and later translated into assembler language, we might become six to 20 times more efficient. However, assembler language code produced by a high-level language is significantly less statically and dynamically efficient, and somewhat less precise, than the best code produced by writing in assembler language, because it generates unnecessary code. Thus in small microcomputers like the 6811, after a high-level language program is written, it may be converted first to assembler language, where it is tidied up, after which the assembler language program is assembled into machine code. As a bonus, the original high-level language can be used to provide comments to the assembler language program. In larger microcomputer systems like the 683xx-based BCC, C can often control the device without being converted to assembler language. This has the advantage of being easier to maintain, because changes in a C program do not have to be manually translated into and optimized in assembler language. Or finally, a small amount of assembler language, the part actually accessing the I/O device, can be embedded in a larger C program. This approach has the advantage of generally being easy to maintain – because most of the program is implemented in C – and yet efficient and precise in small sections where the I/O device is accessed.

We introduce C language rudiments to use the C language as a documentation tool, to access I/O registers in C, or to write the original program in C and translate it to assembler language. We will explain the basic form of a C *procedure*, the simple and the special numeric operators, conditional expression operators, conditional and loop statements, functions, and "*pigeon C*" – useful in documentation. However, we do not intend to give all the rules of C that you need to write good programs.

A C program consists of one or more procedures, of which the first to be executed is called *main*, and the others "subroutines." All the procedures, including *main*, are written as follows:

declaration of global variable;
declaration of global variable;

procedure_name(parameter_1,Parameter_2,....)
declaration of parameter_1;
declaration of parameter_2;

{

    declaration of local variable;
    declaration of local variable;

    statement;
    statement;

}

Each *declaration of a parameter or a variable* and each statement ends in a semicolon (;), and more than one of these can be put on the same line. Carriage returns and spaces (except in names and numbers) are not significant in C programs and can be used to improve readability. The periods (.) in the example do not appear in C programs, but are meant here to denote that one or more declaration or statement may appear.

Parameters and variables used in the 683xx are usually 8-bit (*char*), 16-bit (*int*), or 32-bit (*long*) signed integer types. They can be declared unsigned by putting the word *unsigned* in front of *char, int*, or *long*. More than one variable can be put in a declaration; the variables are separated by commas (,). A vector having *n* elements is denoted by the name and square brackets around the number of elements *n*, and the elements are numbered 0 to *n*-1. For example, the declaration *int a,b[10];* shows two variables, a scalar variable *a* and a vector *b* with ten elements. Variables declared outside the procedure (e.g., before the line with *procedure-name*) are global, and those declared within a procedure (e.g., between the curly brackets after *procedure-name* "{" and "}") are local. Parameters will be discussed in Section 2-4.1. A *caste* redefines a value's type. A caste is put in parentheses before the value. If *i* is an integer, *(char)i* is a character.

Table 2-1. Conventional C Operators Used in Expressions.

=	make the left side equal to the expression on its right
+	add
-	subtract
*	multiply
/	divide
%	modulus (remainder after division)
&	logical bit-by-bit AND
|	logical bit-by-bit OR
~	logical bit-by-bit negation

Statements may be algebraic expressions that generate assembler language instructions to execute the procedure's activities. A *statement* may be replaced by a sequence of statements within a pair of curly brackets "{" and "}". This will be useful in conditional and loop statements discussed soon. Operators used in statements include addition, subtraction, multiplication, and division, and a number of very useful operators that convert efficiently to assembler language instructions or program segments. Table 2-1 shows the conventional C operators that we will use in this book. Although they are not all necessary, we use a lot of parentheses so we will not have to learn the precedence rules of C grammar. We try to avoid programs that cross over page boundaries, so we compact the code, and we put several statements on the same line if they are semantically related, such as a procedure name, the declaration of its arguments, and the opening bracket, or statements to initialize an I/O register. The following simple C procedure *fun* has (signed) 16-bit input parameter *a* and 32-bit local variable *b;* it puts 1 into *b* and then the *a+b* th element of the ten-element unsigned global 8-bit vector *d* into 8-bit unsigned global *c*.

```
unsigned char c,d[10];
fun(a) int a; {
    long b;
    b=1; c = d[a+b];
}
```

We use the THINK C compiler to generate programs in the Macintosh to be downloaded into the BCC. We will show disassembled machine code produced from C procedures compiled by it. The previous procedure is coded in assembler language, as shown below.

```
fun    LINK.W A6,#0xFFFC          ; makes room for (allocates) 4-byte local variable b
       MOVEQ #1,D0                ; creates value 1
       MOVE.L D0,0xFFFC(A6)       ; puts value into local variable b
       MOVEA.W 8(A6),A0           ; gets function parameter a (past saved PC and A6)
       ADDA.L 0xFFFC(A6),A0       ; adds local variable b
       LEA 0xFE7E(A5),A1          ; gets address of global vector d
       ADDA.L A0,A1              ; adds together to get address of element
       MOVE.B (A1),0xFE7D(A5)     ; gets element of array into global variable c
       UNLK A6                    ; removes (deallocates) local varible b
       RTS                        ; returns to caller
```

The procedure is called by pushing the 2-byte parameter *a* and the 4-byte return address on the stack, as we discussed in Section 1-2.4. The procedure's first instruction makes room for *(allocates)* local variables on the stack and the last two instructions remove room for *(deallocates)* local variables on the stack and returns to the calling routine. Note that the LINK instruction puts the stack pointer in register A6 and then adds its (negative) immediate operand to the stack pointer A7. Parameters and local variable will be obtained by index addressing with A6; parameters use a positive offset (accounting for the 4-byte return address) and local variables use a negative offset. Global variables are obtained using register A5. It will be necessary to position A5 correctly to get them. This procedure just indexes the vector *d*, in a manner to be discussed in the next section.

Some very powerful special operators are available in C. Table 2-2 shows the ones we use in this book. For each operator, an example is given together with its equivalent result using the simple operators of Table 2-2. The assignment operator = assigns the value on its right to the variable named on its left and returns the value it assigns so that value can be used in an expression to the left of the assignment operation: the example shows 0 is assigned to *c*, and that value (0) is assigned to *b*, and then that value is assigned to *a*. The increment operator ++ can be used without an assignment operator (e.g., *a++* just increments *a*). It can also be used in an expression in which it increments its operand after the former operand value is returned to be used in the expression. For example, *b=a[i++]* will use the old value of *i* as an index to put *a[i]* into *b*, then it will increment *i*. Similarly, the decrement operator -- can be used in expressions. If the ++ or -- appear in front of the variable, then the value returned by the expression is the updated value; *a[++i]* will first increment *i*, then use the incremented value as an index into *a*. The next row show the use of the + and = operators used together to represent adding to a variable. The following rows show - | *and* & appended to = to represent subtracting from, ORing to, or ANDing to a variable. This form of a statement avoids the need to twice write the name of, and twice compute addresses for, the variable being added to or subtracted from. The last two rows of Table 2-2 show shift left and shift right operations and their equivalents in terms of multiplication or division by powers of 2. However, rather than allowing the use of a slower machine instruction, they force the use of the faster logical shift instructions.

Table 2-2. Special C Operators.

oper- ator	example	equivalent to:
=	a=b=c=0;	a=0;b=0;c=0;
++	a++;	a=a+1;
--	a- -;	a=a-1;
+=	a+ =2;	a=a+2;
-=	a- =2;	a=a-2;
| =	a | =2;	a=a|2;
&=	a & =2;	a=a&2;
<<	a<<3	a*8
>>	a>>3	a/8

Table 2-3.
Conditional Expression Operators.

&&	AND
||	OR
!	NOT
>	Greater Than
<	Less Than
>=	Greater than or Equal
<=	Less Than or Equal
==	Equal to
! =	Not Equal To

A statement can be conditional, or it can involve looping to execute a sequence of statements which are written within it many times. We will discuss these control flow statements by giving the flow charts for them. See Figure 2-1 for conditional statements, 2-2 for case statements, and 2-3 for loop statements. These simple standard forms appear throughout the book, and we will refer to them and their figures.

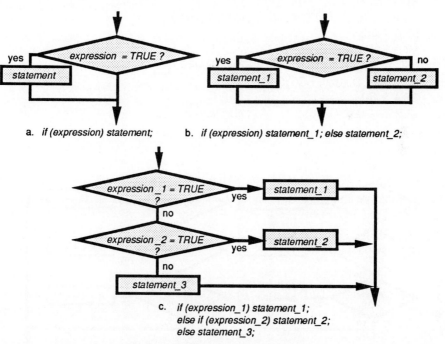

a. *if (expression) statement;*   b. *if (expression) statement_1; else statement_2;*

c. *if (expression_1) statement_1;*
   else if (expression_2) statement_2;
   else statement_3;

Figure 2-1. Conditional Statements.

Simple conditional expressions of the form *if then* (shown in Figure 2-1a), full conditionals of the form *if then else* (shown in Figure 2-1b), and extended conditionals of the form *if then else if then else if then ... else* (shown in Figure 2-1c), use conditional expression operators (shown in Table 2-3). In the last expression, the *else if* part can be repeated as many times as needed, and the last part can be an optional *else*. Variables are compared using *relational operators* (> and <), and these are combined using *logical operators* (&&). For example, *(a>5)&&(b<7)* is true if *a* > 5 and *b* < 7.

Consider a decision tree using conditional expressions, like *if(alpha>0) beta=10; else if(gamma ==0) delta++; else if((epsilon!=0)&&(zeta==1)) beta=beta<<3; else beta=0;* where each variable is of type *int*. We use this example because it contains many operators just discussed. This can be coded in assembler language as

```
       TST.W 0xFFFE(A6)              ; if(alpha>0)
       BLE.S @3
       MOVEQ #0xA,D0                 ; beta=10;
       MOVE.W D0,0xFFFC(A6)
       BRA.S @1
@3     TST.W 0xFFFA(A6)             ; else if(gamma ==0)
       BNE.S @0
       ADDQ.W #1,0xFFF8(A6)         ; delta++;
       BRA.S @1
@0     TST.W 0xFFF6(A6)             ; else if((epsilon!=0)
       BEQ.S @2
       CMPI.W #0001,0xFFF4(A6)      ; &&(zeta==1))
       BNE.S @2
       MOVE.W 0xFFFC(A6),D0
       LSL.W #3,D0                  ; beta=beta<<3;
       MOVE.W D0,0xFFFC(A6)
       BRA.S @1
@2     CLR.W 0xFFFC(A6)            ; else beta=0;
@1     ...
```

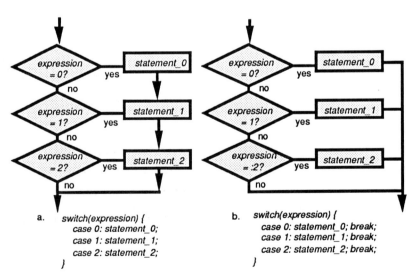

Figure 2-2. Case Statements.

Chapter 2 – Programming Microcomputers

A useful alternative to the conditional statement is the *case* statement. (See Figure 2-2.) An expression giving a numerical value is compared to each of several possible comparison values, then the matching comparison value determines which statement will be executed next. The case statement (such as the simple one in Figure 2-2a) jumps into the statements just where the variable matches the comparison value and executes all the statements below it. The *break* statement can be used (as shown in Figure 2-2b) to exit the whole case statement after a statement in it is executed, in lieu of executing the remaining statements in it.

Consider an expression like *switch(n){ case 1: i=1; break; case 3: i=2; break; case 6: i=3;break;}*. This is compactly coded in assembler language by calling a subroutine to evaluate the case, and providing the cases and addresses below the call as shown below:

```
        JSR 002A(A5)                ; switch(n)
        DC 0003                     ; three cases
@0      DC @1-@0,0001               ; case 1:
        DC @2-@0,0003               ; case 3:
        DC @3-@0,0006,0x0018        ; case 6:
@1      MOVEQ #01,D0                ; case 1: i=1;
        MOVE.W D0,0xFFFE(A6)
        BRA.S @4                    ; break;
@2      MOVEQ #02,D0                ; case 3: i=2;
        MOVE.W D0,0xFFFE(A6)
        BRA.S @4                    ; break;
@3      MOVEQ #03,D0                ; case 6: i=3;
        MOVE.W D0,0xFFFE(A6)
@4      ...
```

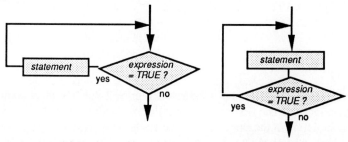

a. *while(expression) statement;*   b.*do statement while (expression);*

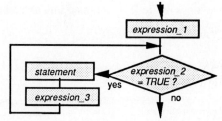

c. *for(expression_1;expression_2;expression_3)statement;*

Figure 2-3. Loop Statements.

Loop statements can be used to repeat a statement until a condition is met. A statement within the loop statement will be executed repeatedly. The expressions in both the following loop statements are exactly like the expressions of the conditional statements, using operators as shown in Table 2-3.

The *while* statement of Figure 2-3a tests the condition before the loop is executed and is useful if, for example, a loop may have to be done 0 times. Assume *i* is initially cleared. Then the *while* statement can clear the array *alpha[10]*. The statement *while(i<10) alpha[i++]=0;* is compiled into assembler language as

```
        BRA.S @1
@0      MOVE.L 0xFFFC (A6),D0
        ADDQ.L #1, 0xFFFC (A6) ;                    i++
        LEA 0xFE7D(A5),A0  ;                   alpha [
        ADDA.L D0,A0
        CLR.B (A0) ;                                      ]=0;
@1      CMPI.L # 0xA,0xFFFC(A6) ; while(i<10)
        BLT.S @0
```

We have indented the comments so the *while* statement can be seen as a whole, because the first expression of the *while* statement is done after the statement within it.

The *do while* statement (shown in Figure 2-3b) tests the condition after the loop is executed at least once, but it tests the result of the loop's activities. It is very useful in I/O software. It can similarly clear *alpha[10]*. Though perhaps less clear, it can lead to more efficient code. The statement *do{alpha[++i]=0;} while (i<10);* is compiled into:

```
@0      ADDQ.L #1, 0xFFFC (A6)  ; do {
        LEA 0xFE7D(A5),A0 ;          alpha [
        ADDA.L 0xFFFC(A6),A0 ;              ++i]
        CLR.B (A0) ;                       =0;}
        CMPI.L # 0xA,FFFC(A6)  ;            while(i<10)
        BLT.S @0
```

The more general *for* statement (shown in Figure 2-3c) has three expressions separated by semicolons (;). The first expression initializes variables used in the loop; the second tests for completion in the same style as the while statement; and the third updates the variables each time after the loop is executed. Any of the expressions in the *for* statement may be omitted. For example, *for(i=0;i<10;i++) alpha[i]=0;* will clear the array *alpha* as the above loops did it. It is compiled into assembler language as follows:

```
        CLR.L 0xFFFC(A6) ;          for(i=0;
        BRA.S @1
@0      LEA 0xFE7D (A5),A0
        ADDA.L 0xFFFC(A6),A0
        CLR.B (A0) ;                                alpha[i]=0;
        ADDQ.L #1,0xFFFC(A6) ;              i++);
@1      CMPI.L #0xA,0xFFFC(A6) ;      i<10;
        BLT.S @0
```

This program segment is not particularly efficient. A more efficient assembler language program equivalent to the C statement *for(i=9;i ! = -1;) alpha[i--]=0;* is

```
        LEA 0xFE86(A5),A0 ; the address of alpha[9] is put in A0
        MOVEQ #9,D0
@0      CLR.B  -(A0)
        DBRA   D0,@0
```

However, the THINK C compiler (version 4.0) does not actually generate the assembler language shown above for the equivalent C code. If you need tight code, you will have to insert the assembler language code into a C procedure, in a manner to be shown in Section 2-3.4. Note also that, as in this example if it were efficiently compiled, the clearest C program does not always lead to the most efficient assembler language program.

The *break* statement will cause the *for, while,* or *do while* loop to terminate just as in the *case* statement, and may be used in a conditional statement. For instance, *for(;;) {i++; if(i==30) break;}* executes the statement *{i++; if(i==30) break;}* indefinitely, but the loop is terminated when *i* is 30.

An important feature of C, extensively used to access I/O devices, is its ability to describe variables and addresses of variables. If *a* is a variable, then *&a* is the address of *a*. If *a* is a variable that contains an address of another variable *b*, then **a* is the contents of the word pointed to by *a*, which is the contents of *b*. (Note that *a*b* is *a* times *b* but **b* is the contents of the word pointed to by *b*.) Whenever you see *&*, read it as "address of," and whenever you see ***, read it as "contents of thing pointed to by." In a declaration statement, the statement *char *p;* means that the thing pointed to by *p* is a character, and *p* points to (contains the address of) a character. In an assignment statement, **p = 1;* means that 1 is assigned to the value of the thing pointed to by *p*, whereas *p=1;* means that the pointer *p* is given the value 1. Similarly, *a=*p;* means that *a* is given the value of the thing pointed to by *p*, while *a=p;* means *a* gets the value of the pointer *p*. Some C compilers will give an error message when you assign an integer to a pointer. If that occurs, you have to use a caste. Write *p = (int *)0x4000;* to tell the compiler 0x4000 is really a pointer value to an integer and not an integer itself.

The final feature of C we need is the comment: anything enclosed by /* and */ . This is useful, in writing "*pigeon C*" programs, to specify an operation at a high level without showing in detail how it is done. For example, we can write a specification for a program that, when getting a number from a keyboard, executes a "go" operation if the number is *1*, a reverse operation if *2*, and a stop operation if *7*:

```
main() {
        char keycode;
        /* get a key into keycode */
        switch (keycode) {
                case 1: /* go */; break;
                case 2: /* reverse */; break;
                case 7: /* stop */; break;
        }
}
```

2-2 Data Structures

Data structures are at least as important as programming techniques, for if the program is one-half of the software, the data and their structure are the other half. When we discuss storage density as an architecture characteristic, we discuss only the amount of memory needed to store the program. We are also concerned about data storage and its impact on static and dynamic efficiency, as well as the size of memory needed to store the data. Prudent selection of the data structures a program uses can shorten or speed up the program. These considerations about data structures are critical in microcomputers.

A data structure is one among three views of data. The *information structure* is the view of data the end user sees. For instance, the end user may think of his of her data as a table, like Table 2-1 in this book. The programmer sees the same data as the *data structure*: strongly related to the way the data are accessed but independent of details such as size of words and position of bits. It is rather like a painter's template, which can be filled in with different colors. So the data structure may be an array of characters that spell out the words in Table 2-1. The *storage structure* is the way the information is actually stored in memory, right down to the bit positions. So the table may appear as an array of 8-bit words in the storage structure.

The data structure concept has been found a bit hard for some to accept. Its usefulness lies in its ability to provide a level of abstraction, allowing us to make some overall observations of how we store things, which can be applied to similar storage techniques. For instance, if we can develop a concept of how to access an array, we can use similar ideas to access arrays of 8-bit or 24-bit data, even though the programs could be quite different. But here we must stress that a data structure is simply a kind of template that tells us how data are stored and is also a menu of possible ways the data can be written or read. Two data structures are different if they have different templates that describe their general structure or if the menus of possible access techniques are different.

Constants are often used with data structures, for instance to declare a size of a vector and to use that same number in *for* loops. They can be defined by *Define* or *enum* statements, put before any declarations or statements, to equate names to values. The *define* statement begins with the characters *#define* and does not end with a semicolon.

#define ALPHA 100

Thenceforth, we can use the label ALPHA throughout the program, and 100 will effectively be put in place of ALPHA just before the program is actually compiled. This permits the program to be better documented, using meaningful labels, and easier to maintain, so that if the value of a label is changed it is changed everywhere it occurs. Another use of *#define* statements for macros will be considered in Section 2-3.1.

A number of constants can be created using the enum statement. Unless reinitialized with an = sign, each member has one greater than the value of the previous member. The first member has value 0.

enum { BETA, GAMMA, DELTA=5};

defines *BETA* to have value 0, *GAMMA* to have value 1, and *DELTA* to have value 5.

The declaration of any scalar variable can be initialized by use of a "=" and a value. For instance, if scalar integers i, j and k have initial values 1, 2 and 3, we write a global declaration:

$$int\ i=1, j=2, k=3;$$

C procedures access global variables using register A5, and initialized global variables are loaded into memory just before the program is started. Upon downloading a program from the Macintosh to the BCC using initialized variables, A5 must be correctly set up and the initial values of the data must be moved from the Macintosh memory to the BCC memory. Initialized local variables of a procedure will generate machine code to initialize them just after they are allocated each time the procedure is called. The procedure

```
fun(){
        int i, j, k; /* allocate local variables */
        i=1; j=2; k=3; /* initialize local variables */
}
```

is equivalent to the procedure

```
fun(){
        int i=1, j=2, k=3; /* allocate and initialize local variables */
}
```

Data structures divide into three main categories: indexable, sequential, and linked. Indexable and sequential, discussed here, are more important. Linked structures are very powerful, but are not as easy to discuss in abstract terms. They will be discussed later.

2-2.1 Indexable Data Structures

Indexable structures include vectors, lists, arrays, and tables. A *vector* is a sequence of elements, where each element is associated with an index i used to access it. To make address calculations easy, C associates the first element with the index 0, and each successive element with the next integer (*zero-origin indexing*). Also, the elements in a vector are considered numbers of the same *precision* (number of bits or bytes needed to store an element). We will normally consider one-word precision vectors, although we soon show an example of how the ideas can be extended to n-word vectors. Finally the *cardinality* of a vector is the number of elements in it. A vector is fully specified if its origin, precision and cardinality are given. A zero-origin, 16-bit, three element vector 31, 17, and 10 is generated by a declaration *int v[3]* and stored in memory as (hexadecimal):

001F

0011

000A

and we can refer to the first element as *v[0]*, which happens to be 31. However, the same sequence of values could be put in a zero-origin vector of three 32-bit elements, generated by a declaration *long u[3]* and stored in memory as:

0000

001F

0000

0011

0000

000A

The declaration of a global vector variable can be initialized by use of a "=" and a list of values, in angle brackets. For instance, the three-element global integer vector *v* can be allocated and initialized by

$$int\ v[3]=\{31,17,10\};$$

The vector *u* can be similarly allocated and initialized by the declaration

$$long\ u[3]=\{31,17,10\};$$

The procedure *fun()* in Section 2.1 illustrated the accessing of elements of vectors in expressions. The expression $c = d[a+b];$ accessed the $a+b$ th element of the 8-bit 10-element vector *d*. The term "vector" is a general term, and similar declarations and statements can be used for 16-bit and 32-bit or other precision, and for other cardinality vectors. The concept of "data structure" is to generalize the storage and access used in one instance to cover other instances of the same kind of data handling technique. When reading the assembly code generated by C, be wary of the implicit multiplication of the vector's precision (in bytes) when calculating offset addresses of elements of the vector. And because C does not check that indexes are within the cardinality of a vector, your C program must be able to implicitly or explicitly assure this to avoid nasty bugs – when a vector's data is inadvertently stored outside the memory allocated to a vector.

A *list* is like a vector, being accessed by means of an index, but the elements of a list can be any combination of different precision words, code words, and so on. For example, the list LIST can have three elements: the 4-byte number 5, the 2-byte number 7, and the 4-byte number 9. This list is stored in machine code as follows:

```
0000
0005
0007
0000
0009
```

The powerful *structure* mechanism is used in C to implement lists. The mechanism is implemented by a declaration that begins with the word *struct* and has a definition of the structure within angle brackets, and a list of variables of that structure type after the brackets, as in

$$struct\ \{\ long\ l1;\ int\ l2;\ long\ l3;\}\ list;$$

A globally defined list can be initialized as we did with vectors, as in

$$struct\ \{\ long\ l1;\ int\ l2;\ long\ l3;\}\ list=\{5,7,9\};$$

The data in a list are identified by "dot" notation, where a dot "." means "element." For instance, *list.l1* is the *l1* element of the list *list*. The *typedef* statement, though it can be used to create a new data type in terms of existing data types, is often used with *structs*. If *typedef a struct struct { long l1; int l2; long l3;} list;* is written, then *list* is a data type, like *int* or *char*, and can be used in declarations such as *list b;* that declares *b* to be an instance of type *list*. We will find the *typedef* statement to be quite useful when a *struct* has to be declared many times and pointers to it need to be declared too. A structure can have *bit fields* which are unsigned integer elements having less than 16 bits. Such a structure as

$$struct\ \{unsigned\ a:1,\ b:2,\ c:3;\}l;$$

has a one-bit field *l.a*, two-bit field *l.b* and three-bit field *l.c*. *if(l.a) l.b=l.c;* is coded:

```
        BTST #07,FFFE(A6) ;            if(l.a)
        BEQ.S @0
        MOVEQ #0x1C,D0 ;                       l.c;
        AND.B 0xFFFE(A6),D0
        LSR.B #2,D0
        ANDI.B #0x9F,FFFE(A6)
        ANDI.B #3,D0
        LSL.B #5,D0
        OR.B D0,FFFE(A6) ;            l.b=
@0
```

A *linked list* structure, a list in which some elements are addresses of (the first word in) other lists, is flexible and powerful and is widely used in advanced software. It is useful in interface applications; its simplicity is concretely discussed in Section 4-2.

An *array* is a vector whose elements are vectors of the same length. We normally think of an array as a two-dimensional pattern, as in

1	2	3
4	5	6
7	8	9
10	11	12

An array is considered a vector whose elements are themselves vectors. The array is stored in *row major* order: in this arrangement a row is stored with its elements in consecutive memory locations. (In *column major* order a column is stored with its elements in consecutive memory locations.) For instance, the global declaration

$$int\ ar1[4][3]=\{\{1,2,3\},\{4,5,6\},\{7,8,9\},\{10,11,12\}\};$$

allocates and initializes a row major ordered array *ar1*, and *a=ar1[i][j];* puts the row-*i* column-*j* element of *ar1* into *a*.

A *table* is to a list as an array is to a vector. It is a vector of identically structured lists (rows). Tables often store characters, where either a single character or a collection of *n* consecutive characters are considered elements of the lists in the table. Index addressing is useful for accessing elements in a row of a table, especially if the table is stored in row major order. If the address register points to the first word of any row, then the displacement can be used to access words in any desired column. Also, autoincrement addressing can be used to select consecutive words from a row of the table.

In C, a table *tbl* is considered a vector whose elements are structures. For instance, the declaration

$$struct\ \{long\ l1;int\ l2;long\ l3;\}\ tbl[3];$$

allocates a table whose rows are similar to the list *list* above. The "dot" notation with indexes can be used to access it, as in

$$a=tbl[2].l1;$$

2-2.2 Sequential Data Structures

The other important class of data structures is sequential structures, which are accessed by relative position. Rather than having an index *i* to get to any element of the structure, only the "next" element to the last one accessed may be accessed in a sequential structure. Strings, stacks, queues, and deques are sequential structures important in microcomputers.

A *string* is a sequence of elements such that after the *i*th element has been accessed, only the (*i*+1)st element, the (*i*-1)th, or both, can be accessed. In particular, a string of characters, stored using the *ASCII code* shown in Table 2-4, is an ASCII *character string* and is used to store text. The ASCII code of a character is stored as a 7-bit code in a *char* variable. Character constants are enclosed by single quotes around the character, as *'A'* is the character A. The special characters are *null* '\0', line feed '\n', form feed '\f' (begin on new page), *cr* carriage return '\r', and ' ' space. Strings are allocated and can be used in C as if they were *char* vectors, are initialized by putting the characters in double quotes, and end in the null character '\0'.(Allow an extra byte for it.)

Table 2-4. ASCII Codes.

	00	10	20	30	40	50	60	70
0	\0			0	@	P	`	p
1			!	1	A	Q	a	q
2			"	2	B	R	b	r
3			#	3	C	S	c	s
4			$	4	D	T	d	t
5			%	5	E	U	e	u
6			&	6	F	V	f	v
7			'	7	G	W	g	w
8			(	8	H	X	h	x
9			)	9	I	Y	i	y
A	\n		*	:	J	Z	j	z
B			+	;	K	[	k	{
C	\f		,	<	L	\	l		
D	\r		-	=	M	]	m	}
E			.	>	N	^	n	~
F			/	?	O	_	o	

One can initialize a global character c to be the code for the letter *a* and a global string s to be *ABCD* with the global declaration :

$$int\ c='a',\ s[5]="ABCD";$$

Strings are also very useful for input and output when debugging C programs; we will discuss the use of strings in these *printf* and *scanf* functions later. However, a source-level debugger for a C compiler provides better debugging tools. Even so, some discussion of string-oriented input and output is generally desirable for human interfacing in applications that mix human and I/O interfacing. This will be done in Section 2-4.6.

Characters in strings can be accessed by indexing or by pointers. An index can be incremented to access each character, one after another from first to last character. Alternatively, a pointer to a character such as *p* can be used; **p* is the character that it points to and **(p++)* returns the character pointed to and then increments the pointer *p* to point to the next character in the string. We will illustrate these techniques shortly.

Strings are so simple that they are hardly worth discussing, but they are so omnipresent that we must discuss them. In particular, we note the ways to identify the length of a string. They are

1. Give the length of the string as a binary number. Put this number in a counter, and count down as each character is read from the string.

2. Get the string's end address. Compare the pointer to the end of the string.

3. Put a special character after the end of the string. Often the ASCII code for a carriage return (0x0D), a null (0), or an END-OF-TEXT (4) is put there. When the character is loaded, say into D0, (and is the low byte of D0, and the high byte is 0) use CMP D0,#0x0D or the equivalent to detect the end of the string. In particular, C uses the null character to terminate strings.

4. Because ASCII codes are seven bits long, set the seventh bit of the last character to 1, the seventh bits of the other characters being 0. After the character is loaded, say into a variable, the end can be detected by a ANDing *0x80* with the variable in a condition for an *if* statement or *while* or *for* loop. The character can be recovered by ANDing *0x7f* with the variable.

The characters you type on a terminal are usually stored in memory in a character string. You can use a typed word as a command to execute a routine, with unique words for executing each routine. A C program to compare a string that has just been stored in memory, and pointed to by *p*, to a string stored in *start_word*, is shown as *main()* next:

```
char *p,start_word[6]={"START"}; /* assume p points to a string stored elsewhere */
main() {
    int i,nomatch;
    for(i = nomatch = 0;i<5;i++){
        if(*(p++) != start_word[i]){ nomatch=1; break;}
    }
    if (nomatch==0) strt(); /* if the string is START then execute the strt proc */
}
```

Inside the loop, we compare a character at a time of the input string against the string *start_word*. If we detect any difference, we set local variable *nomatch* because the user did not type the string *start_word*. But if all five characters match up – the user did type the word *start_word* – the program calls *strt*, presumably to start something.

Besides character strings, bit strings are important in microcomputers. In particular, a very nice coding scheme called the *Huffman code* can pack characters into a bit stream and achieve about a 75% reduction in storage space when compared to storing the characters directly in an ASCII character string. It can be used to store characters more compactly and can also be used to transmit them through a communications link more efficiently. As a bonus, the encoded characters are very hard to decode without a code description, so you get a more secure communications link using a Huffman code. Further, we need to handle data structures and bit shifting using the << and >> operators and bit masking using the & operator in many I/O procedures. Procedures for Huffman coding and decoding provide a rich set of examples of these techniques.

The code is rather like Morse code, in that frequently used characters are coded as short strings of bits, just as the often-used letter "e" is a single dot in Morse code. To insure that code words are unique and to suggest a decoding strategy, the code is defined by a tree having two branches at each branching point (*binary tree*), as shown in Figure 2-4. The letters at each end (leaf) are represented by the pattern of 1s and 0s along the branches from the left end (root) to the leaf. Thus, the character string MISSISSIPPI can be represented by the bit string 111100010001011011010. Note that the ASCII string would take 88 bits of memory while the Huffman string would take 21 bits. When you decode the bit string, start at the root and use each successive bit of the bit string to guide you up (if 0) or down (if 1) the next branch until you get to a leaf. Then copy the letter and start over at the root of the tree with the next bit of the bit string. The bit string has equal probabilities of 1s and 0s, so techniques used to decipher the code based on probabilities won't work. It is particularly hard to break a Huffman code.

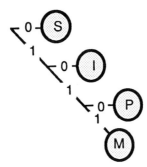

Figure 2-4. A Huffman Coding Tree.

A C program for Huffman coding is shown below. The original ASCII character string is stored in the *char* vector *strng*. We will initialize it to the string *MISSISSIPPI* for convenience, although any string of M I S and P letters could be used. The procedure converts this string into a Huffman coded 48-bit bit string stored in the vector *code[3]*. It uses the procedure *shift()* to shift a bit into *code*. This procedure, shown later, is also used by the decoding procedure shown after it.

```
char strng[12] = "MISSISSIPPI"; /* input code, terminated in a NULL character */
int code[3], bitlength; /* output code and its length */
struct table{ char letter; char charcode[4]; } codetable[4]
        = { 'S',"XX0", 'I',"X10", 'P',"110",'M',"111" };
main(){
        int row, i; char *point, letter;
        for (point=strng; *point ; point++ ){
                for (row = 0; row < 4; row ++)}
                    if (((*point) & 0x7f) == codetable[row].letter)
                        for (i = 0; i < 3; i++){
                                letter = codetable[row].charcode[i];
                                if (letter != 'X') {
                                        shift(); code [2] |=
                                                (letter  &  1);  bitlength++;}
                            }
                }
        }
        i= bitlength; while((i++)<48)shift(); /* shift out unchanged bits */
}
```

```
int shift() {
    int i;
    i=0; if( 0x8000 & code[0]) i=1; code[0] = code[0] <<1;
    if (code[1] & 0x8000) code[0] |=1; code[1] = code[1] <<1;
    if (code[2] & 0x8000) code[1] |=1; code[2] = code[2] <<1;
    return(i);
}
```

Huffman decoding, using *shift()* from the above program, is done as follows:

```
int code[3]={0xf116,0xd000,0},bitlength=21; /* input string and length */
char tbl[3][2] = {{'S',1},{'T',2},{'P','M'}};
char strng[20]; /* output string */
main(){
    int row,entry; char *point;
    point=strng; row =0;
    while((bitlength--)>=0){
        if((entry = tbl[row][shift()]) < 0x20)
            row = entry; /* table entry gives next row to be checked */
        else {row =0; /* we have a character; start over at table row 0 */
            *(point++) = entry &0x7f;
        }
    }
    *point = '\0'; /* terminate C string with NULL character */
}
```

We recommend that you test your ability to read C by studying the procedures above. We also suggest that you compile these procedures and step through them using a high-level debugger, as you can do in THINK C on a Macintosh with at least 2 Megabytes of memory. In this example, we are particularly interested in pointing out that strings may have elements other than characters (here they are bits), or the elements of strings can be themselves strings, provided such data are decipherable.

Now that we have shown how nice the Huffman code is, we must admit a few problems with it. To efficiently store some text, the text must be statistically analyzed to determine which letters are most frequent, to assign these the shortest codes. Note that S is most common, so we gave it a short code word. There is a procedure for generating the best Huffman code, which is presented in many information theory books, but you have to get the statistics of each letter's occurrences to get that code. Nevertheless, though less than perfect, one can use a fixed code that is based on other statistics if the statistics are reasonably similar. Finally, although the code is almost unbreakable without the decoding tree, if any bit in the bit string is erroneous, your decoding routine can get completely lost. This may be a risk you decide to avoid because the code has to be sent through a communications link that is as error-free as possible.

A *deque* is a generalized data structure that includes two special cases: the stack and the queue. A deque (pronounced deck) is a sequence of elements with two ends we call the top and the bottom. You can only access the top or bottom elements on the deque. You can *push an element on top* by placing it on top of the top element, which makes it the new top element, or you can *push an element on the bottom* making it the new bottom element. Or you can *pull (or pop) the top element* deleting the top element from the deque, making the next to top element the top element and putting the old top element somewhere else, or *pull (or pop) the bottom element* in like manner.

Deques are theoretically infinite, so you can push as many elements as you want on either the top or bottom: But practical deques have a maximum capacity. If this capacity is exceeded, we have an *overflow* error. Also, if you pull more elements than you push an *underflow error* exists.

C declarations and programs for initializing, pushing and pulling words from a deque are shown below. The *buffer* is an area of memory set aside for use as the deque expands, and cannot be used by any other data or program code. The programmer allocates as much room for the buffer as appears necessary for the worst case (largest) expansion of the deque. Two indexes are used to read or write on the top or bottom, and a counter is used to detect overflow or underflow. The deque buffer is implemented as a ten-element global vector *deque*, and the indexes as global *unsigned chars top* and *bottom* initialized to the first element of the *deque*, as in the C declaration

unsigned char deque [10], size,error, top=bottom=0;

As words are pulled from top or bottom, more space is made available to push words on either the top or bottom. To take advantage of this, we think of the buffer as a ring or loop of words, so that the next word below the bottom of the buffer is the word on the top of the buffer. That way, as words are pulled from the top, the memory locations can become available to store words pushed on the bottom as well as words pushed on the top, and vice versa. Then to push or pop data into or from the top or bottom of it, we can execute the following procedures:

```
phtop(item_to_push) int item_to_push; {
        if ((size++) < 10){
                if (top ==10) top = 0; deque[top++] = item_to_push;
        }
        else error = 1;
}
int pltop() {
        if ((size - - ) > 0) { if (top==0) top = 10; }
        else error = 1; return(deque[- - top]);
}
psbot(item_to_push) int item_to_push; {
        if ((size++) < 10){
                if (bottom == 0) bottom = 10; deque[- - bottom] = item_to_push;
        }
        else error = 1;
}
int plbot(){
        if ((size - -) > 0){ if (bottom == 10) bottom = 0; }
        else error = 1; return( deque[bottom++] );
}
```

Note that you cannot really associate the ith word from either end of a deque with a particular location in memory. In fact, in a pure sense, you can only access the deque's top and bottom words and cannot read or write any other word in the deque. In practice, we sometimes access the ith element from the deque's top or bottom by using a displacement with the indexes that point to the top and bottom words – but this is not a pure deque. We call it an *indexable deque* to give it some name.

A *stack* is a deque in which you can push or pull on only one end. We have discussed the stack accessed by the stack pointer S, which permits the machine to push or pull words from the top of the stack to save registers for procedure calls, as well as TRAP and hardware interrupts. Now we consider the stack as a special case of a deque. (Actually, the stack A7 in the 683xx can be made a special case of indexable deque using A7 with index addressing.) It is an example of a stack that pushes or pulls elements from the top only. Another equally good stack can be created that pushes or pulls elements only from the bottom of the deque. In fact, if you want two different stacks in your memory, have one that pushes and pulls from the top and another that pushes and pulls from the bottom. Then both stacks can share the same buffer, as one starts at the top of this buffer (lowest address) and builds downward, while the other starts at the bottom (highest address) and builds upward. A stack overflow exists when the top pointer of the stack that builds upward is equal to the bottom pointer of the stack that builds downward. Note that if one stack is shorter, then the other stack can grow longer before an overflow exists, and vice versa. You only have to allocate enough words in the buffer for the maximum number of words that will be in both at the same time.

Programs to push or pull on the two stacks are simpler than the general program that operates on the general deque, because the pointers do not roll around the top or bottom of the buffer.

The final structure that is important in microcomputer systems is the *queue*. This is a deque in which we can push data on one end and pull data from the other end. In some senses, it is like a shift register, but it can expand if more words are pushed than are pulled (up to the size of the buffer). In fact, it has been called an elastic shift register. Or conversely, a shift register is a special case of a queue, a fixed-length queue. Queues are used to store data temporarily, such that the data can be used in the same order in which they were stored. We will find them very useful in interrupt handlers and procedures that interact with them.

One of the rather satisfying results of the notion of data structures is that the stack and queue, actually quite different concepts, are found to be special cases of the deque. The two structures are, in fact, handled with similar programs. Other data structures – such as multidimensional arrays, trees, partially ordered sets, and graphs such as lattices and banyans – are important in general programming. You are invited to pursue the study of data structures to improve your programming skills. However, this section has covered the data structures we have found most useful in microcomputer interface software.

2-3 Writing Clear C Programs

683xx systems are almost always large enough to consider the advantages of writing clear assembler language programs over the expense of writing short programs. There may be reason for concern about static efficiency in smaller microcomputers. The Motorola 6805 has so little memory – 2K words of ROM – that static efficiency is paramount, and the programs are so short that readability is less important to a good programmer, who can comprehend them even if they are unclearly written. When a program is larger than 16K, readability is significant - even for a good programmer - because it may have to be written by several programmers who read each other's code, and may have to be maintained long after the original programmers have gone.

A significant technique for writing clear programs is good documentation, such as using comments and flow charts. Of course, these do not take up memory in the machine code, so they can be used when static or dynamic efficiency must be optimized. Another technique is the use of consistent programming styles that constrain the programmer, thereby reducing the chance of errors and increasing the reader's ease of understanding. Also, a major idea in clear programming methodology is modular top-down design. We also need to develop the concept of object-oriented programming. In order to discuss these ideas, we first need to further refine our understanding of procedures and arguments.

2-3.1 C Procedures and Their Arguments

Conceptually, *arguments* or *parameters* are data passed from or to the calling routine to or from a procedure, like the x in *sin(x)*. Inside the procedure, the parameter is declared as a variable, such as y, as in *sin(y) int y;{ ... }*. It is called the *formal parameter*. Each time the procedure is called the calling routine uses different variables for the parameter. The variable in the calling routine is called the *actual parameter*. For example, at one place in the program we put *sin(alpha)*, in another, *sin(beta)*, and in another, *sin(gamma)*. *alpha, beta,* and *gamma* are actual parameters in these examples.

At the conceptual level, arguments are called by value and result, reference, or name. In *call by value and result*, the formal parameters inside the procedure are usually registers. The values of the actual parameters from the calling routine are really transferred from their memory locations in the calling routine to the registers in the procedure before the procedure begins to execute its operation. The values of formal parameters in the registers are moved to their actual parameters after the procedure is finished. However, any mechanism is called by value and result if the actual values (rather than their addresses) are passed to the procedure or actual results (rather than their addresses) are returned from the procedure. In general, only parameters passed from the calling routine to the procedure are moved before the procedure begins execution, and only the results of the procedure are copied into the calling routine's actual parameters after the end of a subroutine's execution, but the same formal parameter (register) can be used for input and output.

In *call by reference*, the data remain in the calling routine and are not actually moved to another location, but the address of the data is given to the procedure and the procedure uses this address to get the data whenever it needs to. Large vectors, lists, arrays, and other data structures can be more effectively called by reference so they don't have to be copied into and out of the subroutine's local variables. Conceptually, arguments passed in call by reference are evaluated just before the procedure is called and are not reevaluated as the procedure is executed. If an argument is called by reference, you should normally use it only for input, or only for output, and not both, because input arguments are supposed to behave as if they were evaluated just before the procedure call, and are supposed to stay that way throughout the procedure.

The last mechanism, *call by name*, allows complex actual arguments to be passed to a procedure. These actual parameters are effectively (if not actually) inserted into every occurrence of the corresponding formal parameters inside the procedure and are reevaluated each time they are met as the procedure is executed. Call by name is useful when you want to refer to an argument by its address but you change it in the procedure, so it has different values at different times in the procedure. Call by name is also useful when actual parameters are subroutines, for example, as arguments to another procedure. If you wrote a procedure called *plot* to plot a graph, you could pass an argument that would be the address of a procedure like *sin* – as in *plot(sin)* – and *sin* would be reevaluated each time the *plot* routine was ready to plot a new point on the graph. If you used call by reference, the argument *sin* would be evaluated just once, just before the procedure was entered, so your plot would be a straight line. Finally, conceptually, call by name is used to handle error conditions. One argument – the address of a procedure to go to if an error is detected – is only executed if the error occurs and so is a call by name argument.

A procedure in C may be called by another procedure in C as a procedure. The arguments may be the data themselves, which is call by value, or the address of the data, which is call by name. Call by reference is not used in C (it is often used in FORTRAN). Consider the following example: *RaisePower* computes i to the power j, returning the answer in k where i, j and k are integers. The variable i is passed by value, while j and k are passed by name. The calling procedure would have *RaisePower(i,&j,&k);* and the called procedure would have

```
RaisePower (i,j,k) int i,*j,*k; {
    int n;
    *k=1;
    for(n=0;n<*j;n++) *k=*k * i;
}
```

Formal parameters are listed after the procedure name in parentheses, as in (i,j,k), and in the same order they are listed after the procedure name as they would be for a declaration of local variables. However, they are listed before the angle bracket "{".

Call by value, as i is passed, does not allow data to be output from a procedure, but any number of call by value input parameters can be used in a procedure. Actual parameters passed by name in the calling procedure have an ampersand "&" prefixed to them to designate that the address is put in the parameter. In the called procedure, the formal parameters generally have an asterisk "*" prefixed to them to designate that the data at the address are accessed. Observe that call by name formal parameters j or k used inside the called procedure all have a prefix asterisk "*". A call by name parameter can pass data into or out of a procedure, or both. Data can be input to a procedure using call by name, because the address of the result is passed into the procedure and the procedure can read data at the given address. A result can be returned from a procedure using call by name, because the address of the result is passed into the procedure and the procedure can write new data at the given address to pass data out of the procedure. Any number of call by name input/output parameters can be used in a procedure.

A procedure may be used as a function which returns exactly one value and can be used in the middle of algebraic expressions. The value returned by the function is put in a *return statement.* For instance, the function *power* can be written

```
power(i,j) int i,j; {
    int k,n;
    n=1;
    for(k=0;k<j;k++) n=n*i;
    return(n);
}
```

This function can be called within an algebraic expression by a statement $a=power(b,2)$. The output of the function is passed by *call by result*.

In C, the address of a character string can be passed into a procedure, which uses a pointer inside it to read the characters. For example, the string s is passed to a procedure *puts* that outputs a string by outputting one character at a time using a procedure *putchar*. The procedure puts is written

```
puts(s) char *s; {
    while(*s!=0) putchar(*(s++));
}
```

It can be called in either of three ways, as shown side by side:

```
main()                  main()                   main()
{                       {                        {
    char s[6]="ALPHA";      char s[6]="ALPHA";       puts("ALPHA");
    puts(&s[0]);            puts(s);             }
}                       }
```

The first calling sequence, though permissible, is clumsy. The second is often used to pass different strings to the procedure, while the third is better when the same constant string is passed to the procedure in the statement of the calling program. The third calling sequence is often used to write prompt messages out to the user and to pass a format string to a formatted input or output procedure like *scanf* or *printf* described shortly.

A *prototype* for a procedure can be used to tell the compiler how arguments are passed to and from it. At the beginning of a program we write all prototypes, such as

$$extern\ void\ puts(char\ *);$$

The word *extern* indicates that the procedure *puts()* is not actually here but is elsewhere. The procedure itself can be later in the same file or in another file. The argument *char * * indicates that the procedure uses only one argument and it will be a pointer to a character (i.e. the argument is called by name) . In front of the procedure name a type indicates the procedure's result. The type *void* indicates that the procedure does not return a result. After the prototype has been declared, any calls to the procedure will be checked to see if the types match. For instance, a call *puts('A')* will cause an error message because we have to send the address of a character (string), not a value of a character to this procedure. The prototype for the procedure *power()* given above is written

$$extern\ int\ power(int,\ int)$$

to indicate that it requires two arguments and returns one result, all of which are call-by-value 16-bit signed numbers. The compiler will use the prototype to convert arguments of other types if possible. For instance, if x and y are 8-bit signed numbers (of type *char*) then a call *power(x,y)* will automatically extend these 8-bit to 16-bit signed numbers before passing them to the procedure. If a procedure has a *return n* statement that returns a result, then the type statement in front of the procedure name indicates the type of the result. If that type is declared to be *void* as in the *puts()* procedure, there may not be a *return n* statement that returns a result.

At the beginning of each file, prototypes for all procedures in that file should be declared. While writing a procedure name and its arguments twice, once in a prototype and later in the procedure itself, may appear clumsy, it lets the compiler check for improper arguments and, where possible, instructs it to convert types used in the calling routine to the types expected in the called routine. We recommend the use of prototypes.

The *macro* is similar to a procedure, but is either evaluated at compile time or is inserted into the program wherever it is used, rather than being stored in one place and jumped to whenever it is called. The macro in C is implemented as a *#define* construct. As *#defines* were earlier used to define constants, macros are also "expanded" just before the program is compiled. The macro has a name and arguments rather like a procedure. and the rest of the line is the body of the macro. For instance

$$\#define\ f(\ a, b, c)\ a = b * 2 + c$$

is a macro with name f and arguments a,b and c. Wherever the name appears in the program, the macro is expanded and its arguments are substituted. For instance if $f(\ x, y, 3)$ appeared, then $x = y * 2 + 3$ is inserted into the program. Macros with constant arguments are entirely evaluated at compile time, and generate a constant used at runtime.

The *printf* procedure is used for output to a terminal display, and *scanf* is used for input from a keyboard. These very powerful functions require the loading of a lot of machine code along with the program, which may be a serious problem if memory is limited. Simpler procedures *gets* and *puts* can be used to input and output character strings, and *strcpy, strcat,* and *atoi* can be used to manipulate strings being input or output.

The procedure *printf* requires a character string format as its first parameter and may have any number of additional parameters as required by the format string. The format string uses a percent sign "%" to designate the input of a parameter, and the characters following the "%" sign establish the format for the output of the parameter value. While there are a large number of formats, we generally use only a few. The string "%d" will output the value in decimal. For instance, if i has the value 123, then

$$printf("\%d", i);$$

will print on the terminal

123

Similarly, "%X" will output the value in hexadecimal. If i has the value 0x1A, then

$$printf("\%X", i);$$

will print on the terminal

1A

If a number is put between the % and d or X letters, that number gives the maximum number of characters that will be printed. If that number begins in a zero, it specifies the exact number of characters that are printed for the corresponding parameter.

Similarly, "%s" will output a string of characters passed as a parameter. For instance,

char st[6] ="ALPHA";
printf("%s", st);

will print on the terminal

ALPHA

Observe that the integers for decimal or hexadecimal output are passed by value, but the string is passed by name as we discussed at the end of Section 2-4.1. The pair of symbols "\n" signified a carriage return and line feed to end a line. Apart from these special symbols, the symbols in the format string are printed as they appear there. For instance,

printf("Hi There\nHow are you?");

will print on the terminal:

Hi There
How are you?

The procedure *scanf* is the inverse of *printf*. It requires a character string format as its first parameter and may have any number of additional parameters as required by the format string. The additional parameters, being returned values from the *scanf* procedure, must be passed by name. One of the most common errors in C is to try to pass these by value, forgetting to prefix the name with "&". The format string uses a percent sign "%" to designate the input of a parameter, and the characters following the "%" sign establish the format for the output of the parameter value as in *printf*. While there are a large number of formats, we generally use only a few. The string "%d" will input the value in decimal. For instance, if the user types 123 (carriage return), then

scanf ("%d",&i);

will put 123 into *i*. Similarly, %X inputs characters in hexadecimal.

Because *printf* and *scanf* are large procedures, they may take up too much room in a computer with limited memory. Therefore, simpler procedures may be needed. *puts(s);* puts the string *s* out to the screen (automatically appending a carriage return and line feed), and *gets(s);* gets a line from the keyboard, of characters typed up to a carriage return, putting the string into *s* (automatically removing the carriage return).

Character strings input using *gets* can be analyzed and disassembled using indexes in or pointers to the strings. Character strings can be assembled for output using *puts* by the procedures *strcpy* and *strcat*. The procedure *strcpy(s1,s2);* will copy string *s2* (up to the null character at its end) into string *s1*. The procedure *strcat(s1,s2);* will concatenate string *s2* (up to the null character at its end) onto the end of string *s1*. Finally, *i=atoi(s);* puts the numeric value of the string of digits, *s*, into *i*.

We have examined techniques for calling subroutines and passing arguments. We have also learned to use some simple tools for input and output in C. We should now be prepared to write subroutines for interface software.

2-3.2 Programming Style

We conform our programming techniques to some style to make the program easier to read, debug, and maintain. Although this constraint generally produces less efficient code, the use of a consistent style is recommended, especially in longer programs where there is enough memory but not where static efficiency is paramount. For instance we can rigidly enforce reentrancy and use some conventions to make this rather automatic. Another programming style – structured programming – uses only simple conditional and loop operations and avoids GOTO statements. After this we discuss top-down and bottom-up programming. This will lead to an introduction to object-oriented programming.

An element of *structured programming* is the use of single entry point, single exit point program segments. This style makes the program much more readable because, to get into a program segment, there are no circuitous routes which are hard to debug and test. The use of C for specification and documentation can force the use of this style. The conditional and loop statements described in the last section are single entry point, single exit point program segments, and they are sufficient for almost all programs. The *while* loop technique is especially attractive because it tests the termination condition before the loop is done even once, so programs can be written that accommodate all possibilities, including doing the loop no times. And the *for* loop is essentially a beefed-up *while* loop. You can use just these constructs. That means avoiding the use of GOTO statements. Several years ago, Professor Edsger Dijkstra made the then controversial remark, "GOTOs Considered Harmful!" Now, most good programmers agree with him. We heard a story (from Harold Stone) that Professor Goto in Japan has a sign on his desk that says "Dijkstras Considered Harmful!" (Professor Goto denies this.) The only significant exception is the reporting of errors. We sometimes GOTO an error reporting or correcting routine if an error is detected – an abnormal exit point for the program segment. Errors can alternatively be reported by a convention such as using the carry bit to indicate the error status: You exit the segment with carry clear if no errors are found and exit with carry set if an error is found. Thus, all segments can have single exit points.

Top-down design is a program-writing methodology that has produced programs more quickly than ad hoc and haphazard writing. The idea is to write a main program that calls subroutines (or just program segments) without yet writing the subroutines (or segments). A procedure is used if a part of the program is called many times, and a program segment – not a procedure – is used if a part of the program is used only once. The abstract specification is translated into a main program, which is executed to check that the subroutines and segments are called up in the proper order under all conditions. Then the subroutines (or segments) are written in lower-level subroutines (or segments) and tested. This is continued until the lowest-level subroutines (or segments) are written and tested. Superior documentation is needed in this methodology to describe the procedure and program segments so they can be fully tested before they are actually written. "Pigeon C" is a very useful tool for that purpose. Also, the inputs and outputs of subroutines have to be carefully specified. This will be discussed at the end of the next section.

The inverse of top-down design is bottom-up design, in which the lowest-level subroutines or program segments are written first and then fully debugged. These are built up, bottom to top, to form the main program. To test the procedure, you write a short program to call the procedure, expecting to discard this program when the next higher level program is written. Bottom-up design is especially useful in interface design. The lowest-level procedure which actually interfaces to the hardware is usually the trickiest to debug. This methodology lets you debug that part of the program with less interference from other parts. Bottom-up design is like solving an algebra problem with three separate equations, each equation in one unknown. Arbitrarily putting all the software and hardware together before testing any part of it is like simultaneously solving three equations in three unknowns. As the first algebraic problem is much easier, the use of bottom-up design is also a much easier way to debug interfacing software. In a senior level interfacing course at the University of Texas, students who tried to get everything working at once spent 30 hours a week in the lab, while those who used bottom-up design spent less than 10 hours a week on the same experiments.

Combinations of top-down and bottom-up design can be used. Top-down design works well with parts of the program that do not involve interfacing to hardware, and bottom-up design works better with parts that do involve interfacing.

2-3.3 Object-oriented Programming

The concept of object-oriented programming was developed to program symbolic processes, database storage and retrieval systems and user-friendly graphic interfaces. However, it is ideally suited to the design of I/O devices and systems that center on them. It provides a programming and design methodology that simplifies interface design.

The development of object-oriented programming is strongly connected to the language SMALLTALK. We would like to use these object-oriented techniques with those features of C that enable us to control I/O devices about as easily as they can be controlled in assembler language. Standard C cannot be used with all the features of objects. A derivative of C, called C++, has been developed to utilize objects with a syntax similar to that of C. THINK C has been modified to include as many features of object-oriented programming that are strictly compatible with the rules of (ANSI) standard C. The Macintosh interface appears to have been originally written using many object-oriented programming concepts, so there is good reason to make THINK C object-oriented. The THINK class library contains classes of objects, discussed below, for the windows, dialog boxes and menus used in the Macintosh interface.

Object-oriented programming uses data and action in a manner that is sufficiently different from procedural language (normal C) programming that they need new concepts and use different terminology for ideas that are similar to those of procedural languages. In this methodology, the data (called *instance variables* in THINK C, or data members in C++) and the procedures (called *methods* or function members) that operate on this data are *encapsulated* together in an *object*. As you get the data, you automatically get the methods used on it. Simply put, data and the (address of) methods will be declared in C *struct*s. The declaration of one of the *struct*s is called the *class*, which is just a template for the data and methods. For instance, the class for a queue can be declared as:

```
struct Queue :direct {
    unsigned char *QIn, *QOut, *QEnd, QSize, Qlen, error;
    void InitQ (char),Push(long);
    long Pull(void); int Error(void);
}*Q;
```

The data for the queue and pointers are declared in the same manner as are elements of a *struct*. The methods in it are declared in the same manner that prototypes of procedures are declared, as discussed in Section 2-3.1. The use of the type *long*, rather than *char*, in these declarations will be explained later. The essential idea is that an object is declared by a *struct* that declares procedure calls as well as data for the object.

Throughout this text, we will use a procedure *allocate* to provide buffer storage for queues and for an object's instance variables. The global variable *free* is initialized to the high end of a large buffer, which is subdivided into buffers by the *allocate* routine. The type *void ** means a pointer to something, anything; it does not conflict when assigned to other pointers, we don't need a caste when *allocate* is used to initialize a pointer.

char *free=0x10000;
void *allocate(i) int i{ return free -= i; }

A class's methods are written as procedures with the class name in front of two colons and the method name.

void Queue:: InitQ (i) char i;
{ QEnd = (QIn = QOut = allocate(i)) +(QSize = i); Qlen = error = 0; }
void Queue:: Push (i) long i;
{ if((Qlen++)>=QSize) error=1; if(QEnd== QIn) QIn-= QSize; *(QIn++)=i; }
long Queue:: Pull ()
{if((Qlen--)==0) error=1; if(QEnd== QOut) QOut -= QSize; return *(QOut ++); }
int Queue:: Error () { int i; i=error; error=0; return i; }

InitQ's argument is the desired size of the queue. Note that instance variables in the method don't have any special notation indicating their belonging to the object. A variable's name is first matched against local variables. If the name matches, the variable is local. Then the variable is matched against the object instance variables, and finally against the global variables. In a sense, object instance variables are local to the object's methods because they are not (directly) available outside these methods, but are global among the methods because all the object's methods can get to these same variables.

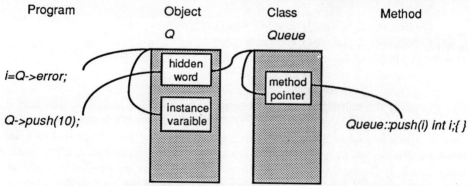

Figure 2-5. An Object and its Pointers.

We declare an object name as we would to a pointer (which we discuss more fully in Section 4-2) to a structure. We can also put (one or more) object names at the end of the declaration of the class, after the *}* and before the *;* on its last line. In order to use an object of a direct class, we use a special function *blessA()* to link up the object to its class(es). Declaring Q and executing the bless procedure is done as follows:

Queue *Q;
Q=blessA(sizeof(Queue),Queue);

It calls *allocate* shown above to provide the object's instance variable buffer, returns the address of the storage area for the object Q into the pointer Q and puts a (hidden) pointer into the instance variable buffer to the storage area for the class *Queue*. Figure 2-5 illustrates the pointers set up by this statement. Pointers to methods are factored out of each object so they do not have to be stored in each. The pointer *Q* to the object directly points to its instance variables (with an appropriate offset) but indirectly accesses the pointers to the methods by means of the link to the class *Queue*. Outside a method, the pointer is always used to access data or send a message to the object; we essentially think of the name of the pointer as the name of the object, as a convenience. When a message is sent to an object, a (hidden) procedure is called (rather like the procedure used in the *case* statement) to follow the pointers to jump to the right method, as illustrated in Figure 2-5.

Another function is provided that can test an object to determine if it is in a particular class or subclass. The procedure *memberD(o, c)* returns true (1) if object *o* is an object of the class c. This function provides a test you can use before using an instance variable of the class or sending a message to a method of the class, in case you do not know whether the variable or method is defined. Other special functions are provided for objects. The THINK C manual, Chapter 15, discusses these functions in more detail. However, in this book we only need *blessA()* and *memberD()*.

Putting all this together, we can write a simple program to use the queue. The program pushes three numbers, 1, 4, and 2, and then pulls them and checks that they appear in first-in-first-out order. Note that the main program uses *blessA()* to link up all the pointers, then it sends the *InitQ* message to *Q*, which executes the method *Queue::InitQ* shown above. Then *Q's Push()* method is executed three times, and *Q's Pull()* method is executed three times. We will test the instance variable *error* after the methods are called to illustrate how they can be accessed outside the object's methods.

```
main() {
    Q=blessA(sizeof(Queue),Queue);Q->InitQ(10);
    Q->Push(1); Q->Push(4); Q->Push(2);
    if(Q->Pull()!=1 || Q->Pull()!=4 ||Q->Pull()!=2) printf("Bad Queue\r");
    if(Q->error!=0) printf("An error occurred\r");
}
```

Sending the message to *InitQ* is executed by a hidden procedure that uses the pointer *Q*, just set up by *blessA*, to get to a hidden word in *Q's* buffer just set up by *blessA*, which is used to get to the pointers stored in class *Queue* where it looks for a pointer to the method *InitQ*. The hidden procedure then begins execution of the method *InitQ*. Similarly the messages sent to push and pull characters are handled through these data structures. Finally, to access *Q's* instance variable *error*, we execute the expression *Q->error*. This merely uses the pointer *Q* with an appropriate offset to get the character within *Q's* buffer, as in any C *struct*.

Objects, initially, just incorporate procedure names with the variables that the procedure uses. To avoid storing the procedure pointers with every object that uses them, the pointers are collected together and put in a different structure, the class. Instance variables are easily accessed by means of the pointer, and methods are almost as easily accessed by means of a pointer to a pointer. However, objects provide much more power.

Other fundamental ideas of object-oriented programming are that of subclasses, inheritance, factoring, and polymorphism. Simply, a class can be a *subclass* (also called *derived class*) of another class. For instance the aforementioned class *Queue* can have a subclass *IntQueue* for *int* variables; it declares different methods such as *Pull* and *Push* for the queue. The *superclass* (also called *base class*) of *IntQueue* is written after its name as *:Queue*. The superclass of *Queue* was written as *:direct* to indicate that it has no superclass (and also that it and its subclasses "directly" use pointers to access it rather than "indirectly" using pointers to pointers – handles – to access it); such a class with no superclass is called a *root class*.

  struct IntQueue: Queue { void Push(long); long Pull(void); };

  void IntQueue:: Push (i) long i;
    { if((Qlen+=2)>QSize) error=1; if(QEnd==QIn)QIn-=QSize; *(int*)QIn=i;QIn+=2; }

  long IntQueue:: Pull ()
    {if((Qlen-=2)==0)error=1;if(QEnd==QOut)QOut-=QSize;QOut+=2;return *((int*)QOut-2); }

InitQ's argument is the desired size of the queue in bytes, which must be even. The subclass defines only the instance variables or methods that are different from its parent's instance variables or methods, and *inherits* the instance variables or methods of the parent that are not redefined in the subclass. Suppose an object *Q1* is blessed as a member of the class *IntQueue* which is defined, as above as a subclass of *Queue* and a message is sent as in *Q1->InitQ(10);* then the method *Queue:: InitQ* is executed because *IntQueue* does not declare a different *InitQ* method. However, if a message *Q1->Push(1);* is sent, then the method *IntQueue:: Push* is executed rather than *Queue:: Push* because the class defines an *overriding* method for messages like *Q1->Push(1);* Although we did not need additional variables in the subclass, the same rules of inheritance and overriding would apply to variables too.

  The root class *Queue* could have a subclass such as *IntQueue* for each size of data to be queued. Following this idea, a hierarchy (tree) of classes will be used for all I/O devices in Section 4.5. The notion of *inheritance* is that an object will have data and methods defined in the superclass(es) of its class as well as those defined in its own class. One restriction applies, however, due to the fact that the compiler does not know how an object will be blessed at run time. If a method appears for a class and is overridden by methods with the same name in its subclasses, the sizes and types of all the arguments must be the same. If they were not, the compiler would not know how to pass arguments to the methods. For this reason, we defined the arguments of *Queue*'s *Push* and *Pull* methods to be *long* rather than *char*, so that the same method name can be used for the *int* version, or a *long* version, of the queue.

  A subclass can also have subclasses, as the class *Int1Queue* is a subclass of *IntQueue*. It merely provides a more obvious way to initialize the queue size.

  struct Int1Queue: IntQueue { void InitQ(char); };

  void Int1Queue:: InitQ (i) char i; { inherited::InitQ(2*i); }

InitQ's argument is the desired size of the queue in words rather than bytes. The statement *inherited::InitQ(2*i);*merely calls the *InitQ* of the class *IntQueue* which is, by inheritance, the method *Queue:: InitQ*.

  The phenomenon we call *factoring* uses inheritance. If you are a typical programmer, you have already faced the frustration of several times rewriting a procedure, such as one that outputs characters to a terminal, wishing you had saved a copy of it and used the earlier copy in later programs. Factoring is common to many disciplines – for instance, to algebra. In programming algebraic expressions, if you have *ab + ac* you can factor out the common term *a* and write *a (b + c)* which is considered more efficient because *a* is referenced just once. Similarly, if a large number of objects use the same method, such a method could be reproduced for each. It would be more efficient to declare such a method in one place, where all the user's programs would be able to use it. Inheritance permits the data and methods common to several classes to be declared in a superclass of them so it can be factored out, declared just once. Factoring is also a key idea in the concept of operating system device drivers, which are discussed in Chapter 10.

Polymorphism means that any two classes can declare the same method name and argument, especially a class and its inherited classes. Polymorphism means that simple intuitive names like *Push* can be used for interchangeable methods of different classes. It will be used later when we substitute one object for another object; the method names and arguments do not have to be changed. Polymorphism further means that a method of a class and its superclass can have the same name. For example in the classes above, both have a method called *InitQ*.

One of the ideas of object-oriented programming that is not compatible with (ANSI) C and is not used in THINK C, is that of *operator overloading*. Overloading means that the same operator symbol generates different effects depending on the type of the data it operates on. The C compiler already overloads its operators. The + operator generates an ADD.B instruction when adding data of type *char*, an ADD.W instruction when adding data of type *int*, and an ADD.L instruction when adding data of type *long*. What C++ does but THINK C cannot do is to overload operators so they do different things when an operand is an object, which depends on the object's definition. In effect, the programmer can provide the part of the compiler that generates the code for symbols, depending on the types of data used with the symbols. For instance, the << operator used for shift can be used for input or output if an operand is an I/O device. The expression *Q<<a* can be defined to output the character *a* to the Q and *a<<Q* can be defined to input a character from the Q and put it into *a*. Overloading can be used to create arithmetic-looking expressions that use methods to evaluate them. While this technique is useful, for instance in defining the operations on complex numbers or matrixes, its utility in handling I/O is rather limited. Without this feature, we simply have to write our messages as *a=Q->Input()* and *Q->Output(a)* rather than *Q<<a* or *a<<Q*. We will not miss operator overloading in this book.

Information hiding is a feature of objects that may or may not be useful. The instance variable *error* in the class Queue can be accessed by a pointer as in *Q->error* or by the method *Error*. A variable that cannot be accessed except by a method is *hidden*. A variable in C++ or in THINK C version 5.0 can be declared *public*, making it available everywhere, as in *Q->error, protected*, making it available only to methods of the same class or a subclass of it, or *private*, making it available only the same class's methods.

C++ or in THINK C version 5.0 also supports constructors, allocators, destructors and deallocators. An *allocator* is used to allocate instance variable storage, a *constuctor* can be used to initialize these variables, a *destuctor* can be used to terminate the use of an object, and a *deallocator* can be used to recover storage for instance variables for later allocation. We do not use these in THINK C version 4.0; they do not significantly impact the use of object oriented programming in interfacing, as described below.

Object-oriented programming has many features that make it very useful in programming a state-of-the-art microcomputer's I/O devices. Encapsulation is extended to include not only instance variables and methods, but also the I/O device, digital, analog, and mechanical systems used for this I/O. An *object* is these parts considered as a single unit. For instance, suppose you are designing an automobile controller. An object (Call it *PLUGS*)might be the spark plugs, their control hardware, and procedures. Having defined *PLUGS*, you define your messages (for instance, *SetRate(10)* to *PLUGS*) that pass between this object and other objects, rather like connecting wires between the hardware parts of these objects. The system takes shape in a clear intuitive way as the messages are defined. In top-down design, you can specify the arguments and the semantics of the methods that will be executed before you write them. In bottom-up design, the object *PLUGS* can be tested by a driver as a unit before it is connected to other objects.

An object can be replaced by another object, if the messages are written the same way (polymorphism). If you replace your spark plug firing system with another, the whole old *PLUGS* object can be removed and a whole new *PLUGS1* object inserted. You can maintain a *library of classes* to construct new products by building on large pretested modules. Having several objects with different costs and performances, you can insert a customer-specified one in each unit. Factoring can be used to save design effort.

Factoring can be used in a different way to simplify programming rather complex 683xx I/O systems. In order to use the 68332's powerful QSPI module for external I/O devices, some basic routines, available in a library of classes, will be needed to initialize it, to repetitively exchange data with the device, or to exchange data with it only on the program's or the device's command. Then as larger systems are implemented, such as *PLUGS*, that use the QSPI, new classes can be defined as subclasses of these existing classes, to avoid rewriting the methods inherited from the classes in the library.

Putting these two notions together might produce an incompatible notion of factoring, but actually appears to work synergetically. The hierarchy of classes at the root end can implement the factoring of routines needed to control a 683xx's I/O system that prevent duplication of code. In this book, we will build up this infrastructure. For instance we will build an object for an I/O device that includes all the methods needed to initialize and use it. The leaf-ward part of the hierarchy can be used to add special functions to the basic I/O system to meet a specific application's requirements. For instance, an object for a robot controller might be coupled to the 683xx system by means of an RS232 serial link as discussed in Chapter 9. The object *ROBOT* can be a member of a newly defined class *ROBOTDevice* that has additional methods, or can use the methods of its superclass(es) to correctly and efficiently handle messages sent to *ROBOT* or received from *ROBOT*. The control of *ROBOT* will be high-level, because all the lower-level operations are invisible to the writer of the messages (information hiding), which should substantially reduce the design cost and improve system reliability.

As defined above, the terminology used in THINK C follows the terminology used in Object PASCAL; corresponding terminology in C++ is: function member for method, data member for instance variable, base class for superclass, and derived class for subclass.

2-3.4 Optimizing C Programs Using Declarations

THINK C is designed to be generally useful but is here used to interface to I/O. We will discuss some of THINK C's techniques that can be used to improve your interface software, and some techniques you can use to get around THINK C's limitations for this application. While the techniques discussed here are specific to THINK C, if you are using another compiler or cross- compiler, similar ideas can be implemented for other systems.

C has some additional declaration keywords. If the word *register* is put in front of a local variable, that variable will be stored in a register. Data variables, declared as in *register int i* or *register char c* are stored in registers D7, D6, ... D3, first declared variable in D7. Pointer variables, declared as in *register int *i* or *register char *c* are stored in registers A4, A3, or A2 (although A4 is not used if objects are used because it is used to access the object instance variables) first declared variable in A4 (or A3 if objects are used). Putting often-used local variable in registers instead of on the stack obviously speeds up procedures. It also puts them in known places that can be used in embedded assembler language discussed in the next subsection. You can check your understanding of the use of these registers by writing a C procedure with embedded assembler language, then using MACSBUG or TSMON to disassemble your program in the Macintosh, or downloading it to the 683xx BCC and disassembling it. Although the latter appears to be more involved, it is easier to understand and to learn from than searching the Macintosh's memory for procedures.

If the word *static* is put in front of a local variable, that variable will initialized, stored, and accessed as a global variable is, but it will only be "known" to the procedure like a local variable is. If the word *static* is put in front of a global variable or a procedure name, that variable or procedure will only be known within the file and not linked to other files. For instance if a THINK C project is composed of several files of source code such as file1.c, file2.c and so on, then if a procedure *fun()* in file1.c is declared static, it cannot be called from a procedure in file2.c. However both file1.c and file2.c can have procedures *fun()* in them without creating duplicate procedure names when they are linked together to run (or download) the procedures. If you use the downloader MacDi, it is only able to download one file at a time and is not able to link them together, so we encourage you to declare all procedures and global variables (except *Aboutxxx()*) as static. Then you can use the same names in different files.

2-3.5 Optimizing C Programs with Assembler Language

Assembly language can be embedded in a C program. It is the only way to insert some instructions like RTE used to end an exception handler, and instructions to modify the status register, for instance to enable interrupts. It can be used to implement better procedures than are produced from C source code by the compiler. For instance, the DBRA instruction can be put in assembler language embedded in C to get a faster *while-loop*. Finally, the DC directive can be used to build the machine code of instructions that are in the 683xx instruction set but are not in the 68000 or 68020 instruction set, and are thus not generated by THINK C or its embedded assembler.

Embedded assembly language is put within the brackets in the expression *asm { }*. Also, to use 68020 instructions that include many of the 683xx instructions not in the 68000, you can write *asm 68020 { }*.

Finally, we may need to insert a (software) breakpoint into a program we are debugging. The BGND instruction is not even available in (68000 or 68020) assembler language because it is an new instruction added to the instruction set of the 683xx. To insert it, we not only have to use the above technique to embed assembler language, but we need to construct machine code using the define constant directive. The machine code for the BGND instruction is *0x4afa*. A software breakpoint can be inserted in a C procedure by putting *asm{ dc 0x4afa}* in the program. Note that a *#define* statement can be used to make this insertion more readable. Use *#define bgnd asm{ dc 0x4afa}* and *#define Bgnd asm{ dc 0x4afa}*. Then each time you need a breakpoint in an assembler language segment, write *bgnd,* and each time you need a breakpoint in a C procedure outside an assembler language segment, write *Bgnd*.

Variable names declared in C can be used in the addressing modes in assembler language instructions. For instance, a procedure *clr()* to quickly clear a block of *N+1* bytes starting at location *A* can be written

> *clr(A,N) register char *A; register int N;{*
> *asm {*
> *@0   CLR.B (A)+*
> *DBRA N,@0*
> *}*
> *}*

The label *A* will generate a reference to A4 because register A4 is the first assigned to a *register* type pointer variable. The first instruction will be coded as CLR.B (A4)+. The label *N* will generate a reference to D7 because that is the first assigned to a *register* data variable. The second instruction will be coded as DBRA D7,@0. Non-register variable names can similarly be used. For instance, a procedure *store()* to put *N* into location *A* can be written

> *clr(A,N) register int *A; int N;{*
> *asm { MOVE.W N,(A) }*
> *}*

The label *A* will generate a reference with appropriate offset (such as 0xC) to A6 because register A6 with a positive offset is used to access arguments of the procedure. The instruction will be coded as MOVE.W 0xC(A6),(A4). Global, local, and object instance variable names, as well as procedure parameter names, can be used as assembler language source or destination addresses provided that the instruction can use index addressing for these addresses. Figure 2-6 illustrates how THINK C treats assembler language variable labels depending on how they are declared.

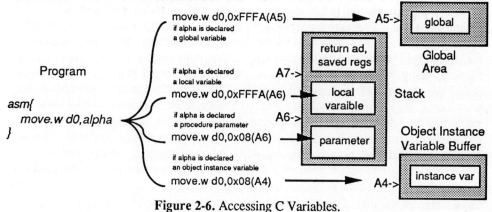

Figure 2-6. Accessing C Variables.

The version 4.0 THINK C manual, Chapter 14, discusses of how assembler language can be embedded in C. The *CPU32 Central Processor Reference Manual (CPU32RM/AD)* Motorola Inc., 1989, should be consulted to understand the machine coding of 683xx instructions an the meaning of instructions. Using these resources, you should be able to insert assembler language and machine code into your C programs.

2-4 Conclusions

In this chapter, we have surveyed some software background needed for microcomputer interfacing. The first section introduced C. It was followed by the description and handling of data structures. C constructs were introduced in order to make the implementation of storage structures concrete. Indexed and sequential structures were surveyed. We then covered programming style and procedure calling and argument passing techniques. We then covered structured and top-down, and bottom-up programming, introduced object-oriented C, and discussed why object-oriented programming is well suited to writing I/O software. Finally, we showed some techniques used to improve C procedures or insert necessary corrections to the code produced by the compiler.

If you found any section difficult, we can recommend additional readings. *The C Programming Language* by Kernighan and Richie, who were the original developers of C, remains the bible and fundamental reference for C. Tutorials on object-oriented programming are available from the IEEE Computer Society Press. An outstanding article, "Object-Oriented Development" by Grady Booch in the IEEE Computer Society Press tutorial *Object-Oriented Computing*, Gerald Peterson, Ed., vol 2. lead us to appreciate the use of objects in the design of embedded microcomputer systems. We recommend that you read it as well as subsequent articles on object-oriented design. Other fine books are available on these topics, and more are appearing daily. We might suggest contacting a local college or university instructor who teaches architecture, microprocessors, or C programming for the most recent books on these topics.

Do You Know These Terms?

See the End of Chapter 1 for Instructions.

procedure, main, declaration of a parameter, declaration of a variable, char, int, long, caste, unsigned, statement, allocate, deallocate, if then (else), relational operator, logical operator, case statement, break statement, while statement, do while statement, for statement, pigeon C, programs, information structure, data structure, storage structure, define statements, enum statement, vector, zero-origin indexing, precision, cardinality, list, structure, linked list, array, row major order, column major order, table, string, character string, ASCII code, null, line feed, form feed, carriage return, space, huffman code, binary tree, deque, push, pull (or pop), overflow, underflow, buffer, indexable deque, stack, queue, arguments, parameters, formal parameter, actual parameter, call by value and result, call by reference, call by name, call by value, return statement, call by result, prototype, extern, macro, structured programming, top-down design, instance variable, method, encapsulation, object, subclass, derived class, superclass, base class, inherit, inheritance, factoring, polymorphism, operator overloading, information hiding, hidden variable, public, protected, private, constructor, allocator, destructor, deallocator, library of classes, register variable, static variable.

3

Bus Hardware and Signals

Understanding data and address buses is critical because they are at the heart of interfacing design. This chapter will discuss what a bus is, how data are put onto it, and how data from it are used. The chapter progresses logically, with the first section covering basic concepts in digital hardware, the next section using those concepts to describe the control signals on the bus, and the final section discussing the important issue of timing in the microprocessor bus.

The first section of this chapter is a condensed version of background material on computer organization and realization (as opposed to architecture and software discussed in earlier chapters) needed in the remainder of the book. They lead to the study of bus timing and control – very important to the design of interfaces. How important can be shown in the following experience. Microcomputer manufacturers have applications engineers who write notes on how to use the chips the companies manufacture and who answer those knotty questions that systems designers can't handle. The author had an opportunity to sit down with Charlie Melear, one of the very fine applications engineers in the Microcomponents Applications Engineering group at Motorola's plant. Charlie told me that the two most common problems designers have are (1) improper control signals for the bus, whereby several bus drivers are given commands to drive the bus at the same time, and (2) failure to meet timing specifications for address and data buses – problems which will be covered in the chapter's last sections. These problems come up so often that studying them in depth can save a lot of frustration in interface design.

This chapter introduces a lot of terminology to provide background for later sections and to enable you to read data sheets provided by the manufacturers. The terminology is as close as possible to that used in industry: Logic diagram conventions conform to those used in *Electronics* magazine and to the Texas Instruments *The TTL Data Book*, and microprocessor notation conforms to that used in Motorola data sheets. However, some minor deviations have been introduced where constructs appear so often in this book that further notation is useful.

This chapter should provide enough background in computer organization for the remaining sections. After reading the chapter, you should be able to read a logic diagram or the data sheets describing microcomputers or their associated integrated circuits, and should have a fundamental knowledge of the signals and their timing on a typical microcomputer bus. This chapter should provide adequate hardware background for later chapters. However, if you find it difficult, additional reading is recommended. As in the last two chapters, references will be mentioned in the Conclusions section of this chapter.

3-1 Digital Hardware

The basic notions and building blocks of digital hardware are presented in this section. While you have probably taken a course on digital hardware design that most likely emphasized minimization of logic gates, microcomputer interfacing requires an emphasis on buses. Therefore, this section focuses on the digital hardware that can be seen on a typical microcomputer bus. The first subsection provides clear definitions of terms used to describe signals and modules connected to a bus. The second subsection considers the kinds of modules you might see there.

3-1.1 Modules and Signals

Before the bus is explained, we need to discuss a few hardware concepts, such as the module and the signal. Because we are dealing in abstractions, we do not use concrete examples with units like electrons and fields.

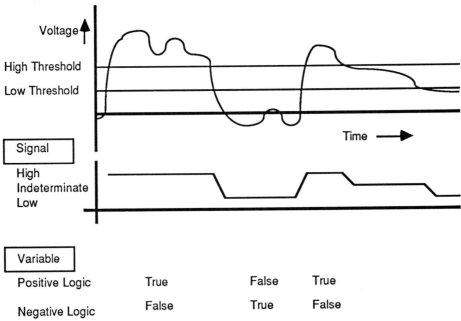

Figure 3-1. Voltage Waveforms, Signals, and Variables.

One concept is the binary *signal*. (See Figure 3-1.) Although a signal is a voltage or a current, we think of it only as a *high* signal, if the voltage or current is above a

Chapter 3 – Bus Hardware and Signals

predefined threshold, or as a *low* signal, if it is below another threshold. We will use the symbols H for high and L for low. A signal is *determinate* when we can know for sure whether it is high or low. Related to this concept, a *variable* is the information a signal carries, and has values *true* (T) and *false* (F). For example, a wire can carry a signal, L, and, being a variable called "ENABLE," it can have a value T to indicate that something is indeed enabled. We use the expression "to *assert a variable*" to mean to make it true, "to *negate a variable*" to make it false, and "to *complement a variable*" to make it true if it was false or make it false if it was true. Two possible relations exist between signals and variables. In *positive logic*, a high signal represents a true variable and a low signal, a false variable. In *negative logic*, a high signal represents a false variable and a low, a true variable. Signals, which can be viewed on an oscilloscope or a logic analyzer, are preferred when someone, especially a technician, deals with actual hardware. Variables have a more conceptual significance and seem to be preferred by designers, especially in the early stages of design, and by programmers, especially when writing I/O software. Simply put, "true" and "false" are the 1 and 0 of the programmer, the architect, and the system designer; and "high" and "low" are the 1 and 0 of the technician and IC manufacturer. While nothing is wrong with using 1 and 0 where the meaning is clear, we use the words true and false when talking about software or system design and the words high and low when discussing the hardware realization, to be clear.

Two types of variables and their corresponding signals are important in hardware. A *memory variable* is capable of being made true or false and of retaining this value, but a *link variable* is true or false as a result of functions of other variables. A link variable is always some function of other variables (as the output of some gate). At a high level of abstraction, these variables operate in different dimensions; memory variables are used to convey information through time (at the same point in space), while link variables convey information through space (at the same point in time). Some transformations on hardware, like converting from a parallel to a serial adder, are nicely explained by this abstract view. For instance, one can convert a parallel adder into a serial adder by converting a link variable that passes the carry into a memory variable that saves the carry. Also, in a simulation program, we differentiate between the types because memory variables have to be initialized and link variables don't.

A *synchronous* signal can be viewed as associated with a periodic variable (for example, a square wave) called a *clock*. The signal or variable is indeterminate except when the clock is asserted. Or, alternatively, the value of the signal is irrelevant except when the clock is asserted. Depending on the context, the signal is determinate either precisely when the clock changes from false to true or as long as the clock is true. The context depends on what picks up the signal and will be discussed when we study the flip-flop. This is so in the real world because of delays through circuitry, noise, and transmission line ringing. In our abstraction of the signal, we simply ignore the signal except when this clock is asserted, and we design the system so the clock is asserted only when we can guarantee the signal is determinate under worst case conditions. Though there are asynchronous signals where there is no associated clock and the signals are supposed to be determinate at all times, most microprocessor signals are synchronous; so in further discussions, we will assume all signals are synchronous. Then two signals are *equivalent* if they have the same (H or L) value whenever the clock is asserted.

The other basic idea is that of the *module*, which is a block of hardware with identifiable input, output, and memory variables. The input variables are the *input ports* and output variables are the *output ports*. Often, we are only interested in the behavior. Modules are *behaviorally equivalent* if, for equivalent values of the initial memory variables and equivalent sequence of values of input variables, they deliver equivalent sequence of values of output variables. Thus, we are not concerned about how they are constructed internally, what the precise voltages are, or what the signals are when the clock is not asserted, but only the signals when the clock is asserted.

In Section 1-1.3, we introduced the idea of an integrated circuit (IC) to define the term microprocessor. Now we discuss more about it. An integrated circuit is a module that is generally contained in a *dual in-line package* or *DIP*. This is a long rectangular plastic or ceramic package with pins along both the long edges (hence the term dual in-line). The pins are the input and output ports. Viewed from the top, one of the short edges has an indent or mark. The pins are numbered counterclockwise from this mark, starting with pin 1. Gates are defined in the next section, but will be used here to describe degrees of complexity of integrated circuits. A *small scale integrated circuit*, or SSI, has about 10 gates on one chip, a *medium scale integrated circuit* (MSI) has about 100, a *large scale integrated circuit* (LSI) has about 1000, and a *very large scale integrated circuit* (VLSI) has more than 10,000. SSI and MSI circuits are commonly used to build up address decoders and some I/O modules in a microcomputer; LSI and VLSI are commonly used to implement 8- and 16-bit word microprocessors, 64K-bit and 128K-bit memory chips, and some complex I/O chips.

A *family* of integrated circuits is a collection of different types made with the same technology and having the same electrical characteristics, so they can be easily connected with others in the same family. Chips from different families can be interconnected, but this might require some careful study and design. The *low-power Schottky* or LS family, and the *complementary metal oxide semiconductor* or CMOS family, are often used with microprocessors. The LS family is used where higher speed is required, and the CMOS family, where lower power or higher immunity to noise is desired. The HCMOS family is a high-speed CMOS family particularly useful in MC683xx system designs because it is fast enough for address decoding but requires very little power and can tolerate large variations in the power supply.

A block diagram was introduced at the beginning of Section 1-3. In block diagrams, names represent variables rather than signals, and functions like AND or OR represent functions on variables rather than signals. An AND function, for example, is one in which the output is T if all the inputs are T. Such conventions ignore details needed to build the module, so the module's behavior can be simply explained.

Logic diagrams describe the realization of hardware to the level of detail needed to build it. In logic diagrams, modules are generally shown as rectangles, with input and output ports shown along the perimeter. Logic functions are generally defined for signals rather than variables (for example, an AND function is one whose output is H if its inputs are all H). It is common, and in fact desirable, to use many copies of the same module. The original module, here called the *type*, has a name, the *type name*. Especially when referring to one module copy among several, we give each copy a distinct *copy name*. The type name or copy name may be put in a logic diagram when the meaning is clear, or both may be put in the rectangle or over the left upper corner. Analogous to subroutines, inputs and outputs of the type name are *formal parameter names*, and inputs and outputs of the copy name are *actual parameter names*. Integrated circuits in particular are shown this way: Formal parameters are shown inside a box representing the integrated circuit, and pin numbers and actual parameters are shown outside the rectangle for each connection that has to be made. Pins that don't have to be connected are not shown as connections to the module. (Figure 3-3 provides some examples of these conventions.)

Connections supplying power (positive supply voltage and ground) are usually not shown. They might be identified in a footnote, if necessary. In general, in LSI and VLSI N channel MOS chips such as microprocessors and input/output chips discussed in these notes, Vss is the ground pin (0 volts) and Vcc or Vdd is usually +5 volts. You might remember this by a quotation improperly attributed to Churchill: "*Ground the SS* ." For SSI and MSI chips, the pin with the largest pin number is generally connected to +5 volts while the pin kitty-corner from it is connected to ground. See Figure 3-3. One should keep power and ground lines straight and wide to reduce inductance that causes ringing, and put a capacitor (.1 microfarad disc) between power and ground to isolate the ICs from each other. When one chip changes its power supply current, these *bypass capacitors* serve to prevent voltage fluctuations from affecting the voltage supplied to other chips, which might look like signals to them. Normally, such a capacitor is needed for four SSI chips or one LSI chip, but if the power and ground lines appear to have noise, more capacitors should be put between power and ground.

In connections to inner modules, negative logic is usually shown by a small bubble where the connection touches the rectangle. In inputs and outputs to the whole system described by the logic diagram, negative logic is shown by a bar over the variable's name. Ideally, if a link is in negative logic, all its connections to modules should have bubbles. However, because changing logic polarity effects an inversion of the variable, designers sometimes steal a free inverter this way; so if bubbles do not match at both ends, remember that the signal is unchanged, but the variable is inverted, as it goes through the link.

A logic diagram should convey all the information needed to build a module, allowing only the exceptions we just discussed to reduce the clutter. Examples of logic diagrams appear throughout these notes. An explanation of Figures 3-2 and 3-3, which must wait until the next section, should clarify these conventions.

3-1.2 Drivers, Registers, and Memories

This section describes the bus in terms of the D flip-flop and the bus driver. These devices serve to take data from the bus and to put data onto it. The memory – a collection of registers – is also introduced.

A *gate* is an elementary module with a single output, where the value of the output is a Boolean logic function of the values of the inputs. The output of a gate is generally a link variable. For example, a three-input NOR gate output is true if none of its inputs are true, otherwise it is false. The output is always determined in terms of its inputs. A *buffer* is a gate that has a more powerful output amplifier and is often used to supply the power needed to put signals onto a bus, discussed soon. And in these cases, the gate may be very simple, so that it has just one input, and the output is the complement of the input (inverting) or the same signal as the input (noninverting).

Your typical gate has an output stage which may be connected to up to f other inputs of gates of the same family (f is called the *fan-out*) and to no other output of a gate. If two outputs are connected to the same link, they may try to put opposite signals on the link, which will certainly be confusing to inputs on the link, and may even damage the output stages. However, a *bus (or buss)* is a link to which more than two gate outputs are connected. The gates must have specially designed output amplifiers so that all but one output on a bus may be disabled. The gates are called *bus drivers*. An upper limit to the number of outputs that can be connected to a bus is called the *fan-in*.

An *open collector gate* or open collector driver output can be connected to a *wire-OR* bus. The bus, in negative logic, must have a *pull-up resistor* connected between it and the positive supply voltage. If any output should attempt to put out a low (true) signal, the signal on the bus will be low. Only when no outputs attempt to put out a low signal will the output be pulled high (false) by the pull-up resistor. Because the wire effects an OR function, but no OR gate is actually used, it is called wire-or. Often, the open collector gate is a two-input AND gate – inputs in positive logic and output in negative logic. A signal, on one of its inputs, is put onto the bus whenever its other input is true. The other input acts as a positive logic *enable*. When the enable is asserted, we say the driver is *enabled*.

A *tristate gate* or tristate driver has an additional input, a *tristate enable*. When the tristate enable is asserted (the driver is enabled), the output amplifier forces the output signal high or low as directed by the gate logic. When the enable is not asserted, the output amplifier lets the output float. Two or more outputs of tristate gates may be connected to a *tristate bus*. The circuitry must be designed to insure that no two gates are enabled at the same time, lest the problem with connecting outputs of ordinary gates arise. If no gates are enabled, the bus signal floats – it is subject to stray static and electromagnetic fields. In other words, it acts like an antenna.

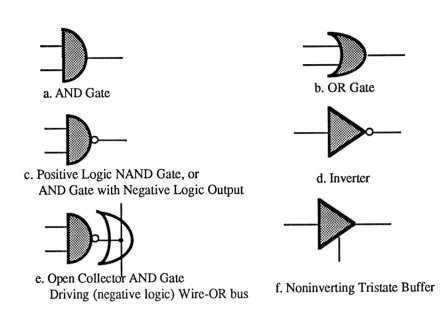

a. AND Gate

b. OR Gate

c. Positive Logic NAND Gate, or
   AND Gate with Negative Logic Output

d. Inverter

e. Open Collector AND Gate
   Driving (negative logic) Wire-OR bus

f. Noninverting Tristate Buffer

Figure 3-2. Some Common Gates.

Chapter 3 – Bus Hardware and Signals

Gates are usually shown in logic diagrams as D-shaped symbols, the output on the round edge and inputs on the flat edge. (See Figure 3-2 for the positive logic AND, NAND, and other gates.) Even though they are not shown using the aforementioned convention for modules, if they are in integrated circuits, the pin numbers are often shown next to all inputs and outputs.

Dynamic logic gates are implemented by passing charges (collections of electrons or holes) through switches; the charges have to be replenished, or they will discharge. Most gates use currents rather than charges and are *static* rather than dynamic. Dynamic logic must be pulsed at a rate between a minimum and a maximum time, or it will not work; but dynamic logic gates are more compact than normal (static) logic gates.

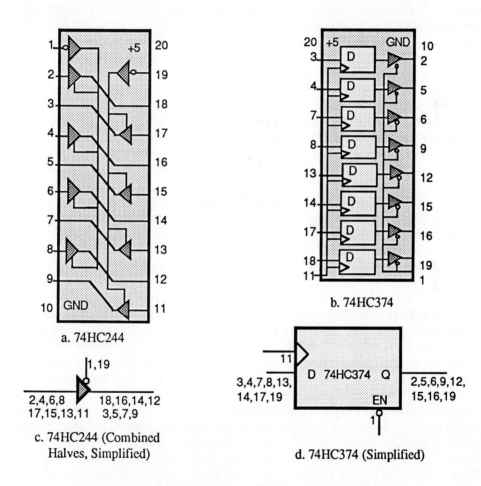

Figure 3-3. Logic Diagrams for a Popular Driver and Register.

Gates are usually put into integrated circuits so that the total number of pins is 14 or 16, counting two pins for positive supply voltage and ground. This yields, for instance, the quad two-input NAND gate, the 7400, which contains four two-input positive logic NAND gates. The 74HC00 is an HCMOS part with the pin configuration of the older 7400 TTL part. The 7404 has six inverters in a chip; it is called a hex inverter, so it is a good treat for Halloween (to invert hexes). A typical microprocessor uses an 8-bit-wide data bus, where eight identical and separate bus wires carry 1 bit of data on each wire. This has, in an IC, engendered octal bus drivers, with eight inverting or noninverting bus drivers that share common enables. The 74HC244 and 74HC240 are popular octal noninverting and inverting tristate bus driver integrated circuits. Figure 3-3a shows a logic diagram of the 74HC244, in which, to clearly show pin connections, the pins are placed along the perimeter of the module exactly as they appear on the dual in-line package. A positive 5-volt supply wire is connected to pin 20, and a ground wire, to pin 10. If the signals on both pins 1 and 19 are low, the eight separate tristate gates will be enabled. For instance, the signal input to pin 2 will be amplified and output on pin 18. If pins 1 and 19 are high, the tristate amplifiers are not enabled, and the outputs on pins 18, 16,..., 9 are allowed to float. This kind of diagram is valuable in catalogues to most clearly show the inputs and outputs of gates in integrated circuits.

To save effort in drawing logic diagrams, if a number n of identical wires connect to identical modules, a single line is drawn with a slash through it and the number n next to the slash. If pin connections are to be shown, a list of n pin numbers is written. Corresponding pins in the list at one end are connected to corresponding pins in the list at the other end. Commonly, however, the diagram is clear without showing the list of pin numbers. Also, if a single wire is connected to several pins, it is diagrammed as a single line, and the list of pins is written by the line. Figure 3-3c, shows how the 74HC244 just discussed might be more clearly shown connecting to a bus in a logic diagram. Note the eight tristate drivers, their input and output links shown by one line and gate symbol. The eight-element vectors indicate the figure should be replicated eight times. The NOR gate output, a single link, connects to all eight bus drivers' enables.

A *D flip-flop*, also called a (1-bit) *latch,* is an elementary module with *data input* D, *clock* C, and *output* Q. Q is always a memory variable having the value of the bit of data stored in the flip-flop. When the clock C is asserted (we say the flip-flop is *clocked*), the value of D is copied into the flip-flop memory. The clock input is rather confusing because it is really just a WRITE ENABLE. It sounds as though it must be the same as the microcomputer system clock. It may be connected to such a clock, but usually it is connected to something else, such as an output of a controller, which is discussed in Section 3-2.1. It is, however, the clock that is associated with the synchronous variable on the D input of that flip-flop, because the variable has to be determinate whenever this clock is asserted. As long as C is asserted, Q is made equal to D. As long as C is false, Q remains what it was. Note that, when C is false, Q is the value of D at the moment when C changed from true to false. However, when C is asserted, the flip-flop behaves like a wire from D to Q, and Q changes as D changes. D flip-flops are used to hold data sent to them on the D inputs, so the data, even though long since gone from the D input, will still be available on the Q output.

A *D edge-triggered flip-flop* is an elementary module like the D flip-flop, except that the data stored in it and available on the Q output are made equal to the D input only when the clock C changes from false to true. The clock causes the data to change (the flip-flop is clocked) in this very short time. A *D master slave flip-flop* (also called a dual-rank flip-flop) is a pair of D flip-flops where the D input to the second is internally

Chapter 3 – Bus Hardware and Signals

connected to the Q output of the first, and the clock of the second is the complement of the clock of the first. Though constructed differently, a D master slave flip-flop behaves the same as the D edge-triggered flip-flop. These two flip-flops have the following property: Data on their Q output are always the former value of data in them at the time that new data are put into them. It is possible, therefore, to use the signal output from an edge-triggered flip-flop to feed data into the same or another edge-triggered flip-flop using the same clock, even while loading new data. This should not be attempted with D flip-flops, because the output will be changing as it is being used to determine the value to be stored in the flip-flops that use the data. When a synchronous signal is input to a D edge-triggered flip-flop, the clock input to the flip-flop is associated with the signal, and the signal only has to be determinate when the clock changes from false to true.

In either type of flip-flop or in more complex devices that use flip-flops, the data have to be determinate (a stable high or a stable low signal) over a range of time when the data are being stored. For an edge-triggered or dual-rank flip-flop, the *setup time* is the time during which the data must be determinate before the clock edge. The *hold time* is the time after the clock edge during which the data must be determinate. For a latch, the setup time is the minimum time at the end of the period when the clock is true in which the data must be determinate; and the hold time is the minimum time just after that when the data must still be determinate. These times are usually specified for worst case possibilities. If you satisfy the setup and hold times, the device can be expected to work as long as it is kept at a temperature and supplied with power voltages that are within specified limits. If you don't, it may work some of the time, but will probably fail, according to Murphy's Law, at the worst possible time.

In most integrated circuit D flip-flops or D edge-triggered flip-flops, the output Q is available along with its complement, which can be thought of as the output Q in negative logic. They often have inputs, set, which if asserted will assert Q, and reset, which if asserted will make Q false. Set and reset are often in negative logic; when not used, they should be connected to a false value or high signal. Other flip-flops such as set-reset flip-flops and JK edge-triggered flip-flops are commonly used in digital equipment, but we won't need consider them in the following discussions.

A *one-shot* is rather similar to the flip-flop. It has an input TRIG and an output Q, and has a resistor and capacitor connected to it. The output Q is normally false. When the input TRIG changes from false to true, the output becomes true and remains true for a period of time T which is fixed by the values of a resistor and a capacitor.

The use of 8-bit-wide data buses has engendered ICs that have four or eight flip-flops with common clock inputs and common clear inputs. If simple D flip-flops are used, the whole module is called a *latch*, and if edge-triggered flip-flops are used, it is a *register*. Also, modules for binary number counting (*counters*) or shifting data in one direction (*shift registers*) may typically contain four or eight edge-triggered flip-flops. Note that, even though a module may have additional capabilities, it may still be used without these capabilities. A counter or a shift register is sometimes used as a simple register. More interestingly, a latch can be used as a noninverting gate or, using the complemented Q output, as an inverter. This is done by tying the clock to true. The 74HC163 is a popular 4-bit binary counter, the 74HC164 and 74HC165 are common 8-bit shift registers, and the 74HC373 and 74HC374 are popular octal latches and registers, with built-in tristate drivers. The 74HC374 will be particularly useful in the following discussion of practical buses, because it contains a register to capture data from the bus, as well as a tristate driver to put data onto the bus.

The following conventions are used to describe flip-flops in logic diagrams. The clock and D inputs are shown on the left of a square, the set on the top, the clear on the bottom, and the Q on the right. The letter D is put by the D input, but the other inputs need no letters. The clock of an edge-triggered flip-flop is denoted by a triangle just inside the jointure of that input. This triangle and the bubble outside the square describe the clocking. If neither appears, the flip-flop is a D flip-flop that inputs data from D when the clock is high; if a bubble appears, it is a D flip-flop that inputs data when the clock is low; if a triangle appears, it is an edge-triggered D flip-flop that inputs data when the clock changes from low to high; and if both appear, it is an edge-triggered D flip-flop that inputs data when the clock input changes from high to low. This notation is quite useful because a lot of design errors are due to clocking flip-flops when the data are not ready to be input. If a signal is input to several flip-flops, they should all be clocked at the same time, when the signal will be determinate.

The logic diagram of the 74HC374 is shown in Figure 3-3b as it might appear in a catalogue. Note that the common clock for all the edge-triggered D flip-flops on pin 11 makes them store data on their own D inputs when it rises from low to high. Note that, when the signal on pin 1 is low, the tristate drivers are all enabled, so the data in the flip-flops are output through them. Using this integrated circuit in a logic diagram, we might compact it using the bus conventions, as shown in Figure 3-3d.

An *(i,j) random access memory* (RAM) is a module with i rows and j columns of D flip-flops, and an address port, an input port, and an output port. A row of the memory is available simultaneously and is usually referred to as a *word,* and the number j is called the *word width.* There is considerable ambiguity here, because a computer may think of its memory as having a word width, but the memory module itself may have a different word width, and it may be built from RAM integrated circuits having yet a different word width. So the word and the word width should be used in a manner that avoids this ambiguity. The output port outputs data read from a row of the flip-flops to a bus and usually has bus drivers built into it. Sometimes the input and output ports are combined. The address port is used to input the row number of the row to be read or written. A *memory cycle* is a time when the memory can write j bits from the input port into a row selected by the address port data, read j bits from a row selected by the address port data to the output port, or do nothing. If the memory reads data, the drivers on the output port are enabled. There are two common ways to indicate which of the three possible operations to do in a memory cycle. In one, two variables called *chip enable* (CE) and *read/write* (RW or R/W) indicate the possibilities; a do nothing cycle is executed if CE is false, a read if CE and RW are both asserted, and a write if CE is asserted but RW is not. In the other, two variables, called *read enable* (RE) and *write enable* (WE), are used; when neither is asserted, nothing is done; when RE is asserted, a read is executed; and if WE is asserted, a write is executed. Normally, CE, RE, and WE are in negative logic. The *memory cycle time* is the time needed to complete a read or a write operation and be ready to execute another read or write. The *memory access time* is the time from the beginning of a memory cycle until the data read from a memory are determinate on the output, or the time when data to be written must be determinate on the input of the memory. A popular fast (20-nanosecond access time) (4,4) RAM is the 74LS670. It has four input ports and four separate output ports; by having two different address ports it is actually able to simultaneously read a word selected by the read address port and to write a word selected by the write address port. A larger, slower (500-nanosecond cycle time) (8K,8) RAM is the 6164. It has an 11-bit address, eight input/output ports, and CE and W variables that permit it to read or write any word in a memory cycle. A diagram of this chip appears in Figure 3-15a, when we consider an example that uses it in Section 3-3.2.

Several cousins to the RAM are used in microcomputers, especially to store fixed data and programs. A *read-only memory* (ROM) is a rather large memory that can be read but can never be written into. The pattern stored in the memory is determined by a mask used in the final stages of manufacturing the chip. This mask is rather expensive; so ROMs are mass-produced using standard patterns and thus are not at all expensive. A *programmable read-only memory* (PROM) is a ROM that can be written into (*programmed*) by the designer by burning fuses inside it for each bit; a fuse is blown if an F is stored, and not blown if a T is stored. PROMs can be programmed by the designer, but he or she cannot unblow a fuse. An *erasable programmable read-only memory* (EPROM) is a PROM that, instead of fuses, uses static charges on a buried conductor in a dielectric insulation layer. A charge on the conductor cuts off the current below it, so it acts like a blown fuse. The charges are programmed similarly to a PROM's, but they can be removed by exposing the insulator to ionizing ultraviolet light. The *electronically erasable programmable memory* (EEPROM) is an EPROM that can be erased by an electrical pulse rather than an ultraviolet light. It is not quite a RAM, however, as it takes ~10 msec. to erase and write. These devices – ROMs, PROMs, EPROMs, and EEPROMs – are often used to store fixed data and programs.

The programmable array logic (PAL) chip has become readily available and is ideally suited to implementing microcomputer address decoders and other "glue" logic. (See Figure 3-4.) A PAL is basically a collection of gates whose inputs are connected by fuses like the PROM just mentioned. The second line from the top of Figure 3-4 represents a 32-input AND gate that feeds the tristate enable of a seven-input NOR gate, which in turn feeds pin 19. Each crossing line in this row represents a fuse, which, if left unblown, connects the column to this gate as an input; otherwise the column is disconnected, and a T is put into the AND gate. Each triangle-shaped gate with two outputs generates a signal and its complement, and feeds two of the columns. The second line from the top can have any input from pins 2 to 9 or their complement, or the outputs on pins 12 to 19 or their complement, as inputs to the AND gate. For each possible input, the fuses are blown to select the input or its complement, or to ignore it. Thus, the designer can choose any AND of the 16 input-output variables or their complements as the signal controlling the tristate gate. Similarly, the next seven lines each feed an input to the NOR gate, so the output on pin 19 may be a Boolean "sum-of-products" of up to seven "products," each of which may be the AND of any input-output or its complement. This group of eight rows is basically replicated for each NOR gate. The middle four groups feed registers clocked by pin 1, and their outputs are put on pins 14 to 17 by tristate drivers enabled by pin 11. The registers can store a state of a sequential machine, which will be discussed further in Chapter 4. PALs such as the PAL16L8 have no registers and are suited to implementing address decoders and other collections of gates needed in a microcomputer system. There is now a rather large family of PALS having from zero to eight registers and one to eight inverted or noninverted outputs in a 20-pin DIP, and there also are 24-pin DIP PALs. These can be programmed to realize just about any simple function, such as an address decoder.

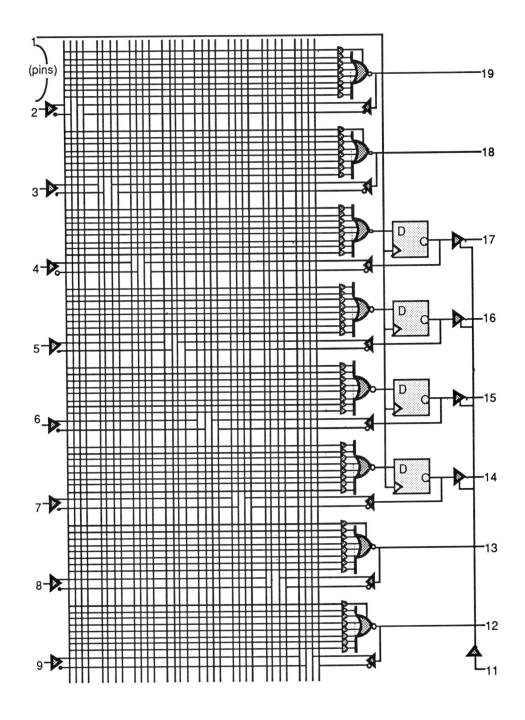

Figure 3-4. 16R4 PAL Used in Microcomputer Designs.

3-2 Control Signals and Their Sequences in a Microprocessor

One of the main problems designers face is how to control bus drivers so two of them will never try to drive the same bus at the same time. To approach this problem, the designer must be acquainted with control signals and the sequences of control signals generated by a microprocessor. This section is devoted to aspects of microprogramming and microcomputer instruction execution necessary for the comprehension and explanation of control signals on the microcomputer bus. The first subsection covers the basics of microprogramming, laying the groundwork for the next subsection. That subsection discusses the way the 683xx actually executes an instruction such as MOVE #5,D0. With this discussion, you should understand the sequencing of control signals, which is at the heart of the aforementioned problem.

3-2.1 Data Transfers, Microprograms, and Pipelines

We now look at the control of a bus by examining the data transfer, microprogram and pipeline. *Microprogramming*, explained in this subsection, is the discipline of writing microprograms to convert instructions read by the computer to the actions that carry out those instructions. It will be used in the next subsection to discuss the timing of signals on the 683xx system address and data buses. Because microprogramming is an extensive subject that can barely be covered in a whole course, this subsection covers only those aspects important in designing microcomputer-based systems. One part of a microprogram deals with the control of the machine, and the other deals with the sequence of control, much the way jump instructions control a program. We will eschew the study of the sequence and concentrate on how the microprogram controls the computer. At this level of detail, one can best explain bus data transfer concepts.

The concept of the data transfer focuses our attention on the data as they move from module to module. This is an orthogonal view of the sequential machine that concentrates on a module as different data are moved into it. For simplicity, we will discuss data transfers on a single bus; and for concreteness, we will describe a bus using the integrated circuits just discussed.

Consider a bus, to which the outputs of several drivers and the D inputs to several registers are attached. The operation of moving data through this bus by enabling exactly one of the drivers and clocking one or more of the registers is a *data transfer*. A data transfer here takes place in a time called a *microstep*. The driver selected to send out the data is enabled throughout almost all of the microstep, and the clocks of the registers selected to receive the data are asserted so that they copy the data near the end of the microstep, while the enable is still asserted. Suppose A and B are registers. The data transfer describes the actual movement of data. We denote a data transfer thus:

$$A \leftarrow B$$

meaning that in this microstep, the value that was in B at its beginning is copied into register A.

We offer to clear up some common misconceptions about data transfers. Some worry about clocking two registers at the same time – that this might drain the signal on the bus, perhaps making it too weak to recognize. Actually, a register uses the same amount of signal output from a driver, whether or not it is clocked. It is only important that the number of inputs physically connected to the bus be less than the fan-out of the bus drivers. Usually, tristate gate enables and latch clocks are in the negative logic relation. That is, when off, they are high, and when on, they are low. The reason for this convention is that TTL decoders, which usually generate these control signals, are easier to build and faster if their outputs are in negative logic. If they are asserted (low) throughout the microstep or at least during as much of the microstep as possible, the driver will put data on the bus throughout the cycle and the data will be clocked into the latch throughout the cycle. The value actually stored there will be that value input at the very end, when its clock input rises from low to high, as the signal changes from true to false. (The register clocks also use negative logic to be interchangeable with latches, but a little gremlin inverts the variable because the register is actually clocked by the beginning of the next cycle. But the explanation is only of interest as a good question for a Master's degree exam. Practically speaking, we make sure that the edge that clocks data into the register occurs at the end of the microstep.)

The enables on the tristate gates and the clocks on the registers are called *control variables* and are generated by a *controller*. A *micro-order* gives value(s) to control variable(s). The driver enable variables should have the following property: that exactly one of them is asserted, while the others are false. A collection of variables in which only one variable is asserted is called *singulary*. For instance, if the variables A, B, and C are singulary, they can have the values TFF, FTF, or FFT. The values TTF or TTT are not permitted (and in a strict sense of the term, FFF is not permitted). The driver enable variables must be singulary, and, although they don't have to be, the register clock variables are often singulary. It is possible to more compactly store and transmit a collection of n singulary variables by *encoding* them in binary; that is, each variable is assigned a number from 0 to n-1, and the binary number of the asserted variable is stored and transmitted. The binary number is called a *code* for the driver or clock that it enables. This way, for instance, three wires can be used in lieu of eight wires. However, ultimately, the code has to be *decoded* so that the singulary variables are individually available to enable each driver or clock each register. A related idea is that of *recoded* control variables. Suppose a module, such as an integrated circuit, has its control variables encoded so that, for instance, eight sources inside the module can put data onto a bus and only three wires or pins are needed to actually send the code into the module to select the source. If the system will only need three of these sources of data, then really only two wires are needed to uniquely identify the source. The n sources are assigned numbers 0 to n-1, and the binary numbers are stored and sent. A *recoder* then converts these into the codes actually used by the device. Encoding and recoding can be used to advantage to reduce the cost of the controller, but their operation can add some time to the microstep, slowing down the processor. This may be unacceptable in some cases.

The controller can be built using one-shots, shift registers, and a mess of gates, or it can be designed around a memory. Because the latter is much easier to describe and becoming more popular, we discuss it here. First, the relatively simple *horizontal microprogram* technique is discussed. A *control memory* C stores a *microprogram*. One row, say row i, is read out during a microstep. Each column, say column j, directly feeds an enable or clock control variable. The bit in row i, column j, is true if the jth enable or clock is to be asserted whenever the ith row is read out. Although it is not essential, a counter can provide addresses to sequentially read each row out of the memory, row $i+1$ right after row i. The microprogram is written for the memory, and the memory is filled with the desired values, so that when it is read out, the data transfers will be executed as desired.

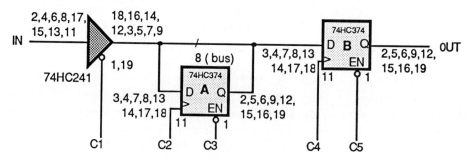

Figure 3-5. Bus with Control Signals.

We now give a concrete example of the data transfer and the horizontal microprogram. Consider a simplified bus. (See Figure 3-5.) Suppose, in one microstep, we wish to transfer the variable IN to the register A (shown in boldface) and, in the next microstep, to transfer the contents of A into B. (The data in B are always output in link OUT.) This is denoted by the transfers written in two successive lines:

$$A \leftarrow IN$$
$$B \leftarrow A$$

To transfer this data, the following micro-orders are given. In the first microstep, C1 and C2 are asserted. This puts the data IN onto the bus and then copies this data into register A. In the second microstep, C3 and C4 are asserted. Consider a slight variation of this microprogram. In one microstep, the data IN are to be sent to both registers A and B. This is denoted

$$A \leftarrow IN; B \leftarrow IN$$

and the two data transfers on the same line are assumed to take place simultaneously in the same microstep. Now, to put IN on the bus, C1 is asserted, and both C2 and C4 are asserted together. By this means, the data are copied simultaneously into both registers.

Some remarks about timing are now noted. When asserted, C1 and C3 should be held low (because they are in negative logic) for the whole duration of the step. When the edge-trigger clocks C2 and C4 are to be asserted, the rising edge of the signal on pin 11 should arrive towards the end of the step, while C1 or C3 are still asserted. Normally, these clock variables are ANDed with a square wave, so they are never asserted during the first half of the microstep; there will thus always be a rising edge at the end of the microstep even if the variable is asserted in two successive microsteps. This rising edge also has to occur when the data are determinate, to satisfy the setup and hold times of all the flip-flops that are loading it. The step's duration must be longer than the delay time for a signal to travel from any output to any input, including the setup and hold times of the flip-flops loading it. This delay time essentially determines the fastest clock that can be used with the system.

To continue our example, horizontal microprograms will be shown for the aforementioned data transfers. Suppose C1, C2, C3, and C4 are output from the respective columns of control memory, the transfer A ← IN is ordered whenever row 5 is read, and the transfer B ← A is ordered whenever row 6 is read. Then the control memory will have the following words in rows 5 and 6, respectively:

TTFF
FFTT

Note that if stored in negative logic, the control memory will have in rows 5 and 6

LLHH
HHLL

We distinguish between the signal and the variable here because, if we were to use 1 and 0 when we write the microprogram on paper, we would write line 5 as 1100, but when we store it in the control memory, we write the same line as 0011. For the second microprogram, if it is executed when row 8 is read, row 8 will be

TTFT

or, if the memory stores variables in negative logic,

LLHL

These concepts are now extended. Suppose a collection of control variables, coming from columns m to n of the control memory, are singulary. (That is, at most, one of the control variables is ever asserted at any given time.) Then we can compress them into fewer variables and columns by encoding them. A decoder module will be needed to decode the codes to obtain the singulary control variables needed for the drivers and registers; the codes are then stored in the compressed columns in lieu of the singulary control signals themselves. Moreover, if recoders are used on the outputs of some columns to further compact the number of columns, the recoded codes are then stored therein. This compaction process can be carried to an extreme, so that only one code is stored on each row of the control memory, and all control variables are derived from it by a collection of decoders and recoders. Such a microprogram is called *vertical* as opposed to horizontal. Note that in a horizontal microprogram, all control variables have their own columns in the control memory, and no decoding or recoding is used. Most microprograms have some decoding and recoding and are thus somewhere between vertical and horizontal microprograms.

We extend our example to show how vertical microprogramming is implemented. Noting that the gate enables C1 and C3 in the previous example must be singulary because only one data word can be put on the bus in a microstep, we can encode them so that the code T orders C1 asserted, and the code F orders C3 asserted. Then if the memory stored this code, followed by the clocks C2 and C4, the first microprogram would be stored thus:

TTF
FFT

Chapter 3 – Bus Hardware and Signals

In general, if n control variables are singulary, they can be encoded into $\log_2 n$ bits to save quite a bit of microprogram storage space. Note that if the clocks were also encoded, another column could be deleted, but the second microprogram would not work because no code would permit both clocks to be enabled simultaneously. A further example is offered to show the concept of recoding. Suppose a microprogram memory has the following rows:

TFTTFT

TTFTTT

FFFFFF

FFTFFT

in which the leftmost two columns and the rightmost two columns have only the patterns TF...FT, TT...TT, FF...FF and FF...FT and never have any other patterns. Because there are only four patterns, they could be replaced by two ($\log_2 4$) columns, and a recoder would be used to recover the original codes. The recoder can be implemented with gates or a small ROM or an equivalent device called a programmable logic array. Suppose we implement the recoder with a ROM having the following pattern:

FFFF

TTTT

TFFT

FFFT

and the original microprogram is then rewritten so that, say, the first two columns generate an address into this ROM, making the ROM generate the control signals from its columns 1 to 4 that were generated from columns 1, 2, 5, and 6 of the original microprogram. Then the new microprogram would look like this:

TFTT

FTFT

FFFF

TTTF

Using recoding, it is possible to generate the hundreds of control signals needed to run a computer from microprograms with word widths of a few tens of bits.

Pipelining is the passing of data through a series of registers and possibly operating on it or modifying it as it passes through each register. Figure 3-6 illustrates a simple 3-stage pipeline. When C1 is pulsed the following transfers occur: A ← IN; B← A; C← B; Pipelining is used in the 683xx controller, so we should understand it before we study the 683xx fetch-execute cycle. It will help us understand how a logic analyser records the 683xx's activities and how cycle timing is to be computed.

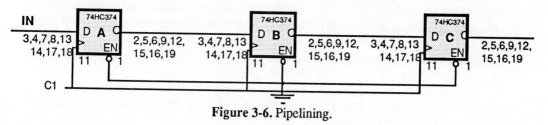

Figure 3-6. Pipelining.

A pipeline serves well to speed up an operation that can be divided into parts and is repeated on a sequence of data. If an operation can be divided into three components, the first component being done on the data as it passes through register A, the second component, as it passes through register B, the third component, as it passes through register C, then as A completes its work on data and the data is shifted into B, new data can be put into A. New data can be put into the pipeline after only 1/3 of the operation is completed. Equivalently, data can be put in at three times the rate that a non-pipelined system could take it. However, when the data to be put into the pipeline is unavailable or the selection of that data depends on decisions made in the third stage of the pipeline, the pipeline can't do any work and "empties out". This is called *flushing* the pipeline.

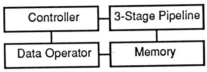

Figure 3-7. 683xx Microprocessor.

As shown in Figure 3-7, the 683xx has a 3-stage pipeline that holds data fetched from memory. The pipeline will try to fetch memory words to fill it up. This is called *prefetching*. This pipeline percolates data from one to the next stage when the next stage is available, rather than simultaneously moving all data as in Figure 3-6. Jump (and similar control) instructions cause the pipeline to be flushed. If the opcode is determined to be a Jump or equivalent type instruction, the pipeline will not attempt to fetch data since that data will not be used. The data operator reads or writes data directly into memory without going through the pipeline. If the data operator must read or write data into memory while the pipeline also needs to prefetch a word from memory, the data operator takes priority and prefetching is deferred until a later memory cycle.

3-2.2 The Fetch-Execute Cycle

Our attention will now focus on the microprocessor's data and address buses. To feel comfortable with the signals we see, we first look at the microprocessor to see how it executes a typical instruction.

We show the pin connections of the BCC because they are substantially the same as the pin connections to the 683xx itself, and it is very difficult to experiment with the 683xx, its pins bein placed 0.025" apart. We present the pins for the M68332 BCC and the M68340 BCC. Two 64-pin "harmonica" connectors on the left and right side of the BCC are marked P1 and P2. For each, there are 64 pins, the even numbered pins on one side. Several pins have two or three different functions designated by slashes between function names, depending on how some control registers in the 683xx are set. For instance, the M68332's P1 pin 49 is either SS (Slave Select) or PCS0 (Peripheral chip select 0). Also the M68340 has an additional connector, P5 on its end, which provide address lines A31 to A19 on pins 7 to 19 (A31 to A24 also are port A bits 7 to 0 and A31 to A18 are IAK bits 7 to 1). We find it somewhat amusing that even with 128 pins on the M68332 BCC, and 130 on the M68340 BCC (and 132 pins on the 683xx chips), we run out of pins and have to use the same pins for more than one purpose. The pins are grouped by background patterns. The light gray pattern ▢ identifies address, data and control signals (RW and ECLK) discussed in this chapter. The patterns such as ▨ are described on the bottom of the figures.

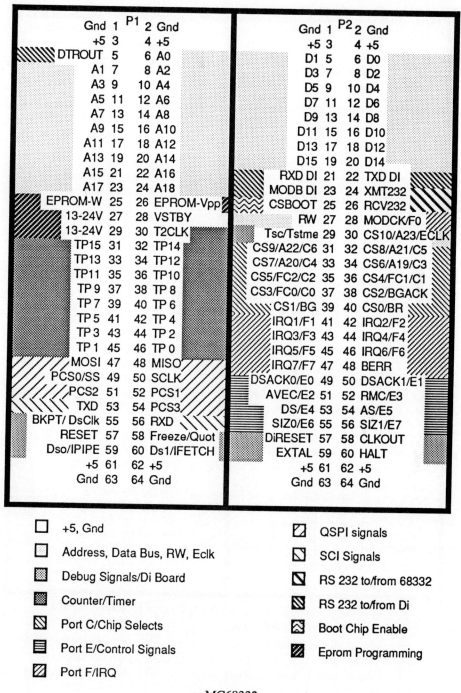

	P1		
Gnd	1	2	Gnd
+5	3	4	+5
DTROUT	5	6	A0
A1	7	8	A2
A3	9	10	A4
A5	11	12	A6
A7	13	14	A8
A9	15	16	A10
A11	17	18	A12
A13	19	20	A14
A15	21	22	A16
A17	23	24	A18
EPROM-W	25	26	EPROM-Vpp
13-24V	27	28	VSTBY
13-24V	29	30	T2CLK
TP15	31	32	TP14
TP13	33	34	TP12
TP11	35	36	TP10
TP 9	37	38	TP 8
TP 7	39	40	TP 6
TP 5	41	42	TP 4
TP 3	43	44	TP 2
TP 1	45	46	TP 0
MOSI	47	48	MISO
PCS0/SS	49	50	SCLK
PCS2	51	52	PCS1
TXD	53	54	PCS3
BKPT/ DsClk	55	56	RXD
RESET	57	58	Freeze/Quot
Dso/IPIPE	59	60	Ds1/IFETCH
+5	61	62	+5
Gnd	63	64	Gnd

	P2		
Gnd	1	2	Gnd
+5	3	4	+5
D1	5	6	D0
D3	7	8	D2
D5	9	10	D4
D7	11	12	D6
D9	13	14	D8
D11	15	16	D10
D13	17	18	D12
D15	19	20	D14
RXD DI	21	22	TXD DI
MODB DI	23	24	XMT232
CSBOOT	25	26	RCV232
RW	27	28	MODCK/F0
Tsc/Tstme	29	30	CS10/A23/ECLK
CS9/A22/C6	31	32	CS8/A21/C5
CS7/A20/C4	33	34	CS6/A19/C3
CS5/FC2/C2	35	36	CS4/FC1/C1
CS3/FC0/C0	37	38	CS2/BGACK
CS1/BG	39	40	CS0/BR
IRQ1/F1	41	42	IRQ2/F2
IRQ3/F3	43	44	IRQ4/F4
IRQ5/F5	45	46	IRQ6/F6
IRQ7/F7	47	48	BERR
DSACK0/E0	49	50	DSACK1/E1
AVEC/E2	51	52	RMC/E3
DS/E4	53	54	AS/E5
SIZ0/E6	55	56	SIZ1/E7
DiRESET	57	58	CLKOUT
EXTAL	59	60	HALT
+5	61	62	+5
Gnd	63	64	Gnd

Legend	
+5, Gnd	QSPI signals
Address, Data Bus, RW, Eclk	SCI Signals
Debug Signals/Di Board	RS 232 to/from 68332
Counter/Timer	RS 232 to/from Di
Port C/Chip Selects	Boot Chip Enable
Port E/Control Signals	Eprom Programming
Port F/IRQ	

a. MC68332

Figure 3-8. Connections to BCCs.

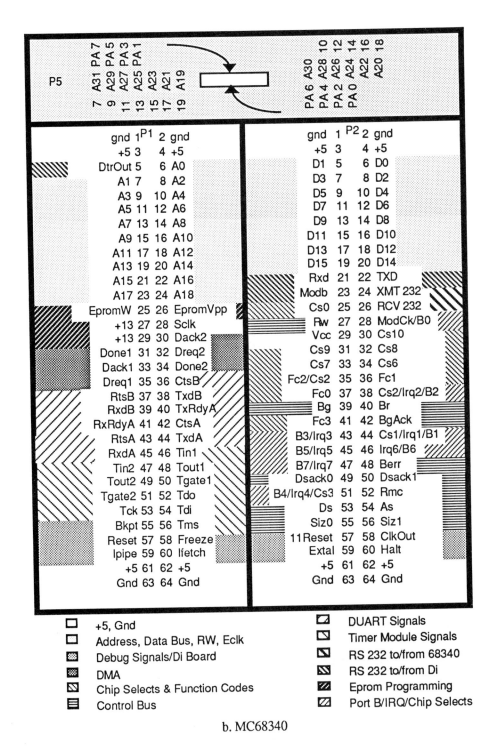

P5	A31 PA7	A29 PA5	A27 PA3	A25 PA1	A23 A21 A19

PA6 A30 / PA4 A28 10 / PA2 A26 12 / PA0 A24 14 / A22 16 / A20 18

7 9 11 13 15 17 19

P1		P2	
gnd 1 2 gnd		gnd 1 2 gnd	
+5 3 4 +5		+5 3 4 +5	
DtrOut 5 6 A0		D1 5 6 D0	
A1 7 8 A2		D3 7 8 D2	
A3 9 10 A4		D5 9 10 D4	
A5 11 12 A6		D7 11 12 D6	
A7 13 14 A8		D9 13 14 D8	
A9 15 16 A10		D11 15 16 D10	
A11 17 18 A12		D13 17 18 D12	
A13 19 20 A14		D15 19 20 D14	
A15 21 22 A16		Rxd 21 22 TXD	
A17 23 24 A18		Modb 23 24 XMT 232	
EpromW 25 26 EpromVpp		Cs0 25 26 RCV 232	
+13 27 28 Sclk		Rw 27 28 ModCk/B0	
+13 29 30 Dack2		Vcc 29 30 Cs10	
Done1 31 32 Dreq2		Cs9 31 32 Cs8	
Dack1 33 34 Done2		Cs7 33 34 Cs6	
Dreq1 35 36 CtsB		Fc2/Cs2 35 36 Fc1	
RtsB 37 38 TxdB		Fc0 37 38 Cs2/Irq2/B2	
RxdB 39 40 TxRdyA		Bg 39 40 Br	
RxRdyA 41 42 CtsA		Fc3 41 42 BgAck	
RtsA 43 44 TxdA		B3/Irq3 43 44 Cs1/Irq1/B1	
RxdA 45 46 Tin1		B5/Irq5 45 46 Irq6/B6	
Tin2 47 48 Tout1		B7/Irq7 47 48 Berr	
Tout2 49 50 Tgate1		Dsack0 49 50 Dsack1	
Tgate2 51 52 Tdo		B4/Irq4/Cs3 51 52 Rmc	
Tck 53 54 Tdi		Ds 53 54 As	
Bkpt 55 56 Tms		Siz0 55 56 Siz1	
Reset 57 58 Freeze		11Reset 57 58 ClkOut	
Ipipe 59 60 Ifetch		Extal 59 60 Halt	
+5 61 62 +5		+5 61 62 +5	
Gnd 63 64 Gnd		Gnd 63 64 Gnd	

☐ +5, Gnd
☐ Address, Data Bus, RW, Eclk
▦ Debug Signals/Di Board
▦ DMA
◪ Chip Selects & Function Codes
▤ Control Bus

◪ DUART Signals
◪ Timer Module Signals
◪ RS 232 to/from 68340
◪ RS 232 to/from Di
▨ Eprom Programming
▨ Port B/IRQ/Chip Selects

b. MC68340

Figure 3-8. Connections to BCCs (continued).

While there are a plethora of pins on this substantial microcomputer, we really only concern ourselves in this chapter with three groups on either BCC – data, address, and memory control – and the data and address bus groups are very simple. The data to or from memory are sent via the 16-bit data bus D[15 to 0]. Generally, we use only the high byte D[15 to 8] for 8-bit I/O devices. M68340's 32-bit address bus A[31 to 0] sends the address to memory and the function FC[2 to 0] sends the memory space (see Figure 1-5), if differentiated spaces are used in the system. Generally, FC[2 to 0] and A[31 to 20] are decoded within the M68332 FC[3 to 0] and A[31 to 20] are decoded within the M68340 and need not be used outside the chip, so we often use only A[19 to 0] to decode addresses. Although some systems can use them in address decoding, pins used for them are shared with chip select or parallel output port functions.

Recall from Section 1-1.2 that an instruction is executed in a period called a fetch-execute cycle, which is composed of several memory cycles. The first memory cycle is called the fetch cycle, and is used to fetch the first word of the instruction (or the first few words, if the instruction takes several words) from memory. Multi-word instructions fetch many words. The next memory cycles decode and execute the instruction.

The bus timing is defined by a 16.7 MHz. clock signal CLKOUT shown in the "debug signals/di board" Section of Figure 3-6. A *fast memory cycle* is four microsteps; in this book they are numbered S0, ... , S3. During a fetch or read memory cycle, the address and function code are sent out their lines from S0 to S3; the memory responds by putting data on the data bus by S2. During a write memory cycle, the address and function code are sent out their lines from S0 to S3; data are sent on the data bus from S1 to S3. Memory writes the data at the location specified by the address lines in S2.

The main control signals are RW, AS, DS, SIZ[1,0] and RMC from the 683xx, and DSACK[1,0] and BERR from the memory or I/O device. See Figure 3-9. RW signals to memory whether the memory is to read or to write a word. Address strobe AS is asserted while the 683xx puts a determinate address on the address bus. Signals SIZ[1,0] indicate the size of the data to be read or written; if LH then we read or write a byte at the address A[23 to 0], otherwise we read or write a word at the address S[23 to 0]. For any other than a fast memory cycle, data strobe DS is asserted low while a word is to be read or a word is to be read or written. (In a fast memory cycle, DS does not get asserted.) RMC is asserted if the instruction executes a read-modify-write cycle. The memory or I/O device responds with DS acknowledge DSACK[1,0] to indicate when it has completed the read or write operation. If an 8-bit memory or I/O device is selected, DSACK[1,0] should be LH, if a 16-bit, then HL. If DSACK[1,0] remains HH too long, the memory cycle is extended by adding more microsteps *(wait states)* to it until either DSACK line becomes asserted low. (In a fast memory cycle, DSACK[1,0] is effectively asserted internally.) An illegal memory access is indicated by asserting bus error BERR.

We now examine the memory cycles and microsteps to execute ADDQ.B #5,(A0) in the 683xx. Assume the operation code (op code) 0x5a10 is at 0x200 in 16-bit memory, and address register A0 has 0x10000, and 0x10000 has 0x12 in an 8-bit memory connected to D[15 to 8]. A word at 0x200 is fetced, a byte at 0x10000 is recalled, 5 is added, then the byte at 0x10000 is written. Assume that the bus signals come directly from registers onto the corresponding buses, to use a register assignment ← as a simple way of showing the time they are asserted and the time they are negated, rather than showing them in a more correct but more involved way. The following discussion is actually how the MC683xx executes the ADDQ.B #5,(A0) instruction.

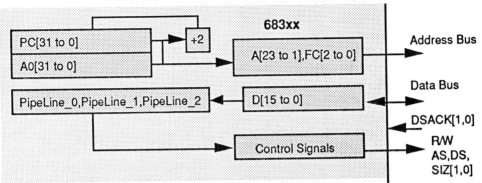

Figure 3-9. Simplified MC683xx Microprocessor.

Microprogram for ADDQ.B #5,(A0)

```
S0   A ← 0x200=PC; FC ← 2; RW ← T; SIZ= HL;
S1   PC ← PC + 2; AS ← L; DS ← L;
S2   D ← 0x5a10;
S3   PipeLine ← 0x5a10; AS ← H; DS ← H;
```

```
S0   A ← 0x10000=A0; FC ← 1; AS ← T; SIZ=LH;
S1   AS ← L; DS ← L;
S2   D ← 0x12??;
S3   AS ← H; DS ← H;
```

```
S0   internally add 5 to D
S1
```

```
S0   A ← 0x10000=A0; FC ← 1;
S1   AS ← L; RW ← L;
S2   D ← 0x1717;
S3   AS ← H; RW ← H;
```

We can see the external address, the external data bus signals, and the RW signal, on a *logic analyzer*. This flexible instrument is capable of storing and displaying a sequence of digital signals. A test pattern is set up in the logic analyzer, and when this pattern is found on the address (or data) buses, the data are stored in the logic analyzer for each consecutive memory cycle until the memory in the logic analyzer is full. Alternatively, the data are stored in the logic analyzer until the test pattern is matched. This is especially useful in identifying the cause of an error that occurs when the test pattern is matched. Then the logic analyzer display can be used to examine this memory to see what happened. This "nonintrusive" observer does not interfere with the timing of the program and is especially valuable for debugging problems with I/O synchronization in general and interrupts in particular, as discussed in Chapter 5.

To efficiently read the display of a simple inexpensive logic analyzer, you should observe the addresses, comparing them to the listing of the program. However, because only instructions are pipelined – prefetching fills the pipeline whenever there is an available memory cycle and is occasionally flushed – but priority is given to data

110   Chapter 3 – Bus Hardware and Signals

requests, memory accesses are often in "scrambled" order. This complicates the task of reading a logic analizer's output. You can observe data recall and write operations in logical order, and instruction fetches occuring somewhere before these data memory cycles. Also the signals IPIPE and IFETCH, discussed in Section 7.3 of the *CPU32 Reference Manual,* can be used to determine when instructions are fetched into the pipeline and when they are advanced through it. Chapter 8 of the *CPU32 Reference Manual* discusses how instruction timing, and by inference, memory cycles observed on a logic analyzer, can be unserstood. More expensive logic analyzers will attempt to disassemble the instructions in memory, printing out mnemonics for op codes, and even symbolic addresses for data references. That makes it easy to debug a program. However, using the concepts discussed here, you can use even a simple inexpensive logic analyzer.

3-3 Interfacing to a Bus

One of the most common problems faced by interface designers is the problem of bus timing and the generation of control signals to the bus. These will be considered in this section. The first subsection considers the analysis of timing information needed to connect a microprocessor to another device. The second subsection shows the techniques used in designing decoders for memories and I/O devices. The third shows the use of the 683xx system integration module (SIM) and the fourth, a simple example of a complete interfacing design to connect a memory to a microcomputer. The next shows how dynamic memories work and how they are used. The last subsection considers the connection of boards to motherboards, the timing of signals through them, and the consideration of control signals that are used to drive this expanded bus. These cover most aspects of bus design.

3-3.1 Address and Data Bus Timing

To connect memory or I/O registers to the microprocessor, the actual timing requirements of the address bus and data bus have to be satisfied. If one uses modules from the same family, such as Motorola 6800-style I/O chips designed to be compatible with the 68000 family, the timing requirements are usually automatically satisfied. However, when mixing modules from different families or when putting heavy demands on the modules' capabilities, one may have to analyze the timing requirements carefully. Therefore, we discuss them here.

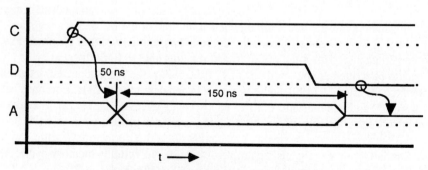

Figure 3-10. Some Timing Relationships.

Timing diagrams are used to show the requirements. A timing diagram is like an oscilloscope trace of the signals, such as is shown in Figure 3-10. For collections of variables, like the 16 address lines shown by the trace labeled A, two parallel lines indicate that any particular address line may be high or low, but will remain there for the time interval where the lines are parallel. A crossing line indicates that any particular line can change at that time. A line in the middle of the high and low line levels indicates the output is floating because no drivers are enabled, or the output may be changing as it tries to reach a stable value. A line in the middle means the signal is indeterminate; it is not necessarily at half the voltage. (Motorola also uses a cross-hatch pattern like a row of X's to indicate that the signal is invalid but not tristated, while a line in the middle means the output is in the tristate open circuit mode on the device being discussed. That distinction is not made in this book, because both cases mean that the bus signal is indeterminate and cannot be used.) Causal relationships, such as a control variable C causing the address lines to change, are shown by arrows from cause to effect. The cause is usually an edge if the change is made by clocking a register, or a level if the effect is a result of enabling a driver. On the left side of Figure 3-10, we indicate that a rising edge of C causes the address lines A to change. Note the circle around the edge showing the cause is the edge. On the right side, we indicate that a low level of signal D causes the address lines to float. Timing is usually shown to scale, as on an oscilloscope, but delays from cause to effect are shown by writing the time by the arrow, and requirements are indicated the way dimensions are shown on a blueprint. On the left, the addresses change 50 nanoseconds after C rises, and, in the middle, we indicate the address should be stable for more than 150 nanoseconds.

We'll show the principles of bus transfers using approximate numbers for timing of a fast memory cycle, which takes four steps S0 to S3, shown in Figure 3-11. We'll refer to the beginning of step Si as « Si and we'll put the time in nanoseconds from the beginning of the memory cycle in parentheses. Using a 16.7 MHz CLKOUT, a microstep is 30 nanoseconds and a memory clock cycle is 120 nanoseconds. Addresses A and function codes FC are on their buses no later than 30 nanoseconds after « S0 (30) and remains until « S0 of the next cycle (120). AS is asserted low no later than 30 nanoseconds after « S1 (60) and rises no later than 30 nanoseconds after « S3 (120) and is further guaranteed to be at least 40 nanoseconds long.

In a fast read cycle as shown in Figure 3-11a, the data strobe DS is asserted low when AS is asserted and the read/write signal RW remains high throughout the cycle. The microprocessor expects valid data on the data bus for 5 nanoseconds before « S3 (85), until 15 nanoseconds after «S3 (105). Memory must provide valid, constant signals during this interval during this setup time and hold time of the MC683xx's registers.

In a fast write cycle as shown in Figure 3-12b, the RW signal becomes low no later than 30 nanoseconds after « S0 (30) and remains until « S0 of the next cycle (120). The data to be written are put on the D bus by the 683xx and are guaranteed determinate 30 nanoseconds after « S2 (90), and is also guaranteed determinate 15 nanoseconds before AS rises (105) and remain stable until 15 nanoseconds after AS rises (135). We note that RW does not have a rising edge whose timing can be depended upon to write data in memory. RW is *not a timing signal*. You cannot depend on it to satisfy setup and hold times. Similarly, address signals are not precisely aligned with the memory cycle. AS is available to time the writing of data into memory. (See Figure 4-1 in Section 4-1.2.)

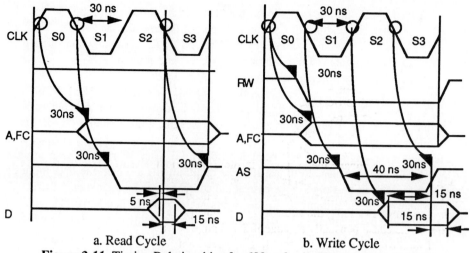

a. Read Cycle   b. Write Cycle

Figure 3-11. Timing Relationships for 683xx family Fast Memory Cycles.

In analyzing timing requirements, one compares the timing of two parts, such as the microprocessor and some memory to be connected. The object is to verify whether data will be available at the receiver when needed. One should be aware that a part may not meet all of its specifications. Some manufacturers just test a few parts from each batch, while others (such as Motorola) test each part for most specifications. A design in which some requirements are not satisfied may still work because some parts may surpass their specifications. In fact, if you are willing to take the time or pay the expense, you can *screen the parts* to find out which ones meet your tighter specifications. However, if the system fails because the design does not meet its parts' specifications, we blame the designer. If the design meets specifications but the system fails, we blame the part manufacturer or the part.

A typical memory has timing requirements that must be compatible with those of the microprocessor. In discussing these, we will give the approximate requirements of the popular 6164, an (8K x 8) RAM which has two chip enables E1 and E2, read/write W, output enable G, a 13-bit address A, and eight data pins D. It is manufactured by different companies and even, with different timing requirements, by the same company. Such variations are designated by letters or numbers added to the name 6164, such as in 6164-A, 6164-45, or MCM6164-45. We discuss the latter, made by Motorola.

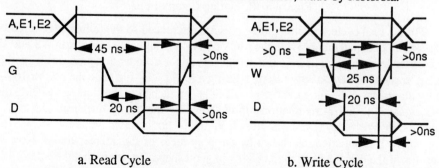

a. Read Cycle   b. Write Cycle

Figure 3-12. Timing Requirements of the Motorola MCM6164-45.

In a read cycle, timing is based on the G signal as shown in Figure 3-12a. The cycle begins when the address bus signal A becomes determinate and stable. Data are available on the data bus pins from the byte addressed by A, 45 nanoseconds after that, and 20 nanoseconds after G falls, whichever is later, and may go away as soon as G rises. A must remain determinate and stable until after G rises.

In a write cycle, timing is based on the W signal. (See Figure 3-12b.) To prevent writing in the wrong word, the W signal should only be asserted when A is determinate and stable. E1 and E2 have to be asserted before W falls, and W should be low for at least 25 nanoseconds. The data input on the data pins should be stable 20 nanoseconds before the rising edge of W and remain stable until after W rises. These are the MCM6164-45's setup and hold times. If these requirements are met, the data input on the data bus pins will be stored in the byte at the address given by A, and only there.

To analyze the requirements to see if this MCM6164-45 is compatible with the 683xx processor, the requirements are compared for the read and write cycles. (See Figure 3-13.) It turns out that the read cycle is satisfied, so we examine it first. The write cycle is not satisfied, as we see later. Even though we have to discard this design, it serves to illustrate how we determine that timing specifications are not met.

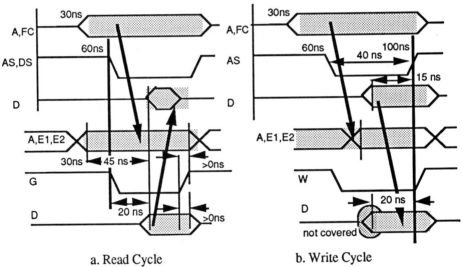

a. Read Cycle b. Write Cycle
Figure 3-13. Timing Comparison.

For the read cycle, the timing diagrams are referenced so the falling edge of 683xx processor's DS signal can provide the MCM6164-45 G signal because both AS and DS are asserted low when the address is determinate and the decoder that produces E1 and E2 can be "trusted" but DS is only asserted during a read cycle. We slide the MCM6164-45 timing diagrams so the time the 683xx DS falls is matched to the time the MCM6164-45 G signal is to fall. This relationship is shown by the heavy line from DS to G in Figure 3-13a. We verify that the address from the 683xx is stable while the MCM6164-45 needs it. It is satisfied, as shown by the gray areas of the address traces. Now we determine if the data get back to the 683xx in good shape. To verify that the MCM6164-45 memory puts out determinate data exactly when the 683xx processor must receive it,

Chapter 3 – Bus Hardware and Signals

we check that the gray area shown in the 683xx D signal is enclosed within the time the MCM6164-45 memory output is determinate, in the MCM6164-45 D trace. It satisfies setup and hold times, so this memory chip apparently can be used.

For the write cycle, the requirements center on the MCM6164-45 W signal. RW needs to be modified to generate W for a MCM6164-45 memory so W occurs at a predictable place, when data are valid. Our initial attempt, which usually works, is to assert W when AS is true to write a word. Assume W is the negative logic AND of AS and RW, using a gate having no delay. The write cycle timing diagram for the MCM6164-45 should be lined up with the 683xx write cycle timing diagram so that the rising edge of W corresponds to the rising edge of 683xx's AS, as shown by the heavy vertical line in Figure 3-13b. We show again that the address is valid to the MCM6164-45 when it is needed. The address needed by the MCM6164-45 does last until its W signal rises (because the 683xx address is stable until well after the 683xx AS signal rises). This is shown by the gray area of the MCM6164-45 address trace A. We do verify that W derived from the 683xx AS signal is low for at least the 25 nanoseconds the MCM6164-45 requires (note it is low for the last 40 nanoseconds), and that the address is determinate before W falls (note that it is determinate 30 nanoseconds before). We have to show the data to the MCM6164-45 are steady when the MCM6164-45 writes them. Figure 3-13b shows that these requirements are not satisfied. The data must be determinate for 20 nanoseconds before the MCM6164-45 W signal rises and stable until after that rising edge. However, the data from the 683xx is only stable 15 nanoseconds, not 20 nanoseconds, before the rising edge of AS (W). This is shown by the gray area of the MCM6164-45 data trace D. The setup time is not satisfied, being 5 nanoseconds too short. Therefore, the memory cannot be used, using AS to generate the W signal.

The problem is generally solved by one of three techniques: Get a faster memory, use a slower 683xx memory cycle by adding wait states, or delay the edge of the W signal that is used to determine the setup and hold times of the memory. To achieve other timing problem solutions, you can often use a faster version of the 6164. Wait cycles can be added to the 683xx by delaying DSACK as we discuss soon. Hardware like a one-shot, shift register, or gate can be used to provide a delayed W signal. One-shots are notoriously susceptible to noise, and a gate's delay is not absolutely reliable, but gates can be screened to get those with the required delay. Assume W is the negative logic AND of AS and RW, using a gate having 5 to 15 nanosecond delay. Observe that data are determinate in the required interval. All other timings remain satisfied. We could use this solution in our design. However, in Section 3-3.4 we use wait states to do that.

It is often necessary to expand a memory cycle to accommodate a slow memory or I/O device. The asynchronous bus timing of the 683xx has a means of doing this, using wait microsteps, by not generating DSACK internally and delaying the assertion of DSACK. A pair of wait microsteps is added after the beginning of S2 if neither DSACK line is low, until one becomes low. Logic to expand the memory cycle by adding wait microsteps is shown in Figure 3-14a, and timing for it is shown in Figure 3-14b. The 74HC164 shifts its input, the inverted address strobe AS, on the falling edge of the CLKOUT signal, which is at the beginning of odd-numbered microsteps. If DSACK is taken from Q2, the output of the second flip-flop in the '164, then DSACK will be high at the end of S2 when it should be low in order to continue the memory cycle without wait microsteps. Because it is high, two wait microsteps are put in the memory cycle and DSACK is sampled again on the falling edge of CLKOUT. The second sample sees

DSACK asserted low, so the memory cycle is resumed until it is completed. When the memory cycle is completed, AS goes high, which resets the shift register, causing DSACK to go high. By taking DSACK from Q3, six wait microsteps are added; by taking it from Q4, eight are added; and so on. Thus, the memory cycle can be extended as needed to read or write data in slow memories or I/O devices in one memory cycle.

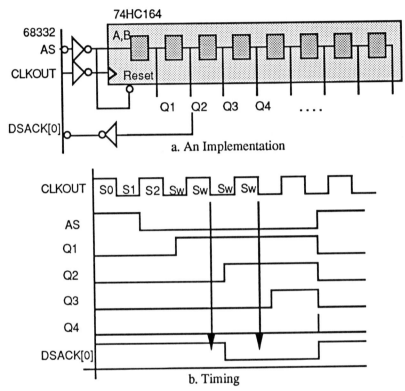

Figure 3-14. Wait Cycle Control Logic.

Instead of a shift register, a PAL like that in Figure 3-4 can be programmed to implement this hardware. However, the 683xx's SIM is even easier to use, as we will shortly observe. We have observed that an analysis of timing requirements can help us select the parts needed to build a system. And, surprisingly, a 45-nanosecond cycle memory does not necessarily have timing characteristics that make it compatible to work with a 120-microsecond memory cycle microcomputer. We reiterate, though, that parts not meeting specifications on paper may work some of the time. However, a designer should satisfy the requirements; then, if the system does not work, he or she can blame the parts supplier rather than personally take the blame.

3-3.2 Address Decoding

The memory of a microcomputer such as the BCC is organized into areas that are random access (RAM) and read-only (ROM) memories and I/O devices according to a memory map (Figure 1-14). The $(n,8)$ RAM memory chip such as the 6164 is very common because it is easy to make a $(m,8)$ memory for an 8-bit processor. An $(n,16)$

memory can be built with two such chips. Two (8K,8) 6164s will implement a (8K,16) memory, having 16K bytes. Similarly, several (8K,8) ROM memory chips such as the MCM68766 are very common. The memory we design for the BCC will add 16K bytes of RAM at location 0x10000 to 0x13FFF.

The purpose of the address decoder is to select, during a read memory cycle, one (possibly a pair of) memories to read data onto the bus, using tristate drivers in them, and to prevent any other (pair of) memories from putting conflicting data on the data bus. Similarly, the purpose of the address decoder is to select, during a write memory cycle, one (pair of) memories to write the data. A chip select E1 of the memory is controlled by the address decoder.

Generally, address decoders are implemented by a small number of SSI gates. The NAND gate can be used to output a negative logic signal that is suited to the negative logic chip enable inputs of a typical memory chip. The memory is enabled when all inputs to the NAND gate are high. If address inputs are attached to these inputs, the chip is enabled when all input address lines are true. If we wish to select the memory when an address bit is false, put an inverter on that address line between the address output of the 683xx and the NAND gate. OR gates can be used as negative logic input- and output-AND gates if most address lines would require inverters. A good logic designer would consider various alternative designs to implement a decoder, and select the design that used the least number of chips (often using parts of chips that are left unused as other parts are used for other functions). Especially when many modules are used, a decoder integrated circuit is used to decode the high-order bits of the address. The 74154 is a popular decoder that can select up to 16 modules; it has 16 different circuits like the NAND gate just discussed to select each module. However, the tendency to use a chip just because it is there should be avoided. A PAL can be programmed to implement a number of gates, including the gates needed in the decoder and other "glue" logic such as the gates used for the W signals of a memory. A *programmable decoder* (Figure 3-15) permits the address to be set by jumper switches S3 to S0, and don't cares to be set by jumper switches S4 to S7. The M68332's SIM implements 12 complete decoders in it, and the M68340's SIM implements four complete decoders in it as we see in the next section.

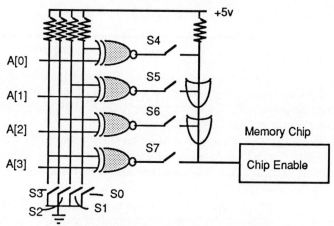

Figure 3-15. A Programmable Decoder.

To put a (8k,16) memory into the memory map of Figure 1-14 in user data space at 0x10000 to 0x13FFF, one could connect a pair of 6164 memory chips as follows. Address lines A[13 to 1] are connected to all 6164 RAMs, the data bus pins from each RAM are connected to an MC68332 data bus pin, and the E1 lines for each memory are connected to different decoders. The decoder checks A[23 to 14] for FFFFFFFTFF and FC[2 to 0] for FFT. More memory modules could be connected to the M68332 this way, to build a 2^{24} byte memory for each user/supervisor program/data space.

Although the principle is the same, the implementation of address decoders in a typical low-cost microcomputer is usually simplified using *incompletely specified decoding*, as is now discussed. Consider the memory map in Figure 1-14 again. If address bit A[14] is disconnected and its input to the decoder gate tied high, this RAM would respond to addresses 0x14000 to 0x17FFF, and the first word in this memory would respond to addresses 0x10000 and 0x14000. If the program uses words 0x10000 and 0x14000, they will in fact be the same words. Similarly, 0x10002 and 0x14002 would be the same words. But if, say, the words from 0x14000 to 0x17FFF are never used in the program, then a simpler decoder without bit A[14] would be adequate. Note from the memory map (Figure 1-14) that no other memory or I/O device needs these addresses, so this is possible. A designer can extend this technique to delete further decoder inputs. In the extreme if only one memory module were used with the M68332, then all inputs could be eliminated using this technique, and E1 could be tied to AS. Then the same word in the module would be selected if the address were 0, 0x10000, 0x14000, 0x18000, and so on. Incompletely specified decoding can eliminate much of the hardware used to decode addresses in a microcomputer. But it should only be used when the program can be trusted to avoid using duplicate addresses. That is because bugs where a program accidentally wrote at 0x14000 and then read that incorrect data from 0x10000 are hard to find. The technique is especially useful for small microcomputers dedicated to execute a fixed program which has no software bugs that might use duplicate addresses. It is not as useful for microcomputers used for software development.

Table 3-1. Address Assignments for the BCC With Extra Memory.

Address line	23	22	21	20	19	18	17	16	15	14	13	12	11	10	9	8	7	6	5	4	3	2	1	0
BCC Ram	F	F	F	F	F	F	F	F	X	X	X	X	X	X	X	X	X	X	X	X	X	X	X	X
Extension Ram	F	F	F	F	F	F	F	T	F	F	X	X	X	X	X	X	X	X	X	X	X	X	X	X
BCC ROM	F	F	F	F	F	T	T	X	X	X	X	X	X	X	X	X	X	X	X	X	X	X	X	X
BCC I/O	T	T	T	T	T	T	T	T	T	T	T	T	T	T	X	X	X	X	X	X	X	X	X	X

We consider an example of an incompletely specified decoder for the memory we add to the BCC using common spaces (ignoring FC[2 to 0]). Table 3-1 shows the preexisting and added module address ranges. Inspection of the permissible addresses indicates that the simplest enable for the extension RAM is when address 16 is T and 17 is F, and no other device is selected when they are TF.

The decoder design can be completed as follows. The upper 6164 whose data lines connect to the M68332's D[15 to 8] has its E1 asserted low when the address is present, and a word is being written (SIZ[1,0] is not 01) or A[0] is L. The lower 6164 whose data lines connect to the M68332's D[7 to 0] has its E1 asserted low when the address is present, and a word is being written (SIZ[1,0] is not 01) or A[0] is H. However the SIM provides a much easier means to implement a decoder. It is introduced next and will be used in all future examples. We examine the simpler M68340, then the M68332.

3-3.3 The M68340 System Integration Module Address Decoder

The previous section illustrated concepts needed to design a decoder using external hardware. Although those techniques are no longer needed in the M68340 except in rather large systems or in very special cases, the M68340's SIM really just integrates them into the M68340 chip, and understanding them makes the SIM's decoder straightforward.

The M68340's SIM contains several parts including subsystems that generate the clock, control the M68340 processor, and handle parallel I/O discussed in the next chapter. The address decoder subsystem is described herein. Locations 0xFFFFF040 to 0xFFFFF05F contain 64-bit data that are associated with each of the 4 chip select devices CS0 to CS3. Figure 3-16 shows two 16-bit registers that control CS3, which we will use in following examples. Further details are provided by the *MC68340 Integrated Processor User's Manual (MC68340UM/AD)* Section 4.3.4.

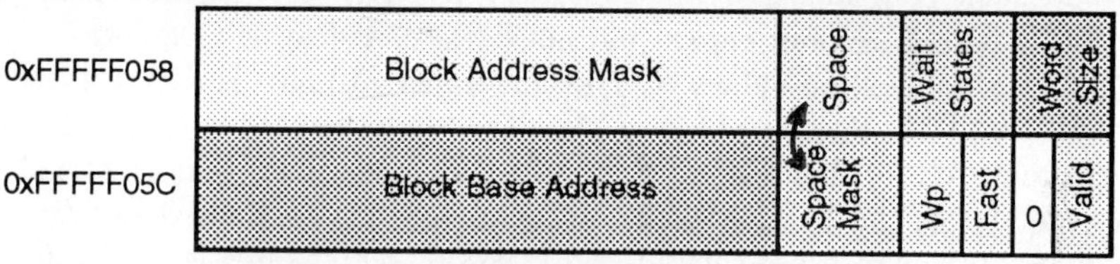

		Space	Wait States	Word Size
0xFFFFF058	Block Address Mask			

		Space Mask	Wp	Fast	0	Valid
0xFFFFF05C	Block Base Address					

Figure 3-16. M68340 Chip Select 3 Registers.

The fields of the chip select registers specify the address and function code and the R/W value that must be present for a valid chip select signal, and the DSACK signals, representing the wait states and word width that must be returned when the address is decoded. The high-order 24 bits of the M68340's 32 bit address are specified by the high order 24 bits of the long word at 0xfffff05c. However, a corresponding mask is put in the high order 24 bits of the long word at 0xfffff058 such that if a mask bit is 1, the address signal is ignored in the decoder. We normally set the low-order bits of this mask field to 1 to ignore low-order address bits, making them don't cares; these low-order address bits might for instance be decode inside a RAM or ROM. The low-order 8 bits of the address and mask fields are not specified by the chip select control register. In effect, these mask bits are always set to 1, making them perminent don't cares. In their place, the information controlling the DSACK signal is put in five fields. The number of wait states (0 to 3) to be used when chip select CS3 is asserted is put in the Wait State field. It essentially chooses the tap on the shift register (Figure 3-14a). If write protect Wp is 1, then the word is read-only; writing into it does not generate chip select or DSACK signals. Otherwise these signals are generated for read or write memory cycles. The (memory) Word Size field is 01 for 16-bit words, 10 for 8-bit words, and 11 for words that generate DSACK externally. In effect, this field is the DSACK signal returned to the processor when the chip select is asserted. However, if the Fast field has a 1, the fast memory cycle is used and the Wait State field and the Word Size field are ignored; the word width being effectively automatically set to 01 (16-bit). The Valid field, initially cleared on reset to prevent accidental matches, must be set to 1 to enable the decoder.

These chip selects have to be initialized whenever a memory or I/O device is to be selected using a chip select pin. In a C program, a macro (Section 2-3.1) can be used to correctly initialize the fields of a chip select control register. The following definitions (put in a header file *di.h*) give the parameters of the macro and the values you should put in them. This macro makes it fairly easy to use the SIM address decoders.

```
enum {wait0=0,rdWr=0,rdOnly,word=1,byte,noDsack,wait1,wait2=8,wait3=0xc,fast=0x10,
    user=0x10,super=0x50};
#define CsAssign(l,a,r,m,w) *((long *)0xffff040+(l<<1))=((0x7fffffff>>(31-r))&0xffffff00)|
((a&user)?0:0xf0)|(m&0xf);  *((long *)0xffff044+(l<<1))=(a&0xfffffff0)|  (w?8:0)|
((m&0x10)?4:0)|l;
```

The macro defined above must be written on one line rather than three lines, so join these lines together if you copy it into a program; it will set up the chip select control registers. CS0 to CS1 are used by the bootstrap ROM and RAM on the BCC. CS2 and CS3 may be used, for instance, for RAM or ROM in the platform card or for I/O devices you design. Then the first parameter of *CsAssign* is the chip select number. We often use chip select 3, so the first parameter of *CsAssign* would be 3.

The second parameter of *CsAssign* is the base address of the memory or I/O device. It should be written as a 32-bit address whose low order eight bits are 0, and may have the constants *user* or *super* (but not both) added to it. (The *enum* statement shown above defines the values of *user* and *super*.) If *user* is added to the address macro argument, the Space and Space Mask fields are assigned to be 1 and 0, enabling the chip select only if the address is in user data space, and if *super* is added to the address, the Space and Space Mask fields are assigned to be 5 and 0, enabling the chip select only if the address is in supervisor data space, and if neither is specified, the Space Mask bits are set to 0xf so the function code bits are ignored, enabling the chip select in any space for common space decoding. This macro does not fully expoit the ability to put don't cares in various bit positions of the Space Mask, which would allow words to appear in different spaces, but only permits the spaces we use in examples in this book.

The third parameter of *CsAssign* is the decoder 's range – the number of low-order bits that are ignored in the decoder. It must be between 8 and 31. The macro does not fully expoit the ability to set masks for don't cares in various bit positions, which would allow words to appear in several disjoint places in the memory map, but only permits low order address bits to be masked out, as we will use it in this book.

The fourth parameter of *CsAssign* is the decoder 's DSACK generation mode. It can be *fast,* to use fast cycles for 16-bit words. Alternatively, it can be the sum of *wait0, wait1, wait2,* or *wait3,* indicating the number of wait states, and *word, byte,* or *noDsack,* indicating the memory word width as 16-bit or 8-bit, or that an external device will return DSACK. Finally, the last parameter is either *rdWr* if the word is readable and writable, or *rdOnly* if it is read-only.

Suppose we wish to make CS3 decode an 8K byte range of RAM (r=13) whose base address is 0x10000 in common space, for 3 wait states and 8-bit word width. The macros for our example is:

$$CsAssign(3,0x10000,13,wait3+byte,rdWr)$$

This generates the following assembler language code:

```
MOVE.L #0x01000E,0x00FFFFF058 Sets up the address and DSACK fileds
MOVEQ #0xF1,D0              Sets up mask and Wp, Fast and Valid fields.
MOVE.L D0,0x00FFFFF05C      THINK  C uses MOVEQ to shorten code
```

Throughout the remainder of this book, whenever we need to use a chip select pin to enable an external memory or I/O device, we will use this simple macro. We will assume the header file *decode.h* is included in the program and we will use its constants.

3-3.4 The M68332 System Integration Module Address Decoder

The M68332's SIM similarly integrates decoder hardware into the M68332 chip; it contains several parts including subsystems that generate the clock, control the M68332 processor, and handle parallel I/O discussed in the next chapter. The address decoder subsystem is described herein. Locations 0xFFFA44 to 0xFFFA47 contain 2-bit fields and locations 0xFFFA48 to 0xFFFA77 contain 32-bit data that are associated with the 12 chip select devices CSBOOT, CS0 to CS10. Figure 3-17 shows the 2-bit and two 16-bit registers that control CS6, which we will use in following examples. Further details are provided by the *68332 SIM User's Manual (SIM32UM/AD)* Section 4.3.

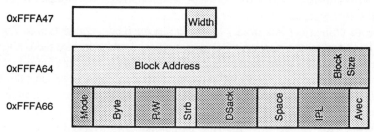

Figure 3-17. M68332 Chip Select 6 Registers.

The two least significant bits of byte 0xFFFA47, the Width field, determine the width of the memory – 10 indicates an 8-bit and 11 a 16-bit wide memory – thus determining which DSACK[1,0] is asserted (Figure 3-14) after the chip is selected. The leftmost 13 bits of the word at 0xFFFA64, the Block Address field, indicate the high-order address values that have to be recognized as if to set the switches in the address decoder in Figure 3-15. The next 3 bits, the Block Size, indicate the number of low-order bits that are ignored in the decoder to handle a block of addresses from 2K bytes (000) to 1Mbytes (111). The Mode bit, leftmost in the word at 0xfffa66, indicates (0) that the block uses 68020-style memory or (1) 6800-style I/O accessing discussed in the next chapter. The next two bits, the Byte field, indicate whether the memory is connected to (10) the upper data bus D[15 to 8] or (01) the lower data bus D[7 to 0] or (11) the whole data bus, to determine whether and how A[0] and SIZ[1,0] are to be decoded, as discussed at the end of the last section. The next two bits, the RW field, indicate whether the chip enable CS6 is asserted when RW is high (01) or low (10) or both (11). The next bit, Strb, determines whether the address or data strobe signals shape the decoder's output. The next two bits, Space, determines whether the memory is to be selected in user (01), supervisor, (10) or common space (11). The last 3-bit and 1-bit fields are used to handle interrupts as discussed in Chapter 5.

These chip selects can be initialized in a C program using a macro, as we did for the M68340. The following definitions (put in a header file *decode.h*) give the parameters of the macro and the values you should put in them to make it fairly easy to use the SIM address decoders.

The three macros defined below will set up the chip select control registers. The first, *pinAssign(csl,w),* puts two bits in the top register of Figure 3-17; the second, *baseAssign(l,a,h),* puts 16 bits in the middle register of Figure 3-17; and the third, *optionAssign(l,q,s,p,i),*puts 16 bits in the bottom register of Figure 3-17. Although this third macro is shown on two lines here, a macro definition must appear on one line in a C program, so join these two lines together if you copy it into a program.

```
enum {cs0=18,cs1=20,cs2=22,cs3=24,cs4=26,cs5=28,cs6=0,cs7=2,cs8=4,cs9=6,cs10=8};
enum {byte=2, word}; /* width w options */
#define pinAssign(csl,w) *((long *)0xfffa44)=(*((long *)0xfffa44)&~(3L<<csl))|((long)w<<csl)
enum {k2,k8,k16,k64,k128,k256,k512,k1024}; /* Height h options */
#define baseAssign(l,a,h) *((int *)0xfffa4c+l*2)=((a&0xfff800)>>8)+(h)
enum {as, ds=1, rd=2, wr=4, lower=8, upper=0x10 }; /* qualifications q options */
enum {fast=14,external,synch}; /* use 0 - 13 or these symbols for s(speed) */
enum {user=1,super}; /* space w options */
#define avec 8 /* interrupt i option enables autovector */
#define optionAssign(l,q,s,p,i) *((int *)0xfffa4e+l*2)=((s&0x10)<<11)|(q<<10)|
    ((s&0xf)<<6)|(p<<4)|((i&8)>>3)|((i&7)<<1)
```

Select a chip select line from 2 to 10, and locate its pin connection in Figure 3-8a. CSBOOT is used by the bootstrap ROM that stores a program like the OS9 operating system, and CS0 to CS1 are used by the RAM on the BCC. Other chip selects may be used, for instance, for RAM or ROM in the platform card that can support the BCC and DI boards. Then the first parameter of *pinAssign* is the letters "cs" concatenated with this pin number, and the first parameters of the other two macros are just this number. We often use chip select 6, so the first parameter of *pinAssign* is *cs6* and the first parameter of *optionAssign* and *baseAssign* is 6. The first parameters "tie together" the macros needed to initialize the chip select control registers for a memory or I/O device.

The second parameter of *pinAssign* is the width of the memory or I/O device. The second *enum* statement shown above defines the values of *byte* and *word*. Use the former if the chip select controls an 8-bit memory or I/O device, and the latter if a 16-bit memory or I/O device. For instance, if an (8K,8) memory is to be enabled for chip select 6, write *pinAssign(cs6,byte);*

The second parameter of *baseAssign* is the base address and the third parameter is the size of the memory block. Write the base address as a 24-bit hexadecimal number, and use the constants *k2, ... ,k1024* to indicate the range of memory space (not the size of the chip) in Kbytes, the first being 2 Kbytes and the last being 1024 Kbytes, which is 1Mbyte. For instance, if the memory for chip select 6 is at 0x10000 and spans a 16 Kbyte range of memory, then write the macro *baseAssign(6,0x10000,k16);*

The second parameter of *optionAssign* is a sum of constants that fill the Bytes, Rw, and Strb fields of Figure 3-17. For Bytes, use *upper* if the memory is attached to D[15 to 8] or *lower* if the memory is attached to D[7 to 0] or *upper+lower* if the memory is attached to D[15 to 0]. For Rw, use *rd* if the memory can be read from, *wr* if it can be written into, and *rd+wr* if it can be both read from and written into. You must also select either the address strobe by adding *as*, or data strobe by adding *ds*, to this parameter to specify the chip select pulse's exact shape. We usually choose the longer address strobe, but the data strobe can be chosen if the chip select is to be valid only when data on the data bus is determinate. If the (8K,8) RAM is attached to D[15 to 8] then the second parameter should be written *upper+rd+wr+as.*

The third parameter of *optionAssign* is the memory's speed, filling the Mode and Dsack fields of Figure 3-17; this determines the delay time when DSACK is generated as in the hardware in Figure 3-14. Use an integer *s* from 0 to 13 to generate that many wait states, which correspond to memory cycle times of 180+60*s nanoseconds. If *as* is selected in the second field, the chip enable is 100+60*s nanoseconds long, and if *ds* is selected in the second field, the chip enable is the same length in a read cycle and 60 nanoseconds shorter in a write cycle. This pulse width should be matched against the required pulse width of the device's enable, as we matched timing in Figure 3-13. Instead of an integer, write in this third parameter the word, *fast* to give a 120 nanosecond memory cycle with a 40 nanosecond pulse width, *synch* to use 6800-style I/O devices described in Chapter 4, or *external* if DSACK is to be generated by some other logic, not by this chip select logic. Writing *synch* in this field will also change the leftmost Mode field of the control register to use 6800-style I/O devices.

The fourth parameter fills the Space field of Figure 3-17; write *user* if the memory is to appear only in user space, *super* if the memory is to appear only in supervisor space or *user+super* if in both spaces. If in our example, memory is to be accessed in either user or supervisor space, we write *user+super*. The fifth parameter fills the IPL and Avec fields of Figure 3-17 and specifies chip select operations used in interrupt acknowledge cycles, and will be explained in Chapter 5. If interrupt acknowledge cycles are not used, put 0 here. The full set of three macros for our example is:

pinAssign(cs6,byte); baseAssign(6,0x10000,k8);
optionAssign(6,rd+wr+upper+as,0,user+super,0);

This generates the following assembler language code:

```
MOVEQ #0xFC,D0           make mask to pick up long word 0xfffa44
AND.L 0x00FFFA44,D0      get the control register
ORI.L #00000002,D0       OR in 2 bits for "byte" width
MOVE.L D0,0x00FFFA44     put back values
MOVE.W #0x0101,0x00FFFA64 put base and height into control register
MOVE.W #0x5830,0x00FFFA66 put all options into control register
```

Note that the *pinAssign* macro sets up the first four instructions in order to preserve the values of the Width field for other chip select modules, and the other macros generate efficient MOVE instructions. If all Width fields are initialized at one time and never changed again, a more efficient *pinAssign* macro can be written to initialize them.

Throughout the remainder of this book, whenever we need to use a chip select pin to enable an external memory or I/O device, we will use these simple macros. We will assume the header file *decode.h* is included in the program and we will use its constants.

3-3.5 The Design of an (8K,16) Memory for a BCC

The design of a memory for a microprocessor illustrates some of the previous sections' principles. We illustrate the initialization of the chip select control registers and the wiring of two MCM6164-45s to implement an (8K, 16) memory at base address 0x10000 in user and supervisor space for the M68340 and then the M68332. The logic diagram for the M68340 is shown in Figure 3-18. The same principles are used in interfacing I/O registers, discussed in the next chapter.

Because 16K words need 14 bits of address, the 13 bits A[13 to 1] of the M68340 connect to the corresponding (address-1) pins of the 6164 (M68340 A[1] to 6164 A[0], and so on.) Each of the data pins of the 6164s is connected to one of the M68340's data bus pins. The "upper" 6164's pins D[7 to 0] are connected to the M68340's D[15 to 8] and the "lower" 6164's pins D[7 to 0] are connected to its data bus D[7 to 0]. Also, connect +5 and ground to pins 28 and 14, and put a .1 μF bypass capacitor between them.

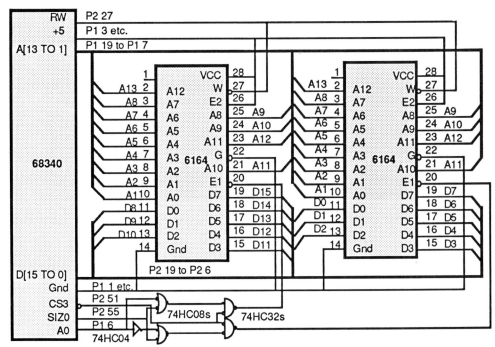

Figure 3-18. An MCM6164-45 Memory System for the M68340.

Having attempted to use the M68340's fast memory cycle in Section 3-3.1 and found that it would not work with the MCM6164-45 without screening parts, we will consider the next fastest timing, using 0 wait states. This six microstep memory cycle produces a 100 nanosecond chip enable pulse. There are several ways to connect the four control signals W, G, E1 and E2 which have different timing requirements. If G is low, E2 is high and W is connected to the M68340's RW line, internally the tristate drivers of the 6164 will be enabled to read data from the chip to the data bus, only when W is high and E1 is low, and the chip writes data only when both W and E1 are low. When E1 is used to control read and write timing of the MCM6164-45, it is the same as in Figure 3-12, except replace G and 20 with E1 and 45 in Figure 3-12a, and W and 25 with E1 and 40 in Figure 3-12b. Using our timing analysis procedure, an E1 pulse greater than 45 nanoseconds can be used, and a 0 wait state pulse width is 100 nanoseconds. Because all other timing requirements are met, we use this timing.

The chip select CS3 will pulse low, following the address strobe timing, when the address lines (and RW and FC) are matched, but the M68340's SIM cannot detect SIZ or address A0 to determine when the low, high or both RAMS should be selected. External logic (inverter and negative-logic OR and AND gates) is needed to enable the RAMs.

The chip select control registers are set for the desired address and the range is set for 14 bits of don't cares because A[13 to 1] is decoded within the RAMs and A0 is decoded to select which RAMs to enable. We select word mode because the memory will read or write 16 bits, and we select 0 wait states as discussed above, and the RAM is clearly a readable and writable device. The *CsAssign* macro we use is shown below:

CsAssign(3,0x10000,14,wait0+word,rdWr)

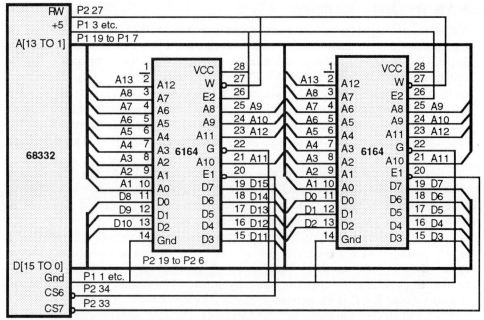

Figure 3-19. An MCM6164-45 Memory System for the M68332.

To build a 16K byte memory for an M68332 system, we can use the same timing analysis as we did for the M68340 system, but the chip selects are organized differently. The M68332, having the ability to decode A0 to determine which RAM to enable, and having 12 decoders, can be used to put all the decoding logic inside the M68332 chip. We will use CS6 and CS7 to decode the high byte and low byte RAM enables as shown in Figure 3-19.

CS6 will be attached to the upper byte, D[15 to 8] of the M68332's data bus. It will be an "upper byte" byte-wide memory occupying 16K bytes of address space starting at 0x10000. It will be enabled for reading writing in user and supervisor states. Its chip select registers are intialized thus:

pinAssign(cs6,byte); baseAssign(6,0x10000,k16);
optionAssign(6,rd+wr+upper+as,0,user+super,0);

CS7 will be attached to the lower byte, D[7 to 0] of the M68332's data bus. It will be a "lower byte" byte-wide memory occupying 16K bytes of address space starting at 0x10000. It will be enabled for reading writing in user and supervisor states. Its chip select registers are intialized thus:

pinAssign(cs7,byte); baseAssign(7,0x10000,k16);
optionAssign(7,rd+wr+lower+as,0,user+super,0);

Having wired the connections shown in Figure 3-19 and initialized both chip enable control registers as shown above, we can use the extra 16K bytes of memory to expand the memory of the BCC. Different memory chips (eg a (32K,8) chip) can be used to expand in larger ranges, and more chips can be added to expand in multiple ranges. Finally, only one chip can be added to expand memory in a byte-wide memory rather than two chips in a word-wide memory, as we did in this example.

3-3.6 Dynamic Memory

A *dynamic memory* is a random access memory that stores data by putting charges on capacitors. A threshold is chosen as a small charge, and a T is a charge greater than the threshold while an F is a charge less than the threshold. The charge dissipates, like the voltage across an RC network. Before a T dissipates to become indistinguishable from an F, the bit must be read and rewritten at a full T charge; this operation is called *refreshing* the memory bit. Because the charge can be stored in a very small area on a chip, dynamic memories are generally larger and cheaper than static memories like the 6164 discussed earlier. In fact, we will discuss the 1-megabit HM511000 in this section as an example of a dynamic memory chip. (See Figure 3-20a.)

Memories, and dynamic memories in particular, are organized into (*n*,1) chips in order to reduce the number of pins. To make up a 16-bit word memory, 16 such chips are connected rather like the two 6164 chips; addresses are sent in identical manner to all of them and data lines are separately connected to each of them.

Refreshing must be done on all bits in a memory in a period of time called a *refresh period.* That is generally in the order of 2 milliseconds (8 milliseconds for the HM511000). In order to refresh 1 million bits in the HM511000 in less than a refresh period, the (1048576,1) memory is internally organized into an array of R rows and C columns so that R x C is the number of bits in the chip (R = 512, C = 2048, R x C = 1 million), and all C bits in a row are simultaneously refreshed together whenever any bit in that row is read or written. (See Figure 3-20b.) Observe that, externally, the chip appears to be a one-bit-wide memory, but internally it is organized by an array. We emphasize that this array structure is only seen inside the chip and is essentially obscured outside the chip. The memory address, say A[19 to 0], is divided into a high address A[19 to 9], called the column address, and a low address A[8 to 0], called the row address, where the row address chooses the row to be read. The row address is needed first and is used to read out a whole row inside each chip. The column address is needed later to choose a bit in the row to read or to be written. In one refresh period, we need to refresh each row once by reading or writing any bit in it. Note that the row address is the least significant part of the address, so consecutive rows are selected by consecutive addresses. We will use 16 of these chips to implement a (1048576,16) memory at 0x80000, which can only be read or written as a word, not as a byte.

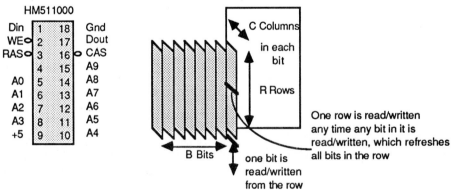

a. Pin Connections   b. Organization of Rows and Columns in a Bit

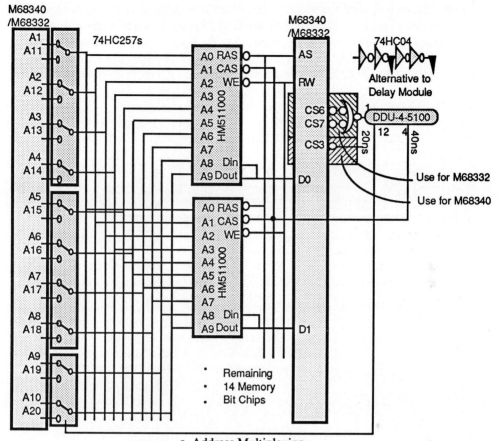

c. Address Multiplexing
Figure 3-20. A Dynamic Memory Chip.

Refreshing can be achieved by reading (or writing) any 512 consecutive words in this memory. In some cases, this can be guaranteed, for instance if the words are read out to a CRT display so that 512 consecutive addresses are always read from memory within a refresh period. Otherwise, the memory must be explicitly refreshed. This can be done by special refresh hardware (a counter chip to generate row addresses and control logic to prevent the M68332 from reading or writing when refreshing is done), or by an interrupt handler or DMA device (discussed in Chapter 5) that reads 512 words every refresh period. The technique that requires the least hardware uses the interrupt handler, which is executed every 8 milliseconds and executes 256 instructions like NOP. In order to use the simplest hardware we will assume it will be used.

Because the row address is needed first and the column address is needed later, they can be time-multiplexed on the same pins in order to put the memory chip in a smaller package. The address is multiplexed so the low addresses are sent first, then the high addresses are sent, over the same bus and pins by means of a multiplexer such as a 74HC257. (See Figure 3-20c.) A *row address strobe* RAS is used to time the row address, and a *column address strobe* CAS is used to time the column address. To make the time multiplexing symmetrical, 10 bits of address, A[10 to 1] are input when RAS falls and 10 bits A[20 to 11] are input when CAS falls, so the internal row is selected by the low-order 9 bits of the address input when RAS falls, and the column is actually selected by the high-order bit when RAS falls and all the bits when CAS falls. For simplicity, we call A[9 to 0] the row address and A[19 to 10] the column address.

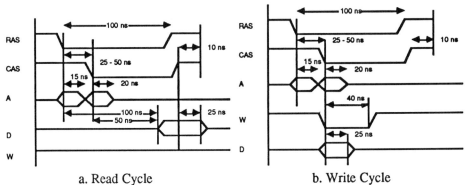

a. Read Cycle   b. Write Cycle

Figure 3-21. HM511000P10 1 Mbit Dynamic Memory Timing.

The timing for a read memory cycle is shown in Figure 3-21a. W is generally high throughout a read cycle. The row address must be put to the memory when RAS falls and for 15 nanoseconds after that. The column address must be put to the memory when CAS falls and for 20 nanoseconds after that. CAS must fall 25 to 50 nanoseconds after RAS falls, and the data are determinate on the Dout pin 100 nanoseconds after RAS falls and 50 nanoseconds after CAS falls, whichever is later. CAS and RAS must be high for 10 nanoseconds at the end of the memory cycle, and data becomes indeterminate on Dout 25 nanoseconds after CAS rises. A write memory cycle is similar, except that W must be low at least before CAS falls and for 40 nanoseconds after CAS falls, and data on Din must be stable for 25 nanoseconds after CAS falls.

A strategy for controlling the HM511000 dynamic memory is shown in the partial logic diagram in Figure 3-20c. We discuss the generation of RAS, CAS, and WE signals, based on the timing diagrams of the memory (Figure 3-21) and the M68332 (see the *MC68332 SIM User's Manual (SIM32UM/AD)* Section 10 Figures 10-2 and 10-3), or for the M68340, the *MC68340 Integrated Processor Unit Techincal Summary (MC68340/D)* to use this memory with that microprocessor.

A dynamic memory is generally selected by asserting or negating CAS using an address decoder. If CAS is false (high) throughout a read cycle, the output Dout is not driven from the chip, and if CAS is false during a write cycle, the bit on Din is not written into the memory. However, the entire row selected by the row address is refreshed, whether or not CAS is asserted, and thus the memory actually reads or writes a bit. Thus, the address decoder decodes high-order address bits and permits CAS to be asserted at the proper time in the memory cycle if this memory is selected. Finally, WE is low exactly when RW is low.

RAS is to be asserted low during a read cycle as soon as the address is stable; AS can be used to directly generate RAS. CAS is asserted low only when the chip is selected, about 40 nanoseconds after RAS is asserted. In order to present the row address and column address to the memory chips, the row address A[10 to 1] is input when RAS is asserted, and the column address A[20 to 11] is to be asserted when CAS is asserted. The multiplexer should switch address inputs between the two edges 20 nanoseconds after RAS is asserted. A delay line such as the DDU-4-5100 can be used to produce the RAS signal delayed 20 nanoseconds to control the multiplexers, and delayed 40 nanoseconds to derive CAS. If a delay line is unavailable, a chain of 74HC04 gates can be used if the chips are screened for delays. In order to satisfy memory read setup timing requirements, 1 wait state is needed.

The M68340 SIM address decoder can decode all the required signals. Chip select CS3 is assigned for the addresses beginning with 0x80000, ignoring the low order 20 bits of the address, for 1 wait state, for 16-bit access, and for reading or writing, as in:

$$CsAssign(3,0x80000,20,wait1+word,rdWr)$$

The maximum address range that the M68332 SIM address decoder is designed to handle is 1 Megabyte, but the (1048576,16) memory at 0x80000 memory requires a 2 Megabyte range of memory, so 2 decoders are needed, and their outputs will be ORed (see Figure 3-20c). These decoders, producing CS6 and CS7, are initialized as in:

$$pinAssign(cs6,word); baseAssign(6,0x80000,k1024);$$
$$optionAssign(6,rd+wr+upper+lower+as,1,user+super,0);$$
$$pinAssign(cs7,word); baseAssign(7,0x100000, k1024);$$
$$optionAssign(7,rd+wr+upper+lower+as,1,user+super,0);$$

Dynamic memories need a refresh mechanism. This can be implemented in hardware by making the address multiplexers three-input multiplexers, the third input coming from a counter that generates consecutive row addresses. Special dynamic memory controller chips have all this logic inside them. However, we can generate these in software, so our hardware is simplified. Finally, small resistances (about 10Ω) are generally connected from fast logic around the memories feeding signals to the memories themselves. These resistors dampen ringing.

3-3.7 Backplanes for Multiboard Computer Systems

A microprocessor has sufficient capability to drive one regular TTL gate, about four gates of the LS family, or around ten CMOS or HCMOS gates or other LSI MOS chips designed to be connected to the microprocessor. When a larger number of gates are connected to a microprocessor line, buffers are usually used to raise the drive capability of that line. Especially when the system is built on several different printed circuit cards, buffers are used to send data between the cards.

Four problems commonly appear in the design of expanded buses. The first is the interconnection pattern of the bus drivers: Without sufficient planning, there is a tendency to design scraggly buses. The second problem is the satisfaction of timing requirements. The third is the prevention of enabling more than one bus driver at any time. And the fourth is the suppression of noise.

It is too easy to let the design of a system sort of grow, so that the signals are improperly distributed. Signals, like the clock, AS, and DS, have edges used as references to capture data on the buses. These edges usually should arrive at every point in the system at precisely − or as close as possible to − the same time. The difference in time between the arrivals of a signal at different points in the system is called the *skew*. If an output can be connected to f inputs, a tree structure with fan-out f is the best way to distribute a signal; the source of the signal drives f buffers, each of these drives f buffers, and so on. All modules using the signals should be at the leaves of the tree, with the same number of buffers between them and the source. Although buffers, even of the same type, can have significantly different delays, this practice reduces the skew to a minimum – however, even this minimum skew may still represent a significant problem.

Although the address bus is less time critical, the 16 address lines are usually distributed using a tree structure, with a pair of octal buffers like the 74HC244 at each branch of the tree. The data bus is not so easy to form, because it carries signals bidirectionally, from microprocessor to memory and from memory to microprocessor. A way to implement this type of bus in a tree is to use a pair of buffers like the 74HC244, connected back-to-back so the inputs of one connect to the outputs of the other. Alternatively, a 74HC245 contains a pair of drivers equivalent to two 74HC241s in the aforementioned configuration. Only one of the two drivers can be enabled at any time, and if several such buffers connect to a node of the tree, only one of the drivers feeding the node may be enabled. To determine which drivers to enable, we use some logic that considers the data's source, which must be either at the root or a leaf of the tree. At most, one source may be selected at any time. If a source on a leaf sends data, all rootward-going drivers between the leaf and the root are enabled, and, in all other branches of the tree, the leafward drivers are enabled. The signal will reach all the nodes on the tree in the shortest possible time. In a trivial bus using only one pair of drivers, the microprocessor is at the root, and all the devices are connected at the other end of the branch, at the only leaf. The RW signal is the only one needed, because, when asserted, data flow rootward, and when not, data flow leafward. While the trivial case is by far the most common, the general case is also very simple.

When buses are expanded using drivers in this way, we must be aware of the delays through these buffers when we check the timing requirements of memories and other devices. Generally, the longest delay for any signal through the expanded bus must be added to the delays for signals using the bus in the analysis of the timing requirements. Also, the edges of the clock and RW ORed with data strobe signals may have to be delayed by the same amount as the signal to cancel the skew caused when the signal is sent through such expanded buses.

The analysis technique of Section 3-3.1 using sliding timing diagrams can be modified to handle expanded buses, but a more general technique uses *interval arithmetic*. In many cases, delays can only be specified as a minimum value and a maximum value, which is an *interval* <min, max>. An arithmetic system has been defined for operating on intervals. For example, if one interval <min1,max1> is added to another interval <min2,max2>, the sum is a new interval <min1 + min2, max1 + max2>. For instance, the sum of <1,5> and <3,4> is <4,9>. The negative of an interval <min,max> is <-max,-min>. For instance, the negative of <-2,5> is <-5,2>.

So, delays can be specified as intervals, and can be added or subtracted using interval arithmetic. Using this tool, skews can be accounted for so we can be assured that, when an edge of a timing signal arrives, the setup and hold times are satisfied.

Consider an example of skewing calculations. Suppose that the data bus from an MC683xx is driven through one 74HC245 and AS passes through one 74HC32, to an MCM6164-45 random access memory chip. Will this satisfy the write cycle timing requirements, as in the earlier analysis of timing requirements? The problem is to determine the time interval that the data from the MC683xx must be stable so they are stable at the inputs of the MCM6164-45 throughout that chip's setup and hold times. Intuitively, we know that the MC683xx must supply stable data for a time (T683xx) to which the delay time through the 74HC245 (T74245) has been added, that covers a greater time interval "⊃" than the setup and hold time interval of the MCM6164-45 (T6164), to which the delay time through the 74HC32 (T7432) is added.

A formula can be checked out intuitively as if all intervals were just ordinary numbers. For each possible time when the memory may need determinate data, the MC683xx must provide determinate data at that time. That is, the set of times in the interval (T7432 + T6164) must be strictly included in the set of times in the interval (T683xx + T74245). The intervals are defined so 0 is the time that an ideal E1 signal rising edge would appear at that point; this memory's reference is AS at the MC683xx. The setup and hold times for a device are <-setup, hold> and the delays are <min delay, max delay>. Suppose the 74HC245 has a delay between 9 and 25 nanoseconds (the interval <9,25>), and the 74HC32 has a delay between 6 and 20 nanoseconds (the interval <6,20>), the M683xx produces data over the interval <-60,15> and the MCM6164-45 needs a setup and hold time of <-20,10> nanoseconds. The source of the data (T683xx +T74245) must make the data stable at least over a minimum interval (T7432 + T6164), relative to the rising edge of AS. Data is correctly written in the MCM6164-45 if

$$\begin{aligned}
\text{T683xx} + \text{T74245} &\quad \supset \quad \text{T7432} + \text{T6164} \\
<-60,15> + <9,25> &\quad \supset \quad <6,20> + <-20,10> \\
<-51,40> &\quad \supset \quad <-14,30>
\end{aligned}$$

So the data on the input of the MCM6164-45 are stable 51 nanoseconds before and 40 nanoseconds after the rising edge of AS signal at the input to the 74HC32. The data on the input of the MCM6164-45 must be stable 14 nanoseconds before and 30 nanoseconds after the rising edge of AS. The data are determinate for the interval <-14,30>, so the hold time is satisfied because of gate delays in the bus.

Intervals can be handled as objects. We show a THINK C program for the Macintosh to illustrate this point. The class *interval* shown below has integer values of the low and high limits. The methods for addition, subtraction and testing within range use *interval* objects as their arguments, and the *init* method is used to set the values of low and high (alternatively these values can be explicitly set; rather than *T683xx->init(-60,15);* one can use *T683xx->low=-60; T683xx->high=15;*.) The overhead associated with objects includes the blessing and the init method. Once this is accomplished, the program reads pretty much like the mathematical expression shown above is written. Once you have written and debugged such a progam, you can use it to verify your timing requirements for a number of different chips, or different families (i.e. 74LS vs 74HC parts), or hypothetical parts, and you can run off tables that verify the set-up and hold times and show margins of safety for each choice.

```
#include "oopsD.c"
typedef struct interval:direct {
    int low,high; int within(interval*);
    void init(int, int),add(interval*, interval*),sub(interval*, interval*);
} indirect;
```

```
char buffer[6][sizeof(interval)];
interval *T683xx, *T74245, *T7432, *T6164;

main(){
        interval *x,*y; int z;
        bless(T683xx=(interval*)buffer[0],interval);
        bless(T74245=(interval*)buffer[1],interval);
        bless(T7432=(interval*)buffer[2],interval);
        bless(T6164=(interval*)buffer[3],interval);
        bless(x=(interval*)buffer[4],interval);
        bless(y=(interval*)buffer[5],interval);
        T683xx->init(-60,15);
        T74245->init(9,25);
        T7432->init(6,20);
        T6164->init(-20,10);
        x->add(T683xx,T74245);
        y->add(T7432,T6164);
        z=x->within(y);
}
void interval::init(i,j) int i,j;{low=i; high=j;}
void interval::add(i,j) interval *i,*j;{ low=i->low + j->low; high=i->high + j->high; }
void interval::sub(i,j) interval *i,*j;{ low=i->low - j->high; high=i->high - j->low; }
int interval::within(i) interval *i;{ return (low<i->low)&&(high>i->high); }
```

The interval arithmetic method is very general and useful in the analysis of skewing and in worst case analysis in general. A complicated system with mezanine boards (such as the BCC board) plugged into boards that plug into backplanes, with several busses and control signals taking different paths, can be easily and reliably handled by means of interval arithemetic. Also, you can use this for other work. Operations for multiplication, division, and complex functions such as SINE and so on can be defined precisely for intervals, and the execution of these operations is mechanical and clean. If you write additional routines for multiplication, division, and so on, you can create a library of interval methods that would be of general use. If you do so for floating point numbers, however, take care to explicitly round down the lower limit and round up the upper limit in your methods to bound any errors made in floating point arithmetic. In using intervals with complex expressions, one must be careful to intuitively check the formula to make sure that the interval's upper and lower bounds really represent the worst cases. Interval arithmetic tends to be pessimistic if two variables appear in two parts of a formula and should cancel. For instance, if the interval A is <1,2>, then, using the rules of interval arithmetic, A - A is evaluated as <-1,1> rather than <0,0>. If possible write the formula so that each variable appears just once, otherwise the answer should be regarded as worse than the real worst case. Also, check the formula with test cases to verify that you really do cover the worst cases.

The bus that interconnects printed circuit boards is often implemented on a board called a *motherboard* or *backplane*, into which the other boards are plugged. This bus can be a standard type so that boards made by different manufacturers can be plugged into it. The *S-100* bus – so named because it has 100 pins – is an old standard type extensively used for Intel 8080 computer systems.

Often, different boards, designed independently of each other, are plugged into the motherboard or backplane, giving rise to the troublesome problem of bus driver control. Unfortunately, it is easy to design the logic that controls the drivers so that a driver from one board is driving the backplane bus exactly when another driver wants to drive the same bus. Although this problem can occur on any bus, it is especially troublesome on the backplane bus because the boards it interconnects are often designed at different times. The solution is good documentation. Each board should be documented to show exactly when it drives signals onto the backplane bus, as a function of the addresses on the address bus or other control signals (such as direct memory access acknowledge signals, discussed in Chapter 5).When a new board is designed, it should be checked to see if it can ever conflict with an existing board. Also, when no explanation can be found for erroneous behavior on the bus, check all boards again to see if two drivers are driving the bus at the same time.

A technique Terry Ritter of Motorola recommends is to design all tristate bus drivers to implement *break-before make* control, using the terminology that describes relay contacts. All tristate address bus drivers should be disabled for the first part of every memory cycle, when the AS signal is high. That way, tristate drivers will not drive the bus in different directions while the address and RW signals are indeterminate.

Many motherboards, especially those for the S-100 bus, use *active terminations*. To reduce the electrical noise and ringing on the signals, each line is *terminated* by connecting it through a (2000-ohm) resistor to a voltage that is half the positive supply voltage. The resistor absorbs the energy that causes the noise. Half the supply voltage is chosen so, whether the driver drives the bus high or low, about the same amount of power is absorbed by the terminator, and thus if several bus lines are terminated together, those that are high will supply current needed by others that are low. This voltage is easily established by an audio amplifier integrated circuit, such as an LM384, because it automatically sets its output to half the supply voltage. Alternatively, if the board is well designed, noise may not be a problem, and active terminations may not be needed.

In this subsection, some of the most common problems in interface design have been discussed. Remember to keep the expanded bus as much like a symmetrical tree as possible. When confirming the timing requirements, use interval arithmetic. Check the logic that determines which drivers are enabled under which conditions, and keep accurate records of these conditions. Finally, use a noise-free motherboard, or supply active terminations on it to suppress noise. By following this advice, you can avoid many of the most common interface design problems.

3-4 Conclusions

The study of microcomputer data and address buses is critical because scanty knowledge in these areas leads to serious interface problems. Before getting on these buses, data inside the microprocessor are unobservable and useless for interfacing. But when data are on the bus, they are quite important in the design of interface circuitry. This chapter has discussed what address, data, and control signals look like on a typical microcomputer bus, supporting that discussion with descriptions of some mechanisms and components that generate those signals. You should now be able to read the data sheets and block or logic diagrams that describe the microprocessor and other modules connected to the bus. You should also be able to analyze the timing requirements on a bus. And, finally, you should have sufficient hardware background to understand the discussions of interface modules in the coming chapters.

If you found any difficulty with the discussion on hardware modules and signals, a number of fine books are available on logic design. We recommend *Fundamentals of Logic Design*, second edition, by C. H. Roth, West Publishing Co., 1990 because it is organized as a self-paced course. However, there are so many good texts in different writing styles, that you may find another more suitable. Computer organization is also covered in a number of fine texts, such as *Fundamentals of Microcomputer Architecture*, by K. L. Doty, Matrix Publishers, Inc. Wilcox's book, *68000 Microcomputer Systems Design and Troubleshooting*, Prentice-Hall, 1987 covers hardware design very thoroughly. Further details on the MC68332 can be obtained from the *CPU32 Reference Manual (CPU32RM/AD)* Motorola Inc., 1989. Further details on the MC68340 can be obtained from the *MC68340 Integrated Processor User's Manual (MC68340UM/AD)* Motorola Inc., 1990. We have not attempted to duplicate the diagrams and discussions in those books because we assume you will refer to it while reading this book; also, we present an alternative view of the subject. You can use either or both views.

Do You Know These Terms?

See the End of Chapter 1 for Instructions.

signal, high, low, determinate, variable, true, false, assert, negate, complement, positive logic, negative logic, memory variable, link variable, synchronous, clock, equivalent signal, module, input port, output port, behaviorally equivalent, dual in-line, small scale integrated circuit, medium scale integrated circuit, large scale integrated circuit, (LSI), very large scale integrated circuit, family, low-power Schottky, complementary metal oxide, logic diagram, bypass capacitor, gate, buffer, fan-out, bus (or buss), bus driver, fan-in, open collector gate, wire-OR bus, pull-up resistor, enable, tristate gate, tristate enable, tristate bus, Dynamic logic, static logic, D flip-flop, latch, D edge-triggered flip-flop, D master slave flip-flop, setup time, hold time, one-shot, latch, register, counter, shift register, (i j) random access memory, word, word width, memory cycle, chip enable, read/write, write enable, memory cycle time, memory access time, read-only memory, programmable read-only memory, erasable programmable read-only memory, electronically erasable programmable memory, microprogramming, data transfer, microstep, control variables, controller, micro-order, singulary, encode, code, decode, recode, horizontal microprogram, control memory, vertical microprogram, pipeline, flushing the pipeline, prefetch, fast memory cycle, wait state, logic analyzer, screen the parts, programmable decoder, incompletely specified decoding, dynamic memory, refreshing the memory, refresh period, row address strobe, column address strobe, skew, interval arithmetic, interval, motherboard, backplane, S-100, bus, break-before make, active terminations, terminate.

4 ——

Parallel and Serial Input/output

The first three chapters were compact surveys of material you really need to know to study interface design. That is why they were a little heavy with concepts and definitions. In the remainder of the book, we will have more expanded discussions and more opportunities to study interesting examples and work challenging problems. The material in these chapters is not intended to replace the data sheets provided by the manufacturers nor do we intend to simply summarize them. If the reader wants the best description of any chip discussed at length in the book, data sheets supplied by Motorola should be consulted. The topics are organized around concepts rather than around integrated circuits because we consider these more important in the long run. In the following chapters, we will concentrate on the principles and practices of designing interfaces with I/O LSI chips in general and in particular with Motorola chips compatible with the M68332 and M68340.

From an I/O device designer's viewpoint, an *I/O device* is a subsystem of a computer that handles the input or output of data. A device can contain in it other devices, but generally it alone accesses and controls one piece of I/O hardware. An *input port* is an input to a computer from an I/O device. An *output port* is an output from a computer to an I/O device. An *I/O port* is an input or output port, or both.

Although this chapter is not the longest, it is the most important chapter in this book. The simple parallel and serial I/O devices are studied, both from a hardware and software viewpoint. These are the most common I/O devices and are key building blocks of all the other I/O devices. So they are exceedingly important to the design of interfaces.

The first section considers some principles of parallel I/O architecture, looking at I/O ports from the programmer's point of view. You have to consider the architectural alternatives before you design either the hardware or the software. This section also shows how to build the simplest parallel I/O ports. The second section introduces some very simple software used with parallel I/O ports. Also, microcomputers are often used to replace the digital logic and relays in obsolete industrial controllers. The software for such controllers is also studied in this section. C procedures are used to control I/O ports. While the software is simple, the memory cycle timing, which is often very important and which we will study carefully, is a little more intricate. The third section introduces the LSI parallel I/O chips. Some general observations are made, and the M6821 and M68230 I/O devices are introduced. We then study the parallel ports in the M68332 and M68340. Indirect I/O is then discussed. Serial I/O devices, considered next, are particularly easy to connect to a computer because a small number of wires are needed, and are useful when the relatively slow operation of the serial I/O port is acceptable. These ports are called *synchronous* because a clock is used. Asynchronous serial ports are discussed in Chapter 8, where communications systems are described. We also discuss how coprocessors like the 68881 floating-point coprocessor are connected to the 683xx. Finally, we show how objects can be used to design I/O devices and their software, and how 683xx I/O device objects can be written in C.

Upon finishing this chapter, the reader should be able to design hardware and write software for simple parallel and serial input and output ports. An input port using a bus driver, an output port using a register, a shift-register-based serial I/O port, a port using an M6821, one employing a MC68230, or using the parallel ports in the M68332 or M68340, should be easy to design and build. Programs of around 100 lines to input data to a buffer, output data from a buffer, or control something using programmed or interpretive techniques should be easy to write and debug. Moreover, the reader will be prepared to study the ports introduced in later chapters, which use the parallel and serial I/O port as a major building block.

4-1 Input/Output Architecture and Simple I/O Ports

We first consider the parallel I/O port's architecture - another way of saying we'll look at such a port from the programmer's viewpoint. One aspect, introduced in the first subsection, is whether I/O ports appear as words in primary memory, to be accessed using a pointer to memory, or as words in an architecturally different memory, to be accessed by different instructions. Another aspect is where to place the port in an address space such as the computer's primary memory. A final aspect is whether the port can be read from or written in, or both. The "write-only memory" is usually only a topic for a computer scientist's joke collection, but it is a real possibility in an I/O port. To understand why you might use such a thing, the hardware design and its cost must be studied. So we introduce I/O port hardware design, which will also be useful in the next section, which introduces the software used with these ports. We then give a summary.

4-1.1 Isolated and Memory-Mapped I/O

There are two major ways in a microcomputer to access I/O, relative to the address space in primary memory. Using the first, *isolated I/O*, the ports are read from by means of *input instructions,* such as IN 5. This kind of instruction would input a word from I/O port 5 into a data register. Similarly, *output instructions* like OUT 3 would output a word from a data register to the third I/O port. Using the second, *memory-mapped I/O*, the port is considered a word in memory, at some location, such as 0x10000. A standard load instruction like MOVE 0x10000,D0 is then an input instruction, and a store instruction like MOVE D0,0x10000 is an output instruction. These can be easily generated in C programs as we show later. There is no need for a separate input or output instruction. Some machines like the 683xx have no separate I/O instructions and exclusively use memory-mapped I/O; other machines have I/O instructions and can use either isolated I/O or memory-mapped I/O.

As we discussed in the last chapter, memory-mapped I/O uses the data and address buses just as memory uses them. The microprocessor thinks it is reading or writing data in memory, but the I/O ports are designed to supply the data read or capture the data written at specific memory locations. As in the memory design in Section 3-3.3, the basic hardware is enabled or clocked by an address decoder that decodes the address on the address bus. The decoder can either be completely specified, built with decoder integrated circuits, or incompletely specified. Generally, though, it must be read from or written into the port when a specific memory address is sent out and must not access it when any other address used by the program is sent out. Isolated I/O is really quite similar in hardware to memory-mapped I/O. To save pins, the port address is sent from the microprocessor on the same bus as the memory address, but some (variable) control signal is asserted when the address is an I/O address and not a memory address. So the memory address decoders must be built to enable or clock the memory only when this variable is false, and the I/O address decoders must be built to enable the port only when this variable is true.

Each technique has some advantages. Isolated I/O instructions, such as are used in the 8-bit INTEL 8080, use a 1-byte op code and a 1-byte port address, while almost all memory-mapped I/O instructions of 8-bit microcomputers tend to be 3 bytes long or tie up an address register to use 2-byte instructions. This extra length can be serious if a program for a dedicated application uses a lot of I/O operations and must fit into the smallest possible size memory to save cost. However, the 683xx has addressing modes such as pointer addressing, which can be used to improve the static efficiency of I/O routines. The port address decoder is simpler, because it need consider only 8, rather than 16 or more, address bits and some control signals. More important, isolated I/O is not as susceptible to software errors as is memory-mapped I/O. In the latter case, especially if the microcomputer has a stack in memory, an error in a loop that has an instruction to push data onto the stack can fill memory with garbage in no time. In our personal experience, this happens all too often. If output ports send signals to turn on motors, say in a tape drive, putting garbage in them could produce interesting effects (spill tape, stretch and change density of tape). Memory-mapped I/O is sometimes awkward when large memories, like the (1048576, 16) memories discussed in Section 3-3.4, occupy the addresses needed for memory-mapped I/O ports. You have to design the address decoder so the memory does not put data on the bus when the input port is read.

Nevertheless, memory-mapped I/O is more popular because most microcomputers have instructions that operate directly in memory, such as ADDQ #1,0x10000, ROL 0x10000, or register to memory instructions such as ADD D0,0x10000. If the program is in read-only memory, indexed addressing can be used to relocate memory-mapped I/O, while isolated I/O may not have this capability. The use of these instructions operating directly on (readable) output ports in memory-mapped I/O is very powerful; their use can also shorten programs that would otherwise need to bring the word into the data register, operate on it, then output it. Finally, conventional C without embedded assembler language can access I/O ports using variable pointers or using constant address pointers.

We do have to worry about accidentally writing over the output ports when we use memory-mapped I/O. Memory-mapped I/O can be protected, however, by a *lock*. The lock is an output port which is itself not locked, so the program can change it. The lock's output is ANDed with address and other control signals to get the enable or clock signals for all other I/O ports. If the lock is F, no I/O ports can be read or written. Before reading an I/O port, the program has to store T in the lock, then store F in the lock after all I/O operations are complete. The Radio Shack Color Computer uses a "Multipack Extension" module that uses a lock. In dedicated microcomputers that execute fully debugged programs, a lock is not needed, but in software development systems, a lock can drastically reduce the ill effects of memory-mapped I/O while allowing most of its advantages.

4-1.2 I/O Ports in an Address Space

The I/O ports in a computer have to be located in an address space of primary memory for memory-mapped I/O, or an equivalent space for isolated I/O. We consider this now.

The port address can be completely or incompletely specified. The 2K byte minimum for a SIM address decoder means that most ports accessed using it will be incompletely specified; never use addresses that accidentally access a memory or port.

We now consider where the port will be addressed by the program in memory. I/O ports are generally put in one place in the memory map (Figure 1-14). (See Figure 4-2a.) This permits the contiguous use of the rest of the memory for RAM or ROM, which is easier for compilers and operating systems to use, as illustrated in Chapter 10. Using the SIM and an external decoder chip, a collection of I/O devices in the same address range can be handled by one address decoder. However, in systems in which an I/O device is on a plug-in board and that board has RAM or ROM on it, RAM, ROM and I/O ports may be bundled together in the address space. The location of ports is a nontrivial problem in systems that are widely reproduced with different combinations of devices in them. Each distinct device should have its own address regardless of which system it is in and which devices are in that system. Alternatively, the address of a port should be easily modified. For instance, the address can be kept in the 683xx's address register, and index addressing can be used to access the port. Finally, the relative location of two ports may simplify programming. For instance, if two 8-bit ports, always read together, are in consecutive bytes, the MOVE.W instruction can be used to read both of them at once.

One of the most common faulty assumptions in port architecture is that I/O ports are 8 bits wide. For instance, in the 683xx, the byte-wide MOVE.B instructions are used in I/O programs in many texts. There are a large number of 8-bit I/O ports on I/O chips that are designed for 8-bit microcomputers. But 8 bits is not a fundamental width. In this book, where we emphasize fundamentals, we avoid that assumption. Of course, if the port is 8 bits wide, the MOVE.B instruction can be used, and used in C by accessing a variable of type *char*. A port can be 1 bit wide. If a 1-bit input port is read in bit 15, reading it will set the N condition code bit, which can be tested by a BMI instruction. Probably most ports read or write ASCII data. ASCII data is 7 bits wide, not 8 bits wide. If you read a 10-bit analog-to-digital converter, you should read a 10-bit port. There are a few 16-bit ports. Whatever your device needs, consider using a port of the right data size. Also, two or more ports may occupy the same word in the 683xx memory. Generally, if an n-bit port ($n<16$) is read, the other bits will be "garbage" and should be stripped off. If the port is not left-justified in the 683xx word, a logical shift instruction can be used to align it, as we will show below.

The *basic input port* is capable of sampling a signal when the microcomputer executes an input instruction (or an equivalent instruction in memory-mapped I/O) and of reading the sample into the data register (or operating on it as if it were a memory word). Because most microcomputers use tristate bus drivers, the port must drive the sample of data onto the data bus exactly when the microprocessor executes a read command with this port's address. A basic 16-bit input port at location 0x10000 is shown in Figure 4-1a, using the M68332 SIM address decoder (Section 3-3.3). The minimum block the SIM address decoder can select is 2K bytes, so the port appears at every word from 0x10000 to 0x107FF. Note that the address is therefore incompletely specified, and care should be taken to avoid other addresses that accidentally access it. CS6 is initialized:

```
pinAssign(cs6,word); baseAssign(6,0x10000,k2);
optionAssign(6,rd+upper+lower+as fast,user+super,0);
```

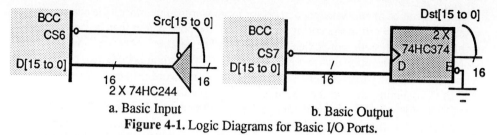

a. Basic Input   b. Basic Output

Figure 4-1. Logic Diagrams for Basic I/O Ports.

The output port usually has to hold output data for an indefinite time – until the program changes it. The *basic output port* is therefore a latch or register which is capable of clocking data from the data bus whenever the microcomputer writes to a location in memory-mapped I/O. The D bus is connected to the D input of the register or latch, and the clock is connected to an address decoder so that the register is clocked when the microprocessor executes a write command at the address selected for this port. Figure 4-1b shows a typical basic output port that will output and hold a 16-bit word of data written at memory location 0x10800. The minimum block the M68332 SIM address decoder can select is 2K bytes, so the port appears at every word in the range 0x10800 to 0x10FFF. Chip select 7 can be used to clock the register; it can be initialized thus:

pinAssign(cs7,word); baseAssign(7,0x10800, k2);
optionAssign(7,rd+wr+upper+lower+as,fast,user+super,0);

For the M68340, the corresponding chip selects CS2 and CS3 can be used for a basic input and a basic output device. The minimum block the M68340 SIM address decoder can select is 256 bytes, so the input port appears at every word in the range 0x10000 to 0x100FF, and the output port appears at every word in the range 0x10800 to 0x108FF. Connect the tristate gate enable of Figure 4-1a to CS2 and the clock of Figure 4-1b to CS3, and use the macros:

CsAssign(2,0x10000,8,fast,rdOnly);
CsAssign(3,0x10800,8,fast,rdWr);

An output port can be combined with an input port at the same address that inputs the data stored in the output port. This *readable output port* is more costly than the basic output port, which is write-only, but is more flexible. A readable output port that can be read from or written in at location 0x10000 is easily designed from the input and output ports shown in Figure 4-1, and is left as an exercise for the reader. However, we emphasize that this readable output port is more costly than the basic output port, and that the basic output port is write-only, and should not be read.

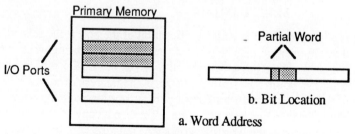

a. Word Address   b. Bit Location

Figure 4-2. Addressing I/O Ports.

Ports can be memory-mapped in one or more words in memory. The address of the lowest addressed word in the port is the address of the port. A port may be only part of a word or of two adjacent words. See Figure 4-2. A "worst-case" 3-bit port, low bit of the word at location 0x10000 and two high bits of 0x10002, might occupy two consecutive words in the memory map (Figure 4-2a) and parts of each word (Figure 4-2b).

In C, assuming we use the declaration *long *p=(long*)0x10000* and *0x10000* is the address of a pair of words containing a 3-bit input port just discussed, the port is read into a variable *d* with *d=(*p>>14)&7*. The declaration, *(long*),* tells the compiler to read or write four bytes at the address pointed to by *p*. The shift operator *>>* is used to move data from the port to the least significant bits of *d*, and the AND operator *&* is used to remove data that is not in the port from the words read from memory. Assuming the pointer p is in A0, this generates the following code:

MOVE.L (A0),D0	*p
ASR.L #14,D0	>>14
ANDI.L #7,D0	& 7
MOVE.L D0,0xFFFC(A6)	d=

Omit the shift operator if the port is aligned so that the least significant bit of the port is the least significant bit of a word. The AND operator is omitted if the port consists of whole words. For instance, assuming pointer *p=(int*)0x10000* is the address of a 16-bit port, *d=*p;* will read a 16-bit port at *0x10000* into d.

Similarly, consider the case where those three bits are a readable output port in words that also contain other readable output ports which must be unchanged. Assume pointer *p=(long*)0x10000* is the address of a pair of words containing a 3-bit output port just discussed. Then *p = *p & 0xFFFE3FFF | ((d << 14) & 0x1C000);* outputs *d* aligned into it. The expression *d << 14* moves the least significant bits of the data in *d* into position to put in the port, *& 0x1C000* removes parts of d that are not to be output, *p & 0xFFFE3FFF* gets data in the words not in the port that must be unchanged, and the OR operator merges the data in *d* to be written into the port and data in the words not in the port together, to put this data into the words at 0x10000 and 0x10002. Assuming the pointer p is in A0, this generates the following code:

MOVE.L # 0xFFFE3FFF,D0	& 0xFFFE3FFF
AND.L (A0),D0	*p
MOVE.L 0xFFFC(A6),D1	(d
LSL.L #14,D1	<< 14)
ANDI.L # 0x1C000,D1	& 0x1C000
OR.L D1,D0	
MOVEA.L 0xFFF8(A6),A0	
MOVE.L D0,(A0)	*p =

If the port is aligned so that the least significant bit of the port is the least significant bit of a word, the shift operator may be omitted, and if the words being written into have no ports other than the port being written, the *p & 0xFE3F |* may be omitted. For instance, assuming pointer *p=(int*)0x10000* is the address of a word, *p = d ;* will write 16-bit data in *d* into a 16-bit output port at location *p*. If the output port is not readable, but the basic output port of Figure 4-1b, then a copy of the data that is output to that and other ports in the words it writes into must be kept in memory, such as in variable *a*. The previous example is modified to save a copy in *int* variable *a* without much effort: $*p = a = a \& 0xFE3F \mid ((d << 14) \& 0x1C0)$; Alternatively, an output port can be at the same address as a word in RAM; writing at the address writes data in both the I/O port and the RAM and reading data reads the word in RAM. This technique is called *shadowed output*.

Some logic function can implemented in hardware upon writing to a port. The data can set bits in a *set port*. A pattern of 1s and 0s is written by the processor; wherever it writes a 1, the port bit is set, wherever it writes a 0, nothing is done. For instance, if the 8-bit set port at the address 0x10000 is to have bits 0 and 3 set, we can use the declaration *char *p=0x10000;* and the statement **p = 9;* The data can clear bits in a *clear port.* Wherever the processor writes a 1, the port bit is cleared, wherever it writes a 0, nothing is done. For instance, if the 8-bit clear port at 0x10000 is to have bits 1 and 4 cleared, we can use the declaration *char *p=0x10000;* and the statement **p = 0x12;* Alternatively, wherever the processor writes a 0, the port bit is cleared, wherever it writes a 1, nothing is done. For instance, if this 8-bit clear port at 0x10000 is to have bits 1 and 2 cleared, we can use the declaration *char *p=0x10000;* and the statement **p = 0xf3;* or the statement **p = ~6;* Set ports and clear ports can be readable; if so the data in the port are read without logic operations being done to them. A clear port is frequently used in devices which themselves set the port bit and the processor only clears the bit. An interrupt request, discussed in the next chapter, is set by the device and can be cleared by the processor writing to a clear port. C and some assembler languages have means to OR or to AND data to memory, so these port functions are redundant. Nevertheless, several I/O chips designed for 683xx systems use set ports or clear ports.

Finally, we introduce three techniques that use the address bus without the data bus to output data. These are the address trigger used in many Motorola I/O devices, and the address output port used in the 68000-based Atari 520ST and the address line output that use techniques based on incompletely specified address decoding. *[≡ a port] 0 – width*

The first is widely used to pulse devices – an *address trigger.* It is a mechanism whereby the address decoder itself provides a pulse that does something. Generating the particular address in the execution of an instruction will cause the address decoder to output a pulse that can be used to trigger a one-shot, clear or set a flip-flop, or be output from the computer. Figure 4-3 shows an example of a trigger on the address 0x11000. Figure 4-3a shows, with a dashed line, an address trigger in a block diagram. This address trigger is shown triggering a one-shot; the one-shot is not part of the address trigger. Figure 4-3b shows how this is implemented in hardware using a SIM address decoder such as M68332's CS6. The address decoder control registers are initialized thus:

pinAssign(cs6,byte); baseAssign(6,0x11000,k2);
optionAssign(6,rd+wr+upper+lower+as fast,user+super,0);

For the M68340, the corresponding chip select CS3 can be used for an address trigger.

CsAssign(3,0x11000,8,fast,rdWr);

Note that if *a* is any variable, the statement *a= (char*)0x11000* does not load data from the one-shot into *a*, nor does *(char*)0x11000=a;* store anything from the data register into it. Either instruction causes the decoder to pulse, causing the one-shot to "fire." An address trigger is, in effect, a port in a word that requires no bits in it. These instructions could simultaneously load or store data in another port even while the address triggers the one-shot in a manner similar to the shadow output port, or they might load garbage into the data register or store the data register into a nonexistent storage word (which does nothing).

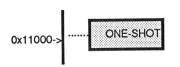 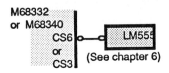

a. Address Trigger Block Diagram Notation   b. Address Trigger Logic Diagram

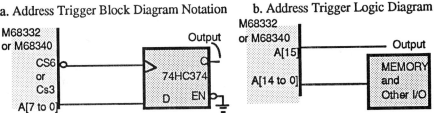

c. Address Register Output Logic Diagram   d. Address Line Output Logic Diagram

Figure 4-3. Address Output Techniques.

Some variations of an address trigger are the *read address trigger*, which produces a pulse only when a memory read operation generates the address, and a *write address trigger*, which generates a pulse only when the address is recognized in a memory write operation. Obviously, in the M68332, to build a read address trigger decoder, put only *rd* into the second parameter of the *optionAssign* macro, and to build a write address trigger decoder, put only *wr* there, instead of *rd+wr*. In the M68340, a read address trigger can be effected by making the last parameter of the *CsAssign* macro *rdOnly*.

The *address register output* technique is used in the 68000-based Atari 520ST because the design of the extension ports support only read-only memories, in order to plug games into the computer. This extension port is suitable for use for an input port. To use the port for 8-bit output, we use the M68332 SIM decoder CS6 for a 2K-byte memory initialized as before, which does not decode the low-order 11 bits, or the M68340 SIM decoder CS3, which does not decode the low-order 8 bits. (See Figure 4-3c.) An output register is clocked whenever the high-order bits of the address are 0x10000; this stores A[7 to 0] in the register. This is easily handled in C; let *a* be a dummy variable, *d* be some *unsigned char* data, and *p* point to the port; the low-order 8 bits of *p* are 0s, *a=*(p+d)* puts the data in *d* into the register.

The last technique, *address line output,* uses a system in which the high-order address bit is a don't care for all memories and I/O ports, to derive a 1-bit output. Software is written so the program counter and effective addresses used in a part of the code are in low memory to output a 0 on A[15], and in equivalent places in high memory, that produce the same low-order addresses, to output a 1 on A[15]. For example, if the program has been running in low memory so A[15] is a 0, the program segment

```
            JMP    L1+0x8000   set bit A[15]
     L1     JMP    L2          clear bit A[15]
     L2     EQU    *           next instruction ...
```

will output a 1 on A[15] for the duration of a JMP instruction at label L1. More output bits can be implemented using more don't cares in the high-order bits of the address. Using this technique, the processor itself provides outputs without the use of any additional hardware. The reader may scoff at this technique and there are some limitations, like avoiding interrupts or DMA when doing this, but many machines like the 68000 have so many address lines that go unused, and these are so cheap (they are free) that this technique warrants consideration in a design.

4-2 Input/Output Software

Software for input and output devices can be very simple or quite complex. In this section, we look at some of the simpler software. We show C programs to make the discussion concrete. The software to use a single input and a single output device to simulate (replace) a wire will be considered first, because it provides an opportunity to microscopically examine what is happening in input and output instructions. We next discuss input to and output from. a buffer. Programmed control of external mechanical and electrical systems is discussed next. We will discuss the control of a traffic light and introduce the idea of a delay loop used for timing. Then, in a more involved example, we'll discuss a table-driven traffic light controller and a linked-list interpreter, which can implement a sequential machine.

The program *main()* following this discussion will move data from a 16-bit input port at *0x10000* (Figure 4-1a) to a 16-bit output port at *0x10800* (Figure 4-1b) repetitively. This program only simulates 16 wires, so it is not very useful. However, it illustrates the reading of input and writing of output ports in C. Observe the manner in which the addresses of the ports are set up. The caste *(int*)* is only needed if the C compiler checks types and objects to assigning integers to addresses. Alternatively, the addresses can be specified when the pointers are declared, as we will show in the next example. This program is worth running, to see how data are sampled and how they are output, using a square-wave generator to create a pattern of input data and an oscilloscope to examine the output data. You may also wish to read the assembler language code that is produced by the C compiler and count the number of memory cycles in the loop, and the number of cycles from when data are read to when they are output (the latency). Its timing is hard to predict for all C compilers, and the best way to really determine it is to run it and measure it.

```
main()
{
    int *src,*dst;
    src = (int*)0x10000; dst= (int*)0x10800;
    while(1) *dst = *src;
}
```

The assembler language generated by this C procedure is shown below:

```
     LINK.W A6,#0xFFF8               Allocate local variables
     MOVE.L #0x00010000,0xFFFC(A6)   Initialize src
     MOVE.L #0x00010800,0xFFF8(A6)   Initialize dst
     BRA.S @1                        Begin while loop
@0   MOVEA.L 0xFFFC(A6),A0           Put src in A0
     MOVEA.L 0xFFF8(A6),A1           Put dst in A1
     MOVE.W (A0),(A1)                Move data from *scr to *dst
@1   BRA.S @0                        End while loop
     UNLK A6                         Deallocate local variable
     RTS                             Return to caller
```

The 683xx actually reads the input port in the middle of the instruction MOVE.W (A0),(A1), and then writes into the output port at the end of the same instruction. This takes only about 300 nanoseconds. Observe that the loop is quite long; it executes in about 2.3 μseconds. A more efficient loop can be created using a *do while* rather than a *while* construct, and declaring the *src* and *dst* pointers to be *register* variables. This loop takes 900 nanoseconds. Note that the timing of the loop is dependent on the compiler's interpretation of the programmer's style. The best way to determine timing is to run the program and measure the chip enable pulses on an oscilloscope.

Alternatively we may wish to input data to a buffer. The declaration *buffer[0x100]* creates a vector of length 0x100 words to receive data from an input port at 0x10000. Observe that the address of the input port is initialized in the declaration of the pointer.

```
main()
{
    int *src=(int*)0x10000, buffer[0x100], i;
    for(i=0;i<0x100;i++) buffer[i] = *src;
}
```

The assembler language generated by this C *for* loop is shown below:

```
        CLR.W 0xFDFA(A6)              for(i=0;
        BRA.S @1
@0      MOVE.W 0xFDFA(A6),D0
        EXT.L D0
        ADD.L D0,D0
        ADD.L A6,D0
        MOVEA.L 0xFFFC(A6),A0
        MOVEA.L D0,A1                           buffer[i] =
        MOVE.W (A0),0xFDFC(A1)                           *src;
        ADDQ.W #1,0xFDFA(A6)         i++;
@1      CMPI.W #0x100,0xFDFA(A6)       i<0x100)
        BCS.S @0
```

Finally we may wish to output data from a buffer. Observe that the address *pnt* of the buffer is initialized in the for loop statement, and is incremented in the *for* loop statement rather than the third expression of the *for* statement, which is missing.

```
main()
{
    int buffer[0x100]; register int *dst=(int*)0x10800,*pnt;
    for(pnt=buffer;pnt<buffer+0x100;) *dst = *(pnt++);
}
```

The assembler language generated by this C *for* loop is shown below:

```
        LEA 0xFE00(A6),A0            for(pnt=buffer;
        MOVEA.L A0,A3
        BRA.S @1
@0      LEA (A3),A0
        ADDQ.L #2,A3
        MOVE.W (A0),(A4)            *dst = *(pnt++);
        CMPA.L A6,A3                note: A6 points to the end of the buffer
@1      BCS.S @0                    pnt<buffer+0x100;)
```

Note the ease of indexing a vector or using a pointer in a *for* loop statement.

Microcomputers are often used for *logic-timer* control. In this application, some mechanical or electrical equipment is controlled through simple logic involving inputs and memory variables, and by means of delay loops. (Numeric control, which uses A/D and D/A converters, is discussed in Chapter 6.) A traffic light controller is a simple example, in which light patterns are flashed on for a few seconds before the next light pattern is flashed on. Using LEDs instead of traffic lights, this controller can be used in a simple and illuminating laboratory experiment. Moreover, techniques used in this example extend to a broad class of controllers based on logic, timing, and little else.

In the following example, a *light pattern* is a collection of output variables that turns certain lights on and others off. (See Figure 4-4.) Each bit of the output port LIGHTS turns on a pair of lights (through a power amplifier, discussed in Chapter 6) if the bit is T. For example, if the north and south lights are paralleled, and the east and west lights are similarly paralleled, six variables are needed; if they are the rightmost 6 bits of a word, then TFFFFF would turn on the red light, FTFFFF would turn on the yellow light, and FFTFFF would turn on the green light in the north and south lanes. FFFTFF, FFFFTF, and FFFFFT would similarly control the east and west lane lights. Then TFFFFT would turn on the red north and south and green east and west lights. We will assume that the basic output port at location 0x10800 (called LIGHTS in the program) is connected so its right 6 bits control the lights as just described. The other 10 bits of the 16-bit output port need not be connected at all. It is constructed as in Figure 4-1b. Also, for further reference, TIME will be a binary number whose value is the number of sixteenths-seconds that a light pattern is to remain on. For example, the pair LIGHT = TFFFFT and TIME = 16 will put the red north and south and green east and west lights on for one second. Finally, a *sequence* will be several pairs of light patterns and associated times that describe how the traffic lights are controlled. In this example, the sequence is a *cycle*, a sequence that repeats itself forever.

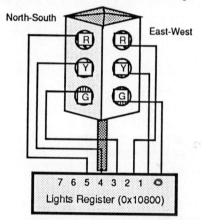

```
main()  {
    int *lights,i;
    lights = (int*)0x10800;
    *lights = 0x21;
    for(i=0;i<0x100;i++);
}
```

Figure 4-4. Traffic Light.

In this technique, as the program is executed, it supplies immediate operands to the output port and immediate operands (as in *lights = 0x21;) to control the duration of the light pattern. A loop, such as *for(i=0;i<0x100;i++);*, is called a *delay loop*. It is used to match the time of the external action with the time needed to complete the instruction. Delay loops are extensively used in I/O interface programs. The usual loop statement after the *for(;;)* and before the ending semicolon (Figure 2-3c) is missing because the control part of the *for* statement provides the required delay. The constant 0x100 that must be put in the statement to get a specific delay in the loop is hard to predict analytically and varies from one compiler to another, but can be determined empirically.

A better way than programming a control sequence using immediate operands is described in the following paragraphs. This method makes it easier to write and modify the control sequences and to store them in a small microcomputer memory. These advantages are so great that the technique introduced in this section is usually recommended for most applications.

An *interpreter* is a program that reads values from a data structure such as a table, a bit or character string, list, or a linked list structure to control something, like drill presses or traffic lights, or to execute interpretive high-level languages like BASIC, APL, or LISP. You might like to scan Section 2-2 to review data structures before looking at interpreters. Table and linked-list interpreters are particularly useful in interface applications. The table interpreter is described first, then the linked-list interpreter is introduced by modifying the table interpreter.

Table 4-1. Traffic Light Sequence.

LIGHT	TIME
TFFFFT	16
TFFFTF	4
FFTTFF	20
FTFTFF	4

A traffic light cycle might be described by Table 4-1. It can be stored in a table or array data structure. Recall from Section 2-2.2 that arrays can be stored in row major order or column major order. C accesses arrays in row major order. The array has two columns – one to store the light pattern and the other to store the time the pattern is output – with one row for each pair. Consecutive rows are read from the array to the output port and to the delay loop.

```
main() {
    int *lights,i,j,k,tbl[4][2];
    lights = (int*)0x10800;
    tbl[0][0]=0x21;tbl[0][1]=16;
    tbl[1][0]=0x22; tbl [1][1]=4;
    tbl[2][0]=0x0c; tbl [2][1]=20;
    tbl[3][0]=0x14; tbl [3][1]=4;
    while(1)
    for(i=0;i<4;i++){
            *lights = tbl[i][0];
            for(j=0; j<tbl[i][1]; j++)for(k=0;k<0xffff;k++);
    }
}
```

Structures can implement tables more efficiently than arrays can, so their columns can have different data types and sizes. You can use a pointer to point to the structure. Pointers are discussed next. We first introduce a very simple link mechanism using the index in an array, and then the use of pointer variables and structures to implement links.

Linked-list interpreters strongly resemble sequential machines. We have learned that most engineers have little difficulty thinking about sequential machines, and that they can easily learn about linked-list interpreters by the way sequential machines are modeled by a linked-list interpreter. (Conversely, programmers find it easier to learn about sequential machines through their familiarity with linked-list structures and interpreters from this example.) Linked-list interpreters or sequential machines are powerful techniques used in sophisticated control systems, such as robot control. You should enjoy studying them, as you dream about building your own robot.

A *Mealy sequential machine* is a common model for (small) digital systems. While the model, described soon, is intuitive, if you want more information, consult almost any book on logic design, such as *Fundamentals of Logic Design*, by C. H. Roth, West Publishing Co., Chapter 14. The machine is conceptually simple and easy to implement in a microcomputer using a linked-list interpreter. Briefly, a Mealy sequential machine is a set S of internal states, a set I of input states, and a set O of output states. At any moment, the machine is in a *present internal* state and has an *input state* sent to it. As a function of this pair, it provides an *output state* and a *next internal* state. The next internal state becomes the present internal state in the next time step.

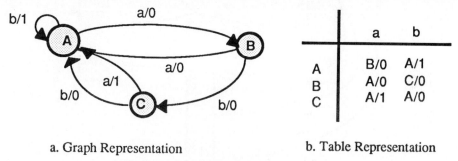

a. Graph Representation   b. Table Representation

Figure 4-5. Mealy Sequential Machine.

The Mealy sequential machine can be shown in graph or table form. (See Figures 4-5a and 4-5b for these forms for the following example.) In this example, the machine has internal states S = {A,B,C}, input states I = {a,b}, and output states O = {0,1}. The graph shows internal states as nodes, and, for each input state, an arc from a node goes to the next internal state. Over the arc, the pair, input state/output state, is written. In the table, each row describes an internal state and each column, an input state. In the table, the pair, next internal state/output state, is shown for each internal state and output state. In this example, if the machine were in state A and received input a, it would output 0 and go to state B; if it received input b, it would output 1 and go back to state A.

Consider a simple example of a sequential machine operation. If the machine starts in internal state A and the input a arrives, it goes to state B and outputs a 0. In fact, if it starts in state A and receives the sequence abbaba of input states, it will go from internal state A through the internal state sequence BCABCA, and it will generate the output state sequence 000001.

The table representation can be stored in a microcomputer in a 3-dimensional array in row major order. The interpreter for it would read an input, presumably from an input port SRC at location 0x10000, and send the output to an output port DST at location 0x10800, as before. The input state 'a' is the value 0x00, when read from the input port, and 'b' is 0x01. The internal state is associated with the row being read. If the initial internal state is A, then the program implements this by initializing an index to row 0 associated with state A and using the next state stored in the table to derive the index to its row. The table is stored and is interpreted by the following program.

```
#define A 0
#define B 1
#define C 2
int tbl[3][2][2]={{{B,0},{A,1}},{{A,0},{C,0}},{{A,1},{A,0}}};
main() {
    int *src,*dst,i,j;
    dst = (int*)0x10800; src = (int*)0x10000;i=0;
    while(1){
        j=*src;
        *dst = tbl[i][j][1]; i = tbl[i][j][0];
    }
}
```

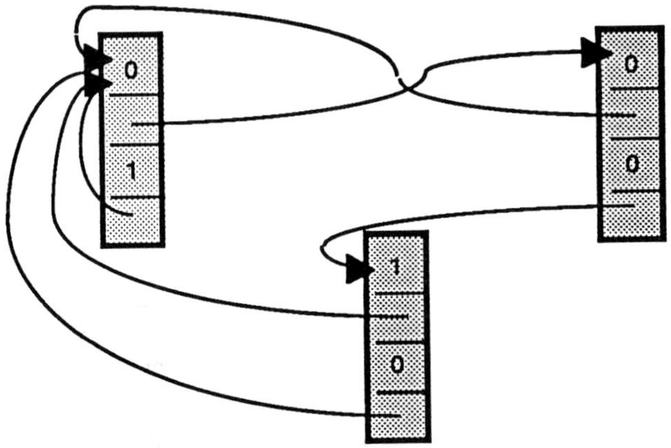

Figure 4-6. A Linked-List Structure.

The program using structures is a bit more complex but it is a more correct use of linked lists in C. In either program, an input port senses the input state and an output port provides the output state to some external system. We introduced the linked-list structure by comparing it to a row of the table. The structure is accessed (read from or written in) by a program, an interpreter. The key idea is that the next row to be interpreted is not the next lower row, but a row specified by reading one of the table's columns. For example, after interpreting the row for state A, if a 'b' is entered, the row for A is interpreted again because the address read from a column of the table is this same row's address. This view of a list is intuitively simple. More formally, a *linked list structure* is a collection of *blocks* having the same *template*. A block is a list like the row of the table and the template is like the column heading. Each block is composed of *elements* that conform to the template. Elements can be 1 bit to 10s of bits wide. They may or may not correspond directly to memory words, but if they do, they are easier to use. In our example, the block (row) is composed of four elements: The first is a 16-bit element containing a next address, the second is an 16-bit output element, and the third and fourth elements are like the first and second. Addresses generally point to the block's first word, as in our example, and are loaded into the address register to access data in the block. Elements are accessed by using the offset in indexed addressing. Another block is selected by reloading the address register to point to that block's first word. Rather than describe blocks as rows of a table, we graphically show them, with arcs coming from address fields to the blocks they point to, as in Figure 4-6. Note the simple and direct relationship between Figure 4-6 and Figure 4-5a. This intuitive relationship can be used to describe any linked-list structure, and, without much effort, the graph can be translated into the equivalent table and stored in the microprocessor memory.

Linked-lists generally have elements that are of different sizes. Also, pointers which are addresses to memory may be needed because they are not multiplied and added to compute memory addresses, as array indexes are, and thus are faster. Such linked-lists should be stored as structures. Recall that in order to point to an element *e* of a structure *s,* we used *s.e* in earlier discussions. If a pointer is moved to different copies of a structure as the current internal state in the sequential machine, we can put it in the structure pointer variable *p,* and *(*p).e* is the element e of the structure pointed to by the pointer *p.* As a shorthand, the operator -> is used; *p->e* is equivalent to *(*p).e* . The previous program can be rewritten:

```
main() {
    int *src=(int*)0x10000,*dst= (int*)0x10800;
    struct state {struct state *next;int out;} A[2], B[2], C[2], *p=A;
    A[0].next=B;A[0].out=0;A[1].next=A;A[1].out=1;
    B[0].next=A;B[0].out=0;B[1].next=C;B[1].out=0;
    C[0].next=A;C[0].out=1;C[1].next=A;C[1].out=0;
    while(1){ p += *src; *dst = p -> out; p = p -> next; }
}
```

Note that a data type, *struct state,* stores the next internal and the output states for a present internal and input state combination. The vector *A[2]* has, for each input state, an element which is of type *struct state,* and the whole vector represents the internal state A. There is such a vector for each internal state. We have to initialize the structures in the program, not in the declaration, because locations of structures must be declared before they are used as entries in a structure. The initial internal state is initialized at the end of the declaration of the structure to be state A. In the while loop, the input number is read from the input port and added to the pointer *p.* If a "1" is read, *p* is moved from *A[0]* to *A[1],* from *B[0]* to *B[1],* or from *C[0]* to *C[1].* Then the structure's element *out* is output, and the structure's element *next* is put in the pointer *p.*

The structure and pointer are very useful in I/O programming. An I/O device may have many ports of different sizes, which can be best described by structures. The address of the device can be put in a pointer *p,* and *p->port* will access the *port* element of it. Linked-list structures are especially useful for the storage of the control of sophisticated machines, robots, and so on. You can model some of the operations as a sequential machine first, then convert the sequential machine to a linked-list structure and write an interpreter for the table. You can also define the operations solely in terms of a linked list and its interpretive rules. Some of our hardware colleagues seem to prefer the sequential machine approach, but our software friends insist that the linked-list structure is much more intuitive. You may use whichever you prefer. They really are equivalent.

The interpreters are useful for logic-timer control. A table is a good way to represent a straight sequence of operations, such as the control for a drill press that drills holes in a plate at points specified by rows in the table. A linked-list interpreter is more flexible and can be used for sequences that change depending on inputs. Interpreters are useful in these ways for driving I/O ports. Their use, though, extends throughout computer applications, from data base management through operating systems, compilers, and artificial intelligence.

4-3 Programmable Parallel Input/Output Devices

Microcomputers often use LSI chips called *programmable parallel input/output devices* that are capable of being both inputs and outputs, selected under software control. The programming of the selection is – how shall we put it? – different. In the first subsection, we will offer you some reasons for having to program these devices in such an illogical manner and introduce the programming ritual used to select these devices' mode of operation. We will introduce the M6821, an 8-bit Motorola 6800-family parallel port, to show how rituals are written. We also discuss the pin connections to this chip, which can be used by other 8-bit M6800-style I/O chips. We then discuss the M68230, a 68000-style parallel I/O chip, and 683xx parallel ports. Finally, we design an I.C. tester to illustrate the programmable I/O device and its software control.

4-3.1 Problems with LSI I/O and the Ritual

The first microcomputers' I/O systems were rather disappointing. Although the microprocessor was put on an LSI chip, the I/O section was implemented with tens of small- and medium-scale integrated circuits, making early microcomputers not much smaller than minicomputers, and quite a bit slower than minicomputers. Semiconductor manufacturers began to develop compact large-scale integrated circuits for I/O.

The first general class of I/O devices that were converted to large-scale integrated circuit chips were the 8-bit-wide parallel I/O devices which we are now discussing. Serial I/O devices and counters were converted later, and these will be the subject of considerable scrutiny in the following chapters. These chips have some quirks that appear at first to be design errors but really are consequences of some unusual characteristics of large-scale integrated circuitry. To reassure the reader, we will review the rationale for these annoying characteristics.

The two key problems for large-scale integrated circuit applications are volume production and pins. The cost of designing such a chip is around a million dollars, but the chip has to sell for around ten dollars. Therefore, they can only be designed if they can be sold in hundreds of thousands. So they are often designed for use in several similar applications, to encompass a sufficient market to pay for the design. For example, the 74HC374 can be used as an output port, of course, and by connecting its outputs to the data bus, it can function as an input port. So one chip can work as either an input or output device. Possibly twice as many chips will be sold if they can be used in both applications, as will be sold if they can only be used in one. To further extend the use of a chip, some pins can be added that determine how it functions. These *parameter pins* are normally connected to positive supply or ground, so a T or F can be constantly input to select a function. The INTEL 8212 is an excellent example of a chip with parameter pins; a mode pin MD is strapped to low to make the chip serve as an input device and to high to make it an output device. The CMOS 4034 is a readable output port that can serve as a shift register using a shift control pin. The Universal Asynchronous Receiver Transmitter (UART), discussed in Chapter 8, is an example of parameterization taken to an extreme. The pins used for parameterization are not cheap. They cannot be used for data input and output. More pins require a larger chip that takes more area on a printed circuit board. Not only is the larger chip more expensive, but the area on the printed circuit board is also costly, as some boards around one square foot can cost a few hundred dollars just for the bare board.

An alternative to the use of parameter pins is to literally put these connections inside the chip itself, with the parameters to be stored in a *control register* or *control port*. This port looks rather like the data port in an I/O chip, in that an output instruction can load it with data. However, the values stored in it are used to set parameters that determine how the chip will function. For example, 1 bit in a control port may determine if the chip is to function as an input port or an output port. This technique solves both the volume production and the pin problem; it permits the same chip to be used in various similar applications, but it does not require a large number of pins to select the specific function the chip performs.

A less important and similar problem is that some LSI chips have too many ports and not enough pins. The address used to select the port is sometimes provided in part by bits that, to avoid using other pins, are stored in other ports inside the chip. The effect of this is that several ports appear at the same location - to be read by an instruction like MOVE 0x10000,D0, for instance - but the port that is actually read depends on some bits in another port, and you have to store an appropriate word in that other port to be able to read the port you want.

Moreover, it seems every solution creates some new problem. The control port has to be *initialized* to set the parameters when the microcomputer is powered on. This must be done before the device is actually used and can be done just before it is used or right after power is turned on. Initializing the control port *configures* the device. The initialization routine is rather like an obscure *ritual* that is hard to explain and understand but is relatively easy to do. The programmer has to determine exactly which bits in the control word have to be set to make the chip perform its specific function, and the correct sequence in which to set these bits. While the initialization ritual is most efficiently done before the device is used, this technique is especially prone to software bugs that do such things as write garbage all over memory, including memory-mapped control ports. Input ports become output ports, interrupts are mysteriously generated, and other marvelous happenings follow. Using some bits of a control port to select a port from a collection of ports is like a magician's hat trick - now you see it, now you don't. When analyzing an erroneous program, it is difficult to know if a program error has changed one of the hidden ports. You have to check them too. The hat trick is one feature of LSI I/O chips that makes life difficult for programmers. Of course, if you can't trust the program, the best thing to do is put a lock on the I/O device decoder to minimize all these calamities.

Improved semiconductor technology permitted the implementation of 16-bit microcomputers like the 68000. The I/O devices for these microcomputers were put in larger dual in-line packages, thus reducing the need for tricky solutions to avoid pins.

4-3.2 The M6821 Input/Output Devices

The M6821 is a large-scale integrated circuit designed for parallel I/O that incorporates a control port to increase its flexibility. This chip is also called a *Peripheral Interface Adapter* or PIA. We really rather use the part name M6821 than the name PIA. The use of names like PIA remind us of alchemy - oil of vitriol, eye of bat, and so on - at least, they smack more of advertising than engineering. We simply don't like them. Besides, Motorola produces two different chips, the M6820 and the M6821, both called PIA. More chips like the PIA will probably be produced, and they may be named PIA, if that is Motorola's wish. So we prefer to use part names like M6821 in this book. But you should know both, and you can use either. We often slip into this jargon ourselves, so we should not complain too loudly if you do.

The chip has two almost identical I/O devices in it; each device has a data port that can be either an input port or an output port, or part input and part output port using a technique we discuss soon. Each device has eight pins, *peripheral data* pins, to accept data from the outside world when the device is an input port or to supply data to the outside world when it is an output device. Each device has hardware to generate interrupts. Its I/O circuitry is discussed now. The interrupt circuitry will be discussed in Chapter 5, after the appropriate concepts have been introduced. The M6821 is fully described in the *Motorola Microprocessor, Microcontroller & Peripheral Data Book Vol 2. (DL139)*.

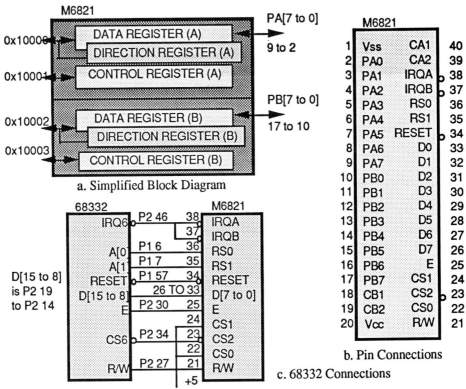

Figure 4-7. The M6821.

Each device in the M6821 has three 8-bit ports – *data, direction,* and *control*. (See Figure 4-7a.) The data port may be an input or a readable output port. The direction port determines, on a bit-by-bit basis, whether a data port bit is treated as an input bit or a readable output bit. In the most common case, the direction bits are all T or all F, which makes the whole data port either an 8-bit readable output port or an 8-bit input port, respectively. These three ports – data, direction, and control – in one device are accessed as just 2 words of memory using a "hat trick." A bit in the control port acts as an extra address bit to select either the data or direction port. For example, these 2 words might be 0x10000 and 0x10001. If the program reads or writes in 0x10001, it always reads or writes data in the control port. If the program reads or writes in location 0x10000, it accesses the direction port if bit 2 of the control port is F, or it accesses the data port if that bit is T. The pin connections for the M6821 are shown in Figure 4-7b for reference later in this chapter. Connections to the M68332 are shown in Figure 4-7c.

The M68332 SIM address decoders have a special mode for selecting 6800-style I/O devices like the M6821. This mode uses the E clock, made available on P2 pin 30 by:

(char)0xfffa46=0; /* output E clock by clearing port C' assignment register bit 7 */

There are several realizations of the M6821 having different speeds indicated by a letter such as B; we can use MC68B21s to use the 500 nanosecond E clock normally provided by the M68332. The E clock can be set to 1 MHz for the M6821 by:

(char)0xfffa05|=0x80;/* output E clock @ 1 MHz by setting SYNCR's bit 7 */

You can only use this slow clock if the bus monitor (SYPCR, 0xfffa21) allows long memory cycles. We will use a byte-wide memory configuration so that the M6821's registers appear in consecutive addresses. Chip select 6 is initialized for synchronous decoding at 0x10000 to 0x10003, and connections shown in Figure 4-7c, as follows:

pinAssign(cs6,byte); baseAssign(6,0x10000,k2);
optionAssign(6,rd+wr+upper+as,synch,user+super,0);

The following ritual will be used to set up device A at 0x10000 and 0x10001 for input. It uses one pointer to the M6821, pia initialized to 0x10000, so the data/direction port is *pia. The control port is *(pia+1).

```
main() {
        char *pia=(char*)0x10000;
        *(pia+1) = 0; /* clear control to access direction*/
        *pia = 0; /* direction is input*/
        *(pia+1) = 4; /* change bit 2 to use data register*/

}
```

Thereafter the data port can be read as in a = *pia. A C program to initialize the M6821 for output is the same as that just shown, except that *pia = 0; is replaced by *pia = 0xff; and data can be output by statements like *pia = a; Because each bit in the data port is selected for input or output by the corresponding bit in the direction port, it is possible to make the same device an input for some bits and an output for others.

A reset pin, if provided, is connected to the M68332's reset pin. When power is first turned on, or when this (negative logic) signal is asserted low (by a panic button reset switch), the M68332 is restarted in a manner discussed in Chapter 5. In this restart program, we can often guarantee that all ports in all I/O chips are cleared, so it is unnecessary to execute a full initialization ritual. In particular, the M6821's direction ports (and the other ports) are cleared, so the device is (almost) configured as an input device. This safely resets an I/O device so two outputs won't be connected to the same line – one driving it high while the other pulls it low until the programmer configures it, which might stress or destroy the gate outputs. But it is necessary to change the M6821's control port so bit 2 is T, or you will actually read the direction port when you think you are reading the input data port. After reset, to configure an M6821 as an input device at location 0x10003, execute *(pia+1) = 4; This is one of the most common errors in using the M6821: Assuming it is configured as an input device when power is applied or the machine is reset. So remember: you must change the control port before you can use the data port as an input. Otherwise, you will be reading the direction port.

As noted in Section 2-3.1, #define directives should be used to generate the constants used in rituals, so the code will be self-documenting or at least as clear as possible. Also, *(pia+i) is exactly equivalent to pia[i] in C. For example, the previous program segment can be written as:

```
#define DatInOut 4
#define PORTA (char*)0x10000
main() {
        char *pia = PORTA ;
        pia[1] = 0; pia[0] = 0; pia[1] = DatInOut;
}
```

The M6821 chip has two almost identical devices called the A and B devices. The B device behaves as we just discussed; the A device has outputs like open collector outputs with pull-up resistors inside the chip, so that, when a bit is configured as an output bit and is read in a program, the data that are read are, in fact, the positive logic AND of the bit stored in the output port and the outputs of any gates driving this bus line. Usually, the A and B devices occupy four consecutive words in memory; for example the A data/direction port is at location 0x10000, the A control port is at 0x10001, the B data/direction port is at 0x10002 and the B control is at 0x10003. However, it is possible and often desirable to connect the address pins to the chip in a different manner. It is possible to put A and B data/direction ports at 0x10000 and 0x10001, respectively, and A and B control at 0x10002 and 0x10003, respectively. Then the 16-bit data ports can be read or written as *int* variables.

4-3.3 The M68230 Parallel Input-Output Devices

The *Parallel Interface/Timer (PI/T)* M68230 is an I/O chip designed to interface directly to the 68000, and includes three parallel I/O devices similar to those in the M6821, among a number of other functions. In this subsection, we focus on the parallel I/O devices in the M68230, and we discuss its connection to an M68332 and an M68340. Other 68000-style I/O devices are connected in the same general manner. The pin connections for the M68230 are shown in Figure 4-8a. This 48-pin package contains logic that interfaces directly with the M68332, connecting correspondingly named pins as in Figure 4-8b. Except that the M68230's CLK must be 8 MHz, and is derived by dividing CLKOUT by 2, these chips are directly connected in an obvious way. The address decoder such as CS6 is initialized with an *external* wait state because the M68230 asserts DSACK to end the memory cycle, and is qualified by data strobe.

> *pinAssign(cs6,byte); baseAssign(6,0x10000,k2);*
> *optionAssign(6,rd+wr+upper+ds,external,user+super,0);*

Similarly, to connect the M68230 to the M68340, chip select CS3 can be configured to let an external device supply DSACK, using the value *noDsack,* as in:

> *CsAssign(3,0x10000,8,noDsack,rdWr);*

The M68340 CS3 signal must be delayed to satisfy M68230 setup times (Figure 4-8d).

The M68230 parallel I/O devices are named A, B, and C; devices A and B are identical, device C being simpler. Suppose *p* and *d* are declared *char d, *p = (char*) 0x10000;* Although you could use *#define* statements to name the ports meaningfully, we here use the vector notation to avoid your having to look at more than one place for definitions, because we do not use the M68230 extensively. Device C has its direction port and behaves exactly like the parallel device in the M6821. To make all bits input, execute *p[4]=0;* and then *d=p[12];* reads pin inputs PC[7 to 0] into *d*. To make all the bits output, execute *p[4]=0xff;* and then *p[12]=d;* outputs *d* to PC[7 to 0]. However, device C shares its pins with M68230's special logic used for interrupts and DMA. If these functions are used, the pins are not available for general I/O. We discuss device A next; device B is analogous.

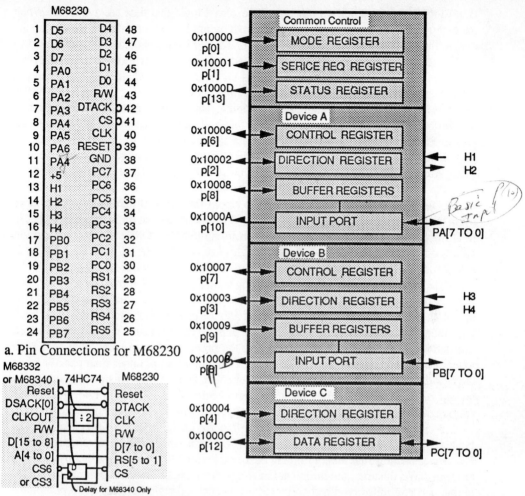

a. Pin Connections for M68230

b. Connections between an M68332/M68340 and an M68230 c. Block Diagram of M68230

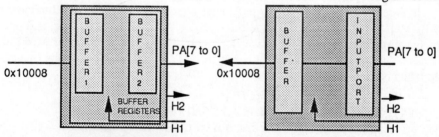

d. Output Double-Buffer   e. Input Double-Buffer

Figure 4-8. The M68230 I/O Device with Parallel I/O.

Device A has a mode to make it function just like device C and a number of modes that feature *double-buffering*. Double-buffering on output is shown in Figure 4-8d. *p[8]=d;* puts data into BUFFER1, which are copied to BUFFER2 as soon as possible. After BUFFER1 is thus freed, another *p[8]=d;* can put more data into it. When BUFFER1 and BUFFER2 are both full, a bit in the STATUS port is set. When at least

BUFFER2 is full, a signal on pin H2 tells external logic that data are available. When the external logic uses the data, it puts an edge on pin H1, which informs the device the data are used. When the edge occurs on H1, if BUFFER1 has data, they are moved to BUFFER2, and the bit in STATUS is cleared because there is room in BUFFER1 for more data. Software can examine the status bit to determine whether or not it can put more data into BUFFER1. This technique is called *double-buffering,* because two buffer registers are used. It is quite similar to pipelining. This is one mode of double-buffering. In a different mode, the status bit indicates that both buffers are empty, rather than just one, to let the program know when all the data have been sent.

Double-buffering on input is shown in Figure 4-8e. An edge on pin H1 (e.g., a rising edge) causes data on the data pins to be stored into a buffer register BUFFER. A bit in the STATUS register can be tested in software, to determine if data are available in BUFFER and pin H2 can be configured to signal the external hardware that no more room is available. *d=p[8];* reads BUFFER and H2 indicates that more data can be put in it. However, *d=p[10];* reads data directly from the INPUT PORT, which is the current values on the pins PA[7 to 0]. Even though only one register is used on input, it is called double-buffering too, because it is symmetric to double-buffered output.

The main advantage of double-buffering is that data can be moved by the processor without precisely synchronizing to the outside world. On input, the outside world fills the BUFFER register and signals the device, and the processor can read it any time later, until more input data must be stored, rather than at the exact time data are to be input. Similarly, on output, double-buffering lets the processor set up some new data even while the old data are still being output before being used up, rather than exactly when the new data are to be output in place of the old data. Double-buffering permits data to be moved between systems which have different timing, at a maximum rate, because an extra register holds the data from the time they are moved until they are used.

A full explanation of all the available features of the MC68230 fills a substantial booklet *(MC68230 Parallel Interface/Timer (PI/T), December 1983, reference ADI-860-R2).* Here, we illustrate the interfacing concepts it embodies with a few examples using device A. We illustrate the initialization rituals for making device A a simple readable output port controlled by direction bits like device C, a double-buffered input port, and a double-buffered output port.

In order to make device A a simple readable output device, we need to clear the MAIN MODE register, store 0x80 into the device A CONTROL register, and put Ts into the direction register where we need outputs. Assuming that the M68230 is addressed starting at 0x10000 and *p* is initialized as before, making all bits (readable) output bits is done by

> **p=0; /* clear MODE reg. for simple 8-bit I/O */*
> *p[6]=0x80; /* device A CONTROL for single buffer */*
> *p[2]=0xff; /*set dev. A DIRECTION reg. for output */*

Then *p[8]=d;* will put *d* out on PA[7 to 0], and *p[8]++* will increment the byte in that output port. All bits can be made input by replacing the last statement by *p[2]=0;,* and some bits can be made input while others are output, as in the M6821.

Double-buffering utilizes handshaking, which is a synchronization mechanism that is studied fully in the next chapter. However, to avoid fragmenting this discussion, we now introduce handshaking using a status port. As the control port is an output to the control of a device rather than to the outside world, *a status port* or *status register* is an input from the logic of the device rather than from the outside world.

In order to make device A a double-buffered output device, we need to clear the MAIN MODE port, store 0x70 into the device A CONTROL port, put Ts into the direction port where we need outputs, and then set bit 4 in MAIN MODE. Making all bits output bits is done by

$$*p=0; p[6]=0x70; p[2]=0xff; *p=0x10;$$

A status port indicates when more data can be sent. When $(p[13]\&1)$ is true, there is room for another word; $p[8]=d;$ puts d into BUFFER1 in Figure 4-8d, and that data are moved to BUFFER2 and appear on PA[7 to 0], and the signal on pin H1 is asserted. The port is not a readable output port. $p[8]++$ reads the BUFFER2 port, increments it, and writes it back into the BUFFER1 port. A true readable output device, such as the simple readable output device, would read BUFFER2 port, increment it, and write it back into BUFFER2. Although it is possible to mix input and output bits using this mode, we do not elaborate on capabilities of the chip that do not illustrate fundamental principles.

In order to make device A a double-buffered input device, we need to clear the MAIN MODE port, store 0x60 into the device A CONTROL port, put 0s into the direction port where we need inputs, and then set bit 4 in MAIN MODE. Making all bits input bits is done by

$$*p=0; p[6]=0x60; p[2]=0; *p=0x10;$$

When $(p[13]\&1)$ is true, another word, input from PA[7 to 0] when the signal on pin H1 is asserted, is stored in BUFFER1; $d=p[8];$ puts it in d. H2 is asserted when a word is put into the BUFFER1 and remains asserted until it is read.

Device B has the same capabilities as device A just discussed. The M68230 is able to coordinate devices A and B together, in order to effect a 16-bit device, and is able to make the same device (either B or both A and B) either input or output, depending on signals on pins H1 to H4 rather than DIRECTION port bits. These devices can generate interrupts or move data using DMA, which is discussed in the next chapter.

The M68230 has a plethora of modes explained in *MC68230 Parallel Interface/Timer (PI/T)*. The first example is called mode 0 submode 1x; the second, mode 0 submode 01; the last, mode 0 submode 00. In the last two cases, we elected to make H2 observe an "interlocked input or output handshake protocol." This chip well illustrates two points we made earlier. I/O chips are designed for as much flexibility as possible to sell them to as many users as possible to recover the design cost. They have to be initialized by a ritual to make them work in a specific manner. The initialization ritual is rather difficult to figure out, but is easy to do, needing only a few statements.

4-3.4 The M68340 and M68332 Parallel Input/Output Devices

In this section, we discuss the M68332 and M68340 parallel ports. While a reader may be interested only in one or the other, both should be studied to generalize the concepts so they can be applied to other systems too. We look at the simpler M68340 first.

The M68340 has two parallel I/O devices – A and B – which are somewhat useful as parallel ports. However, they are also extensively used for other functions – device A for high-order addresses or interrupt acknowledge signals, and port B for interrupt requests or chip selects – that they're not as useful as we might hope for. Figure 4-9 shows the locations of these parallel ports and their control registers.

Both devices have an assignment register as well as a data and a direction register and device A has two assignment registers. For port A, for each bit position, if Port A's assignment register 1 has an F then if its assignment register 2 has an F the pin carries an address signal, else it is an interrupt acknowledge signal; if Port A's assignment register 1 has a T regardless of the value of assignment register 2, the pin is a port A signal. One must put a T in Port A's assignment register 1 to use the device as a parallel port - otherwise it executes an alternative function - and then put T or F into its direction register to make it output or input. *(char*)0xFFFFF015=0xff; *(char*) 0xFFFFF013=0; makes device A a parallel input port so that data on pins A[7 to 0] can be read into d using d=*(char*)0xFFFFF011; and to make it a parallel output port, execute *(char*)0xFFFFF015=*(char*)0xFFFFF013 =0xff; so that data from d can be written to pins A[7 to 0] using *(char*)0xFFFFF011 =d;

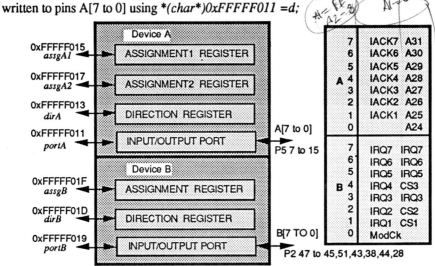

a. Block Diagram   b. Alternate Functions

Figure 4-9. The M68340 Parallel I/O Ports.

Port B is controlled by the full interrupt FIRQ bit, bit 12 of the MCR register, the 16-bit word at 0xffffff000. If FIRQ is F, port B bits 1, 2, and 4 are used for chip selects CS1, CS2 and CS3, leaving only bits 0, 3, 5, 6 and 7 to be used as port B bits or interrupt request bits. If FIRQ is T, then all port B bits are available. Because we generally need CS1 to enable the RAM on the BCC, we will make FIRQ F and use the former assignment of pins. Among those bits that are available, if port B's assignment register bit is T, the pin is used for an interrupt request IRQx, and if F, as a port bit. If FIRQ is F, *(char*)0xFFFFF01f=*(char*)0xFFFFF01d=0; makes bits 0, 3, 5, 6 and 7 of device B a parallel input port so that data on pins A[7 to 5, 3 and 0] can be read into d using d=*(char*)0xFFFFF019; and to make it a parallel output port, execute *(char*)0xFFFFF01f=0; *(char*)0xFFFFF01d=0xff; so that data from d can be written to pins A[7 to 5, 3 and 0] using *(char*)0xFFFFF019=d;

We will use #define statements, kept in the file di.h, to significantly improve the readability of programs in this book written for the M68340. These are:

```
#define portA *((char*)0xfffff011)
#define assgA1 *((char*)0xfffff015)
#define assgA2 *((char*)0xfffff017)
#define dirA *((char*)0xfffff013)
#define portB *((char*)0xfffff019)
#define assgB *((char*)0xfffff01f)
#define dirB *((char*)0xfffff01d)
```

Then for instance *assgA1=0xff; dirA=0;* makes device A a parallel input port so that data on pins A[7 to 0] can be read into *d* using *d=portA;* and *assgA1=dirA=0xff;* makes it a parallel output port so data from *d* can be written to pins A[7 to 0] using *portA =d;*

The M68332 has four parallel I/O devices – C through F – which, like those in the M68340, are somewhat useful as parallel ports. However, they too are extensively used for other functions – device C for chip selects, D for serial I/O, E for control signals like DS and SIZ[1,0], and F for interrupt requests. Moreover they are scattered around the SIM and QSPI modules almost as if to hide them. Figure 4-10 shows the locations of these parallel ports and their control registers.

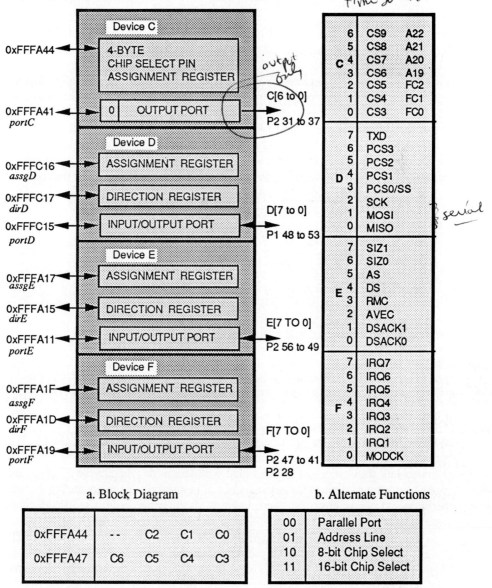

a. Block Diagram

b. Alternate Functions

0xFFFA44	--	C2	C1	C0
0xFFFA47	C6	C5	C4	C3

00	Parallel Port
01	Address Line
10	8-bit Chip Select
11	16-bit Chip Select

c. Device C Assignment Bit-pairs

d. Values of Bit-pairs for Figure c

Figure 4-10. The M68332 Parallel I/O Ports.

Devices D, E and F have an assignment register as well as a data and a direction register. One must put an F in the assignment register to use the device as a parallel port – otherwise it executes an alternative function – and then put T or F into the direction register to make it output or input. However port D bits 7 and 2 are assigned by QSPI control registers, not the port D assignment register. *((char*)0xfffa17) = *((char*)0xfffa15)=0; makes device E a parallel input port so that data on pins E[7 to 0] can be read into d using d=*((char*)0xfffa11); and to make it a parallel output port, execute *((char*)0xfffa17)=0;*((char*)0xfffa15)=0xff; so that data from d can be written to pins E[7 to 0] using *((char*)0xfffa11)=d; Note, however, that port D is used for serial communications, port E bit 4 is used for DS, and port F bit 7 to 0 are used for interrupt requests and port F pin 0 is used for MODCK. DS is used by the DI module for hardware breakpoints, and MODCK determines the mode of clock generation and must be high during reset to use the internal clock to obtain CLKOUT. Both of these should be used with caution.

Port C is only available for output and shared with not only the chip select modules but also the high-order address and function code lines. As noted in Section 3-3.3, chip select modules are controlled by the 32-bit port at 0xFFFA44. To use the pins as parallel output pins, we put the value 00 in the pair of bits that control the chip select modules. The pair for each device C port bit are shown in Figure 4-10c, and their values are shown in Figure 4-10d. In further examples, we assume the following definitions are included in programs that use the parallel ports, in order to self-document the code.

```
#define portC *((char*)0xfffa41)
#define portD *((char*)0xfffc15)
#define assgD *((char*)0xfffc16)
#define dirD *((char*)0xfffc17)
#define portE *((char*)0xfffa11)
#define assgE *((char*)0xfffa17)
#define dirE *((char*)0xfffa15)
#define portF *((char*)0xfffa19)
#define assgF *((char*)0xfffa1f)
#define dirF *((char*)0xfffa1d)
```

Then for instance assgE = dirE =0; makes device E a parallel input port so that data on pins E[7 to 0] can be read into d using d= portE; and assgE = 0; dirE =0xff; makes it a parallel output port so data from d can be written to pins E[7 to 0] using portE =d;

4-3.5 An Example: An IC Tester

In this subsection we consider a design problem to be able to test standard 14-pin ICs, about 30% of the ones we use, at the behavior level. We want to be able to put an IC into a socket, then run a test program that will determine whether the IC provides the correct sequence of outputs for any sequence of inputs; but we are not testing the delays, the input and output electrical characteristics, or the setup, hold, rise, or fall times of signals. Such a tester could be used to check bargain mail-order house ICs.

In principle, there are two design strategies: top-down and bottom-up. In top-down design, you try to understand the problem thoroughly before you even start to think about the solution. This is not easy, because most microcomputer design problems are said to be *nasty*; that means it is hard to state the problem without stating one of its solutions. In bottom-up design, one has a solution – a component or a system – for which one tries to find a matching "problem." This is like a former late-night TV show character, Carnak the Magnificent. Carnak reads the answer to a question written inside an envelope, then he opens the envelope and reads the question. This is bottom-up design. We do it all the time. The answer is microcomputers, now what was the question? Now if you are an applications engineer for Zilog, you are paid to find uses for a chip made by Zilog. But a good design engineer *must* use top-down design!

We now approach the design of this IC tester in a top-down manner. We need 12 I/O bits to supply signals to all the pins and to examine the outputs for all the pins except power and ground. But the pins are not standard from chip to chip. Pin 1 may be an input in one chip and an output in another chip. An M6821, an M68230 or an M68332 port E or F, or M68340 port A or B, would be more suitable than the simple parallel I/O device, because a line to these ports can be made an input or an output under control of software for different chips. Note that this is not always the case, and a simpler I/O device (a basic output device using 74HC374 or a basic input device using a 74HC244) may be indicated because it may be cheaper and use up less board space. The M68230 and M6820 are external chips and cost more than the M68332 ports E and F, or or M68340 port A or B, which are part of the processor. Assuming these ports are available, we choose them. We examine the M68340 first, then the M68332 later.

To choose port bits to connect to the chip being tested, we must consider the alternate uses of the M86340's port A and B bits, and then assign them in a consistent manner that makes it easy to understand and program the test sequences. We will configure the devices so the A data port will input or output data to the low number pins and the B data port, the high number pins. Note that, in the BCC, port B bits 1, 2 and 4 are unavailable. Also, port B bit 0 is ModCk used upon reset to determine whether an internal oscillator on the BCC is used to generate the CLK clock, if ModCk is H, or else an external oscillator will be expected to supply CLK. ModCk must be H when the system is reset, but can be used for a port bit after that. We would therefore prefer not to use it because if a chip being tested pulls this line L during reset, there will be no CLK and the M68340 will not even fetch the first instruction. A rugged socket will be used for 14-pin ICs, with power and ground connections permanently wired to pins 14 and 7, and other pins connected to the M68340's port bits as shown in Figure 4-11a, making it impossible to connect a M68340 output pin to +5 v or ground, which may damage it. The user will plug a 14-pin IC into the 14-pin socket to test it. (Another 16-pin socket will be used for the M68332 design.)

a . M68340 to a 14-Pin Socket b. M68332 to a 16-Pin Socket c. M68332 to a 14-Pin Socket
Figure 4-11.   Port Connections for a Chip Tester.

The general scheme for programming will be as follows. A direction pattern will be set up once, just before the chip is inserted, and a sequence of patterns will be tested, one at a time, to check out the chip. A pattern of T and F values will be put into the direction ports, an F if the corresponding pin is an output from the test IC (and an input to the M68340) and a T if the corresponding pin is an input (output from the M68340). Then a test pattern will be put in the data port to set up inputs to the IC under test wherever they are needed. The test pattern bits corresponding to the IC's output pins are, for the moment, "don't cares." Then the data will be read from the I/O ports, and the bits corresponding to the test chip's output pins will be examined. They will be compared against the bits that should be there. The bits corresponding to the input pins on the test chip are supposed to be exactly the bits that were output previously. The other bits of the pattern, which were don't cares, will now be coded in test pattern to be the expected values output from the IC under test. Summarizing, if an ICs pin is an input, its corresponding port bit's direction bit is T, and its data bit in the test pattern is the value to be put on the test IC's input pin; otherwise, if the IC's pin is an output, its corresponding direction bit is F, and its data bit is the value that should be on the pin if the chip is good. The test sequences are read from a vector by a vector-driven interpreter.

The constants used to test the chip are built up by #define statements and these 16-bit values will finally be put into ports A (low byte) and B (high byte). From Figure 4-11a we construct the definitions:

#define pin1 1	#define pin5 0x10	#define pin10 0x800
#define pin2 2	#define pin6 0x20	#define pin11 0x2000
#define pin3 4	#define pin8 0x40	#define pin12 0x4000
#define pin4 8	#define pin9 0x80	#define pin13 0x8000

We illustrate the general scheme by showing concretely how a quad 2 input NAND gate, the 74HC00, containing four independent gates, can be tested. Figure 4-12a is the truth table for one of the four gates in the 74HC00. We use the above definitions to construct a value to be put in the direction registers and a vector to be tested by the vector interpreter. From the 74HC00 chip pin connections shown in Figure 4-12b, we recognize that the truth table "A" value should be put on pins 1, 4, 10, and 13, the truth table "B" value must be put on pins 2, 5, 9, and 12, and the Z result will appear on pins 3, 6, 8 and 11. So we easily write the #define statements shown to the right:

A	B	Z
L	L	H
L	H	H
H	L	H
H	H	L

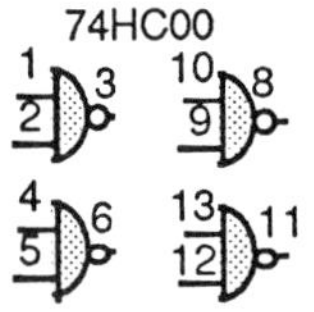

74HC00

#define A (pin1 | pin4 | pin10 | pin13)
#define B (pin2 | pin5 | pin9 | pin12)
#define Z (pin3 | pin6 | pin8 | pin11)

a. Truth Table   b. Pin Connections
Figure 4-12 The 74HC00.

These corresponding constants A, B, and Z, which are actually evaluated to be 0x8809, 0x4092 and 0x2064, construct the vector v, and Z is used in the procedure check(). The first element of v, corresponding to the top row of the truth table, has 1's exactly where Z appears, so we initialize it to the value Z, the second element of v, corresponding to the second row of the truth table, has 1s exactly where B and Z appears, so we initialize it to the value B|Z, and so on. The program sets up ports E and F to be inputs where Z appears, so their direction is initialized to ~Z. Then the vector is read, element by element, the values of bits A and B are output and the value returned is checked to see if it matches the element value. For a particular element, the vector value is output; wherever the direction bit is T the element's bit is output and wherever the direction bit is T the element's bit is ignored. The ports are read, and wherever the direction bit is T the element's bit is compared to the bit from the port. The procedure *check()* returns 1 if the chip agrees and 0 if it fails to match the patterns in *v*.

```
/* for the M68340 */
unsigned v[4]={ Z,B| Z,A| Z,A| B}; /* construct the test vector for the 7400 */
check(){ register unsigned bits, i;
    assgA1=0xff; assgB=0; dirA=~Z; dirB=(~Z)>>8; /* initialize ports A and B */
    for(i=0; i<4; i++){ /* for all 2**2 rows of truth table */
        portA = bits = v[i]; portB = bits>>8; /* output bits to chip */
        bits=portA| (portB<<8); /* get back bits from chip */
        if((bits & Z)!=(v[i] & Z)) return 0; /* if no match, exit returning 0 */
    }
    return 1; /* if all match, return 1 */
}
```

The procedure above tests the 74HC00 chip. Other combinational logic chips can be tested in an almost identical manner. Tests of other 14-pin chips will, of course, only require different vectors *v*. Chips with memory variables require initialization of these variables and more care in testing. Also, a thorough test of any chip can require a lot of patterns. If a combinational chip has *n* input pins, then 2^n patterns must actually be tested. However, our simple test can be used to detect almost all the bad chips.

We now discuss the design for the M68332. Its ports E and F have a few more available bits, so 16-pin chips can be tested as well as 14-pin chips. To choose port bits to connect to the chip, we again consider their alternate uses, and then assign them to easily understand and program the test sequences. We will configure the devices so the F data port will input or output data to the high number pins and the E data port, the low number pins. However, port E bit 4 is also DS which is used by the Di board to qualify the hardware breakpoint comparator; using it will prevent our using hardware breakpoints. Port E bit 5, also AS, can be used for breakpoints too, and port F bit 7 is used as MODCLK during reset; if it is low during reset the M68332 assumes an external clock is being used and it doesn't run. So we would prefer to avoid these bits. A rugged socket will be used for 16-pin ICs, with power and ground connections permanently wired to pins 16 and 8, and other pins connected to the M68332's port bits as shown in Figure 4-11b, making it impossible to connect a M68332 output pin to +5 v or ground, which may damage it. Another rugged socket will be used for 14-pin ICs, with power and ground connections permanently wired to pins 14 to 7, and other pins connected to the M68332's port bits as shown in Figure 4-11c. The user will plug a 16-pin IC into the 16-pin socket and not put anything in the 14-pin socket to test a 16-pin IC, or plug a 14-pin IC into the 14-pin socket and nothing into the 16-pin socket to test it.

We use the same general scheme as in the M68340. The equivalent *#define* statements for the pins are shown below. A similar set can be written for 16-pin chips.

#define pin1 1	#define pin5 0x40	#define pin10 0x800
#define pin2 2	#define pin6 0x80	#define pin11 0x1000
#define pin3 4	#define pin8 0x200	#define pin12 0x2000
#define pin4 8	#define pin9 0x400	#define pin13 0x4000

For testing the 74HC00, the same analysis of the chip leads to the same *#define* statements for *A*, *B* and *Z*, shown to the right of Figure 4-12, but for the M68332 the constants *A*, *B*, and *Z*, will become *0x4809*, *0x2442* and *0x1284*. Almost the same procedure is used for the M68332 as we used for the M68340:

```
/* for the M68332 */
unsigned v[4]={ Z,B| Z,A| Z,A| B}; /* construct the test vector for the 7400 */
check(){ register unsigned bits, i;
        assgE=0x30;assgF=0;  dirE=~Z; dirF=(~Z)>>8; /* initialize ports E and F */
        for(i=0; i<4; i++){ /* for all 2**2 rows of truth table */
                portE = bits = v[i]; portF = bits>>8; /* output bits to chip */
                bits=portE| (portF<<8); /* get back bits from chip */
                if((bits & Z)!=(v[i] & Z)) return 0; /* if no match, exit returning 0 */
        }
        return 1; /* if all match, return 1 */
}
```

A very powerful message brought home by this example is the ability of high level languages to abstract and simplify a design. By *#define* statements that are in turn defined in terms of other *#define* statements, we are able to utilize the rather awkward ports of the M68332 and M68340 in a manner that is easy to understand and debug. Also note that most of the design carried over from the M68340 to the M68332. High-level languages make it easier to port a solution from one machine to another.

4-4 Input/Output Indirection

When studying single-chip microcomputers, we found it easy to use parallel ports on them to simulate the control signals on a memory bus, flipping them around in software. The kind of I/O considered up to now is analogous to direct memory addressing. The use of a parallel port to simulate a memory bus is like indirect addressing. Shift register connected I/O is further indirection. And a coprocessor becomes an I/O device that is read or written in microcode, which is one level below normal I/O, analogous to immediate addressing. In this section, we examine these different levels of I/O indirection and examine some issues a designer should consider regarding I/O indirection. We will cover indirect I/O in the first subsection, followed by serial I/O, and will conclude with a discussion of design issues.

4-4.1 Indirect Input/Output

We now come to a somewhat surprising technique that is particularly suited to single-chip microcomputers, as well as 683xx systems. You might have a personal computer, which you might be reluctant to open up to get to the memory address and data buses, but it may have an M6821 (often used to connect to a printer). Up to now, the I/O device has been attached to the address and data buses. We shall call this *direct I/O*. Alternatively, the address, data, and control pins of an I/O device can be connected to a parallel I/O device's I/O port pins, such as ports C and F of the M68332 or ports A and B of the M68340. Explicit bit setting and clearing instructions can raise and lower the control signals for the I/O chip.

We call the use of one I/O device to control another device *indirect I/O*. Although indirect I/O is slow, and therefore cannot be used in some applications, it is very easy to debug because we do not interfere with the integrity of the memory bus and we thus have a working computer that supports a debug monitor. Indirect I/O is thus a good way to experiment with an LSI I/O chip. Indirect I/O is also a good way to implement some completed designs. We will give an example of the use of indirect I/O, using an MC6818A time-of-day clock chip, and then discuss its limitations and advantages.

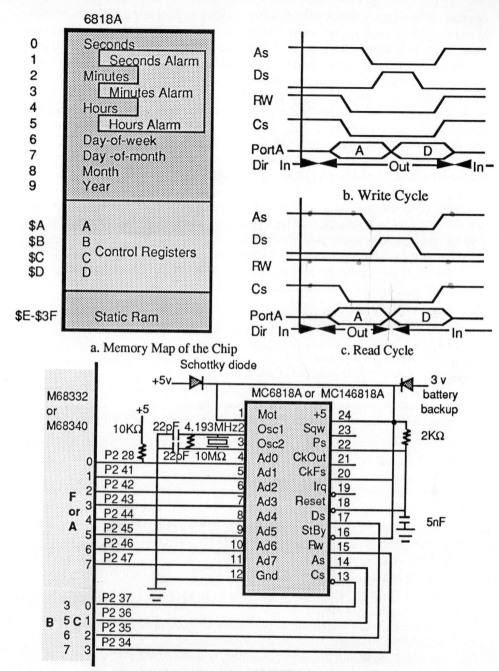

a. Memory Map of the Chip

b. Write Cycle

c. Read Cycle

d. Connecting an M6818A Time-of-Day Chip Using Indirect I/O

Figure 4-13. M6818A Time-of-Day Chip.

We want to keep track of the time of day, so we choose the MC6818A or MC146818A time-of-day clock chip to do this even when the microcomputer is turned off. Figure 4-13a shows the memory organization of the MC6818A. The current time is in locations 0 to 9, except for locations 1, 3, and 5, which hold an alarm time to generate an interrupt. Control ports at locations 0xA to 0xD allow different options. Locations 0xE to 0x3F are just some CMOS low-power RAM. After an initialization ritual, which puts 0xF into control port F, the time may be loaded into locations 0 to 9, and then 0x8 is put into control port C to start the timekeeping. These locations 0 to 9 can be read after that to get the current time of day.

The MC6818A can be connected to M68340 ports A and B or M68332 ports C and F, as shown in Figure 4-13d. The timing of control signals and the sequence of supplying address and data to the M6818A is shown in Figure 4-13b for the write cycle and in Figure 4-13c for the read cycle, as taken from Motorola data sheets. Control signals (address strobe As, data strobe Ds, read-write RW, and chip select Cs) are set high or low in the M68332 port C, or the M68340 port B, to write a word. They are initially high, except for Ds which is low. We first raise As high, put address A to port F, make Cs and RW low, drop As low, make Ds high, put data to port F, drop Ds low, and raise Cs, RW, and As high. The read procedure is essentially the same, except that RW remains high and data are read from port F.

We next examine a program to write the time of day. We first show the M68332 implementation, using ports E and F, and then the M68340 implementation, using ports A and B. The pins (e.g. P2 28) shown in Figure 4-13d are for the M68332.

```
/* for the M68332 */
enum { cs=1, as=2, ds=4, rw=8};
main() {
    int yr,mo,dm,dw,hr,mn,se;
    assgF = dirF = 0; /* make port F an input */
    *((long*)0xfffa44) &= 0xc0ffffc; /* port C bits 3 to 0 are output */
    outa(0x80,0xb);outa(0xf,0xa);outa(yr,9);outa(mo,8);
    outa(dm,7);outa(dw,6);outa(hr,4);outa(mn,2);outa(se,0); outa(8,0xb);
}

outa(d,a) int d,a; {
    portC = as+rw+cs; dirF = 0xff; /* make port F an output */
    portF = a; portC = as+cs; portC = as; /* output the address a */
    portC = 0; portC = ds; portF = d; portC = 0; /* output the data d */
    portC = as+rw+cs; dirF = 0; /* make port F an input */
}

/* for the M68340 */
enum { cs=8, as=0x20, ds=0x40, rw=0x80};
main() {
    int yr,mo,dm,dw,hr,mn,se;
    dirB=assgA1=0xff; assgB=dirA=0; /* make port A input and port B output */
    outa(0x80,0xb);outa(0xf,0xa);outa(yr,9);outa(mo,8);
    outa(dm,7);outa(dw,6);outa(hr,4);outa(mn,2);outa(se,0); outa(8,0xb);
}

outa(d,a) int d,a; {
    portB = as+rw+cs; dirA = 0xff; /* make port F an output */
    portA = a; portB = as+cs; portB = as; /* output the address a */
    portB = 0; portB = ds; portA = d; portB = 0; /* output the data d */
    portB = as+rw+cs; dirA = 0; /* make port a an input */
}
```

Either C procedure *outa* accesses the chip. It is shown following the main program that calls it up. Observe that *outa* rather tediously, but methodically, manipulates the MC68181A's control signals. A statement *(dst+a) =d;* in direct I/O is simply replaced by a procedure call *outa(d,a)* in indirect I/O that does the same thing. High-level language programs are easy to write. It is generally possible to write the procedure *outa* in assembler language, while the main program is in C, to regain some speed but keep most of the advantages of high-level languages. While the program shows how MC6818A's memory can be written into, similar routines can read it.

The main point of this section is the concept of indirect I/O, which we now elaborate on further. Besides being a good way to connect complex I/O devices to a single-chip computer, indirect I/O is a very good way to experiment with an I/O chip. The main advantage is that the connections to the chip are on the "other side" of an I/O port, rather than directly on the 683xx's address and data buses. Therefore, if you short two wires together, the 683xx still works sufficiently to run a program. You have not destroyed the integrity of the microcomputer. You can then pin down the problem by single-stepping the program and watching the signals on the ports with a logic probe. There is no need for a logic analyzer.

We used this technique to experiment with a floppy disk controller chip and a CRT controller chip set in Chapter 9. We got these experiments to work in perhaps a quarter of the time it would have taken us using direct I/O. That experience induced us to write a whole section on this technique here in Chapter 4. There is a limitation to this approach. Recall from Chapter 3 that some chips use "dynamic" logic, which must be run at a minimum as well as a maximum clock speed. The use of indirect I/O may be too slow for the minimum clock speed required by dynamic logic chips. However, if the chip is not dynamic, this indirect I/O technique is very useful to interface to complex I/O chips.

4-4.2 Synchronous Serial Input/Output

Except when already wired in a personal computer, parallel registers and their address decoders take a lot of wiring to do a simple job. Just wire up an experiment using them, and you will understand our point. In production designs, they use up valuable pins and board space. Alternatively, a serial signal can be time-multiplexed to send 8 bits of data in eight successive time periods over one wire, rather than sending them in one time period over eight wires. This technique is limited to applications in which the slower transfer of serial data is acceptable, but a great many applications do not require such a fast parallel I/O technique. Serial I/O is similar to indirect I/O covered in the last section, but uses yet another level of indirection, through a parallel I/O port and through a serial shift register, to the actual I/O device.

This subsection considers the serial I/O system that uses a clock signal in addition to the serial data signal; such systems are called synchronous. Asynchronous serial communication systems (Chapter 8) dispense with the clock signal. Relatively fast (100 kilobits per second) synchronous serial systems are useful for communication between a microcomputer and serial I/O chips or between two or more microcomputers on the same printed circuit board, while asynchronous serial systems are better suited to slower (9600 bits per second) longer distance communications. We first examine some simple chips that are especially suited for synchronous serial I/O. We then consider the use of a parallel I/O port and software to communicate to these chips.

Although serial I/O can be implemented with any shift register, such as the 74HC164, 74HC165, 74HC166, and 74HC299, two chips − the 74HC595 parallel output shift register and the 74HC589 parallel input shift register − are of special value.

The 74HC589 is a shift register with an input port and a tristate driver on the serial output of the shift register. (See Figures 4-14b and 4-14d.) Data on the parallel input pins are transferred to the input port on the rising edge of the register clock RCLK. Those data are transferred to the shift register if the load signal LD is low. When LD is high, data in the shift register are shifted left on the rising edge of the shift clock SCLK and a bit is shifted in from IN, as in the 74HC595, but the data shifted out are available on the OUT pin only if EN is asserted low; otherwise it is tristated open.

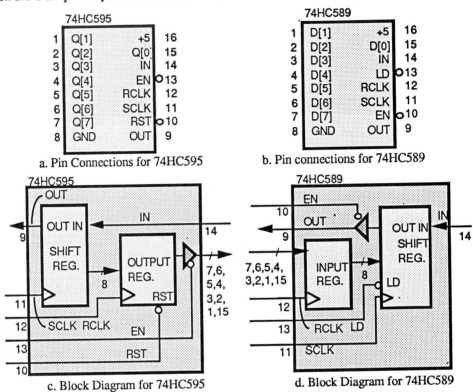

a. Pin Connections for 74HC595   b. Pin connections for 74HC589

c. Block Diagram for 74HC595   d. Block Diagram for 74HC589

Figure 4-14. Simple Serial Input/Output Ports.

The 74HC595 is a shift register with an output port and tristate driver on the parallel outputs. (See Figures 4-14a and 4-14c.) We consider the shift register to shift left rather than right. A shift occurs on the rising edge of the shift clock SCLK. A bit is shifted in from IN and the bit shifted out is on OUT. On the rising edge of the register clock RCLK, the data in the shift register are transferred into the output port. If the output enable EN is asserted low, the data in the output port are available to the output pins; otherwise they are tristated open.

These chips can be connected in series or parallel configurations. (See Figure 4-15.) The 74HC589 can be connected in a series configuration to make a longer register, as we see in the Figure 4-15a 24-bit input port. The outputs OUT of each chip are connected to the inputs IN of the next chip to form a 24-bit shift register. Each chip's RCLK pins are connected to an M68332 port D pin to clock the input ports together, each chip's LD pins are connected to a M68332 port D pin to load the shift registers together, and each chip's SCLK pins are connected to an M68332 port D pin to clock the shift registers together. The EN pins are connected to ground to enable the tristate drivers. In the software considered later, we will load the input ports at one time to get a consistent "snapshot" of the data, then load this into the shift register at one time by making LD low, and then, with LD high, send 24 pulses on SCLK to shift the data into the M68332. For the M68340, substitute port A for the M68332's port D.

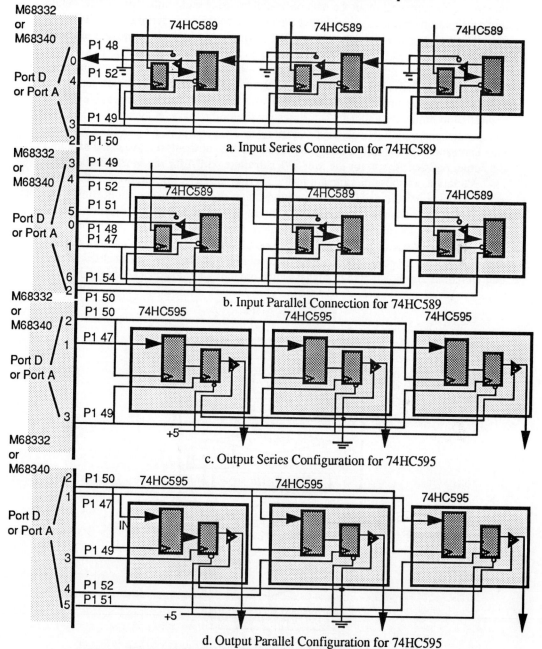

a. Input Series Connection for 74HC589

b. Input Parallel Connection for 74HC589

c. Output Series Configuration for 74HC595

d. Output Parallel Configuration for 74HC595

Figure 4-15. Configurations of Simple Serial Input/Output Registers.

The 74HC589 can be connected in a parallel configuration to make several separate input ports, as we see in the three 8-bit input ports of Figure 4-15b. The outputs OUT of each chip are connected to a common tristate bus line, and the tristate enables EN of each chip are connected to different M68332 port D pins, but the other pins are connected as in Figure 4-15a. Any of the input ports may be selected by asserting its tristate enable low, the others being negated high. Then a sequence similar to that discussed in the previous paragraph will input the data on that chip, using eight pulses on SCLK. While this configuration requires more output pins on the M68332, it permits the software to choose any chip to read its data without first having to read the chips in front of it in a series shift register. For the M68340, substitute port A for the M68332's port D.

Figures 4-15c and 4-15d show the corresponding series and parallel configurations for the 74HC595. Reset can be connected to the M68332 reset pin which resets the system when it is turned on or when the user chooses. The output enable EN is connected to ground to assert it. The series configuration makes a longer shift register. The parallel configuration makes separate ports that can output data by shifting the same data into each port, but only pulsing the RCLK on one of them to transfer the data into the output register. Again, for the M68340, substitute port A for the M68332's port D.

Variations of these circuits are useful. Series-parallel configurations, rather than simple series or simple parallel configurations, may be suited to some applications. The 74HC595 RCLK signals can come from the logic associated with the data's source, rather than from the microcomputer, to acquire data when the source determines it is ready. The 74HC589 output enable EN can be used to connect the output to a parallel data bus, so it can be disabled when other outputs on that bus are enabled. These configurations are shown here to suggest some obvious ways to connect serial ports.

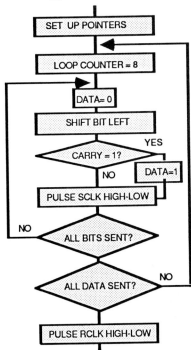

Figure 4-16. Flow Chart for Series Serial Data Output.

Serial I/O chips can be controlled by software, using parallel I/O port bits to control the lines to the chips. We discuss the general principles after we consider this example: sending 24 bits of data to a series configured output, as shown in Figure 4-15c.

A C program to control the 24-bit serial output is based on the flow chart in Figure 4-16 and is listed below for the M68332 and then the M68340. We will use the M68332's port D. The shift register clock is connected to port D bit 2, and the data out are connected to bit 1. The output buffer register clock is connected to bit 3. We initialize the D port to be output by:

```
/* for the M68332 */
assgD=0xF1; /* assignment register bits 3,2,1 set for parallel I/O */
dirD=0xE; /* direction register set for output */
```

The outer loop of the procedure *serial_out()* below reads a word from a buffer and an inner loop shifts 1 bit at a time into the D port output, clocking the SCLK after each bit is sent, and then pulsing the RCLK line to put the data into the output buffer register. Procedures for the other configurations in Figure 4-15 are similar to this one. The basic concept is that the individual signals needed to control the external chips can be manipulated by setting and clearing bits in parallel I/O ports. It is easy to write programs that will interface to serial I/O devices via a parallel I/O port.

```
/* for the M68332 */
enum {data=2, sclk=4, rclk=8}
serial_out(buffer) char *buffer; { int i,j,k;
    for(k=0; k<4; k++) {
        j = buffer[k]&0xff;
        for(i=7; i>=0; i--){
            portD = 0;
            if ((0x100 & (j = j <<1))==0x100) portD| = data;
            portD |= sclk; portD & = ~ sclk; /* pulse shift clock */
        }
    }
    portD |= rclk ; portD & = ~ rclk; /* pulse output register clock */
}
```

We will use the M68340's port A. The shift register clock is connected to port D bit 2, and the data out are connected to bit 1. The output buffer register clock is connected to bit 3. We initialize port A to be output by:

```
/* for the M68340 */
assgA1=dirA=0xE; /* assign bits 3,2,1 and set direction for output */
```

The outer loop of the procedure *serial_out()* essentially just duplicates the procedure *serial_out()* above for port A.

```
/* for the M68340 */
enum {data=2, sclk=4, rclk=8}
serial_out(buffer) char *buffer; { int i,j,k;
    for(k=0; k<4; k++) {
        j = buffer[k]&0xff;
        for(i=7; i>=0; i--){
            portA = 0;
            if ((0x100 & (j = j <<1))==0x100) portA| = data;
            portA |= sclk; portA & = ~ sclk; /* pulse shift clock */
        }
    }
    portA |= rclk ; portA & = ~ rclk; /* pulse output register clock */
}
```

4-4.3 The M68332 QSPI Module

The M68332 was designed with the intent of exploiting serial modules like the 74HC589 and 74HC595. It incorporates a *Queued Serial Peripheral Interface* (QSPI) Module in the QSM that takes care of shifting serial data to and from these chips, essentially implementing the procedure of the last section entirely in hardware. This hardware can also implement an I/O queue to store data that has been moved or is to be moved. In this section we introduce the QSPI module, performing essentially the same function as the procedure above, and also scanning a keyboard.

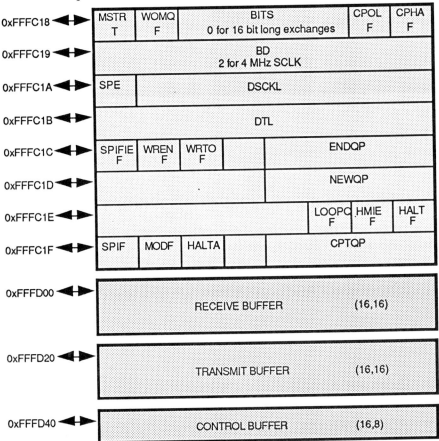

Figure 4-17. QSPI Control and Status Registers.

Figure 4-17 shows the control and status ports used by the QSPI module. The port D registers in Figure 4-9 and some additional QSM control registers discussed in the next chapter are also used to control the QSM. These ports, 1 to 8 bits wide, are conveniently handled in C using bit-field structures. Compare the following *type* definition of the structure *QSPI* with Figure 4-17.

```
typedef struct QSPI {
    unsigned mstr:1,womq:1,bits:4,cpol:1,cpha:1,bd:8,spe:1,dsckl:7,dtl:8;
    unsigned spifie:1,wren:1,wrto:1,:1,endqp:4,:4,newqp:4;
    unsigned :5,lcopq:1,hmie:1,halt:1,spif:1,modf:1,halta:1,:1,cptqp:4;
} QSPI;
```

In the following discussion, we use a global pointer *qspiPort* to this structure, initialized as *QSPI *qspiPort=(QSPI *)0xfffc18;* We also use three buffers built into the M68332's QSPI hardware, receive *R[0 to 15]*, transmit *T[0 to 15] and* control *C[0 to 15]*, which are considered vectors of 16-bit, 16-bit and 8-bit elements. These can be declared as pointers *char *C=(char *)0xFFFD40; unsigned *R=(unsigned *)0xFFFD00, *T=(unsigned *)0xFFFD20;* and used as vectors. Generally, *T[i]* is sent to external shift register chips as data recieved from external shift register chips is put into *R[i]*, under the control of *C[i]* in one *exchange*. A sequence of consecutive elements, *T[i]* and *R[i]*, *T[i+1]* and *R[i+1]*, *T[i+2]* and *R[i+2]*, ... can be exchanged in one *operation*. *Wraparound* can be used to send and receive them continuously; when an operation is completed it is automatically repeated, without software intervention.

The QSPI uses seven of the port D pins and is controlled by port D's assignment, direction and data registers (see Figure 4-9). The shift clock SCLK pin (port D[2]) clocks the shift registers. The master-in-slave-out MISO pin (D[0]) inputs to the M68332 serial data from an external chip and the master-out-slave-in MOSI pin (D[1]) outputs data. All pins used by the QSPI must be assigned to it by writing T in the associated bits of the assignment register, although the SCLK pin (port D[2]) is automatically assigned to the QSPI whenever it is in operation. The direction bits must be T or F to make the pins outputs or inputs whether or not they are used by the QSPI, and the port D data port determines the values of output pins when the QSPI is not in operation. The output peripheral chip select pins PCS[3 to 0] (D[6 to 4]), can be determined by a nibble in *C[i]* to generate RCLK or EN signals for the external chips. The pins we used for software control of serial chips using the parallel port D in Figure 4-17 happen to be pins that can be used for automatic operation of them using the QSPI.

C[i] is initialized for each *T[i]* or *R[i]* that will be used later. The low nibble can be output during an exchange for the row as the value PCS[3 to 0]. Note that when no exchange occurs, default values in port D[6 to 3] can be sent out on these pins. Bit 7, CONT is set to 1 if PCS[3 to 0] is to remain output, instead of D[6 to 3], between exchanges in an operation, and is cleared if D[6 to 3] is to be output between exchanges in an operation. Bit 6, BITSE, is set to 0 if 8 bits are sent, and to 1 if from 8 to 16 are exchanged (a *long exchange*).

Although the M68332 can also act as a slave to another computer, it is usually a master and we will consider it so until the end of this section. Thus the *mstr* control port bit must be T as shown in Figure 4-17. The *womq* bit determines whether the QSPI's pins are wire-or and is usually F. The nibble *bits* determines the number of shift clocks in a long exchange, and will be 0 to get 16 pulses. The bits *cpol* and *cpha* determine the shape of the shift clock SCLK pulse. The value FF is suitable for positive-edge clocked registers like the 74HC589 or 74HC595. The 8-bit *bd* determines the shift clock rate. The aforementioned chips can use a fast 4.19 MHz shift clock, generated when *bd* is 2. The key control bit *spe* is set to start the QSPI module. It can be read to see if the module is still running or has been stopped after a single shift operation has been requested, and it can be cleared to turn off the module, although a safer method uses bits described below. The 7-bit *dsckl* and byte *dtl* will not be used in the following examples. The bit *spifie* enables interrupts when a transfer is complete. We leave it F in this chapter. The bit *loopq* is used for testing and should be F. The bit *modf* indicates a master-slave mode fault has occurred, and will be ignored.

A QSPI operation can be safely halted by setting the bit *halt*. Setting *halt* will stop the QSPI after the current operation is completed, whereas clearing *spe* may prematurely abort a serial transfer leaving the external chips in an uncertain state. We leave these bits F in this book. The bit *hmie* enables an interrupt after an operation is halted, and the bit *halta* can be read and tested to determine when it is halted.

The nibbles *endq* and *newqp,* establish the range of words to be sent or received. The beginning *i* and end *j* of the operation are put in the *newqp* and *endq* control ports and the nibble status port *cptqp* indicates the last word that has been completely exchanged. The bit *wren* enables wraparound, and *wrto* determines whether wraparound goes to *newqp* or 0. The bit *spif* indicates that a QSPI transfer is finished (even though another transfer may have automatically begun in wraparound mode).

The QSPI can be easily used to output a byte to a 74HC595. Suppose that the chip is connected so that its SCLK (pin 11) is connected to the M68332's SCLK (P1 50), IN (pin 14) is connected to the M68332's MOSI (P1 47), RCLK (pin 12) is connected to the M68332's PCS[0] (P1 49), its RESET (pin 10) is tied to +5, and EN (pin 13) is grounded, as the leftmost 74HC595 is in Figure 4-15d. Assuming *qspiPort* is globally declared as before, to output one byte, after reset has initialized most of the QSPI control registers, just configure port D, set the *mstr* bit and clear *cpha* and *C[0]*:

assgD = dirD = 0xE; portD = 8;
qspiPort->mstr = 1; qspiPort->cpha = *((char*)0xfffd40) = 0;

To output a byte *d,* assuming the *spe* bit is 0, put the byte into *T[0]* and set *spe*:

*((unsigned *)0xfffd20)=d; qspiPort->spe=1;

We now consider a procedure *serial_out_3()* and its initialization *init3()* that implements a 24-bit serial output using the connections in Figure 4-15c, and is equivalent to the procedure *serial_out()* in the last section. The procedure *serial_out_3()* will put two bytes into *T[0]* as a 16-bit word and one byte into *T[1]*, and then output the word and byte. *init3()* sets up the port D assignment, direction, and data registers to use SCLK, MOSI, and PCS[0] and to outputs T on PCS[0] between operations. The values of QSPI control registers are initialized as shown in Figure 4-17, *cpha* is cleared, the baud rate is initialized to 2, and the queue end pointer is initialized to 1; other fields are assumed to be left as they are upon resetting the M68332. *C[0]* is initialized with CONT and BITSE set to output 16 bits and L continuously on PS[0], and *C[1]* is initialized for 8 bits as before. Assume *qspiPort* is globally allocated.

```
init3(){
        register char *C=((char*)0xfffd40); qspiPort = (qspi *)0xfffc18;
        assgD=dirD=0xE; portD=8; /* bits 3,2,1 set for QSPI out */
        qspiPort->mstr = qspiPort->endqp = 1; qspiPort->bd = 2; qspiPort->cpha=0;
        C[0]=0xc0; C[1]=0; /* set up command rows 0 and 1 */
}
```

The procedure *serial_out_3()* implements a 24-bit serial output of 3-bytes pointed to by its argument. It merely puts the bytes into *T[0]* and *T[1]*, checks to see if *spe* is 0 in the statement *while(qspiPort->spe);* and then sets the *spe* bit to make it run. After that, the QSPI ouputs the data independently of the M68332 program.

```
serial_out_3(buffer) char *buffer;{
        register unsigned *T=(unsigned *)0xfffd20;
        while(qspiPort->spe); /* wait for spe low, then load buffer and start QSPI */
        T[0]=((buffer[0])<<8)+buffer[1]; T[1]=buffer[2]; qspiPort->spe=1;
}
```

The procedures above can be trivially modified to input data from three 74HC589s, connected as in Figure 4-15a, while simultaneously outputting data as they are now. Port D[4] has to be pulsed to move data from the 74HC589s' input pins into their parallel holding register before the *out3* procedure is executed; *out3* will put that data into *R[0]* and *R[1]* as it outputs the data from *T[0]* and *T[1]*.

Parallel input or output connections can be implemented using similar procedures. Parallel output (Figure 4-15d) can get data to only one output register, without taking the time to shift data through all of them, as the serial connection requires. The port D register should be initialized to also assign D[5,4] to the QSPI and output T on them. The value of *endqp* is made 0 so that only row 0 is output. *C[0]*s upper nibble should be cleared to cause high outputs on PCS[2 to 0] between exchanges and its lower nibble should select the external register that is being input or output. Put 0xe into *C[0]* and start the QSPI; the low byte from *T[0]* is sent to the leftmost 74HC595. Parallel input (Figure 4-15b) is handled similarly. Up to 15 parallel inputs and outputs can be handled by considering PCS[3 to 0] as a binary number and using an external decoder chip to decode it, to get the RCLK and EN control signals for each of the shift registers.

We now consider procedures to scan a coincident select keyboard (Figure 4-18). Although the 74HC589 and 74HC595 can be used, their extra parallel registers that buffer the shift registers are not needed and make these chips more awkward than simple shift registers like the 74HC164 and 74HC165. The keys (normally open switches) are logically arranged in an (8,8) array, although they may be physically arranged like a typewriter keyboard. The 74HC164's 8-bit output sends a pattern of all H except for one bit that is L, on row wires. The 74HC165 inputs, having pull-up resistors on column wires, senses the row for an L for a closed switch indicating a key is pressed at the coincidence of the bit's column and the row that is made L. The 74HC165's parallel inputs and serial input are wired so that all 8 bits of row *i* are put into *R[i]*.

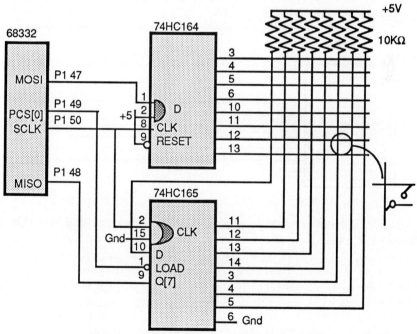

Figure 4-18. A Coincident Select Keyboard.

The procedure *initkbd()* shown below implements a 64-bit serial output and input. It sets up the QSPI module in wraparound mode, just once, and thereafter the software can merely examine *R[0 to 7]*. Each key is sensed every 25 μseconds and its value is put into that buffer. A bit *j* in word *i* will be an L if the key in row *i* column *j* is pressed.

The QSPI will send out a word in *T[0 to 7]* which puts H on all the outputs of the 74HC164 chip except one, and will simultaneously input a word into *R[0 to 7]*. The word that was input is the pattern that resulted from the previous output. Therefore the outputs are arranged, and the *T[0 to 7]* is initialized, so that row *i* in it has a L in bit *i+1*. Then *R[i]* is the pattern picked up from the inputs of the 74HC165 chip when row *i* was L. The low-order bytes of *R[0 to 7]* are an exact image of the keyboard array.

The main difference from the previous example is that *T[0 to 7]* is initialized with a scan pattern, wraparound is enabled, and words 0 to 7 are exchanged rather than words 0 and 1. The control bytes have CONT cleared and make PCS[0] H during the transfer while port D's data register makes it L between exchanges. This L pulse loads data into the 74HC165 chip. Having started the QSPI, the program need not do anything more. Slow devices like keyboards can be easily handled in the M68332 using serial I/O devices and the QSPI.

```
initkbd(){
    register unsigned i,j, *T=(unsigned *)0xfffd20;
    register char *C=((char*)0xfffd40); register QSPI *qspiPort=(QSPI *)0xfffc18;
    assgD=0xF; dirD=0xE; portD=0; /* portD */
    qspiPort->mstr = qspiPort->wren = j = 1; qspiPort->bd = 2; qspiPort->endqp = 7;
    for(i=0;i<8;i++) { T[i]= ~(j=j<<1); C[i] = 1; } T[7]=0xfe; C[7] = 1;
    qspiPort->spe=1;
}
```

This example will be further developed in the next two chapters to accommodate interrupts and key debouncing. This first step of the example exhibits a lot of the power of the QSPI module of the M68332's QSM.

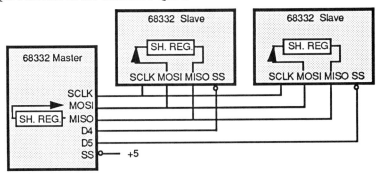

Figure 4-19. Multicomputer Communication System Using the SPI.

The QSPI interface can be used to communicate among several M68332s. (See Figure 4-19.) One M68332 is made a master, and all the others are *slaves*. The PCS[0] pin is used as a slave select SS input. The SCLK pins are connected together, as are the MOSI (Master Out, Slave In) and MISO (Master In, Slave Out) pins. The master has its *mstr* bit in the control register set, while the slaves have that bit clear and port D direction bit 3 clear. The master controls the slaves through some parallel output port like port D or the PCS[3 to 1] bits by making exactly one slave SS input low. The SS input on the master must be high. Then the SPI exchanges the data of the master SPI shift register with the data in the selected slave SPI shift register using a program like

Chapter 4 – Parallel and Serial Input/Output

that just shown. The slave can monitor its *spif* bit, status register bit 7, to detect when data have been exchanged, using synchronization techniques discussed in the next chapter. It is also possible for several M68332s to cooperate as equals, with any one of them being a master at any time. To detect errors, this requires a protocol, discussed in Chapter 8, and the use of the *modf* status bits we have not discussed here.

The serial port is a valuable alternative to the parallel port. It requires substantially less hardware. The M68332's SPI interface makes it easy to use these devices, but, with a modest amount of software, any parallel I/O register can be used to control them. However, a parallel port is required where speed is needed, because the serial port, especially using software control, is considerably slower than the parallel port.

4-4.4 Coprocessors as I/O Devices

A *coprocessor* can be considered as an extension of a main processor like the Motorola 68020, or an I/O device. In this section we consider a coprocessor as a conventional I/O device. We look at 68020 coprocessor ports and access cycles to understand the floating-point coprocessor, to show how it can be controlled by a 683xx system.

Simply put, a coprocessor appears as an I/O device to the *microcode* of the main processor. In the sense of I/O indirection, it is at an immediate level of indirection, in contrast to the direct and indirect levels considered above. If indirect I/O uses software to emulate the control signals as we observed in Section 4-4.1, then in a coprocessor, microcode is used in place of I/O instructions to access the device. As a rule, indirect I/O is an order of magnitude slower than conventional I/O, and a coprocessor should be an order of magnitude faster than a conventional I/O device.

For the Motorola 68020 coprocessors, a coprocessor is assigned an ID number from 0 to 7. The ID number 0 is reserved for the MC68851 memory management unit and 1 is used for the MC68881 floating-point coprocessor. The numbers 6 and 7 are assigned to user designed coprocessors.

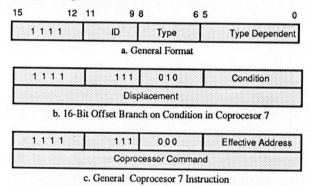

Figure 4-20. Coprocessor Instructions.

The general format of coprocessor instructions is shown in Figure 4-20a. The ID field is the ID number of the coprocessor, the type is the instruction type - general (cpGEN), conditional branch (cpBcc), decrement and conditional branch (cpDBcc), set on coprocessor condition (cpScc), context conditional trap (cpTRAPcc), context save (cpSAVE) or context restore (cpRESTORE) - and the type dependent field is of course dependent on the instruction type. A typical coprocessor instruction, branch on condition (cpBcc) in coprocessor 7, is shown in Figure 4-20b. Here, the type dependent field specifies the condition to be tested. A word following the op code is the displacement for this branch instruction. Another coprocessor instruction, a general instruction (cpGEN) in coprocessor 7, is shown in Figure 4-20c. Here, the type dependent field specifies the effective address used in the instruction. A word following the op code is the command for the coprocessor. We will consider cpGEN and cpBcc in this section.

The 68020 microcode accesses the coprocessor by means of the same address and data bus as it uses to access memory and I/O devices. The pins are connected about the same as in any I/O device. However, the function code FC[2 to 0] is the "special" code 7 for coprocessor access cycles rather than 1 for user data memory access cycles. If the function code is ignored in decoders (using common spaces as in Figure 1-5), then the ports in it can be accessed as if they were I/O ports in the address range 0x00020000 to 0x0002E000 as well as coprocessor ports, and we must not have memory or I/O ports in the address range used by coprocessors. Inputting the function code into all decoders in the system (using differentiated spaces) makes the coprocessor invisible to the normal 68020 memory read and write instructions like MOVE D0,ALPHA, and prevents coprocessor accesses from conflicting with memory and I/O ports. Figure 4-21 shows the address map of coprocessors in common or differentiated memory.

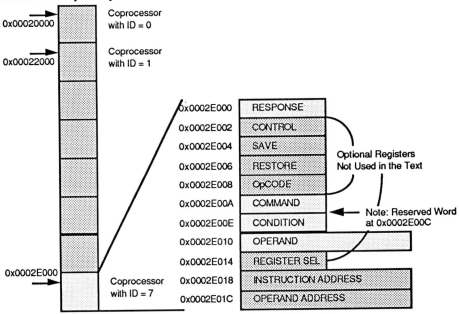

Figure 4-21. Coprocessor Port Address Map.

A coprocessor instruction is executed by the processor's handshake, reading and writing in the coprocessor's ports (shown light gray in Figure 4-21.) The *COMMAND* port is written in general instructions (cpGEN) and the *CONDITION* port is written in conditional branch instructions (cpBcc), and the *OPERAND* port is read or written.

The *RESPONSE* port is the means by which the coprocessor asks the main processor to get or to give some data, or the coprocessor gives back a result to the main processor. Figure 4-22a shows the general format of responses in this port, and Figure 4-22b shows a partial list of functions the 68020 will carry out, using "pigeon C" to describe these activities. In Figure 4-22a, CA is the "come-again" bit; if it is set, the 68020 should read the RESPONSE port again for another request, otherwise it is free to execute the next instruction. The main processor continues to execute the coprocessor instruction, responding to requests in the RESPONSE port, as long as the "come-again" bit is 1. (The PC bit requests that the current program counter value be sent to the instruction address port in the coprocessor. We do not discuss this further.) The DR bit is the direction of transfer; a 0 means move data to the coprocessor and a 1 means move from coprocessor. The FUNCTION field identifies the function that the coprocessor requests of the main processor as shown in Figure 4-22b, and the PARAMETER field supplies a parameter for the function, depending on the function.

a. Port Format

```
While(CA==1){
    if (DR==0) { /* transfers to coprocessor */
        switch(FUNCTION){
            case 1: OPERAND <- M (PARAMETER bytes), as in the 68020 MOVEM
                    instruction; break; /* Transfer Multiple Coprocessor Registers */
            case 2: OPERAND <- 68020 STATUS REGISTER; break;
            case 5: OPERAND <- M (PARAMETER bytes), at the address given by
                    OPERAND ADDRESS; break; /* Take Address, Transfer Data */
            case 6: OPERAND <- 68020 registers D0 to A7, as specified by
                    REGISTER SEL; break; /* Transfer Multiple 68020 Registers */
            case 7: Op-CODE <- OP Code; break;
            case 8: (Coprocessor signals 68020) switch (PARAMETER){ /* Null */
                    case 0: "The response is false"; break;
                    case 1: "The response is true";break;
                    case 2: case 3: "I'm not busy"; break;
                    } break;
            case 10: OPERAND ADDRESS <- Effective address; break;
            case 12: OPERAND <- 68020 Address/Data register [PARAMETER]; break;
            case 13: OPERAND <- 68020 Control register [PARAMETER];break;
            case 15: OPERAND <- M (PARAMETER bytes) from instruction stream;
                    break; /* Transfer Immediate Operands From Instruction Stream */
            case 21: case 22: OPERAND <- (M or reg) (PARAMETER bytes) from effective address; break;
            case 28: OPERAND <- (PARAMETER bytes) popped from stack; break;
        }
    }
    else { /* transfers from coprocessor */
        switch(FUNCTION){
            case 1: M <- OPERAND(PARAMETER bytes), as in the 68020
                    MOVEM; break; /* Transfer Multiple Coprocessor Registers */
            case 2: 68020 STATUS REGISTER <- OPERAND; break;
            case 4: "I'm busy - you have to reinitialize me."
            case 5: M <- OPERAND(PARAMETER bytes), at the address given by
                    OPERAND ADDRESS; break; /* Take Address, Transfer Data */
            case 6: 68020 registers D0 to A7 <- OPERAND, as specified by
                    REGISTER SEL; break; /* Transfer Multiple 68020 Registers */
            case 12: 68020 Address/Data register [PARAMETER]<- OPERAND; break;
            case 13: 68020 Control register [PARAMETER] <- OPERAND;break;
            case 21: case 22: (M or reg) <- OPERAND (PARAMETER bytes) using effective address; break;
            case 28:M <- OPERAND push (PARAMETER bytes) to stack; break;
        }
    }
}
```

b. Responses

Figure 4-22. Coprocessor Response.

The 68020 continuously reads the RESPONSE port and performs the actions that are indicated in it. Three actions are shown with dark background in Figure 4-22b, which are used in the following operations. A "null" response (case 8) indicates the 68020 should do nothing. It is mainly used in the execution of a conditional branch instruction to inform the 68020 of some test done in the coprocessor. Cases 21 or 22 are highlighted for moving data into the coprocessor. It requests the 68020 to evaluate the effective address, using the least significant 6 bits of the op code of a general instruction (Figure 4-20c), in the same way as the effective address is evaluated for a MOVE instruction, and then a number of bytes indicated by the PARAMETER field are input from that and consecutively higher addresses into the coprocessor, writing them into the OPERAND port. If the PARAMETER field is less than 5 and the address mode specifies data or address register contents, this case can be used to move data from the indicated register in the 68020 to the OPERAND port. A corresponding case for moving data from the coprocessor, case 23, writes the data at the effective address and consecutively higher addresses. However, using case 23 to read as well as write data might cause an address register to be autoincremented twice. So transfers from the coprocessor have a case 0, which outputs a number of bytes indicated by the PARAMETER field to the same address used in a previous transfer without recomputing the effective address.

A quick perusal of the cases shown in Figure 4-22b indicates that the OPERAND port in the coprocessor is like a bidirectional data port used to move data into or out of the coprocessor. The data can be moved to or from the memory word or address or data register "pointed to" by the effective address, to or from an address or a data register not explicitly identified by the effective address, to or from the 68020 status register that contains the condition codes, to or from other "control" registers in the 68020 such as those shown on the bottom of Figure 1-2, to or from the top of the stack, or from immediate operands. The OPERAND port is 32 bits wide. If fewer than 4 bytes are to be transferred, they are left-justified in the OPERAND port. If more are to be transferred, the OPERAND port is used repeatedly to transfer up to 4 bytes at a time.

To begin execution of a conditional branch instruction, the processor merely places the rightmost six bits of the op code, the "condition" shown in Figure 4-20b, in the CONDITION port. Writing in that port triggers the coprocessor to evaluate a condition in it. The meaning of these "condition" bits is entirely determined by the coprocessor; the 68020 simply takes them from the op code and places them in the CONDITION port. It expects a "null" response back (case 8), with a PARAMETER that indicates the evaluation of the condition. For simple cases where the condition is determined within a memory cycle, the response is returned to tell the 68020 whether or not to take the conditional branch. A PARAMETER of 0 in the "null" response indicates the result is false and execution should continue to the next instruction below the conditional branch instruction. A PARAMETER of 1 indicates the result is true and execution should continue at the address specified by the conditional branch instruction. While the 68020 expects a "null" response back, other responses listed in Figure 4-20b can be sent to the 68020 to get it to do some work on behalf of the coprocessor in order to execute the instruction. Other conditional instructions, decrement and conditional branch (cpDBcc), set on coprocessor condition (cpScc) and context conditional trap (cpTRAPcc), operate in the same way as far as the coprocessor is concerned.

The general class of coprocessor instructions can be used to perform operations entirely within the coprocessor, like a 683xx MOVE D0,D1 is done entirely in the 683xx, between the coprocessor and memory, like MOVE D0,ALPHA or MOVE ALPHA,D0, or in memory like MOVE ALPHA,BETA. The 68020 begins execution of a general instruction by merely placing the word following the op code, the "coprocessor command" shown in Figure 4-20c, in the COMMAND port, triggering the coprocessor to execute it. The meaning of these "command" bits is entirely determined by the coprocessor; the 68020 simply takes them from below the op code and places them in the COMMAND port. Upon decoding them, the coprocessor may use any of the requests shown in Figure 4-22b, to get the 68020 to help it execute the operation in its own hardware. A typical read-modify-write coprocessor instruction, with one memory cycle used to do some work within the coprocessor, would be executed as follows: In the first memory cycle, the coprocessor returns a code for case 23, to get data specified by the effective address of the instruction. It then returns a "null" (case 8) response while it works alone. Finally it returns a code to output using case 0, to write the data where it came from. As long as it expects to need another request from the 68020, it asserts the "come-again" bit CA, as it would on all but the output request, case 0, in our example. The last request, output case 0, negates that bit. The coprocessor can actually continue working within itself after negating CA, as long as it doesn't need anything from the 68020. (Synchronization mechanisms discussed in the next chapter are used to prevent the coprocessor from doing two instructions simultaneously.)

The two types just discussed, the conditional branch and general coprocessor instructions, are really very simple. From the point-of-view of the coprocessor, each begins with a write to a port, either the CONDITION or the COMMAND port. The conditional branch instruction is completed by the coprocessor putting its answer in the RESPONSE port. The general instruction continues with a request, written by the coprocessor in the RESPONSE port, with "come again" CA = 1 until the last response when CA = 0, and each such request except the "null" response, causes the 68020 to read or write some data, usually in the OPERAND port. The coprocessor generally moves data between the OPERAND port and its own internal ports as the instruction indicates.

The coprocessor save instruction, cpSAVE, and the corresponding restore instruction cpRESTORE are used to save and restore the contents of the coprocessor when, for example, an interrupt occurs and the state of the machine is to be saved, and when the interrupt is over and the state is to be restored. These instructions let the 68020 ask the coprocessor how much data have to be saved, and the 68020 saves and restores the amount of data indicated by the coprocessor in an efficient manner. The save instruction reads the SAVE port and thus triggers the save sequence in the coprocessor. The contents of the port tell the 68020 how much is to be saved. Different amounts of data can be saved when the coprocessor is in different situations. Those data from the SAVE port are also saved on the stack to be used when the state is to be restored. The restore instruction writes that word back to the RESTORE port in the coprocessor. That triggers the coprocessor to run its restore sequence, using the data in the RESTORE port to indicate how much is restored and where to resume execution.

We now look at a particular coprocessor, the MC68881 floating-point coprocessor. The floating-point coprocessor is assigned ID = 1 and appears at addresses 0x00022000 to 0x0002201F. The coprocessor ports in it appear as in Figure 4-21, with the address nibble E replaced by a 2. The programmer does not see these ports, but sees in the 68881 eight 80-bit registers FP0 - FP7 that act like the data registers, a status register that acts like the status register in the 68020, and some other registers. Figure 4-23a shows how it is connected, using common memory spaces so it can be used as a coprocessor and as an I/O device. We assume that all other memory and I/O devices are below 0x00020000 or above 0x100030000 in order to simplify the incompletely specified address decoder. We study the execution of FBEQ ALPHA (a cpBcc type) and

FMOVE.W 0x1000,FP0 (a cpGEN type) instructions. We will first show the microcode memory cycles that are used to access the coprocessor, and then we will show the use of normal 68020 MOVE instructions that treat the coprocessor as an I/O device.

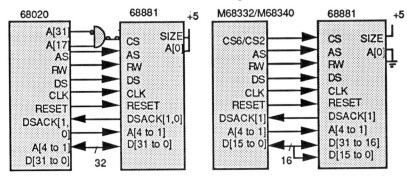

a. To the 68020 as a Coprocessor   b. To the 683xx as an I/O device

Figure 4-23. Connecting the 68881 Floating-Point Coprocessor.

The FBEQ ALPHA instruction is encoded as two words: 0xF281 and 0x0014. All coprocessor instructions begin with an op code 0xFxxx. The 2 specifies coprocessor ID = 1. Following it, the bits specify a 16-bit conditional branch. The FUNCTION field specifies a branch on equal, one of 64 possible conditional branches. The 16-bit displacement to address APLHA, 0x0014, is the second word of the instruction. Figure 4-24a shows the sequence of memory cycles used to execute this instruction. Each horizontal line is a beginning of a new memory cycle, the left column is the contents of the 68881 RESPONSE port each time it changes, the middle column shows what the 68881 is doing, and the right column is the 68020 activity.

After the FBEQ instruction is decoded by the 68020, and it is found to be a cpBcc instruction to coprocessor 1, the 68020 writes the rightmost 6 bits of that op code (0x1) into the CONDITION port at memory location 0x0002200E. The 68881 reads this port, examines its condition codes, and determines if the answer is "yes" to cause the 68020 to take the branch or "no" to cause it to continue executing the next instruction.

We consider the execution of the FMOVE.W 0x100,FP0 instruction. It reads the 16-bit word at location 0x100 as a 2's complement integer; it converts that word to an extended precision floating-point number and puts it into floating point register FP0 in the coprocessor. The instruction is coded as 0xF238, 0x5000, and 0x0100. The first word identifies this as a cpGEN type instruction to coprocessor 1, and the rightmost 6 bits identify the address mode, a 16-bit direct address. The next word tells the floating-point coprocessor that this is a move of a 16-bit word (which is an integer) from the 68020 or memory to register FP0, and the last word of the instruction gives the 16-bit address of the source word.

The 68020 fetches and decodes the op code, determining it is a cpGEN type instruction to coprocessor 1. It has already prefetched the next word, 0x5000, so it sends that word to the 68881 COMMAND port at 0x0002200A in the next memory cycle. The 68881 reads and decodes this command to determine that it is a MOVE to FP0 from the 68020 or memory. The 68020 continues to read the RESPONSE port and do what is requested, until the "come again" bit CA is 0. The first response value is a request of case 23 in Figure 4-22b, which is a request to evaluate the effective address determined by the rightmost 6 bits of the op code and read the 2 bytes at that location. The 68020 reads this request and determines what to do next to evaluate it.

Contents of RESPONSE	Activity of 68881	Activity of 68020
Null, CA=0, PARAMETER =2		Decode Instruction Determine it is (cpBcc type)
	Read CONDITION register, determine result	Write 6-bit condition code in CONDITION register
Null, CA=0 PARAMETER =0 or 1	Write RESPONSE, Null, CA=0,PARAMETER =0 or 1	Read "yes" (PARAMETER =1) or "no" (PARAMETER =0) response
		If "yes", add displacement to PC else fetch next instruction

a. An FBEQ Instruction

Contents of RESPONSE	Activity of 68881	Activity of 68020
Null, CA=0 PARAMETER =2		Decode Instruction Determine it is (cpGEN type), fetch second word, = command
	Read COMMAND decode it	Write 16-bit command in COMMAND register
code 23, CA=1 PARAMETER =2	Write RESPONSE, code 23 CA=1,DR=0, PARAMETER =2	Read response, determine it is a request to evaluate EA, read word
Null, CA=1 PARAMETER =0	Write RESPONSE, Null, CA=1, PARAMETER =0	Evaluate effective address (can take more than one cycle)
		Read a word from locations $100, $101
	Read the OPERAND register	Write the word in the OPERAND register (left justified)
		Read response, determine it is a Null with CA = 0
	convert integer to floating-point and put in register FP0 ▼ (several memory cycles)	Execute next instruction
Null, CA=0 PARAMETER =2		

b. An FMOVE Instruction

Figure 4-24. Execution of Floating-Point Coprocessor Instructions.

Complex address calculations can take many cycles. This one just needs to read the third instruction word to get the effective address. In the next cycle the 68020 reads the word at 0x0100 into itself. In the next cycle, the 68020 writes the word into the 68881. The RESPONSE port is read in the next cycle to see if any further operations are needed. The RESPONSE port was written several cycles back to indicate there is no further need of the 68020 to complete the instruction, so the 68020 is now free, and it fetches the next op code. Meanwhile the 68881 has to convert the 16-bit 2's complement integer to an 80-bit floating-point number, which is put into port FP0. That takes several cycles, but it happens while the main processor is doing something else. (Floating-point hyperbolic arctangent FATANH takes about 230 memory cycles to completion inside the 68881, and some instructions take twice as long.) When the 68881 is finished, it puts a "null" response with CA=0, PARAMETER=2, in the RESPONSE port. Observe now the contents of the RESPONSE port. It is a "null" response with CA=0, PARAMETER=2 whenever the 68881 is free to execute a new command, otherwise the 68881 is busy. Microcode can use this to wait for a completion of a previous 68881 instruction if the 68020 attempts to use the 68881 again before it is complete.

We now consider using the 68881 as an I/O device, using first the M68332 and then the M68340 to access the coprocessor ports as I/O ports, assuming a common address space. The chip is connected as in Figure 4-23b. We present two procedures which will be used to execute cpGEN or cpBcc instructions. For simplicity, the cpGEN procedure requires that the effective address be calculated prior to entering the procedure.

The M68332's chip select CS6 (or the M68340s chip select CS2) is first initialized to recognize the 68881 at 0x22000. We qualify the M68322's decoder for 16-bits with address strobe as, and use "external" wait states because the 68881 will assert DSACK[1]. The coprocessor will be initialized at this point using *initM68881*.

```
unsigned FP_error,*M68881;
void initM68881(){ /* for the M68332 */
    pinAssign(cs6,word); baseAssign(6,0x22000,k2);
    optionAssign(6,rd+wr+upper+lower+as,external,user+super,0);
    M68881=(unsigned *)0x00022000; M68881[1] = FP_error = 0;
}

void initM68881(){ /* for the M68340 */
    CsAssign(2,0x220000,8,noDsack,rdWr);
    M68881=(unsigned *)0x00022000; M68881[1] = FP_error = 0;
}
```

The FBEQ ALPHA instruction can be replaced by using the *cpBcc* procedure with an argument 1. We pass the 6-bit condition code, wait for a response of T or F, and return that response. This method works in both the M68332 and M68340.

```
int cpBcc(condition) int condition; { unsigned i; /* for both implementations */
    do i = M68881[0]; while ((i & IA) || !(i & PF));/* Wait until completed instr. */
    M68881[7] = condition; /* Write condition code into the condition register */
    do i = M68881[0]; while (i & CA); return((int)(i & 1)); /* then get response */
}
```

The FMOVE 0x100,FP0 instruction can be replaced by executing the *cpGEN* procedure with an arguments 0x5000 and 0x100, in both the M68332 and M68340.

```
void cpGEN(instruction, memory) unsigned instruction; unsigned long *memory; {
    register unsigned i; unsigned j,length; /* for both implementations */
    if (FP_error == 1) return; /* if FP_error you can run initM68881 to clear error */
    do i = M68881[0]; while ((i & IA) || !(i & PF));/* Wait for the MC68881 */
    M68881[5] = instruction; /* Load the instruction into the MC68881 */
    do i = M68881[0]; while ((i == 0x0802) || (i == 0x8900));/* Wait for the Resp. */
    length = i & PARAMETER; /* Check resp. to verify correct information */ j = 0;
    if ((i & DR) == 0) /* NOTE: all transfers to/from memory are LONG words !!! */
        while (length>0){*(long*)(memory + j++)=*(long*)(M68881+8);length -= 4; }
    else while (length>0){*(long*)(M68881+8)=*(long*)(memory + j++);length -= 4; }
    do i = M68881[0]; while (i & CA); if ((i != 0x900) && (i != 0x0802)) FP_error = 1;
}
```

From these two examples, you can see that coprocessor operation is faster than I/O device operation. Though generally an order of magnitude faster, these two cases are perhaps five to six times faster. The program segments can, of course, be implemented in the 16-bit 68000 system or even the 8-bit MC68008 or other microcomputers. The use of coprocessor instructions is recommended when using the 68881 in the 68020, even though I/O program segments are possible here too, because coprocessor operation is built into the microprocessor and is faster.

4-4.5 Design Considerations with Regard to Indirection

We now summarize the design alternatives regarding I/O indirection and recommend some guidelines for the designer. Although most I/O devices are direct, we need to consider the other alternatives because they are more suitable from time to time.

Indirect I/O is a mode where one I/O device is used to provide the address, data, and control signals for another I/O device. Software emulates the microprocessor controller and generates its signals to the I/O device. It is generally an order of magnitude slower than direct I/O. But it is very useful when a parallel I/O device is available anyhow, such as in single-chip microcomputers like the 6811, or in personal computers that have a parallel port – often used for a printer. It is not necessary to attach devices to the address, data, and control buses within the computer, which might destroy the integrity of the computer and make operating systems and debuggers unavailable.

Coprocessors use an immediate mode, where the microcode of the main processor accesses the I/O device. If the main processor has coprocessor mechanisms, then coprocessors can be an order of magnitude faster than direct I/O. The coprocessor generally has to be more intelligent, often being designed around a microsequencer and microcode, but can be as simple as a regular simple input device.

The main factor affecting the design decision is the speed of the I/O device. Sometimes the speed is dictated by the external system's speed, as when data are sent to or from a fast communication network using light pipes, as we consider later; and sometimes it is dictated by the process technology used to build the chip, as when dynamic logic is used, and requires a maximum time between events. Generally, the slower the required speed, the simpler the system. Many I/O devices are overdesigned with respect to speed. You should carefully determine the minimum allowable speed for the device and then choose the technique that fits that requirement. Then look at the system and determine if it has the needed mechanisms – a parallel port of sufficient width for indirect I/O or a coprocessor mechanism for coprocessor immediate I/O. We suspect that a lot of cases where indirect I/O is suitable and available are designed around direct I/O, which significantly increases their design and maintenance costs.

4-5 Object-Oriented Parallel and Serial I/O

Although a high-level language goes a long way towards making I/O interfacing easy, objects further simplify this task by standardizing the general ideas of encapsulation, information hiding, polymorphism, and inheritance. In this section, we show how these concepts related to objects can be used in parallel and serial I/O devices.

Objects can be used as part of the core of a program, as well as for I/O interfacing. The original idea of an object was to tie together a data structure with all the operations that can operate on it. For instance, we define the array data structure, and we tie to it the operations like array multiply, array addition, array inversion, and so on. Interpreters such as the traffic light controller that interprets an array, discussed in Section 4-2 and the chip tester that interprets a vector of test patterns in Section 4-3.5, are essentially operations that can be applied to the data structures that store the patterns. The data structures and their (interpreter) operations can be encapsulated like arrays and their operations are often encapsulated, using objects. Further, and independently, the I/O software they use can be organized in terms of objects. We will illustrate the traffic light controller object in the following example, after we show how I/O objects are used.

The I/O device can be encapsulated into an object, as discussed in Section 2-3.3. The main program or (traffic light or IC tester) interpreter does not have I/O statements in it, but rather sends messages to I/O object methods (calls I/O procedures), which actually have those I/O statements in them. Recall from Section 4-4.1 that we handled indirect I/O to the M6818 time-of-day chip by means of a call to procedure *outa*. In effect, we will handle all our I/O operations to parallel direct, parallel indirect, or serial I/O devices using object methods (procedure calls). Since all these alternative techniques can now be implemented in the same way, it becomes easy to replace a device using one technique with a device using another technique. We can separate the design into a part having to deal with interpreting a data structure, and a part having to deal with the I/O, and test each part separately, or mix and match different alternatives of both parts of the design at will. We can make I/O operations *device-independent,* meaning that they are written at compile time in the main program exactly the same way (as sending messages to I/O objects), regardless of the technique (parallel direct or indirect or serial) used to implement them. By using different arguments to procedures that bless and initialize an I/O object, a different I/O device that uses the same techniques or one that uses different techniques can be substituted. When this can be done at run time, this is *I/O redirection.*

Both device-independence and I/O redirection are also key ideas of device drivers in operating systems like OS-9, discussed in Chapter 10. Device drivers appear to be better suited to complex I/O devices like terminals that may need to recognize special characters such as backspace, and disks that need directories and allocation bit maps. Objects appear better suited to simple I/O devices: parallel I/O ports, and A-to-D converters. These can well use device-independence and I/O redirection, but a device driver is too complex.

We can define classes of objects for I/O devices in many ways, having increased power and sophistication. We can get as sophisticated as a device driver. However, this sophistication also increases overhead. When a class has a method with the same name as a method of its superclass, the class's method over-rides the superclass's method, as discussed in Section 2-3.3. However, the compiler generally loads both methods into memory, because it may be unable to determine if the superclass's methods will ever get used. We must be cautious about what we put into classes and superclasses or we will fill memory with a lot of unnecessary methods. (By the way, a similar kind of overhead appears when we use device drivers.) Having tried a number of different approaches in the 683xx, we have concluded that the following rules should be used for I/O objects.

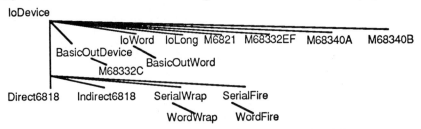

Figure 4-25. A Library of I/O Classes In Section 4-5.

Chapter 4 – Parallel and Serial Input/Output

1. There will be a hierarchical library of classes that use the same number and size of arguments for interchangeable I/O devices. See Figure 4-25.
2. There should be an *Init, Input, Output,* and *Terminate* method for every 8-bit, 16-bit and 32-bit I/O device, to enable device-independence and I/O redirection among them. A *chip* long word, used as a pointer to designate where the port is in memory, and an 8-bit *error,* that can, and should, be tested after every I/O operation, so that complex devices' errors can be reported with little overhead, should be instance variables in every I/O device. *Init* should have parameters to specify the address of the port and to specify a byte of control for programmable I/O or QSPI devices. These methods and instance variables will be defined for a root class *IoDevice;* all 8-bit, 16-bit and 32-bit I/O devices are objects of this class or of its subclasses.
3. The initialization of the chip selects for external I/O chips should not be part of the I/O device's *Init* method, because it makes that method have too many arguments. Rather, this initialization should be part of the reset handler discussed in Section 5-3.5 The *Init* method's argument will just be the port's address and a control byte.

We now show the object classes for I/O devices discussed in this chapter. The root class *IoDevice* and its methods are defined below:

```
struct IoDevice :direct { /* a direct root class */
      char error; long chip;
      void Init(long, unsigned);
      long Input(void);
      void Output(long);
      void Terminate(void);
};

void IoDevice::Init(p,m) long p; unsigned m;{ /*m is used later */
      chip=p;error=0; /* initialization needed in most devices */
}

long IoDevice::Input() { /* default input method used by most devices */
      return *(char*)chip;
}

void IoDevice::Output(d) long d;{ /* default output method */
      *((char*)chip) = d;
}

void IoDevice::Terminate() {} /* default terminate does nothing */
```

We can make all 8-bit readable output ports or basic input ports members of the class *IoDevice* because there is nothing else to define for them. The basic input port could be defined as members of this class or as members of a separate class with a method *Output* that makes the variable *error* some value to indicate that the operation was not completed, but a programmer can simply not use the method *Output* for basic input ports. A basic output port needs to save data output so that it can be read by an input method to maintain device-independence. We may have a statement that reads the value of an output port, modifies (e.g. increments) it, and writes it back. It has to work the same way for a readable output port as for a basic output port. A basic output port would be made a member of the class *BasicOutDevice* defined below:

```
struct BasicOutDevice :IoDevice { /* This class has slightly modified methods */
    long value;
    long Input(void);
    void Output(long);
};
void BasicOutDevice::Output(d) long d;{ /* save values being output */
    *((char*)chip) = value = d;
}
long BasicOutDevice::Input() { /* just read saved value */
    return value;
}
```

If an object is a member of the class *IoDevice* then sending an *Input* message to it will cause the method *IoDevice::Input* to be executed. If an object is a member of the class *BasicOutDevice* then sending an *Input* message to it will cause the method *BasicOutDevice::Input* to be executed because the subclass over-rides its superclass's *Input* method. We can show that a read-modify-write operation on either a basic or a readable output device can be written in exactly the same way sending messages to the *Input* and *Output* methods.

Sixteen-bit ports can be objects of the class *IoWord*, which is a subclass of *IoDevice*. This class and its noninherited methods are defined below:

```
struct IoWord :IoDevice { long Input(void); void Output(long); };
long IoWord::Input() { return *(int*)chip; }
void IoWord::Output(d) long d;{ *((int*)chip) = d; }
```

Ports that are 32-bits wide can be objects of the class *IoLong*, which is also a subclass of *IoDevice*. This class and its noninherited methods are defined analogously to *IoWord*, using *long* in place of *int* in the castes in the methods *Input* and *Output*. Basic 16-bit output ports can be defined by the class *BasicOutWord* shown below and basic 32-bit output ports can be defined by the class *BasicOutLong* in similar manner:

```
struct BasicOutWord : BasicOutDevice { void Output(long); };
void BasicOutWord::Output(d) long d;{ *((int*)chip) = value = d; }
```

Consider the procedure that simulated 16 wires (Section 4-2). A 16-bit wire can be simulated using objects, assuming the classes defined above, as shown below:

```
IoWord *Src; BasicOutWord *Dst; /* (pointers to) objects */
main() {
    Src=blessA(sizeof(IoWord), IoWord); /* allocate and link object Src */
    Dst=blessA(sizeof(BasicOutWord), BasicOutWord); /* allocate, link Dst */
    Src->Init(0x10000,0); Dst->Init(0x10800,0xff);
    while ((Src->error ==0) && (Dst->error ==0)) Dst->Output(Src->Input());
    Src->Terminate(); Dst->Terminate ();
}
```

Observe that the objects are in fact referenced by pointers *Src* and *Dst*, which are declared and globally allocated in the first line of this example. The instance variables are actually stored in buffers which are allocated in high memory. The first two lines in the program bless the objects, which set up the linkages in the storage for the instance variables to the storage for the classes, so that messages can be sent to the right methods. The *Init* methods set up the port addresses and clear the error indicator.

Although no errors occur in these simple objects, if more complex devices that report errors are substituted for them, then the program will respond to errors that they indicate in a correct manner by terminating the *while* loop. Note that the *Init* method is always used just once at the beginning of the use of the device and the *Terminate* method is used at the end of its use. The *Input* or *Output* methods are repetitively used each time a byte is to be input or output.

Polymorphism and inheritance provide for device-independence and I/O redirection. If a programmer wanted to use a 16-bit basic input device at a different location in place of the one at 0x10000, then the argument to *Src->Init* can be made the address of that device. If a programmer wanted to put a 16-bit readable output device at 0x10800 instead of a basic output device that is there in the current example, then the argument to *Dst =blessA(sizeof(BasicOutWord),BasicOutWord);* can be changed to *Dst=blessA(sizeof(IoWord),IoWord);* These substitutions can always be done at compile time (device-independence) and can generally be done at run time (I/O redirection). Encapsulation is clearly enforced in objects. All the data and methods needed to handle an I/O device are grouped together. Some information hiding is also evident, as the address *chip* maintained in the object is used only by methods of the object and is not visible to any other software. However, we make the instance variable *error* visible to external procedures; if we really enforced information hiding we would get to error by a root class method *geterror*. We think a method is unnecessary and inefficient. Directly accessing the instance variable *error* is completely general and more efficient.

Objects make programmable I/O devices like the M6821 and M68230 interchangeable with 8-bit basic input and output, and readable output devices. Direction registers of programmable devices need to be initialized; a control byte parameter in all *Init* methods has been included to use in this class to initialize them. The object class *M6821* and its *Init* method is given below. The reader should try writing similar object classes *M68230A, M68230B,* and *M68230C* for unbuffered I/O in the M68230.

struct M6821 : IoDevice {void Init(long, unsigned);};

void M6821::Init(p,m) long p; unsigned m;{ /* Init for M6821 */
    inherited:: Init(p,0); /* call up IoDevice's Init, clear error, fix chip address */
    ((char)chip+1)=0; *(char*)chip=m; *((char*)chip+1)=4; /* configure direct. port */
}

Methods *Init, Input, Output,* and *Terminate* of *M6821* are fully interchangeable with the methods of the same name for objects of the class *IoDevice.* Either *M6821* or *IoDevice* can be used as the class for an 8-bit input device, such as in an 8-bit version of our wire simulation example. Similar classes can be defined for M68230's port C, or for its ports A or B.

We can define the object class *M68332EF* and its *Init* method for M68332 port E or port F:

    struct M68332EF : IoDevice { void Init(long, unsigned);};

    void M68332EF::Init(p,m) long p; unsigned m;{
        inherited:: Init(p,0); /* call up IoDevice's Init, clear error, fix chip address */
        ((char)chip+6)=0; *((char*)chip+4)=m; /* config assignt and dir port */
    }

The objects for port E will be initialized with address *0xfffa11* and objects for port F will be initialized with address *0xfffa19.* Similar classes for M68332 ports C and D can be defined.

```
struct M68332C : BasicOutDevice { void Init(long, unsigned);};

void M68332C::Init(p,m) long p; unsigned m;{ register long *cfg=(long*)0xfffffa44;
    inherited:: Init(p,0); if (m&0x40) *cfg &= ~0xc0;
    if (m&1) *cfg &= ~0x3000000; if (m&0x20) *cfg &= ~0x30;
    if (m&2) *cfg &= ~0xc000000; if (m&0x10) *cfg &= ~0xc;
    if (m&4) *cfg &= ~0x30000000; if (m&8) *cfg &= ~3;
}

struct M68332D : IoDevice { void Init(long, unsigned);};

void M68332D::Init(p,m) long p; unsigned m;{ /* bits 2, 7 not always useable */
    inherited:: Init(p,0); /* call up IoDevice's Init, clear error, fix chip address */
    *((char*)chip+1)=0; *((char*)chip+2)=m; /* config assignt and dir port */
}
```

We can define the object class *M68340A* and its *Init* method for M68340 port A:

```
struct M68340A : IoDevice { void Init(long, unsigned);};

void M68340A::Init(p,m) long p; unsigned m;{ /* p should be set to 0xfffff011 */
    inherited:: Init(p,0); /* call up IoDevice's Init, clear error, fix chip address */
    *((char*)chip+4)=0xff; *((char*)chip+2)=m; /* config assignt and dir port */
}
```

We can define the object class *M68340B* and its *Init* method for M68340 port B:

```
struct M68340B : IoDevice { void Init(long, unsigned);};

void M68340B::Init(p,m) long p; unsigned m; {/* p should be set to 0xfffff019 */
    inherited:: Init(p,0); /* call up IoDevice's Init, clear error, fix chip address */
    *((char*)chip+6)=0; *((char*)chip+4)=m; /* config assignt and dir port */
}
```

Note that all the above classes are so defined that they are interchangeable, to effect device-independence and I/O redirection. They all use the basic *Init* parameter *p* and instance *long* variable *chip* to be the address of the data port so they can all use the inherited *Input* and *Output* methods of the root class *IoDevice*.

In the middle of this chapter we studied I/O indirection. Indirect I/O can be more naturally handled when all devices are objects than when they are handled as pointers, because we now handle all I/O operations by executing methods (procedures). An object and its methods, for direct I/O for the M6818 chip in Section 4-4.1, appears as follows:

```
struct Direct6818 :IoDevice { /* specific I/O device */
    char Inputa(char); void Outputa(char,char);
};
char Direct6818::Inputa(a) char a; { return *((char*)chip+a);}
void Direct6818::Outputa(d,a) char d,a ;{*((char*)chip+a) = d;}
```

Note that the *IoDevice::Init(p)* method inherited from the superclass *IoDevice* is used whenever an *Init* message is sent to a device of class *Direct6818* because it inherits its superclass's methods which are not over-ridden. This *Init* method need not be written again for the subclass because it is identical to the same method used for the superclass. The names of the input and output method are different than the names for them for the root class because different arguments are used; we use the same name for methods only if the methods are fully interchangeable, including the number and type of their parameters. The technique that access the M6818 using indirect I/O via port F (or A) can now be defined using a class *Indirect6818* and its output method, as shown below:

struct Indirect6818 :IoDevice { char Inputa(char); void Outputa(char,char); };

void Indirect6818::Outputa(d,a) char d,a ;{ /* save values being output */
      portC = as+rw+cs; dirF = 0xff; portF = a; portC = as+cs; portC = as;
      portC = 0; portC = ds; portF = d; portC = 0; portC = as+rw+cs; dirF = 0;
}

Port F (or A) is accessed here by pointers as we did in earlier sections; it could also be accessed less efficiently using I/O device object methods, as described above in this section.

The following three pages, up to the traffic light controller, apply only to the M68332. They can be skipped if you are studying the M68340.

Serial I/O using a parallel I/O port rather than the M68332 QSPI can be handled as objects in a manner similar to indirect I/O, because the former is really a special case of the latter. The procedure *serial_out* in Section 4-4.2 is made a method just like the indirect I/O procedure *outa* was made the method *Indirect6818::Outputa(d,a)* in the previous example. Serial I/O using the QSPI can be implemented using objects in a simple manner, or a very general manner. Simply, the procedure *serial_out3* in Section 4-4.3 is made a method just like *serial_out* in Section 4-4.2 is made a method. The procedure *init3* is also made an *Init* method.

However, the M68332 QSPI can be further handled using objects, by classifying all serial I/O devices into two groups and having classes for each group. This complex QSPI device becomes transparently equivalent to a parallel port using objects. In fact, this reduction in complexity is one of the main reasons why we like object-oriented I/O interfacing for the M68332. One group, *SerialWrap*, like the keyboard scanning device and the serially connected devices like the 74HC589 and 74HC595 accessed repetitively and continuously by the QSPI (in wraparound mode) would be used for all devices that must be continuously scanned. The other group, *SerialFire*, which are the devices that are selected explicitly by software for input or output (i.e. "fired"), would be best connected in a parallel hardware configuration (figures 4-154b or 4-15d), and the methods would select them when they are accessed and only when they are accessed.

The class for M68332 QSPI 8-bit I/O, *SerialWrap* and its methods are:

struct SerialWrap : IoDevice { /* special case of 8-bit I/O */
      QSPI *qspiPort; void Init(long, unsigned), Terminate(void);
};

void SerialWrap::Init(p,m) long p;unsigned m;{
      qspiPort=(QSPI *)0xfffc18; /* initialize pointer to QSPI registers */
      if(! qspiPort->mstr){ /* if this is the first time the QSPI is initialized */
          portD=assgD=0x7F; dirD=0x7E; qspiPort->mstr = 1; qspiPort->bd = 2;
      }
      inherited::Init(p,0); p=(p&0x1f)>>1; if(p>qspiPort->endqp) qspiPort->endqp = p;
      ((char)0xfffd40+p) = m; qspiPort->wren = 1; qspiPort->spe=1;
}

void SerialWrap::Terminate() { /*halt it, wait for it to halt, turn off wraparound*/
      qspiPort->halt =1; while(! qspiPort->halta); qspiPort->wren = 0;
}

A serial 8-bit input device like the 74HC589 can be in an object of the class *SerialWrap;* the address parameter *p* of *Init* will be an odd address from *0xfffd01* to *0xfffd1f*. An 8-bit output device like the 74HC595 can be in an object of this class initialized with odd address *p* from *0xfffd21* to *0xfffd3f*. This parameter *p* is the actual location of the byte read or written in the QSPI receive and transmit buffers. An input byte is read from the low byte of receive buffer *R[i];* an output byte is written into the low byte of transmit buffer *T[i]*, where *i* is bits 4 to 1 of the address *p*. The control byte, which is put into *C[i]*, will be the second parameter *m* of *Init*. Its most significant nibble should generally be 0 and its least significant nibble is the chip select value put out on pins PCS[3 to 0] when the device is selected. This value should match the value the hardware decodes PCS to enable the chips. An input and output device can have the same value *i,* so they use corresponding elements *R[i]* and *T[i],*if they have the same value of the *Init* parameter *m* which is put into *C[i]*.

A serial 16-bit input device like a pair of 74HC589s or a 16-bit output device like a pair of 74HC595s can be in an object of the class *WordWrap*:

struct WordWrap :: SerialWrap { long Input(void); void Output(long); }

long WordWrap::Input() { return *(int*)chip; }

void WordWrap::Output(d) long d;{ *((int*)chip) = d; }

This class inherits the *Init* and *Terminate* methods of the wraparound serial 8-bit class, but uses *Input* and *Output* methods similar to those of 16-bit parallel I/O devices. Wraparound 16-bit input devices should have address parameter *p* of *Init* be an even address from *0xfffd00* to *0xfffd1e* and wraparound 16-bit output devices should have address parameter *p* of *Init* be an even address from *0xfffd20* to *0xfffd3e*. The high-order nibble of the control parameter *m* of *Init* should be 4 to enable a long exchange, and its low-order nibble is the chip select value put out on pins PCS[3 to 0] when the device is selected. Again, an input and output device can have the same value *i,* which use corresponding elements *R[i]* and *T[i]*, if they have the same *Init* parameter *m* which is put into *C[i]*. A similar set of 32-bit devices can be styled as objects.

Finally, 8-bit, 16-bit and 32-bit devices can be used together in wraparound mode, especailly to handle serially configured shift registers. For efficient scanning by the QSPI, the values *p,* for several 16-bit devices serially configured, should be consecutive even numbers, starting at *0xfffd00* for input devices and starting at *0xfffd20* for output devices. If an odd number of 74HC589s or 74HC595s is connected in series, an 8-bit device can be used with the 16-bit devices. If, say, a 24-bit serial shift register is connected as before (Figure 4-15a or 4-15c), consider it an 8-bit and a 16-bit port. The *Init* parameter *m* of the device with lower numbers *i* should have the CONT bit (most significant bit of *m*) set, and the *Init* parameter *m* of the device with highest number *i* should have the CONT bit cleared, so the values of PCS[3 to 0] remain steady between scanning each device but switches when all devices have been scanned, as they should for series configuration serial shift registers. Up to 16 words (256 bits) can be continuously scanned using wraparound. The port data transparently moves to and from the QSPI buffers, and this transfer delay is only ~ 5 μsec (8-bit) to ~ 160 μsec (256-bit).

The procedure *serial_out* of Section 4-4.2 can be implemented using objects defined above. We illustrate its use in a *main* procedure that initializes the objects.

```
WordWrap *D1; SerialWrap *D2; /* (pointers to) objects */ char b3[3];
void main() {
      D1=blessA(Sizeof (WordWrap), WordWrap); D1 ->Init(0xfffd20,0x40);
      D2 =blessA(sizeof (SerialWrap), SerialWrap); D2 ->Init(0xfffd23,0);
      serial_out(b3);    D1 ->Terminate(); D2 ->Terminate ();
}
serial_out(buffer) char *b;{
      D1 ->Output((b[0] <<8) + b[1]) ;D2 ->Output( b[2]) ;
}
```

In the example above, note that *Init*'s first operands are transmit buffer addresses: *D1*'s is even (word) and *D2*'s is odd (byte). Its second operands set *C[]* to send 16 or 8 bits.

Shift registers are generally connected in parallel (Figures 4-15b or 4-15d) because there is a need to access them individually without shifting data throughout all the shift registers. They appear to be best handled by objects which *"fire"* the QSPI when the devices need to be accessed. The class for 8-bit I/O, *SerialFire* and its methods, useful for shift registers configured in parallel, is shown below. The basic difference is that wraparound is not enabled, and the input or output method has to enable the QSPI each time it is used. This class assumes that devices of class *SerialWrap* are not also being used; if they are being used concurrently then to execute an operation in a device of this class, a device using the *SerialWrap* class has to be terminated, this has to be initialized, input or output done and terminated, then the device of the class *SerialWrap* has to be initialized again, to prevent interaction. Otherwise *error* is set to 1, meaning the operation could not be done. A more general class able to handle both wraparound and fired devices, without reinitialization, will be described after interrupts are discussed.

```
struct SerialFire : IoDevice { /* special case of 8-bit I/O */
      QSPI *qspiPort;
      void Init(long, unsigned),Output(long); long Input(void);
};

void SerialFire::Init(p,m) long p; unsigned m;{
      qspiPort=(QSPI *)0xfffc18; /* initialize pointer to QSPI registers */
      if(qspiPort->wren) { error=1; return; }  inherited::Init(p,0); p&=0x1f;
      if( ! qspiPort->mstr){
            assgD=0xF; dirD=0xE; /* config port D */
            portD=0; qspiPort->mstr = 1; qspiPort->bd = 2;
      }
      *((char*)0xfffd40+(p>>1)) = m;
}

long SerialFire::Input() {
      qspiPort->endqp = qspiPort->newqp = (chip&0x1f)>>1;
      qspiPort->spe=1; while ( qspiPort->spe=1); return *((char*)chip);
}

void SerialFire::Output(d) long d;{
      qspiPort->endqp = qspiPort->newqp = (chip&0x1f)>>1;
      *(char*)chip = d; qspiPort->spe=1; while ( qspiPort->spe=1);
}
```

Fired 16-bit serial I/O can be handled by an object of the class *WordFire* which is a subclass of *SerialFire* that has its own *Input* and *Output* methods.

```
struct WordFire : SerialFire { /* special case of 8-bit serial fire I/O */
       long Input(void); void Output(long);
};
long WordFire::Input() {
       qspiPort->endqp = qspiPort->newqp = (chip&0x1f)>>1;
       qspiPort->spe=1; while ( qspiPort->spe==1); return *((int*)chip);
}
void WordFire::Output(d) long d;{
       qspiPort->endqp = qspiPort->newqp = (chip&0x1f)>>1;
       *(int*)chip = d; qspiPort->spe=1; while ( qspiPort->spe==1);
}
```

Of course, use an even address *p* for words. The class *WordFire* can be adapted for 24-bit and longer devices, by initializing all elements of the control vector *C[i]* in the *Init* method and changing *endqp* in the *Input* and *Output* methods.

The fired QSPI ports can be initialized all at the same address (same element of *T*, *R*, and *C*) or at any address. Any number of ports can be initialized, and then read or written in any order, before any are terminated. Up to 16 words (256 bits) can be fired at one time to and from serial I/O devices under explicit program control. Up to 15 groups (3840 bits) of I/O devices can be controlled this way.

The objects defined in this section are simple and interchangeable. However, the QSPI is a more complex and flexible port than the other ports and we may need to utilize features that are special to the QSPI. For instance, if we have serial devices whose maximum shift clock (SCLK) rate is 1 MHz, we may need to set the QSPI baud rate to 8. To accommodate these extra features, we can directly access the QSPI registers by executing *(char*)0xfffc19 = 8*, or we can access it using the instance variable *qspiPort* of object *P* by executing *P->qspiPort->bd = 8*. We prefer the use of object instance variables if there were several QSPIs in a computer and we wanted to set the baud rate of only the one that is associated with the object *P*. This technique also seems somewhat clearer. However, because of device-independence and I/O redirection, *P* could be blessed in another class, e.g. *M68332EF*. The procedure *memberD(P, SerialWrap)* returns 1 (true) if *P* is a member of *SerialWrap* or a subclass of it. We can write *if(memberD(P, SerialWrap)) P->qspiPort->bd = 8;* to set the baud rate only when it can be set, and to omit setting it when that statement is illegal.

We now return to the traffic light controller, to show how objects can be used for interpreters and the I/O devices they use. The array interpreter traffic light controller of Section 4-2 is now defined as an object of a class *traffic_table* as follows:

```
struct traffic_table :direct { /* a direct root class */
       unsigned tbl[4][2],row; void Build(char, char, char ), Execute(void);
};
void traffic_table:: Build (a,p,t) char a,p,t;{ tbl[a][0]=p; tbl[a][1]=t; }
void traffic_table:: Execute () { int j,k;
       P->Output(tbl[row][0]);
       for(j=0; j<tbl[row][1]; j++) for(k=0;k<0x100;k++);
       if((row++)==3) row=0;
}
```

The main routine, using an 8-bit basic output device runs now as follows:

```
BasicOutDevice *P; traffic_table *T;
main(){
        T=blessA(sizeof(traffic_table),traffic_table);
        P=blessA(sizeof(BasicOutDevice),BasicOutDevice);
        T-> row=0;
        T->Build (0,0x21,16);T->Build (1,0x22,4);
        T->Build (2,0x0c,20);T->Build (3,0x14,4);
        P->Init (0x10000,0);
        while(P->error == 0) T->Execute ();
        P->Terminate ();
}
```

Simply by changing the *blessA(sizeof(BasicOutDevice),BasicOutDevice);* procedure parameters, we can substitute the basic output device with a M6821, a parallel port in the M68332, or the QSPI. The methods that interpret the traffic light array need not be altered in the least. This separates the interpreter from the I/O devices, permitting them to be independently tested and interchanged, because objects facilitate device-independence and I/O redirection.

THINK C version 5.0 and C++ have additional concepts which are of some value in I/O programming. A *constructor* can be used to implement the *Init* method. However, THINK C's version 5.0 implementation of constructors does not provide for arguments, and we utilize two arguments to set the devices address and its direction register. These arguments would have to be provided via global variables, which is poor style. However, the *allocator* can implement the *allocate* procedure in the BCC and the *destructor* can implement the *Terminate* method without problems.

We observe that most I/O devices can be implemented as objects. This makes them suited to object-oriented design of systems, where the device, its software and data, and the mechanical system and analog and digital hardware outside the microcomputer are treated as a single entity able to be replaced or to be debugged as a unit. We do observe, however, that there is loss of both static and dynamic efficiency when we use objects. The objects and methods take up more room in memory, and are slower than straightforward I/O using pointers, as we did for the first four sections of this chapter. When efficiency is needed, that simpler approach is recommended. However, object-oriented I/O has significant advantages supporting clarity, correctness and modularity.

4-6 Conclusions

The parallel I/O device is the most flexible and common I/O device. When designing a parallel I/O device, the first step is to decide on the architecture of the port. Select the address and I/O capability. The hardware can be implemented using simple TTL MSI chips or an LSI chip like the M6821. This chapter showed how to use the popular 74HC244 and 74HC374 medium-scale integrated circuits to implement these ports. This approach is really very simple and is often desired because it uses less board space and cheaper ICs than the other approach discussed; that of using a large-scale parallel I/O chip like the M6821. We saw some I/O software that moved data through a microcomputer, moved data into a buffer, and implemented a traffic light controller using the simple I/O devices. Because timing is important to them, we studied the timing of such program segments. The M6821, M68230 and parallel ports in the M68332 were introduced and shown to be more flexible. These chips are often used in printed circuit card microcomputers that are mass-produced and intended for a wide variety of applications. They can be configured by the appropriate ritual for almost any parallel I/O device. The M6821, for instance, can also be used to implement two I/O devices on one (large) chip rather than on (two) smaller chips. This can be attractive if the devices are readable outputs, because it takes more (small) chips to build both the input and output parts of the device. If the device is changed from input to output under software control, the programmable parallel output chips, are better. The designer has to consider indirection. An indirect I/O technique was presented, which is especially useful for experimenting with most LSI I/O chips but which is usually an order of magnitude slower than direct I/O. A slight variation of this idea using serial I/O was shown to be quite attractive because there are special chips designed to be used this way. A coprocessor is suitable for a 68020 system, and was found to provide about an order of magnitude speedup over direct I/O. We showed how the 683xx can use the floating-point coprocessor chip as an I/O device. Finally, we saw some details on how objects can be used to provide simple parallel and serial port device-independence and I/O redirection.

Programming decisions generally affect clarity and often affect efficiency. I/O devices can be accessed with constant pointers, as in *d=(char*)0x10000;*, with variable pointers, as in *char p=(char*)0x10000; d=*p;*, with vector indexing, as in *char p=(char*)0x10000; dp[0];*, and with pointers to structures, as in *qspiPort->bd=2;* , and by *#define* statements that use one of the above, but provide self-documenting code. We have shown several examples of each. Constant pointers seem to be useful where an I/O port is accessed once or twice. Vector indexing seems to be clearer than variable pointer access, but the latter is useful when a long integer or a pointer is recast. Structure pointer access is very useful for devices with many ports of assorted sizes. Finally, any long program can likely benefit from the intelligent use of *#define* statements to rename these constructs to be meaningful port names.

Objects provide a mechanism to efficiently implement the capabilities of device drivers such as device independence and I/O redirection. They achieve a major fraction of the capabilities of I/O device drivers with a small fraction of the overhead.

The interfacing of a microcomputer to almost any I/O system has been shown to be simple and flexible, using parallel and serial I/O devices. We can use the same approach to designing an IC or an I/O system as we can for studying it, and thus develop an understanding of why it was designed as it was and how it might be used. In the remaining chapters, these techniques are extended to analog interfacing, counters, communications interfacing, and display and magnetic recording chips.

Do You Know These Terms?

See the End of Chapter 1 for Instructions.

input port, output port, I/O port, synchronous port, isolated I/O, input instruction, output instruction, memory-mapped I/O, lock, basic input port, basic output port, readable output port, read address trigger, write address trigger, address register output, address line output, logic-timer control, interpreter, mealy sequential machine, linked list structure, block, template, element, programmable parallel input/output device, parameter pin, control register, control port, initialize, configure, ritual, peripheral interface adapter, reset pin, parallel interface/timer, double-buffering, nasty design problem, direct I/O, indirect I/O, queued serial peripheral interface, exchange, wraparound, long exchange, slave, coprocessor, device-independent, I/O redirection, fire mode, wrap mode.

5

Interrupts and Alternatives

The computer has to be synchronized with the fast or slow I/O device. The two main areas of concern are the amount of data that will be input or output and the type of error conditions that will arise in the I/O system. Given varying amounts of data and different I/O error conditions, we need to decide the appropriate action to be taken by the microcomputer program. This is studied in this chapter.

One of the most important problems in the design of I/O systems is timing. In Section 4-2.1, we saw how data can be put into a buffer from an input device. However, we ignored the problem of synchronizing with the source of the data, so we get a word from the source when it has a word to give us. I/O systems are often quite a bit slower, and are occasionally a bit faster, than the computer. A typewriter may type a fast 30 characters per second, but the computer can send a character to be typed only once every 133,333 memory cycles. So the computer often waits a long time between outputting successive characters to be typed. Behold the mighty computer, able to invert a matrix in a single bound, waiting patiently to complete some tedious I/O operation. On the other hand, some I/O systems, such as hard disks, are so fast that a microcomputer may not take data from them fast enough. Recall that the time from when an I/O system requests service (such as to output a word) until it gets this service (such as having the word removed) is the latency. If the service is not completed within a maximum latency time, the data may be over-written by new data and be lost before the computer can store them.

Synchronization is the technique used to get the computer to supply data to an output device when the device needs data, get data from an input device when the device has some data available, or to respond to an error if ever it occurs. Over ten techniques are used to match the speed of the I/O device to that of the microprocessor. Real-time synchronization is conceptually quite simple; in fact we have already written a real-time program in the previous chapter to synchronize to a traffic light. Gadfly synchronization requires a bit more hardware, but has advantages in speed and software simplicity. Gadfly was actually used in synchronizing to the 68881 and the QSPI. Three more powerful interrupt synchronization techniques – polled, vectored, and real-time – require more hardware. Direct memory access and context switching are faster synchronization mechanisms. Shuttle, indirect, time-multiplexed, and video memories can be used for very fast I/O devices. These synchronization techniques are also discussed in this chapter.

5-1 Synchronization in Slow I/O Devices

We first study the synchronization problem from the I/O device viewpoint, introducing busy/done states and terminology. An example of a paper tape reader, illustrating the collection of data from a tape into a buffer will be used to illustrate the different approaches to I/O synchronization. Paper tape (See Figure 5-1a.) is used in environments like machine shops, whose dust and fumes are hostile to floppy disks.

Data from the data port can be read just as in the previous chapter and will be put into a buffer, as we now discuss. The pattern of holes across a one-inch-wide paper tape corresponds to a byte of data; in each position, a hole is a true value, and the absence of a hole is a false value. Optical or mechanical sensors over each hole position connected to the port pins signal an H (T) if the sensor is over a hole. We will read data from port E in an M68332 (see Figure 5-1b), and from port A in an M68340 (see Figure 5-1c), to realize this collection in 683xx systems. At any time, the values of such a pattern of holes under the paper tape head can be read by an instruction like *d=portA;* in the M68340, or *d=portE;* in the M68332. It can be put in a buffer by a statement like: *for(pnt=buffer; pnt<buffer+0x100;) *(pnt++)=portA;* However, in the last chapter we ignored, and in this chapter we focus on, the problem of getting the data at the right time, when the hardware presents it. The user can advance the paper manually. In this example, we have to read one byte of data from the pattern of holes when the sprocket hole sensor finds a sprocket hole.

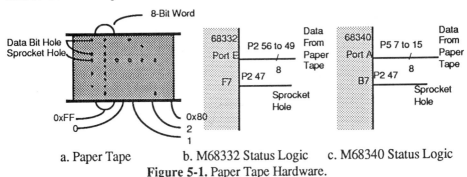

a. Paper Tape   b. M68332 Status Logic   c. M68340 Status Logic

Figure 5-1. Paper Tape Hardware.

A simple but general model (a Mealy sequential machine) of the device is used to describe how we synchronize a computer with an I/O device so it can take data from it or send data to it. (See Figure 5-1.) In this model, the device (or equivalently, its object) has three states: the *IDLE, BUSY,* and *DONE states.* The device is in the IDLE state when no program is using it. When a program begins to use the device, the program puts it in the BUSY state. If the device is IDLE, it is free to be used, and, if BUSY, it is still busy doing its operation. When the device is through with its operation, it enters the DONE state. Often, DONE implies the device has some data in an output port that must be read by the program. The state transition from BUSY to DONE is associated with the availability of output from the device to the program. When the program reads this data, it puts the device into IDLE if it doesn't want to do any more operations, or into BUSY if it wants more operations done. An error condition may also put the device into DONE and should provide some way for the program to distinguish between a successfully completed operation and an error condition. If the program puts the device into BUSY or IDLE; this is called, respectively, *starting* or *stopping* the device. The device enters DONE by itself. This is called *completing* the requested action. When the device is in DONE, the program can get the results of an operation and/or check to see if an error has occurred.

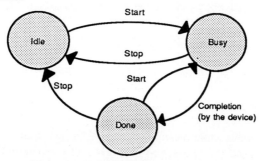

Figure 5-2. State Diagram for I/O Devices.

The IDLE state indicates the paper tape reader is not in use. The user starts the paper tape reader, putting it into the BUSY state. In that state, he or she pulls the paper tape until the next pattern is under the read head that reads a word from the tape. When the sprocket hole is under the tape reader or no paper is left, the reader reads a byte and enters the DONE state. The computer recognizes that when the reader is in the DONE state, data from the pattern should be read through the data port and put into the buffer in the next available location, or that an error condition might exist. Once read, if the program intends to read the next pattern because more words are needed to fill the buffer, it puts the reader back into the BUSY state to restart it. If another pattern should not be read because the buffer is full, the device goes to the IDLE state to stop or to ignore it. If an error condition is signaled, the device is left in the DONE state so it won't be used until the error is read and possibly fixed or reported. To read three bytes, the tape reader might pass through the following states: IDLE, BUSY, DONE, BUSY, DONE, BUSY, DONE, IDLE. (See Figure 5-2.) Data are read each time the paper tape reader goes into the DONE state. Note that there is a difference between the IDLE state and the DONE state. In the DONE state, some data in the input port are ready to be read, and the I/O device is requesting the computer to read them, or an error has rendered the device unusable; while in the IDLE state, nothing is happening, and nothing need be done.

In some I/O systems which do not return values or error messages back to the computer, however, DONE is indistinguishable from IDLE, so only two states are required. Consider a paper tape punch. IDLE corresponds to when it is not in use. BUSY corresponds to when the program has put a byte out to it but the byte has not yet been completely punched. DONE corresponds to when the holes are punched, and another byte of data can be sent out. In this case, with no error conditions to examine in DONE, the DONE and IDLE states are indistinguishable, and we can say the device has just two states: IDLE and BUSY.

A typical microcomputer having several I/O devices has as many busy-done sequential machines, one for each device, and possibly a busy-done sequential machine for every buffer being emptied and filled. The general problem of synchronization is to attend to a device or buffer when it enters its DONE state, in order to get input data, check for and respond to errors, or initiate an activity for future work.

Throughout this section, we will consider the synchronization techniques in simple C procedures and then apply them to I/O objects of the class *TapeReader*, which will be redefined in each section. *TapeReader* will be a subclass of *M68332EF* with *p= 0xfffffa11* for the M68332, and of *M68340A* with *p= 0xffffff011* for the M68340. The general environment of each object will be the following program:

```
char buffer[0x100];
TapeReader *PtRdr; /* (pointer to) tape reader object */
main() {
    (PtRdr =blessA(sizeof(TapeReader), TapeReader);)->Init(0x10000,p);
    for(i=0;(i<0x100) && (PtRdr->error ==0) ;i++) buffer[i] = PtRdr ->Input();
    PtRdr->Terminate();
}
```

There are several ways a microcomputer can synchronize with a slower I/O device, as discussed in this section. Two ways, real-time and gadfly synchronization, are simple but less efficient than the other ways; single, polled, vectored, and real-time interrupts. Each is studied in a subsection, and then the particular synchronization features of the 683xx and parallel I/O chips are discussed in the next section. Six alternatives, which require additional hardware for even faster synchronization, are introduced in Section 5-3.

5-1.1 Real-time Synchronization

Real-time synchronization uses the timing delays in the program to synchronize with the delays in the I/O system; specifically to either equal or exceed the time a device is in BUSY. See Figure 5-3a. Two cases are: (1) using a procedure's process delays, and (2) using a wait loop or other time-consuming statements to "pad" the processor's delay to match or exceed the I/O device's BUSY state time. To illustrate the first case, a simple program *main* shown below that inputs the data from the M68340's port A (or the M68332's port E) picks it up at the rate that the *for* loop executes. If that happens to be the rate at which the paper tape is pulled, and the procedure is started so as to pick up the first pattern of holes, putting it into buffer[0], (a preposterous idea) the processor is synchronized with the device. Because required program statement timing delays already synchronize the processor to the tape reader, we are using real-time synchronization. Assume port A is already configured for input (in the M68332 substitute port E).

```
main() {char buffer[0x100]; int i;
    for(i=0;i<0x100;i++) buffer[i] = portA;
}
```

To illustrate the second case, we insert a delay loop as we did in the traffic light application in Section 4.2. We can modify the procedure as follows:

```
main() {char buffer[0x100]; int i,j;
    for(i=0;i<0x100;i++) {buffer[i] = portA; for(j=0;j<N;j++);}
}
```

The delay loop, *for(j=0;j<N;j++);}* is empirically adjusted, by defining constant *N*, so that the rate that the *for* loop executes is the rate at which the paper tape is pulled. If the procedure is started so as to pick up the first pattern of holes, putting it into buffer[0], (a non-trivial challenge) the processor is synchronized with the device. Because required program statement timing delays already synchronize the processor to the tape reader, we are also using real-time synchronization.

Real-time synchronization can be implemented in objects by using the delay of sending the object a message and other programming delays, or by putting a delay loop inside the *Input* method, as shown below:

```
void M68340A::Input() { int j;
    for(j=0;j<N;j++); return *(char*)chip;
}
```

In real-time synchronization, the device has IDLE, BUSY, and DONE states, but the computer may have no way of reading them from the I/O device. Instead, it starts operations and keeps track of the time in which it expects the device to complete the operation. Busy-done states can be recognized by the program segment being executed in synchronization with the device state. IDLE is any time before we begin reading the tape; the delay loop corresponds to BUSY; and DONE is when *buffer[i] = portA;* is executed. The device is started, and the time it takes to complete its BUSY state is matched by the time a program takes before it assumes the device is in DONE. While an exact match in timing is occasionally needed, usually the microcomputer must wait longer than the I/O device takes to complete its BUSY state. In fact, the program is usually timed for the longest possible time to complete an I/O operation.

Real-time synchronization is considered bad programming by almost all computer scientists. In 16- and 32-bit microcomputers that use high-level languages, real-time synchronization can be messy. Dynamic memories can require refresh cycles, interrupts, and DMA cycles discussed later in this chapter, which can occur at unpredictable times. A cache memory supplying instructions or data can speed up the execution of instructions, thus affecting delays based on their execution. If timing delays are implemented in high-level languages such as a *for* loop in C, the delay time can change when a later version of the compiler or operating system is used. It is difficult to provide a delay of a fixed time by means of delays inherent in instruction execution. The effort in writing the program may be the highest because of the difficulty of precisely tailoring the program to provide the required time delay, as well as being logically correct. This approach is sensitive to errors in the speed of the I/O system. If some mechanical components are not oiled, the I/O may be slower than what the program is made to handle. The program is therefore often timed to handle the worst possible situation and is the slowest of the techniques for synchronizing to an I/O system.

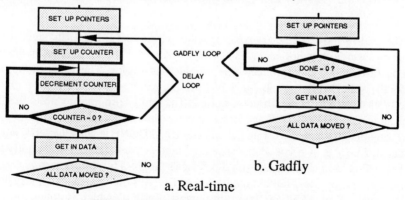

Figure 5-3. Flow charts for Programmed I/O.

However, real-time synchronization requires the least amount of hardware of all the approaches to the synchronization problem. It can be used with a basic input or output device, without the need for further hardware. Real-time synchronization is a practical alternative in some primitive microcomputers that are dedicated to one application, such as in a single-chip microcomputer that implements the traffic light controller discussed in 4-2.2 or a microcomputer that is dedicated to control a printer.

5-1.2 Gadfly Synchronization

The sprocket hole input can be sensed in the *gadfly* synchronization technique to pick up the data exactly when they are available. The program continually "asks" one or more devices what they are doing (such as by continually testing the sprocket hole sensor). This technique is named after the great philosopher, Socrates, who, in the Socratic method of teaching, kept asking the same question until he got the answer he wanted. Socrates was called the "gadfly of Athens" because he kept pestering the local politicians like a pesky little fly until they gave him the answer he wanted (regrettably, they also gave him some poison to drink). This bothering is usually implemented in a loop, called a *gadfly loop*, in which the microcomputer continually inputs the device state of one or more I/O systems until it detects DONE or an error condition in one of the systems. See Figure 5-3b. Gadfly synchronization is often called polled synchronization. However, polling means sampling different people with the same question – not bothering the same person with the same question. Polling is used in interrupt handlers discussed later; in this text, we distinguish between a polling sequence and a gadfly loop.

To illustrate gadfly synchronization, a simple program *main* shown below inputs the data from the M68340's port A (or the M68332's port E) when the sprocket hole just passes under its sensor. To detect that, M68340's port B bit 7 (or the M68332's port F bit 7) is directly connected to the sprocket sensor; a T is read if the sprocket hole is under it. As it changes from F to T, the data are read. See Figures 5-1b and 5-1c. The processor is synchronized with the device to read every row of holes into corresponding elements of the buffer. Assume port A and port B bit 7 are already configured for input (in the M68332 substitute port E for port A and port F bit 7 for port B bit 7).

```
main() {char buffer[0x100]; int i;
    for(i=0;i<0x100;i++) {while (portB>=0); buffer[i] = portA; while (portB < 0); }
}
```

The gadfly loop, *while (portB≥0);* waits while port B bit 7 (its sign bit) is F, while a sprocket hole is not under its sensor. Data are picked up as soon as the test in this loop fails; when the sprocket hole is under its sensor. The gadfly loop, *while (portB<0);* waits while port B bit 7 is T, to prevent the program from picking up another data byte until a new hole is sensed. The gadfly program exhibits the IDLE, BUSY, and DONE states. IDLE and DONE are the same as in real-time synchronization. IDLE is any time before we execute the procedure and DONE is when *buffer[i] = portA;* is executed. BUSY is in effect when executing (either, except the very last) gadfly loop.

The gadfly loop above checks on the device's progress by reading a *status register,* which is an input port that returns the BUSY or DONE state in some way, Usually this state is in a flip-flop called an "interrupt request flip-flop" which is automatically set when the device is done, and is cleared by the program using an address trigger or a clear port. We will see examples of this mechanism in our discussions of the M6821 and M68230. In this very simple example, we merely read the sprocket hole sensor to determine the BUSY-DONE status of the paper tape reader. While this example reduces the status logic to an extreme, it highlights the fundamental idea of a status register; moreover it is a useful technique in monitoring control switches and position sensors.

Gadfly synchronization can be implemented in objects by putting the gadfly loop(s) inside the *Input* method, as shown below. An *Input* method for the M68332 uses PortF in place of PortB.

```
long TapeReader::Input() { char d; /* for the M68340 */
    while (portB>=0); d=*(char*)chip; while (portB < 0); return d;
}
```

While gadfly synchronization is more efficient than real-time synchronization, because the gadfly loop terminates exactly when BUSY is left while the delay loop must delay for the worst-case time the device is in BUSY, real-time synchronization requires no hardware in addition to the basic I/O port, while gadfly synchronization requires hardware to sense when the device is in the BUSY or DONE states. Many of the I/O devices in the 683xx already have this hardware, so that gadfly is clearly better than real-time synchronization for them. Moreover, both techniques tie up the processor in a loop while the device is in BUSY, and that can be a long time for slow I/O devices. The interrupt techniques discussed below can free the processor to do other things while it waits for a device to become DONE.

5-1.3 Single Interrupts

In this section, we consider interrupt hardware and software. *Interrupt* software can be very tricky. Nevertheless, based on what we have learned from the last chapter and the previous sections, we should find interrupt software quite easy to use. At one extreme, some companies actually have a policy never to use interrupts, but instead to use the gadfly technique. At the other extreme, some designers insist on using interrupts just because they are readily available in microcomputers like 683xx systems. We advocate using interrupts when necessary but using simpler techniques whenever possible.

Interrupt techniques can be used to let the I/O system interrupt the processor when it is DONE, so the processor can be doing useful work until it is interrupted. Also, latency times resulting from interrupts can be less than latency times resulting from a large gadfly loop that tests many I/O devices, or a variation of the gadfly approach, whereby the computer executes a procedure, checks the I/O device, next executes another procedure, and then checks the devices, and so on – and that can be an important factor for fast I/O devices. Recall the basic idea of an interrupt from Chapter 1: that a program P currently being executed can be stopped at any point, then a "handler" program D is executed to carry out some task requested by the device and the program P is resumed. The device must have some logic to determine when it needs to have the processor execute the D program, and a wire to the microprocessor to inform it that the device needs service. P must execute the same way whenever and regardless whether D is executed. Therefore, D must somehow save all the information that P needs to resume without error. Hardware saves the registers that cannot be saved easily by software. The interrupt saves the status register and program counter and the RTI instruction restores these registers. A MOVEM instruction can be used to save or restore additional registers or memory words that might be used by D. When D is finished, it must execute some instruction like a subroutine return instruction that resumes P exactly where it left off.

Interrupts can be requested by devices outside the M68332 by the IRQ1 to IRQ7 pins, which are shared by port F bits in the M68332, and the M68340 by the IRQ3, IRQ5, IRQ6 and IRQ7 pins, which are shared by port B bits in the M68340. To use one of these inputs for interrupt requests, the port's assignment bit for that input must be set. While for all levels from 1 to 6 interrupts are requested by a low signal on inputs IRQ 1 to IRQ6, level 7 is special; a level 7 interrupt is *nonmaskable*. It cannot be disabled and it is requested by a falling edge (rather than a low level) on the IRQ7 pin. It has been used as a means to stop a runaway computer, to enable the examination of the stack and other variables to determine why the program went wild.

In this subsection, we will consider a 683xx microcomputer that has just one interrupt (IRQ6). We will examine the use of only that interrupt, considering the sequence of actions leading to an interrupt that counts occurrences of a pattern input form a paper tape reader. Then we will consider the *Init* and *Input* methods for the paper tape reader. We gloss over some details in order to concentrate on the principles of the single interrupt. In the next subsections, the details will be discussed as the multiple interrupt case will be studied, using two techniques called polling and vectored interrupts. These will be simple extensions of the single interrupt case.

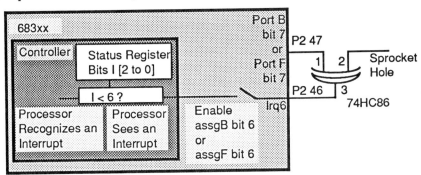

Figure 5-4. Interrupt Request Path.

Inside the 683xx, an interrupt line from the paper tape reader can send a signal to the controller. See Figure 5-4. If the paper tape were pulled though the reader, the sprocket hole signal SH would be a 256-pulse square wave, which is H each time a hole is under the sensor. SH and a parallel port bit B7 (port B bit 7 for the M68340 or port F bit 7 for the M68332) are applied to a 74HC78 exclusive-OR gate, whose output IRQ6 is L if its two inputs are the same. If B7 is H and SH is L, IRQ6 becomes L when SH becomes H. If B7 is L and SH is H, IRQ6 becomes L when SH becomes L.

The seven-step sequence of actions that lead to an interrupt and that service it are outlined below.

1. When the external hardware determines it needs service either to move some data into it or out of it or to report an error, we say an *the device requests an interrupt*. This occurs in the paper tape reader when IRQ6 becomes L.

2. If the IRQ6 pin had been assigned (in the assgB or assgF register) to sense interrupts rather than to be a port I/O bit, we say *IRQ6 interrupts are enabled*.

3. The microprocessor's status register's I[2 to 0] bits are compared to the value 6 for IRQ6. When I is 0, we say the *microprocessor is enabled for all interrupts.* When I is 7, the *microprocessor is masked* (or the *microprocessor is disabled*) for all interrupts (except the non-maskable interrupt). When I is less than 6, we say the *microprocessor is enabled for level 6 interrupts.* When I is greater than or equal to the level 6, the *microprocessor is masked* (or the *microprocessor is disabled,* or the *interrupt is inhibited) for level 6 interrupts.* If the value from (any) device, sent to the controller, is greater than I then we say the *microprocessor sees a request,* or *a request is pending,* and an interrupt will occur, as described below. (These bits I are also controlled by hardware in the next step.)

4. Most microcomputers cannot stop in the middle of an instruction. (The 683xx is capable of processing interrupts to handle page faults in the middle of an instruction, but we will not use this mechanism in this book.) Therefore, if the microprocessor recognizes an interrupt, it *honors an interrupt* at the end of the current instruction. When the 683xx honors an IRQ6 interrupt, it saves the status register and the program counter on the supervisor stack, sets the supervisor bit and clears the trace bits, and loads the long word at 0x78 into the program counter to process this interrupt. Importantly, I[2 to 0] is changed to the device's level, 6, after the former value of it is saved on the stack; it is called the *current processor priority.*

5. Beginning at the address specified by 0x78 is a routine called a *handler.* (When we consider multiple sources of interrupts, we will distinguish between the interrupt handler and the interrupt request handler, but for now we refer to it as a handler.) The handler is like a "subroutine" which performs the work requested by the device. It may move a word between the device and a buffer, or it may report or fix up an error. One of a handler's critically important but easy to overlook functions is that it must explicitly remove the cause of the interrupt (by making the interrupt request IRQ6 H) unless the hardware does that for you automatically.

6. When it is completed, the handler executes an RTE instruction; this restores the status register and program counter to resume the program where it left off.

Some points about the interrupt sequence must be stressed. As soon as it honors an interrupt seen on a line, the 683xx, like most computers, sets I[2 to 0] in the status register to 6 to prevent honoring another interrupt from the same device. If it didn't, the first instruction in the handler would be promptly interrupted – an infinite loop that will fill up the stack. You do not have to worry about returning it to its value before it was changed, because step 6 in the preceding sequence restores the program counter and the status register and its current priority, to the values they had before the interrupt was honored. However, a handler can change that level using a MOVE, AND or OR to status register instruction to permit honoring interrupts, or change the value of I[2 to 0] before the handler is finished. Note that the I/O device is generally still asserting its interrupt request line because it doesn't know what is going on inside the microprocessor. If the RTE is executed or I is otherwise set to a number lower than the devices's level, this same device will promptly interrupt the processor again and again – hanging up the machine. Before the handler executes RTE or changes I, it *must* remove the source of the interrupt! (Please excuse our frustration, but this is so simple yet so much of a problem.)

Section 5-1 Synchronization in Slow I/O Devices

To handle the paper tape reader's interrupts, we need to put the handler's address in the long word at 0x78. The mechanism that puts an interrupt handler's address where the interrupt mechanism needs to find it is specific to THINK C but similar mechanisms will have to be used if you use another compiler. Getting an address of a program segment like an interrupt handler is easier in embedded assembler language than in C. Assume the handler starts at an address whose (assembler language) label is *@0*. If a program's register variable such as *hndaddr* is a pointer to an integer then the assembler language statement *asm{lea @0,hndaddr}* puts the address of an assembler language label *@0* (using relative addressing) into an address register and *(int **)0x78 = hndaddr;* puts that address into location 0x78, where the interrupt mechanism needs to find it. The label *@0* is local to a procedure, being unknown outside it, so the label and the statement *asm{ lea @0,hndaddr }* must be in the same procedure; the handler can be put in an expression in *if(0) { }*, or alternatively it can be put after a *return* statement or a *while(1);* infinite loop, in a procedure, so it is never actually executed as part of that procedure. In this text, we show the handler's entry point with a triangle and write the handler on a gray background. Note also that a handler must end in RTE, which is not generated by any C statement; it must be generated by embedded assembler language.

We initially assume that all interrupts are disabled (I is 7). The *main* procedure will set up the pointer to the buffer, which will be used in the interrupt handler to collect the data, then assign port B in the M68340 (port F in the M68332) so its most significant bit is an output bit, and so that the next bit is assigned to be IRQ6. Then the handler address is put into 0x78. We then enable level 6 interrupts by changing I to 5, and wait for the buffer's pointer to reach its end. Then we disable interrupts and exit.

The strategy used in this paper tape reader is to output a value on the parallel port's bit 7 B7 which is the value on the sprocket hole SH that we wish to wait for and be interrupted when that arrives. While we wait for that, IRQ6 is H. When that value arrives and IRQ6 goes L, we request an IRQ6 interrupt; in the handler we invert B7 to make IRQ6 go H (remove the source of the interrupt) and exit the handler. Note that we get interrupts both when SH falls and when it rises. We collect a byte of data into the buffer when SH rises, which is when B7 was H; we do nothing when SH falls.

We first implement the M68340 paper tape reader using the interrupt technique. The M68340 has a control register at 0xfffff006 (AVL) discussed in the next section; we need to put 0x40 in it to handle a single interrupt on IRQ6 using the vector at 0x78.

```
char buffer[0x100], *p;
main() { register int *hndlr;        /* for the M68340 */
    p=buffer; /* set pointer */ assgB=0x40; dirB=0x80; /*asgn irq6, PortB 7 output*/
    *(char*)0xfffff006 |=0x40; /* set (bit6) IRQ6 autovector */
    asm{lea @0,hndlr} *(int **)0x78=hndlr; /* put level 6 handler address in 0x78 */
    asm{and #0xfdff,sr} /* make I[2 to 0] 5 to enable interrupts above level 5 */
    while (p<(buffer+0x100)); /* wait for the buffer to fill up */
    asm{or #0x200,sr} return; /* disarm interrupts and exit */
 ▶  asm{@0 movem.l d0/a0,-(a7)}/* sprocket int hnd */
    if(portB&0x80) *p++=portA; portB ^=0x80;
    if( p==(buffer+0x100) ) assgB=0;
    asm {movem.l (a7)+,d0/a0 } asm {rte}
}
```

Note that the interrupt handler saved some registers and restored them. These are determined empirically. We compile the procedure and download it into an M68340 system, and then disassemble it. We save all the registers we find used in the handler.

The M68332 paper tape reader procedure *main* using interrupts will be quite similar to the M68340 procedure above. We substitute port E for port A and port F for port B. However, the M68332 uses the chip select hardware (CS6) to generate autovectors which we use in this simple interrupt example. These will be explained in a later subsection. We have to include these *pinAssign, baseAssign,* and *optionAssign* macros shown in the program, rather than initializing the AVL register.

```
main() {  register int *hndlr;     /* for the M68332 */
    assgF=0x40; dirF=0x80; /*asgn irq6, PortF 7 output*/
    pinAssign(cs7,byte);baseAssign(7,0xffffff,k2); /* to get IRQ6 interrupts at 0x78 */
    optionAssign(7,rd+upper+ds,fast,0,6+avec); /* we have to set up autovector 6 */
    asm{lea @0,hndlr} *(int **)0x78=hndlr; /* put level 6 handler address in 0x78 */
    asm{and #0xfdff,sr} /* make I[2 to 0] 5 to enable interrupts above level 5 */
    while (p<(buffer+0x100)); /* wait for the buffer to fill up */
    asm{or #0x200,sr} return; /* disarm interrupts and exit */
►  asm{@0 movem.l d0/a0,-(a7)}/* sprocket int hnd */
    if(portF&0x80) *p++=portE; portF^=0x80;
    if( p==(buffer+0x100) ) assgF=0;
    asm {movem.l (a7)+,d0/a0 } asm {rte}
}
```

The procedures above show some of the mechanisms used in interrupt handlers, but these examples are poor examples because the program wastes its time gadflying on the buffer pointer. Unless the microprocessor can do something else in the meantime, gadfly synchronization would be simpler, have lower latency, and be easier to debug. Interrupt handlers generally use queues to pick up the data while the microprocessor is doing something else. The object-oriented interrupt handler below will illustrate the use of queues. We use an object *Q* of the class *Queue* defined in Section 2-3.3; (a pointer to) it is declared in the class *TapeReader,* shown with the simple *Input* method below.

```
struct TapeReader:M68340A /* for the M68340 */
    { Queue *Q; void Init(long,unsigned), Terminate (void); long Input(void); };
void TapeReader::Input() { while (Q-> Qlen); errorl=Q->Error(); return Q->Pull(); }
```

The *Init* method has to initialize the queue (to 10 bytes), and initialize the device and interrupt handler as the procedure main did above. Some observations follow *Init*.

```
long SaveA4;
long TapeReader::Init() { register int *hndlr;
    inherited::Init(p,0);(Q=blessA(sizeof(Queue),Queue))->InitQ(10);
    assgB=0x40; dirB=0x80; *(char*)0xffff006 l=0x40;
    asm { move.l a4,SaveA4} /* save pointer to access instance variables later */
    asm{lea @0,hndlr} *(int **)0x78=hndlr; asm{and #0xfdff,sr} return;
►  asm{@0 movem.l d0/a0/a4,-(a7)} asm{move.l SaveA4,A4}
    if(portB&0x80) Q->Push( portA ); portB ^=0x80;
    asm {movem.l (a7)+,d0/a0 /a4} asm {rte}
}
```

Notice the use of address register A4. The handler uses A4 whenever an object is referenced in it. Therefore, it must be saved and restored along with the other registers used in the handler, and loaded from global variable *SaveA4* (global variables are always accessible via A5, even in interrupt handlers) which was saved when A4 pointed to the object (such as in *Init*). If there are several objects (e.g. *TapeReader, Kbd, AtoD,....*) used in interrupt handlers, use a different pointer (e.g. *TapeReaderA4, KbdA4, AtoDA4,....*) for each, or use a vector *SaveA4[3]* and use a different element (e.g. *SaveA4[0], SaveA4[1], SaveA4[2],....*) for each.

The *Terminate* method disables the interrupt. If you do not do that, more paper tape or noise can generate more interrupts and the paper tape's queue will overrun.

void TapeReader::Terminate (){ assgB ^= ~ 0x40; / disable IRQ6 interrupts */ }*

The M68332 object-oriented interrupt handler follows the same strategy, but substitutes ports E and F for ports A and B, and uses M68332's autovector mechanism.

struct TapeReader:M68332EF / for the M68332 */*
    *{ Queue *Q; void Init(long,unsigned), Terminate (void); long Input(void); };*

void TapeReader::Input() { while (Q-> Qlen); error!=Q->Error(); return Q->Pull(); }

long SaveA4;

*long TapeReader::Init() { register int *hndlr;*
    pinAssign(cs7,byte);baseAssign(7,0xffffff,k2); / to get IRQ6 interrupts at 0x78 */*
    optionAssign(7,rd+upper+ds,fast,0,6+avec); / we have to set up autovector 6 */*
    inherited:: Init(p,0); (Q=blessA(sizeof(Queue),Queue))->InitQ(10);
    assgF=0x40; dirF=0x80; asm {move.l a4,SaveA4} / save instance variable ptr */*
    *asm{lea @0,hndlr} *(int **)0x78=hndlr; asm{and #0xfdff,sr} return;*
    ➤ *asm{@0 movem.l d0/a0/a4,-(a7)} asm{move.l SaveA4,A4}*
    if(portF&0x80) Q->Push(portE); portF^=0x80;
    asm {movem.l (a7)+,d0/a0 /a4} asm {rte}

}

void TapeReader::Terminate (){ assgF ^= ~ 0x40; / disable IRQ6 interrupts */ }*

As in previous discussions of synchronization methods, we will discuss the busy-done states of the devices using the interrupt synchronization method. The paper tape reader is IDLE until after the *Init* method sets it up to input *chars*, and after the *Terminate* method disables interrupts from the paper tape reader. It becomes BUSY after the *Init* method sets it up. The DONE state is entered when every other interrupt occurs and data are moved from port A or port E to the input queue. When the data are moved, the device goes into the BUSY state.

A very important issue about interrupts is the correct implementation of critical sections. A *critical section* is part of a procedure or method, which, if interrupted, can cause incorrect results. An example, in *Queue's Pull* method called by *TapeReader's Input* method, might be the statement *if((Qlen--)==0) error=1;* If this is coded in assembler language so that *Qlen* is copied from its memory location to a register like D0, decremented there, and put back, if an interrupt occurs between the time *Qlen* is read until it is rewritten and the interrupt handler's *Queue Push* method increments *Qlen*, then the interrupted program will overwrite the value changed by the handler, putting its decremented value in *Qlen*, thus cancelling the change made by the handler. For instance, if *Qlen* were 3, indicating there are 3 words in the output queue, and the

Input method pulled a word, it would decrement *Qlen* to 2. But if, while *Qlen* is effectively moved to D0, an interrupt occurs and the interrupt handler saw a request to output a word for that interrupt request, it would push a word. It would increment the value of *Qlen* that was in memory, changing it from 3 to 4. When the interrupted program that was decrementing Q->Qlen is resumed, it will write the number 2 in the memory variable *Qlen*. That is an error because there are now 3 words in the queue, not 2. Subsequent size checking will be faulty. The chances of this happening are small. But if you believe in Murphy's law, such an error will occur at the worst possible time. Therefore, to write correct programs, you must avoid any possibility of such an error.

Critical sections exist whenever a variable changed in an interrupt handler is changed (in a register) in the critical section. They are correctly implemented by inhibiting all interrupts that can affect the variables in these sections. When a critical section is being executed, the current processor priority $I[2 \text{ to } 0]$ is made equal to or larger than the priority of any interrupts whose handlers change the variable in the critical section, and when it is left, the current processor priority is restored to what it was before the critical section was entered. To change $I[2 \text{ to } 0]$ in a C procedure, assembler language statements AND #K,sr, OR #K,sr, or MOVE #K,sr have to be embedded in C, and these privileged instructions must be executed in the supervisor state. Thus, any program having a critical section should be executed in supervisor state.

We must look at the assembler language generated by a C procedure to determine if a variable is actually moved to a register. In the examples above, the variable Q->Qlen is decremented in memory as in SUBQ.W #1,8(A4). Because an instruction cannot be interrupted until it is completed, there can be no error and there is no critical section.

We distinguish between enabling and arming interrupts, even though our example does not show this distinction. Most I/O devices will use an interrupt request flip-flop, IRQ, that is set when the device requests service. There are two switches, the arm/disarm in the path from the device to the IRQ flip-flop, and the enable/disable in the path from IRQ to the processor. A disarmed interrupt is completely ignored. A device is disarmed when it will externally request an interrupt but you are not going to honor it. A disabled interrupt is postponed but not ignored. Disable an interrupt if it can't be honored right now but will be honored later. Disarming prevents IRQ from becoming set. Disabling takes place, in effect, after IRQ is set, so it is still set if the device or the microcomputer is later enabled. However, IRQ can be cleared just before the interrupt is enabled. This *software disarm* is occasionally necessary because we do not know the state of such a flip-flop when we enable the interrupt, so we must prevent the possibility of getting an interrupt right away before we are expecting it.

This example shows that interrupts are really not that complicated. A few more techniques are needed to handle more than one interrupt on a line, but these are also quite simple, as we now show.

5-1.4 Polled Interrupts

The handlers become a bit more complicated for multiple interrupts. The *interrupt handler* just finds out which interrupt request needs service. Each different interrupt has its own *interrupt request handler* that actually services the interrupt. In the previous section where there is but one interrupt that can cause a handler, whose address is in 0x78, to be executed, these two handlers merge into one (or one can say the interrupt handler becomes trivial or disappears). In this case, when the interrupt handler, whose address is in 0x78, is executed, it *polls* the possible interrupts to see which one caused the interrupt. The polling program checks each possible interrupt, one at a time, in *priority* order, highest priority interrupt request first, until it finds a device that requested service, and then it jumps to, or calls, the device handler for it.

To extend our running example in order to show techniques for polled interrupts, we will contrive an unrealistic but illustrative system that has two devices, one of which is our paper tape reader and the other of which will count the number of sprocket holes by means of the interrupt generated when SH falls, as the sprocket hole passes out of the sensor. This counter, similar to frequency and voltage meters, simply maintains a count, which is read and cleared whenever input is requested from the device. Of course, this example would be more practical if the second device counted some other events than sprocket holes, but that would take more hardware, whose description would get in the way of the study of synchronization techniques. When an interrupt occurs, we will have to determine whether we will pick up data to be put into the buffer or queue, or increment the count. We have found it the to have the IRQ6 interrupt handler call procedures which are the device handlers, which are normal C procedures.

For our simpler main procedure, we will assume that the buffer is to be filled with data from the paper tape and that the count of the number of holes is to be read at the end of the program. This procedure is a simple extension of the single interrupt procedure:

```
char buffer[0x100], *p; long count;
main() { register int *hndlr;       /* for the M68340 */
    p=buffer; /* set pointer */ assgB=0x40; dirB=0x80; /*asgn irq6, PortB 7 output*/
    *(char*)0xffffff006 |=0x40; /* set (bit6) IRQ6 autovector */
    asm{lea @0,hndlr} *(int **)0x78=hndlr; /* put level 6 handler address in 0x78 */
    asm{and #0xfdff,sr} /* make I[2 to 0] 5 to enable interrupts above level 5 */
    while (p<(buffer+0x100)); /* wait for the buffer to fill up */
    asm{or #0x200,sr} return; /* disarm interrupts and exit */
    asm{@0 movem.l d0/a0,-(a7)}/*  IRQ6 interrupt handler */
    if(portB&0x80) moveData();   else incCount();
    asm {movem.l (a7)+,d0/a0 } asm {rte}
}

void moveData(){ *p++=portA; portB &=~0x80; if( p == (buffer+0x100) ) assgB=0; }
void incCount(){ count++; portB |=0x80; } /* device handler for the event counter */
```

Note that the IRQ6 interrupt handler saved some registers and restored them as in the paper tape interrupt handler. However, it actually just determines whether to enter the paper tape reader device handler or the counter device handler. Generally, the interrupt handler polls the devices in an *if ... else if ... else ...* like that shown in this handler. (See Figure 5-5.) Device handlers do what is required by the devices. This paper tape interrupt handler reads data into the buffer and this counter interrupt handler increments the count. Moreover, device handlers clear the source of the interrupt that they service. In our example, *moveData* clears bit B7 and *incCount* sets bit B7. They return to the IRQ6 handler, which has the RTE instruction, which resumes the interrupted program.

The M68332 paper tape reader procedure *main* using interrupts substitute port E for port A, port F for port B, and chip select CS7's for AVL's initialization.

```
main() { register int *hndlr;  /* for the M68332 */
    pinAssign(cs7,byte);baseAssign(7,0xffffff,k2); /* to get IRQ6 interrupts at 0x78 */
    optionAssign(7,rd+upper+ds fast,0,6+avec); /* we have to set up autovector 6 */
    asm{lea @0,hndlr} *(int **)0x78=hndlr; /* put level 6 handler address in 0x78 */
    assgF=0x40; dirF=0x80; asm{and #0xfdff,sr} /*asgn irq6, PortF 7 out, enable int.*/
    while (p<(buffer+0x100)); /* wait for the buffer to fill up */
    asm{or #0x200,sr} return; /* disarm interrupts and exit */
```

> ```
  asm{@0 movem.l d0/a0,-(a7)}/* IRQ6 interrupt handler */
    if(portB&0x80) moveData();   else incCount();
    asm {movem.l (a7)+,d0/a0 } asm {rte}
```

```
}
```

```
void moveData() {
  *p++=portE;
  portF &=~0x80;
  if(p == (buffer+0x100) assgF=0;
}
```

Figure 5-5. Flow Chart for Interrupt Polling.

```
void incCount()
  { count++; portE |=0x80; }
```

The polling routine for polled interrupt objects can be put in the *Init* method of (only) the first device that is opened, and send messages to each *Hndlr()* method using an *if(O1->Hndlr1() || O2->Hndlr2() || ...*) statement. For example, the tape reader may have the two interrupts to read the tape when the sprocket hole is entered and to count when it has left. For each handler method such as *O1::Hndlr1()*, if its device caused the interrupt, it removes the interrupt source and returns 1, otherwise it returns 0. Note that *if((O1&&O1->Hndlr1()) || (O2&&O2->Hndlr2()) || ...*) sends messages to methods from left to right until one returns true. Assuming object pointers *O1, O2* are initially clear, testing a pointer for zero before calling the interrupt method prevents calling it before it is initialized. Note that we do not save A4 in *saveA4* in *Init* because sending a message to a method sets up A4. However, the interrupt handler saves and restores A4 because sending a *moveData* or *IncCount* message to *TpRdr* changes A4.

```
long TapeReader::Init() { /* for the M68340 */
    inherited::Init(p,0);(Q=blessA(sizeof(Queue),Queue))->InitQ(10);assgB=0x40;
    dirB=0x80;*(char*)0xffffff006 |=0x40;
    asm{lea @0,hndlr} *(int **)0x78=hndlr; asm{and #0xfdff,sr} return;
```

> ```
  asm{@0 movem.l d0/a0/a4,-(a7)}/* IRQ6 interrupt handler */
    if((TpRdr&&TpRdr->moveData()) || (TpRdr&&TpRdr->IncCount()));
    asm {movem.l (a7)+,d0/a0/a4} asm {rte}
```

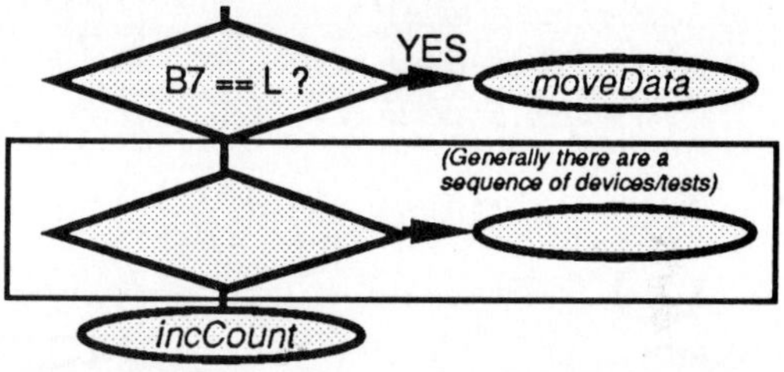

```
}
```

```
TapeReader::moveData(){
    if(portB&0x80) return 0;
    *p++=portA; portB &=~0x80; if( p == (buffer+0x100) ) assgB=0; return 1;
}
```

```
TapeReader:: incCount(){count++; portB |=0x80; } /* device handler counts events */
```

The M68332 object-oriented interrupt handler is similar, but substitutes port E for port A, port F for port B, and M68332's chip select autovector mechanism for AVEC.

```
long TapeReader::Init() { /* for the M68332 */
    inherited::Init(p,0);(Q=blessA(sizeof(Queue),Queue))->InitQ(10);assgF=0x40; dirF=0x80;
    pinAssign(cs7,byte);baseAssign(7,0xffffff,k2); /* to get IRQ6 interrupts at 0x78 */
    optionAssign(7,rd+upper+ds,fast,0,6+avec); /* we have to set up autovector 6 */
    asm{lea @0,hndlr} *(int **)0x78=hndlr; asm{and #0xfdff,sr} return;
    asm{@0 movem.l d0/a0,-(a7)}/* IRQ6 interrupt handler */
    if(TapeReader->moveData()  || TapeReader->IncCount());
    asm {movem.l (a7)+,d0/a0 } asm {rte}
}
TapeReader::moveData(){
    if(portF&0x80) return 0;
    *p++=portE; portF &=~0x80; if( p == (buffer+0x100) ) assgF=0; return 1;
}
TapeReader:: incCount(){count++; portF |=0x80; } /* device handler counts events */
```

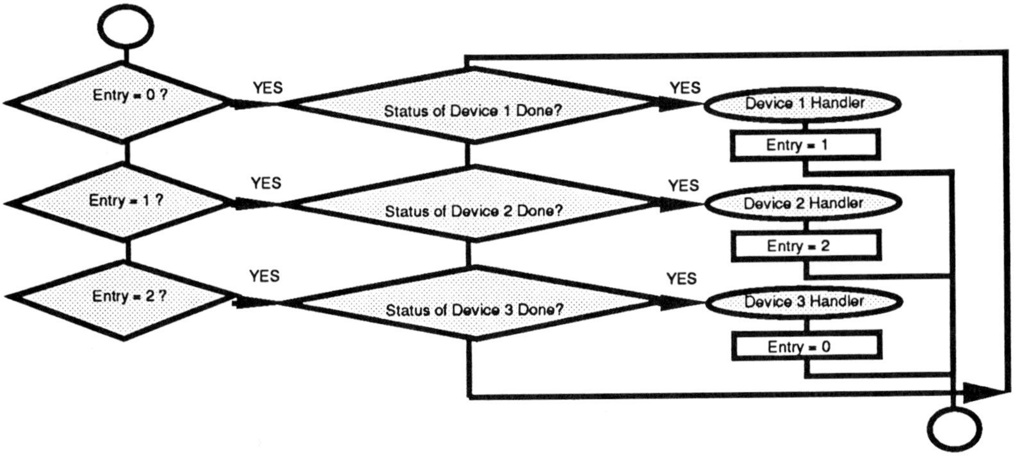

Figure 5-6. Flow Chart for Round-robin Interrupt Polling.

The polling technique just described checks the interrupt requests in priority order. The program should first check the interrupt requests that need service fastest. The first interrupt flag bit tested in the polling sequence should be associated with the fastest or the most critical I/O system. Lower priority interrupt requests are handled after the higher priority interrupt request handlers clear the interrupt source that masks the lower priority interrupt, all of which happens only after the higher priority interrupt is fully handled. An alternative scheme is called a *round-robin* priority scheme. Here, the polling program is arranged as an infinite program loop. When the ith interrupt request in the priority order gets an interrupt and is serviced, the i+1th interrupt request assumes the highest priority; and whenever an interrupt occurs, the polling program starts checking the i+1th interrupt request first. A round-robin polling handler is shown below, and its flow chart is given in Figure 5-6. A global variable *entry* determines which interrupt request bit to test first. It is set by the last interrupt that was honored, so that the interrupt request below it will be tested first when the next interrupt occurs.

Chapter 5 – Interrupts and Alternatives

> ▶ *asm{@0 movem.l d0-d2/a0/a1,-(a7)}*
> *l1 : switch (entry) {*
> *case 0: if (StatusRegister1&Done) {hndll1(); entry = 1; break;}*
> *case 1: if(StatusRegister2&Done) {hndll2(); entry = 2; break;}*
> *case 2: if(StatusRegister3&Done) {hndll3(); entry = 0; break;}*
> *entry=0; goto l1;*
> *}*
> *asm{movem.l d0-d2/a0/a1,-(a7)} asm {rte}*

Polling in the same priority order is useful when some interrupt requests clearly need service faster than others. Democratic round-robin priority is especially useful if some interrupt request tends to hog the use of the computer by frequently requesting interrupts.

5-1.5 Vectored Interrupts

The previous example shows how multiple interrupts can be handled by polling them in the interrupt handler. Polling may take too much time for some interrupt requests that need service quickly. A *vectored interrupt* technique can be used to replace the interrupt handler software by a hardware device, so that the interrupt request handler is entered almost as soon as the device requests an interrupt.

The basis of vectored interrupts in the 683xx is that there is a seven-valued signal within the chip and seven pins IRQ1 to IRQ7 on which an interrupt can be requested. Internal devices like the M68332 QSPI have a LEVEL register, they make this internal signal its LEVEL register value, and external devices assert one of the IRQ pins low to request an interrupt of level ℓ. When an interrupt is honored in step three (Section 5-1.3), the 683xx encodes ℓ as an "address"; the interrupting device responds by asserting a signal AVEC or by sending the value of its VECTOR register. This produces an *address vector*, which gives the actual address of the routine that handles the interrupt, in a manner discussed below. If different interrupt requests are attached to different IRQ lines or have different VECTOR register values, their handlers are immediately started when the interrupt occurs. Thus, the interrupts are vectored to their handlers. The 683xx's interrupt vectors are located in low memory as shown in Table 5-1. The *vector number*, multiplied by 4, gives the long word *vector address,* which should contain the location of the first instruction of the handler.

The 683xx has two classes of vectored interrupts – autovectored and explicitly vectored. *Explicitly vectored* interrupts utilize a VECTOR register in the I/O device. If an I/O device has such a register, then when it requests an interrupt, VECTOR is "read" back to the 683xx when ℓ is sent as an "address". I/O devices internal to the 683xx, such as the QSPI, utilize a VECTOR register, and thus belong to this class. The SIM chip select module can decode the level ℓ for external I/O devices to make them "read" back their VECTOR value. The vector address at VECTOR << 4 is put into the program counter. Explicitly vectored interrupts use *User Interrupts* ($64 \leq$ VECTOR ≤ 255); the addresses of their handlers would thus be in locations 0x100 to 0x3ff. An example of explicitly vectored interrupts appears in the next subsection.

Autovectored interrupts do not have this VECTOR register, but their interrupt level determines their vector address, as shown in Table 5-1. If a device interrupt level is level 6, then its vector number is 30 and its handler's address is at 0x78.

Table 5-1. Exception Vectors in the 683xx.

Vector Number	Vector Address	Description
0	0	Reset - Initial A7
-	4	Reset - Initial PC
2	8	Bus Error
3	0xC	Address Error
4	0x10	Illegal Instruction
5	0x14	Zero Divide
6	0x18	CHK Instruction
7	0x1C	TRAPV Instruction
8	0x20	Privilege Violation
9	0x24	Trace
10	0x28	Line $A Emulator
11	0x2C	Line $F Emulator
12	0x30	Hardware Breakpoint
14	0x38	Format Error
15	0x3C	Uninitialized Interrupt
24	0x60	Spurious Interrupt
25	0x64	Level 1 Interrupt
26	0x68	Level 2 Interrupt
27	0x6C	Level 3 Interrupt
28	0x70	Level 4 Interrupt
29	0x74	Level 5 Interrupt
30	0x78	Level 6 Interrupt
31	0x7C	Level 7 Interrupt
32-47	0x80-0xBF	TRAP Instructions
64-255	0x100-0x3FF	User Interrupt

In the M68340, bits of the control register at 0xfffff006, AVL, determine whether each IRQ uses autovector or is explicitly vectored. If bit i is 1, IRQi is autovectored.

In the M68332, the SIM chip select module can be used to acknowledge autovector interrupts. CS7 will acknowledge level 6 interrupts if the macros below are executed.

pinAssign(cs7,byte); baseAssign(7,0xffffff,k2); /* match 1st argument in all macros */
optionAssign(7,rd+upper+ds,fast,0,6+avec); /* acknowledge autovector level 6 */

The leftmost argument of each macro should match as discussed in Section 3-3.3. The rightmost *optionAssign* argument specifies that CS7 will acknowledge level 6 interrupts and will assert AVEC internally. Other macro arguments should be copied directly from this example. When a level 6 interrupt is honored, the long word at location 0x78 will be put in the program counter to begin execution of the handler.

We illustrate the use of autovectored interrupts by implementing an *X-10 decoder*. The controllers and modules, originally designed and sold by BSR Inc. to control lamps and appliances in the home by means of a signal sent over household 110 volt 60Hz "power wiring", have lately been distributed by Radio Shack and Sears. One or more controllers, costing about $20, and up to 16 modules, costing about $10, are plugged into power wiring sockets, without the need for any other wiring. A controller sends commands as bursts of 100 KHz signals over the power wiring to the modules. One bit is sent each half-cycle of the *60Hz* signal. An F bit is no burst, and a T bit is three 100

KHz bursts. We can build a detector, described in Figure 6-3, which outputs a squared-up *60Hz* wave and a *signal* which is an L only when a 100KHz burst is present; it will output the signals shown in Figure 5-7a for a T followed by an F bit. Figure 6-3c is used to derive *signal*. Figure 6-3b's +12 volt power is obtained from the BSR module's chip (PICO78570) pin 2, its GndA from pin 18, and its Sig from pin 11. The +5 and GndB are derived from the 683xx supply, and the output is the *60Hz* signal.

The program uses the exclusive-OR gate as we did for the sprocket signal in the paper tape reader. The *60Hz* and *signal* waveforms, shown in Figure 5-7a, are applied to exclusive-OR gates (74HC85) to generate IRQ6 and IRQ5 interrupts. The IRQ6 *signal* interrupt handler is to increment *tickCount* each time *signal* either rises or falls. The IRQ5 *60Hz* interrupt handler is to increment *hist[tickCount]* and then clear *tickCount*. These handlers interrupt the main program which is gadflying on *hist[0]*, the number of F bits found, until it reaches 1200. During the ~ 10 seconds this takes, you should press a controller button to send a message, to count the number of *tickCount*s in each *60Hz* half-cycle in the message.

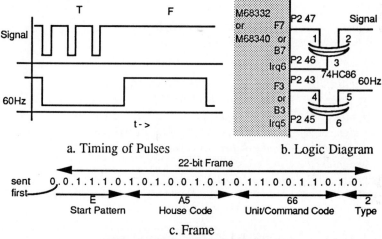

a. Timing of Pulses   b. Logic Diagram

c. Frame

Figure 5-7. X-10 Code Receiver.

The modules are identified by a "house" and a "unit" code, by 16-position rotary switches on the module, and the controller is identified by a "house" code, by 16-position rotary switches on the controller. The house codes, from "A" to "P", are generally the same for the controller and all the modules in the same house; a different house code is to be used by other houses that share the same power wiring. Each module in the house is assigned a different unit code. The controller buttons select a unit number and give commands. For instance, by pressing the buttons "1" and "on", you can turn on module 1. Pressing the "1" button sends a message, and pressing the "on" button sends a message. Each message is a 22-bit frame which is sent twice for reliability; a frame consists of a start pattern (0xe), an 8-bit house code, an 8-bit unit or command code, and a 2-bit type code (Figure 5-7c). We discuss the decoding of this frame later.

We first implement a program to count the number *tickCount* of *signal* pulses that occur in a 60 Hz half-cycle period. Each such period, element *hist[tickCount]* is incremented, until *hist[0]* reaches 1200 (~ 10 seconds). This gives us a *histogram* of the *signal* to determine its quality. (This is a nice experiment to see an interrupt request on an oscilloscope, to see the latency to handle it, and to see handling it to remove the source of the interrupt. However, the 16-channel M68332 TPU and 2-channel M68340 Timer can interrupt on *signal* edges without any additional hardware.) The M68340 procedure is shown first, then the M68332 procedure is shown for histograms.

```
int tickCount,hist[10]; /* global variables used in interrupt handlers */
main() { register int *hndlr; /* for the M68340 */
        assgB=0x60; dirB=0x88; /*asgn irq6, irq5, Port B 7, 3 output*/
        *(char*)0xffff006 |=0x60; /* set (bit6) IRQ6 IRQ5 autovector */
        asm{lea @0,hndlr} *(int **)0x74=hndlr; /* put level 5 handler address in 0x74 */
        asm{lea @1,hndlr} *(int **)0x78=hndlr; /* put level 6 handler address in 0x78 */
        asm{and #0xfcff,sr} /* make I[2 to 0] 4 to enable interrupts above level 4 */
        while(hist[0]< 1200); /* gadfly on count of F bits for about 10 seconds */
        assgB=0; asm{or #0x300,sr} return; /* disarm interrupts and exit */
    asm{@0 movem.l d0/a0,-(a7)}/* 60 Hz int hnd, level 5 portB 3 */
    portB ^=8 if(tickCount<10) hist[tickCount]++;
    tickCount=0; asm{movem.l (a7)+,d0/a0} asm {rte}

    asm{ @1 } /* X10 interrupt handler, level 6, B 7 */
    portB ^=0x80; tickCount++; asm { rte}

}
```

```
int tickCount,hist[10]; /* global variables used in interrupt handlers */
main() { register int *hndlr; /* for the M68332 */
        assgF=0x60; dirF=0x88; /*asgn irq6, irq5, PortF 7, 3 output*/
        pinAssign(cs6,byte); baseAssign(6,0xffffff,k2);
        optionAssign(6,rd+upper+ds fast,0,5+avec); /* autovector 5 */
        pinAssign(cs7,byte);baseAssign(7,0xffffff,k2);
        optionAssign(7,rd+upper+ds fast,0,6+avec); /* autovector 6 */
        asm{lea @0,hndlr} *(int **)0x74=hndlr; /* put level 5 handler address in 0x74 */
        asm{lea @1,hndlr} *(int **)0x78=hndlr; /* put level 6 handler address in 0x78 */
        asm{and #0xfcff,sr} /* make I[2 to 0] 4 to enable interrupts above level 4 */
        while(hist[0]< 1200); /* gadfly on count of F bits for about 10 seconds */
        assgF=0; asm{or #0x300,sr} return; /* disarm interrupts and exit */
    asm{@0 movem.l d0/a0,-(a7)}/* 60 Hz int hnd, level 5, cs 6, portF 3 */
    port F ^=8; if(tickCount<10) hist[tickCount]++;
    tickCount=0; asm{movem.l (a7)+,d0/a0} asm {rte}

    asm{ @1 } /* X10 interrupt handler, level 6, chip select 7, F 7 */
    portF^=0x80; tickCount++; asm { rte}

}
```

Main's first line sets up port B's or port F's assignment register so that bits 5 and 6 are used instead as IRQ5 and IRQ6 interrupt inputs, and the port's direction port is initialized so bits 3 and 7 are outputs. Note that this particular device uses two vectored interrupts; we therefore put two handlers in the same procedure *main* (or the same object's *Init* method). The next lines set up autovectoring for IRQ5 and IRQ6. The next two lines set up the addresses of the handlers, and the next line enables level 5 and level 6 interrupts by changing the current priority I[2 to 0] from 7 to 4, then gadflies until *hist[0]* reaches 1200. Interrupts are then disarmed and disabled, and *main* terminates.

Note the interrupt handlers below the *return* statement. The last two lines handle autovector level 6 interrupts, and are entered when IRQ6 becomes low. Besides incrementing *tickCount,* it complements port F bit 3; by means of the exclusive-OR gate this complements IRQ6 which removes the source of the interrupt. This interrupt then occurs on either a rising or falling edge of *signal,* so *tickCount* is the number of either rising or falling edges that have occurred since it was last cleared. The *60Hz* interrupt handler, shown above the *signal* interrupt handler, similarly is entered upon either rising or falling edges of the *60Hz* waveform, and that interrupt is removed by complementing port F bit 7. In it, we increment the *tickCount* element of *hist* (provided that *tickCount* is less than the size of *hist*) and then we clear *tickCount.*

The previous example uses two different vectored interrupts. Note that if a *60Hz* edge is detected and its handler is entered, the current priority I[2 to 0] is set to 5, which still allows honoring a level 6 *signal* edge interrupt. Higher levels should thus be used for higher precedence interrupts. The output bit and exclusive-OR gate illustrates the concept of removing the source of the interrupt in a more general sense than earlier examples, which merely cleared a status flip-flop to remove the source of the interrupt.

A class *X10Device* can be developed from the histogram program described above. We assume that M68332 chip selects or M68340 AVL have been initialized before this device is used, to autovector 5 and 6, as shown in the *main* procedure above. (They should be initialized in the reset handler.) The *signal* interrupt handler increments *tickCount* as before, but the *60Hz* handler's second line shifts the T (1) or F (0) bits leftward into a long word *Frame* to collect a 22-bit frame (Figure 5-7c). If ~ 0 edges occur, the bit is an F, and if ~ 6 edges, a T. The next two lines maintain the global variable *bitCount,* indicating the number of bits collected. If *bitCount* is 0, indicating no message is present, it is left to be 0 unless a T bit is detected, thereafter it is incremented. However, if the first four bits found are not 0xe, *bitCount* is returned to 0 to indicate a false start. When *bitCount* is 22, a full frame has been read into *Frame;* it is saved in long word *saveFrame.* When *bitCount* is 44, a second full frame, and thus the entire message, has been read; if *Frame* is different from *saveFrame,* an error is recorded, otherwise, *Frame* is pushed onto a stack, to be popped by the *Input* method when this value is desired in the program. In either case *bitCount* is reset to begin looking for a next message. Finally, *tickCount* is cleared and *60Hz*'s interrupt source is removed by inverting port F bit 1.

We illustrate the M68340 class; for the M68332, merely change the portB to portF.

```
long SaveA4; int tickCount,bitCount;

struct X10Device : IoDevice { /* an I/O device class */
    long Frame, saveFrame; LongQueue Q; /* LongQueue is a 4-byte queue (like IntQueue) */
    void Init(long, unsigned), Terminate(void); long Input(void);
};

void X10Device::Init(p,m) long p; unsigned m;{ register int *hndlr;
    inherited::Init(p,0); (Q=blessA(sizeof(LongQueue), LongQueue))->InitQ(40);
    asm{lea @0,hndlr} *(int **)0x74=hndlr; asm{lea @1,hndlr} *(int **)0x78=hndlr;
    assgB=0x60; dirB=0x88; asm{move.l a4,SaveA4} asm{and #0xf4ff,sr} return;
```

▶ `asm {@0 movem.l d0-d2/a0/a1/a4, - (a7)} asm { movea.l SaveA4,a4 } /* 60Hz */`
`Frame = (Frame <<1) + (tickCount>3);`
`if(bitCount) bitCount++; else if(tickCount>3) bitCount++;`
`if((bitCount==4)&&((Frame&0xf)!=0xe)) bitCount==0; /* check if frame starts o.k. */`
`if(bitCount==22) saveFrame = Frame; /* when first frame is received, save it */`
`if(bitCount==44){ /* when second frame, and thus the whole message, is received */`
`  if((Frame &0x03fffff)!=(saveFrame &0x03fffff)) error|=1; /* if both frames are same */`
`  else{ Q->Push(saveFrame); error|=Q->Error(); } /* push */`
`  bitCount = 0; /* reset to begin looking for next message */`
`}`
`PortB^=8; tickCount=0; asm {movem.l (a7)+,d0-d2/a0/a1/a4 } asm {rte }`

▶ `asm{ @1 } portB^=0x80; tickCount++; asm { rte} /* sig handler */`
`}`

The *Terminate* method disarms interrupts by reassigning the IRQ inputs as port bits.

`void X10Device::Terminate() { assgB=0; } /* disarm IRQ6, IRQ5 interrupts */`

The *Input* method shown below not only pops data from its queue, but also decodes the data to deliver a more useful pattern to the calling routine. The pattern that was pushed on the stack by the interrupt handler appears as in Figure 5-7c. The frame type is first analysed; the two permissible values are TF (give command) and FT (select unit number). Bit 8 of the method's returned data is 1 if the message is the selection of a unit number, which results from pressing a key like "1" in the controller. If the frame is bad, an error is reported. Then the frame bits giving the house code are extracted from the data popped from the stack, and are converted into a binary number using a *for* loop implementing a linear search of the conversion vector *cnvt*. The *i*th element of this vector is initialized to the code for house *i* (house "A" is house binary number 0, house "B" is house binary number 1, etc.)

```
long X10Device::Input() { unsigned char house,unit; long code, ans; int i;
  static unsigned char cnvt[16]=
    {0x69,0xa9,0x59,0x99,0x56,0x96,0x66,0xa6,0x6a,0xaa,0x5a,0x9a,0x55,0x95,0x65,0xa5 };
  code=Q->Pull(); ans=0; if((code&3)==1) ans=0x100; else if((code&3)!=2) error=3;
  house=code>>10;for(i=0;i<16;i++) if(cnvt[i]==house)break;if(i>0xf)error=5;else ans+=i<<4;
  unit=code>>2; for(i=0;i<16;i++) if(cnvt[i]==unit)break;if(i>0xf)error=4;else ans+=i;
  return ans; /* ans = thhhhuuuu: t is type, hhhh is house, and uuuu is unit/command */
}
```

For instance, house code "A" (*i*=0) is 0x69. In Figure 5-7c, the house code 0xa5 is for house 0xf which is house "P". Bits 3 to 0 of the method's returned data are this binary house number. The same *cnvt* vector and algorithm is used to decode the unit number or code. If the frame type was for a unit, this pattern is the unit number to select that unit, otherwise it is the command to be given to preselected units. The command values are 2 (on), 4 (all on), 6 (bright), 0xa (off), 0xc (all off), and 0xe (dim). In Figure 5-7c, because the type, 10, is for a command, the unit code 0x66 corresponding to binary number 6 represents the command "bright". Bits 7 to 4 of the method's returned data are the command or unit number. When the pattern in Figure 5-7c is received, the method returns the value 0x06f to indicated it is a command to "bright" the lights (of units previously selected) in house "P".

The above example illustrates that operations on data can be done in the interrupt handler or in the *Input* method. The latter is a better place to execute complex procedures. The handler should do the minimum amount of work. The handler above merely verifies that the first and second frames of a message were identical before one of them was pushed onto a queue. Doing this requires saving only a 22-bit frame on the stack, which is easily done by pushing a long word on it, rather than trying to save a 44-bit message on the stack. This concept will occur again in device drivers, where the interrupt handler does only what must be done there, and the operating system's input system call does much more work.

The main point of this section is that by using vectored interrupts, because the addresses of different handlers are at different locations and there is no polling routine to go through, the specific interrupt request handler is executed without the delay of a polling routine. In effect, the polling routine is executed very quickly in hardware, and the winning handler is jumped to right after the registers are saved on the stack.

5-1.6 Real-time Interrupts

The 683xx system integration module (SIM) has a *periodic interrupt* (PI) timer, which illustrates explicitly vectored interrupts, that can cause interrupts every 122 μseconds to every 15.9 seconds. Its interrupt handler can be used to synchronize I/O transfers to or from the outside world. In this section, we discuss means to control the PI device in a simple way and then in a manner similar to time-sharing, and its use in timing operations, using the traffic-light controller example.

The PI device has five registers, as shown in Figure 5-8. The low nibble of the CONFIG register is the hardware priority of the SIM, including the PI module, relative to other modules such as the 683xx processor (which has the lowest priority 0). This must be set to a level different from the level of any other CONFIG register, and different from 0, the processor's priority. The LEVEL register determines the interrupt level of the PI module; its interrupt is honored if the 683xx status register I is lower than LEVEL. The VECTOR register is multiplied by 4 to get the address of the long word that stores the address of the PI interrupt handler. The TIME and PRESCALE registers determine the time between interrupts; if PRESCALE is 0, the period is TIME/8196, otherwise it is TIME/16. However, if TIME is 0 the interrupt is disabled. A value of PRESCALE = 1, TIME = 0x10 gives an interrupt each second.

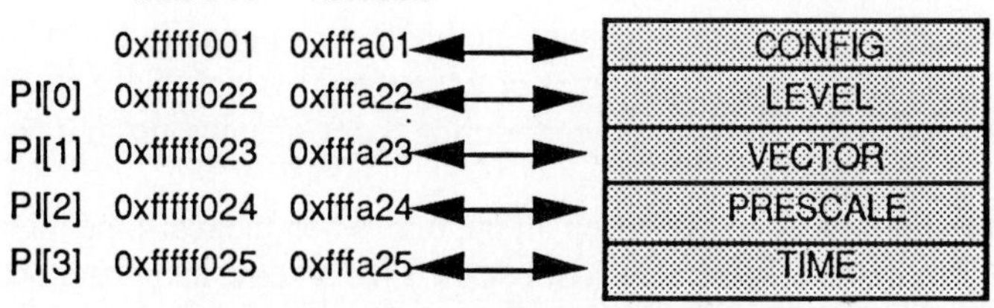

	M68340	M68332		
	0xfffff001	0xfffa01◄──►		CONFIG
PI[0]	0xfffff022	0xfffa22◄──►		LEVEL
PI[1]	0xfffff023	0xfffa23◄──►		VECTOR
PI[2]	0xfffff024	0xfffa24◄──►		PRESCALE
PI[3]	0xfffff025	0xfffa25◄──►		TIME

Figure 5-8. Periodic Interrupt Device.

After each time-out the PI interrupt handler is executed. The handler can directly input or output data, or it can set a global variable bit that another program continually checks (in a gadfly loop) that causes data to be input or output. The handler need not remove the source of this interrupt. Hardware removes it automatically.

The second technique can be used to implement a more accurate traffic light controller. The class *traffic_table* and its *Build* method are the same as at the end of Section 4-5, and the beginning of *main* is similar, but calls a procedure *PiInit*, shown below, to initialize the real-time interrupt. The traffic light controller's *Execute* method is slightly modified to use the variable *TimeUp* to time out the execution of the interpreter. The global variable *TimeUp* is set in the handler in *PiInit*, and tested and cleared in the traffic light's *Execute* method. This procedure is for the M68332; for the M68340, change *0xfffa22* to *0xffff022* (line 1) and *0xfffa01* to *0xffff001* (line 2).

```
PiInit(){ register int hndaddr; register char *PI=0xfffa22;
    *(char)0xfffa01 =0xe; PI[0]=6; PI[2]=1; PI[3]=0x10;
    PI[1]=0x42; asm{lea @0,hndaddr} *((int **)0x108)=hndaddr; asm{and #0xfaff,sr} return;
▶   asm {@0 ADDQ.W #1,TimeUp} asm { rte }
}
```

4*42=108

```
void traffic_table:: Execute () { /* this executes the interpreter - it is called up repetitively */
    int j,k; P->Output(tbl[row][0]);
    for(j=0; j<tbl[row][1]; j++) {while (! TimeUp); TimeUp=0;} if((row++)==3) row=0;
}
```

The *Execute* method is generally executing its gadfly *while* loop, because *TimeUp* is 0. Once each second, the handler makes *TimeUp* 1, which lets the method execute one more *for* loop. Thus the entire *for* expression delays *tbl[row][1]* seconds. Note that, in place of a wait loop that uses possibly uncertain real-time program delays to time the lights, this method gadflies on the *TimeUp* variable synchronized to the more accurate PI timer interrupt. This real-time interrupt version is thus more accurate.

This example still ties up the processor by waiting for a *TimeUp* signal change in a gadfly loop. A more useful *multi-thread* scheduling technique, which is a primitive form of task scheduling done in a multi-tasking multi-user operating system like OS-9, would be to permit some other work to be done while this routine waits for real-time interrupts. We will generate real-time interrupts once every *tick*, where a tick is about 1/100th second, rather than once every second. We will maintain several different threads, where a *thread* is a part of the program that is independent of other threads and that can be executed to do useful work. A thread can be executed for one tick, and then another thread might be executed for a tick, and so on. We can put a thread to *sleep* for a number of ticks; the other threads will be able to execute without competition from a sleeping thread. Rather than gadflying all of the time when waiting for the next light change, after using part of a tick to change the lights we can gadfly for the rest of a tick, and then sleep for the remaining number of ticks, until the next light change is to take place. The 683xx can do other useful work during those sleeping ticks; it does not spend all its time in a gadfly loop.

The execution of a thread is frozen after a tick, when the real-time interrupt occurs, by saving all its registers on the supervisor stack. (We assume here that control registers USP, VBR, SFC, and DFC are not used.) Several threads will have their registers saved this way. The real-time interrupt handler, saving registers for one thread, may end by restoring these registers, but restore the registers for a different thread than the one that was just saved. That way a different thread can execute for the next tick.

We decide which thread will be executed by its *sleepTime, priority,* and *age* variables. If *sleepTime* is nonzero, *sleepTime* is decremented each tick, otherwise, among all the non-sleeping threads *(sleepTime=0)*, one thread will be executed. A thread can be made to sleep *N* ticks by making *sleepTime* equal to *N*. A thread will be going to sleep in the next tick if *sleepTime* is made non-zero. Among non-sleeping threads, a thread with the oldest *age* will be executed. The *age* of each non-executing thread is incremented (up to 0xffff), but the *age* of the thread being executed is reset to its *priority*. The *priority* is thus the initial value of *age*. Non-sleeping threads will share processing time "proportional" to their *priority* values. If all threads are given the same *priority*, they will share processing time equally, when they are not sleeping. If a thread has a much lower *priority* than all the other threads, it will execute when all the other threads are sleeping, or will execute very infrequently when they are not; such a thread is called a *background* thread. If a thread has a much higher *priority* than all the other threads, it will hog processing time; such a thread is called a *high-priority* thread.

The information about a thread is maintained by an object of the class *Thread*. Up to 10 threads can be maintained by a vector of ten objects *thread[10]*. Instance variables of each object keep track of *sleepTime*, *priority*, and *age* as well as the location of the *stack*. A thread is started by a *Fork* method, which sets up the thread's entry point, size of its stack, and its priority. We illustrate with an example below. The class, objects, buffers, the real-time interrupt handler, and the *Fork* method are given before the *main* procedure is listed, which uses them. Finally, two threads *main1* and *main2* are listed.

```
struct Thread :direct {
    unsigned age, priority, *stack; long sleepTime;void Fork(unsigned *, unsigned, unsigned);
} *thread[10], *curThread;

int *TimeMgr(void){ register int i,j; register int *iPtr; register Thread *p;
    asm{lea @0,iPtr} return iPtr;/* return address of real-time handler */
    asm{ @0 movem.l d0-d7/a0-a6,-(a7) /* handler: save registers on stack */
    move.l a7,iPtr /* save stack pointer */
    }
    curThread->stack=iPtr; curThread->age=curThread->priority;
    for(curThread=i=j=0;(i<10)&&(p=thread[i]);i++){
    if((p->sleepTime)&&(p->sleepTime!=0xffffffff)) p->sleepTime--;
    if(!p->sleepTime){
    if(p->age!=0xffff) p->age++;/* increase age */
    if(p->age>=j) {j=p->age; curThread=p;} /*find max age */
    }
    }
    iPtr=(int*)curThread->stack;
    asm{
    movea.l iPtr,a7
    movem.l (a7)+,d0-d7/a0-a6
    rte /* use stacked registers to get going again */
    }
}
```

Executing the procedure *TimeMgr* above merely returns the address of @0, the entry point of the real-time interrupt handler in this procedure. The procedure *TimeMgr* will be executed in *main* to get the handler's address into location 0x108, so it can handle real-time interrupts. After an interrupt is honored, which saves the status register and program counter, as will be shown in Figure 5-13a, the handler begins by saving the registers with a MOVEM instruction. Then the location of stack register A7 is saved in the current thread's instance variable *stack*. We reset the current thread's age to its priority, to be used after further ticks. Then we search the thread objects for the next thread to become the current thread. If a thread is sleeping, unless *sleepTime* is maximum, we decrement its *sleepTime*. (Maximum *sleepTime* will be used in Section 5-2.1) Otherwise, we increment its age and obtain the thread with the greatest age. We will ensure, using a dummy thread that never sleeps, that a thread will be selected for each tick. We put its *stack* instance variable into stack register A7, and then restore the registers with a MOVEM instruction, and the status register and program counter with an RTE instruction, thus resuming execution of the selected thread.

A thread is started by sending a *Fork* message to it. The *Fork* method below requires parameters to specify the thread's starting address, priority and stack size. This method initializes the thread's instance variables and then sets up the stack in the same way that it would be saved at the beginning of the real-time interrupt when the thread is frozen. Then that handler will properly start it when its *age* is greatest.

```
void Thread::Fork(location, newPriority, stackSize) int *location, newPriority,stackSize;{
    register int *stackpointer;
    sleepTime=0; age=priority=newPriority;
    stack=allocate(17*4+stackSize); stackpointer=stack+=stackSize/2;
    stackpointer[30]=0x2500; stackpointer[31]=(long)location>>16;
    stackpointer[32]=(long)location; stackpointer[33]=0x108;
    asm{ movem.l d0-d7/a0-a6,(stackpointer) }
}
```

The *main* procedure, listed below, initializes the real-time interrupt as in the last example, but with a ~ 1/100th second period, and initializes port E to provide output pulses observable on an oscilloscope. It then calls *TimeMgr* to put the address of the handler in it in 0x108, where real-time interrupts will vector. The procedure then blesses the thread objects and *Forks* them. Finally, it executes a loop, until the first tick occurs, which will become thread 0. Note that the real-time interrupt is disabled from the beginning of this procedure until its end because the objects and their variables modified in this critical section are used in the handler. This procedure is for the M68332; for the M68340, change *0xfffa22* to *0xffff022* and *0xfffa01* to *0xffff001* (line 3).

```
main(){
    asm{or #0x700,sr} /* be sure interrupts are disabled while forking */
    *(char*)0xfffa01=0xe; *(long*)0xfffa22=0x6420052;
    *((unsigned int **)0x108)=TimeMgr();
    curThread=thread[0]=blessA(sizeof(Thread),Thread); thread[0]->Fork(0,0,100);
    thread[1]=blessA(sizeof(Thread),Thread); thread[1]->Fork(main1(),500,100);
    thread[2]=blessA(sizeof(Thread),Thread); thread[2]->Fork(main2(),500,100);
    thread[3]=0; asm{and #0xf8ff,sr} while(1);
}
```

A dummy thread at the end of the above procedure *main*,never sleeps but loops indefinitely. Two threads executed in the procedures *main1* and *main2* are shown below. For simplicity, *main1* outputs a 1.03 Hz square wave on bit 7, and *main2* outputs a 0.501 Hz square wave on bit 6, of port F. We will shortly use the traffic light controller in lieu of the later thread. Note that *main1* and *main2* threads sleep most of the time; *main* will be in its *while* loop using up ticks not used by the other threads. This procedure is shown for the M68332; for the M68340, change *assgF* to *assgB*, *dirF* to *dirB*, and *portF* to *portB*.

*unsigned int *main1(){ register unsigned int *iPtr; asm{lea @0,iPtr} return iPtr;*
> *asm{@0} assgF &=~ 0x80; dirF |=0x80;*
> *while(1) {portF ^=0x80; thread[1]->sleepTime=50;while(thread[1]->sleepTime);}*
}

*unsigned int *main2(){ register unsigned int *iPtr; asm{lea @0,iPtr} return iPtr;*
> *asm{@0} assgF &= ~ 0x40; dirF |= 0x40;*
> *while(1){portF ^=0x40; thread[2]->sleepTime=100;while(thread[2]->sleepTime);}*
}

The last thread can execute the traffic light routine instead of generating the ~ 1/2 Hz waveform. This routine, using a *BasicOutDevice* object, is coded as follows.

struct traffic_table :direct { / a direct root class */*
   unsigned int tbl[4][2],row;
   void Build(unsigned,unsigned, unsigned), Execute(void);
};

void traffic_table:: Build (a,p,t) unsigned int a,p,t;{ tbl[a][0]=p; tbl[a][1]=t; }

void traffic_table:: Execute () { / executes the interpreter each second */*
   P->Output(tbl[row][0]); if((row++)==3) row=0;
   *thread[2]->sleepTime= tbl[row][1]*100; while(thread[2]->sleepTime);*
}

*BasicOutDevice *P; traffic_table *T;*

*unsigned int *main2(){ register unsigned int *iPtr; asm{lea @0,iPtr} return iPtr;*
> *asm{@0} P=blessA(sizeof(BasicOutDevice) BasicOutDevice); P->Init (0x10000);*
> *T=blessA(sizeof(traffic_table),traffic_table); T-> row=T-> timeLeft=0;*
> *T->Build (0,0x21,16);T->Build (1,0x22,4) T->Build (2,0x0c,20);T->Build (3,0x14,4);*
> *while(! P->error)T->Execute (); /* loop forever, unless an I/O error occurs */*
> *P->Terminate (); thread[2]=0; /* remove thread 2 from scheduling */*
> *while(1); /* waste rest of tick time */*
}

Observe that any program gadflying on variables set in the real-time interrupt handler can be inserted in place of the threads *main1* and *main2*, and more threads could be added. The programs need only be modified by replacing those gadfly loops with statements to set the *sleepTime* variable and then gadfly for the remainder of the tick time that the thread remains running. In a later section, we will show that threads can be switched within a tick time to avoid wasting even that time, but from this section we have shown that real-time interrupt efficiently synchronizes to slow-speed devices.

5-2 Special Device Interrupt Mechanisms

We now look at interrupts in parallel I/O chips, the M6821 and M68230, and the M68332 QSPI. While this section does not cover fundamental concepts of synchronization, which have been covered in the previous section, it covers applications of them for parallel I/O chips and the serial I/O system in the M68332.

Before looking at these chips, we note that in the M68332 the basic input and output devices can use the TPU, discussed in Chapter 7, to generate interrupts for them. Most modes, in particular its discrete I/O input mode, can generate interrupts when an edge occurs, and this can be used to signal entry into the done state.

5-2.1 The M6821 Interrupt Mechanism and its M68332 Interface

The interrupt mechanism in the M6821 is typical of 6800-style I/O chips, so we introduce a little more of it here. Recall that control bit 2 is used to determine whether the direction port or the data port can be accessed, if that bit is, respectively, F or T. We now explore the use of the other control bits.

Each of the two devices in the M6821 has a primary interrupt mechanism and another mechanism that can be configured either as a secondary interrupt mechanism or else as an output bit. The status of the interrupt mechanisms can be read from a two-bit read-only status port. The six-bit readable control port of either the A or B device governs a primary interrupt request mechanism, as shown in Figure 5-9a. The control port and status port are in the same word in the device.

Bit 7 of the control port is the read-only output of the D edge-triggered flip-flop IRQA1. When it is set, we say *IRQA1 recognizes an interrupt*. A pin, CA1, and a control port bit, 1, determine when IRQA1 is set. If bit 1 is false, IRQA1 is set on a high to low transition of the signal on the CA1 pin; if true, IRQA1 is set on a low to high transition of the CA1 pin's signal. Because the IRQA1 bit is read-only, writing in the control port does not change it. However, because an interrupt usually requires reading the data from the data port, IRQA1 is cleared to false when the data port in that device is read. That is, a read address trigger is used, so reading the data port also clears the IRQA1 flip-flop. One of the common errors in using the M6821 is to try to clear the IRQA1 flip-flop by writing 0 into the control port. It must be cleared by reading the data port. (Similarly, reading the direction port will not clear IRQA1, so you have to set control bit 2 before you can read the data port to clear IRQA1.) Control port bit 0 is ANDed with IRQA1, the output going in negative logic to the IRQA pin. This output can be sent through a negative logic wire-OR bus to a 683xx microprocessor IRQ pin (such as IRQ6). Alternatively, the IRQA pin can be left disconnected or can even be connected to some light or alarm if that is useful.

The primary interrupt mechanism is always armed for use. A second part of the control logic can be used to implement a secondary interrupt mechanism, or one of three different 1-bit output mechanisms, depending on the values of control bits 5 to 3. (See Figures 5-9b to 5-9e.)

If the other part is to be used as a second interrupt, then the user makes control bit 5 false. Then control bits 6, 4, and 3 function for this part exactly as control bits 7, 1, and 0 function for the device interrupt we discussed earlier. (See Figure 5-9b.) That is, the IRQA2 flip-flop can always be read as bit 6. It is set if bit 4 is false and the CA2 input has a high to low transition, or if bit 4 is true and CA2 has a low to high transition, and is cleared when the data port is read. Writing in the control port does not change the read-only bit, bit 6, just as it doesn't change bit 7. The value of IRQA2 is ANDed with control bit 3, and ORed into the wire-OR bus through the same IRQA pin used by the IRQA1 flip-flop.

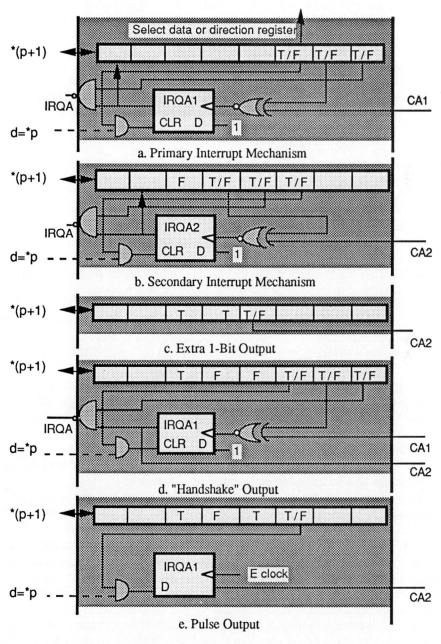

Figure 5-9. M6821 Device A Interrupt/Output Mechanisms.

Three modes are available to use CA2 as an output if control bit 5 is T. If control bit 4 is also a T, then control bit 3 is output in positive logic on the CA2 pin to give an extra output bit. This mode is simply called the *extra one-bit output* mode. (See Figure 5-9c.) For example, if control bits 0 and 1 are supposed to be false, and we want to access the data port, then storing 0x34 in the control port will output a low signal on the CA2 pin, and storing 0x3C in the control port will output a high on that pin. This extra output bit can be changed by the program. For instance in a printer, a motor can advance the print head as long as this output is low. After ASCII character data is written in an output port and a character is printed, the motor is started by outputting L, to move the print head, and then stopped by outputting H.

If control bits 5 to 3 are T F F, CA2 is essentially the contents of the IRQA1 flip-flop. This mode is called *handshaking* because this is the same principle, called by the same name, as is used in asynchronous communication, which will be introduced in Chapter 8. The external logic sets IRQA1 via CA1 and CA2 can output the value of this flip-flop to control external hardware.

If control bits 5 to 3 are T F T, CA2 is normally high and drops for just one memory cycle when the data port is read. This mode is called *pulse* for obvious reasons. (See Figure 5-9e.) This is an example showing the address trigger available as an output to control an external part of the I/O system. This can be used to trigger an external one-shot to make a printer motor move one character position.

The two devices in an M6821 are almost identical. There are control pins for each; CA1 and CA2, which are the control pins for the A device, correspond to control pins CB1 and CB2 for the B device. Separate interrupt signal outputs IRQA and IRQB are used for each device so they can be wired to different buses discussed later, or one can be connected while the other is not. The logic associated with CA1 and CB1 is identical. The logic associated with CA2 is as discussed above, but the logic associated with CB2 is just a bit different. The logic for the B device is designed to make it more useful for output, while the A device is designed to be more useful for input. CB2 is pulsed with a negative signal when control bits 5 to 3 are T F T, and the data port is written in, rather than read from, as is CA2. (That is, replace read address trigger $d=*p;$ with write address trigger $*p=d;$ in Figures 5-9d and 5-9e for the B device.) CB2 is not quite the value of the IRQB1 flip-flop in the B device; it becomes high when IRQB1 is set, but it becomes low when the data port is written in, while the IRQB1 port is cleared when the data port is read from. (In the A device, CA2 is the positive logic output of IRQA1.) With these minor differences, which are easy to forget, the two devices in an M6821 are very flexible and can be used for almost any parallel I/O requirement.

We will show the use of the M6821 by implementing a "Centronics" parallel printer port as an I/O object in a multi-thread environment discussed in Section 5-1.6 for an M68332 (only). This example, adapted from an OS-9 device driver, not only illustrates M6821 interrupts but also a thread sleeping until an interrupt occurs.

Figure 5-10a shows the "Centronics" parallel printer connector. A character is printed by putting its ASCII code on the data lines, and asserting Stb low for at least 1 μsecond. When the printer accepts the character, it pulses Ack low (Figure 5-10b). A printer usually has a buffer in it, and can quickly put the character in the buffer, but if the buffer is full of data, the printer must wait milliseconds for a character to be printed before it can store the incoming character in the buffer. Thus, the time from Stb to Ack will be a few microseconds if the buffer is not full, or a few milliseconds if full.

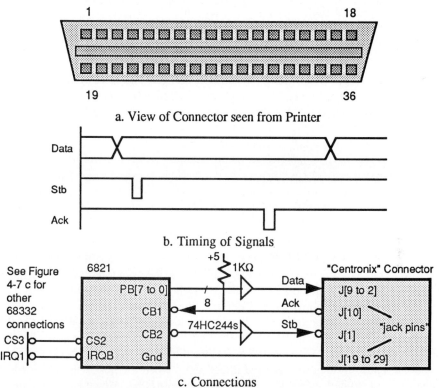

a. View of Connector seen from Printer

b. Timing of Signals

c. Connections

Figure 5-10. "Centronics" Parallel Printer Port.

We connect the printer to an M6821's port B, and connect Ack to CB1, and Stb to CB2 (Figure 5-10c). The 74HC244s are needed to drive about 5 milliamps through the printer cable into a 1KΩ load, because the M6821 is able to drive only ~ 1.6 milliamps.

The M68332 is set up as in Section 4-3.2, using CS3 to select the M6821. The macro

> *pinAssign(cs3,byte); baseAssign(3,0x10000,k2);*
> *optionAssign(3,rd+wr+upper+as,synch,user+super,0);*

is used to initialize CS3. Also, CS4 will be used to acknowledge interrupts, autovectoring to level 1 (our example's multi-thread's real-time interrupts use level 6):

> *pinAssign(cs4,byte); baseAssign(4,0xffffff,k2);*
> *optionAssign(4,rd+upper+ds,fast,0,1+avec);*

The *Init* method of class *CentronicsB*, a subclass of *M6821*, calls its parent's *Init* to set output direction. Disabling interrupts, it sets the M6821 port B control register for falling edge triggered pulse mode (0x2d) and, because the M6821 may have IRQB1 set at the time it is being initialized, generates an address trigger to remove the IRQB1 interrupt using the peculiar statement *i=*chip;* The M68332's IRQ1 input is assigned for interrupts and the address vector for level 1 interrupts is written with the address of *CentronicsBs* handler, the pointer to the process that is sleeping is cleared, and interrupts are enabled. The *Terminate* method clears the M6821's control register.

```
struct CentronicsB : M6821
    {Thread *sleepT; void Init(long, unsigned),Output(long),Terminate(void); }*Printer;

void CentronicsB::Init(p,m) long p; unsigned m;{ register int *hndlr,i;
    inherited::Init(p,0xff);
    asm{or #0x700,sr} *((char*)chip+1)=0x2d; asm{ move.l a4,saveA4} assgF=2;
    i=*(char*)chip; /* "read" the data reg to generate add. trigger in order to remove int.*/
    asm{lea @0,hndlr} *(int **)0x64=hndlr; sleepT=0; asm{and #~0x700,sr}; return;
▶   asm{@0 movem.l a0-a4/d7,-(a7)} asm{move.l saveA4,a4}
    i=*(char*)chip;/* remove interrupt */ sleepT->sleepTime = 0;
    asm{movem.l (a7)+,a0-a4/d7} asm{rte};
    }

void CentronicsB::Terminate() { *((char*)chip+1)=0; }
```

The handler and the *Output* method interact as we discuss below. Data are output by *M6821*'s inherited output method. Writing to M6821's port B will produce a negative pulse on pin CB2 which pulses Stb, which should cause the printer to assert Ack low, to put a falling edge on CB1. Recalling that the printer might respond quickly or slowly, the *Output* method checks IRQB1 right after data are sent, as in a gadfly loop. Interrupts are disabled while IRQB1 is checked, for if they were enabled, the interrupt handler would be entered before the *Output* method could see IRQB1 set. If the printer responded quickly and IRQB1 is set, then the *Output* method reenables interrupts and is completed. Otherwise, as in the multi-thread example in Section 5-1.6, the current thread's *sleepTime* is set to make the thread sleep when the next tick occurs and the current tick is wasted using a gadfly loop on *sleepTime*. However, the real-time interrupt handler in Section 5-1.6 does not decrement a maximum value *sleepTime* set here. The thread appears to sleep forever. However, because the current thread's object pointer *curThread* has been copied into *CentronicsBs sleepT*, when the IRQB1 interrupt occurs, the handler clears *sleepT*'s *sleepTime*, thus waking up the thread. Sleeping forever avoids the possibility that decrementing *sleepTime* will restart the thread when the printer has not responded. Of course this will hang up the thread if the printer is not on and does not respond. The user is supposed to recognize this and fix it.

```
void CentronicsB::Output(d) register long d;{ int i;
    asm{or #0x700,sr} /* disable interrupts to check IRQB1*/ inherited::Output(d);
    if(*((char*)chip+1)&0x80) { i=*(char*)chip; asm{and #~0x700,sr} return; }
    (sleepT=curThread)->sleepTime = 0xffffffff; asm{and #~0x700,sr} while(curThread->sleepTime);
}
```

A thread[1]'s procedure *main1* prints the line "Hello world" as shown below:

```
char s[14]="Hello World\r\n", *p;
main(){
    int *s; free=(char*)0x10000;
    *(char *)0xfffa01=0xe;*(long *)0xfffa22=0x6420052; *((int **)0x108)=TimeMgr();
    (curThread=thread[0]=blessA(sizeof(Thread),Thread))->Fork(0,0,100);
    (thread[1]=blessA(sizeof(Thread),Thread))->Fork(main1(),500,100);
    thread[2]=0;s=thread[0]->stack; asm {movea.l s,a7} asm{and #0xf8ff,sr}while(1);
}
```

int *main1(){ register int *iPtr; asm{lea @0,iPtr} return iPtr;

▶ *asm{@0}   *(char*)0xfffa05/=0x80; /* output E clock @ 1 MHz */*
(Printer=blessA(sizeof(CentronicsB), CentronicsB)) ->Init(0x10002,0); p=s;
while (*p && (Printer->error ==0)) Printer->Output(*p++);
Printer->Terminate();OutString("Done\r");curThread->sleepTime=0xffffffL;
while(1);

}

A parallel printer port can use M6821's port A, but its CA2 output needs to be controlled by the "one-bit output" technique. *Init* must initialize the M6821 control register to 0x3d, and after outputting the data, *Output* must put 0x35 and 0x3d in it. However, this port A is better suited to devices requiring data input than is port B.

The M6821, an early I/O chip, has proven itself flexible and useful for many years and for many different processors, but has some unusual characteristics, such as different read and write address triggers to assert or negate interrupt requests or output lines.

Observe also that "sleeping forever" lets other threads use ticks when a thread waits for an interrupt. In this example, the printer may return its ack signal a few seconds after the data has been sent to it. This may occur if the printer has to execute a slow carriage return when its buffer is full. The thread outputting data to the printer will "sleep forever", not requesting ticks, until the printer is ready to accept the next character.

External devices like the M6821 can request interrupts on the 683xx IRQ1 - IRQ7 pins that share port F. Several such devices can be connected to the same pin, and an interrupt sensed when that pin is asserted (low) will cause a handler to be executed. That handler will poll all the (6821) devices to determine which one caused the interrupt. The interrupt flag and interrupt enable should be checked to see if both are asserted. However, this simple test makes maintenance a bit more difficult than a slightly more complex test. If the first M6821 is burned out or is removed from the microprocessor, an attempt to read any word at its address will probably read 0xFFFF. The handler would read this word, so the test for T's in the enable and interrupt flag would pass and its handler would be executed. Unfortunately, because there is no chip here, attempts to remove the source of the interrupt will again be futile, so the interrupt will be recognized just as soon as the handler is executed, ad nauseam. To correct this troublesome problem, all that we have to do is also check for an F in the control word. Any F will do. If this condition is not satisfied, the next device is tested, and, if it does not satisfy the test, the next is tested, then the next and the next, until all are tested.

5-2.2 Synchronization Mechanisms for the M68230 Parallel Devices

Parallel devices in the M68230 are able to use synchronization mechanisms like the M6821. The M68230 is very useful when two parallel devices are needed, and is a more flexible successor to the M6821. It can be easily connected to the M68332 or M68340.

Figure 5-11 shows the three parallel devices of the M68230 parallel interface/timer, which have been described in Section 4-3.3. The ports in Figure 4-11b are arranged in consecutive address order and the control ports are shown with their fields, in Figure 5-11a. The devices A and B have similar control mechanisms, and part of device C is used to implement these control mechanisms so it has no control mechanisms itself. The

Mode port has a 2-bit Main Mode field that specifies one of four main modes for both devices A and B together. Mode 0 makes both devices independent 8-bit ports, each of which may be double-buffered on either input or output, but not both, or double-buffered on neither. Mode 1 makes both devices into one 16-bit device, which may be double-buffered on either input or output, but not both. Mode 2 makes device B into an 8-bit device, which may be double-buffered on both input and output, leaving device A without control logic or double-buffering capability. Mode 3 makes both devices into a 16-bit device, which may be double-buffered on both input and output. We will discuss mode 0 in device A. Device B can be used in an identical manner in mode 0, and both devices can be used in a similar manner in mode 1.

The Mode, Service Req and Status ports are used in common to both devices. We first discuss the bits in these ports. The corresponding bits and fields apply to device B, replacing A with B, 1 with 3, and 2 with 4.

The status port has inputs that read the pins directly. Bit H1 is the signal on "handshake" pin H1 and bit H2 is the signal on pin H2. Figures 5-11b to 5-11e show upward arrows from these inputs indicating these inputs can be read into the 683xx. This port also contains the interrupt request flip-flop values IRQ1 and IRQ2. These flip-flops can always be read, are changed by hardware, and can be cleared by software by writing a T in them. In Figures 5-11b and 5-11c, the downward arrow to IRQ1 and IRQ2 has a phrase "Clear 1" to indicate this. That is, the Status ports are "clear ports." The IRQ flip-flops in the M68230 are cleared by writing a T in them; writing an F does not change them. The 683xx clears its "clear ports" by writing an F in them, writing a T does nothing. Although different conventions are used, neither is really better than the other, and with the 683xx AND-to-memory instruction, neither are necessary. We have to live with these little anomalies.

The ArmA bit in the Mode port can disarm Device A's control logic if it is F. Figures 5-11b and 5-11c show the ArmA flip-flop feeding an AND gate to control inputs, and a comment indicates that when ArmA is cleared, IRQ1 and IRQ2 are cleared. Pin H1 is always an input, like CA1 in the M6821. The Edge1 bit in the Mode port permits software to select the edge of the signal on input pin H1 that sets interrupt request bit IRQ1; a T causes IRQ1 to set on a rising edge and an F causes IRQ1 to set on a falling edge. Note that Edge1 feeds an exclusive-NOR gate. Pin H2 can be an input or output, like CA2 in the M6821. The Edge2 bit in the Mode port permits software to select the edge of the signal on input pin H2 that sets interrupt request bit IRQ2 in a similar manner. When H2 is an output, Edge2 inverts the F output signal: If Edge2 is F the output is high (negative logic), and if Edge2 is T the output is low (positive logic).

The Pin 34 Sel field of the Service Req port will be discussed in Section 5-5.1, and the Priority field will be discussed in Section 5-4.2. The P35S bit determines whether pin 35 is device C bit 5 (if P35S is F) or the interrupt request line to the 683xx, and P36S determines whether pin 36 is device C bit 6 (if P36S is F) or the interrupt acknowledge signal from the 683xx. Pin 35 is needed as an interrupt request if interrupts are to be used with the parallel devices, and pin 36 is needed as an interrupt acknowledge if vectored interrupts are to be used, as discussed in Section 5-2.6. If these features are not implemented, the pins can be used for parallel device C bits 5 and 6. The timer portion of the M68230 has separate interrupt and input-output lines that share port C bits.

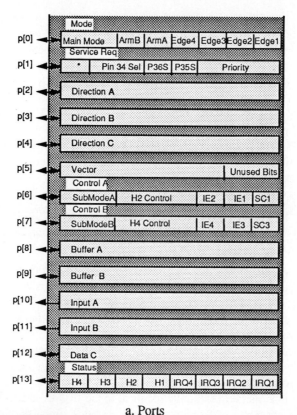

a. Ports

b. Primary Interrupt Mechanism
(Device A, Main Mode 0, SubModeA = 0)

c. Secondary Interrupt Mechanism
(Control A bit 5 = 0)

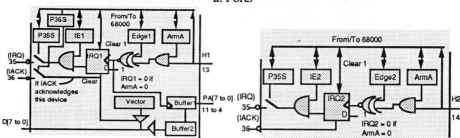

d. Extra 1-Bit Output Mechanism
(Control A bits 5, 4 = TF)

e. Handshake and Pulse Output Mechanism
(Control A bits 5, 4 = TT)

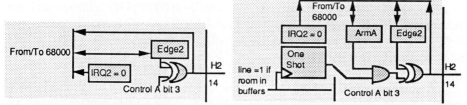

Figure 5-11. Synchronization Mechanisms for the M68230 Parallel Devices.

The M68340's IACK signal, on the same pin as a port A signal, can assert the parallel port interrupt acknowledge (pin 36) to use the external vector interrupt method. If the chip select is set up as in that section, IRQ6 is connected to pin 35, IAK6 is connected to pin 36, P35S and P36S are T, and bit 6 of port A's assignment1 register is cleared, and bit 6 of its assignment2 register is set. This IACK signal acts like a chip select, being asserted only when an interrupt level 6 is honored, and if connected to the M68230's IACK pin, causes the M68230 to send out its LEVEL register value to establish the interrupt vector.

The M68332's chip select mechanism can be used to assert the M68230 chip select pin (pin 41) as discussed in Section 4-3.3, and another chip select can assert the parallel port interrupt acknowledge (pin 36) to use the external vector interrupt method. If the chip select is set up as in that section, IRQ6 is connected to pin 35, CS7 is connected to pin 36, and P35S and P36S are T, the macro for interrupt acknowledge is:

pinAssign(cs7,byte); baseAssign(7,0xffffff,k2); /* match 1st argument in all macros */
optionAssign(7,rd+upper+ds,external,0,6); /* acknowledge external vector level 6 */

Compared to the autovectored method, the constant *avec* is not added to *optionAssign*'s last parameter, so the Avec field of the chip select control register (Figure 3-16) is not set. This inhibits the SIM form asserting the AVEC line, so the interrupt is not handled by autovectoring. Instead, when pin 36 is asserted by CS7, the M68230 supplies its Vector register value p[6] in the external vector method.

The Control A port has a SubModeA field that determines the mode of device A only, if the Main Mode is 0. Submode 2 or 3 makes device A a simple device controlled by a direction port like device A in the M6821 and permits the IRQ1 and IRQ2 flip-flops to be used in a manner essentially identical to the IRQA1 and IRQA2 flip-flops in the M6821. The examples of Section 4-3.3 utilized this simple mode; we will utilize the connections shown in Figure 4-8b for all the examples in this subsection. Compare Figures 5-11b through 5-11e to Figure 5-9. The primary interrupt mechanism is available for all the following cases, and is shown in Figure 5-11b, except that the Buffer1 and Buffer2 registers are not used for double-buffering. IRQ1 is set on the edge of H1 if ArmA is T, and can be read (in the Status port) or cleared (by writing a T) as just discussed. If IE1 and P35S are T, then the IRQ line on pin 35 is asserted low, which can cause an interrupt if connected to one or more interrupt priority level (IPL) lines of the 683xx.

The use of H2 depends on the H2 Control field and IE2 bit of the Control A port. If H2 Control is Fxx (Control A bit 5 is F), IRQ2 is a secondary interrupt sensing the signal on H2 and controlled by IE2 but sharing the ArmA and P35S flip-flops with the primary interrupt mechanism. However, if Control A bit 5 is T, H2 is an output. Edge2 determines the logic level of this output; if Edge2 is T then H2 is a positive logic, and if F, H2 is a negative logic signal. If Control A bit 4 is F, then the output value is Control A bit 3. That is, if H2 Control is TFF, H2 is F and if H2 Control is TFT, H2 is T. This is essentially the same mechanism as in the M6821.

If the SubModeA field is 1, then device A is double-buffered for all bits in which the direction is "output," and handled as in the M6821 for all bits that are "input". The edge that sets IRQ1 in the primary interrupt mechanism also causes the bits last put into Buffer2 to be replaced by the bits in Buffer1. Bits in Buffer2 are output from this port. IRQ1 remains set as long as there is room for a byte in either Buffer1 or Buffer2, so both bytes can be written by the 683xx and will be output in correct order. See Figure 4-8d. The secondary interrupt and the one-bit output mechanisms are available in this submode as in the submode 2. A "handshake" output in this mode puts a T on H2 whenever data are available on port A output pins until H1 is asserted to indicate the data are used by the external hardware, or it pulses H2 as new data become available in the pins, by direct analogy to the input handshake of submode 2.

We illustrate this submode in the M68340 using gadfly synchronization for the Centronics printer example (Figure 5-10). The negative logic Centronics signals, Ack and Stb are connected to H1 and H2. For the M68332, use the *pinAssign, baseAssign,* and *optionAssign* macros shown in Section 4-3.3, in place of the *CsAssign* macro.

```
char s[12]="hello world",*sp;
main(){ register char *cp=(char*)0x10000;register int i; register char c;
    CsAssign(3,0x10000,8,noDsack,rdWr); /* enable chip select 3 to select M68230 */
    sp=s; cp[0]=0; /* disable port: change registers */ cp[2]=0xff; /* direction: output */
    cp[6]=0x72;/* submode 01; H1 is output request, H2 handshake output */
    cp[0]=0x12;/* enable port a, H2 handshake output is normally high */
    while(*sp){
        while((cp[0xd]&1)==0); /* gadfly on H1 edge */
        cp[8]=*sp++; /* output data */ cp[0xd]=1; /* clear IRQ1 */
    }
}
```

If the SubModeA field is 0, then device A is double-buffered for all bits in which the direction is "input," and handled as in the M6821 for all bits that are "output." The edge that sets IRQ1 in the primary interrupt mechanism also causes any data bits to be put in Buffer1 and moved to Buffer2 whenever another edge occurs before the 683xx reads this device. IRQ1 remains set as long as there is a byte in either Buffer1 or Buffer2, so both bytes can be read in correct order. The secondary interrupt and the one-bit output mechanisms are available in this submode as in the submode 2. A "handshake" output is also available in this mode. If the H2 Control field of the Control A port is TTF, H2 is T if there is any room left in either input buffer. Edge2 again determines the logic level of H2. This can be used by an external device to determine whether more data can be sent into device A. The "handshake" output can be a pulse that occurs whenever room becomes available, if the H2 Control field of the Control A port is TTT. The pulse is essentially four cycles long, where a cycle is the clock cycle on the CLK pin.

We illustrate this submode in the M68340 using externally vectored interrupt synchronization for the paper tape reader example (Figure 5-1). The negative logic Centronics signal, SprocketHole, is connected to H1, M68230's PC5/PIRQ is connected to M68340's portB6/IRQ6 and M68340's PC6/PIACK is connected to M68340's portA6/Iack6. For the M68332, use the *pinAssign, baseAssign, and optionAssign* macros shown in Section 4-3.3, in place of the *CsAssign3* macro, use the *pinAssign, baseAssign, and optionAssign* macros shown above in this subsection, in place of the *CsAssign3* macro, connect the M68230's PC5/PIRQ to the M68332's portF6/IRQ6 and the M68340's PC6/PIACK to M68332's CS7. This example should be studied with some care if you are studying the M68340 and you will be interested in DMA in Section 5-5-4.1; we will extend it to use the M68230 for DMA.

```
main(){ register char *cp=(char*)0x10000; register int *hndlr;
    CsAssign(3,0x10000,8,noDsack,rdWr); /* enable chip select 3 to select M68230 */
    assgB=assgA2=0x40; assgA1=~0x40; /* assign irq6 request and iack6 acknowledge */
    sp=s; cp[0]=0;/* set general mode to 0, disable ports a and b to change registers */
    cp[1]=0x18;/* permit int req on pin C5 and int ack on pin C6 */
    cp[2]=0;/* direction input */
    cp[5]=0x40;/* interrupt vector */
    cp[6]=0x32;/* submode 0 H2 is not interrupt (is output) request H1 enabled */
    cp[0]=0x10;/* set mode 0 again, enable port a (H2 is normally low) */
    asm{lea @0,hndlr} *(int **)0x100=hndlr; /* put handler address for vector 0x40 */
    asm{and #0xfdff,sr} /* make I[2 to 0] 5 to enable interrupts at level 6 */
    while(sp!=(s+12));Exit(); /* wait for all characters to output, then exit to debugger */
asm {@0 movem.l a0/d0,-(a7)} /* interrupt handler */
    *sp++=cp[8]; /* input data */ cp[0xd]=1; /* remove interrupt */
    if(sp==(s+12)) {cp[0]=0; asm{or #0x700,sr}} /* if done, disable interrupt */
    asm{movem.l (a7)+,a0/d0} asm{rte};
}
```

We will use mode 0 in device A in an example in this chapter. Other MainModes and the B device have similar behavior. Consult the *MC68230 Parallel Interface/Timer* data book (ADI-860-R2) for detailed information on the other modes. This data book is primarily written for those who are experts in designing with Motorola chips. Note that the H1S flip-flop in that document is the device A primary interrupt flip-flop, which is the same as the IRQ1 flip-flop in this text. Similarly, H2S is IRQ2, H3S is IRQ3, and H4S is IRQ4.

5-2.3 Synchronization Mechanisms for the M68332 QSPI

The QSPI is a powerful device, and demands some programming techniques to utilize it fully. In Chapter 4, we learned how to use it for fire and for wrap devices, but not for both fire and wrap devices. In this section, we will develop techniques to simultaneously use the QSPI for both fire and wrap devices. Proceeding to this goal in small steps, we will first discuss how a byte from a 74HC589 will be shifted in, and then compared to a constant, 0x55. If the value equals the constant, a global variable will be incremented. We will make the SCLK (baud) rate large (*baud = 0xff* gives 33KHz) so that the slowed QSPI can well use interrupts to smooth out data movement. We study this contrived example to illustrate how interrupts are handled, before we look at using the QSPI for "fired" serial data transfer because we need to focus on the interrupt mechanism without the further problems associated with queues. This counting program is shown below.

The first three lines of the counting program initialize three QSM control registers, which we will discuss in Section 5-2.3, to control interrupts in both the QSPI and SCI modules in the QSM. The QSPI will be enabled when I[2 to 0] is less than 6, and since the VECTOR is 0x40, the QSM's SCI interrupt handler is at 0x100 (see Section 8-3.6) and the QSM's QSPI interrupt handler address is immediately under it at 0x104.

The QSPI is initialized as we have done it before, except that the SPI finish interrupt enable SPIFIE is set to enable interrupts each time a serial transfer is finished. The QSM interrupt arbitration level in the CONFIG register must be changed from its reset value of 0 to any nonzero value, or no interrupts will be generated. The QSPI LEVEL (6) and VECTOR (0x40) must be set up, as we discussed earlier in this section, so that the M68332 will know when the QSPI interrupt is enabled, and where the location of its handler is to be found. The QSPI must be not only turned on (SPE) but its interrupt must be enabled (SPIFIE), and the processor's interrupt level, normally 7, must be reduced to 5 to permit QSPI interrupts at level 6.

The handler is entered each time (all the) data has been shifted in and out of the buffers. This handler increments the global variable *count* if the received byte is 0x55, and will then clear the source of the interrupt, and return to the interrupted routine with an RTE instruction. The SPIF bit must be cleared by reading it and then putting a 0 in it. The bclr instruction executed by the C statement *qspiPort->spif=0;* does just that.

```
long count=0;
main(){ register int *hndaddr;
    *((int*)0xfffc00)=0xe; /* set QSM interrupt arbitration to 14 */
    *((char*)0xfffc04)=0x30; /* set QSPI interrupt LEVEL to 6 */
    *((char*)0xfffc05)=0x40; /* set QSM VECTOR so 0x104 has address of handler */
    asm{ lea @0,hndaddr } *((int **)0x104)= hndaddr; /* put @0 into location 0x104 */
    portD=assgD=0x7F; dirD=0x7E;
    qspiPort=(QSPI*)0xfffc18;qspiPort->mstr=qspiPort->wren=1; *((char*) 0xfffd40)=0;
    asm{ and #0xfdff,sr } /* change I[2 to 0] to 5 to permit QSPI's level 6 interrupt */
    qspiPort->bd = 0xff; qspiPort->spifie=1; qspiPort->spe=1; qspiPort->cpha=0;
    while(1); /* you really should do some useful work, rather than loop forever */
    asm{ @0} /* label for lea */
    if(*((char *)0xfffd01) == 0x55) count++; /* if incoming 0x55, inc global */
    qspiPort->spif=0; /* clear interrupt source */
    asm {rte } /* return to interrupted program */
    /* note the label and rte must be in assembler language, but the rest can be in C */
}
```

We now consider the QSPI using interrupts to move data from the processor when an external device requests data. These are fundamental concepts that apply to many I/O devices. A queue (Section 2-2.3) is used so that the outside world can be given data long after the program has generated it, permitting the program to get ahead of the output system. The processor need not be forced to loop, waiting for a "fire" device to become DONE. Interrupt-based I/O devices will use queue objects (Section 2-3.3) to factor out the common code used in their queues.

Assume there are one or more "wrap" QSPI I/O device(s) requiring a total of up to $N \leq 14$ words of the QSPI buffers R, T and C and only one word "fire" QSPI output device, and that we continually input and output data to the "wrap" devices, outputting data from the "fire" QSPI device upon request from the outside world. See Figure 5-12 for an example of such a connection.

The "wrap" devices' *Init*'s first parameter is the memory address of the element of T or R they use, and the low nibble of their second parameter is m, the value of PCS[3 to 0], 0xe. The "fire" device's value of PCS[3 to 0] is 0xd, the low nibble of its *Init*'s second parameter m. The outside world requests data by applying a positive edge of some signal, called the device's transfer request bit, like a bit on port F, a basic input device, or a bit of one of the serial input "wrap" devices. The least significant nibble of the fire device's *Init*'s first parameter *p* will be the bit number, and the rest of it is the memory location of this bit. We will assume that the transfer request's port is initialized elsewhere in the program. For Figure 5-12, because port F is at *0xfffa19*, the value of *p* would be *0xfffa190*.

The QSPI simultaneously and repetitively inputs and outputs its "wrap" I/O device data, using *R[0 to N-1]*, *T[0 to N-1]*, and *C[0 to N-1]* using *WordWrap* objects (Section 4-5). The fire device uses its *Output* method to send data. Its *Input* method will read the last word that was output, as in a basic output device. If a positive edge appears on the output device's transfer request and there are data in the object's queue, the QPSI will send a "fire" QSPI word popped from the object's queue using *T[N]*, and *C[N]*. *C[N]* will be initialized to provide PCS[3 to 0] for this "fire" output device. When the QSPI SPIF interrupt occurs indicating that all words previously put in *R* and *T* have been shifted in or out, and there is a transfer request from the output device, and its queue is not empty, a word popped from the queue is put in *T[N]* and the QSPI's ENDQP is set to N. Otherwise, QSPI's ENDQP is made N-1 to move only "wrap" data.

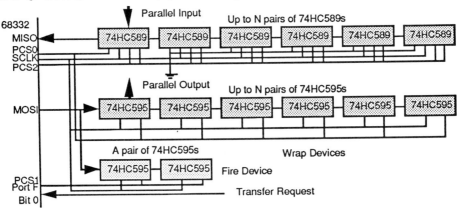

Figure 5-12. Multiple Wrap Devices and an Output Fire Device.

The object *Q* maintains a queue for 16-bit words and *qspiPort, flag,* and *error* and *chip* inherited from *IoDevice* handle the QSPI. The *Output* method merely pushes data into the queue. The interrupt handler will pull data out of this queue.

```
struct WordFire : BasicOutWord { /* special case of 16-bit basic output device */
    QSPI *qspiPort; IntQueue *Q; char flag,i; void Init(long, unsigned),Output(long);
};
    void WordFire::Output(d) long d; { Q->Push(value=d); error l = Q->Error(); }
```

The interrupt handler is in the *Init* method. If the transfer request bit was 0 and is now 1, and the queue is not empty, the interrupt handler pops a word from the queue into *T[N]* and sets ENDQP to N; otherwise it sets ENDQP to N-1 to input and output only the "wrap" data. It then clears the source of the interrupt and returns to the interrupted program. The *Init* method sets up the queue, and initializes the QSPI about the same as in the counting program above. However, to use objects in the handler, it must save address register a4, which is used to access instance variables, in a global variable *SaveA4,* and recover its value in the handler.

```
void WordFire::Init(p,m) long p;unsigned m;{
    qspiPort=(QSPI *)0xfffc18; (Q=blessA(sizeof(Queue),Queue))->InitQ(10);
    inherited::Init(p,0); portD=assgD=0x7F; dirD=0x1E;
    qspiPort->mstr = qspiPort->wren = 1; qspiPort->bd = 0xff;
    *((char*)fffc05)=0x40; asm{ lea @0,hndaddr } *((int **)0x104)= hndaddr;
    asm { move.l a4,SaveA4} /* save pointer to access instance variables later */
    *((char*) 0xfffd40+N) =m; /* initialize control for "fire" output */
    *((char*)fffc04)=0x30; *((int*)0xfffc00)=0xe;
    asm{and #0xfaff,sr} qspiPort->spifie=1; qspiPort->spe=1; return;
    asm {@0 movem.l d0-d2/a0/a1/a4, - (a7)} asm { movea.l SaveA4,a4 }
    i=(*(char *)(chip>>4) >> chip&7) &1; /* get input request bit */
    if (Q->len && i && !flag ){ /* if Q nonempty, old req 0, new req 1 (pos't edge)*/
        ((int *) 0xfffd20+N) =Q->Pull(); qspiPort->endqp= N;
    }
    else qspiPort->endqp= N-1;
    flag = i; qspiPort->spif=0; asm {movem.l (a7)+,d0-d2/a0/a1/a4} asm{rte }
}
```

We next consider the QSPI using interrupts to input data to the processor when an external device requests inputting data. A queue is used for input so that data can be sent before the program is ready to use it, permitting the input to get ahead of the program. This is similar to the previous case, but after a request is made and an interrupt occurs, the QSPI will be set up to get the word. However, the word will actually be brought in when the next interrupt occurs. That word can then be put into the queue. The program requests input data by sending messages to the *Input* method. If a word is available in the queue, it is returned, otherwise the method "gadflies" until a word is pushed. We will assume the program never outputs to an input device. The outside world requests to input data by a positive edge transfer request signal, identified as in the previous class.

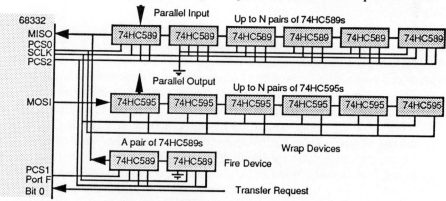

Figure 5-13. Multiple Wrap Devices and an Input Fire Device.

The QSPI simultaneously and repetitively inputs and outputs its "wrap" I/O device data as before. If a positive edge appears on the input device's transfer request, the QPSI will use *T[N]*, and *C[N]* to input a "fire" QSPI word. The control vector element *C[N]* will be initialized to provide PCS[3 to 0] for this "fire" input device. The devices are connected in almost the same way as the previous example's devices were connected

(Figure 5-13) and the "fire" and "wrap" *Init*'s parameters are the same. When the QSPI SPIF interrupt occurs indicating that all words previously put in *R* and *T* have been shifted in or out, and a transfer request positive edge occurs, QSPI's ENDQP is set to N for the next operation, and a variable *InFor* is set. Otherwise, QSPI's ENDQP is set to N-1 to move only the "wrap" I/O data, and *InFor* is cleared. After that, if *InFor* is set, the word in *R[N]* is pushed into the queue.

```
struct WordFireIn : IoWord {
   QSPI *qspiPort;IntQueue *Q;char flag,InFor,i;void Init(long, unsigned);long Input(void);
};
```

The interrupt handler is again in the *Init* method. However, if the queue is full an input request results in an error. The queue's error is copied into the device'e error. The *Init* method initializes the queue and QSPI about the same as in the class above.

```
void WordFireIn::Init(p,m) long p;unsigned m;{
   qspiPort=(QSPI *)0xfffc18; Q=blessA(sizeof(IntQueue), IntQueue); Q->InitQ(10);
   inherited::Init(p,0); portD=assgD=0x7F; dirD=0x7E;
   qspiPort->mstr = qspiPort->wren=1; qspiPort->bd = 0xff;*((char*)0xfffd40+N) =m;
   *((char*)fffc05)=0x40; asm{ lea @0,hndaddr } *((int **)0x104)= hndaddr;
   asm { move.l a4,SaveA4} *((char*)fffc04)=0x30;*((int*)0xfffc00)=0xe;
   asm {and #0xfdff,sr} qspiPort->spifie=1; qspiPort->spe=1; return;
▶  asm {@0 movem.l d0-d2/a0/a1/a4, - (a7)} asm { movea.l SaveA4,a4}
   if(InFor) {Q->Push((int *)0xfffd00+N); error |= Q->Error();InFor=0;}
   if( (i=(*(char *)(chip>>4) >> chip&7) &1) && ! flag ) /* if rising edge */
   { qspiPort->endqp= N; InFor=1;} /* expand buffers for an input word */
   flag = i; qspiPort->spif=0; asm {movem.l (a7)+,d0-d2/a0/a1/a4;} asm {rte }
```

}

The *Input* method gadflies until the queue is empty. While this wastes time, the user can check *WordFireIn*'s Q->Qlen, to skip *Input* if the queue is empty.

```
long WordFireIn::Input() { return Q->Pull(); }
```

We finally consider the QSPI using a single interrupt for requesting that I/O data be moved to or from the QSPI buffers *R* and *T* when the data have been shifted in or out. This is typical of more complex interrupt-based I/O devices that use queues to improve performance, and approaches the operating system device driver in power and sophistication. Generally there can be several "wrap" QSPI I/O devices (requiring a total of N words of the QSPI buffers *R, T,* and *C*, N<16) and several "fire" QSPI I/O devices (say M different devices, M < 15) whose maximum length is (16-N) words long, and that we need to continually input and output data to the "wrap" devices, while inputting and outputting data to and from the "fire" QSPI devices upon request from the program and from the outside world. In this example, we will assume that the length of all "fire" devices is 1 word to simplify our methods. A *WordFireInOut* device can be either input or output but not both. The value of PCS[3 to 0], the low nibble of *Init*'s second parameter *m*, is different for each device. We will call this the device "*path number*" *n*. See Figure 5-14. The low bits of PCS are decoded, the two "fire" input devices using 74HC589s are selected when these bits are 0 or 1, the two "fire" output devices using 74HC595s are selected when these bits are 2 or 3, the "wrap" devices using 74HC589s and 74HC595s are selected when these bits are 4. PSC bit 3 is used to pulse the 74HC589 LOAD and RCLK pins as in the "fire" input device above.

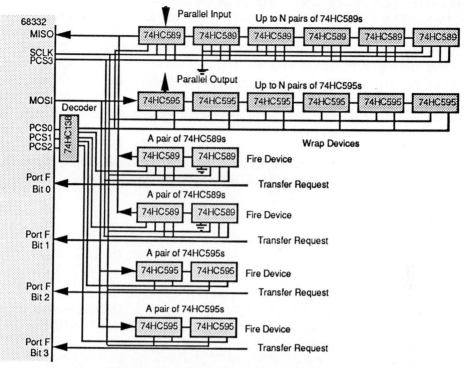

Figure 5-14. Multiple Wrap and Fire Devices.

To simplify the program, assume that the "fire" *n*s are consecutive numbers from 0 to M-1 where input devices have their *n*s below K and output devices have their *n*s at K and above, and the "wrap" QSPI I/O devices' *n* is the number 0xf, where M and K are fixed at compile time. In the example shown in Figure 5-14, the value of K is 2, and the value of M is 4. The objects for the "fire" devices will be accessed by a global M element vector F allocated by *WordFireInOut *F[M]*. For a "fire" device having path number *n*, the index in vector F used to get its object's pointer will be *n*. Delayed input is identified by a global index *InFor*, which is 0xf when nothing is requested.

The program requests transfers by sending messages to *Input* and *Output* methods. To input a word from path *i* into *d* we send the message by a statement such as *d=F[i]->Input();* and to output a word *d* to path *i*, we send the message by a statement such as *F[i]->Output(d)*. We will assume the program never inputs form an output device or outputs from an input device to simplify our methods. This restriction can be overcome by subclasses like BasicOut. The outside world requests transfers by applying a positive edge on the device's transfer request bit as before.

The QSPI will simultaneously input and output its "wrap" I/O device data, using *R[0 to N-1]*, *T[0 to N-1]*, and *C[0 to N-1]* as in Section 4-5. If a positive edge appears on an input device's transfer request, and that device's length is L words, the QPSI would use *R[0 to L+N-1]*, *T[0 to L+N-1]*, and *C[0 to L+N-1]* to send data in and out, elements 0 to N-1 used for "wrap" data and elements N to L+N-1 used to input "fire" data which will be pushed onto the object's queue. In our simplified program, L=1. Similarly, If a positive edge appears on an output device's transfer request and there is data in the object's queue, and that device's length is L words, the QPSI will use *R[0 to L+N-1]*, *T[0 to L+N-1]*, and *C[0 to L+N-1]* to send data in and out, elements 0 to N-1 used for "wrap" data and elements N to L+N-1 for "fire" data popped from the object's queue. Again, in our simplified program, L=1. When the QSPI interrupt occurs, if there is a transfer request from an input device, or if there is a transfer request from an output device and its output queue is not empty, we set up the QSPI to input or output it by altering the QSPI's ENDQP and setting the control vector elements *C[N to L+N-1]* (only *C[N]* in this program), and for output, putting the data in *T[N to L+N-1]* (only *T[N]* in this program) used for this device.

```
struct WordFireInOut : IoWord {
    QSPI *qspiPort; char flag, control; IntQueue *Q;
    void Init(long, unsigned),Output(long),Terminate(void); long Input(void);
};
long WordFireInOut::Input() {return QIn->Pull(); }
void WordFireInOut::Output(d) long d; { QOut->Push(d); error | = Q->Error(); }
```

The *Init* method sets up the queue each time an object uses it, and initializes the QSPI only the first time it is used. Its assembler language handler just calls *hndlr()* below it.

```
void WordFireInOut::Init(p,m) long p;unsigned m;{
    inherited::Init(p,0);qspiPort=(QSPI*)0xfffc18;Q=blessA(sizeof(Queue),Queue);Q->InitQ(10);
    if( qspiPort->mstr) return; /* only initialize the QSPI the first time */ InFor=0xf;
    control =m; portD=assgD=0x7F; dirD=0x7E;*((int*)0xfffc00)=0xe;
    *((char*)fffc04)=0x30; *((char*)fffc05)=0x40; qspiPort->mstr = qspiPort->wren = 1;
    qspiPort-> hmie=1; qspiPort->bd = 0xff; asm{lea @0,hndaddr}*((int**)0x104)=hndaddr;
    asm{and #0xfdff,sr}qspiPort->spifie=1; qspiPort->spe=1; return;
    asm {@0 movem.l d0-d2/a0/a1/a4,-(a7)}
    if (qspiPort->spif && qspiPort->spifie) hndlspif();
    else if(qspiPort->halta && qspiPort->hmie) hndlhalta();
    asm{movem.l (a7)+,d0-d2/a0/a1/a4} asm {rte}
    }
}
```

The QSPI actually has three interrupts; the SPIF interrupt when data in the buffers has been moved, a MODF interrupt when a mode fault occurs in processor-processor communications, and a HALTA interrupt when the QSPI is told to halt and does halt. If any of these interrupts occur and are honored, the processor will load the same address, obtained from VECTOR, and execute the same handler. We will not need the MODF interrupt handler unless we are using the QSPI in a multicomputer system where another master could conceivably cause a mode fault. However, we poll the QSPI status register to distinguish between SPIF and HALTA interrupts, reading the QSPI's status port at *0xfffc1f*. It can test these in *if()* *then* statements to execute the actual C procedures *hndlspif()* or *hndlhalta()* that are the specific handlers that correctly responds to each possible interrupt. Note that two or more QSPI interrupts could be simultaneously requested, or one interrupt request could occur while another is being serviced. The rather substantial interrupt handler will be a conventional C procedure called from within the *Init* method. It will explicitly reference the instance variables of the many objects it needs to access using the vector of object pointers, as in *F[i]->error*.

```
void hndlr(){ int i,j;
    qspiPort->spif=0; /* clear inter. */ F[0]->qspiPort->endqp= N-1; /* assume no fire */
    if(InFor<0xf ){ /* if last exchange requested an input */
        F[InFor]->Q->Push(*(int *)0xfffd00+N); InFor=0xf; /* push on object's queue*/
        F[InFor]->error |= F[InFor]->Q->Error(); /* copy error */
    }
    for(i=0;i<M;i++) { /* look at all M objects until one is found requesting transfer */
        if ((j=(*(char *)(F[i]->chip>>4)>>F[i]->chip&7)&1) && ! F[i]->flag ){
            *((char *)0xfffd40+N)=F[i]->control; F[i]->qspiPort->endqp=N;
            if(i<K) { InFor=i;F[i]->flag = j; break; }/* if input dev requests xfer, remember it */
            else if(F[i]->Q->Qlen){ /* if out dev requests xfer, output queue nonempty */
            (int *) 0xfffd20+N) = F[i]->Q->Pull(); F[i]->flag = j; break; /*pop byte */
        }
        F[i]->flag = j;
}}
```

The *Terminate* method just sets the halt request *qspiPort-> halt=1.*

```
    void WordFire::Terminate(){ qspiPort-> halt =1;}
```

The *hndlhalta()* procedure will respond to halting the QSPI and clear the *halta* bit.

▷ *hndlhalta() { qspiPort->spe=qspiPort->spifie=qspiPort->hmie=0; }*

Because *qspiPort-> hmie* is set enabling interrupts HALT and MODF, the *hndlhalta()* procedure will be entered when *qspiPort-> halta* becomes set, to actually stop the QSPI. The Terminate method might request halting the QSPI, possibly while it is in an exchange. This would fail to completely shift in or shift out the data. The halt acknowledge interrupt actually shuts down the QSPI when done, when the data is completely shifted, by disarming it.

We briefly discuss the QSPI keyboard scanning routine of Section 4-4.3 for hardware shown in Figure 4-17, relative to interrupts. Each time the keyboard is scanned and the SPIF bit is set, generating an interrupt, the keys, represented by their bits in *R[0 to 7]* can be examined to see if one has just been closed. This is the same idea as checking for a rising edge on a transfer request bit input. When such a closure is detected, we may construct an ASCII code for the key and push the code into a queue, to be used by the program as a character of a command string. However, there is a problem with most keyboards, called bouncing. Pressing a key once will often cause multiple rising edges to be detected, so typing "GO" might generate the command string "GGGGOOO" in the input queue. The techniques used for debouncing are discussed in the next chapter, so we will discuss the interrupt-based keyboard scanning routine there.

5-3 Other 683xx Exceptions

In this section we discuss some exceptions specific to the 683xx, which are like interrupts, but are not used for synchronization. We first discuss exceptions that respond to malfunctions. Then we examine the operations done after reset. Finally we discuss the trap and line emulator instructions. The latter section also further explores the 683xx's supervisor and user states.

5-3.1 Error Exceptions

The 683xx handles various error conditions in a manner similar to the way it handles interrupts. The error exceptions vector to locations in low memory as shown in Table 5-1. These are discussed below.

A negative logic pin BERR (*bus error*) should be asserted low by external hardware if no memory or I/O device responds in a reasonable time. If the BERR signal is asserted during normal read/write memory cycles (FC not 7), the *Vector* 2 is used to handle this exception. Whereas only the status register and program counter are saved on the stack during most exception processing (Figure 5-15a), the bus error saves additional information which enables software to diagnose the cause of the error (Figure 5-15b). The bus error handler should remove the fourth word, whose most significant nibble distinguishes the type of exception. The BERR handler is entered if that nibble is 0xc. The handler may try to correct the error. An RTE instruction at the end of that handler can be used to resume processing if the error is corrected.

To *trace* instruction execution, a debugger sets the trace bit T of the status register SR (SR[15]). The T bit, if set, permits the execution of exactly one instruction and then generates an exception that uses *Vector* 9. If SR[14] is set instead, the exception is executed only when the instruction changes program flow, on branch, rts, and similar instructions. In the business card computer (BCC), MacDi puts a BGND instruction in the handler for trap exceptions. When the exception is processed, MacDi is called. You can change register or memory contents as if a breakpoint had occurred to put you in MacDi.

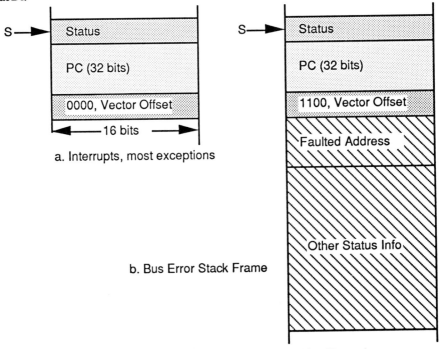

a. Interrupts, most exceptions

b. Bus Error Stack Frame

Figure 5-15. State Saved on Stack when Processing Exceptions.

Double-bus faults are considered catastrophic. In the BCC, these catastrophic errors cause the 683xx to enter the background mode to let the debugger examine the cause of the error.

Six exceptions are caused by inadvertent software activities. *Address error (Vector 3)* is caused when a word is fetched with an odd value of the program counter or a word or long word is recalled or memorized with an odd address. Even addresses are needed to read full 16-bit words from the 16-bit-wide memory. An *illegal instruction* exception *(Vector 4)* is caused when a word is fetched and decoded as an instruction but does not correspond to a legal 683xx instruction. *Zero divide (Vector 5)* is obviously caused when a divide instruction is attempted with a zero divisor. A *CHK* exception *(Vector 6)* is taken when the CHK instruction is executed and the word being checked is out of the bounds supplied to the instruction. A *TRAPV* exception *(Vector 7)* is taken when a TRAPV instruction is executed and the V condition code bit is set. A *privilege* exception *(Vector 8)* is taken when a privileged instruction is executed in the user mode, as we discuss later. It is rather like an illegal instruction exception for users.

The handler for error exceptions can attempt to fix the error, or just report it. In the Macintosh, the handler displays a bomb on the screen, In the BCC, the handler executes a BGND instruction to call the debugger. In multi-thread environments, it should terminate the thread, and possibly inform another supervisor thread of the failure.

5-3.2 An M68332 Reset Handler

In the M68332, RESET must be asserted low for the first 100 milliseconds after power is first applied and reaches 4.5 volts. Also, if the RESET pin is asserted low at any time for at least 590 clock cycles, processing stops (a kind of ultimate interrupt). The RESET line is generally connected to RESET pins on all I/O devices; it normally clears all I/O ports and initializes the M68332's I/O registers. The M68332 RESET instruction also causes this pin to be asserted low, but does not reset the M68332 itself.

When the RESET signal rises again, the long word at location 0 is put into the stack pointer A7, and the long word at location 4 is put into the program counter. This starts the M68332 at the location specified by the contents of long word 4 with the stack pointer A7 initialized to handle exceptions or subroutines. These long words and the reset handler or the bootstrap program are normally in read-only memory, for if we didn't have these locations and programs in memory before executing the first instruction, we would have no way to start the machine. (You may laugh at this, but machines proposed even in learned papers have had this problem – that they can't be started.) A ROM, PROM, EPROM, or similar nonvolatile memory must be enabled to read out the initial value of the program counter and stack pointer, and must remain available to fetch instructions from it until the bootstrap loads programs into RAM. However, it may be desirable to effectively remove that nonvolatile memory from the low end of the memory map after the bootstrap program in it has served its purpose, so that exception vectors in low memory can be written in RAM. The concept of including a memory or device in the memory map and then excluding it from the memory map is called *phantoming* the memory.

The M68332 BCC has a special chip select, CSBOOT, that is connected to a (64K, 16) EPROM, and is initialized upon reset to select the EPROM for any address in the first 1Mbyte of memory. Using incompletely specified addressing, this EPROM reappears in eight 128K byte blocks from 0 to 1Mbyte. In particular, it appears at location 0, to read out the stack pointer and program counter as discussed above, and at 0x60000, to read out the program in the EPROM, as shown in the BCC memory map, Figure 1-14. Shortly, this chip select's control registers are rewritten to select the EPROM only at 0x60000 to 0x7ffff, and CS0 to CS2 are initialized to select the BCC's RAM from 0 to 0xffff. This implements the phantoming of the EPROM.

The program that is entered handles the initialization ritual after a reset, so we call it the *reset handler*. The reset handler configures the M68332 and many of the I/O devices not already configured as desired by the RESET signal on their RESET pins and not to be configured later as part of the program that uses the device. In earlier discussions, we said that the rituals to be run just after power is applied are all put in this reset handler. The System Integration Module (SIM) is initialized; MacDi's ritual initializes *((int*)0xfffa00= 0x62cf;* to initialize its module configuration register, *((int*)0xfffa04=0x7f08;* to initialize the clock synthesizer, and *((int*)0xfffa20 = 0x0006;* to generate BERR signals when no chip select responds in 16 clock cycles. If you implement a stand-alone BCC, you should write these control registers in your reset handler. For further information on writing these and similar registers upon reset, consult Chapter 4 of the *MC68332 SIM User's Manual (SIM32UM/AD)*.

Whether or not you initialize the BCC using MacDi, you should set the chip select control registers of all the chip selects you will need for external memories and I/O chips in the reset handler. We attempted to initialize these control registers in the devices's *Init* methods, but found that to require too many arguments for external devices, which were unused for internal devices, so we recommend that these chip select modules be initialized in the reset handler. Put all the *baseAssign* and *optionAssign* macros in this reset handler. The CSBOOT registers (written if the macros' first parameter are -1) should be initialized so that the 2-wait state 128K EPROM appears at 0x60000, enabled to be read in upper and lower bytes in user/supervisor space, CS0 is the write enable for the upper RAM, CS1 is the write enable for the lower RAM, and CS2 is the read enable for both RAMs. The last three are set for zero-wait state 64K supervisor/user at location 0. However, rather than use the *pinAssign* macro several times, once for each chip select, you can initialize long word 0xfffa44 just once. This long word contains the pin assignement for all chip selects, for address bus lines or for port C output bits, in the pattern of bit pairs: 00 CS5 CS4 CS3 CS2 CS1 CS0 CSBOOT 00 00 00 CS10 CS9 CS8 CS7 CS6, where each bit pair CSi is a port C, address line or chip select pin control, and is 0 to make it a port C bit, 1 to make it an address line, 2 to make it an 8-bit chip select, and 3 to make it a 16-bit chip select. See the *MC68332 SIM User's Manual (SIM32UM/AD)* Table 4-5 and accompanying description for more detail. For instance, to make CS2, CS1, CS0, and CSBOOT 16-bit ports to control BCC chips, and CS7 and CS6 8-bit ports for your external I/O chips, write the statement: *((long*)0xfffa44)= 0x00ff000a;*

When using interrupts, whether or not you initialize the BCC using MacDi, you must set the interrupt arbitration IARB control registers of each module that can generate interrupts. The least significant nibble of the SIM's module configuration register, set to 0xf in the discussion above, the least significant nibble of the QSM's module configuration register at word 0xfffc00, and the least significant nibble of the TPU's module configuration register at word 0xfffe00, must be set to different non-zero values, so that simultaneous interrupts in each module will be hardware-arbitrated; if two modules request an interrupt, an interrupt from the module with the higher value will be honored. Since these values are interdependent, they should be initialized together, in the reset handler. These IARB control registers are generally initialized at the time that the entire module configuration registers are initialized, so the module configuration register should be initialized in the reset handler. While the values will depend on the specific use of these modules as explained in Sections 4.1.1 and 5.4.2.1 of the *MC68332 SIM User's Manual (SIM32UM/AD), and* Section 2.1.1 of the *MC68300 Family TPU Time Processor Unit Manual, (TPURM/AD),*we used *((int*)0xfffa00= 0x62cf; *((int*)0xfffc00= 0xe; and *((int*)0xfffe00= 0x8d; in our examples. A sample reset handler for a stand-alone BCC system, which uses CS6 and CS7, appears as follows:

```
RestHandlr() {
    *((int*)0xfffa00= 0x62cf; *((int*)0xfffc00= 0xe; *((int*)0xfffe00= 0x8d;
    *((int*)0xfffa04=0x7f08;*((int*)0xfffa20=0x0004;*((long*)0xfffa44)= 0x00ff000a;
    baseAssign(-1,0x60000,k128);optionAssign(-1,rd+upper+lower+as,2,user+super,0);
    baseAssign(0,0,k64);optionAssign(0,wr+upper+as,0,user+super,0);
    baseAssign(1,0,k64);optionAssign(0,wr+lower+as,0,user+super,0);
    baseAssign(2,0,k64);optionAssign(0,rd+upper+lower+as,0,user+super,0);
    baseAssign(6,0x10000,k16);optionAssign(6,rd+wr+upper+as,0,user+super,0);
    baseAssign(7,0x10000,k16);optionAssign(7,rd+wr+lower+as,0,user+super,0);
}
```

The handler may also run diagnostic programs to check the microprocessor, memory, or I/O devices or clear all or part of memory or initialize some variables. This handler might be a *bootstrap program* whose purpose is to load into memory and then execute the program that follows, or an *operating system* to manage memory and time resources for a microcomputer. Operating systems will be described in Chapter 10.

5-3.3 An M68340 Reset Handler

The M68340 BCC has a special chip select, CS0, that is connected to a (64K, 16) EPROM, and is initialized upon reset, and until the valid bit CS0's control register is set, it selects the EPROM for any address in memory. Using incompletely specified addressing, this EPROM reappears in every eight 128K byte block. In particular, it appears at location 0, to read out the stack pointer and program counter as discussed above, and at 0x60000, to read out the program in the EPROM, as shown in the BCC memory map, Figure 1-14. Shortly, this CS0's control registers are rewritten to select the EPROM only at 0x60000 to 0x7ffff, and CS1 is initialized to select the BCC's RAM from 0 to 0xffff. This implements the *phantoming* of the M68340 EPROM.

The I/O registers internal to the M68340 can be positioned anywhere in memory. A special register, the Module Base Register MBR at location 0x3ff00 in CPU space (Function Code FC{2 to 0]=7) is written with the desired address, but the least significant 12 bits are written as 0s. The least significant bit of this register is a valid bit, which must be set to 1. The MBR must be written in before any other register, such as the chip select register, is written in. Being in CPU space, it can only be written into using the special MOVES instruction, after the destination function code register DFC is made to be 7.

The program that is entered handles the initialization ritual after a reset, so we call it the *reset handler*. A reset handler configures the M68332 and many of the I/O devices not already configured as desired by the RESET signal on their RESET pins and not to be configured later as part of the program that uses the device. In earlier discussions, we said that the rituals to be run just after power is applied are all put in this reset handler.

The System Integration Module (SIM) is initialized using a pointer *int *p=0xffffff00;* MacDi's ritual initializes *p[0]=0x62cf;* to initialize its module configuration register and *p[0x10]=0x0004;* to generate BERR signals when no chip select responds in 64 clock cycles. The initial CLK clock rate is set to 8.387 MHz. To run at 16.666 MHz, we need to write the clock synthesizer control register *p[2]=0x7f00.* Write these control registers in your reset handler in a stand-alone BCC. For further information on writing these and similar registers upon reset, consult Chapter 4 of the *MC68340 Integrated Processor User's Manual (MC68340UM/AD).*

Whether or not you initialize the BCC using MacDi, you should set the chip select control registers of all the chip selects you will need for external memories and I/O chips in the reset handler. We attempted to initialize these control registers in the devices's *Init* methods, but found that to require too many arguments for external devices, which were unused for internal devices, so we recommend that these chip select modules be initialized in the reset handler. Put all the *baseAssign* and *optionAssign* macros in this reset handler. The CS0 registers should be initialized so that the 2-wait state 128K EPROM appears at 0x60000, enabled to be read in user/supervisor space, CS1 is the write enable for the RAM, and if the BCC platform board is used, CS2 is the enable for the M68881, and CS3 is the read enable for external ROMs or RAMs on the platform board. See the *MC68340 Integrated Processor User's Manual (MC68340UM/AD)* Table 4-5 and accompanying description, and Section 4.3.4, for more detail.

When using interrupts, whether or not you initialize the BCC using MacDi, you must set the interrupt arbitration IARB control registers of each module that can generate interrupts, which are the least significant nibble of their module configuration register). The SIM's IARB is set to 0xf in the discussion above, the TM's at word *p[600]*, the DMA's Serial I/O's and Timer's at word *p[0x300]*, *p[0x380]*, *p[0x3c0]*, and *p[0x3e0]*, must be set to different non-zero values, so that simultaneous interrupts in each module will be hardware-arbitrated; if two modules request an interrupt, an interrupt from the module with the higher value will be honored. Because these values are interdependent, they should be initialized together, in the reset handler. These IARB control registers are generally initialized at the time that the entire module configuration registers are initialized, so the module configuration register should be initialized in the reset handler.

In this reset handler, the chip selects for I/O devices used in all the procedures should be initialized. For instance, as in Section 4.2, we enable a read-only input port at 0x10000 and a read-write output port at 0x10800. The *CsAssign* macros for these chip selects should be in the reset handler. A sample reset handler for a stand-alone BCC system appears as follows:

```
RestHandlr() { register int *p=0xffffff00;
    p[0]= 0x62cf; p[0x10]=0x0004; p[2]=0x7f00;
    p[0x300] = 0xa; p[0x380] = 0xb; p[0x3c0]= 0xc; p[0x3e0] = 0xd;
    CsAssign(0,0x60000,17,word+3,rdOnly);CsAssign(1,0,16,fast,rdWr);
    CsAssign(2,0x10000,8,fast,rdOnly); CsAssign(3,0x10800,8,fast,rdWr);
}
```

5-3.4 Traps, Line Emulators, and Special Instructions

In this subsection we discuss some interrelated instructions and mechanisms, related to exception processing, that can be used to support operating systems. At the end of this subsection, the multi-thread environment of Section 5-1.8 will be expanded into a simple multi-tasking operating system using these instructions and mechanisms.

The TRAP #n (n = 0 to 15) instructions and line 0xA and line 0xF emulators are exceptions that are deliberately executed as instructions. They all save the program counter and status register like an interrupt does (see Figure 5-15a) and jump to an address using an exception vector number as in Table 5-1. The TRAP #n instructions use *Vector* numbers 32 to 47, the line 0xA emulator uses *Vector* 10, and the line 0xF emulator uses *Vector* 11. We will discuss the use of TRAP #n instructions later.

The line 0xF emulator trap is executed whenever the instruction is 0xFxxx where x is a don't care hexadecimal number. Instructions designed for the floating-point coprocessor 68881 and memory management unit 68851 that work with the 68020 have op codes of the type 0xFxxx. If you replace your 683xx with a 68020 and connect the appropriate coprocessors, these op codes will be executed by the coprocessors. You can write the line 0xF emulator trap exception handler to perform the same function the coprocessor would perform were it there. In fact, in the 683xx you can use the 68881 as an I/O device in that handler, to carry out its operations almost directly. That way, software written with such code would correctly run on a 68020 with the coprocessor, but the exception handler would produce the same result, albeit more slowly, otherwise. That is why line 0xF emulator traps are called emulator traps. Therefore, such op codes should be avoided for any other purpose than to emulate the coprocessor instructions.

The use of 0xA line emulator traps and TRAP #n instructions depends upon the operating system. The line 0xA emulator trap is executed whenever the instruction is 0xAxxx where x is a don't care hexadecimal number. The Macintosh uses these 0xA line emulator traps to call "subroutines" usually put in ROM that implement commonly used operations like drawing figures on the screen (QuickDraw) or inputting or outputting data to a disk or modem. These 0xA line emulator traps are shorter than subroutine calls using JSR, and the source code can remain unchanged if different ROMS are used that have these "subroutines" in different locations, provided that the address at vector 10 points to where the different "subroutines" are sorted out in a manner similar to how interrupts are polled.

The supervisor state, indicated when the status register S bit (SR[13]) is set, is often used by operating systems. The user state, indicated when the status register S bit (SR[13]) is clear, is used by user programs. The supervisor state is entered (S is set) upon reset or the processing of any exception. The user state is entered when the S bit is cleared by an instruction that changes the high byte of the status register or by restoring the status register from the stack such that the S bit is cleared. The supervisor and user states can have different memory spaces if differentiated spaces are used (Figure 1-12). The supervisor stack pointer is different from the user stack pointer. The supervisor stack pointer is used to push or pull return addresses or data (using A7) when in the supervisor state; the user stack pointer is used to push or pull return addresses or data (using A7) when in the user state. Certain instructions that change the high byte of the status register or MOVE to/from the user stack pointer can be executed in the supervisor state but cause a privilege violation exception in the user state.

A TRAP #n instruction is often used to call an operating system subroutine. In addition to being a short one-word instruction, whose "subroutine" address is in low memory and therefore the caller's instruction code does not change if the subroutine is put somewhere else, this instruction, an exception, also changes the 683xx to supervisor mode. This permits user programs to call subroutines which can execute privileged instructions. The user programs themselves can be in user mode, where they are prevented from executing these privileged instructions. If privileged instructions include all those instructions that can make one thread interfere with another in a multi-thread environment, several such user threads can be prevented from interfering with each other. The user can be prevented from accidentally destroying the operating system or another user's code or data. These totally independent threads are called *tasks,* and the operating system is called *multi-tasking.* Privileged instructions are needed only by the operating system. So the operating system is often entirely treated as a collection of "TRAP #n called subroutines". The OS-9 operating system, discussed in Chapter 10, uses TRAP #0 to call the operating system, and the remaining TRAP #n instructions to link to common library routines at execution time.

Differentiated memory spaces can be used to allow the program being debugged the use of only the user data and user program spaces. A user is prevented from affecting the supervisor program or data spaces, where the operating system is running. Similarly the user stack is different from the supervisor stack, so incorrect operation of the user stack pointer should not affect the operating system's correct use of the supervisor stack pointer. These features are useful in the BCC if the operating system's supervisor data space can be put in the 2K RAM that is inside the M68332 rather than the 64K RAM that is on the BCC outside the M68332 chip. The latter memory can be divided into user *task spaces* of sizes 2K, 4K, 16K, or 32K. The operating system can modify the SIM's CS0, CS1 and CS2 control registers to enable one of these task spaces at a time, to run one user task at a time. For instance, executing *baseAssign(0,0,k2); baseAssign (1,0,k2); baseAssign(2,0,k2);* will permit only the lowest 2K bytes of RAM to be read or written. When one task is running in its task space, the other task spaces are not accessible because the chip selects will not be enabled for addresses that correspond to other task spaces, to prevent that task from accessing the other task spaces.

STOP #n puts n into the status register and waits for an interrupt, rather like the infinite wait loop in the count program in Section 5-1.3. The 683xx goes to "sleep," to be "awakened" by a reset or interrupt. If an interrupt is requested and its level is higher than I[2 to 0], as set by STOP #n, the 683xx honors the interrupt, so an interrupt signal will start the 683xx but will not execute the interrupt handler. STOP #0 will honor any interrupt, and then resume normal execution after the STOP instruction. STOP #0x700 will not honor any interrupts (except nonmaskable level 7 interrupts). This permits an interrupt signal to merely resume normal execution. LPSTOP is a special 683xx instruction similar to STOP. When it is executed, the processor shuts down as completely as possible. A "sleeping" 683xx consumes only 500 μamp, instead of the 125 ma. required by a running 683xx. This is like an infinite wait loop executed in microcode. However, if we use the real-time interrupt in a multi-thread environment, LPSTOP partially shuts down that module's counters to conserve power. Conserving power results in a tick-time being stretched about 40%. That makes the "sleep time" 40% longer when the LPSTOP instruction is executed than when another task runs the computer during a tick. This is a "feature" of the current M68332 chip (mask F) we are using. A "feature" is a characteristic of a product that is actually a design error, but the company being unable to fix it, may try to convince the buyer that this "feature" is desirable. If you can't fix it, advertise it as a "feature". However, we hope this anomaly will soon be corrected. Presently, we use STOP #*n* if the BCC is not battery powered, because the tick period can be used for real-time interrupt synchronization.

5-3.5 Multitasking in the M68332

A simple multi-tasking operating system using special 683xx instructions and mechanisms in the M68332 is now presented. We will assume the operating system, including its classes, objects, methods and exception vectors, is entirely located in the (1K,16) RAM located inside the M68332, and that two user programs are running in 0x4000 to 0x7fff and 0x8000 to 0xbfff, respectively. We assume the two user programs initialize their register a4 to access global variables but do not show this step. Before running the operating system, we assume the program *RestHandlr()* is executed, and that, in addition, that RAM is located at 0xfff000 which is defined to be *VBASE*, effected by executing *(long*)0xfffb02) = 0x100fff0;* (See Chapter 6, *MC68332 SIM User's Manual*). User programs call the operating system for input-output and time and space management.

A user program calls the operating system with TRAP #0. To pass it parameters, this program, in user memory, will use a procedure that consists only of this TRAP #0 instruction. Its *register* parameters can be easily passed to the system.

long System6(procPath,d6,d5,d4,d3,d2)
    register unsigned int procPath; register long d6,d5,d4,d3,d2;{asm{trap #0}}

The operating system has a similar procedure in supervisor memory (0xfff000 to 0xfff7ff), which contains in it the trap #0 handler:

static long System(procPath,d6,d5,d4,d3,d2)
    register unsigned int procPath; register long d6,d5,d4,d3,d2; {
asm{ lea @0,a0
    move.l a0,VBASE+0x80 / trap #0 handler address vector */*
    return
▶ *@0...*
    }
}

The code after the label @0 is executed when a trap #0 instruction is executed. Because both these procedures have identical lists of register variables, the user's call to *System6* will put the variables in registers d7 to d3, and the program in supervisor space, which executes the trap #0 handler, will find these variables in the same registers (e.g. procedure parameter d6 will be in data register d6). While one to six arguments can be passed this way, system calls with one or two arguments can be more efficiently implemented as in *long System1(procPath) register unsigned int procPath;{asm{trap #0}}* and *long System2(procPath,d6) register unsigned int procPath; register long d6;{asm{trap #0}}*, which put the argument *procPath* in data register d7. They all put the argument *procPath* in data register d7, and *System* will use *procPath* to identify the system call. User programs can use *System1, System2,* or *System6,* whichever passes enough arguments, and the handler in *System* will examine *procPath* to determine what to do, and therefore how many parameters to use.

The 16-bit parameter *procPath* will be used to pass a system call number in its high byte and a constant in its low byte, depending on the call. For illustration, we will assume that the operating system calls will initialize an I/O device (high byte 0), input data (1) output data (2) and terminate (3) it. These I/O calls will use a path number, which is an index into a vector of I/O device objects as we used them in the class *WordFire* in Section 5-1.3, which will be encoded into the low byte of *procPath*. The path number will be an index into a vector of I/O objects. It will also determine, in the *System* TRAP #0 handler, which class a device is in. The I/O classes, objects (with instance variables) and methods will be in supervisor space to protect them against user program errors. Thus, directly accessing an instance variable from a user program, as we read the variable *error* in previous examples, will generate a bus error. We will use a system call (high byte 4) to return the error value to the user and then automatically clear it to zero. In general, I/O object instance variables (like queue pointers read to see if the queue is empty) as well as I/O device control registers and status registers will be in supervisor space and will not be directly accessible to the user; a system call like the one just discussed will be used to read or write them. Finally, time management, such as putting a process to sleep for a number of ticks, will be implemented by a system call (high byte 5). Other operating system functions, such as this, can be added. We can use macros to make the generic system call descriptive and easier to use for each of these:

```
#define Init(i,j,k) System6(0+i,j,k,0,0,0)
#define Input(i) System1(0x100+i)
#define Output(i,j) System2(0x200+i,j)
#define Terminate(i) System1(0x300+i)
#define Error(i) System1(0x400+i)
#define Sleep(i) System2(0x500,i)
```

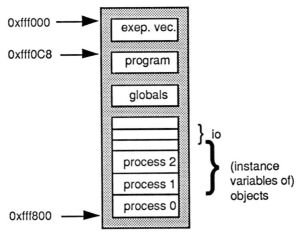

Figure 5-16. Supervisor Memory Map.

A task, whose code and data are stored between 0x4000 and 0x7fff, and which initializes an input device, an output device, and moves a byte from input to output, terminates both devices and then sleeps, might look thus:

```
main(){
    Init(0,0xfffa11,0xff);Init(1,0xfffa19,0);
    Output(0,Input(1));
    Terminate(1);Terminate(0);Sleep(0xffffffff);
}
```

The allocation procedure assigns supervisor data buffer space for process and I/O object (instance variables) from high to low memory, while the exception vectors, program and global variables are loaded into low memory, as shown in Figure 5-16. The program assumes that the process objects are allocated together and that process 0 (that never sleeps) is allocated first, at highest memory location.

We now discuss time management that uses real-time interrupts. As we forked threads (different parts of one program that are compiled at the same time, that share global variables, and that each can run the processor for a tick time) in the multi-thread environment (Section 5-1.6) we now fork processes (that are compiled at different times and share no data, except for data passed though the operating system). The class *Process* includes time-management instance variables *age* and *priority* and methods *InitP* for initializing the real-time clock and *Fork* for forking processes.

```
struct Process :direct {
    unsigned age, priority, base; long sleepTime, savedUsp, registers[15],StatusReg;
    long ProgCount, unsigned Vect;
    void InitP(void),Fork(long, unsigned int, unsigned int, unsigned int);
};
```

The *InitP* method starts the real-time clock and contains its interrupt handler. It will be called early in the initialization of the operating system; it calls *Fork* to set up process 0 that never sleeps, and sets up the exception vectors, and the vector address for the real-time interrupt. *TICK* is elsewhere defined as the address vector of the real-time interrupt handler. It then starts the real-time clock and returns to the rest of the initialization of the operating system.

The handler will be executed each 10 milliseconds. It saves all the registers in a buffer within instance variables *registers* and *savedUsp* of the object for the process. The MOVEM instruction saves all data and address registers, except a7, in *registers* and saves the user stack pointer in *savedUsp* (note that the handler executes in supervisor space, but the user's stack pointer must be saved to resume the user process). The extra two long words of the instance variable *registers* will have been filled with the stack frame that results from an exception (see Figure 5-15a). At the end of the handler, like the handler for threads, the registers will be restored from the instance variables, but from the object of the process that is chosen to use the next tick. The handler decrements *sleepTime* of sleeping processes, increments *age* of non-sleeping processes, and chooses the process with oldest *age* to run during the next tick time.

However, the handler also implements a memory management protection mechanism that uses the chip select control registers. As noted earlier, chip selects CS0, CS1, and CS2 control registers can be altered to restrict the range of RAM that can be accessed. An instance variable *base,* set by a *Fork* parameter, provides the value of that control register. When a process is run, only the memory it uses is enabled. Memory outside that range is not enabled, so that any attempt to access it will cause a bus error. That way, one process cannot accidentally or maliciously interfere with another process.

```
void Process::InitP(void) { register long vector,i,j; /* set up real-time interrupts */
    Fork(0xfff190,0,0,3); /* set up process 0 which never sleeps */
asm{move.l #VBASE,a0 /* set vector base register */
    movec a0,vbr /* to low end of supervisor ram */
    lea @0,a1 /* put address of real-time handler */
    move.l a1,TICK(a0) /* in vector address */
    movem.l a4-a5,VBASE /* save global, object pointer */
    move.b #0xe,0xfffa01 /* set up rt clock */
    move.l #0x6000052+(((long)TICK/4)<<16),0xfffa22
    return /* return to main */
```
▶
```
    @0 movem.l d0-d7/a0-a6,-(a7) /* handler: save registers on ssp */
    move.l 16*4(a7),vector /* save vector to distinguish rt tick from trap #0 */
    movec usp,i /* save usp pointer */
    movem.l VBASE,a4-a5 /* get object, global pointers */   }
    savedUsp =i; age=priority; asm{lea 0xfff800-sizeof(Process),a4}
    for(i=j=0;i<NPROCS;i++){
        if(((vector&0xfff)==TICK)&&(sleepTime)&&(sleepTime!=0xffffffff)) sleepTime--;
        if(!sleepTime)
        {if(age!=0xffff) age++; if(age>=j) {j=age; asm{move.l a4,VBASE}} }
        asm{lea -sizeof(Process)(a4),a4}
    }
    asm{move.l VBASE,a4}i=savedUsp; /* use chosen process */
    *((int *)0xfffa4c)=*((int *)0xfffa50)=*((int *)0xfffa54)=base;
    asm{
    lea registers(a4),a7
    movec i,usp
    movem.l (a7)+,d0-d7/a0-a6
    rte /* use stacked registers to get going again */
    }
```
}

The *Fork* method merely initializes instance variables *priority*, *base*, and
sleepTime, sets up *savedUsp* (which is 0) and *registers* to be the same as they are left
when the real-time interrupt handler stops and saves the state of a process. A minor note,
process 0's instance variables *savedUsp* and *registers* are put by *allocate* where the
system stack will be located when *Fork* is executed, so we let its values be initialized
later when the first real-time clock interrupt occurs, to avoid crashing this method.

```
void Process::Fork(location, newPriority, stackLoc, decodeValue)
    long location;unsigned int newPriority,stackLoc,decodeValue;{
    sleepTime=0; age=priority=newPriority;base=decodeValue;
    if(!(savedUsp=stackLoc)) return;
    StatusReg=0; ProgCount=location; Vect=TICK;
    asm{ movem.l d0-d7/a0-a6,registers }
}
```

The operating system's *main* procedure merely initializes the TRAP #0 handler by
calling *System* and the real-time interrupt handler (and process 0 that never sleeps) by
sending an *InitP* message and other processes by sending them a *Fork* message. It
enables interrupts and loops forever, using the STOP #n (or LPSTOP #n) instruction.

```
main(){ Process *p;
    free=(char*)0xfff800; asm{lea 0xfff800,a7 } System(0,0,0,0,0,0);
    p=blessA(sizeof(Process),Process); p->InitP();
    p=blessA(sizeof(Process),Process); p->Fork(0x4000,100,0x8000,0x42);
    p=blessA(sizeof(Process),Process); p->Fork(0x8000,500,0xc000,0x82);
    asm{and #0xf8ff,sr} while(1) asm{stop #0x2000};
}
```

Finally we come to the TRAP #0 handler that executes all system calls. As previously explained, it gets its parameters from a similarly structured procedure such as *System6* executed in a user program. The high byte of the *procPath* parameter determines, in a *case* statement, what is to be done. Note that, for all I/O calls (*Init, Input, Output, Terminate,* and *Error*) the low byte is an index into the vector *IO,* whose elements are elsewhere defined to be (pointers to) objects of type *IoDevice,* and for object *Init* calls, this number further determines which class the object belongs to. For this example, we assume that paths 0 and 1 belong to the class *M68332EF* and path 2 to the class *IoDevice.* The *if then else* statements at the beginning of *System*'s *case 0* save the (pointer to the) I/O class in *class,* to provide the required class for each path. We did this for simplicity (and because we ran out of room in the 2K byte supervisor memory). However, you would probably use a multi-tasking capability with interrupt-based I/O devices rather than simple I/O devices and you would explicitly rewrite this code to provide the desired classes for each of your program's paths. Note also that the local variable *device* is preloaded with the contents of one of the (pointers to) I/O objects *IO[i]* to avoid having to do that for each I/O case, even though it is not needed for other cases (such as the *Sleep* call).

The *Sleep* system call is similar to the statement *curThread->sleepTime=n;* used in the multi-threaded environment to put a process to sleep for a number of ticks. However, after assigning a parameter value to the instance variable *sleepTime,* this call falls into the real-time interrupt handler by executing *asm{movea.l VBASE+TICK,a0} asm{jmp (a0)}.* This "fakes" a real-time interrupt to give up the rest of the current tick period. We do not have to execute the statement *while(curThread->sleepTime);* that we used in the multi-threaded environment to waste the rest of the current tick period. However, this "fake" tick interrupt does not cause the sleeping processes to decrement their *sleepTime* because TRAP #0 stack frame's last word is different from the real-time interrupt stack frame's last word, and that is tested before decrementing *sleepTime.*

The very useful *Sleep* call gives up the current tick to non-sleeping processes. A process sleeps "forever" while waiting for a device to enter its done state, as in the Centronics class (Section 5-2.1), or when an *Input* method waits for its queue to fill or an *Output* method waits for its queue to get some room. "Waking up" clears *sleepTime* and resumes execution of the task. When different tasks use only the time that other tasks would waste while waiting for these events, each task will appear to have full use of the machine, as if the other tasks weren't even there.

Putting a process to sleep indefinitely, without waking it up, effectively stops it. The process no longer competes for, and therefore does not get, any tick periods to execute its code. In the user's *main* procedure, the last statement puts the process to sleep indefinitely to stop it.

```
static long System(procPath,d6,d5,d4,d3,d2)
    register unsigned int procPath; register long d6,d5,d4,d3,d2; {
    register void *class;register IoDevice *device;
asm{ lea @0,a0} asm{move.l a0,VBASE+0x80} return;
▶    asm{ or #0x700,sr /* disable interrupts */
     @0 movem.l a3-a5,-(a7)
     move.l 0xfff004,a5
     }
     device=IO[procPath&0xff]; switch(procPath>>8){
     case 0: f((procPath&0xff)==2) class=IoDevice; else class=M68332EF;
        device=IO[procPath&0xff]=blessA(sizeof(IoDevice),class); device->Init(d6,d5); break;
     case 1:d6=device->Input(); break;
     case 2:device->Output(d6); break;
     case 3:device->Terminate(); break;
     case 4:d6=device->error; device->error=0; break;
     case 5: (*(Process **)VBASE )->sleepTime=d6;
        asm{ movem.l (a7)+,a3-a5
             movea.l VBASE+TICK,a0
             jmp (a0) /* give up tick */
        }
     }
     asm{movem.l (a7)+,a3-a5
     move.l d6,d0
     rte
     }
}
```

We also put the classes *IoDevice* and *M68332EF* and objects *IO[3]* of the class *IoDevice* in supervisor space. The resulting program worked. However, were we to reprogram the EPROM to store supervisor and user programs, there would be much more room in the 2K byte RAM inside the M68332 to store more exception vectors and instance variables of objects.

You should review this example because it illustrates many operating system principles in a compact and concrete example. Examine the task scheduling mechanism. It is the same as the thread scheduling mechanism. Then study the use of the supervisor and user states, and their effect on parameter passing mechanisms needed to call supervisor state procedures. Though this section requires effort, that effort will pay off.

In Chapter 10, we expand the ideas in this section towards a full multi-tasking operating system. This section provides the key mechanisms of that system, and we will refer back to it later. Moreover, it can be used in lieu of a full operating system to provide many of the latter's features, such as time management and memory protection. The operating system provides much more powerful time and memory management capabilities than these simple objects give, but OS-9 requires up 128K bytes of EPROM to do that. So these object-oriented programs provide an alternative to a full operating system, and you can use as many of these capabilities as your application needs.

5-4 Fast Synchronization Mechanisms

In the previous section, we discussed the synchronization mechanisms used for slower I/O devices. There are six mechanisms used for faster devices. These are direct memory access, context switching, coprocessing, and shuttle, indirect, time-multiplexed, and video memory. They are briefly outlined in the last section.

The first two subsections discusses three I/O synchronization techniques for that are faster than interrupts. *Direct memory access* (DMA) is a well-known technique, whereby an I/O device gets access to memory directly without having the microprocessor in between. By this direct path, a word input through a device can be stored in memory, or a word from memory can be output through a device, on the device's request. It is also possible for a word in memory to be moved to another place in memory using direct memory access. The second technique, *context switching*, is actually a more general type of DMA. The *context* of a processor is its set of accumulators and other registers (as Texas Instruments uses the term) and the instruction set of the processor. To switch context means to logically disconnect the existing set of registers – bringing in a new set to be used in their place – or to use a different instruction set, or both. *Coprocessing* can be considered a form of context switching in which the main processor lets the coprocessor execute exactly one instruction with its context before the main processor resumes its execution using its context. These three techniques are now studied.

5-4.1 M68340 Direct Memory Access

One of the fastest ways to input data to a buffer is direct memory access. Compared to techniques discussed earlier, this technique requires considerably more hardware and is considerably faster. A *DMA channel* is the additional logic needed to move data to or from an I/O device. The M68340 microprocessor has two identical DMA channels, 1 and 2. (See Chapter 6, *MC68340 Integrated Processor User's Manual (MC68340UM/AD)*.) We discuss channel 1. Pins DREQ1, DACK1 and DONE1 handshake between channel 1 and an external I/O device. See Figure 1-15.

In DMA, a word is moved from the device to a memory in a *DMA transfer*. The device requests transferring a word to or from memory; the microprocessor CPU, which may be in the middle of an operation, simply stops what it is doing for one to five memory cycles and *releases control* of the address and data bus to its memory by disabling its tristate drivers that drive these buses; the I/O system including the DMA channel is then expected to use those cycles to transfer words from its input port to a memory location. Successive words are moved this way into or from a buffer.

Two DMA techniques are available for the M68340. An internal I/O device or an external I/O device can use DMA. If an external I/O device wishes to input or output data, it asserts an M68340 pin control signal (DREQ1) which *steals a memory cycle* to transfer one word in *cycle steal mode* or it halts the microprocessor to transfer one or more words in *burst mode*. The cycle steal technique is designed to respond to an edge of DREQ1 and generally will transfer only one byte, word, or long word before the processor resumes its operation. In this mode, the device can only steal a cycle, then give the processor a cycle, and so on. The burst DMA lets the I/O device and DMA channel control the system for many cycles. If DREQ1 is asserted (low), and as long as it is asserted, the I/O device will transfer data in consecutive memory cycles until it is done. Many words can be input from the input device to consecutive memory words; greater throughput is achieved because this mode permits the device to transmit as many words as it wants in successive memory cycles. When the channel transfers data, it asserts an M68340 pin control signal (DACK1). When all transfers are done, an M68340 input-output pin signal (DONE1) is asserted, or it can be asserted to end DMA.

For each mode just discussed, there are two modes of transferring a word from an input device to memory or vice versa. The *single-address DMA transfer* uses the address bus to select a memory word that is to be written into, while DACK1 causes the device to put a word on the data bus. In one memory cycle, DACK1 signals the device, which puts data on the data bus; while in the same memory cycle, the M68340 DMA module puts the address on the address bus and puts a write signal on the RW line to memory to cause the data to be written at the address. The *dual-address DMA transfer* uses the address bus twice in two consecutive memory cycles to move a word on the data bus from a device to a memory location; first to select the I/O device to read a word from it into the M68340, and second to select a memory word that is to be written into from the M68340. A holding register in the DMA module holds the word from the first memory cycle to the second. The single-address transfer is more common among DMA systems in most microcomputers, but the dual-address transfer can be used with the M68340. While DMA can be used for input, output, or memory-to-memory moves, it will be described in the following for memory-to-memory moves. It can be easily adapted to input or output operations. We will utilize the dual-address transfer to move a block of memory in the following example and in the paper tape reader example that follows it.

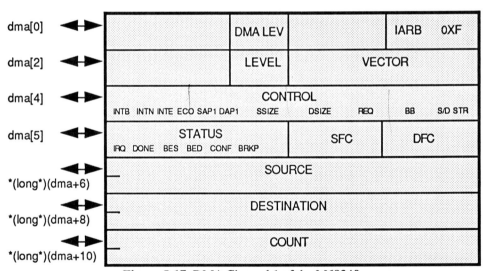

Figure 5-17. DMA Channel 1 of the M68340.

We focus on the ports used in the simplest dual-address memory-to-memory block transfer using channel 1, whose block move is synchronized using a gadfly technique. Assume *(int*)dma* points to the location of the first word of the M68340 channel 1, as shown in Figure 5-17. Channel 1 has 32-bit address registers SOURCE (and function code SFC) to get the data from memory in the first cycle and DESTINATION (and DFC) to supply the memory address where the data are to be written in the second cycle of a dual-address transfer. Each address is incremented after a word is moved so the next word will be read from and written in the next location. Also, as a number of bytes are to be moved, a 32-bit register COUNT is needed to keep track of how many words remain to be moved. As each word is moved, this counter is decremented by the number of bytes moved. Channel configuration is specified by a CONTROL register. Finally, DMA requires interrupt and done flags that can be read in the 6-bit STATUS register.

To simplify the correct setting of fields for the CONTROL register, a collection of *#define* and *enum* statements should be included in each program using DMA. Note that *enum* statements lists alternatives of which one should be chosen, and can fill in several fields; for instance the constant *BURSTW* means use burst mode for external transfers, and assert the DACK1 signal during the memory cycle when data are written. One of these constants and the constant *START* must be in each assignment to the CONTROL register. Other constants, *#define*d in the following list, may or may not be included as the situation calls for. Finally, if DMA interrupts are used, the IARB field of *dma[0]* must be initialized to a nonzero value different from other M68340 IARB fields.

```
#define INTB 0x8000
#define INTN 0x4000
#define INTE 0x2000
#define SAPI 0x800
#define DAPI 0x400
#define SOURCE 8
#define DESTINATION 6
enum {LONG,BYTE,WORD};
enum {INTERNAL25,INTERNAL50=4,INTERNAL75=8,INTERNAL100=0xC,       100 C
BURSTW=0x20, CYCLESTEALW=0x30,BURSTR=0x1020,CYCLESTEALR=0x1030};
enum {DUAL,SINGLE=2};       ?                                    ?
#define START 1
```

DMA block transfers have IDLE, BUSY, and DONE states. An IDLE state indicates that no DMA activity is in progress, a BUSY state generally indicates that a word will be transferred whenever the device needs it, and a DONE state indicates that all words in the buffer have been transferred. To use DMA, the program must initialize the SOURCE DESTINATION (and SFC, DFC) to the address where data are read and written, and must initialize COUNT to the number of bytes that will be moved. A gadfly loop can be used to monitor the DONE state of the DMA system to determine when all words are transferred. DMA requires extra hardware – an address port, a counter, and a busy-done mechanism – but permits data to be moved at a rate of one data word per memory cycle from an input device to memory.

To transfer 128 bytes from 0x1000 to 0x2000, the DMA controller is initialized in the procedure *main* below. First, bit 0 of the control register, STR, which indicates the DMA channel is started, must be cleared to change any registers. The DMA LEV register, which prevents DMA when the current processor interrupt level is greater than DAM LEV, should be set to 7 to permit DMA regardless of that level. The program then clears status bits and writes the function codes 5, writes 0x1000 to SOURCE, 0x2000 to DESTINATION, 128 into COUNT, and a word into CONTROL. While that part is easy and obvious, a ritual, which we briefly explain for our example, sets CONTROL so you can select the options you want for the transfer: interrupt enables, single or dual address and size and incrementing of source and destination addresses, and external control of transfers. The four most significant bits of the control word, INTB, INTN and INTE, used to enable interrupts, and ECO, to control external transfers, are negated F. The bits, SAPI and DAPI, are T to increment source and destination addresses after each transfer. The next two pairs of bits, SSIZE and DSIZE, used to designate the size of each data transfer, are set to 1 for byte transfers. The next bits, REQ and BB, used to designate how requests are to be made, are set for internal requests using the bus 100% of its bandwidth. The next bit, S/D, used to designate single or dual address transfers, is set to F, indicating dual address. The program starts the DMA by setting STR, CONTROL's least significant bit. Control is written with the pattern FFFF TTFT FTFF TTFT (0x0d4d). The program gadflies until the second most significant bit of the status port, DONE, is set, when all 128 bytes are moved.

```
main(){ register int *dma=(int*)0xffff780;
    dma[4]=0; dma[0]=0x780; /* stop DMA, set interrupt mask to allow DMA anytime */
    dma[5]=0x7f55; /* clear all status bits, interrupts, set function codes sup. data*/
    *(long*)(dma + 6)=0x1000; /* source */ *(long*)(dma + 8)=0x2000; /* destination */
    *(long*)(dma + 10)=0x80; /* number of bytes to be moved */
    dma[4]=DAPI+SAPI+(BYTE<<SOURCE)+(BYTE<<DESTINATION)+
        CYCLESTEALR+ DUAL+START;0xd4d; /* set control bits to 0xd4d */
    while( ! (dma[5] & 0x4000)); /* gadfly until DONE */
}
```

We illustrate DMA for input using the M68230 in our paper tape example. (Please forgive us for using a fast synchronization technique for the very slow paper tape reader, but again we reuse this example to avoid introducing more extraneous material.) The M68230 connections will be the same as in Figure 4-8b, but in addition, port C bit 4/DMAREQ is connected to the M68340's DREQ1 pin. The procedure *main* will first initialize the M68230 and then the M68340 DMA controller module 1. The M68230 initialization ritual in the first half of *main* closely follows the ritual used to initialize it for externally vectored interrupts shown at the end of Section 5-2.2. The M68340 DMA controller initialization ritual in the second half of *main* closely follows the ritual used above for the memory block move. Note how simple the M68340 DMA controller is to use, both in hardware and software.

```
main(){ register char *cp=(char*)0x10000;register int *dma=(int*)0xffff780;
    CsAssign(3,0x10000,8,noDsack,rdWr); /* enable chip select 3 to select M68230 */
    cp[0]=0;/* set general mode to 0, disable ports a and b to change registers */
    cp[1]=0x40;/* binary x1000000 permit dma req on pin C4 */ cp[2]=0;/* input */
    cp[6]=0x32;/* submode 00 H2 is not interrupt (is output) request H1 enabled */
    cp[0]=0x10;/* set mode 0 again, enable port a (H2 is normally low) */
    dma[4]=0; /* stop DMA */ dma[0]=0x780; /* permit DMA at any interrupt level */
    dma[5]=0x7f55; /* clear all status bits, interrupts, set function codes sup. data*/
    *(long*)(dma + 6)=0x10008; *(long*)(dma + 8)=0x2000; /* source, destination address */
    *(long*)(dma + 10)=3; /* number of bytes to be moved */
    dma[4]=(BYTE<<SOURCE)+(BYTE<<DESTINATION)+DAPI+CYCLESTEALR+
        DUAL+START;
    while( ! (dma[5] & 0x4000)); /* gadfly until DONE */
}
```

Chapter 5 – Interrupts and Alternatives

This sequence of events happens when an external dual cycle DMA request is made:

1. A falling edge on the M68230 H1 pin sets IRQ1. Because cp[1] is 0x40, this causes port C bit 4/DMAREQ to be asserted, rather than an interrupt on portC bit 5/PIRQ; DMAREQ is connected to the M68340's DREQ1 pin.
2. In the DMA controller, if it is on (START is 1) and COUNT is nonzero, two memory cycles are stolen from the 683xx processor; in the first (read) cycle the SOURCE address is sent.
3. The M68340 CS3 is asserted which asserts the M68230's chip select and its port A's data register is selected by the low bits of the address. A byte from port A moves, via the data bus, to a holding register in the DMA controller, and the M68230's IRQ1 is cleared by an address trigger.
4. In the second memory cycle, the byte is written into memory using the DESTINATION address. Because DAPI is T, that address is then incremented.
5. The COUNT value is decremented. If it becomes 0, the DONE status bit is set. The program is gadflying on this DONE bit, and is resumed when it is set.

There is a two-level busy-done state associated with DMA, as with any I/O transfer that fill or empties a buffer, as discussed at the beginning of this chapter. The low-level busy-done state is associated with the transfer of single words. BUSY is when a word is requested from an input device and has not been input, or is sent to an output device and has not been fully output (the hardware is punching the paper, in the paper tape example). The high-level busy-done state is associated with the transfer of the buffer. BUSY is when the buffer is being written into from an input device and has not been completely filled, or the buffer is being read from into an input device and has not been completely emptied. The DMA channel synchronizes to the low-level busy-done state to move words into or out of the I/O device. The computer can synchronize with the high-level busy-done state in the ways discussed so far. A real-time synchronization would have the processor do some program or execute a wait loop until enough time has elapsed for the buffer to be filled or emptied. Gadfly synchronization was used in the example given above. An interrupt could be used to indicate that the buffer is full

All previously discussed object classes can be expanded to input or output whole buffers. Simple I/O devices would just repeatedly send byte input and output messages.

```
struct IoDevice :direct { char error; long chip; long Input(void);
     void Init(long, unsigned),Output(long),Terminate(void),
     InputB(char*,long),OutputB(char*, long);
};
void IoDevice::Init(p,m) long p; unsigned m;{ chip=p;error=0; }
long IoDevice::Input() { return *(char*)chip; }
void IoDevice::Output(d) long d;{ *((char*)chip) = d; }
void IoDevice::Terminate() {} /* default terminate does nothing */
void IoDevice::InputB(p,n) char *p; long n;{ for (;n>0;n- - ) *p++=Input(); }
void IoDevice::OutputB(p,n) char *p; long n;{ for (;n>0;n- - ) Output(*p++); }
```

DMA I/O devices can be written to primarily input or output whole buffers, and input or output individual bytes as special cases of buffer input and output. The class *TapeReader* for DMA synchronization is shown below (we omit *Output* and *OutputB*). We use interrupts and sleep while the buffer is transferred. The use of interrupts requires that we set up IARB in dma[0] to be nonzero and different from any other IARB, that we set up LEVEL and VECTOR in dma[2], that we put the address of the interrupt handler in the exception vector associated with VECTOR, and that we save A4 in a global variable *long saveA4,* as we did for the peiodic interrupt (Section 5-1.6). The normal interrupt is enabled (INTN) in dma[4] but the start bit (START) is not set until a buffer is to be input. The IRQN bit will be asserted when DMA is DONE.

```
struct TapeReader : IoDevice
    {Thread *sleepT; long Input(void); void Init(long, unsigned), InputB(char*,long); };
long TapeReader::Init(p,m)long p;unsigned m;{
    register int *hndlr;register int *dma=(int*)0xffffff780;
    cp[0]=0; cp[1]=0x40; cp[6]=0x32; cp[0]=0x10;dma[4]=0;
    dma[0]=0x78f; dma[2]=0x644; dma[5]=0x7f55; *(long*)(dma+6)=0x10008;
    dma[4]=INTN+(BYTE<<SOURCE)+(BYTE<<DESTINATION)+DAPI+
        CYCLESTEALR+DUAL;
    asm{lea @0,hndlr} *((int **)0x110)=hndlr; asm{and #0xfdff,sr} return;
asm{@0 movem.l d0/a0l-a4,-(a7)} asm{move.l saveA4,a4} sleepT->sleepTime = 0;
    *(char*)0xffffff78a=0x7f; asm{movem.l (a7)+,d0/a0/a4} asm{rte}
}
void TapeReader::InputB(p,n) char *p; long n;{
    *(long*)(dma+8)=(long)p;*(long*)(dma+10)=n; dma[4]|=START;
    (sleepT=curThread)->sleepTime = 0xffffffff; while(curThread->sleepTime);
}
long TapeReader::Input() { char c; InputB(&c,1); return c; }
```

I/O used in high-level languages is often *buffered* or *cached*. For input, a buffer or *cache* is maintained, and filled with more data than are needed. In *lazy* buffer management, the buffer is filled with data only when some data input is requested, but more data is put into the buffer than is requested in order to take data from the buffer, rather than from the input device, when some more data is needed later. In *eager* buffer management, the buffer is filled with data before some data input is requested, so that it will be in the buffer when it is requested. This technique makes the I/O device faster.

Finally, DMA can be used to synchronize to the high-level busy-done state; a kind of DMA[2]. In larger computers such as an IBM mainframe, such a pair of DMA channels is called an *I/O Channel*. In an I/O channel, a second DMA that synchronizes the high-level busy-done state of the first DMA channel will refill the COUNT, SOURCE, DESTINATION, and CONTROL of the first DMA channel that moves words synchronizing to the low-level busy-done state. Thus, after one buffer is filled or emptied by the first DMA channel, the second DMA channel sets up the first DMA channel so the next buffer is set up to be filled or emptied. The second DMA channel's buffer is conceptually a program called the *I/O channel program*. This channel itself has busy-done states. BUSY occurs when some, but not all, buffers have been moved, and DONE occurs when all buffers have been moved. How can this busy-done state synchronizing the high-level busy-done states be synchronized? Here we go again. It can be synchronized using real-time, gadfly, interrupt, or DMA synchronization. However, DMA[3] is not very useful; DMA would not be used to reload the COUNT, SOURCE, DESTINATION, and CONTROL of the second DMA channel.

Direct memory access requires more hardware and may restrict the choice of some hardware used in I/O systems. The DMA channel must be added to the system, and the other I/O chips should be selected to cooperate with it. However, the amount of software can be less than with other techniques because all the software does is initialize some of the ports and then wait for the data to be moved. The main attraction of DMA is that the data can be moved during a memory cycle or two anytime, without waiting for the M68340 to use software to move the data.

5-4.2 Context Switching and Memory Buffer Synchronization

An interesting variation to DMA, uniquely attractive because it is inexpensive, is to use two or more microprocessors on the same address and data bus. One runs the main program. This one stops when a device requests service, as if a DMA request were being honored, and another microprocessor starts. When the first stops, it releases control over the address and data buses, which are common to all the microprocessors and to memory and I/O, so the second can use them. The second microprocessor, which then can execute the interrupt request handler, is started more quickly because the registers in the first are saved merely by freezing them in place rather than saving them on a stack. The registers in the second could already contain the values needed by the interrupt request handler, so they would not need to be initialized. DMA using a DMA chip is restricted to just inputting a word into, or outputting a word from, a buffer; whereas the second microprocessor can execute any software routine after obtaining direct memory access from the first microprocessor.

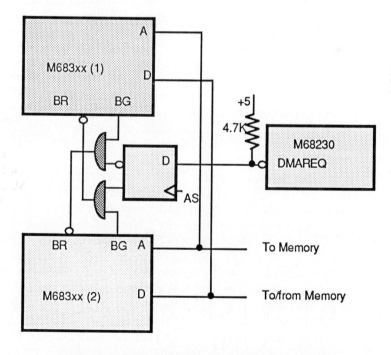

Figure 5-18. Connections for Context Switching.

A complex operation is easy to do with context switching, while ordinary DMA cannot do this operation, and context switching is quite a bit faster than ordinary interrupt synchronization because, not only are the registers not saved, but also they remain in the second 683xx, so they usually don't have to be initialized each time an interrupt occurs.

Finally, any set of microcomputers having DMA capability can be used in this manner; the one operating the main program need not be the same model as the one handling a device. This means you can put a new microprocessor in your old microcomputer. The old microprocessor is turned on to run programs left over from earlier days, and the new microprocessor is turned on to execute the new and better programs. This is an alternative to simulation or emulation in microprogramming. It is better because the best machine to emulate itself is usually itself. And putting two microprocessors in the same microcomputer hardly has an impact on the system's cost.

A coprocessor, such as the floating-point 68881, essentially uses the same concept as context switching. Whenever the main processor detects an instruction that should be executed in the coprocessor, such as a floating-point add that should be executed in the 68881, it gives up the bus to the coprocessor which does one instruction, and then the main processor resumes decoding the next instruction. A one-instruction context switch makes the main processor and coprocessor appear to be part of a processor having the main processor's instructions plus the coprocessor's instructions. While coprocessors can be designed to handle I/O, they usually handle data computation.

Though this technique is not used often by designers because they are not familiar with it, it is useful for microcomputers because the added cost for a microprocessor is so small and the speed and flexibility gained are the equivalent of somewhere between those attained by true DMA and vectored interrupt, a quality that is often just what is required.

The last techniques we will consider that synchronize fast I/O devices involve their use of memory, which is not restricted by memory conflicts with the microprocessor. One technique uses a completely separate and possibly faster memory, called a *shuttle memory*. A variant of it uses an I/O device to access memory, like indirect I/O, and is called an *indirect memory*. Another uses the same memory as the microprocessor, but this memory is fast and can be *time-multiplexed*, giving time slices to the I/O device. In a sense, these techniques solve the synchronization problem by avoiding it, by decoupling the microprocessor from the I/O by means of a memory that can be completely controlled by the I/O device.

Figure 5-19a shows a shuttle memory. The multiplexer connects the 16 address lines that go into the shuttle buffer and the 16 data lines that go to or from the buffer to the microprocessor or the I/O device. The buffer memory is shuttled between the microprocessor and the I/O device. When the buffer is connected to the I/O device, it has total and unrestricted use of the shuttle memory buffer whenever I/O operations take place. The microprocessor can access its primary memory and I/O at this time without conflict with the I/O's access to its shuttle memory because they are separate from the shuttle memory used by the I/O device. The multiplexer switches are both in the lower position at that time. Then when the microprocessor wishes to get the data in the shuttle memory, the multiplexer switches are put in the upper position, and the microprocessor has access to the shuttle memory just as it has to its own primary memory. The buffer appears in the memory address space of the microprocessor. The microprocessor can load and store data in the shuttle memory using *p++ = *q++;. The synchronization problem is solved by avoiding it. Synchronization is required as data are moved to and from the I/O device from and to the shuttle memory; but the buffer memory is wholly controlled by the I/O device, so that synchronization is not too difficult. The microprocessor can move data to and from the shuttle memory at leisure. It can even tolerate the delays that result from handling an interrupt at any time, when it moves data from one location in its memory to another location in it. There is no need for synchronization in that operation.

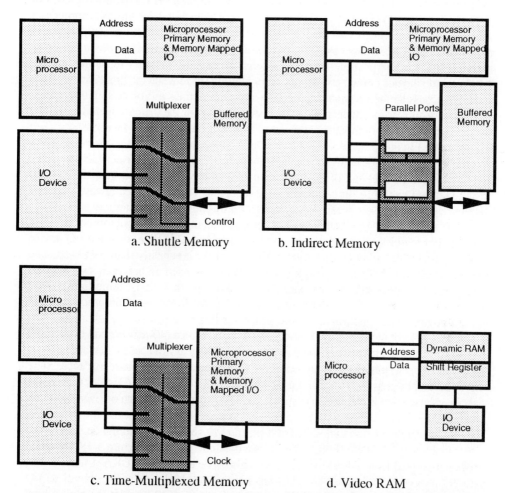

a. Shuttle Memory   b. Indirect Memory

c. Time-Multiplexed Memory   d. Video RAM

Figure 5-19. Fast Synchronization Mechanisms using Memory Organizations.

We built a parallel computer called TRAC, which used shuttle memories. The shuttle memories were connected to one processor or another processor. Once connected to a processor, the shuttle memory behaved like local memory and did not experience memory contention. Caches were simple to use with this variation of a shared memory. In I/O devices discussed in this book, the shuttle memory similarly removes the problem of memory contention from the synchronization problem.

A variation of a shuttle memory uses a parallel I/O device like an M6821 in place of the multiplexer. (See Figure 5-19b.) The external port pins of an I/O device connect to the address and data buses of the memory. The processor writes an address to a parallel output port and then reads (or writes) the data to (or from) another port to access the memory. The only way to read or write in the buffer is to send addresses and data to or from the I/O device, just as we accessed an indirect I/O device in Section 4-4.1, so we call it *indirect memory*. The CMOS static RAM at 0xE to 0x3F in the M6818A is an indirect memory. The buffer memory is completely separate from the microprocessor primary memory. When the (fast) memory is not controlled by the microprocessor through the I/O ports, it can be completely controlled by the I/O device, so it can synchronize to fast I/O devices. Only the memory-mapped parallel I/O device takes up memory space in the primary memory, whereas the shuttle memory technique has the whole shuttle memory in the primary memory address space when the processor accesses it. But to access the buffer memory, you use slow subroutines as you do in indirect I/O.

A very similar mechanism uses the same memory for the primary memory and the buffer memory, but that memory is twice as fast as is necessary for the processor. (See Figure 5-19c.) In one processor memory cycle, the memory executes two memory cycles – one for the processor and one for the I/O device. The multiplexer is switched to the I/O device (for the first half of the memory cycle) and to the processor (for the last half of the memory cycle) to time-multiplex the memory. The I/O device always gets one memory cycle all to itself because the processor only uses the other memory cycle.

The time-multiplexed memory uses the same memory as the microprocessor, but this memory is twice as fast, and the processor gets one time slice, then the I/O device gets one time slice, in an endless cycle. It is obviously less costly than the shuttle and indirect memories because a single large memory is used rather than two smaller memories. Its operation is very similar to DMA. In fact, it is sometimes called *transparent DMA*. However, the memory must be twice as fast as the processor, and the I/O device must synchronize to the processor (CLK) clock in this technique. The shuttle and indirect memories are more costly, but a very fast (40-nanosecond cycle time) memory can be used in the buffer and run asynchronously at full speed when accessed by the I/O device, but run about the speed of the CLK clock when the processor accesses it. All three techniques provide for faster synchronization to the I/O device than the techniques discussed in the previous subsection. They can transfer data on every memory cycle, without handshaking with the processor to acquire memory or use the processor. They find considerable use in CRT, hard disk, and fast communication I/O devices.

Finally a video RAM (Figure 5-19d) is a dynamic memory (Figure 3-18) in which a row can be read from DRAM into a shift register, or written into DRAM from a shift register, in one memory cycle. The shift register can then shift data into or out of an I/O device. The TMS48C121 is a (128K, 8) DRAM with a (512,8) shift register, which chan shift data into or out of an I/O device at 30 nanoseconds per byte.

One of the main points of this section is that extra hardware can be added to meet greater synchronization demands met in fast I/O devices. While DMA is popular, it is actually not the fastest technique because handshaking with the microprocessor and the cycle time of the main memory slow it down. Shuttle or indirect memories that use fast static RAMs can be significantly faster than DMA. Moreover, for all of these techniques, the controlling software can usually be quite slow, and thus can be coded in C without loss of performance compared to programs coded in assembler language.

5-5 Conclusions

We have discussed over ten alternatives for solving the synchronization problem. Each has some advantages and some disadvantages. Figure 5-20 summarizes the techniques presented in this chapter.

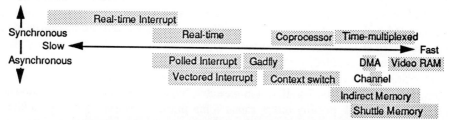

Figure 5-20. Synchronization Mechanisms Summarized.

Real-time synchronization uses the least hardware and is practical if an inexpensive microcomputer has nothing to do but time out an I/O operation. However, it can be difficult to program. Gadfly programs are easier to write, but require that the hardware provide an indication of DONE. Also, a computer generally cannot do anything else when it is in a gadfly loop, so this is as inefficient as real-time synchronization. Real-time interrupt synchronization provides for long delays, giving up the processor to other threads or processes. Real-time and real-time interrupt synchronization are synchronous, in that the external timing is determined by processor timing. Gadfly is asynchronous, in that the I/O device's timing is not synchronized to the processor's timing but the processor locks onto its timing when data are to be transferred.

The interrupt-polling technique and the vectored interrupt technique require more hardware to request service from the processor. The 683xx provides for autovectored and for external vectored interrupts. They are useful when the device needs service in a shorter time. However, the tendency to use them just because they are available should be avoided. Although interrupt-polling only requires an interrupt bus line from device to processor, if the gadfly approach is exclusively used, this line invites the mayhem of an unrecognizable interrupt if a software error rewrites the control port in the device. Also, the interrupt technique can be used together with the gadfly technique. With the gadfly technique, the interrupts are all disabled by setting the status port current priority, as in the OR #0x700,SR instruction, or by clearing control bit 0 in an M6821 device. Then the program can loop as it tests the device, without fear of being pulled out by an interrupt. When used together, gadfly is used for careful, individual stepping of an I/O system; and interrupt, for automatic, rapid feeding of data.

The DMA technique is useful for fast devices that require low latency. This technique can only store data in a buffer or read data from a buffer. DMA[2] (the I/O channel) can restart a DMA transfer a little bit faster than simple DMA. A variation of DMA, context switching, is almost as fast and flexible as the interrupt technique. A coprocessor uses a similar mechanism, and although it is generally used to execute data computation, it could be used for I/O. Shuttle, indirect, and time-multiplexed memories can be used for the fastest devices. What is somewhat surprising, DMA, which requires a fair amount of extra and expensive hardware, actually is most desirable for a rather limited range of synchronization timing. Indirect and shuttle memories can be used for much faster synchronization, and context switching for slightly slower synchronization.

Do You Know These Terms?

See the End of Chapter 1 for Instructions.

synchronization, idle, busy, done, starting the device, stopping the device, completing the requested action, real-time synchronization, gadfly synchronization, gadfly loop, interrupt, external interrupt is requested recognize an interrupt, request an interrupt, microprocessor is enabled, microprocessor is masked, microprocessor is disabled, microprocessor sees a request, request is pending, honor an interrupt, vector register, current processor priority, handler, nonmaskable interrupt, polled interrupt, interrupt request, handler, poll, priority order, round-robin priority, vectored interrupt, address vector, vector number, vector address, explicitly vectored interrupt, user interrupt, autovectored interrupt, X10 code, decoder, histogram, real-time interrupt, multi-thread scheduling, fork, extra one bit, output, handshaking, pulse mode, Centronics, trace, address error, illegal instruction, zero divide, chk exception, trapv exception, privilege exception, phantoming, reset handler, bootstrap program, operating system, multi-tasking, task spaces, direct memory access, context switching, context, coprocessing, DMA channel, DMA transfer, steal a memory cycle cycle, steal mode, burst mode, single-address DMA transfer, dual-address DMA transfer, device address port, memory address port, count port, control ports, status port, buffered I/O, cached I/O, cache, lazy management, eager management, I/O channel program, shuttle memory, indirect memory, time-multiplexed memory, transparent DMA.

6

Analog Interfacing

Analog circuits are commonly used to interconnect the I/O device and the "outside world." This chapter will focus on analog circuits commonly used in microcomputer I/O systems. In this chapter, we will assume you have only a basic knowledge of physics, including mechanics and basic electrical properties. While many of you have far more, some, who have been working as programmers, may not. This chapter especially aims to provide an adequate background for studying I/O systems.

Before analog components are discussed, some basic notions of analog signals should be reviewed. In an *analog* signal, voltage or current levels convey information by real number values, like 3.1263 volts, rather than by H or L values. A *sinusoidal alternating current* (AC) signal voltage (or current) has the form $v = A \sin (P + 2\pi Ft)$ as a function of time t, where the *amplitude* A, the *phase* P, and the *frequency* F can carry information. The *period* is $1/F$. (See Figure 6-1a.) One of the most useful techniques in analog system analysis is to decompose any *periodic* (that is, repetitive) waveform into a sum of sinusoidal signals, thus determining how the system transmits each component signal. The *bandwidth* of the system is the range of frequencies which it transmits faithfully (not decreasing the signal by a factor of .707 of what it should be). A square wave, shown in Figure 6-1b, may also be used in analog signals. Amplitude, phase, and frequency have the same meaning as in sinusoidal waveforms.

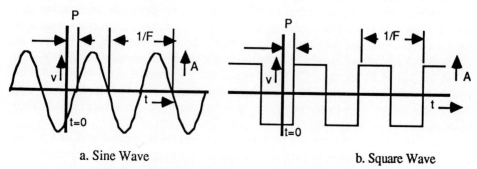

a. Sine Wave   b. Square Wave

Figure 6-1. Waveforms of Alternating Voltage Signals.

Two kinds of analog signals are important. These correspond to AM and FM radio. In this chapter, we consider analog signals whose amplitude carries the value, whether the signal is a direct current or an alternating current signal, as AM radios carry the sound. In the next chapter, we consider analog signals whose frequency or phase carries the value of the signal, as FM radios carry the sound. Amplitude analog signals are more pervasive in interface design. It is hard to find examples of interface hardware that do not have some analog circuitry (we had to search long and hard to find some decent problems for Chapter 3 that did not have analog circuits in them). It is even hard to discuss frequency analog circuits without first discussing amplitude analog circuits. So we study amplitude analog circuits here, and frequency analog circuits in Chapters 7 and 8.

Analog signals are converted to digital signals by *analog-to-digital converters* (A-to-D converters), and digital signals are converted to analog by *digital-to-analog converters* (D-to-A converters) such that the digital signal – usually a binary or binary coded decimal number – corresponds in numerical value to the analog signal level. Analog signals are also converted to a single digital bit (H or L) by a *comparator*, and digital signals control analog signals by means of *analog switches*. The frequency of an AC signal can be converted to or from a voltage by *voltage-to-frequency converters* (V-to-F converters) or by *frequency-to-voltage converters* (F-to-V converters). Finally, analog signals are generated by *transducers* that change other measurements into voltages or currents, such as temperature to voltage transducers, and are amplified and modified by *operational amplifiers* (OP AMPs).

A basic theme of this chapter is that many functions can be performed using digital or analog hardware, or using software. The smart designer determines the best technique from among many alternatives to implement a particular function. Thus, the designer should know a little about analog circuitry. On the one hand, a basic understanding of analog circuits' operation and use is essential in making intelligent hardware-software tradeoffs and is quite useful even for programmers who write code to interface to such devices. So we want to include the required material in this chapter. On the other hand, to use them well, one can devote an entire year's study to these devices. We have to refrain from covering that much detail. Therefore, our aim is to give enough detail so readers can make good hardware-software tradeoffs in the design of microprocessor-analog systems and to encourage those who seek more detail to read some of the many excellent books devoted to the topic of analog signal processing.

In the following sections, we will discuss conversion of physical quantities to voltages and from voltages, the basics of operational amplifiers and their use in signal conditioning and keyboard/display systems, digital to analog conversion, analog to digital conversion, and data acquisition systems. Much of the material is hardware oriented and qualitative. However, to make the discussion concrete, we discuss in some detail the use of the popular CA3140 operational amplifier and the 4066 and 4051 analog switches. Some practical construction information will be introduced as well. The reader might wish to try out some of the examples to understand firmly these principles.

This chapter should provide enough background on the analog part of a typical microcomputer I/O system so the reader is aware of the capabilities and limitations of analog components used in I/O and can write programs that can accommodate them.

6-1 Input and Output Transducers

A *transducer* changes a physical quantity, like temperature, to or from another quantity, often a voltage. Such a transducer enables a microcomputer that can measure or produce a voltage or an AC wave to measure or control other physical quantities. Each physical property – position, radiant energy, temperature, and pressure – will be discussed in turn, and for each we will examine the transducers that change electrical signals into these properties and then those that change the properties into electrical signals.

6-1.1 Positional Transducers

About 90% of the physical quantities measured are positional. The position may be linear (distance) or angular (degrees of a circle or number of rotations of a shaft). Of course, linear position can be converted to angular position by a rack and pinion gear arrangement. Also, recall that position, speed, and acceleration are related by differential equations: If one can be measured at several precise times, the others can be determined.

A microcomputer controls position by means of *solenoids* or *motors*. A *solenoid* is an electromagnet with an iron plunger. As current through the electromagnet is increased, an increased force pulls the plunger into its middle. The solenoid usually acts against a spring. When current is not applied to the solenoid, the spring pulls the plunger from the middle of the solenoid; and when current is applied, the plunger is pulled into the solenoid. Solenoids are designed to be operated with either direct current or alternating current, and are usually specified for a maximum voltage (which implies a maximum current) that can be applied and for the pulling force that is produced when this maximum voltage (current) is applied. A *direct current motor* has a pair of input terminals and a rotating shaft. The (angular) speed of the shaft is proportional to the voltage applied to the terminals (when the motor is running without being loaded), and the (angular) force or torque is proportional to the current. A *stepping motor* looks like a motor, but actually works like a collection of solenoids. When one of the solenoids gets current, it pulls the shaft into a given (angular) position. When another solenoid gets current, it pulls the shaft into another position. By spacing these solenoids evenly around the stepping motor and by giving each solenoid its current in order, the shaft can be rotated a precise amount each time the next solenoid is given its current. Hence the term stepping motor. The *universal motor* can be given either direct current or alternating current power. Most home appliances use these inexpensive motors. Their speed, however, is very much dependent on the force required to turn the load. *Shaded pole motors* require alternating current, and the shaft speed is proportional to the frequency of the AC power rather than the voltage. The torque is proportional to the current. These inexpensive motors often appear in electric clocks, timers, and fans. *Induction motors* are usually larger power AC motors, and their speed is proportional to frequency, like the shaded pole motor. Finally, the *hysteresis synchronous motor* is an AC motor whose speed is accurately synchronized to the frequency of the AC power. These are used to control the speed of Hi-Fi turntables and tape decks.

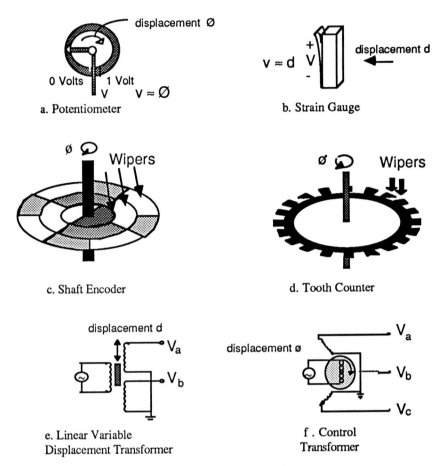

Figure 6-2. Position Transducers.

In inexpensive systems, linear position or angular position is usually converted into a resistance, which determines a voltage level in a voltage divider circuit, or which determines a frequency of some kind of RC oscillator. A *potentiometer* converts angular position to resistance. (See Figure 6-2a.) A *slide potentiometer* converts linear position to resistance. Both transducers are inexpensive but are prone to inaccuracy as the wiper arm in the potentiometer wears down the resistor or as a coat of dirt or oil builds up on the resistor. Also, these transducers are sensitive to vibration. Overall accuracy is limited to about 3%. Minute position displacements can be measured by piezo-electric crystals, such as in commercial *strain gauges*. A crystal phono cartridge uses the same mechanism. (See Figure 6-2b.) The angular position of a disk can be converted directly into a digital signal by *shaft encoders*, which use mechanical wipers or photodetectors to read a track on the disk, the tracks being laid out so that the wipers or detectors read a digital word corresponding to the angle of rotation ø of the disk. (See Figure 6-2c.) Also, a pair of wipers or detectors can sense the teeth of a gear or gear-like disk in a *gear-counter*, so they can count the teeth as the gear turns. (See Figure 6-2d.) Two wipers are needed to determine both the motion and the direction of motion of the teeth.

A *mouse* on a Macintosh computer is basically a pair (x-direction and y-direction) of gear-counters. Finally, the most accurate and reliable position transducer is the *linear variable displacement transformer*. (See Figure 6-2e.) In this device, a transformer having a primary winding and two secondary windings has a movable slug. As the slug moves, the two secondary windings of the transformer producing V_1 and V_2 get more or less alternating current from the primary winding, and the relative phase of the sine waves output from the windings changes. Either the voltage level of the sine wave or the relative phase difference between the sine waves may be used to sense the position of the slug. The linear variable displacement transformer is the most accurate device for measuring linear distances because it is not affected by dirt, wear, or vibration as other devices; however, it is the most expensive. Angular position can be measured by a *control transformer* using the same kind of technique. (See Figure 6-2f.) This device's rotor has a primary coil that can be turned by a shaft, and secondary windings in the housing, which is held stationary, that surrounds the rotor. The angular position of such a device's rotor determines the amount and phase of a sine wave that is picked up by the secondaries of the transformer.

Velocity and acceleration can be determined by measuring position using one of the aforementioned transducers, and then differentiating the values in software or using an electrical circuit that differentiates the voltage. Also, a *direct current tachometer* is a direct current generator. Being an inverse of a DC motor, its output voltage is proportional to the rotational speed of the shaft. An AC tachometer is an AC motor run as a generator; its output frequency is proportional to the (angular) speed of its shaft. Finally, acceleration can also be measured by producing a force F as a mass m is accelerated at rate a ($F = m \times a$), then letting the force act against a spring, and then measuring the displacement of the spring. This type of device, an *accelerometer*, can convert the acceleration into a position using mechanical techniques, thereby measuring acceleration at the output of the transducer. This is an alternative to measuring position, then using software to differentiate the values to determine acceleration. Conversely, an accelerometer can be used to measure acceleration, which can be integrated by a software program to derive velocity, or integrated twice to get position. This is the basis of an inertial guidance system. The examples in this paragraph show that functions can be done by mechanical, analog, digital, or software methods, or a combination of these.

6-1.2 Radiant Energy Transducers

Radiant energy – light and infrared – can be produced or controlled by a microprocessor using lamps, *light emitting diodes* (LEDs), and *liquid crystal displays* (LCDs). The terms used for light and infrared radiant energy are those used for radio waves. In a continuous wave (CW) or pulse-coded mode (PCM), the radiant energy is either on (high) or off (low). In an amplitude-modulated mode (AM), the amplitude of the radiation varies with a signal that carries analog information. In frequency-modulated mode (FM), the frequency varies with an analog signal. The common incandescent lamp is lit by applying a voltage across its terminals. The radiant energy is mostly uniformly distributed over the light spectrum and includes infrared energy. Gas discharge lamps and fluorescent lamps work in a similar fashion but require current limiting resistors in series with the lamp and usually need higher voltages. Their radiant energy is confined to specific wavelengths which are determined by the material in the lamp. While these are sometimes used with microprocessors, their usefulness is limited by their relatively high voltage and current requirements and the electrical noise generated by gas discharge lamps and fluorescent lamps. More popular are the LEDs and LCDs. An LED is basically a diode which will emit light if about ten milliamperes are sent through it. The light is generated in specific wavelengths: Red and infrared are the easiest to generate, but green, yellow, and orange are also widely available. Current passing through an LED drops about 1.7 to 2.3 volts, depending on the diode material. LEDs are often used in displays to indicate some output from a microcomputer and are also used in communications systems to carry information. Inexpensive LEDs can be pulse-modulated at better than ten kiloHertz, and special ones can work at around a gigaHertz. An LCD is electrically a capacitor which is clear if the (RMS) voltage across it is less than about a volt and is opaque if above about two volts; it consumes very little power. The voltage across an LCD must be AC, however, because DC will polarize and destroy the material in the LCD. Usually, one terminal has a square wave signal. If the other terminal has a square wave signal in phase with the first, the display is clear, and if it has a square wave signal out of phase with the first, the display is opaque.

Radiant energy is often measured in industrial control systems. A *photodetector* converts the amplitude to a voltage or resistance for a given bandwidth of the very high frequency sine wave carrier. Often this bandwidth covers part of the visible spectrum and/or part of the infrared spectrum. The *photomultiplier* can measure energy down to the photon – the smallest unit of radiation – and has an amplification of about one million. However, it requires a regulated high-voltage power supply. The *photodiode* is a semiconductor photodetector able to handle signals carried on the amplitude of the radiant energy around ten megaHertz. The current through the diode is linearly proportional to the radiation if the voltage drop across it is kept small. This is done by external circuitry. However, it is inefficient because a unit of radiant energy produces only 0.001 units of electrical energy. A photodiode might be used in a communication linkage to carry a signal on a light beam because of its high bandwidth and ease of use with integrated circuits. If the diode is built into a transistor, a *phototransistor* is made that relates about one unit of electrical energy to one unit of radiant energy, but the signal carried on the amplitude is reproduced up to about 100 kiloHertz. Finally, a *photoresistor* is a device whose resistance varies with the intensity of the light shone upon it. While this device is also temperature sensitive, has poor frequency response, and is quite nonlinear, it can be used to isolate a triac, as we discuss later.

Photodiodes, phototransitors, photoresistors, and other detectors are often used with LEDs or lamps to sense the position of objects or to isolate an external system from the microcomputer. Photodetectors are commonly used with an LED light source to detect the presence or absence of an object between the light source and the photodetector. To sense the pattern on the disc under the contacts, a shaft encoder or tooth counter can use this kind of sensor in place of a mechanical contact. Similar techniques place an LED and a photodiode or phototransistor inside an integrated circuit package, called an *opto-isolator*, to isolate the circuitry driving the LED from the circuitry connected to the detector so that they can be kilovolts apart and so that electrical noise in the driver circuitry is not transmitted to the detector circuitry. The opto-isolator, an LED and photodiode, appears in Figure 6-3a. An opto-isolator like the 4N28 can be used to get the X-10 signals of Figure 5-8 discussed in section 5-1.5, as shown in Figures 6-3b and 6-3c, and will be discussed in later sections.

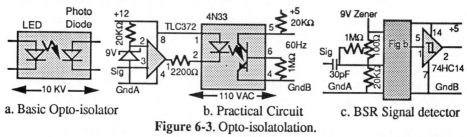

a. Basic Opto-isolator   b. Practical Circuit   c. BSR Signal detector

Figure 6-3. Opto-isolatolation.

Temperature is controlled by means of heaters or air conditioners. To control the temperature of a small component, such as a crystal, the component is put in an *oven*, which has a resistive heater and is fairly well insulated. As more current is passed through the heater, it produces more heat; as less current is passed, the natural loss of heat through the insulated walls brings down the temperature. The temperature of a large room or building is controlled by means of a furnace or air conditioner, of course. Because these usually require AC power at high currents and voltages, the microcomputer has to control a large AC current. An interesting problem in controlling air conditioners is due to the back pressure built up in them. If the air conditioner has just been running, is then turned off, and is quickly turned on, the motor in it will stall because it cannot overcome the back pressure in it. So in controlling an air conditioner, if it is turned off, it must not be turned on for an interval of time, which is long enough for the back pressure to drop off.

Temperature is often sensed in a microprocessor system. Very high temperatures are measured indirectly, by measuring the infrared radiation they emit. Temperatures in the range -250 degrees centigrade to +1000 degrees centigrade can be measured by a *thermocouple*, which is a pair of dissimilar metals (iron and constantan, for instance), where the voltage developed between the metals is around 0.04 millivolts times the temperature. Note that such a low-level signal requires careful handling and amplification before it can be used in a microprocessor system. The most popular technique for measuring temperatures around room temperature is to put a constant current through a diode (or the diode in the emitter junction of a bipolar transistor) and measure the voltage across it. The output voltage is typically 2.2 millivolts times the temperature in Kelvin. This voltage level requires some amplification before conversion to digital values is possible. Provided the current through the diode is held constant (by a constant current source), the transducer is accurate to within 0.1 degrees Kelvin. While a common diode or transistor can be used, a number of integrated circuits have been developed that combine a transistor and constant current source and amplifier. One of these (AD590) has just two pins and regulates the current through it to be one microampere times the temperature in Kelvin. Converting to and then transmitting a current has the following advantage: The voltage drops in wires whose sensor is a long distance from the microprocessor, or in switches that may have unknown resistance, and thus does not affect the current. The current is converted to a voltage simply by passing it through a resistor. Finally, temperature can be sensed by a temperature sensitive resistor called a *thermistor*. Thermistors are quite nonlinear and have poor frequency responses, but relatively large changes in resistance result from changes in temperature.

6-1.3 Other Transducers

Pressure can be produced as a by-product of an activity controlled by a microcomputer. For instance, if a microcomputer controls the position of a valve, it can also control the flow of liquid into a system, which changes the pressure in the system. Pressure is sometimes measured. Usually, variations in pressure produce changes in the position of a diaphragm, so the position of the diaphragm is measured. While this can be implemented with separate components, a complete system using a Sensym chip in the LX1800 series of chips (formerly a National Semiconductor series) can measure absolute or relative pressure to within 1% accuracy. Motorola also makes a fine series of pressure sensors. These marvelous devices contain the diaphragm, strain gauge position sensor, compensation circuits for temperature, and output amplifier on a hybrid integrated circuit. Finally, weight is normally measured by the force that gravity generates. The weighing device, called a *load cell*, is essentially a piston. Objects are weighed by putting them on top of the piston, and measuring the fluid pressure inside the piston.

Other properties – including chemical composition and concentration, the Ph of liquids, and so on – are sometimes measured by transducers. However, a discussion of these transducers goes beyond the scope of this introductory survey.

6-2 Basic Analog Processing Components

Basic analog devices include power amplifiers, operational amplifiers, and analog switches. These will be discussed in this section. The first subsection discusses transistors and SCRs, the next discusses OP AMPs and analog switches in general, and the last discusses practical OP AMPs and analog switches.

6-2.1 Transistors and Silicon-controlled Rectifiers

To convert a voltage or current to some other property like position or temperature, an amplifier is needed to provide enough power to run a motor or a heater. We briefly survey the common power amplifier devices often used with microcomputers. These include power transistors, darlington transistors, and VFETs for control of DC devices (motors, heaters, and so on) and SCRs and triacs for control of AC devices.

The *(bipolar) transistor* is a device which has terminals called the collector, base, and emitter. (See Figure 6-4a.) The collector current I_c is a constant (called the *beta*) times the base current I_b. Small currents such as from a photodiode (Figure 6-3a) are amplified by a transistor (the transistor's emitter diode is the photodiode) to get useful currents, such as in Figure 6-3b. The *power transistor* can be obtained in various capacities: able to handle up to 100 amperes, and up to 1000 volts. These are most commonly used for control of DC devices. A *darlington transistor* has a pair of simple transistors connected internally so it appears to be a single transistor with very high beta. (See Figure 6-4b.) Power darlington transistors require less base current I_b to drive a given load, so they are often used with microprocessor I/O chips that have limited current output. *Field effect transistors* (FETs) can be used in place of the more conventional (bipolar) transistor. In an FET, the current flowing from drain to source is proportional to the voltage from gate to source. Very little current flows into the gate, which is essentially a capacitor with a small leakage current. (See Figure 6-4c.) However, a *vertical field effect transistor* (VFET) is faster than a standard FET and can withstand larger voltages (about 200 volts) between drain and source. The VFET is therefore a superb output amplifier that is most compatible with microcomputers. Suffice to say for this survey, a power transistor, a darlington, or a VFET is usually required to drive a DC device like a motor, heater, or lamp.

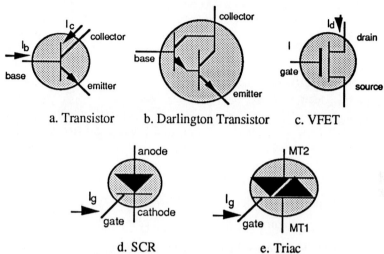

a. Transistor   b. Darlington Transistor   c. VFET

d. SCR   e. Triac

Figure 6-4. Power Output Devices.

An AC device like an AC motor uses a *silicon-controlled rectifier* (SCR) or a *triac* to amplify the voltage or control signal output from a microcomputer. The SCR has anode, cathode, and gate terminals, as in Figure 6-4d. When sufficient current I_g (about 50 milliamperes) flows into the gate through the anode, the device looks like a diode, passing positive current from anode to cathode but inhibiting flow from cathode to anode. That is why it is called a controlled rectifier, because a rectifier is an older name for a diode. Moreover, the SCR has memory; once turned on, it remains on, regardless of the current through the gate, until the current through the anode tries to reverse itself and is thus turned off. The gate controls only half a cycle, because it is always turned off for the half cycle when current tries to but cannot go from cathode to anode; and it is turned on only when the gate is given enough current and the current will then flow from anode to cathode. To correct this deficiency, two SCRs are effectively connected "back to back" to form a triac. (See Figure 6-4e.) The power current flows through main terminal one (MT1) and main terminal two (MT2) under the control of the current I_g through the gate and MT1. If the gate current is higher than about 50 milliamperes either into or out of the gate, MT1 appears shorted to MT2 and continues appearing as such regardless of the current through the gate until the current through MT1 and MT2 passes through zero. Otherwise, MT1 and MT2 appear disconnected. SCRs and triacs handle currents from half an ampere up to 1000 amperes and can control voltages above 800 volts.

SCRs and triacs control motors, heaters, and so on, by controlling the percentage of a cycle or the number of cycles in which full power is applied to them. The types of control are discussed next in terms of triacs, but they also apply to SCRs.

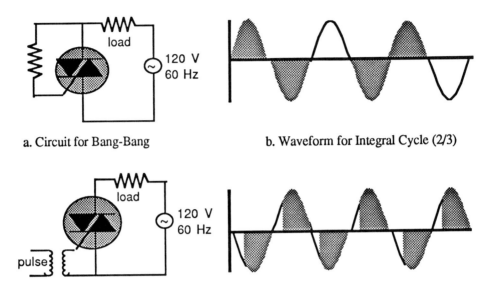

a. Circuit for Bang-Bang

b. Waveform for Integral Cycle (2/3)

c. Circuit for Proportional Cycle

d. Waveform for Proportional Cycle

Figure 6-5. Triac Control Techniques.

In *on-off,* or "*bang-bang,*" control, the triac applies either full power or no power to the motor. To do this, either full current or no current is applied to the gate. A simple variation of this technique applies gate current from MT2 through a resistor, so that if the resistance is low, when voltage on MT2 begins to build up, current flows through the resistor to turn on the triac. (See Figure 6-5a.) As soon as it is turned on, however, the voltage on MT2 disappears. Thus, the current through the resistor stops as soon as it has done its work. This reduces the power dissipated in the resistor. If the resistance is large, no current flows through the gate, so the triac is off. The resistor can be a photoresistor, coupled to an incandescent lamp or an LED in an optocoupler. When the LED or lamp is lit, the photoresistor has a low resistance, which turns the triac on. Otherwise, the resistance is high and the triac is off. This configuration is particularly suited to on-off control of large AC loads by means of triacs.

A simple variation is called *integral cycle control.* Here, the triac is turned on for *n* out of every *m* half-cycles. (See Figure 6-5b.) The gate current has to be turned on at the beginning of each half-cycle when the triac is supposed to be on. A final variation is called *proportional cycle control.* A pulse generator of some kind is commonly used to send a current pulse through the gate at a precise time in each half-cycle. (See Figure 6-5c.) For a fraction F of each half-cycle, the triac is turned on. (See Figure 6-5d.) Full power is applied to the device for the last F*th* of the cycle. Roughly speaking, the device gets power proportional to the fraction F. A pulse transformer is often used to isolate the controller from the high voltages in the triac circuitry. (See Figure 6-5c.) The controller provides a short (five-microsecond) voltage pulse across the primary winding (shown on the left) of the transformer, which provides a current pulse to the triac to turn it on. The controller has to provide this pulse at the same time in each half-cycle. If the pulse is earlier, more current flows through the triac and more power goes to the load.

On-off control is used where the microprocessor simply turns a device on or off. A traffic light would be controlled like this. Bang-bang control is commonly used in heating systems. You set your thermostat to 70 degrees. If the temperature is below 70 degrees, the heater is turned on fully, and, if above 70 degrees, the heater is completely off. Integral cycle control is useful in electric ranges, for instance, to provide some control over the amount of heating. Finally, variable duty cycle control is common in controlling lighting and power tools, because the other types of control would cause the light to flicker perceptibly or the tool to chatter. However, this type of control generates a lot of electrical noise whenever the triac is turned on fully in the middle of a half-cycle. This kind of noise interferes with the microcomputer and any communications linkages to and from it. So variable duty cycle control is normally used when the other forms generate too much flicker or chatter.

6-2.2 Basic Linear Integrated Circuits

The basic module used to process analog signals is the operational amplifier, or OP AMP. It is used in several important configurations, which we will discuss here. We will then discuss the analog switch, which allows convenient microprocessor control of analog signals, and consider several important applications of this switch.

The OP AMP has two inputs labeled + and -, and an output. (See Figure 6-6.) The output voltage signal Vout is related to the signals V+ on the + input and V- on the - input by the expression

$$Vout = A (V+ - V-)$$

where A is a rather large number, such as 100,000. The OP AMP is in the *linear mode* if the output voltage is within the range of the positive and negative supply voltages, otherwise it is in the *saturated mode* of operation. Clearly, to be in the linear mode, V+ has to be quite near V-.

The first use of the OP AMP is the *inverting amplifier*. Here, the + input is essentially connected to ground, so V+ is zero, and *feedback* is used to force V- to zero volts, so the OP AMP is in the linear mode. In Figure 6-6a, if Vin increases by one volt, then V- will increase by a small amount, so the output Vout will decrease 100,000 times this amount, large enough to force V- back to zero. In fact, Vout will have to be

$$Vout = - (Rf/Rin) Vin$$

in order to force V- to zero. The *amplification* of this circuit, the ratio Vout/Vin, is exactly Rf/Rin and can be selected by the designer as needed. In a slight modification of this circuit, one or more inputs having signals Vin1, Vin2, ... can be connected by means of resistors Rin1, Rin2, ... (as in Figure 6-6b) and the output voltage is then

$$Vout = - (((Rf/Rin1) Vin1) + ((Rf/Rin2) Vin2) + ...)$$

in a circuit called a *summing amplifier*.

Another classical use of an OP AMP is integration of a signal. A capacitor has the relation of current through it, i, to voltage across it, v, as follows:

$$i = Cf \, dv/dt$$

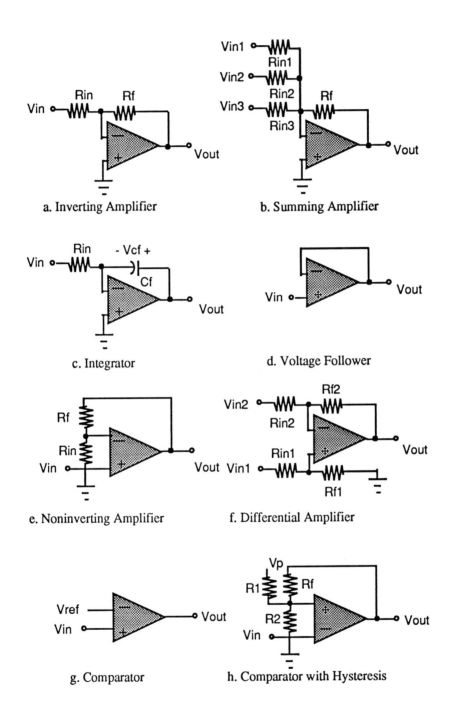

a. Inverting Amplifier

b. Summing Amplifier

c. Integrator

d. Voltage Follower

e. Noninverting Amplifier

f. Differential Amplifier

g. Comparator

h. Comparator with Hysteresis

Figure 6-6. Operational Amplifier Circuits.

where Cf is the capacitance. In Figure 6-6c, if Vin increases by one volt, then Vout will have to change by one volt per second so the current through the capacitor can offset the current through Ri to force V- to zero. Generally, the relationship of an *integrator* is

$$\text{Vout} = \text{Vcfi} - (1 / (\text{Ri Cf})) \int_{t_0}^{t} \text{Vin dt}$$

where Vcfi is the initial voltage across the capacitor.

In these three techniques, the voltage V- is forced to zero. V- is called a *virtual ground*. Of course, it cannot really be connected to ground or no current would be available for the OP AMP V- input. However, complex circuits, such as amplifiers, integrators, differentiators, and active filters, are analyzed using circuit analysis techniques, assuming that V- is effectively grounded.

A different use of the OP AMP puts the incoming signal on the + input and uses feedback to try to force V- to the same voltage as V+. The *voltage follower* (shown in Figure 6-6d) does this by connecting V- to Vout. The noninverting amplifier uses the same principle (as shown in Figure 6-6e) and satisfies the relationship

$$\text{Vout} = (1 + (\text{Rf} / \text{Rin})) \text{ Vin}$$

and the output voltage has the same polarity as the input voltage. Combining the ideas underlying the *summing amplifier* with those of the noninverting amplifier, we have the differential amplifier (shown in Figure 6-6f.) One or more inputs such as Vin1 are connected via resistors like Rin1 to the + input of the OP AMP, and one or more inputs such as Vin2 are connected via resistors such as Rin2 to the - input of the OP AMP. The output is then

$$\text{Vout} = K1 \text{ Vin1} - K2 \text{ Vin2}$$

$$\text{where} \quad K1 = \frac{\text{Rf1}}{\text{Rin1}+\text{Rf1}} \left(1 + \frac{\text{Rf2}}{\text{Rin2}} \right) \quad \text{and} \quad K2 = \frac{\text{Rf2}}{\text{Rin2}}$$

In this circuit, if more than one input Vin is connected to the + OP AMP input via a resistor Rin, it appears like the term for Vin1 adding its contribution to Vout; and if connected to the - input, it subtracts its contribution to Vout like the term for Vin2.

A final technique used in the OP AMP is to depend on the finite output range it has using the saturation mode of operation. The *comparator* has the connections shown in Figure 6-6g. Here, the output is a high logical signal, H, if Vin > Vref, else it is L. A CMOS comparator such as the TLC372 (Figure 6-3b) can be used to output a squared-up wave which is high if Sig is greater than Vref, which is set to 9v by a Zener diode. This high impedance CMOS device also requires very little Sig current. The comparator can be reversed, so that Vref is on the + input and Vin is on the - input. Then Vout is high if Vin < Vref. Also, Vref can be derived from a voltage divider: Vref = Vp R2/(R1+R2), where Vp is an accurate voltage. Finally, feedback can be made to change the effective Vref a little. Using this variation, the comparator can be made insensitive to small changes in Vin due to noise. By connecting the output to V+ (as shown in Figure 6-6h) the effective Vref can be changed so it is higher when the output is H than when the output is L, so that the output remains H or L even when the input varies a bit. Suppose, for instance, that the input is low and the output is high. The input must exceed the higher reference before the output goes low. The output remains low until the input drops below the lower reference. When the input finally drops below the lower reference and the output goes high, the input has to exceed the higher reference again before the output can go low, and so on. This stubborn-like mechanism is called *hysteresis* and is the basis of the *Schmitt trigger* gate used to ignore noise in digital systems. The 74HC14 is a hex inverter in which each gate is also a Schmitt trigger; Figure 6-3c illustrates its use in "squaring up" a slow-rising or jagged signal from an optoisolator.

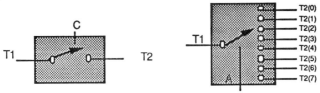

a. Analog Switch   b. Analog Multiplexor
Figure 6-7. Analog Switches.

The analog switch is implemented with field-effect transistors and has a control C and two terminals T1 and T2. (See Figure 6-7a.) If C is high, T1 is connected to T2 and the switch is said to be *on*, else they are disconnected and the switch is *off*. Some number (eight) of such switches can be connected at the T1 terminal, and a decoder with (three-bit) address A can be on a chip. The A*th* switch can be turned on by the decoder, the others being turned off. This chip then behaves like an (eight-) position rotary switch that is controlled by the address input. (See Figure 6-7b.) This kind of chip is an *analog multiplexor*. Single analog switches and analog multiplexors are valuable as ways to control analog signals from a microcomputer.

6-2.3 Practical Linear Integrated Circuits

We now consider an operational amplifier, the CA3140, which is particularly suitable for microprocessors. This device has CMOS inputs, which use almost no current, and it has bipolar transistor outputs which can supply plenty of current. Its characteristics are listed in Table 6-1 and will be discussed here.

In this book, Vs+ is the positive supply voltage and Vs- is the negative supply voltage. The first two table entries indicate that the total supply voltage may not be greater than 36 volts nor less than four volts. Two very common connections are the *dual supply*, where Vs+ is exactly the negative of Vs- (for example, Vs+ = +15 volts, Vs- = - 15 volts), and the *single supply*, where either Vs+ or Vs- is zero (for example, Vs+ = 5 volts, Vs- = zero volts). A ± 15-volt dual supply is useful when almost maximum output voltage range is needed, and a single +5-volt supply is useful when the only power supply is the one supplying five volts to the logic part of the system. A good OP AMP for microcomputer applications should be capable of operating in either of the preceding cases. Clearly, both connections are within the specifications listed in the first two rows of Table 6-1 for the CA3140. To make the information in the table more concrete, we will consider its significance for a single-ended +5-volt supply application. The reader is invited to consider the significance of these parameters for a ±15-volt dual supply application.

Table 6-1. Characteristics for the CA3140.

Characteristic	Value
Maximum (Vs+ - Vs-)	36 V
Minimum (Vs+ - Vs-)	4 V
Maximum (V+ or V-)	Vs+ + 8
Minimum (V+ or V-)	Vs- - .5
Max common mode input	Vs+ - 2.5
Min common mode input	Vs- -.5
Input resistance	1 TΩ
Input capacitance	4 pF
Input current	2 pA
Input offset voltage	5 mV
Input offset current	.1 pA
Output resistance	60Ω
Maximum output voltage	Vs+ - 3 v
Minimum output voltage	Vs- +.13 v
Maximum sourcing current	10 mA
Maximum sinking current	1 mA
Amplification	100,000
Slew rate	7 v/µs
Gain bandwidth product	3.7 MHz
Transient response	80 ns
Supply current	1.6 mA
Device dissipation	8 mW

The next four entries indicate the range of input voltages. The maximum and minimum values of V+ and V- should not be exceeded or the OP AMP may be destroyed. For example, if Vs+ is five volts and Vs- is zero volts, then neither the + nor the - input should have a voltage higher than 13 volts, nor lower than -0.5 volts. The full range of voltages can be used in the saturated mode of operation. This OP AMP has adequate capabilities using a +5-volt single supply for comparator applications. However, if the linear mode of operation is used, the input voltages should be kept within the maximum and minimum *common mode* voltages. For our previous example, using the same supply voltages, the inputs should be kept within 2.5 volts and -0.5 volts for operation in the linear mode. Note that inputs above 2.5 volts will pull the OP AMP out of the linear mode, and this can be a problem for voltage follower, noninverting amplifiers or for differential amplifiers. However, because the common mode voltage range includes both positive and negative voltages around zero volts, inverting amplifiers, summers, and integrators can be built using a single +5-volt supply. This is a very attractive feature of a modern OP AMP like the CA3140.

The next five lines of the table show the input characteristics that cause errors. The + and - inputs appear to be a resistor, a capacitor, and a current source, all in parallel. The equivalent input resistance, one teraohm, is very high. This high input resistance means that a voltage follower or noninverting amplifier can have such high input resistance, which is especially important for measuring the minute currents output from some transducers like pH probes and photodetectors. Moreover, it means that quite large resistors (100,000-ohm) and quite small capacitors (.01-microfarad) can be used in the circuits discussed earlier, without the OP AMP loading down the circuit. Especially when the rest of the system is so miniaturized, larger capacitors are ungainly and costly. The input capacitance, four picofarads, is very low, but can become significant at high frequencies. The current source can cause some error, but is quite small in this OP AMP, and the error can often be ignored. The + and - inputs have some current flowing from them, which is less than two picoamperes according to the table. If the + input is just grounded but the - input is connected by a one MΩ resistor to ground, this input current causes two microvolts extra, which is multiplied by the amplification (100,000) to produce an error of 0.2 millivolts in Vout. The error due to input current can be minimized by making equal the resistances that connect the + and - inputs to ground. In Figure 6-6a, a resistance equal to Rin in parallel with Rf can be connected between the + input and ground, just to cancel the effect of the input current on the output voltage. However, this particular OP AMP has such low input current that the error is usually not significant, and the + input is connected directly to ground.

The offset voltage is the net voltage that might be effectively applied to either the + or the - inputs, even when they are grounded. The offset current is the current that can be effectively applied to either input, even when they are disconnected. These offsets have to be counterbalanced to get zero-output voltage when no input signal is applied. An *offset adjustment* is available on OP AMPs like the 3140 to cancel the offset voltage and current.

The next five entries describe the output of the OP AMP. The output resistance is the effective resistance in series with the output of the amplifier considered as a perfect voltage source. In this case, it is 60 ohms. A high output resistance limits the OP AMP's ability to apply full power to low resistance loads, such as speakers. However, the effective output resistance of an amplifier is substantially decreased by feedback. The output voltage can swing over a range of from two to 0.13 volts, if the power supply Vs+ is five volts and Vs- is zero volts. This means that for linear operation the amplifier can support about a 1.8-volt peak-to-peak output signal, but this signal has to be centered around 1.07 volts. Note that the output range is a serious limitation for a comparator whose output drives a digital input, because a high signal is usually any voltage above 2.7 volts. An external (10,000-ohm) pull-up resistor, from the output to +5 volts, can be used such that whenever the OP AMP is not pulling the output low, the output is pulled up to nearly five volts. The output can source (supply) ten milliamperes and can sink (absorb) one milliampere to the next stage. It can supply quite a bit of current to a transistor or a sensitive gate triac because these devices require current from the output of the OP AMP. However, this OP AMP's ability to sink only one milliampere restricts its use to low-power (CMOS, LSTTL, microprocessor NMOS) digital inputs; and it cannot sink 1.6 milliamperes reliably as is required to input signals to conventional TTL gates.

Recall that the bandwidth of an amplifier is the range of frequencies over which the gain is at least (1/√2) times the maximum gain. If the bandwidth of an amplifier is 100,000 Hertz, then any small signal sine wave whose frequency is between direct current and 100,000 Hertz will be correctly amplified. Moreover, any complex periodic waveform can be decomposed into a sum of sine waves. To correctly amplify the waveform, all the component sine waves must be amplified correctly. (The phase delays also must be matched for all components.) Generally, a square wave of frequency F will be reproduced fairly accurately if the amplifier bandwidth is at least ten F.

For most OP AMPs, the bandwidth decreases as the gain increases, so the product is constant. In the 3140, this constant is 3.7 MHz. That means that if the circuit amplification is 1, the bandwidth is 3.7 MHz. For an OP AMP (shown in Figure 6-6a) with an amplification of ten, the bandwidth is 370,000 Hertz. The bandwidth is an important limitation on the OP AMP's ability to amplify small high-frequency signals. The slew rate is the maximum rate at which the output can change (due to a sudden change on the input). The slew rate usually limits the effective bandwidth of large signals less than the available bandwidth of small signals, because the output cannot change fast enough. This OP AMP has a very good slew rate; the output can change at a rate of seven volts in one microsecond. The transient response is the time delay between a sudden change in the input and the corresponding change in the output. A related parameter, the *settling time,* is the time it takes for the output to reach the desired voltage. It is not specified in the table because it depends on the external component configuration and on what we mean by reaching the desired voltage. The transient response and settling time can be of concern to a programmer who must compensate for such delays. In circuits where a digital device interfaces with an OP AMP, the slew rate and transient response may be the limiting factor on the use of an OP AMP.

Finally, the power requirements of the device are given. It dissipates about eight milliwatts when operated using a single 5-volt supply, taking 1.6 milliamps from the power supply under normal conditions. It takes about six milliamperes and dissipates about 180 milliwatts when operated from dual ±15-volt supplies. This parameter determines how big the power supply has to be to supply this device and can be significant when little power is available.

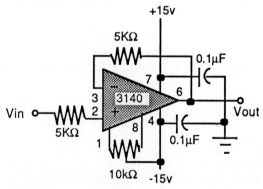

Figure 6-8. A Practical Voltage Follower.

Figure 6-8 shows the pin connections for a CA3140 and some practical considerations in using it for a dual supply voltage follower. To avoid noise input and unwanted oscillation, 0.1-microfarad capacitors, called *bypass capacitors*, are connected between the Vs+ pin and ground and between the Vs- pin and ground. The connection should be made as close to the pin as possible. Wherever practical, every OP AMP should be bypassed in this manner. The 10,000-ohm potentiometer between pins one and eight is used to counterbalance the voltage offset. The inputs (to the whole circuit, not the OP AMP) are connected momentarily to ground, and this potentiometer is adjusted to output zero volts. Although the voltage follower needs no resistors (as in Figure 6-6d), resistors are put in the feedback loop and the input to prevent excessive currents from flowing when the OP AMP is driven out of its linear mode of operation. Because the inputs have very high resistance in normal operation, these resistors have no effect in that mode. However, they should be put in if the OP AMP can enter a saturation mode of operation. Note that if the power to this OP AMP is off and a signal is applied to the input, excessive current can flow unless these resistances are put in because that operation will be in the saturated mode.

Some other considerations are offered. When handling devices with such high input resistances, tools, soldering irons, and hands should be connected via a large (15,000,000-ohm) resistance to ground. Such a device should never be inserted or removed from a socket when power is on, and signals should not be applied to inputs (unless a series resistor is used, as in the voltage follower recently described) when power is off. Especially if high (one-megohm) resistances are used, keep them clean, keep the leads short, and separate the components on the input of an OP AMP as far as possible from the output circuitry. A sheet of metal connected to ground provides some isolation from electrical noise, and all components and wires should be close to this *ground plane*. However, the ground reference points for such high-gain OP AMPs should be connected at one single point, running separate wires from this point to each "ground" point, to avoid so-called *ground loops*. If this advice is ignored, the OP AMP may become an oscillator because the minute voltages developed across the small but finite resistance of a ground wire could be fed back into an input of the OP AMP.

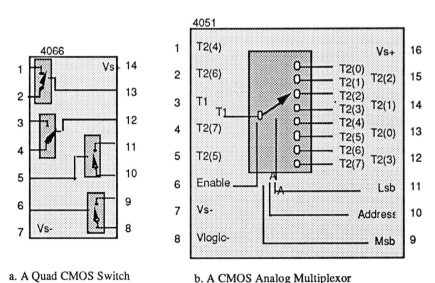

a. A Quad CMOS Switch   b. A CMOS Analog Multiplexor

Figure 6-9. Practical Analog Switches.

We now turn to some practical aspects of using CMOS analog switches. The analog switch is almost perfect: Its bandwidth is about 40 MHz, when closed it is almost a short-circuit, and when open it is almost an open circuit. We now focus on the meaning of "almost." Look at Figure 6-9, wherein the 4066 and the 4051 are shown.

We consider the problem of supplying control signals that are compatible with the voltage levels on the terminals of the switch. The maximum Vs+ - Vs- voltage across the 4066 is 15 volts. Sometimes, a dual ± 7.5-volt supply is used. If so, the control signals on pins 5, 6, 12 and 13 must be around -7.5 volts to be considered low enough to open the corresponding switch, and around +7.5 volts to be considered high enough to close the switch. Control signals from a microcomputer are normally in the range of zero to five volts and must be translated to control the switch. However, the 4051 has some level translation ability. The logic signals to address and enable the switches are referenced to Vs+ and pin 8, so a high signal is close to Vs+ and a low signal is close to the voltage level on pin 8. However, the analog levels on the switch's terminals can be between Vs+ and Vs-, which is on pin 7. Commonly, Vs+ is +5 volts, pin eight is grounded, and Vs- is -5 volts, to directly use control signals from a microcomputer, yet provide some range of analog voltages on the terminals.

When a switch is closed, it appears as a small resistance, about 80 ohms for the 4066 or about 120 ohms for the 4051. This resistance is not exactly linear, varying over a range of two to one. The resistance is more linear if Vs+ - Vs- is as large as possible. However, if used with external resistances around 10,000 ohms in series with the switch, less than 0.5 percent distortion is introduced by the nonlinear resistance of the 4066, even for Vs+ - Vs- = 5 volts.

When the switch is open, each terminal appears to be a small current source, about 100 nanoamperes for the 4066 and about 500 nanoamperes per analog switch in the 4051. This small current increases substantially with temperature and can be a serious source of error if the associated circuitry has very high resistance. To minimize it, we sometimes see a *heat sink* (a metal attachment to a transistor or integrated circuit to dissipate the heat) on an analog switch, and it is sometimes placed away from heat-producing components. Finally, a substantial amount of unwanted current flows from the power supply to the terminals if the voltage from a terminal to Vs- is greater than 0.6 volts and positive current flows from pin 3 of the 4051, or from pins 2, 3, 9, or 10 in the 4066. One should insure that positive current flows into these pins or that the voltage drop across the switch is never more than .6 volts. In summary, the 4066 has a bit better performance, lower "on" resistance and lower "off" current, and may be used individually; but the 4051 incorporates eight switches into one chip and translates the control signal level from 0 to 5 volts to control signals between ± 5 volts.

6-3 Signal Conditioning Using OP AMPs and Analog Switches

OP AMPs and analog switches are often used with microcomputers to condition analog signals before converting them to digital signals, to control analog signals used for other purposes, or to clean up or modify analog signals generated by D/A converters. The four main aspects of conditioning a signal are the filtering of frequency components, the selection of inputs, the amplification or scaling of input levels, and the nonlinear modification of signal voltages. These are now considered in turn.

6-3.1 Filters

Recall that any periodic waveform can be considered a sum of sine waves. Frequency filtering is commonly done when the signal of interest is accompanied by unwanted noise, and most of the noise is at frequencies other than those of the signal's sine wave components. If the signal frequencies are low and the noise frequencies are high, a *low-pass filter* is used. (See the amplitude versus frequency characteristic of a low-pass filter in Figure 6-10a and the circuit diagram in Figure 6-10b.) Intuitively, we see that capacitor C1 tends to integrate the signal, smoothing out the high-frequency components, and capacitor C2 further shorts out the high-frequency components to ground. Some D/A conversion techniques generate high-frequency noise, so a low-pass filter is commonly used to remove the noise from the signal. If the signal frequencies are higher than the noise frequencies, a *high-pass filter* is used to reject the noise and pass the signal. (See Figure 6-10c for the amplification characteristics and 6-10d for a high-pass filter circuit.) Intuitively, we see that the capacitors pass the high-frequency components, bypassing the low-frequency components through the resistors. A signal from a light pen on a CRT gets a short pulse every time the electron beam inside the CRT writes over the dot in front of the light pen. The signal has high-frequency components, while the noise – mostly a steady level due to ambient light – is lower in frequency. A high-pass filter passes the signal and rejects the noise. Finally, a *bandpass filter* can reject both higher- and lower-frequency components, passing only components whose frequencies are between the lower and upper limits of the band, and a *notch filter* can reject frequencies within the upper and lower limits of a band. (See Figures 6-10e through 6-10h for the amplification characteristics and circuit diagrams of these filters.)

A filter can be implemented around other components without the need for a separate OP amp for the filter. Figure 6-3c's input circuit shows a high-pass filter that feeds a comparator. It is designed to pass the 100 KHz BSR signals to the comparator, while eliminating the 60Hz and direct current components of the input signal Sig.

Compound filters can be used to reject various frequencies and emphasize other frequency components. Two techniques can be used: in one, the output from one filter feeds the input to the next filter to *cascade* them in a chain configuration; and in the other, the signal is fed to both filters and the outputs are added by a summing amplifier in a *parallel* configuration. For instance, a bandpass filter can be made from a low-pass filter that rejects components whose frequency is above the band, cascaded into a high-pass filter that rejects components whose frequency is below the band. A notch filter can be made by summing the outputs of a parallel high-pass and low-pass filter. Compound filters can be used to more sharply attenuate the signals whose frequencies are above the low-pass band or below the high pass band. The best way to cascade n low-pass filters to more sharply attenuate high-frequency components and thus get a *2 nth order filter* is a nice mathematical study and three types of filters have been shown mathematically optimal in one sense or another. The *butterworth* filter has the flattest amplification versus frequency curve in the low-frequency band where we pass the signal in a low-pass filter. However, the phase delays are quite different for different components. A square wave comes out with a few notches and humps. The *bessel* filter has the most linear relationship between frequency and phase delay and is especially useful for processing signals whose information is carried, in part, by the phase of its components and its pulse edges and shapes. The *chebyshev* filter is characterized by a designer-specified irregularity in the amplification versus frequency curve in the low-frequency band and maximum rejection just outside this band in a low-pass filter. All these filters look alike, but differ in the precise values of the components. These precise values can be obtained from tables, using simple transformations on the values in the tables, or by means of commonly available computer programs. Finally, while the preceding discussion concentrated on low-pass filters, the same terms and concepts apply to high-pass filters. And high-pass filters can be cascaded with low-pass filters to get bandpass filters or paralleled to get notch filters.

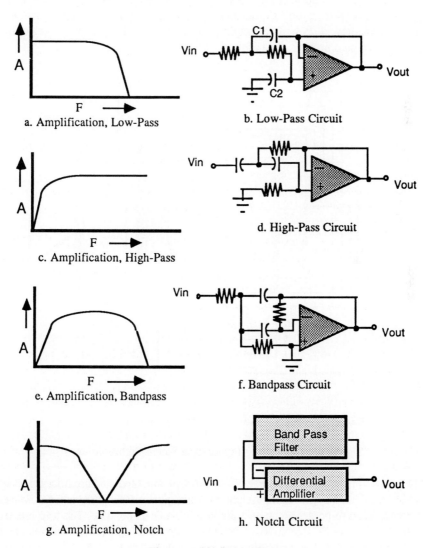

Figure 6-10. Some Filters.

6-3.2 Selection of Inputs and Control of Gain

The selection of inputs and distribution of outputs is normally accomplished by means of analog switches under the control of a microcomputer parallel output device. The individual analog switches of a 4066 can be controlled, each by a bit from an output device, to obtain maximum flexibility throughout the system being controlled. Alternatively, the 4051 can select from one of eight inputs, or distribute to one of eight outputs, using three bits from a parallel output device.

Microcomputers are appearing in almost every electronic product. They are useful in a stereo system, for example, because the listener can program a selection of music for a day or more. The microcomputer acts as a very flexible "alarm clock." Analog switches can be used to control the selection and conditioning of analog signals in the preamplifier. We now discuss an example of the use of 4051 switches for selection of inputs to a stereo preamplifier. (See Figure 6-11.)

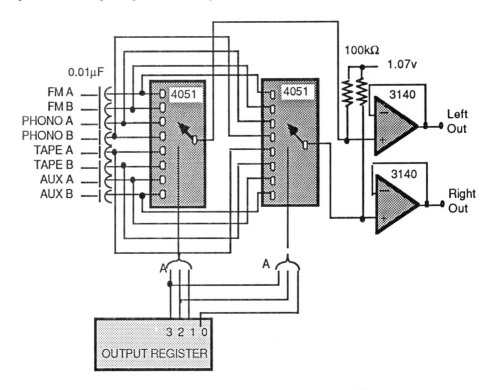

Figure 6-11. Selecting Inputs for a Stereo Preamplifier.

This preamplifier has four sources (FM radio, phono, tape, and auxilliary) and each source has two channels (for example, phono A and phono B). All signals are no larger than 1.5 volts peak-to-peak and are as close to that range as possible. The four bits from the output device control the two switches such that the high-order two bits are the high-order bits of the addresses of both switches, but the lowest-order bit is the low bit of the address of one of the switches, and the next lowest-order bit is the low address bit of the other switch. The two high-order bits select the source: FF selects the tuner, FT selects the phono, TF selects the tape input, and TT selects the auxilliary input. The two low-order bits select the mode: FF puts the A channel into both speakers, FT puts the A input channel into the A speaker and B input channel into the B speaker (stereo), TF puts the A input into the B speaker and the B input into the A speaker (reverse stereo), and TT puts the B input into both speakers. To select the phono inputs in the stereo mode, the program would put the value 0x5 into the output device.

We note some fine points of the hardware circuit in Figure 6-11. Using a single +5-volt supply both for the analog switches and the OP AMP makes level conversion of the control signals unnecessary. To achieve this, the direct current component of the analog signal must be *biased* by adding a constant to it. The OP AMP has its + input connected to a voltage midway between the limits of the input and output voltage of the CA3140 to keep it in its linear mode of operation. The inputs are connected through capacitors to shift the input signal so it is between 0.2 volts and 2.5 volts.

Figure 6-3c's input circuit shows a bias circuit that feeds a comparator. It is designed to set the two inputs to the comparator to nearly the same value (9 volts set by the Zener), such that a small 100KHz signal will trip the comparator.

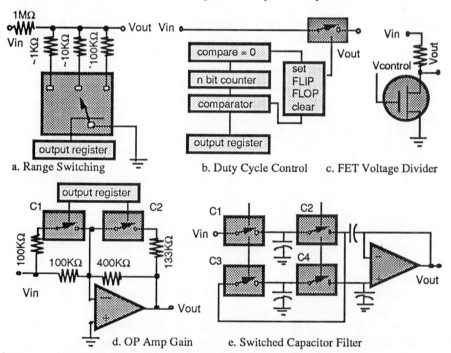

Figure 6-12. Computer Control of Amplification and Filtering.

The analog signal often has to be conditioned either by amplifying or scaling down its magnitude. This is often required because, to get maximum accuracy, A-to-D converters require a voltage range as wide as possible without exceeding the range of the converter; and D-to-A converters produce an output in a fixed range which may have to be amplified or reduced before it is sent out of the system. Two techniques for scaling down a signal are discussed first, then a technique for amplifying a weak signal at an amplification selected by the computer is discussed. (At the end of this subsection, we briefly discuss a related technique, the switched-capacitor filter.) The first and fourth techniques are not unlike the selection of inputs discussed earlier; the scale factor is selected by a switch. The second and final techniques use a fast switch to sample the input at a given duty cycle. We will discuss examples of these techniques now. Then we explain how the amplification of a signal can be controlled by a computer.

We now consider a mechanism for reducing an analog signal by a factor controlled by an output device of a microcomputer. This mechanism is used to select the range of a microcomputer-controlled digital meter (the MAX 134 – see Figure 6-21). Suppose an input voltage in the range of zero to 500 volts is to be reduced to a voltage in the range zero to 0.5 volts to be used in the next stage of the meter. (See Figure 6-12a.)

The 4051 selects one of the resistors, connecting it to ground. That resistor becomes part of the voltage divider that reduces the input voltage to be within the range needed by the next stage. The other resistors not selected by the 4051 are effectively connected to very large resistors (turned-off analog switches), so they disappear from the circuit. The voltages across all the switches are kept within 0.6 volts because the computer will select the appropriate resistor to divide the input voltage so the next stage gets a voltage within its range. Thus, the analog switch is not corrupted by unwanted current flow, as we worried about in the last section. This technique can be used to reduce the magnitude of incoming analog signals under the control of a microcomputer.

Another very useful technique is to open and close a switch at a very fast rate, about ten times the maximum frequency of the analog signal being processed. (See Figure 6-12b.) If the analog switch is closed, the amplification is unity. If open, the amplification is zero; if open 50% of the time, the amplification is one-half. The microcomputer can control the duty cycle of the switch (the percentage of the time the switch is closed) to control the scaling of the analog signal. The output of this switch has a fair amount of high-frequency noise, which can be eliminated by passing it through a low-pass filter. Because an analog switch can operate well at ten MHz, making the control signal frequency as high as possible eases the requirements on the low-pass filter. A simple way to control the duty cycle is to use an n bit binary counter, a comparator fed from an output device, and a set-clear flip-flop. The counter should be clocked fast enough so that it completes its $2**n$ count cycle in about ten times the maximum frequency of the analog signal, because that will determine the frequency of the switch control. When the counter passes zero, the flip-flop is set. When the value in the counter is equal to the value in the output register, as determined by the comparator, the flip-flop is cleared. Its output controls the switch, so the duty cycle of the switch is proportional to the number in the output register. A single counter can be used with a number of comparator /flip-flop/switches to control several analog signals. For instance, an octave filter used in sophisticated stereo systems has a bandpass amplifier for each octave so the listener can compensate for irregularities in the reproduction of each octave. Ten comparator/flip-flop/switches can control the amplification of each octave from a microcomputer. This would enable a microcomputer to automatically "calibrate" a stereo system by adjusting the amplification of each octave as tones are generated and responses are measured under its control.

Two other techniques useful for scaling an analog signal deserve mention. (See Figure 6-12c.) A field effect transistor (FET) behaves like a fairly linear resistor, provided the voltage across it, from drain to source, is not too high. The resistance is proportional to the voltage from gate to drain. Alternatively, the resistance of a light sensitive FET is proportional to the light shone on it. Used in an opto-isolator, a light sensitive FET can be used as any resistor in a voltage divider or an operational amplifier circuit. (See Figure 6-12c.) Finally, some operational amplifiers (like the CA3180) have a pin whose voltage controls the amplification. These devices can be controlled by a microcomputer sending out a voltage to adjust the light of the opto-isolator FET or by the gain of a suitable operational amplifier. Finally, the level of a signal can be determined and used to adjust the amplification of these devices automatically, in an *automatic gain control* (AGC) circuit. An AGC circuit is sometimes useful to adjust the input voltage to a filter to prevent saturating it.

Amplification (greater than one) must be done with an OP AMP, but can be controlled with analog switches. By effectively connecting or disconnecting a resistor R1 in parallel with another resistor R2, the resistance can be changed from R2 to (R1 R2)/(R1 + R2). The two resistors in an inverting amplifier can be switched by this method to alter the gain. (Consider Figure 6-12d.) If control signals C1 and C2 are HL, the amplification is 1; if LL, the amplification is 2; if HH, 4; and if LH, 8. A second stage, cascaded onto this one, could be built to have amplification 1, 16, 256, or (a rather high) 4096, and so on; so the computer can select the amplification by setting these control signals to the analog switches. Amplification ratios lower than 2 provide closer control and can be obtained by appropriate resistors in the circuit.

The resistors in a filter can be implemented by switches in a manner similar to Figure 6-12b. (See Figure 6-12e.) Switches C1 and C3 together, and C2 and C4 together at a different phase, are toggled at a high frequency, which controls the filter's cut-off frequency. The *switched capacitor filter,* that results from replacing the resistors in a filter with these switches, uses small capacitors and is easily implemented in a chip.

6-3.3 Nonlinear Amplification

The final type of signal conditioning is the nonlinear modification of analog signals. A number of fascinating circuits have been advanced to multiply and divide one analog signal by another or to output the square root, log, or sine of an analog signal. Unless the signal is too fast, however, hardware-software tradeoffs usually favor doing this processing in the microcomputer. Three cases often favor conditioning using analog circuits; absolute value, logarithmic function, and sample-and-hold. (See Figure 6-13.)

A diode is capable of extracting the *absolute value* of a waveform, and this is the basis of the AM radio detector. An accurate absolute value function is sometimes very useful if, for example, an input voltage whose range is over ± one volt is to be measured by an analog-to-digital converter that can only measure positive signals and perhaps has only a single-ended 5-volt supply. Figure 6-13a puts the diode into the feedback loop of an OP AMP to increase the linearity of the absolute value function. For positive inputs, the diode disconnects the OP AMP so the output is connected to the input via the feedback resistor R2. For negative inputs, the OP AMP simply inverts the input to get the output. Using a CA3140, this circuit can derive the absolute value of sine waves even beyond 100,000 Hertz.

The logarithm of an input voltage is sometimes obtained using analog signal conditioners, because audio levels, light levels, and so on are logarithmically related to voltages measured by transducers. Conditioning the analog signal by a *logarithmic* function drastically compresses the range of signal that must be converted by an analog-to-digital converter. The transistor's emitter current I is related to its emitter voltage V by the exponential law

$$I = (e^{V/a} - 1)$$

where a is a constant. It can be put into a feedback circuit of an OP AMP to derive a logarithmic function signal conditioner. (See Figure 6-13b.) The output Vout is related to the input Vin by

$$Vout = A \log (Vin/B)$$

where A and B are constants that depend on the resistor in the circuit and on the transistor and its temperature.

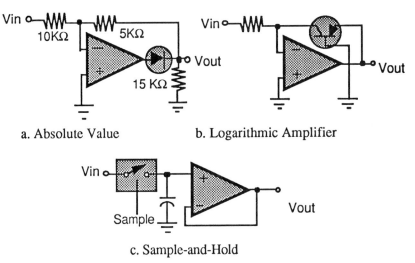

a. Absolute Value   b. Logarithmic Amplifier

c. Sample-and-Hold

Figure 6-13. Nonlinear Signal Conditioning.

The last of the nonlinear signal conditioners of particular use in microcomputer systems is the sample-and-hold circuit. Sometimes used by itself to sample an input signal at a precise time, it is also an important building block in digital-to-analog converters, covered in Section 6-5, and in multiple output data acquisition systems. (See Figure 6-13c.) The signal is input through an analog switch. When the switch is on, the voltage on the capacitor quickly approaches the input voltage. When off, the voltage across the capacitor remains steady. The voltage follower makes the output voltage equal to the voltage across the capacitor without changing its voltage by taking current from the capacitor, even though the output may have to supply considerable current to the device it feeds. Turning the switch on causes this circuit to *sample* the input. A microcomputer output device can control the switch to sample an incoming waveform at a precise time so the output voltage from the sample-and-hold circuit can be converted to a digital value.

6-4 A Keyboard and LED Display Module

We now consider the design of a typical keyboard and light emitting diode (LED) display module. This example illustrates some alternatives in analog and digital hardware and in software for solving the problem of contact bounce. This design is also important as a module you'll see in many microcomputer systems.

This example was partially introduced in Chapter 4 as an application of parallel I/O. However, parallel I/O is just a small part of the design; analog circuits or functions which can be performed by analog, digital, or software techniques are also part of the design. So we extend this discussion here, after analog circuits have been introduced. Besides, it offers an opportunity to review parallel I/O, which we have been ignoring in introducing other concepts. It is a good opportunity to tie together the material of the previous three chapters.

6-4.1 Key Debouncing

A keyboard is a collection of switches. Switches have some imperfections, including electrical noise and *contact bounce*. The former is the false signal picked up by the wires due to motors, fluorescent lights, lamp dimmers, and so on; it is more likely a problem in a keyboard module mounted where the user wants to have it than in a microcomputer properly enclosed and isolated from noise. The latter is due to the dynamics of a closing contact. Though a contact appears to close firmly and quickly, at the computer's fast running speed, the motion is comparatively slow, and, as it closes, the contact bounces like a ball. This generates a ragged signal, as we soon observe.

A single switch is normally connected as in Figure 6-14a. The resistor serves to pull the voltage V to high if the switch is open; the voltage drops to low if the switch is closed. Because we normally think of a variable associated with such a switch as true when the switch is closed, the signal V is in negative logic. This choice is due to the nature of TTL logic, which requires a low resistance connection to ground to reliably input a low signal. Therefore, the resistor is connected to +5 volts, and a switch is connected to ground. This configuration is not necesssary but is usually used for MOS integrated circuits so they can be compatible with TTL in case an existing design using TTL is converted to a microcomputer implementation. This signal can be attached to any input device, such as a 68332 port F bit configured as an input, or the 74HC244 discussed earlier. In the following example, we connect it to the most significant bit of port F because that bit can be easily tested in the program.

The noise and contact bounce problem can be solved in analog or digital hardware or in software. The signal V resulting from closing the switch shown in Figure 6-14a is shown in Figure 6-14b. The signal falls and rises a few times within a period of about five milliseconds as the contact bounces. Because a human cannot press and release a switch faster than 20 milliseconds, a *debouncer* will recognize that the switch is closed, after the voltage is low for about ten milliseconds and will recognize that the switch is open after the voltage is high for about ten milliseconds.

The bouncing problem can be reduced by using a good switch. A mercury switch is much faster, and an optical switch (whereby a beam of light from an LED to a photodetector is interrupted) or a hall effect switch (whereby the magnetic flux by a semiconductor is changed) are essentially free of bounce. However, it is not difficult to eliminate bounce. Hardware solutions include an analog circuit using a resistor and capacitor to integrate the voltage and two digital solutions using set-reset flip-flops or CMOS buffers and double throw switches. These are discussed next.

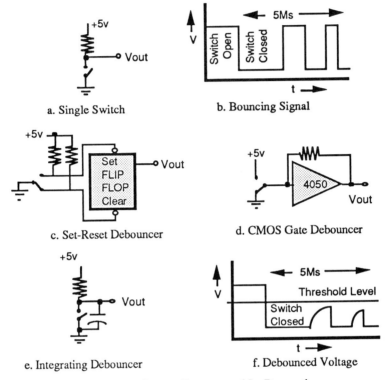

a. Single Switch

b. Bouncing Signal

c. Set-Reset Debouncer

d. CMOS Gate Debouncer

e. Integrating Debouncer

f. Debounced Voltage

Figure 6-14. Contact Bounce and Its Prevention.

In the commonly used *set-reset debouncer* (Figure 6-14c), the switch wiper sets or clears a flip-flop when it contacts the top or bottom plate, respectively. When the switch wiper is up (the flip-flop output is therefore high) and the wiper is moved down, the output remains high because the (negative logic) set and clear signals are false. The first instant the wiper hits the bottom plate, it clears the flip-flop by asserting the clear input. As it bounces (it does not bounce up enough to make contact with the top plate) it continually clears the already cleared flip-flop, so the output remains low. A similar effect occurs when the wiper is moved to the top plate, and the flip-flop is repetitively set on each bounce. In either case, the output changes just once when the wiper is moved to the other plate, so the output is debounced.

A better way uses a noninverting CMOS gate with a high-input impedance, as shown in Figure 6-14d. The wiper normally holds the gate input, and thus the gate output, high or low when it is resting on the top or bottom plate. When the wiper is moving, the resistor tends to hold the input where it was. On the first bounce, the output changes and remains at that level as the wiper leaves the plate, because of the resistor. Successive bounces do not change the output. Thus, the output is debounced.

Chapter 6 – Analog Interfacing

Several analog debouncers are possible. We will look at the integrating debouncer because it leads to the software technique that we advocate. Figure 6-14e shows how easy an integrating debouncer can be implemented. The input circuit functions like an analog comparator; the input to the microcomputer is high if the voltage sensed by the comparator is above a threshold level. The waveform for the voltage across the capacitor and the threshold is shown in Figure 6-14f. While a comparator can be used to precisely sense the voltage level, any gate and a 68332 input port in particular can be used as a not-too-accurate comparator. Then an integrating comparator can be implemented by simply connecting 68332 input port bit 7 through a capacitor to ground.

Software solutions include the *wait-and-see* technique and the software simulation of the *integrating debouncer* just discussed. In the wait-and-see technique, when the input drops indicating the switch might be closed, the program waits ten milliseconds and looks at the input again. If it is still low, the program decides that the key has indeed been pressed. If it is high, the program decides that the input signal was noise, or that the input is bouncing – which will later certainly show that the key has been pressed. In either case, the program returns to wait for the input to drop. We will use this method in a keyboard scanning program in the next subsection.

The integrating debouncer can be simulated by keeping a binary number *count* that represents the voltage across the capacitor in the hardware approach. If the input is low, indicating the switch is closed, *count* is incremented; otherwise *count* is decremented. This count more or less simulates the voltage across the capacitor. The key signal is input to the most significant bit of a 68332 port F whose data port is at location *0xFFFA19*. Suppose *count* is initially set to one and the input is sampled every millisecond. The key is certainly pressed when *count* is above ten; when that happens, we should call a procedure *proc()* to do what the key indicates. This technique is shown in the following program.

```
main(){
    int delay,count=1; char *p=(char *)0xFFFA19;
    *(p+6)=(*(p+4)=0);
    while(1){
        for(delay = 0; delay <0x14; delay ++); /*wait 1 msec */
        if((*p)&0x80) { if(count==0xf4) {count=1;} else if(count!=0) count- -; }
        else {if(count==0x10) {proc(); count=0xff;} else if(count!=0xff) count++;}
    }
}
```

The declaration initializes *count* to one. In a continuous *while* loop, the *for* loop provides a one-millisecond delay and port F is then input. If its leftmost bit (the switch value) is high, indicating the switch is not pressed, *count* is decremented, otherwise it is incremented. Note that upon incrementing and decrementing, we guard against *count* cycling through the threshold value of ten; otherwise we would produce the same effect as that of a keyboard repeat key. Moreover, we also simulate hysteresis, which improves noise immunity much as a schmitt trigger comparator in hardware improves the integrating debouncer. When the key is sensed closed and *count* reaches ten, *count* is changed to 0xFF, so that if noise decrements it after it has been sensed it will not be affected. If *count* is decremented and reaches 0xF4, which indicates the switch has been open for ten milliseconds, *count* is reset to one. This simulated hysteresis makes the switch highly immune to noise and quite usable with cheap, bouncy, switches.

A single key is sometimes all that is needed. The preceding hardware and software approaches are often used; the best one depends on cost analysis, as in any hardware-software tradeoff. But we are often in need of tens of switches, as in a typewriter keyboard. The next section will consider sensing multiple switches. Again, there are both hardware and software approaches, and they are mutually analogous.

6-4.2 Debouncing Keyboard Scanning Techniques

Keyboards are arranged in arrays for the sake of describing the connections, although physically they can be arranged for the user's convenience. Using terminology from core memory arrays, a *coincident select* or *matrix* keyboard (shown in Figure 4-17 and Figure 6-15) uses two decoding and selecting devices to determine which key was pressed by coincidental recognition of the row and column the key is in. (A *linear select* keyboard has only a one-dimensional array of keys.) Only one normally open switch is closed, in column i and row j of the coincident select keyboard; exactly one code word $(i<<3) + j$ is to be output from a procedure or method that read this keyboard, each time this key is pressed.

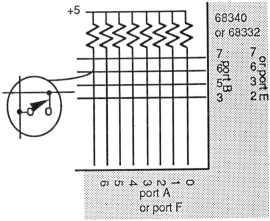

Figure 6-15. A Coincident-select Keyboard Array.

We first consider the use of parallel ports to *scan* the keyboard. On the M68332, port F is suitable, and on the M68340, port A is suitable, for an 8-bit input port, and on the M68332, port E bits 7,6,3 and 2 are suitable, and on the M68340, port B bits 7 to 5 and 3 are suitable, for a 4-bit output port. The 683xx presents a pattern on the output port in which exactly one of its bits is low, and reads the input bits; if a switch is closed in the row whose output is shorted low byt the output port, the pattern read from the input port will be something other than 0xFF; the low bit indicates which column the pressed key is in. Each of the four rows are scanned one after another to check if a key is pressed in them.

The class *KeyBd* below is shown for the M68340; for the M68332 substitute port E for port B, port F for port A, and use *char pattern[4]={0x4C,0x8C,0xC4,0xC8};*

```
struct KeyBd : IoDevice
{char flag, step; char b[4][4]; Queue *Q; void Init(long, unsigned); long Input(void);}*K;
long saveA4; char pattern[4]={0x68,0xa8,0xc8,0xe0};
void KeyBd::Init(p,m) long p; unsigned m;{ register int i,j,k,*hndaddr;
    assgA1=0xFF; dirA=0; assgB=0x17; dirB=0xe8; error=flag=step=j=0;
    (Q=blessA(sizeof(Queue),Queue))->InitQ(10); for(i=0;i<4;i++) b[0][i]=0;
    *(char *)0xffff001=0xe; *(long *)0xffff022=0x640000f; asm{move.l a4,saveA4}
    asm{lea @0,hndaddr} *((int **)0x100)= hndaddr; asm {and #0xfdff,sr} return;
```

▷
```
    asm {@0 movem.l d0-d2/d5-d7/a0-a1/a4, -(a7)}
    asm{move.l saveA4,a4}
    for(i=0;i<4;i++) { /* look at all 4 rows */  k=0xff; /* init accumul */
    for(j=0;j<4;j++) if(j==step) k&=b[j][i]; else k&=~ b[j][i];
    portB=pattern[i];
    if( k&= ~ portA ){ /* if row has a 1 */
    for(j=0;j<8;j++) {if (k&1) break; k=k>>1;} /* find column */
    Q->Push((i<<3) + j);
    }
    b[step][i]=portA; /* save history */
    }
    step=(step+1)&3;
    asm { movem.l (a7)+,d0-d2/d5-d7/a0-a1/a4} asm { rte }
```

```
}
long KeyBd::Input() { while(Q->Qlen==0); return Q->Pull();}
```

The object has, in addition to the usual queue, a *buffer* that holds the last four inputs from the keys and its index *step*. The keys are sampled in its interrupt handler every 1.8 msec. by outputting a pattern from the global vector *pattern* to port B, and examining the input from port A. After each sample, the previous values in the buffer are saved and the inputs from port A are moved into the buffer. We "wait-and-see" if the input remains down (L) for 4 samples. If the current key and 4 previous samples of it are all L, and the sample previous to that was up (H), then the key is considered pressed and the code for it is pushed onto the queue. The *Input* method merely pops a key code.

The preceding technique assumes that only one key is pressed at a time. If we allow two keys to be pressed simultaneously — as is often done by proficient keyboard users who press a new key before releasing the key being pressed — the program might keep picking up the first key, not seeing the new key while the first is in its scan. Any technique that can correctly recognize a new key even though n-1 keys are already pressed and are still down is said to exhibit *n-key rollover*. Two-key rollover is a common and useful feature that can be achieved with most keyboards, but for larger numbers one must guard against sneak paths through the keys. Sneak paths appear when three keys at three corners of a rectangle are pushed, and the fourth key seems to have been pushed because current can take a circuitous path through the pressed keys when the fourth key is being sensed. This sneak path current can be prevented by putting diodes in series with each switch, but this is rather expensive and n-key rollover is not that useful.

The hardware approach for keyboard scanning and debouncing actually uses the same principles as the software approach does. A special purpose integrated circuit connects to the keyboard and executes routines like those just described; the microprocessor connects to an output from them, from which the code for the key appears. Though this takes all the effort out of keyboard interfacing, it adds another large chip to the hardware; in addition, the microprocessor may anyhow be twiddling away in a delay loop while awaiting a command entered through the keyboard. The software approach to scanning and debouncing is therefore rather commonly used.

The keyboard mechansim used in this example utilizes scarce resources (the parallel ports). A better alternative uses the M68332 QSPI and shift register chips to reduce the use of scarce pins on the M68332 chip. This is considered in the next subsection.

6-4.3 Keyboard Scanning Using the M68332 QSPI

The coincident select keyboard was scanned by the QSPI, after it was set up by the procedure *initkbd()* in section 4-4.3, to determine which key is pressed. We now write a keyboard object that can input codes for keystrokes from a keyboard shown in Figure 4-17. A scanning program searches for the pressed key as in section 4-4.3, then the previous subsection's wait-and-see debounce routine verifies that the key is closed.

QSPI's baud rate is slowed to where its interrupts occur each 2 milliseconds, and the keys are sampled in its interrupt handler; after each sample, the previous values in the buffer are saved and the inputs from the QSPI are tested and moved into the buffer.

```
struct KeyBd : IoDevice { QSPI *qspiPort; char flag, step; int b[4][8]; Queue *Q;
    void Init(long, unsigned); long Input(void);
};
void KeyBd::Init(p,m) long p; unsigned m;{
    register int i,j,k, *T=(int*)0xfffd20,*hndaddr; register char *C=((char *)0xfffd40);
    Q=blessA(sizeof(Queue),Queue); Q->Init(10); for(i=0;i<8;i++) b[0][i]=0;
    *((int *)0xfffc00)=0xe; *((char*)0xfffc04)=0x30; *((char*)0xfffc05)=0x40; /* QSM */
    assgD=0xF; dirD=0xE; portD=0; /* portD */ qspiPort=(QSPI *)0xfffc18;
    qspiPort->mstr = qspiPort->wren = j = 1; qspiPort->bd = 0xff; qspiPort->endqp = 7;
    for(i=0;i<7;i++) {T[i]=~(j=j<<1); C[i]=1; for(k=0;k<4;k++) buffer[j][i]=0;}
    T[7]=0xfe; C[7]=1; error=0; qspiPort->spifie=1; qspiPort->spe=1; flag=step=0;
    asm{move.l a4,saveA4} /* save so that handler can access object instance variables */
    asm{lea @0,hndaddr} *((int **)0x104)= hndaddr; asm {and #0xfdff,sr} return;
▷   asm {@0 movem.l d0-d2/d5-d7/a0-a1/a4, -(a7)}
    asm{move.l saveA4,a4} qspiPort->spif=0;
    for(i=0;i<8;i++) { /* look at all 8 rows */  k=0xff; /* init accumul */
        for(j=0;j<4;j++) if(j==step) k&=b[j][i]; else k&=~ b[j][i];
        if( k&= ~ *(int *)(0xfffd00+(i<<1)) ){ /* if row has a 1 */
            for(j=0;j<8;j++) {if (k&1) break; k=k>>1;} /* find column */
            Q->Push((i<<3) + j); }
    }
    b[step][i]=*(int *)(0xfffd00+(i<<1)); /* save history */
    }
    step=(++step)&3; /* next step */
    asm { movem.l (a7)+, d0-d2/d5-d7/a0-a1/a4} asm { rte }
}

long KeyBd::Input() { while(Q->Qlen==0); return Q->Pull();}
```

6-4.4 Displays

We now extend the example to include a display for the keyboard. The hardware and software to support the keyboard and display are quite similar and can be shared. These two modules are both used very often for user input/output. We'll study the LED, the LED display, and the scanned display, giving concrete examples, including those for the very convenient MC14499 LED display and 145000 LCD display chips.

Recall that an LED is a diode that emits light if about ten milliamperes of positive current flow from anode to cathode. These diodes can be arranged in the form of a block 8, a diode per bar in the Figure 8. To save pins, either the cathodes or the anodes are tied together internally. The first is called a *common cathode* LED display, and the cathode is connected to ground. (See Figure 6-16a.)

To display a digit, the LEDs are turned on or off in each segment. Using the lettering system shown in Figure 6-16a, which is widely used in practice, a *seven-segment code* covers the values variables a through g. The seven-segment code for the number 2 is TTFTTFT. The representation of the number in the computer is hexadecimal (or binary-coded decimal). This representation must be recoded into its seven-segment form, and the seven-segment variables must be applied to the display to turn on the LEDs. This can be done in hardware or software. In the hardware approach, a *seven-segment decoder-driver* integrated circuit chip is used. The hexadecimal number from the computer output device is input to this chip, and its output is attached to the display LEDs. In the software approach, the hexadecimal number is converted by a routine – usually a table lookup routine – into the desired seven-segment code, which is then output to the LEDs. However, because the output device may be able to supply about one milliampere, a *segment driver* integrated circuit amplifies the signal. Figure 6-16a diagrams a popular segment driver, the 75491, which was designed for the high-volume calculator market. To use it with a microcomputer, a pull-up resistor on its input is often needed. If the input to the 75491 is high, current flows through the transistor. This current, limited by the small (100-ohm) current limiting resistor, goes through the LED to light it.

A typical program to generate the seven-segment code for a display uses table lookup. Suppose a table *char tbl[10];* is initialized to have the seven-segment codes for the digits; the i*th* row is the code for the i*th* digit. The hexadecimal number *n* is displayed through parallel port *p* by the simple statement *p=tbl[n];*

A single display may be needed in some applications, but we are often in need of several displays. Just as the concepts used for the single switch can be easily expanded to a keyboard, the preceding technique can be easily expanded to handle multiple displays. One way to handle multiple displays is to have one output device for each display. Alternatively, the displays can be *multiplexed*. Multiplexing is usually used because it saves the cost of several output devices; but sometimes it generates noise which might be intolerable, for instance, if a sensitive radio is near the display. In that case, separate displays must be used.

In multiplexed displays, the cathode of a common cathode display is connected to ground through a transistor. If the transistor is turned off, no current can flow through any of the LEDs in the display, so it appears dark regardless of the signals applied to the anodes. Suppose n displays are connected, with corresponding anodes connected to a segment driver as in the previous example and the transistors connected to a second output device so that only one is turned on. If the first transistor is turned on and the preceding program is executed, the number in D0 is displayed on the first display. If another number is put in D0 and the second display is turned on, that number is displayed in the second display, and so on. The number can be read from a table, for instance. The displays are turned on one at a time as the numbers to be displayed are picked up from the table by a table interpreter and are entered through putting them in D0 and executing the preceding program. Each is turned on for the same amount of time. Note that each display is on for 1/*nth* of the time. The current limiting resistor is made smaller so that n times as much current is sent through the LED, thus ensuring it is as bright as if driven as a single display. (See Figure 6-16b.)

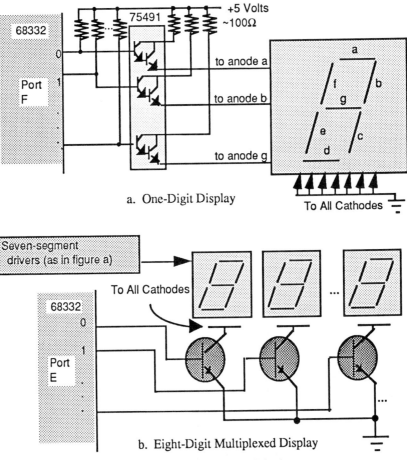

a. One-Digit Display

b. Eight-Digit Multiplexed Display

Figure 6-16. Seven-Segment Displays.

Multiplexed displays are widely used in calculators. The *digit driver* 75492 integrated circuit has six transistors capable of being used in the cathode line of these displays; and *peripheral drivers* like the 75451 have two NAND gates, each connected to

Chapter 6 – Analog Interfacing

a transistor, that can be used in this application. Multiplexing is useful for up to about ten displays; beyond that, too much current must be put through the LEDs for the small percentage of the cycle in which they are scanned. Even with six displays, if something goes wrong while one display is being driven so it remains on for longer than one-sixth the scan time, it can be burned out by the rather large currents flowing through it.

Other types of displays are used. A liquid crystal display is configured like an LED display, except that the bars are capacitors. A digit is displayed by putting voltages across the appropriate bars, much as in the LED display. However, if an LCD display has direct current across the capacitor, it weakens due to polarization of the chemical in it. An alternating voltage must be imposed to darken it. If the root mean square (RMS) voltage is below about one volt, the display is clear, and if above about two volts, it is opaque. The control circuitry supplies a voltage of 0, 1, 2, or 3 volts to the plates of the capacitors. The common connection analogous to the cathode in the LED display is sent a square wave of one volt alternating with two volts if the digit is not selected, and of zero volts alternating with three volts if the digit is selected. The connection analogous to the anode in the LED display is also sent a square wave. If the segment square wave is two volts whenever the common connection of a selected segment is at zero volts, and is one volt whenever it is at three volts, then the segment in the selected digit will have enough RMS voltage to darken. If the segment square wave is one volt when the common connection of a selected terminal is zero volts, and two volts when it is three volts, the segment does not have quite enough voltage across it to darken. Note too that none of the segments of the nonselected digits have enough RMS voltage to darken. When one digit is selected, all the segments to be darkened in it are given a signal that will darken them. One digit is scanned at a time. This technique provides the required alternating voltage free of DC to protect the LCDs. However, if the number of digits scanned this way increases, the RMS voltage of the segments to be darkened decreases so the ratio of the clear to dark levels gets too small to work reliably. So LCDs can be multiplexed, but only about three or four can be multiplexed together. The technique is to multiplex half the seven-segment display, consisting of four segments, at the same time the other half is multiplexed, and do this for each segment. In effect, the multiplexing is done orthogonally to the way it is done in LED displays – by scanning down half a segment rather than across all the segments. Finally, incandescent, gas discharge, and fluorescent seven-segment displays are also used, and self-scanning PANAPLEX displays can be used for user messages.

One can see that there is a similarity between the keyboard scan and the display scan hardware and software. Indeed, the decoder that selects the column of the keyboard can also select the digit to be displayed, and, as the rows are read from the keyboard the segments can be driven to display the digit through another output device. One can feast the imagination on all the variations of this technique that can be implemented.

The MC14499 and MC145000 are two chips that use the serial interface technique introduced in Section 4-4.2. Serial interfacing uses a small number of I/O pins, such as the data, clock, and enable pins, and is suitable for rather slow I/O devices, such as displays that cannot be read by the eye any faster than one pattern every few seconds. As discussed in that section, series and parallel configurations of these chips are possible, so they very effectively solve the display problem for microcomputer systems such as one having the M68332.

The MC14499 seven-segment LED display with serial interface is a very convenient package. (See Figure 6-17a.) One chip can multiplex four digits (and chips can be serially cascaded to handle more digits). Data on the data pin are shifted on the falling edge of the clock input Ck into a 20-bit shift register when the enable input En is low, to specify four digits and four decimal points, as illustrated in Figure 6-17b. The decimal points (1 = ON) are sent first, and that for digit one is sent first. Then the binary-coded digits are sent in, digit one first and most significant bit first. When all bits are sent in, the En input is made high, which causes the data in the shift register to be transferred to the register that drives the LED display. The chip multiplex timing frequency is set by a capacitor on pin six.

The MC145000 is a multiplexed LCD driver with serial interface capable of driving up to six seven-segment digits, (and can be cascaded to handle more). LCD displays are not uniformly configured, but Figure 6-17c shows one way (used on the General Electric LXD69D3F09KG LCD display). Data are shifted into a 48-bit shift

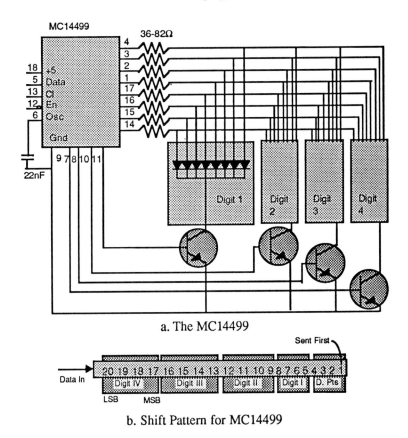

a. The MC14499

b. Shift Pattern for MC14499

Figure 6-17. Special Serial Interface Chips for LED and LCD Displays.

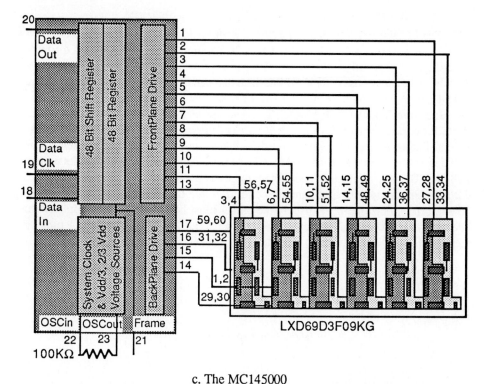

c. The MC145000

Figure 6-17. Special Serial Interface Chips for LED and LCD Displays (continued).

register on the falling edge of the data clock. When the LCD display is fully updated, an output pulse appears on the frame pin (pin 21), and the contents of the shift register is transferred to the output register, which determines what will be displayed in the next display period. The first eight bits shifted in will govern the least-significant digit location, one bit per segment (d first, then e, g, f, decimal point, c, b, and a). The next eight bits govern the next digit in like manner, and so on. The chip multiplex timing frequency is set by a resistor between pins 22 and 23, whose value depends on the LCD display. Whereas the LED display gets the bcd data and decodes them in the chip, the actual segment pattern is sent to the MC145000, so a translation routine like the simple statement *p=tbl[n]; is needed.

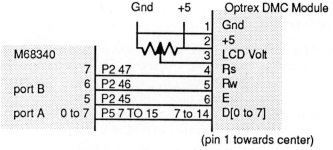

Figure 6-18. LCD Display Module Connections

The LCD displays such as OPTREX's DMC series can display a 16 column 1 row, a 16 column 2 row, a 20 column 1 row, a 20 column 2 row, a 20 column 4 row, or a 40 column 2 row ASCII message. We show procedures for the 16 column 1 row display. All displays use a standard interface that can be connected to the M68340's port A and port B, as shown in Figure 6-18, or to the M68332's port F and port E. To use the procedure below for the M68332, substitute *dirF* for *dirA*, *portF* for *portA*, and *portE* for *portB*, and substitute *assgF=0; dirF=0; assgE=0xf0; dirE=portE=0xe;* for the second line of *main*. The *main* procedure has an initialization ritual to select cursor blinking and movement. Its second line duplcates a command to configure its input port to 8 bits. The *wait* procedure gadflies on the LCD controller chip's busy indicator. The *out* procedure outputs a command or a character and the *outS* procedure outputs up to 16 characters. For a 16-by-1 display the cursor must be moved after 8 characters have been moved with the statement *if(i==7) waitOut(0xa8,0);*. To control other size displays, this statement must be modified to move the cursor appropriately.

```
#define rs 0x80
#define rw 0x40
#define e 0x20

main(){ int i;
      assgA1=0xff;dirA=0;assgB=0x1f;dirB=portB=0xe0;
      out(0x38,0);for(i=0;i<100;i++);out(0x38,0);
      waitOut(0xf,0);waitOut(1,0);waitOut(6,0);
      outS("Hello Family!");
}

void waitOut(c,a) char c,a; { wait(); out(c,a);}

void out(c,a) char c,a; {
   portB=rw+a;portB=a; dirA=0xff; portA=c; portB=e+a; portB=a;portB=rw+a;dirA=0;
}

void wait(){char c; do{ portB=rw; portB=rw+e; c=portA; portB=rw; } while(c&0x80);}

void outS(s) char *s;{ int i,j;
   waitOut(0x80,0);for(i=0;*s;i++) {waitOut(*(s++),rs);if(i==7)waitOut(0xa8,0);}
}
```

6-5 Converters

We often convert analog signals into digital signals and vice versa. Also, we convert analog amplitude signals into analog frequency signals and vice versa. The first subsection describes the digital-to-analog converters that are commonly available for microcomputer I/O systems. The next subsection describes analog-to-digital converters. Though they seem to be more common than digital-to-analog converters, we discuss them later because some analog-to-digital converters use digital-to-analog converters inside them. Finally, the timer, frequency-to-voltage, and voltage-to-frequency converters are discussed.

The following are some important concepts that cover the various converters. In general, the analog input is either sampled, using a sample-and-hold circuit or its equivalent, or integrated, using an integrator circuit or its equivalent. Analog output is either produced in samples or is output from an integrator. Integration smooths out the signal, reducing noise, but limits the upper-frequency signal components. Sampling provides a "snapshot" of the data and also the noise. In sampling converters, another problem is caused by high frequencies. The *sampling rate* is obviously the rate at which the data samples are taken. The *Nyquist rate* is one-half the sampling rate. Components of the signal that have higher frequency than the Nyquist rate "beat against" the frequency of the sampling rate in the same manner as radio frequency signals are "beat against" the frequency of a local oscillator in a radio, generating *alias* frequency components. For example, if a component has a frequency equal to the sampling rate, it will appear as a direct current component. To eliminate the generation of these alias components, a low-pass filter is used to eliminate all frequencies above the Nyquist rate.

6-5.1 Digital-to-analog Converters

Three basic digital-to-analog converters (D-to-A's) are introduced now: the summing amplifier, the ladder, and the exponential superposition D-to-A's. The summing amplifier converter most readily shows the basic principle behind all D-to-A converters, which is that each digital bit contributes a weighted portion of the output voltage if the bit is true and the output is the sum of the portions. The ladder converters are easier to build because the resistors in a ladder network can be trimmed precisely without much effort. Ladder networks for these D-to-A converters are readily available, quite fast, and inexpensive. The exponential superposition converter is quite a bit slower and less accurate, but doesn't need precision components, so it would be very useful in microcomputer-based toys or appliance controllers. A convenient package of 6-bit D-to-A converters, the MC144110 will be considered at the subsection's end.

The summing amplifier can be used in a D-to-A converter, as in Figure 6-19a. Keeping in mind that the output voltage is

$$\text{Vout} = - \text{Rf} (\text{V1/R1} + \text{V2/R2} + ...)$$

if $V1 = V2 = ... = 1$ volt, and Ri is either infinity (an open switch) or a power of two times Rf (if the corresponding switch is closed), then the output voltage is

$$\text{Vout} = \text{C1} / 2 + \text{C2} / 4 + \text{C3} / 8 + ...$$

where Ci is T if the switch in series with the *ith* resistor is closed; otherwise it is F. An output device can be used to control the switches, so the *ith*-most significant bit controls the *ith* switch. Then the binary number in the output register, considered as a fraction, is converted into a voltage at the output of the summing amplifier. Moreover, if the reference input voltage is made v volts rather than one volt, the output is the fraction specified by the output register times v volts. V can be fixed at a convenient value, like ten volts, to *scale* the converter. Usually, a D-to-A converter is scaled to a level, so for largest output value the summing amplifier is nearly, but not quite, saturated, to minimize errors due to noise and to offset voltages and currents. Alternatively, if V is itself an analog signal, it is multiplied by the digital value in the output register. This D-to-A converter is thus a *multiplying D-to-A converter*, and can be used as a digitally controlled voltage divider – an alternative to the range switch and duty cycle control techniques for amplification control.

Although conceptually neat, the preceding converter requires using from eight to 12 precision resistors of different values, which can be difficult to match in the 2-to-1 ratios needed. An alternative circuit, an *R-2R ladder* network, can be used in a D-to-A converter that uses precision resistors, all of which have values R or 2R ohms. This network can be used as a voltage divider or a current divider; the former is conceptually simpler, but the latter is more commonly used. (See Figure 6-19b for a diagram of a current ladder D-to-A converter.) A pair of analog switches for each "2R" resistor connects the resistor either into the negative input to the OP AMP or to ground, depending on whether the control variable is high or low, respectively. The current through these switches, from left to right, varies in proportion to 1/2, 1/4, 1/8, ..., as can be verified by simple circuit analysis. If the ith control variable is true, a current proportional to $2^{**}-i$ is introduced into the negative input of the OP AMP, which must be counterbalanced by a negative current through Rf to keep the negative input at virtual ground, so the output voltage proportional to $2^{**}-i$ is generated. The components for each input i are added, so the output is proportional to the value of the binary number whose bits control the switches. Like the previous D-to-A converter, this can be scaled by appropriately selecting the voltage Vin and can be used as a digitally controlled amplification device. It, too, is a multiplying D-to-A converter.

A program for outputting a voltage by means of either a summing or an R-2R D-to-A converter is very simple. One merely stores the number to be converted onto an output register that is connected to the converter.

A ladder network for a converter can be obtained as an integrated circuit for six to 12 bits of accuracy. The chip contains the switches and the resistors for the circuit. The output settles to the desired voltage level in less than a microsecond in a typical converter, so the programmer usually does not have to worry about settling time.

The last converter uses a sample-and-hold circuit to sample a voltage that is the sum of exponential voltages corresponding to bits of the digital word being converted. The circuit, in Figure 6-19c, is simplicity itself. We first offer some observations on an exponential waveform and the superposition principle. Consider an exponential waveform as shown in Figure 6-19d. Note that for such a signal there is a time T (not the time constant of the network, though) at which the signal is 1/2 the initial value of the signal. And at times 2 T, 3 T, 4 T, and so on, the signal level is 1/4, 1/8, 1/16 of the initial value, and so on. Furthermore, in a linear circuit, the actual voltage can be computed from the sum of the voltages of each waveform. This is called superposition. Now if a sample-and-hold circuit samples a voltage that is a sum of exponential voltages, an exponential waveform that was started T time units before will contribute 1/2 its initial value; one that was started 2 T time units before will contribute 1/4 its initial value; one started 3 T units before will contribute 1/8 its initial value; and so on. Thus, by generating or not generating each of the exponential waveforms from left to right in Figure 6-19d, the voltage sampled will or will not have a component of 1/8, 1/4, 1/2, and so on. These waveforms are generated by asserting control variable P if the shifted bit is true, as the least significant bits are shifted out each T time units. This closes the switch if the bit shifted out is true, so that the current source pumps a charge into the capacitor to generate the exponential that contributes its component of the sampled voltage. The control variable S is asserted to sample the waveform after all bits have been shifted out. The sampled voltage is the desired output of the D-to-A converter. The output can be scaled by selecting an appropriate current source, but this D-to-A converter doesn't make a good multiplying converter because dynamically changing the input current level will destroy its accuracy.

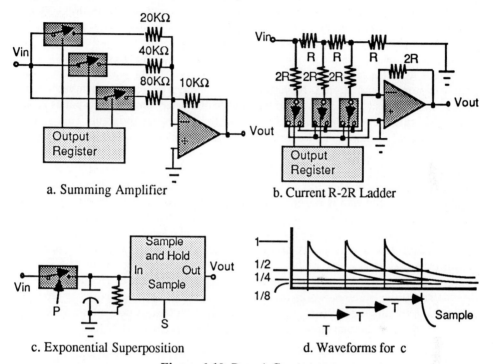

a. Summing Amplifier

b. Current R-2R Ladder

c. Exponential Superposition

d. Waveforms for c

Figure 6-19. D-to-A Converters.

The following M68332 program to convert an 8-bit number *a* to a voltage first makes port F a readable output device. It assumes bit zero is connected to control the switch via control variable P (see Figure 6-19c.) and that chip select CS6 supplies an address trigger (as discussed in Section 4-1.2) to assert the S control signal and thus sample the data whenever the address 0x10000 is generated in a read or write operation. A similar M68340 procedure would substitute its port A for port F.

```
put(a) unsigned char a;{
    assgF=0; dirF=0xff; pinAssign(cs6,byte); baseAssign(6,0x10000,k2);
    optionAssign(6,read+write+upper+lower+as fast,user+super,0);
    portF=a; /*put number in output register, output lsb to a/d converter */
    port =portF >>1; /* next lsb to a/d control */ portF=portF >>1; portF=portF >>1;
    portF=portF>>1portF=portF>>1;portF=portF>>1;portF=portF>>1;*(char*)0x10000;
}
```

The first three lines initialize port F to output the least significant bit of the data port and make the other bits act like a read/write memory word (that is, also make them "output" bits). In the next two lines, chip select CS6 is set up to supply an address strobe. The data to be converted are stored into the data port. Note that this will cause the least significant bit to be sent to the D-to-A converter to generate an exponential signal if the bit is true. Then the number to be converted is shifted seven times to generate the other seven exponential waveforms. Finally the address 0x10000 is generated, so the address decoder will output a pulse to the S line to cause the sample-and-hold module to sample the waveform. As explained earlier, this waveform contains components from each output bit if that bit was true, and the component generated by the most significant bit is twice as big as the component for the next, and so on.

Accuracy of this simple converter is limited to just a few bits. The sample-and-hold circuit loads the capacitor, and the current source doesn't supply a fixed current if its output is stopped and started. Nevertheless, this converter requires a minimum of adjustment. The resistor is adjusted so the exponential decay time T corresponds to the time to execute the *p=*p>>1; statement in the preceding program. This simple converter would be most suitable, for instance, where a microcomputer runs a toy train by controlling a voltage supplied to the motor.

The last D-to-A converter we discuss is the MC144110, a serial interface chip that has six 6-bit converters. (See Figure 6-20.) A serial interface requires fewer pins than a parallel interface and also is easier to isolate using opto-isolators if the analog voltage must be on a different ground system than the microcomputer. The data are shifted in from the data pin serially, left to right (msb first), on the falling edge of the bit clock Ck, when En is low. When 36 bits have been shifted in, En should rise and the data will be put in the register, where each six bits will govern the analog output of a D-to-A converter; the register bit switches the bottom of the 2R resistor to ground or to +5v. The outputs of the ladder networks (pins three, five, and so on) can be used as inputs to FET OP AMP voltage followers. The transistors in each D-to-A converter can be used as emitter follower current amplifiers for low-impedance bipolar OP AMPs.

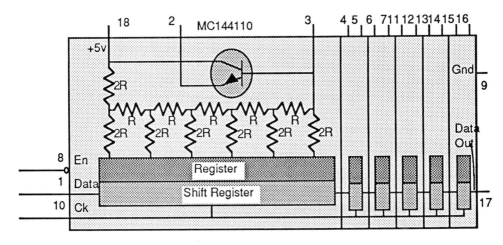

Figure 6-20. The MC144110.

6-5.2 Analog-to-digital Converters

In a manner like that of the previous subsection, six analog-to-digital converters (A-to-Ds) are introduced, which have different costs, accuracies, and speeds. We discuss them in approximate order of decreasing speed and cost. Parallel and pipeline converters are fastest, followed by the delta, successive approximation, and ramp converters.

The *parallel* A-to-D converter uses comparators to determine the input voltage and can be made to operate almost as fast as the comparators. One avoids using too many comparators because they are expensive, so this converter's accuracy is limited by the number of its comparators. Figure 6-21a illustrates a typical three-bit converter that has, for ease of discussion, a range of zero to seven volts. The resistor divider network establishes reference voltages for each comparator, from top to bottom, of 0, 1, 2,...,7 volts. If the input voltage Vin is between i-1 and i volts, the i bottom comparators output a true value. A priority encoder module encodes this set of values to a binary number that is the most prior true input address, which is i.

A variation of the parallel converter, a *pipeline converter*, consists of n identical stages of a comparator and differential amplifier (see Figure 6-21b and Figure 6-21c) to achieve n bits of accuracy. In a typical stage illustrated in Figure 6-21b, the signal Vin is sent to the input, and the output Vout of the differential amplifier on the right of the stage is then sent to the input of the next stage to the right. Suppose the voltage range is Vmax. The output of the comparator on the left of the stage is either Vmax if the V+ input is higher than the V- input of the comparator or it is zero volts. If the input is above half Vmax, then half Vmax is subtracted from the input and then doubled – otherwise the input is just doubled – in the differential amplifier that feeds the output Vout. If a steady signal is fed into the input Vin, then as the signal flows through the stages, bits from most significant bit are obtained from each stage, being true if half Vmax was subtracted, otherwise being false. Moreover, the conversion is actually done as the leading edge of the analog signal flows through each stage. It is possible, then, to begin the next conversion when the first stage has settled, even though later stages may yet be settling. Its rather like oil flowing through a pipeline. This kind of system is then called a pipeline. Several years ago, an experimental six-bit converter was reported to have an incredible eight-gigaHertz conversion rate. Digital oscilloscopes, anyone?

Successive approximation, delta, and ramp converters can be implemented with the hardware illustrated in Figure 6-21d. The programs differ for each method. For *delta* or *servo* conversion, a D-to-A converter outputs a voltage Vcomp which is compared to Vin. If Vcomp > Vin, then Vcomp is diminished; otherwise Vcomp is increased by a small amount. Assuming Vin changes slower than Vcomp can change, Vcomp should "track" Vin in the manner of a feedback control or servo system. By another analogy to communications systems, the digital output changes by delta increments, as in delta modulation systems. Figure 6-21e shows a varying Vin and a tracking Vcomp for a delta converter. The following M68332 procedures *init()* and *get()* for an 8-bit delta converter assumes that port F is an output port, whose output is converted by the 8-bit D-to-A converter to Vcomp, and port E is an input port, whose sign bit is true if Vin > Vcomp. The M68340 procedures substitute ports A and B and their initialization ritual.

init();{char assgF=assgE=0; dirE=0x7f; assgF=0xff;}
unsigned char get();{ if(portE<0) return portF++ else return portF- -;}

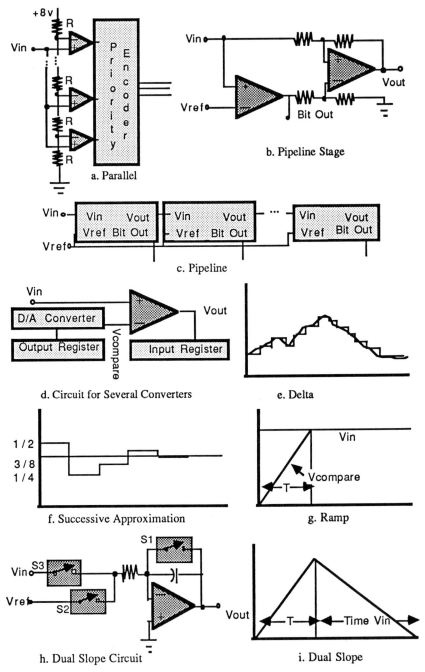

Figure 6-21. A-to-D Converters.

The number in port F, which tracks the input voltage, is to be read by continuously calling *get*. Each time it is called, the output voltage becomes a little closer to the input, to "track" it. A digital hardware servo converter can also be built, so a processor is not tied up in the loop, but the technique is identical. Servo converters are as fast as the comparator, D-to-A converter, and up-down counter that track the input. However, like OP AMPs, they have a slew rate limitation that may be unacceptable.

A *successive approximation* converter uses the same circuit but requires a program that embodies a different principle – the principle of divide-and-conquer. We observe the same technique in long division. Suppose the input is in the range zero to Vmax. The D-to-A converter is so loaded as to output Vmax/2. If the comparator senses Vin > Vmax/2, then the D-to-A converter is set to output Vmax 3/4, otherwise it is set to output Vmax/4. Note that this is done by either adding or subtracting Vmax/4 from the current output, depending on the result of comparing this output with Vin. In successive trials, Vmax/8, then Vmax/16, Vmax/32,... are added or subtracted from the value output to the D-to-A converter. The comparison voltage Vref approaches Vin, as shown in Figure 6-21f. The following M68332 procedure *success* will be called in a program in Section 6-6. A similar M68340 procedure would substitute ports A and B.

```
init();{dirE=0x7f; assgE=assgF=0; dirF=0xff;}

unsigned char success();{unsigned char pattern=0x80;
    portF=pattern;
    do {
        pattern = pattern >>1; if(portE<0) portF += pattern; else portF - = pattern;
    } while (pattern);
    return portF;
}
```

Data in the output port are initialized to half the range so the D-to-A converter will initially try Vcomp = Vmax/2. In the *do while* loop, the adjustment value *pattern* is divided by two, so that in the first execution of the loop, Vmax/4 will be added to or subtracted from the comparison voltage; in the second execution of the loop, Vmax/8 will be added or subtracted, and so on. At the end of the loop, the adjustment value is examined; if it has become zero the conversion must be complete. Successive approximation converters are quite fast, because each execution of the loop determines one more digit of the result. Moreover, by implementing this technique in hardware (called a successive approximation register), the computer can concentrate on other things as the voltage is being converted.

A *ramp* analog-to-digital converter can use the same circuit as in Figure 6-21d or a simpler circuit as in Figure 6-21h. Simply, in Figure 6-21d, the comparator voltage Vcomp is initialized to zero by clearing port F, then is gradually increased by incrementing it until Vcomp > Vin is sensed by the comparator. (See Figure 6-21g.) The circuit illustrated in Figure 6-21h uses a *dual slope* technique that is shown in Figure 6-21i. The output voltage from the integrator, sensed by the comparator, is initially cleared by closing only switch S1. Then, by closing only S2 for a specific time T, the reference Voltage – Vref is integrated, charging the capacitor in the integrator. Lastly only S3 is closed, so that the voltage Vin is integrated to discharge the capacitor. The capacitor discharge time is proportional to Vin. Moreover, the time is proportional to the average value of Vin over the time it is integrated, which nicely reduces noise we don't want to measure; and the accuracy of the converter does not depend on the values of the components (except Vref), so this converter is inexpensive. However, it is the slowest converter. It finds great use, nevertheless, in digital voltmeters, multimeters, and panel meters, because it can achieve about 12 bits (three-and-a-half digits) of accuracy at low cost, and it is faster than the eye watching the display.

The MAX 134 Digital Multimeter chip, made by a fairly new company, MAXIM, is essentially a digital multimeter that is controlled by a microcomputer (see Figure 6-22a). The microcomputer, using a 4-bit data bus and 3-bit address, sets register values (Figure 6-22b) to select the range and function. For instance, to measure a DC voltage (4v maximum), 10-1 (register 2 bit 0) and DC (register 3 bit 3) are set. After conversion is complete (EOC is asserted) the value can be read, register 0 having the low-order BCD digit, and so on. This 4 1/2 digit converter's accuracy is limited mainly by analog noise.

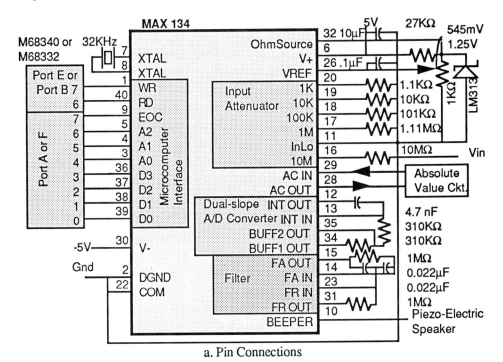

a. Pin Connections

Address	D3	D2	D1	D0	Data Read
0	Hold	HiFreq	BeeperOn	Sleep	Ones
1	10-0	FilterShort	Div5	50Hz	Tens
2	10-4	10-3	10-2	10-1	Hundreds
3	DC	ExAC	Divider	Ohms R/2	Thousands
4	Current	X2	ReadZero	FilterOn	10Thousands
5					Status

b. Control and Data Registers

Figure 6-22. MAX 134 Digital Multimeter.

We illustrate the control of a complex I/O chip, the Max134, with the M68340 gadfly-synchronized class *Max134*, using ports A and B as shown in Figure 6-22a. This example illustrates the utility of objects in handling the control bits shown in Figure 6-22b. As with other classes, an object such as *M* would be blessed, then initialized using the method *initMeter*. The method *setMeter* sets bit fields for a command, its argument, chosen from a list on the *enum* statement below, and then outputs the register values using the method *outa*. The 4v. voltage is selected using *M->setMeter(dcVlotage); M->setMeter(1);* It is read by sending the *M->Input();* message. That method uses the method *ina* to actually read the chip.

```
#define EOC 0x80        #define Read 0x40        #define Write 0x80
enum {beepOff=5,beepLow,beepHigh,calibrate,acVoltage,dcVoltage,acCurrent,
    dcCurrent,ohms};

struct Max134:direct {
    char settings[2];
    unsigned :4,hold:1,highF:1,beep:1,sleep:1,:4,ten0:1,filterS:1,div5:1,Hz50:1,
        :4,ten4:1,ten3:1,ten2:1,ten1:1,:4,dc:1,ac:1,divideS:1,ohmsR2:1,
        :4,amps:1,x2:1,readZero:1,filterOn:1,
        :4,alwaysOne:1, continuity:1, notHolding:1, lowBat:1;
    long offset;
    long Input(void); char ina(char);
    void outa(char,char),initMeter(void),setMeter(int);
};

void Max134::initMeter(){ int i;
    assgA1=0xff;portA=dirA=0x70;assgB=0;dirB=portB=Read+Write;
    for(i=0;i<7;i++) settings[i]=0; setMeter(calibrate); Input(); filterOn=1;
}

char Max134::ina(a) char a;{ char d;
    portA=((a<<4) & 0x70); portB &= ~Read; for(d=0;d<4;d++);
    d=portA & 0xf; portB |= Read; return d;
}

void Max134::outa(a,d) register char a,d;{
    dirA=0x7f; portA=((a<<4) & 0x70) + (d&0xf);
    portB &= ~Write; portB |= Write; dirA=0x70;
}

void Max134::setMeter(command)int command;{ int i;
    if(command<beepOff){
        ten0=ten1=ten2=ten3=ten4=0;
        switch(settings[0]=command){
            case 0:  ten0=1;break; case 1: ten1=1;break; case 2: ten2=1;break;
            case 3:  ten3=1;break; case 4: ten4=1;break;
        }
    }
```

```
    else{
        switch(settings[1]=command){
            case beepOff: beep=0;break; case beepLow: beep=1;highF=0;break;
            case beepHigh:  beep=highF=1;break;
            case calibrate:    readZero=1;divideS=ac=dc=0;break;
            case acVoltage:  divideS=ac=1;readZero=dc=0;break;
            case dcVoltage:  divideS=dc=1;readZero=ac=0;break;
            case acCurrent:  amps=ac=1;readZero=divideS=dc=0;break;
            case dcCurrent:  amps=dc=1;readZero=divideS=ac=0;break;
            case ohms: ohmsR2=dc=1;readZero=ac=divideS=0;break;
        }
    }
    hold=1; outa(0,settings[2]); while(!(portA & EOC));
    hold=0;for(i=6;i>1;i--) outa(i-2,settings[i]);
}

long Max134::Input(){ int i;register long result=0;
    while(portA & EOC); while(!(portA & EOC)); settings[7]=ina(0);
    for(i=4;i>=0;i--) result = (result<<3) + (result<<1) + ina(i);
    if(result>40000) result -= 100000;
    if(readZero) offset=result; else result-=offset;
    if(div5) asm 68020{ divs.l #5,result}
    if(ten4) asm 68020{ muls.l #10000,result}
    if(ten3) asm 68020{ muls.l #1000,result}
    if(ten2) asm 68020{ muls.l #100,result}
    if(ten1) asm 68020{ muls.l #10,result}
    if(ohmsR2) result>>=1;
    if(x2) result<<=1;
    return result;
}
```

This example requires considerable skill in both analog and digital design. While it illustrates the utility of objects, it was not satisfactorally tested. Measurements had considerable error and we only tested the D.C. voltage function. We had to take care to read the output of the MAX134 using port A, because this low-power chip was unable to drive port B, which has 5 KΩ pull-up resistors. We did not provide for sufficient grounding. However, we offer it as a good starting point for a very interesting project.

6-5.3 Frequency Generators and Converters

In this section, we discuss frequency converters and generators. A timer generates a square wave whose period is proportional to a resistance, capacitance or an input voltage, a voltage-to-frequency converter (VFC) generates a square wave whose frequency or period is proportional to an input voltage, and a frequency-to-voltage converter (FVC) generates a voltage proportional to the frequency of an input signal. Finally we discuss the phase locked loop (PLL) used to generate higher frequencies. These are useful building-blocks that can be used with the next chapter's counter-timers.

A timer outputs a periodic signal whose period is proportional to the value of a resistor and a capacitor connected to it. (Often, the period can be adjusted by a control voltage, but the voltage to frequency converter discussed below is generally better.) The timer allows resistor-based transducers to generate AC signals, where the information is carried by the frequency (period). Such signals are easy to handle and measure, as we will see in the next chapter. The ubiquitous 555 is the most popular and least expensive timer. (See Figure 6-23a for the circuit that generates repetitive signals.) In Figure 6-23b we see a graph that gives the period of the signal as a function of the resistance, which is the value R1+2R2 in Figure 6-23a, and the capacitance, which is the value of C1.

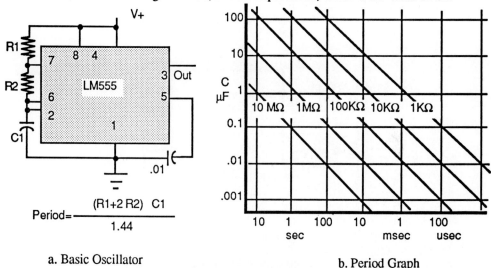

a. Basic Oscillator　　　　　　　　　　b. Period Graph

Figure 6-23. 555 Timer.

The *voltage-to-frequency converter* (VFC) generates a square wave whose frequency or period is proportional to the input voltage Vin. (See Figure 6-24a.) Internally, Vin is integrated, until the integrated voltage reaches a reference voltage Vref, when the integrated voltage is cleared. An output pulse, occurring as the integrator is cleared, has a frequency that is proportional to the input Vin. If desired, this can be fed to a toggle flip-flop to square the signal as its period is doubled. By reversing the role of the reference and input voltage so the reference voltage is integrated and compared to the input voltage, the period of the output is proportional to the voltage Vin. So this makes a voltage-to-period converter. But noise on Vin is not averaged out in this technique. Other circuits are used for VFCs, but the principles are similar to those discussed here. VFCs can be quite accurate and reasonably fast; the Teledyne 9400 (see Figure 6-24b) accurately converts voltage to frequency to about 13 bits of accuracy and remains equally accurate after two cycles have occurred on the output wave. That means the converter is faster for higher voltages, because they result in higher frequencies, than for lower voltages. Used in an integrating mode, moreover, the VFC can reduce noise the way the dual ramp converter does. The VFC is of particular value where the microprocessor has a built-in counter to measure frequency, especially because the frequency carrying signal is easy to handle, being carried on only one wire.

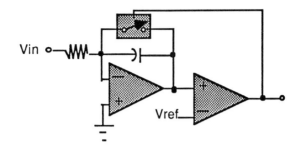

a. Basic Mechanism

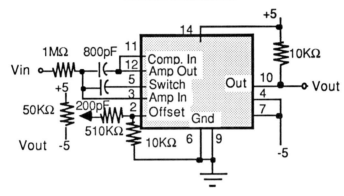

b. Teledyne 9400

Figure 6-24. Voltage-to-Frequency Conversion.

Related to the digital-to-analog converter, a *frequency-to-voltage converter* (FVC) outputs a voltage that is proportional to the input frequency. For high frequencies, an FM detector serves this function. Several integrated circuits are available for detecting FM signals. For a broad range of frequencies, a phase-locked loop can be used. The error voltage used to lock the oscillator in it to the frequency of the incoming signal is proportional to the difference between the frequency to which the oscillator is tuned and the frequency of the incoming signal. For audio frequencies, a common technique is to trigger a one-shot with the leading edge of the input signal. The output is a pulse train, where the pulses are of constant width and height and occur with the same frequency as the input signal. (See Figure 6-25a.) This signal is passed through a low-pass filter to output a signal that is proportional to the area under the pulses, which is in turn proportional to the frequency. The LM3905 is especially suited to this application, as it is a one-shot (monostable) with built-in voltage reference and an output transistor that is capable of producing output pulses of precise height. (See Figure 6-25b.) Another way to convert frequency to voltage is to use an integrated circuit specially made for the vast automobile market to implement a tachometer, because a tachometer senses spark pulses whose frequency is proportional to engine speed, and it outputs an analog level to a meter to display the engine speed. This technique can be used with subaudio frequencies, because it is designed to measure low-rate spark pulse trains. Frequency-to-voltage converters have the advantage that information is carried by the frequency of a signal on a single wire, which can be easily opto-isolated, and is remarkably immune to noise and degradation due to losses in long wires from microcomputer to output. However, the signal they carry has to pass through a low-pass filter, so its maximum frequency must be much lower than that of the carrier which is being converted to the voltage.

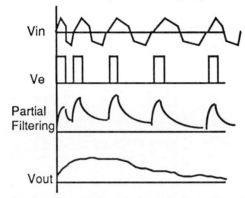

a. Frequency-to-Pulse-Train-to-Voltage Conversion

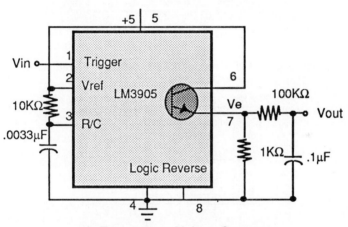

b. Frequency-to-Voltage Converter

Figure 6-25. Frequency-to-Voltage Conversion.

The *phase-locked loop* (PLL) is used to generate higher frequencies than can be achieved by a microcomputer using a TPU. (See Figure 6-26.) Figure 6-26a shows the digital part and Figure 6-26b shows the analog part of a PLL that can generate almost any frequency within a wide range. Figure 6-26a diagrams one of several chips that use a serial input and that can handle the digital logic for a PLL. Serial input is desirable to save pins because the frequency of the oscillator is not changed that often and changes do not have to be prompt. The chip contains two down-counters: one divides the variable frequency of a signal Fin on pin nine by N, where N is a fourteen-bit number sent from the computer, while the other divides a reference frequency of a signal generated by an oscillator on pin seventeen by R, where R is chosen by the levels on pins two, one, and eighteen. The number N is shifted in, using the techniques discussed in Section 4-4.2. Actually, the low-order fourteen bits of the sixteen bits shifted in (most significant bit first) are N; the high-order two bits are output as signals on pins thirteen and fourteen, which are "open collector" outputs that can be used in any way the designer needs to use two control bits. The average voltage on the phase detector output PD (pin 6) is raised if the variable frequency divided by N is less than the reference frequency divided by R, and it is lowered if the variable frequency divided by N is greater than the reference frequency divided by R. Other outputs ør, øv, and lock detect LD can be used in more advanced PLLs.

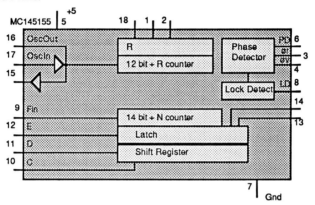

a. The MC145155 Serial Input PLL Frequency Synthesizer

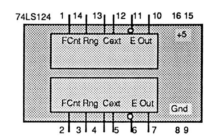

b. A Dual Voltage-Controlled Oscillator

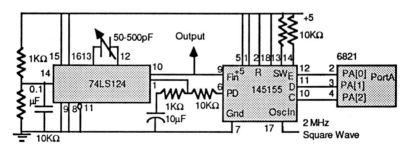

c. A Simple Circuit
Figure 6-26. Phase-Locked Loop.

Figure 6-26b is the analog part of the PLL. The chip contains two variable-frequency oscillators (VCOs). We describe the upper one here. The capacitor Cext between pins twelve and thirteen sets the nominal frequency of the oscillator – about (500/Cext) MHz, where Cext is in picoFarads. The frequency of the output on pin ten is proportional to the voltage on pin one. The range control Rng on pin fourteen sets the sensitivity; the larger Rng voltage makes oscillator frequency changes more sensitive to input voltage changes. The enable E must be low for the output to oscillate.

Figure 6-26c shows a simple application. Some new chips require unusual clock frequencies. For example, the author found a very interesting voice-output chip needing a 3.123-MHz crystal, but could not find the crystal. The PLL just mentioned could be used to generate frequencies in the range of one to eight-MHz in place of a crystal. It is a feedback control system of the kind that will be described in Section 6-6.3 that uses voltage analog and frequency analog signals. The 145155 compares a frequency on input Fin to one generated by the OscIn input, and outputs a voltage on PD that is proportional to the difference. This voltage, passed through a low-pass filter, is put into FCnt of the 74LS124 VCO to generate a frequency Fin. When stable, the voltage PD is just the right voltage to generate the frequency Fin that is (R/N) times the frequency of the signal OscIn. In this example, OscIn is generated from some 2-MHz clock, and R is set to $8192 = 2^{13}$. To set up the oscillator at frequency F, the connection from pin six of the 145155 to pin one of the 74LS124 is broken, a voltage of 2.5 volts is put on pin one, the VCO capacitor Cext is set to cause oscillations at about the desired frequency F, and then a number $N = (F/2MHz) * 8192$ is shifted into the 145155 so that the output PD is about 2.5 volts. Then the broken connection is put back. The output signal should have frequency F. The design of the low-pass filter is quite involved: whole books are available on this topic. In the preceding circuit, the resistor connected to output PD determines the frequency of oscillation of the locking error, and the resistor connected to the ten μF capacitor determines its damping; these can be twiddled to get acceptable results. This technique is useful in generating high frequencies up to about 15-MHz. Note that the frequency can be changed (over a 2:1 range) by changing the number in the shift register, so the pitch of the voice-output chip can be altered to get a more natural speech. A similar technique is used with FM and TV tuners and a divide-by-sixteen prescaler to control the frequencies of oscillators up to the 300-MHz range used by FM radios and television sets.

6-6 Data Acquisition Systems

A *data acquisition system* (DAS) consists of switches, a D-to-A converter, and signal conditioning circuits so that several inputs can be measured and several outputs can be supplied under the control of a microcomputer. In the first subsection, we consider the basic idea of a data acquisition subsystem. Then we consider the MC145040 A-to-D converter that is the input part of a data acquisition system. The final subsection considers how these data acquisition systems can be used in control systems.

6-6.1 Basic Operation of a Data Acquisition System

A DAS can be purchased as a printed circuit board, or even as a (hybrid) integrated circuit module. Such a DAS would be better to use than the system we discuss, but we introduce it to show how such a system works and to bring together the various concepts from previous sections. Finally, in this section, we will show how a DAS can be used to implement a digital filter or feedback control system.

The DAS described in this section is diagramed in Figure 6-27. From left to right, an analog switch selects from among eight inputs an input for the comparator. This is used to measure the input voltages. The D-to-A converter is used, with the comparator, for prompting the A-to-D converter to measure the inputs and for supplying the output voltages. The analog switch and voltage followers on the right implement sample-and-hold circuits, which act like analog flip-flops, to store the output voltages after they have been set by the microcomputer. In the following discussion, port F will be an output port to the D-to-A converter, port E will be an input whose sign bit is true if Vin (selected by the analog switch) is greater than Vcomp. Port C will be a readable output port that addresses both the analog switches. If, for instance, three is put in this port, then input three is sent to the comparator (as Vin), and the output of the D-to-A converter is made available to the sample-and-hold circuit that supplies output three. Finally, the analog switch is enabled by an address trigger. If the microcomputer addresses location 0x10000, as it does when executing *(char *)0x10000; the address decoder will provide a short pulse which will enable the analog switch for about 60 nanoseconds. Recall that, when enabled, the addressed input is connected to the output of the switch, but when not enabled, all inputs and the output are not connected.

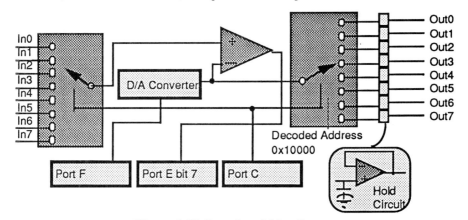

Figure 6-27. Data Acquisition System.

The DAS is controlled by a program, shown soon, which will be called as a subroutine whenever the inputs are to be measured and the outputs are to be adjusted. Eight output values are stored in an 8-element vector *outputs,* so that *outputs[0]* is converted to a voltage on output zero; *outputs[1]* on output one; and so on. *outputs* is loaded with the desired values just before this subroutine is called. After returning from the subroutine, the eight inputs are, to keep things simple, converted and stored in *inputs. inputs[0]* will store the number equal to the voltage on input zero; *inputs[1],* that equal to the voltage on input one; and so on.

We assume that the routines *init* and *success* for the successive approximation A-to-D converter shown in section 6-5.2 are used. For the M68332, *Init* is executed to set up ports E and F, chip select CS6 is configured as follows:

> *pinAssign(cs6,byte); baseAssign(6,0x10000,k2);*
> *optionAssign(6,read+write+upper+lower+as,fast,user+super,0);*

and port C is initialized so that the three least significant bits are outputs. For the M68340, *Init* is executed to set up ports A and B, chip select CS3 is configured as:

> *CsAssign(3,0x10000,8,fast,rdWr)*

In the loop, a number is read from the table to the D-to-A converter via output port F, and then the output analog switch is enabled by executing **((char *)0x10000;* The address trigger technique discussed in Section 4-1.1 is used here. At that time, the output of the D-to-A converter is sampled by the sample-and-hold circuit that feeds output zero, because the analog switch addresses the top position. The voltage output from the D-to-A converter is now sampled, and will remain on this output until it is changed when this subroutine is called again. Thus, the sample-and-hold behaves rather like an analog storage register. Next, a successive approximation subroutine like that discussed in the previous section is called. The subroutine converts the top input, because port C is 0, to a digital value that is put in *inputs[0]*. When all rows are output and input, this subroutine is left.

```
char inputs[8],outputs[8];
DAS(){ int i;
for(i=0;i<8;i++) { portC=i; portF=outputs[i]; *((char *)0x10000=i; inputs[i]=success(); }
}
```

The M68340 doesn't have 17 parallel I/O bits for this exact design. the reader might attempt to design a reduced version, with port A for the D-toA, port B bit 7 for comparator input, and port B's four other bits to select one of four inputs or outputs.

6-6.2 The MC145040 Chip

A very convenient way to measure analog voltages in the 68332 microcomputer is with the 145040 chip. (See Figure 6-28.) It is similar to a data acquisition system (DAS) in that it uses an analog multiplexor (mux) to select a number of inputs for the converter.

A serial interface is desirable for an A-to-D converter because it uses fewer pins than a parallel interface and thus can be easily isolated using opto-isolators. The MC145040 is one of the better serial interface A-to-D converters.

Data are shifted into and out of the 145040 at the same time, using the "exchange" technique discussed in Section 4-4.3. During bit movement, CS must be low and should rise after all bits are moved because that edge transfers the data to the mux address register and begins the conversion. An input "address" is sent first (to select input i, $i=0$ to 11, send $i<<4$, msb first), and each bit is clocked in on the rising edge of SClk. Conversion is done with the A/D Clk using the successive approximation technique, with Vref as the maximum and VAG as the minimum reference voltage. If the "address" is 0xB, then a voltage (Vref+VAG)/2 is input and should convert to a value of 0x80; this can be used for a check. Wait 32 A/D Clk pulse cycles, and then input the eight-bit digital value, msb first, that was converted from the *ith* analog input. Data are sent from the chip on the falling edge of SClk. The "address" for the next conversion can be output while the previous conversion's data are being input, in an exchange operation.

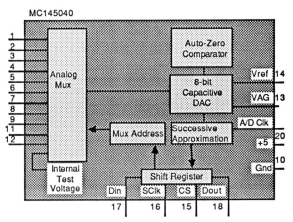

MC145040

Figure 6-28. Serial Interfaced A-to-D Converter.

As this book goes to press, another A-to-D and D-to-A converter has become available. This 13-bit serial interfaced chip, the MC145402, can be controlled using indirect I/O. But to reach its full speed, 64 KHz., requires substantial additional logic.

6-6.3 Data Acquisition Systems in Control Systems

The DAS and subroutine in Section 6-6.1 or the A-to-D converters in 6-6.2 and D-to-A MC144110 converter in 6-5.1 can be used in control systems. The three main applications are the collection and generation of analog data and feedback control.

The microcomputer is admirably suited for collecting analog data. The DAS and subroutine recently discussed can collect a sample of up to eight analog inputs. The collected data could be stored in a table, transmitted across a data link, or operated on. The programs for these operations should be simple enough, so that they are not spelled out here. However, it should be stressed that data collection using microcomputers has a unique advantage over simpler techniques: Its software can execute functions on the incoming data. In particular, functions can, as we discuss, correct errors in the measurement apparatus.

Suppose the incoming data actually has value x, but the measurement apparatus reports the value as $y = F(x)$. The function F can be empirically obtained by inputting known values of x, then reading the values of y. Suppose F is an invertible function and the inverse function is G; then $x = G(y)$. The software can read y from the measurement apparatus, then compute $G(y)$ to get the accurate value of x.

A number of techniques can be used to evaluate some arbitrary function $G(y)$, such as might be obtained for correcting errors. The well-known Taylor series expansion is sometimes useful; but to evaluate such a polynomial may take a long time and accumulate a lot of rounding error. A better technique is to evaluate $G(y)$ as a continued fraction $G(y) = A / B + G'(y)$, where $G'(y)$ is either y or a continued fraction. The most suitable for microcomputers, however, is the *spline* technique. Just as a complex curve is often drafted by drawing sections of it with a "French curve," the complex function $G(y)$ is approximated by sections of simpler functions (called splines) like parabolas. (See Figure 6-29.) Given a value y, we determine which section of $G(y)$ it is in, to choose which spline to evaluate. We do this by comparing y against the values y_i that separate the splines. A fast way is to test y against the middle yi, then if y < yi, check y against the yi a quarter of the way across the scale; otherwise, check against the yi three-quarters of the way; and so on in the same manner as the successive approximation technique for A-to-D conversion. Once the section is determined, evaluate the function by evaluating the spline. If the spline is a parabola, then X = A y**2 + B y + C for some constants A, B, and C. The values yi for the boundaries and the constants A, B, and C can be stored in a table. Software for searching this table to select the correct spline and for evaluating the spline is quite simple and fast on a microcomputer.

Analog signals can be converted to digital values, then filtered using digital techniques, rather than filtered using OP AMPs, as discussed earlier in this chapter. The following is a discussion of digital filtering as a feedback control technique.

In a manner similar to that just discussed, if analog values are to be output from a microcomputer, errors in the output apparatus may be corrected in software. If the true output value is y but x is sent to the output, the output is actually y = F(x); then if F is invertible and G is the inverse of x (x = G(y)), the microcomputer can evaluate G(y) and send this value to the output system. The program that evaluates G(y) compensates ahead of time for the error to be made in the output apparatus.

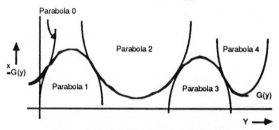

Figure 6-29. The Spline Technique.

A test system might be designed using the preceding techniques to output some analog voltages to the object being tested, then to measure the voltages it returns. While these systems are important, the feedback control system is even more important and interesting. Figure 6-30 shows the classic model of the feedback control system. The entire system has a stimulus x (or a set of stimulae considered as a vector) as input, and an output z (or a set of outputs, a vector z). The system that outputs z is called the *plant*. The plant usually has some deficiencies. To correct these, a *feedback system* is implemented (as diagramed in Figure 6-30), which may be built around a microcomputer and DAS. The output of this system, an error signal, is added to the stimulus signal x, and the sum of these signals is applied to the plant. A feedback control system is used in phase locked loops, as described in Section 6-5.3. Feedback control systems like this have been successfully used to correct for deficiencies in the plant, thus providing stable control over the output z.

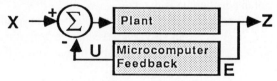

Figure 6-30. Feedback Control.

Three techniques have been widely used for feedback control systems: the proportional integral differential, the linear filter, and multi-input-output controllers.

The simplest and most popular controller is called the *proportional integral differential* controller (PID). Its form is easy to implement on a microcomputer. The output of the feedback system U is a weighted sum of the current input to the feedback E, the integrated value of E, and the differential value of E:

$$U = A E + B \int E(t) \, dt + C \, d(E(t))/dt$$

Integration is nicely approximated in a microcomputer by adding each input value to a number in memory each time the inputs are sampled. If the feedback control system is working correctly, the inputs will be positive and negative, so this running sum will tend to zero. The differential is simply approximated by subtracting the current value of the input from its last value.

A more general kind of controller can be implemented as a digital version of a filter. (As a filter, it can be used to correct errors in analog measurement and output systems, as we previously discussed.) A *digital filter* is defined by a *Z-transform*, which is an expression like this:

$$D(z) = \frac{U(z)}{E(z)} = \frac{A0 + A1\,Z^{**}\text{-}1 + A2\,Z^{**}\text{-}2 + \ldots + An\,Z^{**}\text{-}n}{1 + B1\,Z^{**}\text{-}1 + B2\,Z^{**}\text{-}2 + \ldots + Bn\,Z^{**}\text{-}n}$$

An example of a digital filter given to us by R.W. Strum, a Chebychev bandpass filter passing 20 to 40 Hz with 0.5 dB ripple, passing 17 to 46 Hz at -3 dB, for a sampling frequency of 1000 Hz is

$$D(z) = \frac{0.00517 - 0.01034\,Z^{**}\text{-}2 + 0.00517\,Z^{**}\text{-}4}{1 - 3.75422\,Z^{**}\text{-}1 + 5.35079\,Z^{**}\text{-}2 - 3.43194\,Z^{**}\text{-}3 + 0.83628\,Z^{**}\text{-}4}$$

The general expression is evaluated in a microcomputer as follows. Call the input at time k Ek and the output at time k Uk. Then the output Uk at any given time is just the weighted sum of the inputs and outputs of the n prior times:

$$Uk = A0\,Ek + A1\,Ek\text{-}1 + \ldots + An\,Ek\text{-}n$$
$$- B1\,Uk\text{-}1 - \ldots - Bn\,Uk\text{-}n$$

For the preceding example, every millisecond we compute

$$Uk = 0.00517\,Ek + - 0.01034\,Ek\text{-}2 + 0.00517\,Ek\text{-}4$$
$$+ 3.75422\,Uk\text{-}1 - 5.35079\,Uk\text{-}2 + 3.43194\,Uk\text{-}3 - 0.83628\,Uk\text{-}4$$

The program should keep the vectors A, B, E, and U. Each time it updates the most recent output value Uk, it can shift all values of E and U back one place so Uk-1 becomes the value Uk-2, Uk becomes the value Uk-1, etc., used at the next time k.

A particularly suitable technique is the *multi-input multi-output controller*, which has a mathematical definition as follows. Let E be an (eight-variable) input and U be an (eight-variable) output, and S be an (n-variable) state vector, stored in a table in memory. **A, B, C,** and **D** are matrixes having suitable dimensions. Then the controller is defined by matrix multiplication equations that give the next value of the state vector S in terms of the current value of the state vector and the input E:

$$S = A S + B E$$

and that give the output values in terms of the current value of the state vector and the input:

$$U = C S + D E$$

These equations can be implemented by subroutines that perform matrix multiplication and vector addition, together with the subroutine that exercises the DAS to get the input vector X and to output the values of Z.

These techniques show how simply a microcomputer with a DAS can, with programs to correct for nonlinear errors or to digitally filter the data or with one of several feedback controllers, implement multiple input analog measurement systems or multiple sources of analog output voltages. All we have to do is determine the coefficients for the aforementioned formulas. That is a nontrivial problem, but it is treated in many excellent texts on control theory. Our only intent in this chapter is to show that, once a desired control system has been defined, it can be implemented easily in a microcomputer.

6-7 Conclusions

This chapter has covered a lot of ground. We studied transducers, analog devices, and a keyboard and display system. The A-to-D, D-to-A converters and the data acquisition system were surveyed and software techniques for them were discussed.

In general, most I/O devices have some analog circuitry. On one extreme, some analog controllers use only OP AMPs without a microprocessor. This often is the best way if the frequencies of the signal are higher than the Nyquist rate of an economically acceptable microprocessor-based system. On the other extreme, everything can be implemented in software, thus minimizing the analog hardware. This appears attractive where flexibility is valuable and the signal rates are not higher than the Nyquist rate of the system. In between, just about every design has some analog hardware, some software, and some digital hardware. A good designer must therefore be aware of the analog devices and circuits and must be aware of the advantages of the different ways to implement some functions in analog or digital hardware, or in software.

This chapter should provide sufficient background for understanding what the analog circuitry in an I/O device is supposed to be doing, and for sorting out many of the analog, digital, and software alternatives for implementing important I/O functions. If you want further information, we recommend Garrett's *Analog Systems for Microprocessors and Minicomputers,* Reston Publishing Company. Many of the concepts we've introduced in this chapter were inspired by that fine book. A more recent edition of his book has appeared as *Computer Interface Engineering for Real-Time Systems,* Prentice Hall, 1987. We think that Vanlandungham's *Introduction to Digital Control Systems,* Macmillan Publishing Co., 1985 is an excellent modern coverage of the theory of digital control. *First Principles of Discrete Systems and Digital Signal Processing,* by R.D. Strumm and D. E. Kirk, Addison Wesley, 1988, presents practical aspects of digital filters, and *Digital Filters, 3rd Ed.,* by R. W. Hamming, Prentice Hall, 1989 covers the theoretical basis of them. Applications notes from linear integrated circuits manufacturers, and even catalogues from some of them, have a wealth of useful information about how to use the chips they make. The catalogue for Analog

Devices Incorporated and linear device catalogs from Motorola and National are good sources of information. Further information on Motorola analog interface chips is available in Motorola data sheets such as the *CMOS/NMOS Special Functions Data*, (DL130). Circuit Cellar Ink has many useful articles; our description of the MAX 134 multimeter chip was derived from their October 1990 article.

For further reading on phase-locked loops, we recommend *Digital PLL Frequency Synthesis Theory and Design*, by U. L. Rohde, Prentice-Hall 1983, and Motorola data sheets such as the *CMOS/NMOS Special Functions Data* (DL130) and applications notes such as the *Electronic Tuning Address System* (SG-72).

You should now be ready to use analog circuits in microcomputers. We now turn our attention to frequency analog signals, and then to communication systems and storage and display systems that use frequency analog signals.

Do You Know These Terms?

See the End of Chapter 1 for Instructions.

sinusoidal alternating current signal, amplitude, phase, frequency, period, periodic, bandwidth, analog-to-digital converter, digital-to-analog converter, comparator, analog switch, voltage-to-frequency converter, frequency-to-voltage converter, transducer, operational amplifier, solenoid, motor, direct current motor, stepping motor, universal motor, shaded pole motor, induction motor, hysteresis synchronous motor, potentiometer, slide potentiometer, strain gauge, shaft encoder, gear-counter, mouse, linear variable displacement transformer, control transformer, direct current tachometer, accelerometer, light emitting diode, liquid crystal display, photodetector, photomultiplier, photodiode, phototransistor, photoresistor, opto-isolator, oven, thermocouple, thermistor, load cell, (bipolar) transistor, beta, power transistor, darlington transistor, field effect transistor, vertical field effect transistor, silicon-controlled rectifier, triac, on-off control, bang-bang control, integral cycle control, proportional cycle control, linear mode, saturated mode, inverting amplifier, feedback, amplification, summing amplifier, integrator, virtual ground, voltage follower, summing amplifier, comparator, hysteresis, Schmitt trigger, analog multiplexor, timer, dual supply, single supply, common mode, offset adjustment, settling time, bypass capacitor, ground plane, ground loop, heat sink, high-pass filter, bandpass filter, notch filter, cascade filter, parallel filter, 2 nth order filter, Butterworth filter, Bessel filter, Chebyshev filter, biased analog signal, automatic gain control, switched capacitor filter, sample a signal, contact bounce, debouncer, wait-and-see, integrating debouncer, linear select, coincident select, analog switch, scanned keyboard, n-key rollover, common cathode LED display, seven-segment code, seven-segment decoder-driver, segment driver, multiplexed display, digit driver, peripheral driver, sampling rate, Nyquist rate, alias frequency component, multiplying D-to-A converter, R-2R ladder network, parallel A-to-D converter, pipeline A-to-D converter, successive approximation converter, ramp A-to-D converter, dual slope A-to-D converter, frequency-to-voltage converter, data acquisition system, spline, feedback system, proportional integral differential, digital filter, Z-transform, multi-input multi-output controller.

7

M68332 Time Processor Unit

As an alternative to voltage analog signals, frequency analog signals can be generated or measured using the M68332 Time Processor Unit (TPU) or the M68340 Timer Module (TM). These two modules perform almost identical functions; however, their techniques are not at all identical. The M68332 Time Processor Unit is internally microprogrammed, and data are put into a shared memory much as arguments are passed to a subroutine. The M68340 Timer Module is hard-wired with control ports attached to the counters, which requires a different style of programming. We attempted to write a chapter that described both modules, sharing the common description of the experiment, but that was hard to digest. We find it best to separately describe these modules, repeating the description of the experiment in each, so you can read one without the other at all. In this chapter, we discuss the M68332 Time Processor Unit, and in the next, the M68340 Timer Module. You will probably read one or the other.

The 16-channel M68332 Time Processor Unit is one of the most flexible modules that can be put in a microcomputer. A channel can generate a square wave, sine wave, or any periodic wave, used in cassette tape recorders, telephone systems (touch-tone), and signals to the user (bleeps). It can be used to generate single-shot pulses to control motors, solenoids, or lights. It can itself provide interrupts to coordinate a program to effect an instruction step or a real-time clock. It can be used to count the number of events (falling edges of a signal input to the module) and thus the number of events in a fixed interval of time (the frequency). It is also capable of measuring pulse width and period; voltage, resistance, or capacitance can be converted to the period, which can be measured by a channel. TPU channels were designed for these purposes.

The TPU is the principal component, then, in interfacing to frequency analog signals. These "FM" signals are easier to handle and more noise-free than "AM" signals. We observe that amplitude analog signals are still pervasively used in interface circuits; but we believe that frequency (or phase) analog signals are becoming equally important.

The primary objective of this chapter is to explain the principles of using the TPU module. To make these principles concrete, the TPU is introduced first. Then sections will be devoted to each application of this powerful module. A further objective is to review various synchronization mechanisms introduced in Chapter 5. The TPU clearly illustrates applications of many of these techniques.

This chapter should acquaint you with the hardware and software of the TPU in the M68332. Upon finishing the chapter, you should be able to connect a TPU to external hardware, and write C procedures or object-oriented C methods to generate square waves or pulses, or measure the frequency or period of a periodic wave or the pulse width of a pulse. With these techniques, you should be able to interface to I/O systems that generate or use periodic signals or pulses, or to interface through voltage-to-frequency or frequency-to-voltage converters to analog I/O systems.

7-1 TPU Organization and Registers

The TPU has 16 channels, which share control registers including the Module Configuration and Interrupt Configuration registers (See Figure 7-1a). The former has fields that control two counters (See Figure 7-1b). TCR1P and PSCK control the prescaler of a free-running timer; PSCK selects either a ~4MHz or ~500 KHz count rate, which is divided by 2^{TCR1P}. TCR2P and T2CG control the prescaler and gate of another counter that is controlled by an M68332 pin signal TCR2; if T2CG is 0, then positive edges of TCR2 increment the second counter, otherwise it is incremented when T2CG is high at ~2 MHz; this count is then divided by 2^{TCR2P}. The SUPV bit is set if the TPU's registers are only accessible in the supervisor state. The Module Configuration register IARB field and Interrupt Configuration register LEVEL field and VECTOR field are used to establish interrupt priorities and vectoring as the similar registers are in the QSPI modules, except that, whereas each channel will usually generate interrupts requiring different responses, the vector's high bits are derived from the VECTOR register, and its low bits are the channel number. For instance, if VECTOR is 4, and channel 3 generates an interrupt, then the effective vector number is 0x43, and the vector address is 0x10c.

Each channel has a set of register fields and a *parameter memory*. A curious "feature" of all these registers and memory words (except the interrupt status register) is that they cannot be accessed in byte mode; MOVE.B #0x8d,0xFFFE01 doesn't work correctly. It is especially important to verify that code generated by the C compiler accesses word or long word units in TPU's registers. Any C statement whose assembler language code reads or writes a byte to one of TPU's registers must be avoided.

A channel's register fields are the 1-bit *interrupt enable* INTEN, the 4-bit *channel function select* CFS, the 2-bit *host sequence request* HSQ, the 2-bit host *service request* HSR, the 2-bit *channel priority* CPR, and the 1-bit *interrupt status* ISTAT. The sixteen channel's 1-bit INTEN bits are in one 16-bit word at location 0xFFFE0A; channel 15 in most significant bit and channel 0 in least significant bit. In a similar manner, the ISTAT bits are in the word. The sixteen channel's 2-bit HSQ bits are in one 32-bit long word at location 0xFFFE14; channel 15 in most significant two bits and channel 0 in least significant two bits. Similarly, the HSR and CPR are each in long words at 0xFFFE18 and 0xFFFE1C. Finally the sixteen channel's 4-bit CFSs are in one 64-bit "word" at location 0xFFFE0C; channel 15 in most significant four bits and channel 0 in least significant four bits. The interrupt enable and interrupt status obviously are used to enable and to test for interrupts.

The TPU is controlled by a microprogrammable *"microengine"*. The channel function select, host sequence and service request control the microprogram, and channel priority controls the scheduling of the microprogram to service channels when more than one requires action. These fields will be explained as various functions are described.

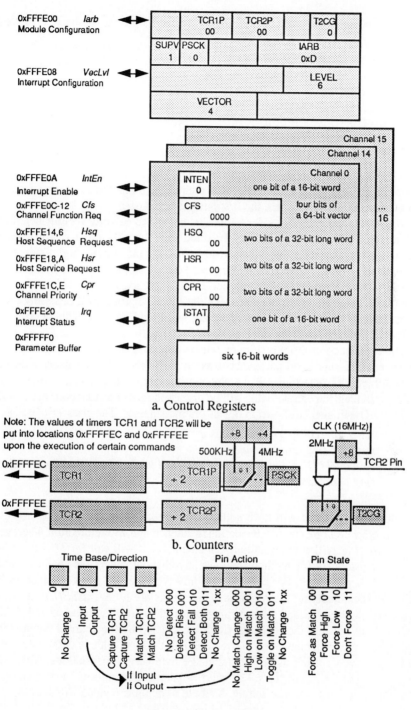

a. Control Registers

b. Counters

c. Channel Control Fields

Figure 7-1. TPU Registers.

In subsequent procedures, we use the following definitions for the TPU registers:

```
#define Iarb *(int *)0xfffe00
#define VecLvl *(int *)0xfffe08
#define IntEn *(int *)0xfffe0a
#define Cfs *(int *)0xfffe12
#define Hsq *(int *)0xfffe16
#define Hsr *(int *)0xfffe1a
#define Cpr *(int *)0xfffe1e
#define Irq *(int *)0xfffe20
```

Note that, for *Cfs, Hsq, Hsr,* and *Cpr,* these definitions apply only to channel 0. Other channels will use a lower address if their control bits are in another word. Note also in this set of definitions that the first letter is capitalized.

The parameter memories for each channel *n* are 6-word vectors beginning at location 0xFFFF00 + *n* * 0x10. Each function uses them differently. For instance, if channel 0 generates a repetitive wave, word 0xffff04 is the output's high time, and word 0xffff06 is its period. Parameter memory can be read or written in word or long word mode, but not byte mode, as noted earlier. Long word accesses are *coherent;* the TPU will not access parameter memory between the M68332 processor's accessing the high-order word and the low-order word of a long word read or write. This is occasionally necessary to avoid irregular timing problems.

The channel control fields (Figure 7-1c), in the first word of a channel's parameter memory, contain some short parameters used in most functions. For instance the second most significant bit determines if the channel is input or output, rather like a parallel port's direction register. These fields will be discussed further as functions are described.

TPU I/O will also be shown in object-oriented classes. The class *TPU* is:

```
struct TPU :direct { /* a direct root class */
    unsigned char error, channel;
    void InitTPU(unsigned,unsigned,unsigned,unsigned,unsigned,unsigned );
    void Terminate(void);
};
```

Subclasses of *TPU* will have additional methods such as *Init, Input* and *Output* similar to other I/O objects, for device independence and I/O redirection wherever that makes sense. *Init* will actually initialize a channel, but will call *InitTPU* to set up the channel's registers. *TPU*'s methods can use any channel, where the channel number is *InitTPU*'s first parameter. For concreteness however, we will show channel 0's bits in the figures accompanying the routines. If interrupts are used, *InitTPU* first initializes the common registers needed for interrupts, unless they are already initialized. *InitTPU*'s parameters are put into the registers' fields as selected by the channel parameter. The former value of each parameter is cleared out, and the new value is ORed into the field. This C code avoids using assembler language byte access instructions, which do not work correctly in the TPU's control registers or parameter memory. The channel priority field is initialized last, because setting this field to a nonzero value will start the device. *The Terminate* method, shown first, disables interrupts and clears the channel priority to prevent it from being scheduled by the microengine.

```
void TPU::InitTPU( chan, cfs, hsq, hsr, cpr, inten)
    unsigned chan, cfs, hsq, hsr, cpr, inten; {
    register long *p1=(long *)0xfffe00,*p2;
    if(inten&&((p1[0] &0xf0000)==0) /* if not previously initialized, set SUPV=1 */
        { *(int *)p1=0x8d;*((int *)p1+4) =0x640; /* IARB= 0x8d, lev 6, vect 4 */ }
    *(((int *)p1)+5) = (~ (1<<chan) & *(((int *)p1)+5)) | ( inten<<chan);
    p1[5] = (~ (3L<<(chan<<1))&p1[5]) | (((long)hsq)<<(chan<<1));
    p1[6] = (((long) hsr)<<(chan<<1));
    error=0; p2=p1+4; if((channel=chan)&8) p2- -;
    (*p2) = (~(0xfL<<(chan<<2)) & (*p2)) | (((long) csf) <<(chan<<2));
    p1[7] = (~ (3L<<(chan<<1)) & p1[7]) | (((long) cpr)<<(chan<<1));
}
void TPU::Terminate()
    {Inten &=~(1<< channel); *((long *)0xfffe1c)&=~(3L<<(channel<<1));}
```

7-2 Signal Generation

We want to cover the generation of level outputs, square waves and pulses first because you can implement these examples as experiments and see results on the output pins. Later, we look at frequency measurement techniques, which can be studied using a microcomputer to generate the signals using techniques introduced in this section. We can also generate interrupts for the microcomputer that can be used to time operations, which include the timing of output signals. This section covers the generation of signals with the TPU. We begin by describing the hardware used in generating a level output as a one-bit parallel output port. We then generate square waves and pulses. The generation of square waves and subsequent generation of arbitrary repetitive waveforms will be considered in the second subsection. The next subsection covers the techniques for pulse generation. The last subsection shows how to generate time-based interrupts, which could be used to implement real-time clocks.

7-2.1 One-bit Parallel Output

We may need to output a 0 or 1 on a TPU pin, for instance to test the hardware or to force an output value. A procedure to output a 1 on channel 0 is shown below. Figure 7-2 shows what it puts into the registers and parameters to implement a one-bit parallel output port. This function is chosen when CFS=8 and HSR is 01 or 10. The channel priority (01 - low, 10 - medium, 11 - high) determines how prompt the TPU microcontroller will attend to this channel. It must be set to nonzero for the channel to do anything. Writing a non-zero value in the host service request (HSR) sends the microcontroller a message that "fires" it to act. Writing a zero value in it does nothing harmful. Generally, a long word write can write many channel HSR fields to initiate simultaneous operations, and will write zeros in the HSR fields of those channels that are not to be initiated. This procedure outputs a 1 as it initializes the channel. To output a 0, change the last statement to *Hsr=2;* We can later output a 0 by setting HSR to 10, and we can output a 1 by setting HSR is 01. The bit just output is stored in the most significant bit of the word below the Channel Control (after the word's other bits are shifted right). This word will have a history of the last 16 bits that have been output, earlier bits to the right.

```
main(){ /* output a 1 on pin TP0 */
    Cfs = 8; /* channel function select: parallel I/O */
    Cpr = 1; /* channel priority low */
    Hsr = 1; /* host service request HSR written to output 1 */
}
```

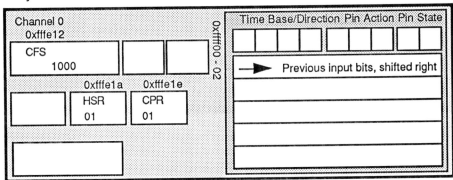

Figure 7-2. One-bit Parallel Output.

The one-bit output class *BitOut*'s *Init* method initializes the channel specified by its second parameter to output the bit which is its first parameter. Thereafter the *Output* method outputs the least significant bit of its parameter to the pin. Mainly for device independence, *BitOut*'s *Input* method can obtain the last bit output from the most significant bit of the word below the Channel Control fields, although this *Input* method would not be all that useful.

struct BitOut : TPU {void Init(long,unsigned),Output(long);long Input(void);};

void BitOut::Init(p,m) long p; unsigned m;
    *{if(p) p=1; else p=2;InitTPU(m,8,0,p,1,0);} /*chan, csf, hsq, hsr, cpr, int*/*

long BitOut::Input() { return ((unsigned *)(0xffff02+(channel<<4)))>>15;}*

void BitOut::Output(d) long d;
    *{if(d) d=1; else d=2; *((long *)0xfffe18)=(d<<(channel <<1)); }*

7-2.2 The Square Wave Generator

A square wave can be generated by several TPU functions. One of the easiest ways is to use the *Pulse Width Modulation* (PWM) mode, whose channel command value is 9. Figure 7-3 shows the values put into the registers and parameters to implement a variable duty cycle "square-wave" output port. Below Channel Control are put the time the output is high Th, and the period P of the waveform. We can later change the waveform by changing these words. Putting 10 into HSR starts the waveform. When we change the waveform we can force the end of the old waveform by putting 01 into HSR.

A simple procedure to generate a square-wave with period p and high time h is given below. If TCR1 is clocked at 520.833 KHz (SCK=16MHz, TCR1P=PSCK=0), then to get frequency f set P to 520833 / f and set Th to P/2. (Note: P-Th must be ≤ 0x8000.) Setting Th > P results in a high output, and setting Th = 0 results in a low signal. The high time and period are coherently written as a long word, to avoid timing glitches. This procedure has to set up the channel control word. The pin state (11) indicates the output pin value is not changed when the channel is initialized, and pin action (100) indicates writing the channel control word does not change the pin action bits. The time base/direction bits (0100) denote that the pin is an output (as we noted earlier), and its two low-order bits indicate we are using TCR1 as a match time reference.

```
main(){ /* generate a square wave */
    *(unsigned *)0xffff00 = 0x93; /* channel control word */
    *(long *)0xffff04 = 0x7fffffff; /* high- and period width- timing */
    Cfs = 9; Hsr = 2; Cpr = 1;
}
```

When Tnhl matches the free-running count TCR1, Tnhl is put in Tphl, P is added to it, and the output goes high. When Tphl + Th = TCR1, the output goes low.

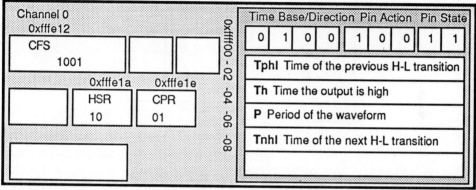

Figure 7-3. Square-wave Output.

The class *PWM* generalizes *main* above. Its *Init* method initializes the channel specified by its second parameter to the value of its first parameter, whose 16 most significant bits are the high time and 16 least significant bits are the period. Thereafter the *Output* method changes the waveform, using the same parameter format.

```
struct PWM : TPU {void Init(long,unsigned),Output(long);long Input(void);};
void PWM::Init(p,m) register long p; unsigned m;{
    *(long *)(0xffff00+(m<<4))=0x93; /* channel control */
    *(long *)(0xffff04+(m<<4))=p; /* high-, period width- timing */
    InitTPU(m, 9, 0, 2, 1, 0); /* chan, csf, hsq, hsr, cpr, int */
}
long PWM::Input() { return *(long *)(0xffff04+(channel<<4));}
void PWM::Output(d) long d;{
    *(long *)(0xffff04+(channel<<4))=d; /* put high time, period */
    *((long *)0xfffe18)=(1L<<(channel <<1)); /* (optional) output 1 to HSR field*/
}
```

We now consider an application of this generator to the production of touch-tone signals. A *touch-tone* signal is a pair of sine waves having frequencies that represent the digits used in dialing a telephone. A touch-tone generator can generate these signals so that the microcomputer can dial up on the telephone, and it can generate such tones to be sent via radio remote control or to be stored on cassette tape, and so on. In a top-down design, one must consider all the relevant alternatives. One possibility is integrated circuits that output touch-tone signals in response to keyboard contact closings, but these would require the microcomputer to act like the keyboard to such a chip. Another is analog switches in place of the keys that can be controlled by an output device. (A few other alternatives are also possible.) However, the number of chips needed in any of the latter alternatives would be at least two, if not more. The TPU has two channels 0 and 1, which can generate the tones using a CMOS 4015 shift register making two four-stage *Johnson counters*, to implement the tone generator using one chip. So we consider generating a square wave using TPU channels 0 and 1 and a 4015.

Table 7-1. Touch-Tone Codes.

Digit	Coding
0	R4,C2
1	R1,C1
2	R1,C2
3	R1,C3
4	R2,C1
5	R2,C2
6	R2,C3
7	R3,C1
8	R3,C2
9	R3,C3

Code	Hertz	Counter
R1	697	93
R2	770	84
R3	852	76
R4	941	69
C1	1209	53
C2	1336	48
C3	1477	44
C4	1633	39

a. Codes for Digits   b. Frequencies for Codes

A touch-tone signal consists of two simultaneous sine waves. Table 7-1 shows the tones required for each digit that can be sent. Table 7-1a shows the mapping of digits to frequencies shown in Table 7-1b, and Table 7-1b shows the frequencies in Hertz and the corresponding values of n to be put into the TPU module to generate the desired frequencies, as they will be used later in the example. Thus, to send the digit 5, send two superimposed sine waves with frequencies 770 Hertz and 1336 Hertz.

To send a sine wave, a Johnson counter is almost ideal. This counter is actually just a shift register whose output is inverted, then shifted back into it. (See Figure 7-4.) A four-bit Johnson counter would have the following sequence of values in the flip-flops:

```
L L L L
H L L L
H H L L
H H H L
H H H H
L H H H
L L H H
L L L H
```

As described in Don Lancaster's marvelous little book, *The CMOS Cookbook*, Howard Sams Inc., these counters can be used to generate sine waves simply by connecting resistors of value 33 KΩ to the first and third stages and 22 KΩ to the second stage of the shift register. (See Figure 7-4.) Although the wave will look like a stair-step approximation to a sine, it is free of the lower harmonics and can be filtered if necessary. Moreover, using more accurate values of resistors and a longer shift register, it is possible to eliminate as much of the low-order harmonics as desired before filtering. In this case, if we want a sine wave with frequency f, we clock the shift register with a square wave whose frequency should be $8 * f$.

Consider now the approach to generating a sine wave with frequency F using the TPU system, with E clock one-MHz, to drive a four-stage Johnson counter. We set the channel's period to 520833 / (8 * f) and set its high time to half that value. The values, are shown in the right half of Table 7-1b for the touch-tone codes. For instance, to send the digit 8, we put the numbers 76 and 48 into the two TPU periods, which will each generate a sine wave to comprise the signal.

Two channels are used to generate the two sine waves required by the touch-tone signal. The external connections are shown in Figure 7-4. Note that the CLEAR control on the shift register is connected to the microcomputer RESET bus line to ensure that the shift register does not have some unusual pattern in it after power is applied. The desired signal is simply the sum of the sine waves produced by two shift registers and is obtained by merely connecting to the common points of the resistors. The procedure *sendTone* below will send the touchtone signal using this circuit. It uses two objects *Ch0* and *Ch1* of the class *PWM* described above. After blessing these objects, it merely initializes them to begin sending the touch-tone code, then waits for a while and then terminates the channels. Note *Init*'s use of array *tt1* that implements Table 7-1a to establish the pair of frequencies to be sent, and of vector *tt2* that implements Table 7-1b to establish the period values that are sent to each channel to get those frequencies.

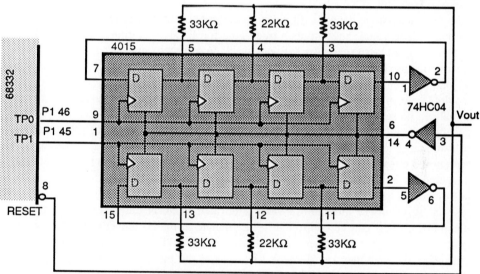

Figure 7-4. A Touch-Tone Generator.

```
#define hp(i) i+(((long)i<<15)&0xffff0000)
PWM *Ch0,*Ch1; unsigned char b1[sizeof(PWM)], b2[sizeof(PWM)];
unsigned tt1[10][2]={{3,5},{0,4},{0,5},{0,6},{1,4},{1,5},{1,6},{2,4},{2,5},{2,6}};
long tt2[8]={hp(93),hp(84),hp(76),hp(69),hp(53),hp(48),hp(44),hp(39)};

static void sendTone(n) int n;{ int l;
    Ch0 =blessA(sizeof (PWM ), PWM); Ch0 ->Init( tt2[ tt1[n][0] ], 0);
    Ch1 =blessA(sizeof (PWM ), PWM); Ch1 ->Init( tt2[ tt1[n][1] ], 1);
    for(l=0;l<0xffff;l++); /* wait loop */ Ch0 ->Terminate();Ch1 ->Terminate();
}
```

A slight variation of this technique can be used to generate any periodic waveform. The square wave can be used to increment a counter which supplies an address to a read-only memory. It can output words to a D-to-A converter and can store the desired pattern to be developed. Thus, generating a square wave can generate other periodic waves. Finally, as discussed in the previous chapter, a square wave can be integrated to get a ramp signal, and this can be shaped by nonlinear analog techniques. Also, as in music generation, a periodic signal can be shaped by attenuating it under control of an output device to apply attack and decay characteristics in a music synthesizer.

The TPU system is seen as a valuable tool in generating square waves, which can be used to generate other periodic waves using Johnson counters or read-only memories and D-to-A converters. However, the designer must not always assume that the TPU is so much better than any other generator. Waveforms can be generated using hardware approaches discussed in Section 6-5.3 and software approaches using various synchronization mechanisms discussed in Chapter 5. The designer should consider the software approach as well as the hardware approaches for generating frequencies, and pick the best one for his application.

7-2.3 The Pulse Generator

Like the square wave generator, a pulse generator has many uses. The device normally outputs a false value, but outputs a true value for a specified time after it actually is triggered. It can be triggered by software or by an external signal. And, like the square wave generator, there are software and hardware techniques to implement it. The software technique to supply a pulse triggered by software merely outputs a true, waits the required time, and then outputs a false value. To react to an external signal, the external signal can be sensed in a gadfly loop or can generate an interrupt so that the pulse is generated when the signal arrives. But, like the software square wave generator, the software pulse generator is susceptible to timing errors due to interrupts, direct memory access, and dynamic memory refresh cycles. A 555 timer can act like a pulse generator, triggered by a microcomputer or an external signal; and the length of the pulse, determined by the value of a resistor and a capacitor, can be controlled by selecting of the resistor by means of an analog switch controlled from an output device. One-shot integrated circuits can be controlled in like manner. Finally, the TPU can be used to generate pulses when the computer starts them (or started by an external signal and then sensed by the computer, as discussed later), and the pulse length can be computer controlled, as we now discuss.

This subsection considers the use of the TPU to generate pulses. The *Output Compare* function (OC) whose channel function code is 0xe, can do this in many ways. In the example below, the channel control word's time base/direction bits (0100) make it an output which matches using timer TCR1. When the M68332 processor puts 01 into HSR, the channel control word's pin state (01) causes a rising edge on the output pin upon initialization, the output goes high, and remains for P TCR1 clock cycles, and the pin action bits (010) make it low when the next match occurs. The pulse width P is put into the word following the channel control; if we clock TCR1 at 520.833 KHz (SCK=16MHz, TCR1P=PSCK=0), to generate a pulse p μseconds long, set P to about $p * 0.5208$. (Note: P must be $\leq$ 0x8000.)

The reference address Ref1 requires some discussion. When the M68332 processor puts 01 into HSR, Tnm is put into Tlm, the output is set as indicated by the pin state, and a value is added to P to get Tnm; when TCR1 = Tnm the output is set as indicated by the pin action. What is usually added to P is the current time TCR1, although we may wish to add values such as the time of another's next high-to-low transition (Tnhl) in Figure 7-3 to synchronize the falling edge of this channel's pulse to another signal. We could first read that value in software, then add it to P and write it to Tnm. However, we can let the faster microcontroller in the TPU do it for us if this value happens to be in parameter memory. We pass in R1 the low-order byte of the address of the data to be added. If the pulse's falling edge is to be based on the current time, then the low byte (0xec) of TCR1's address is put in R1. Then, TCR1 + P will be put in Tnm.

```
main(){ /* generate a pulse */
    *(unsigned *)0xffff00 = 0x89; /* channel control word */
    *(unsigned *)0xffff02 = 0x7fff; /* offset */
    *(unsigned *)0xffff04 = 0xec;/* ref1 */
    Cfs = 0xe; Cpr = Hsr = 1;
}
```

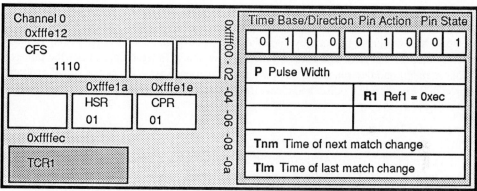

Figure 7-5. Single-Shot Pulse Generator.

The class *Pulse* generalizes the procedure above. Its *Init* method initializes the channel specified by its second parameter to the value of its first parameter, whose 16 least significant bits are the pulse width. Thereafter the *Output* method fires another pulse, whenever it is executed, whose width is its parameter, in the same format.

```
struct Pulse : TPU { void Init(long ,unsigned ),Output(long); long Input(void); };

void Pulse::Init(p,m) register long p; unsigned m;{
    *(long *)(0xffff00+(m<<4))=0x89; /* channel control */
    *(unsigned *)(0xffff02+(m<<4))=p; /* pulse width */
    *(unsigned *)(0xffff04+(m<<4))=0xfe; /* Ref1 */
    InitTPU(m, 0xe, 0, 1, 1, 0); /* chan, csf, hsq, hsr, cpr, int */
}
long Pulse::Input() { return *(unsigned *)(0xffff02+(channel<<4));}
```

```
void Pulse::Output(d) long d;{
    *(long *)(0xffff02+(channel<<4))=d; /* put pulse width */
    *((long *)0xfffe18)=(1L<<(channel <<1)); /* output 1 to HSR field*/
}
```

We illustrate the use of TPU channel 0 to fire a TRIAC using proportional cycle control (Figure 6-5d). We use the edge detector of Chapter 5, although we shall soon discover that the TPU has better means to detect edges than we used in Chapter 5. Interrupt requests on IRQ5's pin occur each time the household 110 volt 60Hz "power wiring" signal passes through zero (Figure 5-8). A positive-going pulse is generated such that its falling edge will fire the TRIAC at a time in the 60Hz cycle that corresponds to the end of the pulse. A small pulse width fires the TRIAC early in each cycle, making it conduct most of the time to apply full power to the load; a large width fires it late, making the TRIAC open most of the time to turn off the power to the load.

The program sets up port F bit 1 to send its signal to the exclusive-OR gate of Figure 5-8b, sets up IRQ5 to receive the output of the gate, and sets up chip select CS6 to recognize level-6 autovector interrupts, as described in Section 5-1.5. Then TPU channel 0 is configured to generate pulses as described above. We arbitrarily turn on the light fully by making the initial value of the pulse width small (8). After enabling interrupts, we execute while(1) in lieu of some program that does useful work. The latter program can set the pulse width to w by executing *(unsigned *)0xffff02=w; at any time. (This could also be done by an *IoWord* object whose address is 0xffff02.) It need not reinitialize the TPU, nor send commands to channel 0's HSR field to fire the pulses. The interrupt handler sends the HSR value 01 to it each time the 60Hz signal crosses through 0 to generate a pulse, and clears the source of the interrupt.

```
main() {
    register int *hndlr;
    *((char *)0xfffa1f)=0x20; *((char *)0xfffa1d)=2; /* asgn irq5 pin, output port F bit 1 */
    pinAssign(cs6,byte); baseAssign(6,0xffffff,k2);optionAssign(6,read+upper+ds fast,0,5+avec);
    asm{lea @0,hndlr} *(int **)0x74=hndlr; /* put level 5 handler address in 0x74 */
    *(unsigned *)0xffff00=0x89; *(unsigned *)0xffff02=8; *(unsigned *)0xffff04=0xec;
    Cfs = 0xe; Cpr = 1; asm{and #0xfcff,sr} while(1); /* enable interrupts, do something */
►   asm{@0  move.w #1,0xfffe1a} *((char *)0xfffa19) ^=2; asm {rte}
}
```

Initialization of the OC function will always cause internal timers TCR1 and TCR2 to be copied into the parameter memory locations 0xffffec and 0xffffee so that they can be accessed by the relative address R1 in Figure 7-5. At other times, these words in parameter memory do not change even as the internal timers TCR1 and TCR2 change. If the heretofore unused host sequence field HSQ is 10 when an output compare function is initialized (when we set HSR to 01), then internal timers TCR1 and TCR2 are copied into the parameter memory, but a pulse is not initiated. This can be used to simply examine the current values of these counters. HSQ is here seen as a kind of initialization parameter passed to the TPU microcontroller, to modify its function.

In the TPU, the pulse width is timed to within ~ two microseconds, which is not affected by processor interrupts, dynamic memory refresh requests, or other subtle real-

338   Chapter 7 – M68332 Time Processor Unit

time problems. This is quite useful in automobile engine control, where the pulse width controls the amount of gasoline injected into the engine, the spark timing, and other key factors in running the engine. The TPU, with 16 channels, can measure input signals and compute the values of the pulse widths for the timers. In fact, the M68332 with its TPU was developed for the vast automobile industry.

7-2.4 Timer Interrupts

Using a configuration almost identical to that used for a square-wave, periodic interrupts can be generated. Using a configuration almost identical to that used for a pulse generator, interrupts can be generated to execute procedures at an interval of time after another procedure is executed. In this section we'll cover these applications.

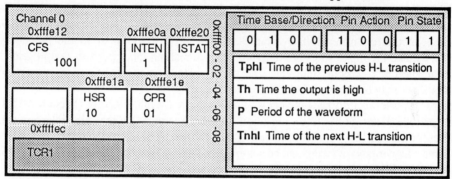

Figure 7-6. Periodic Interrupt.

The procedure *main* below will set up TPU channel 0 as a square-wave generator with period *n* (where *n* is a local variable), as in Section 7-2.1, putting values in the TPU's fields as shown in Figure 7-6. This will put the square-wave signal on pin TP0 whether we need it or not. This procedure further enables interrupts by setting INTEN to 1. If interrupts are enabled, the TPU's IARB, VECTOR and LEVEL registers must be set up to handle them, like the QSPI's registers were set up. The interrupt handler is entered each time the output waveform drops from high-to-low, every *n* TRC1 clock ticks. The interrupt handler clears the interrupt source by clearing ISTAT, and then executes some procedure.

As an example of such a procedure, consider a time-of-day clock that keeps track of the time in global *struct{int ticks,hrs,mins;} timer;* using TPU channel 0 to generate periodic interrupts. We generate interrupts every 1/16 second by setting *n* to 520833 / 16 = 32552. The interrupt handler will count down *ticks* by 16 * 60 = 960. Each minute, *hrs* and *mins* is updated.

```
struct{int ticks,hrs,mins;} timer;
main(){ /* generate periodic interrupts */
    register int *p1=(int *)0xfffe00;unsigned n=32552;
    p1[0]= 0x8d; p1[4]=0x640; /* set IARB, VECTOR, LEVEL */
    asm{ lea @0,p1 } *((int **)0x100)= p1; /* set up interrupt addr. */
    *(int *)0xffff04=0x93; *(long *)0xffff04=n+(((long)n<<15)&0x7fff0000);
    Cfs =9; Hsr =2; Cpr =1; /* prepare chan 0 */
    IntEn =1; asm{ and #0xfdff,sr } while(1); /* enable interrupts */
```

```
asm{@0  movem.l d0/d1/a4,-(a7)
move.w  #0xfffe,0xfffe20 /* remove interrupt */ }
if((++timer.ticks)==960){ /* an example of a procedure */
   timer.ticks = 0; if((++timer.mins) == 60){
      timer.mins=0; timer.hrs++;
   }
}
asm{movem.l (a7)+,d0/d1/a4} asm{ rte}
```
}

This real-time interrupt, or any interrupt that causes things to happen when an interrupt occurs, can be viewed as a Mealy model sequential machine. The state transition occurs when there is an interrupt. The internal state of the sequential machine is kept in one or more global variables, like *ticks, hrs* and *mins* in the preceding example, and the input states are determined from reading input ports or the program's global variables. Output states may be put in output ports or the program's global variables or may be programs that are executed.

The *periodic interrupt* is very similar to the real-time interrupt (Section 5-1.6). The periodic interrupt has finer resolution for short intervals; the real-time interrupt can be set for periods like 62.5 milliseconds or 125 milliseconds, but no intermediate value, whereas the periodic interrupt can be set to any value ± 1 µsecond. However, the TPU is not in all M683xx-family processors, so the periodic interrupt may not be available.

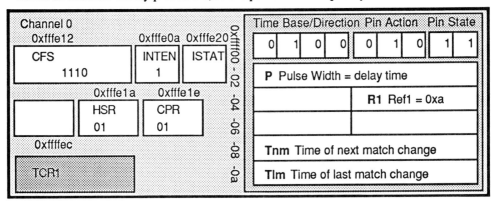

Figure 7-7. Time Delay Interrupt.

Analogous to the previous example, we will generate an interrupt after a fixed time after a procedure is executed that fires the TCU. The OC function pulse generator is used, but with INTEN set to 1. See Figure 7-7. We also set R1 to point to the channel's own Tlm word, as explained later. A pulse is generated on pin TP0 whether we need it or not. However, an interrupt is also generated when the pulse is finished.

As an example of the use of *time delay interrupts,* we consider the design of a microcomputer control of a telephone that uses a rotary dialer, such as was common before touch-tone phones became available. In a rotary dialer, a relay connected in series with the dialer contacts will be pulsed to dial the number. Assume the relay is connected to bit 0 of port F. The telephone standards require the relay to be closed for at least 40 milliseconds and then opened for at least 60 milliseconds for each pulse, and the number of pulses corresponds to the number being dialed. 600 milliseconds is needed between each number being dialed. We will use a global *state* that is decremented upon each interrupt; if *state* is 0, no futher interrupts are requested, if *state* is below 10 or is even, the output is low, opening the relay, and the time to the next interrupt is set to 60 milliseconds, otherwise the output is high, closing the relay, and the time to the next interrupt is set to 40 milliseconds. The initial value of *state* determines the number of pulses to be sent; to send *n* pulses, *state* is initialized to (2 * *n*) + 10. Note that for the number 0, however, 10 pulses are sent.

```
unsigned char state;
main(){ /* rotary dialer to send number "0" */
    register int *hndaddr; register i,j;
    AssgF=0;DirF=1; /* init port F */
    Iarb=0x8d; VecLvl=0x640; /* set IARB, VECTOR, LEVEL */
    asm{ lea @0,hndaddr } *((int **)0x100)= hndaddr; /* set up interrupt addr. */
    *(unsigned *)0xffff00=0x8b; *(unsigned *)0xffff02 =20832; /* offset */
    Cfs =0xe; Hsr = Cpr =1; /* chan 0 OC */
    *(unsigned *)0xffff04 = 0xc; /* ref1 */ state=30; /* send number 0 = 10 pulses */
    IntEn =1; asm{ and #0xfdff,sr } while(1); /* enable interrupts */
▶   asm {@0 movem.l d6-d7,-(a7) }
    *((int *)0xfffe20)=0xfffe; /* remove interrupt */
    if(state){
        if((((state - - )&1)==0 )||(state<10)){ i=0; j=31248; }
        else { i=1;j=20832; }
        *(unsigned *)0xffff02 =j; /* set time to next interrupt (pulse width) */
        *((int *)0xfffe1a)=1; /* set channel 0 HSR to fire another pulse */
        *((char *)0xFFFA19)=i; /* data to port F */
    }
    asm {movem.l (a7)+,d6-d7} asm {rte}
}
```

We initialize port F so that the least significant bit is output, and then set up TPU's IARB, VECTOR and LEVEL registers, set up the interrupt address, and prepare channel 0 for pulse generation as in the previous example. Reference register R1 is set to the address of this channel's own time of last match, so that will be added to the pulse width to get the next interrupt time, thus maintaining accurate timing.

This example gives me an opportunity to relate one of the truly great stories in electronics – the invention of the dial telephone. In the 1880s Almond B. Strowger, one of two undertakers in a very small town, couldn't get much business. His competitor's wife was the town's telephone operator. When someone suffered a death in the family, they called up to get an undertaker. The wife naturally recommended her husband, diverting callers from poor Almond. Necessity is the mother of invention. With a celluloid shirt collar and some pins, he contrived a caller operated mechanism, using a stepping relay mechanism that would connect the caller to the desired telephone, so that calls for his business would not go through his competitor's wife. It worked so well that it became the standard mechanism for making calls all over the world. Even today, about a quarter of all telephones use this "step-by-step" or *Strowger system.*

An instruction trace can be implemented using the time delay interrupt. In Chapter 1 we explained that a monitor is a program used to help you debug programs. The monitor behaves like a trap handler, because it may be "called up" by a breakpoint, which is a trap instruction, so it is left by an RTE instruction. Although the M68332 has trace bits in its status register able to trace instruction execution, other processors do not have this capability and they can use counter-timer interrupts to trace a program. To "trace" a user program, we can leave the monitor to execute just one instruction, then reenter the monitor to see what happened. Just before we leave the monitor, we put a number N into a counter latch, after which we execute RTE. The user program will be given enough time to execute just one instruction, and N will be chosen to permit that to happen. Then an interrupt will occur and the monitor will be reentered to display the changes wrought by the executed instruction.

7-3 Frequency Analog Measurement

Converse to generating square waves or pulses, one may need to measure the frequency or period of a square wave or repetitive signal, or the width of a pulse. Many important outputs carry information by their frequency: tachometers, photodetectors, piezo-electric pressure transducers. The voltage-to-frequency converter integrated circuit can change voltages to frequencies economically and with high accuracy. The frequency of output from a timer chip like the 555 timer is inversely proportional to the resistance and capacitance used in its timing circuit. Therefore, a by-product of measuring frequency is that one can easily obtain measurements of resistance or capacitance. Better yet, the period of the signal is linearly proportional to resistance and capacitance. Period can be measured directly. Moreover, for high frequencies, frequency is easier and faster to measure, while for low frequencies, period is easier and faster. The M68332 is quite capable, if necessary, of inverting the value using its DIVU and DIVS instructions. For nonrepetitive waveforms, pulse width measurement is very useful. This can be measured too. Also, the time between two events can be measured by using the events to set, then clear, a flip-flop. The pulse width of the output of this flip-flop can be measured. Sometimes the microcomputer has to keep track of the total number of events of some kind. The event is translated into the rising or falling edge of a signal, and the number of edges is then recorded. Note that the number of events per second is the frequency. Thus, events are counted in the same way as frequency is measured, but the time is not restricted to any specific value.

In this section, we first study one-bit parallel input and generation of interrupts based on its edges. Then we discuss the measurement of frequency. The counting of events is similar to this, and even though it won't be discussed explicitly, it can be done in the same way as the measurement of frequency. We next describe the period measurement, after which we include a short example that shows how period measurement can be used to read the positions of several potentiometers. We then describe pulse width measurement. In a final subsection, we summarize the modes of the TPU subsystems in the TPU .

7-3.1 One-bit Parallel Input

From time to time an input signal normally used by the TPU, for instance to measure a frequency, will have to be examined directly by software as in a one-bit parallel input. We may wish to record a sequence of bits taken from a single input at a fixed rate. We also may wish to generate interrupts upon receiving an edge on TPU inputs. The simple input function is provided for these possibilities.

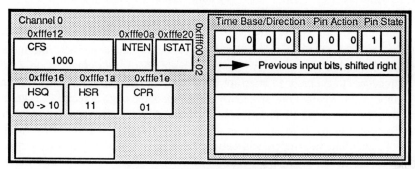

Figure 7-8. One-bit Parallel Input.

A class *BitIn* to input a bit on channel 0 is shown below. Figure 7-8 shows what it puts into the registers and parameters to implement a one-bit parallel input port. This function is selected by initializing CFS=8, HSR is 11 and HSQ is 00, and then HSQ is changed to 10. When HSQ is 10, writing 11 into HSR puts a bit from pin TP0 into the most significant bit of the word below the Channel Control (after the word's other bits are shifted right). This word will have a history of the last 16 bits that have been input, earlier bits to the right.

struct BitIn : TPU {void Init(long,unsigned);long Input(void);};

void BitIn::Init(p,m) long p; unsigned m;{
    *((int *)0xffff00) = 3; InitTPU(m, 8, 0, 3, 1, 0); /* chan, csf, hsq, hsr, cpr, int */
    Hsq = 2; /*HSQ is now made 10 to record inputs when HSR is made 11 */
}

long BitIn::Input() { /*make host service request HSR 11 to input */
    Hsr = 3; return (*(unsigned *)(0xffff02+(channel<<4)))>>15;
}

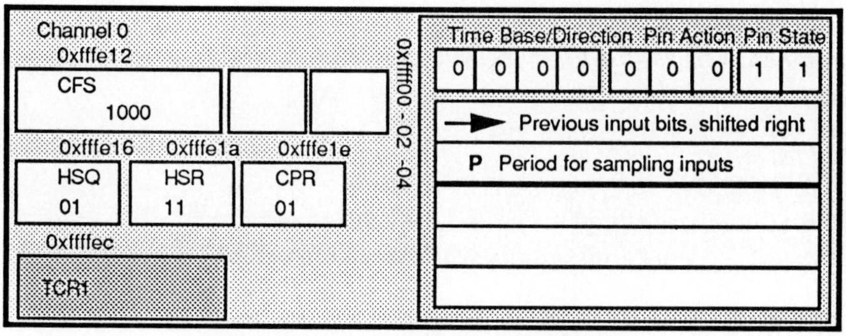

Figure 7-9. One-bit Sequential Input.

A procedure to record a sequence of bits taken from a single input at a fixed rate on channel 0 is shown below. Figure 7-9 shows the register and parameter values to implement this function. It is selected by initializing CFS=8, HSR is 11 and HSQ is 01, and the rate of input is put in P, the second word below the Channel Control.

```
main() { int m=0x30;
    Cfs = 8; Cpr = Hsq = 1; /* init cfs, cpr, hsq */
    *((int *)0xffff00) = 3; *((int *)0xffff04) = m; Hsr = 3; /*HSR*/
}
```

The input is sampled every P TCP1 clock cycles, and the bit is shifted into the word below the Channel Control. Another channel could generate periodic interrupts at a rate of M /16 (Section 7-2.3) to move the 16-bit word, that is thus collected, to a buffer.

A procedure to generate an interrupt when a rising, falling or either edge occurs on a single input TP0, which more efficiently implements the edge detector of Figure 5-8, is shown below. Figure 7-10 shows what it puts into the registers and parameters to interrupt on either edge. This function is selected by initializing CFS=8, HSR is 11 and HSQ is 00, enabling interrupts, and setting the Channel Control so that pin action selects either edge. The most significant bit of the word below the Channel Control is the bit received, which can be read to determine whether the edge was a rising or falling edge. The pin action field could alternatively be set to interrupt on only rising edges or on only falling edges.

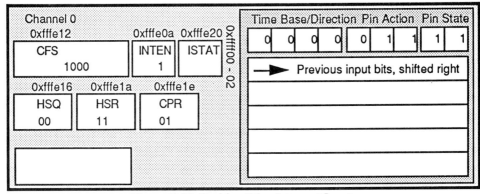

Figure 7-10. Positive Edge Interrupt Input.

```
main() {
    register int *p;
    Iarb=0x8d; VecLvl =0x640; /* set IARB, VECTOR, LEVEL interrupt regs */
    Cfs = 8; Cpr = 1; Hsq = 0; /* init cfs, cpr, hsq chan. */
    Irq =0xfffe; /* remove any exisiting interrupt */
    asm{ lea @0,p } *((int **)0x100)= p; /* set up interrupt addr. */
    *((int *)0xffff00) = 0xf; /* chan cont */ Hsr = 3;
    IntEn =1; asm{ and #0xfdff,sr } while(1); /* enable interrupts */
    asm {@0 } *((int *)0xfffe20)=0xfffe; /* do some procedure */ asm {rte}
}
```

7-3.2 Frequency Measurement

A TPU channel can be used to count input transitions, and thus to measure frequency, using the input capture/input transition counter (ITC) function whose function code is 0xa. It is initialized by writing 01 in HSR; at that time HSQ determines which among several modes are implemented. Having 01 there implements a continuous mode, which is described here.

The ITC function in continuous mode will increment the count C on each edge, as determined by the Pin Action field, until the count reaches the maximum count Mc. On that occurence, the TCR1 count value is strored in the final time Tf; on all other occurences of edges, the count value is stored in Tn, over and over again. Also on that occurence, an interrupt is generated. The interrupt handler can increment a global variable to extend the count. If Mc is set to 0x8000 (the largest power of 2 that can be used) then the full count is the global variable, shifted left 15 bits, catenated with the value in field C. If this count is obtained during a fixed time such as 1 second, the count is the frequency of the waveform. If the count is obtained for another interval of time, say 1/10 seconds, then the value of global variable catenated with the value in field C should be multiplied by 10 to get the frequency.

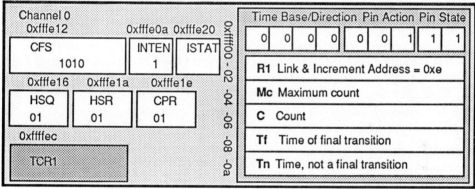

Figure 7-11. Transition Counter or Frequency Measurement.

The procedure *frequency* first sets up TPU channel 0's control to count rising edges, then it initializes the maximum count Mc to 0x8000, and clears count C (these should be accessed coherently). Then it sets up the TPU interrupt mechanism and control registers as before. The function field is made 0xa to request the ITC function, priority hsq, hsr are set as shown in Figure 7-11. Upon each interrupt, software increments the global variable *count*, which is the high-order word of the count of the number of positive edges that have occured because *frequency* began. We use the inefficient and inexact real-time synchronization method here because it is clear (assume N is set to delay 1 second), but we will shortly use the periodic interrupt to time out one second.

```
unsigned int count;
long frequency() {
    register int *p=0xffff00;
    *p=7; *(p+1) = 0xe; *((long *)(p+2)) = 0x80000000; /* chn ctl, R1, Mc and C */
    Iarb=0x8d; VecLvl =0x640;    Cfs = 0xa; Cpr = Hsq = 1; Hsr = 1;
    Irq =0xfffe; /* remove any exisiting interrupt */
```

```
asm{ lea @0,p } *((int **)0x100)= p; /* set up interrupt addr. */
IntEn =1; asm{ and #0xfdff,sr } /* enable interrupts */
for(l=0;l<N;l++); /* real-time program delay for 1 second */
IntEn =0; return (((long)count<<15)+*(unsigned int *)0xffff06);
▷   asm {@0}  count++;  Irq=0xfffe; asm {rte}

}
```

A useful class *FreqIn* that incorporates the periodic interrupt PI (Section 5-1.6) and the TPU ITC function is shown below. Each second, the frequency is read by a periodic interrupt, and put in instance variable *value*. When the program sends an *Input* message, it gets *value*, the most current frequency that was measured. The *Init* method initializes the TPU as in the previous procedure, and also the PI module as in Section 5-1.6. One interrupt handler takes care of count overflow, and another reads frequency.

struct FreqIn : TPU { long value; unsigned count; void Init(long,unsigned);long Input(void);};

```
void FreqIn::Init(p,m) long p; unsigned m;{
    register int *pt=0xffff00; *p = 7; /* chan cnl */
    *(pt +1) = 0xe; *((long *)(pt +2)) = 0x80000000; /* parameters */
    Iarb =0x8d; VecLvl =0x640; /* IARB, VECTOR, LEVEL */
    Irq =0xfffe; /* remove interrupt */
    InitTPU(m, 0xa, 1, 1, 1, 1); /* chan, csf, hsq, hsr, cpr, int */
    asm{ lea @0, pt } *((int **)0x100+(m*4))= pt; /* set up TPU interrupt addr. */
    *(char *)0xfffa01=0xe; *(char *)0xfffa22=6; *(int *)0xfffa24=0x110; /* PI set to 1 sec. */
    *(char *)0xfffa23=0x50; asm{ lea @1, pt } *((int **)0x140)= pt; /* PI int. addr. */
    Irq=0xfffe; asm{move.l a4, saveA4} IntEn =1; asm{ and #0xfdff,sr } /* enable int. */ return;
▷  asm {@0 move.l  a4,-(a7)} asm {move.l saveA4,a4} count++;
    Irq=0xfffe; asm {move.l  (a7)+,a4} asm { rte }
▷  asm{@1 movem.l a4,-(a7)} asm {move.l saveA4,a4}
    value=((long)count<<15)+*(unsigned int *)0xfffe06;
    count=*(unsigned int *)0xfffe06=0; asm{ movem.l (a7)+,a4} asm {rte}

}
```

long FreqIn::Input() { return value;}

7-3.3 Period and Pulse Width Measurement

We now turn to the direct measurement of the period of a waveform. The TPU measures period using the period/pulse-width accumulator (PPWA) function. (See Figure 7-12.) The control word 0xf is put in the channel function field, HSQ is cleared, pin action is selected for falling edge, max count is set to 1, update rate is set to a large value, and HSR is set to 10 to initialize the channel. The interrupt status bit becomes set when the number of edges found (which the TPU puts in Pc) equals the max count Mc. While running, at a rate specified by R, the TPU writes La and A to indicate the current count. Though this might be useful in other procedures, we do not read La and A here; because these values are not used, so R is made large to reduce this overhead of reading the counts into La and A. In this program we test the status bit with a gadfly loop. Then the (24-bit) period can be read from W.

```
long period() { register int *p=(int*)0xffff00;
    p[0]=0xb; p[1]=0x100; p[4]=0xff00; /* large R */
    Cfs = 0xf; Cpr = 1; Hsq = 0; Hsr = 2;
    while((Irq&1)==0); /* gadfly loop*/ Irq=0xfffe; /* clear status bit */
    return (*((long *)0xffff08)&0xffffff;
}
```

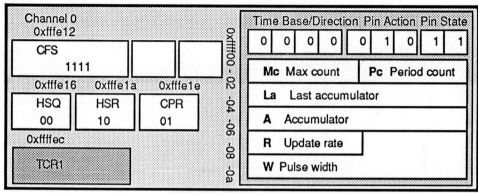

Figure 7-12. Period Timer.

The *pulse width* of a signal is the time from a rising edge to the next falling edge (that is, as the width of a positive pulse). If a negative pulse is to be measured, in hardware it is inverted and measured as a positive pulse. Pulse width is measured by a TPU in a manner similar to period measurement, using the period/pulse-width accumulator (PPWA) function. See Figure 7-13. The differences are: the HSQ field is 10 and the pin action is selected to detect a rising edge.

```
long pulseWidth() {  register int *p=(int*)0xffff00;
    p[0]=7; p[1]=0x100; p[4]=0xff00; /* large R */
    Cfs = 0xf; Cpr = 1; Hsq = Hsr = 2;
    while((Irq&1)==0); /* gadfly loop*/ Irq=0xfffe; /* clear status bit */
    return (*((long *)0xffff08)&0xffffff;
}
```

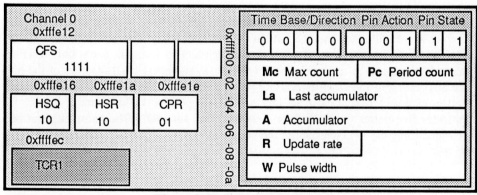

Figure 7-13. Pulse Width Timer.

We illustrate a class *PulseIn* that measures each pin TP0 pulse's width, pushing that number on a queue, to be read by sending an *Input* message. A class *PeriodIn* would be similar to it, as the *period* procedure was similar to *pulseWidth*. This class uses a queue of long words to save the 24-bit pulse widths. The *Init* method configures channel *m*. First, the queue is initialized, then the parameter memory for channel *m*, the TPU interrupt registers, the TPU channel *m* registers, and the interrupt location for channel *m* are initialized.

```
struct PulseIn : TPU { LongQueue Q; void Init(long,unsigned);long Input(void); };

void PulseIn::Init(p,m) long p; unsigned m;{
    register int *pt; register int i;
    (Q=blessA(sizeof(LongQueue),LongQueue))->InitQ(10);
    pt=(int *)0xffff00+(m<<4); pt[0]=7; pt[1]= 0x100; pt[4] = 0xff00;
    Iarb=0x8d; VecLvl=0x640;
    InitTPU( m, 0xf, 2, 2, 1, 1);/* channel, csf, hsq, hsr, cpr, inten */
    asm{lea @0,pt}*((int **)0x100)=pt; /* set up interrupt addr. */ IntEn |=1<<m;
    asm{move.l a4,saveA4} asm{ and #0xfdff,sr } while(1);
    asm {@0 movem.l d0-d2/d7/a0/a1/a4, - (a7)
        movea.l saveA4,a4 /* get a4 for the channel */
        }
    Irq=~(1<<channel);
    Q->Push(*((long *)(0xffff08+(i<<2)))&0xffffff);
    asm {movem.l (a7)+,d0-d2/d7/a0/a1/a4} asm {rte}
}

long PulseIn::Input() { return Q->Pull();}
```

You may question why we might want to measure pulse width when we can already measure period, or vice versa. Usually the signal being measured is an analog signal, and this is converted to a digital signal by an analog comparator. Normally, the period is independent of the comparator's threshold, so it should be measured. The pulse width can depend on the comparator's threshold because the comparator outputs a high signal when the input is above the threshold; so the pulse width depends on the shape of the input and the threshold. The pulse width has to be measured if the waveform is not repetitive; in such a case, period could not be measured.

Initializing the SCI is an illustration of the use of pulse width measurement. In Chapter 8, we will study the SCI, which is used to communicate over a serial link. It requires a baud rate that matches the rate at which bits arrive on the serial link. A TPU channel, configured to measure period, is suited to automatic determination of the bit rate and setting of the clock rate, using pulse width measurement. The sender should send the capital U character – ASCII code 0x55 – repetitively. Each time it is sent, it generates five pulses (or six pulses if the parity is set even). The pulse rate can be measured using the TPU to establish the SCI's baud rate.

7-4 Multiple Channels and Special Functions

Beyond the primitive functions described in sections 7-2 and 7-3, the TPU is capable of more complex operations. One way to extend the TPU's operation is to link channels together. This is described in the first subsection. Another is to build a complex function within the microprogrammed TPU. We consider that possibility later.

One of the key themes of this book is that an object encapsulates the procedures (methods) and data, and also the I/O devices and external hardware associated with an I/O device. Objects rather nicely extend to encapsulate more than one TPU channel. They also adapt well to accommodate special functions implemented in the TPU's microcode. These objects may or may not conform to the model of an I/O object introduced in Chapter 4 and extended up to this point. They may include more parameters or methods than I/O objects, but they do sensibly encapsulate all the data, methods, channels, microcode and I/O hardware needed to execute a more complex function, as we discuss in this section.

7-4.1 Linked Channels

Channels executing variations of some of the functions we have so far described can be linked within the TPU. A *link* is rather like an interrupt executed entirely within the TPU, without any involvement of the M68332 processor, whereby one channel can fire an activity in another channel. Channels executing functions: ITC (used for frequency measurement), PPWA (used for period or pulse width measurement) or SPWM which is a variation of PWM (used for generating square waves) can generate links, and channels executing OC or PPWA (used for generating square waves) can be fired by links.

Linked channels will be illustrated by showing how a channel executing an ITC function can control up to eight OC channels. The OC channels must be consecutively numbered, but each channel can have different parameters. We will only illustrate one ITC channel, channel 0, and one OC channel, channel 1, in the example below. A single rising edge on pin TP0 will start a square-wave output on pin TP1.

Generating a link requires a small extension to the ITC function used to count transitions, as previously discussed in Section 7-3.2. The ITC function will be initialized with HSQ value 2, rather than 1, to generate a link only on the occurrence of the first edge of its input, and the channel control fields are set to detect a rising edge. For HSQ set to 2, this channel's parameter memory's second word contains the start and count of links to be generated, and is here set to start linking channel 1, and to link 1 channel. The third word is set to count 1 edge and then generate the link. When a rising edge occurs on pin TP0, a link is generated to fire channel 1 described below.

Channel 1, executing an OC function, is initialized with HSR value 3, rather than 1, as previously discussed in sections 7-2.3 or 7-2.4. In this mode, the channel waits until a link is received, and then generates a symmetric square wave, rather than a single pulse, as in the previous cases. The rising edge and the width of (both high and low) pulses are established by references R2 and R3, which are the low byte of the addresses of words W2 and W3 in TPU parameter memory whose values are used. W1 becomes the time to be matched to TCR1 to begin the square wave, and W2 * R, where the ratio R is a binary fraction, becomes the width of positive and the width of negative pulses of the symmetric square wave that is generated on output pin TP1.

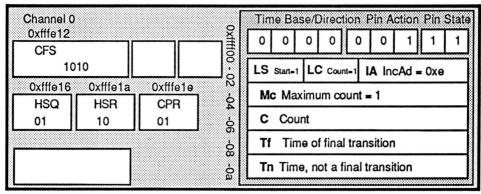

a. ITC Channel

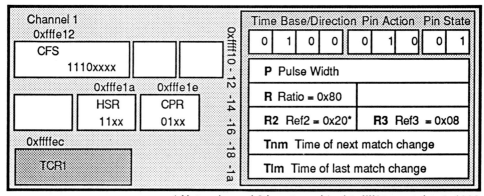

* Note: channel 2 is not used and 0xffff20 contains 0x1000

b. OC Channel

Figure 7-14. Linked Channels.

The procedure *link* initializes channel 0's parameter memory as shown in Figure 7-14a first, then it initializes channel 1's parameter memory as shown in Figure 7-14b. The channel registers are simultaneously initialized in the last line, utilizing the fact that channel 1's fields are immediately to the left of channel 0's fields in each word. For instance, channel 1's CFS field 0xe is catenated to channel 0's CFS field 0xa, to derive the constant 0xea that is written into the CFS word at 0xfffe09.

```
link() {
    register int *p=0xffff00; *p=7; *(p+1)=0x110e; *(p+2)=1;
    p=0xffff10; *p=0x89; *(p+2)=0x8000; *(p+3)=0x2008; *(int *)0xffff20=0x1000;
    Cfs = 0xea; Hsq = 1; Cpr = 5; Hsr = 0xe;
}
```

The functions that can be fired by a link appear to be useful only in special applications. We have not found a way to generate a single pulse in response to an edge of a signal on an input pin (a useful function), nor have we found many useful examples of the use of a link in the applications that we have studied. But the automotive industry uses these special features to reduce the processor load by replacing processor-intensive functions with special-purpose TPU functions.

7-4.2 Special Functions

The TPU executes a number of rather specialized functions for automobile control applications, and can be user-microprogrammed for further specialized functions. The PMA (period measurement with additional transition) and PMM (period measurement with missing transition) functions are used to track engine timing where a fly-wheel has teeth to establish it, and an extra tooth or a missing tooth to establish a reference time. The PSP (position-synchronized pulse generator), another specialized function for automobile control, can be coupled with one of the aforementioned functions, using the timer TCR2, to inject fuel and fire spark plugs in an automobile. These specialized functions, and the microprogramming of the TPU, are beyond the scope of this book. However, we find the SM (stepper motor) to be a useful example of a specialized TPU function, and will describe it herein. The example in this section sets up a class *Stepper* for a half-stepping two-phase stepper motor (Figure 7-15a) whose first step when accelerating is 4 milliseconds and which runs at a rate of 2 milliseconds per step.

This class's *Init* method is derived from the example given in the *M68300 TPU Time Processor Unit Reference Manual Preliminary Edition, July 1990*, sections 1.10.1 and 3-9. Their use of channels 4 to 7 and TCR1 clock rate of 10 µseconds is changed to channels 0 to 3 and 2 µsecond rate to conform to our earlier examples. We do not attempt to generalize the procedures for arbitrary channels, although that is possible. The TPU channel 0 to channel 3 registers and parameter memory are set up as shown in Figure 7-15b. The parameters used in this method would be determined from the characteristics of the stepper motor being run by the TPU. This class's *Output* method puts the desired stepper motor position into parameter memory and requests movement to that position, and this class's *Input* method returns the current stepper position.

struct Stepper : TPU
{void Init(long,unsigned),Output(long);long Input(void);};

void Stepper::Init(p,m) long p; unsigned m;{
    register int *p=0xffff00; Cfs = 0xdddd; /* SM function */
    pt=(pt+0x10)=0x81; *(pt+8)=*(pt+0x18)=0x82; /* channel control */
    (pt+1)=0xe0e0;(pt+9)=0x0e0e;*(pt+0x11)=0x8383;*(pt+0x19)=0x3838; /*pin pattn */
    (pt+2)=0x8000;/ presumed mid-point */ *(pt+4)=1;/* mod count, next step rate */
    (pt+5)=0x3a;/ last chan., # step rates */
    (pt+0xa)=100;/ step control 0: 200µsec. */ *(pt+0xb)=2200;/* step control 1: 4 msec. */
    pt=0xffff10; *pt=0x89; *(pt+2)=0x8000; *(pt+3)=0x2008; /* set parameters in sec. ch. */
    Irq =0x1000; Hsr = 0xaa; /* HSR */ Cpr = 0x55; /* low priority */
}

long Stepper::Input() { return *((int *)0xffff04) }

void Stepper::Output(d) long d;
    {*((int *)0xffff06) = d; /* desired position */ Hsr = 3; /* start microengine */ }

The TPU stepper motor function takes care of all the pulsing needed to run a stepper motor. It is easily controlled as an object, using an *Init* method to initialize it, an *Output* method to command the motor to move to a desired position, and an *Input* method to determine the current position of the stepper motor. Once these methods are written, the TPU is as easy to use as any I/O device.

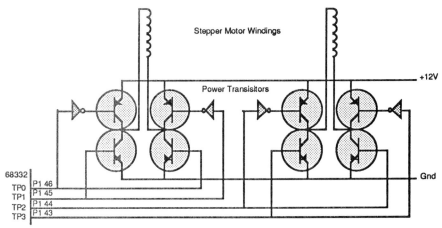

a. Connection of a Stepper Motor

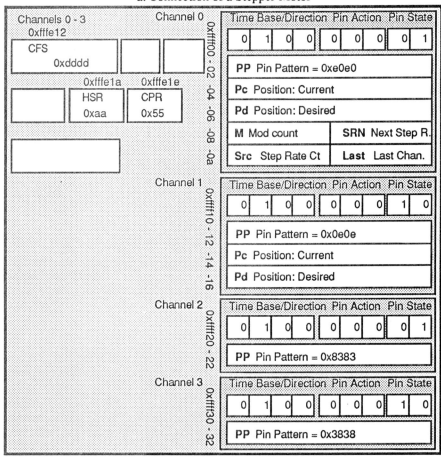

b. TPU Registers and Parameter Memory

Figure 7-15. Stepper Motor Control.

7-5 Conclusions

Frequency or phase analog signals are often generated naturally – by an AC tachometer, for instance – and may be used directly, in firing a TRIAC, for instance. Even when the signal is first an amplitude analog signal, conversion to frequency analog or phase analog signal simplifies the noise isolation and voltage level isolation between transducer and microcomputer. Moreover, several hardware and software techniques, including those that use a module like the TPU, can be used to measure or generate frequency analog signals.

The TPU is a very useful and attractive I/O device for measuring or generating frequency or phase analog signals. It is useful in generating square waves, pulses, and timing interrupts; it can measure events, frequency, period, and pulse width; and it can monitor period or pulse width to interrupt the computer if too long a value is noticed. It is very attractive because a single wire sends the signal to or from the TPU. To the chip designer, it means that an I/O device can be put on a chip or inside a microcomputer chip without using a lot of pins. While counters take up a nontrivial amount of area on the chip, that area is comparatively cheap, while pins are in much shorter supply. Moreover, to the system designer, a single wire is easy to isolate with an optical isolator, to prevent the voltages of the system under test from getting to the microcomputer and the user, as well as to isolate noise generated in that system, to prevent it from getting into the microcomputer.

The TPU was introduced to illustrate the discussion of the TPU module. (There are counter/timers with quite different architectures, useful in different applications, but space limitations restrict what can be covered in one chapter.) The TPU also illustrated how a single chip can be made more flexible when the devices in it are configured by setting the control word. This chapter prepares us for similar techniques in communication modules covered in Chapter 9 and display and secondary storage chips, covered in Chapter 10. You should now be familiar with the TPU in general and with the TPU in particular. Connecting their pins and writing software to initialize and use them should be well within your grasp.

Further information on the TPU is available in the *8-Bit Microprocessor & Peripheral Data Catalog (DL 133)*. As noted earlier, we have not attempted to duplicate the diagrams and discussions in that book because we assume you will refer to it while reading this book; and, because we present an alternative view of the subject, you can use either or both views.

Do You Know These Terms?

See the End of Chapter 1 for Instructions.

parameter memory, interrupt enable, channel function select, host sequence request, host service request, channel priority, interrupt status, microengine, coherent access, pulse width modulation, output compare, periodic interrupt, time delay interrupt, Strowger system, frequency measurement, period measurement, pulse width measurement, link, stepper motor.

8

M68340 Timer Module

The M68340 dual Timer Module (TM), discussed in this chapter, can be used to generate and measure signals like the M68332's TPU discussed in the previous chapter. A timer can generate a square-wave, a sine wave, or any periodic wave, used in cassette tape recorders, telephone systems (touch-tone), and signals to the user (bleeps). It can be used to generate single-shot pulses to control motors, solenoids, or lights. It can itself provide interrupts to coordinate a program to effect an instruction step or a real-time clock. It can be used to count the number of events (falling edges of a signal input to the module) and thus the number of events in a fixed interval of time (the frequency). It is also capable of measuring pulse width and period; voltage, resistance, or capacitance can be converted to the period, which can be measured by a timer. TM timers were designed for these purposes.

The TM is the M68340's principal interface for frequency analog signals. These "FM" signals are easier to handle and more noise-free than "AM" signals. We observe that amplitude analog signals are still pervasively used in interface circuits; but we believe that frequency (or phase) analog signals are becoming equally important.

The primary objective of this chapter is to explain the principles of using the TM module. To make these principles concrete, the TM is introduced first. Then sections will be devoted to each application of this powerful module. A further objective is to review M68340's various synchronization mechanisms introduced in Chapter 5. The TM clearly illustrates applications of many of these techniques.

This chapter should acquaint you with the hardware and software of the TM in the M68340. Upon finishing the chapter, you should be able to connect a TM to external hardware, and write C procedures or object-oriented C methods to generate square waves or pulses, or measure the frequency or period of a periodic wave or the pulse width of a pulse. With these techniques, you should be able to interface to I/O systems that generate or use periodic signals or pulses, or to interface through voltage-to-frequency or frequency-to-voltage converters to analog I/O systems.

8-1 Timer Organization and Registers

The Timer Module has two timers. Timer 1 is illustrated in Figure 8-1 and is used in most examples in this chapter. Timer 2 is identical, but all addresses are 0x40 higher.

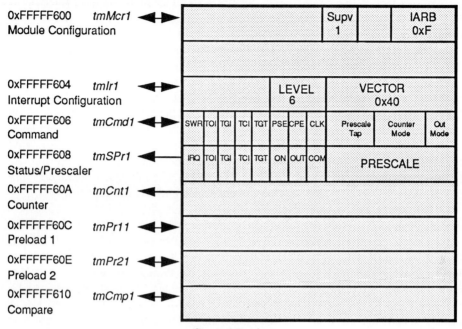

a. Control Registers

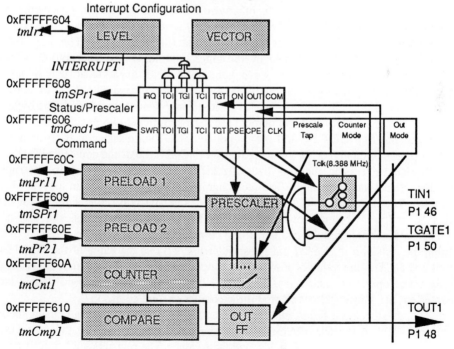

b. Counter logic
Figure 8-1. TM Registers.

In this section, we enumerate the registers and their fields for your reference. In later sections, we will show examples of their use, and explain some subtleties regarding them. For now, we suggest the reader merely "get the lay of the land".

The 16-bit counter *tmCnt1* (0xffffff60a), optionally fed by an 8-bit prescaler at 0xffffff09 (the low byte of *tmSPr1*), is decremented by either the 16.777 MHz system clock divided by 2 (called Tclk), or by the TIN1 signal. An H on TGATE1 can disable counting, or a falling edge can be used to generate interrupts. Interrupts use the interrupt LEVEL and VECTOR of *tmIr1* and the IARB field of the module configuration register *tmMcr1* as in the M68340 periodic timer (Section 5-1.6). The counter can be initialized to or loaded with 0, or the 16 bit preload values in registers *tmPr11* or *tmPr21* (0xffffff60c and 0xffffff60e) depending on the timer function. An output flip-flop OUT FF, whose value appears on TOUT1, can be changed when the counter *tmCnt1* "times out" (becomes 0) or *tmCnt1* equals the compare value *tmCmp1* (0xffffff610).

The command register *tmCmd1* (0xffffff06) has bits and fields to control the module. The most significant bit of *tmCmd1*, denoted *SWR*, is called software reset, but is used to turn the counters on when T, and to enable simple I/O when F. The next three most significant bits, denoted *TOI*, *TGI*, and *TCI*, are interrupt enables to permit interrupts when the timer "overflows" (counts down through 0), when the gate input falls, and when the compare register matches the counter. The next bit, *TGT*, enables the gate input to control the counter; if *TGT* is F or TGATE1 is asserted low the prescaler and counter run, otherwise they stop. The next bit, *CPE*, enables the prescaler, which is controlled by the Prescale Tap field; if *CPE* is F, the counter decrements at the rate of TIN or Tclk, otherwise the counter decrements every time the prescale bit falls, selected by the Prescale Tap *PsTf* field (i.e. essentially at (the rate of TIN or Tclk)/ 2^{PsTf}, except that if *PsTf* is 0, at (the rate) / 2^8). The next field determines the function performed by the timer module; 0 is input capture, output compare, 1 is symmetric square-wave generation, 2 is asymmetric square-wave generation, 3 is pulse generation, 4 is pulse width measurement, 5 is period measurement, 6 is event counting useful in frequency measurement, and 7 is bypass useful in simple parallel input and output. The least significant two bits determine how the output flip-flop OUT FF and the output bit TOUT1 are changed each time the counter passes through 0 or the compare register *tmCmp1* equals the counter *tmCnt1*.

The status register, the high byte of *tmSPr1* (0xffffff608), indicates interrupt, processing state, and pin status. The most significant bit, *IRQ* is 1 if an interrupt has occurred. The next three bits denoted *TOI*, *TGI*, and *TCI*, are status signals that the timer "overflows" (counts down through 0), that the gate input falls, and that the compare register matches the counter. If the corresponding bits in *tmCmd1* are T, then setting the status bit in *tmSPr1* causes an interrupt. *TGT* is the value of the TGATE1 input and OUT is the value of the TOUT1 output pin. *ON* is T if the module is busy doing some operation, and *COM* is T if the compare register *tmCmp1* equals the counter *tmCnt1;* however, it is cleared if the counter *tmCnt1* counts to 0.

The registers, their fields, and their values can be easily handled in C using these constants (kept in the file TM.h). In subsequent procedures, we use the following definitions for the TM registers, fields, and their values. The registers are listed first for both timer 1 and timer 2. The fields and values are shown below these values. We will illustrate examples of the use of these fields and values after their definitions are given.

```
#define tmMcr1 *((int*)0xfffff600)        #define tmMcr2 *((int*)0xfffff640)
#define tmIr1 *((int*)0xfffff604)         #define tmIr2 *((int*)0xfffff644)
#define tmCmd1 *((int*)0xfffff606)        #define tmCmd2 *((int*)0xfffff646)
#define tmSPr1 *((int*)0xfffff608)        #define tmSPr2 *((int*)0xfffff648)
#define tmCnt1 *((unsigned*)0xfffff60a)   #define tmCnt2 *((unsigned*)0xfffff64a)
#define tmPr11 *((int*)0xfffff60c)        #define tmPr12 *((int*)0xfffff64c)
#define tmPr21 *((int*)0xfffff60e)        #define tmPr22 *((int*)0xfffff64e)
#define tmCmp1 *((int*)0xfffff610)        #define tmCmp2 *((int*)0xfffff650)
```

The command register uses the following bit field values:

```
#define SWR 0x8000        #define TGT 0x800
#define TOI 0x4000        #define CPE 0x200
#define TGI 0x2000        #define CLK 0x100
#define TCI 0x1000
```

The status register uses the following bit field values, as well as the values of *TOI, TGI, TCI,* and *TGT* also used for the command register:

```
#define IRQ 0x8000        #define ON 0x400
#define OUT 0x200         #define COM 0x100
```

The Prescale Tap field of the command register uses the following constants to indicate the prescale division factor (if no value is given, the default *Div1* is used):

```
enum{Div1,Div2=0x420,Div4=0x440,Div8=0x460,Div16=0x480,Div32=0x4a0,
Div64=0x4c0,Div128=0x4e0,Div256=0x400};
```

The Counter Mode field of the command register uses the following constants to indicate the timer function:

```
enum{IcOc,Squ=4,VdSqu=8,SSht=0xc,Pw=0x10,Prd=0x14,EvC=0x18,ByPs=0x1c};
```

Finally, the Out Mode field of the command register uses the following constants to indicate the function that controls OUT FF, generating the output signal TOUT1:

```
enum{TriState,Tgl,Zero,One};
```

These definitions will be used in examples in the following sections. For instance, we will write:

```
tmPr21=3;
```

to denote that 3 is put in timer prescale register 2 of timer 1. The command register can be set up to set bit 15 (SWR) and put 7 *(ByPs)* into the Counter Mode field and 2 *(Zero)* into the Out Mode field in:

```
tmCmd1=CPE+ByPs+Zero;
```

They will make easy the control of the timer modules in C procedures. Object-oriented C methods will access the registers by means of indexes into vectors, which correspond to the offsets in Figure 8-1a. For instance, if *(int*)p* is *(int*)0xfffff600* for timer 1, or *(int*)0xfffff640* for timer 2, then the module configuration register is denoted **p*, the interrupt configuration register is *p[2]*, the command register is *p[3]*, the status/prescaler is *p[4]*, the counter is *p[5]*, the preload 1 register is *p[6]*, the preload 2 register is *p[7]*, and the compare register is *p[8]*. This makes the object-oriented methods adaptable to either timer 1 or timer 2.

8-2 Signal Generation

We want to first cover the generation of level outputs, square waves, pulses, and interrupts that can result in changes to output signals, because you can implement these examples as experiments and see results on the output pins. Later, we look at frequency measurement techniques, which can be studied using timer module 2 to generate the signals using techniques introduced in this section. We begin by describing generating a level output as a one-bit parallel output port. We then generate square waves and pulses. The last subsection shows how to generate time-based interrupts, which could be used to implement real-time clocks.

8-2.1 One-bit Parallel Output

We may need to output a 0 or 1 on a TOUT pin, for instance to test the hardware or to force an output value. Figure 8-2 shows to put into the command register to implement a one-bit parallel output port. This function is chosen when Counter Mode is 7 if SWR is 0 and CPE is 1. The Out Mode determines what will be put on TOUT1. Putting 2 *(zero)* into this field outputs an L signal, and putting 3 *(one)* into this field outputs an H signal. In effect, if the second least significant bit of Out Mode is 1, its least significant bit is output. The procedure *BitOut* below outputs an L on TOUT1 and an H on TOUT2.

BitOut() { /* produce a 0 on TOUT1 and a 1 on TOUT2 */
    tmCmd1=CPE+ByPs+Zero; tmCmd2=CPE+ByPs+One;
}

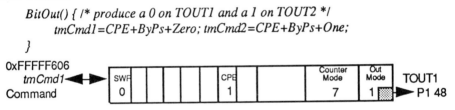

Figure 8-2. One-bit Parallel Output.

The one-bit output class *BitOut's Init* method initializes the timer specified by its second parameter (values 1 or 2). The *Init* methods of most later classes use this same timer selection parameter. Thereafter the *Output* method outputs the T or F value of its parameter to the pin. Mainly for device independence, *BitOut's Input* method can obtain the last bit output from the timer command fields, although this *Input* method would not be very useful.

struct BitOut:IoDevice
    {void Init(long,unsigned),Output(long);long Input(void);}*Bit0,*Bit1;

void BitOut::Init(p,m) long p; unsigned m;
    { inherited::Init(0xfffff606+((m-1)<<6),0);}
long BitOut::Input() { return *(int*)chip&1;}
void BitOut::Output(d) long d;
    { if(d) *(int*)chip=CPE+ByPs+One; else *(int*)chip=CPE+ByPs+Zero;}

This 1-bit output mode is only available when the Counter Mode is Bypass (7) and SWR is F. However, this mechanism is not designed to be used to preset TOUT1 for another mode like pulse mode because initializing the next mode for toggle or clear output always clears TOUT1 when the command register is loaded.

8-2.2 The Square-Wave Generator

A square wave can be generated by several TM functions. One of the easiest ways is to use the *Square-Wave* mode, whose timer command value is 1. Figure 8-3 shows the values put into the registers and parameters to implement a symmetric "square-wave" output port. SWR is cleared to write any data into the command or any other register, and is set to start the square wave. The clock prescale enable (CPE) must be 1, the Counter Mode must be 1 to generate symmetric square waves and the Out Mode is 1 to toggle on each timeout. The input is selected by the CLK bit of the command register; if CLK is T then it is the TIN1 input, otherwise it is half the 16.77 MHz system clock, which is 8.389 MHz, after initialization. The prescaler divides this input by 1 if PRE is F, by 2 if PRE is T and the Prescale Tap is 1, by 4 if PRE is T and the Prescale Tap is 2, . . . , by 128 if PRE is T and the Prescale Tap is 7, and by 256 if PRE is T and the Prescale Tap is 0. The output will be high and will be low, repetitively, each for *tmPr11*+1 clock periods where *tmPr11* is the value in the preload 1 register.

A simple procedure to generate a ~ 2 MHz square wave on TOUT1 is given below.

SqWave(){ tmCmd1=0; tmCmd1=CPE+Div1+Squ+Tgl; tmPr11=1; tmCmd1+=SWR;}

Note that SWR is first cleared to permit the registers to be written in, and then set after they have been written, to start the counter. The *tmCmd1* register is initialized to enable the prescaler clock and set the Counter and Output Modes to 1, and may be set to choose different prescaler values (we bypass the prescaler in out example). If TGE is T, then counting stops when TGATE1 is negated high; it can be used to start the square wave in synchrony with some external signal, but it can also stretch the square wave after the square-wave generation is started, which may not be desirable. The square wave's "half-period" is put into the PRELOAD1 register as discussed at the end of the previous paragraph. The current value of TOUT1 can be read in Status bit OUT (and the current TGATE1 input can be read in status bit TGT, as we discuss in Section 8-3.1).

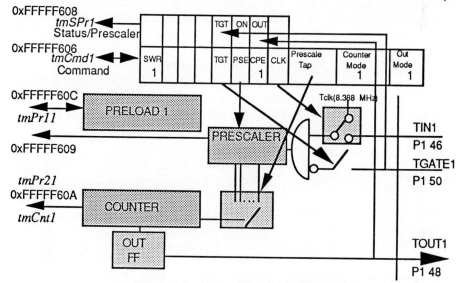

Figure 8-3. Symmetric Square-wave Output.

We now consider an application of this generator to the production of touch-tone signals. A *touch-tone* signal is a pair of sine waves having frequencies that represent the digits used in dialing a telephone. A touch-tone generator can generate these signals so that the microcomputer can dial up on the telephone, and it can generate such tones to be sent via radio remote control or to be stored on cassette tape, and so on. In a top-down design, one must consider all the relevant alternatives. One possibility is integrated circuits that output touch-tone signals in response to keyboard contact closings, but these would require the microcomputer to act like the keyboard to such a chip. Another is analog switches in place of the keys that can be controlled by an output device. (A few other alternatives are also possible.) However, the number of chips needed in any of the latter alternatives would be at least two, if not more. The TM has two timers 1 and 2, which can generate the tones using a CMOS 4015 shift register making two four-stage Johnson counters, to implement the tone generator using one chip. So we consider generating a square wave using TM timers 1 and 2 and a 4015.

Table 8-1. Touch-Tone Codes.

Digit	Coding
0	R4,C2
1	R1,C1
2	R1,C2
3	R1,C3
4	R2,C1
5	R2,C2
6	R2,C3
7	R3,C1
8	R3,C2
9	R3,C3

Code	Hertz	Counter
R1	697	752
R2	770	680
R3	852	615
R4	941	557
C1	1209	434
C2	1336	392
C3	1477	355
C4	1633	321

a. Codes for Digits   b. Frequencies for Codes

A touch-tone signal consists of two simultaneous sine waves. Table 8-1 shows the tones required for each digit that can be sent. Table 8-1a shows the mapping of digits to frequencies shown in Table 8-1b, and Table 8-1b shows the frequencies in Hertz and the corresponding values of n to be put into the TM module to generate the desired frequencies, as they will be used later in the example. Thus, to send the digit 5, send two superimposed sine waves with frequencies 770 Hertz and 1336 Hertz.

To send a sine wave, a Johnson counter is almost ideal. This counter is actually just a shift register whose output is inverted, then shifted back into it. (See Figure 8-4.) A four-bit Johnson counter would have the following sequence of values in the flip-flops:

```
L L L L
H L L L
H H L L
H H H L
H H H H
L H H H
L L H H
L L L H
```

As described in Don Lancaster's marvelous little book, *The CMOS Cookbook*, Howard Sams Inc., these counters can be used to generate sine waves simply by connecting resistors of value 33 KΩ to the first and third stages and 22 KΩ to the second stage of the shift register. (See Figure 8-4.) Although the wave will look like a stair-step approximation to a sine, it is free of the lower harmonics and can be filtered if necessary. Moreover, using more accurate values of resistors and a longer shift register, it is possible to eliminate as much of the low-order harmonics as desired before filtering. In this case, if we want a sine wave with frequency f, we clock the shift register with a square wave whose frequency should be $8 * f$.

Consider now the approach to generating a sine wave with frequency F using the TM system, with system clock 16.667 MHz, to drive a four-stage Johnson counter. We set TM's preload register to $(4,194,444 / (8 * f)) - 1$. The values, are shown in the right half of Table 8-1b for the touch-tone codes. For instance, to send the digit 8, we put the numbers 304 and 194 into the two TM half-periods, which will generate an 852 and a 1336 Hz sine wave to comprise the signal.

Two timers are used to generate the two sine waves required by the touch-tone signal. The external connections are shown in Figure 8-4. Note that the CLEAR control on the shift register is connected to the microcomputer RESET bus line to ensure that the shift register does not have some unusual pattern in it after power is applied. The desired signal is simply the sum of the sine waves produced by two shift registers and is obtained by merely connecting to the common points of the resistors. The procedure *sendTone* below will send the touchtone signal using this circuit. It uses both timers using the procedure described above for timer 1. It merely initializes them to begin sending the touch-tone code, then waits for a while and then terminates the timers. Note *Init*'s use of array *tt1* that implements Table 8-1a to establish the pair of frequencies to be sent, and of vector *tt2* that implements Table 8-1b to establish the period values that are sent to each timer to get those frequencies.

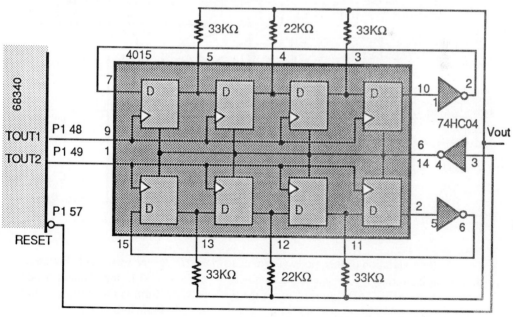

Figure 8-4. A Touch-Tone Generator.

```
struct TTone:BasicOutDevice
    { void Init(long,unsigned),Output(long),Terminate(void); };
unsigned tt1[10][2]={{3,5},{0,4},{0,5},{0,6},{1,4},{1,5},{1,6},{2,4},{2,5},{2,6}};
long tt2[8]={752,680,615,557,434,392,355,321};
void TTone::Init(p,m) register long p; unsigned m;
    { tmCmd1=0; tmCmd1=CPE+Squ+Tgl; tmCmd2=0; tmCmd2=CPE+Squ+Tgl;}
void TTone::Output(d) long d; {
    value = d; tmPr11=tt2[tt1[d][0]]; tmCmd1|=SWR;
    tmPr12=tt2[tt1[d][1]]; tmCmd2|=SWR;
}
void TTone::Terminate() { tmCmd1=tmCmd2=0; }
```

A slight variation of this technique can be used to generate any periodic waveform. The square wave can be used to increment a counter which supplies an address to a read-only memory. It can output words to a D-to-A converter and can store the desired pattern to be developed. Thus, generating a square wave can generate other periodic waves. Finally, as discussed in the previous chapter, a square wave can be integrated to get a ramp signal, and this can be shaped by nonlinear analog techniques. Also, as in music generation, a periodic signal can be shaped by attenuating it under control of an output device to apply attack and decay characteristics in a music synthesizer.

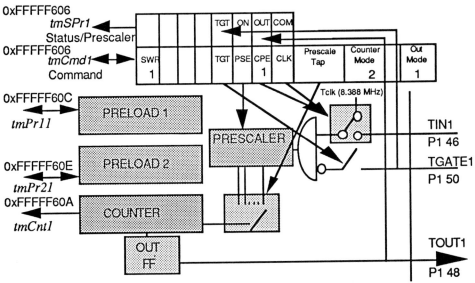

Figure 8-5. Asymmetric Square-wave Output.

A slight variation of this mode generates *asymmetric square waves*. See Figure 8-5. The variable duty-cycle square-wave mode, with *VdSqu* (2) in the Counter Mode register, uses PRELOAD1 *tmPr11* to set the time the wave-form is low, minus 1, and PRELOAD2 *tmPr21* to set the time the wave-form is high, minus 1. *aSqWave* produces an asymmetric square wave that is low for three and high for two ticks:

aSqWave ()

{ tmCmd1=0; tmCmd1=CPE+Div1+VdSqu+Tgl; tmPr11=2; tmPr21=1; tmCmd1+=SWR;}

An object-oriented class *SquWv* shown below sets the low time to the most significant 16 bits and high time to the 16 least significant bits of *Output*'s long parameter. This general object can set up either or both timers (m=1 or m=2) for symmetric or asymmetric wave generation.

struct SquWv:IoDevice{ void Init(long,unsigned),Output(long),Terminate(void);};

void SquWv::Init(p,m) register long p; unsigned m;{ register int *t;
  inherited::Init(0xffff60c+((m-1)<<6),0);t=(int*)chip;
  t[-3]=0; t[-3]=CPE+Div1+VdSqu+Tgl; *t=p-1; t[-3]+=SWR;
}
void SquWv::Output(d) long d; {*((long*)chip)=d-0x10001;}
void SquWv::Terminate(){*(((int*)chip)-3)=0;}

The TM system is seen as a valuable tool in generating square waves, which can be used to generate other periodic waves using Johnson counters or read-only memories and D-to-A converters. However, the designer must not always assume that the TM is so much better than any other generator. Hardware approaches discussed in Section 6-5.3 and software approaches using various synchronization mechanisms discussed in Chapter 5 should be considered by a design engineer, and the most suitable technique selected.

8-2.3 The Pulse Generator

Like the square-wave generator, a pulse generator has many uses. The device normally outputs an F, but waits a specified time and outputs a T for a specified time after it is triggered. It can be triggered by software or by an external signal. And, like the square-wave generator, there are software and hardware techniques to implement it. The software technique to supply a pulse triggered by software merely outputs a T, waits the required time, and then outputs an F. To react to an external signal, the external signal can be sensed in a gadfly loop or can generate an interrupt so that the pulse is generated when the signal arrives. But, like the software square-wave generator, the software pulse generator is susceptible to timing errors due to interrupts, direct memory access, and dynamic memory refresh cycles. A 555 timer can act like a pulse generator, triggered by a microcomputer or an external signal; and the length of the pulse, determined by the value of a resistor and a capacitor, can be controlled by selecting of the resistor by means of an analog switch controlled from an output device. One-shot integrated circuits can be controlled in like manner. Finally, the TM can be used to generate pulses when the computer starts them (or started by asserting an external signal low on TGATE1), and the pulse length can be computer controlled, as we now discuss.

This subsection considers the use of the TM to generate pulses. The *Variable Width Single-Shot* is like the square wave mode, but *SSht* (3) is put in Counter Mode, the low time, minus 1, is put in *tmPr11* and the high time, minus 1, in *tmPr21*. The sequence can be initiated when TGATE1 falls if TGE is T. A procedure to produce a ~1/4 µsec pulse ~1/4 µsec after initialization, when *tmCmd1* is written, is shown below.

main()
  { tmCmd1=0; tmCmd1=CPE+SSht+Tgl ;tmPr11=1; tmPr21=1; tmCmd1|=SWR; }

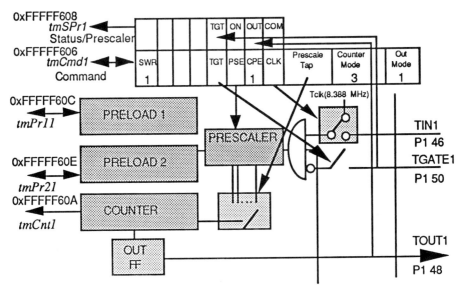

Figure 8-6. Single-Shot Pulse Generator.

The class *Pulse* generalizes the procedure above. Its *Init* method initializes the timer specified by its second parameter (0 initializes timer 1, and 1 initializes timer 2). Thereafter the *Output* method fires a pulse, whenever it is executed, after a delay specified by the most significant 16 bits whose width is specified by the least significant 16 bits of its long parameter, in the same format.

struct Pulse:IoDevice{ void Init(long,unsigned),Output(long),Terminate(void);} ;

void Pulse::Init(p,m) register long p; unsigned m;{ register int *t;
    inherited::Init(0xffff60c+((m-1)<<6),0);t=(int*)chip;
    t[-3]=0; t[-3]=CPE+Div1+SSht+Tgl;
}

void Pulse::Output(d) long d;
    { *(((int*)chip)-3)&=~SWR;*((long*)chip) =d-0x10001; *(((int*)chip)-3) |=SWR;}

void Pulse::Terminate(){*(((int*)chip)-3)=0;}

We illustrate the use of TM timer 1 to fire a TRIAC using proportional cycle control (Figure 6-5d). We use the edge detector of Chapter 5, although we shall soon discover that the TM has better means to detect edges than we used in Chapter 5. Interrupt requests on IRQ5's pin occur each time the household 110 volt 60Hz "power wiring" signal passes through zero (Figure 5-8). A positive-going pulse is generated such that its falling edge will fire the TRIAC at a time in the 60Hz cycle that corresponds to the end of the pulse. A small pulse width fires the TRIAC early in each cycle, making it conduct most of the time to apply full power to the load; a large width fires it late, making the TRIAC open most of the time to turn off the power to the load.

The program sets up port B bit 7 to send its signal to the exclusive-OR gate of Figure 5-8b, sets up Irq6 to receive the output of the gate, and sets up level-6 autovector interrupts, as described in Section 5-1.5. Then TM timer 1 is configured to generate pulses as described above. We arbitrarily turn on the light fully by making the initial value of the pulse width small (8). After enabling interrupts, we execute while(1) in lieu of some program that does useful work. The latter program can set the pulse width to *w* by executing *tmPr11 = w;* at any time. (This could also be done by an *IoWord* object whose address is 0xfffff60c). It need not reinitialize the TM, nor send commands to the timer to fire the pulses. The interrupt handler clears and sets SWR to refire the pulse each time the 60Hz signal crosses through 0, and clears the source of the interrupt.

```
main() { register int *hndlr;
      tmCmd1=0; tmCmd1=CPE+SSht+Tgl ;tmPr11=8; tmPr21=1; tmCmd1|=SWR;
      assgB=0x40; dirB=0x80; /*asgn irq6, Port B 7 output*/
      *(char*)0xfffff006 |=0x40; /* set (bit6) IRQ6 autovector */
      asm{lea @0,hndlr} *(int **)0x78=hndlr; /* put level 6 handler address in 0x78 */
      asm{and #0xfdff,sr} while(1); /* enable level 6 interrupts, do something */
➤    asm{@0 ) tmCmd1 &=~SWR; *tmCmd1 |=SWR; portB ^=0x80; asm {rte}
}
```

In the TM, the pulse width is timed to within ~ 1/4 microsecond, and this time is not affected by processor interrupts, dynamic memory refresh requests, or other subtle problems that affect the timing of real-time programs. This is quite useful in process control, where for instance the pulse width controls the amount of gasoline injected into the engine, the spark timing, and other key factors in running the engine. The dual TM can measure input signals and compute the values of the pulse widths for the timers.

8-2.4 Timer Interrupts

Using a configuration almost identical to that used for a square-wave, periodic interrupts can be generated. Using a configuration almost identical to that used for a pulse generator, interrupts can be generated to execute procedures at an interval of time after another procedure is executed. In this section we'll cover these applications.

The procedure *main* below will set up TM timer 1 as a square-wave generator with half-period *0x8001*, as in Section 8-2.1, putting values in the TM's fields as shown in Figure 8-6. This can put the square-wave signal on pin TOUT1 if Out Mode is 1 *(Tgl)*. This procedure further enables interrupts by setting command bit TOI to T. If interrupts are enabled, the TM's IARB, VECTOR and LEVEL registers must be set up to handle them, like the PI's registers were set up (Section 5-1.6). The interrupt handler is entered each time the output waveform changes, every *0x8000* +1 clock ticks. Note that the prescaler sets the clock tick to 8.38 MHz / 256. The interrupt handler clears the interrupt source by writing 1 into status register bit TOI; it could then execute some procedure.

```
main(){ register int *hndlr; /* interrupt periodically */
      tmMcr1=0x8d; tmIr1=0x640; tmSPr1=TOI; /* clear overflow interrupt if it was set */
      tmCmd1=SWR+TOI+CPE+Div256+Squ; tmPr11=0x8000;
      asm{ lea @0,hndlr } *((int **)0x100)= hndlr; asm{ and #0xfdff,sr } while(1);
➤    asm {@0} tmSPr1=TOI; /* clear timer overflow interrupt */ asm {rte}
}
```

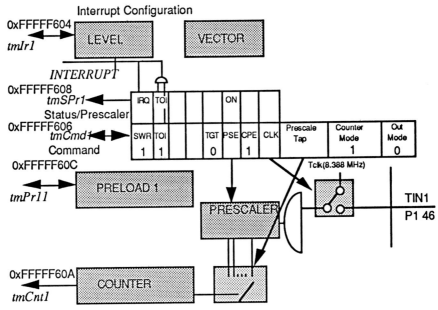

Figure 8-7. Periodic Interrupt.

As an example of such a procedure, consider a time-of-day clock that keeps track of the time in global *struct{int ticks,hrs,mins;} timer;* using TM timer 1 to generate periodic interrupts. We generate interrupts every second by setting the prescaler to divide by 256 and *tmPrll* to (4,194,444 / 256) = 16,385. The interrupt handler will count down *secs* by 60, then *mins* by 60, then *hrs.*

```
struct{int secs,hrs,mins;} timer;
main(){ register int *hndlr; /* interrupt periodically */
    tmMcr1=0x8d; tmIr1=0x640; tmSPr1=TOI; tmCmd1=SWR+TOI+CPE+Div256+Squ;
    tmPrll=16385;
    asm{ lea @0,hndlr } *((int **)0x100)= hndlr; asm{ and #0xfdff,sr } while(1);
►   asm{@0  movem.l d0/d1/a4,-(a7)}
    tmSPr1 = TOI; /* remove interrupt */ }
    if((++timer.secs) == 60){ /* an example of a procedure */
    timer.secs =0;
    if((++timer.mins) == 60){
       timer.mins=0; timer.hrs++;
    }
    }
    asm{movem.l (a7)+,d0/d1/a4} asm{ rte}
}
```

This real-time interrupt, or any interrupt that causes things to happen when an interrupt occurs, can be viewed as a Mealy model sequential machine. The state transition occurs when there is an interrupt. The internal state of the sequential machine is kept in one or more global variables, like *secs, hrs,* and *mins* in the preceding example, and the input states are determined from reading input ports or the program's global variables. Output states may be put in output ports or the program's global variables or may be programs that are executed.

The *periodic interrupt* is very similar to the real-time interrupt (Section 5-1.6). (See Figure 8-7.) The periodic interrupt has finer resolution for short intervals; the real-time interrupt can be set for periods like 62.5 milliseconds or 125 milliseconds, but no intermediate value, whereas the periodic interrupt can be set to any value ± 1/8 μsecond. However, the TM is not available in all systems such as the M68330.

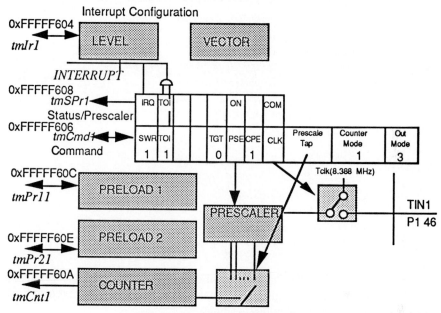

Figure 8-8. Time Delay Interrupt.

Analogous to the previous example, we will generate an interrupt after a fixed time after a procedure is executed that fires the TM. The pulse generator function is used, but with TGI set to 1. See Figure 8-8. A pulse can be generated on pin TOUT1 if OutMode is set to *Tgl* (1). An interrupt would generated both times the counter decrements to 0, so we clear the interrupt enable when the first interrupt occurs.

```
IntDelay{ register int *hndlr; /* interrupt after a delay */
    tmMcr1=0x8d; tmIr1=0x640; tmSPr1=TCI; tmCmd1=SWR+TCI+CPE+Div1+EvC;
    tmCmp1=0x8000; asm{ lea @0,hndlr } *((int **)0x100)= hndlr; asm{ and #0xfdff,sr }
    while(!flag); asm{ or #700,sr } return;
    asm {@0} tmCmd1=0; flag=1; asm {rte}
}
```

As an example of the use of *time delay interrupts*, we consider the design of a microcomputer control of a telephone that uses a rotary dialer, such as was common before touch-tone phones became available. In a rotary dialer, a relay connected in series with the dialer contacts will be pulsed to dial the number. Assume the relay is connected to bit 0 of port F. The telephone standards require the relay to be closed for at least 40 milliseconds and then opened for at least 60 milliseconds for each pulse, and the number of pulses corresponds to the number being dialed. 600 milliseconds is needed between each number being dialed. We will use a global *state* that is decremented upon each interrupt; if *state* is 0, no further interrupts are requested, if *state* is below 10 or is even, the output is low, opening the relay, and the time to the next interrupt is set to 60 milliseconds, otherwise the output is high, closing the relay, and the time to the next interrupt is set to 40 milliseconds. The initial value of *state* determines the number of pulses to be sent; to send *n* pulses, *state* is initialized to (2 * *n*) + 10. Note that for the number 0, however, 10 pulses are sent.

```
main(){ /* rotary dialer to send number "0" */ register int *hndlr;
    assgA1=dirA=1; tmMcr1=0x8d; tmIr1=0x640; tmSPr1=TOI;
    tmCmd1=SWR+TOI+CPE+Div8+Squ;
    tmPr11=20832; asm{ lea @0,hndlr } *((int **)0x100)= hndlr;
    state=30; /* send number 0 = 10 pulses */
    asm{ and #0xfdff,sr } /* enable interrupts */
    while(state); asm{ or #0x700,sr } return;
```

⮞
```
    asm {@0 movem.l d0/d6-d7,-(a7) }
    tmSPr1=TOI;
    if(state){
        if(((state -- )&1)&&(state>=10)){portA=1; tmPr11=31248;}
        else {portA=0; tmPr11=20832;}
    }
    asm {movem.l (a7)+,d0/d6-d7} asm {rte}
```

```
}
```
We initialize port A so that the least significant bit is output, and then set up TM's IARB, VECTOR and LEVEL registers, set up the interrupt address, and prepare timer 1 for pulse generation as in the previous example.

This example gives me an opportunity to relate one of the truly great stories in electronics – the invention of the dial telephone. In the 1880s Almond B. Strowger, one of two undertakers in a very small town, couldn't get much business. His competitor's wife was the town's telephone operator. When someone suffered a death in the family, they called up to get an undertaker. The wife naturally recommended her husband, diverting callers from poor Almond. Necessity is the mother of invention. With a celluloid shirt collar and some pins, he contrived a caller operated mechanism, using a stepping relay mechanism that would connect the caller to the desired telephone, so that calls for his business would not go through his competitor's wife. It worked so well that it became the standard mechanism for making calls all over the world. Even today, about a quarter of all telephones use this "step-by-step" or *Strowger system*.

An instruction trace can be implemented using the time delay interrupt. In Chapter 1 we explained that a monitor is a program used to help you debug programs. The monitor behaves like a trap handler, because it may be "called up" by a breakpoint, which is a trap instruction, so it is left by an RTE instruction. Although the M68340 has trace bits in its status register able to trace instruction execution, other processors do not have this capability and they can use counter-timer interrupts to trace a program. To "trace" a user program, we can leave the monitor to execute just one instruction, then reenter the monitor to see what happened. Just before we leave the monitor, we put a number N into a counter latch, after which we execute RTE. The user program will be given enough time to execute just one instruction, and N will be chosen to permit that to happen. Then an interrupt will occur and the monitor will be reentered to display the changes wrought by the executed instruction.

8-3 Frequency Analog Measurement

Converse to generating square waves or pulses, one may need to measure the frequency or period of a square wave or repetitive signal, or the width of a pulse. Many important outputs carry information by their frequency: tachometers, photodetectors, piezo-electric pressure transducers. The voltage-to-frequency converter integrated circuit can change voltages to frequencies economically and with high accuracy. The frequency of output from a timer chip like the 555 timer is inversely proportional to the resistance and capacitance used in its timing circuit. Therefore, a by-product of measuring frequency is that one can easily obtain measurements of resistance or capacitance. Better yet, the period of the signal is linearly proportional to resistance and capacitance. Period can be measured directly. Moreover, for high frequencies, frequency is easier and faster to measure, while for low frequencies, period is easier and faster. The M68340 is quite capable, if necessary, of inverting the value using its DIVU and DIVS instructions. For nonrepetitive waveforms, pulse width measurement is very useful. This can be measured too. Also, the time between two events can be measured by using the events to set, then clear, a flip-flop. The pulse width of the output of this flip-flop can be measured. Sometimes the microcomputer has to keep track of the total number of events of some kind. The event is translated into the rising or falling edge of a signal, and the number of edges is then recorded. Note that the number of events per second is the frequency. Thus, events are counted in the same way as frequency is measured, but the time is not restricted to any specific value.

In this section, we first study one-bit parallel input and generation of interrupts based on its edges. Then we discuss the measurement of frequency. The counting of events is similar to this, and even though it won't be discussed explicitly, it can be done in the same way as the measurement of frequency. We next describe the period measurement, after which we include a short example that shows how period measurement can be used to read the positions of several potentiometers. We then describe pulse width measurement. In a final subsection, we summarize the modes of the TM subsystems in the TM .

8-3.1 One-bit Parallel Input

From time to time an input signal normally used by the TM, for instance to measure a frequency, will have to be examined directly by software as in a one-bit parallel input. We may wish to record a sequence of bits taken from a single input at a fixed rate. We also may wish to generate interrupts upon receiving an edge on TM inputs. The simple input function is provided for these possibilities. This procedure reads the signal on the input TIN1 into variable i. See Figure 8-9.

main() { register int i; tmCmd1=CPE+ByPs; i=(tmSPr1>>11)&1; }

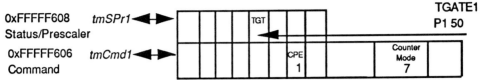

Figure 8-9. One-bit Parallel Input.

A class *BitIn* to input a bit on a timer's TIN is shown below. Figure 8-9 shows what it puts into the registers and parameters to implement a one-bit parallel input port.

struct BitIn:IoDevice{void Init(long,unsigned);long Input(void);};

void BitIn::Init(p,m) long p; unsigned m;
    *{ inherited::Init(0xfffff608+((m-1)<<6),0); *(int*)(chip-2)=CPE+ByPs;}*

long BitIn::Input() { return ((int*)chip>>11)&1;}*

A procedure to generate an interrupt when a falling edge occurs on a single input TIN1, which more efficiently implements the edge detector of Figure 5-8, is shown below. Figure 8-10 shows what it puts into the registers and parameters to interrupt on either edge. This function is selected by initializing TGI, TGT and CPE to 1 and, enabling interrupts, and setting LEVEL and VECTOR as usual. It is available in all the other modes too; Status TGT can be read at any time to determine the level of TGATE1.

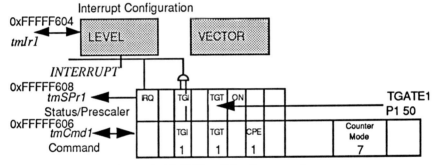

Figure 8-10. Falling Edge Interrupt Input.

*main(){ register int *hndlr;*
    tmMcr1=0x8d; tmIr1=0x640; tmSPr1 =TGI; tmCmd1=TGI+TGT+CPE+ByPs;
    *asm{ lea @0,hndlr } *((int **)0x100)= hndlr; /* set up interrupt addr. */*
    asm{ and #0xfdff,sr }while(!flag);
▶   *asm {@0} mSPr1=TGI; flag=1; asm {rte}*
}

8-3.2 Frequency Measurement

A TM timer can be used to count input transitions, and thus to measure frequency, using the event count function whose Counter Mode code is 7. It is initialized by setting SWR and CPE in *tmCmd1* which initializes the prescaler to 0xff and the counter to 0. The prescaler and counter decrement on each tick of the 8.388 MHz Tckl or the TIN1 pin.

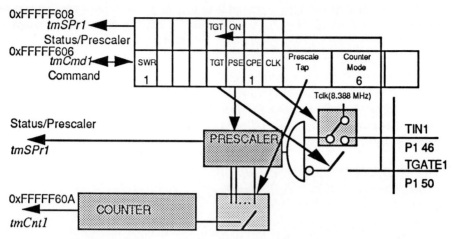

Figure 8-11. Transition Counter or Frequency Measurement.

The prescaler can be used to extend the counter to 24 bits, by setting PRE to 1 and the prescale tap to 0. To get the count value, we have to read both, and then negate the bits because the counters count down instead of up. However, the prescaler is initialized to 0xff, while the counter is initialized to 0. Therefore the count is actually the catenation of *(~tmSPr1)&0xff* (low byte) with *-tmCnt1* (high two bytes). Further, there is a possible timing problem, because the counter and prescaler are read in two different memory cycles (even if one uses a long word read), whereby the counter could be read and then be incremented when the prescaler is read, or alternatively the prescaler could be read and then the counter is incremented and then read. This problem is handled in hardware in most counter-timer systems; in this module we handle the problem in software - by reading the counter, then the prescaler, and if the prescaler is in the early part of its count, then reading the counter again. This way, we get a compatible pair of reads the avoids the possibility that the propagating carry will give a false count.

This event counter can be used to monitor the performance of software on the M68340, as Bill Highsmith of Motorola suggested to us. Before a procedure, we start the counter, counting the system clock (divided by 2), and after it, we read the count. Twice this number gives the time the procedure takes to be executed, in clock cycles. We also count TIN1 edges over a fixed time (1 second) in order to measure frequency.

The procedure *frequency* first sets up TM timer 1's command to count falling edges. Note that the prescaler is used to extend the count to 24 bits. We use the inefficient and inexact real-time synchronization method here because it is clear (983546 is set for a delay of 1 second), but we will shortly use the periodic interrupt to time out one second. We then read the 24-bit count into variable *l* using the technique above.

frequency (){ register long l; register unsigned i;
  tmCmd1 =0; tmCmd1 =SWR+CPE+CLK+Div256+EvC;
  for(l=0;l<983546;l++); / real-time program delay for 1 second */*
  l=-tmCnt1; i=0xff&~(tmSPr1);if(i>128)l=-tmCnt1; l=(l<<8)|i;
}

A better method of delaying 1 second is to use the periodic interrupt (Section 5-1.6). Its interrupt handler sets a global variable *TimeUp* which is cleared in the program and gadfly tested to make sure the counter counts events for 1 second.

```
int count, val, TimeUp;
main(){ register long l,n;register unsigned i;
    register int *hndaddr;register char *PI=(char*)0xffff022;
    *(char*)0xffff001 =0x8e; PI[0]=6; PI[1]=0x42; PI[2]=1; PI[3]=0x10;
    asm{lea @0,hndaddr} *((int **)0x108)=hndaddr; asm{and #0xfaff,sr};
    tmCmd1=0; for(TimeUp=0;TimeUp==0;); tmCmd1=SWR+CPE+CLK+Div256+EvC;
    for(TimeUp=0;TimeUp==0;);tmCmd1&=~CPE;/* stop counter */
    l=((-tmCnt1)<<8)/(0xff&(~(tmSPr1&0xff)));
▶    asm{ @0 ADDQ.W #1,TimeUp } asm{rte}
}
```

A useful class *FreqIn* is shown below. Each second, the frequency of TIN1 is read by a periodic interrupt, and put in instance variable *value*. When the program sends an *Input* message, it gets *value*, the most current frequency that was measured. The *Init* method initializes the PI module (Section 5-1.6) and the TM as above.

```
struct FreqIn :direct
    { char error,flag; unsigned long value; void Init(long, unsigned); long Input(void);};

void FreqIn::Init(p,m) long p; unsigned m;{register int i,*hndlr;
    *(char *)0xffff001=0xe; *(long *)0xffff022=0x6500110; /* PI set to 1 sec. */
    asm{ lea @0, hndlr } *((int **)0x140)= hndlr; asm{move.l a4, saveA4}
    tmCmd1=0;tmCmd1=SWR+CPE+CLK+Div256+EvC;
    asm{ and #0xfdff,sr } return; /* enable interrupts */
▶    asm{@0 movem.l a4/d7,-(a7)} asm {move.l saveA4,a4}
    value=-tmCnt1 ;i=0xff&(~(tmSPr1&0xff));if(i>128)value=-tmCnt1;
    value=(value<<8) |i;flag=1;
    tmCmd1&=~SWR; tmCmd1|=SWR;
    asm{ movem.l (a7)+,a4/d7} asm {rte}
}
long FreqIn::Input() { return value;}
```

8-3.3 Period and Pulse Width Measurement

We now turn to the direct measurement of pulse width and period of a waveform. The TM measures pulse width using the pulse width function. The command word 4 is put in the Counter Mode field, SWR, TGT and CPE are enabled. The prescaler and counter should count the number of Tckl ticks while the TGATE1 signals is low. They do not decrement when TGATE1 is high. There is a feature of the TM in this mode (with mask set B of the silicon). The prescaler and timer begin decrementing as soon as the command register is written, rather than after the falling edge of TGATE1 after the command register is written in. Therefore we must make sure TGATE1 is high before we write in the command register. We gadfly on TGT until that input is low and then until that input is high. Then we initialize the command register, which begins to decrement the prescaler and counter when TGATE1 becomes low. We gadfly on ON which becomes clear when the timer is finished executing the pulse width mode, when the rising edge of TGATE1 appears. Then the (24-bit) period can be read from the prescaler and counter as in the event mode. If the prescaler and counter began decrementing when TGATE1 fell after the command register was initialized, the gadfly loops *while(!(tmSPr1&TGT)); while(tmSPr1 & TGT);*would not be necessary. Perhaps a future revision of the silicon will correct these "features" of the current version in mask set B. Also, we were unable to read period using interrupts in this version.

```
main() { register unsigned long n;
    tmCmd1=0; while(!(tmSPr1&TGT)); while(tmSPr1&TGT);
    tmCmd1=SWR+TGT+CPE+Div1+Pw; while(tmSPr1&ON);
    n=14-tmCnt1;
}
```

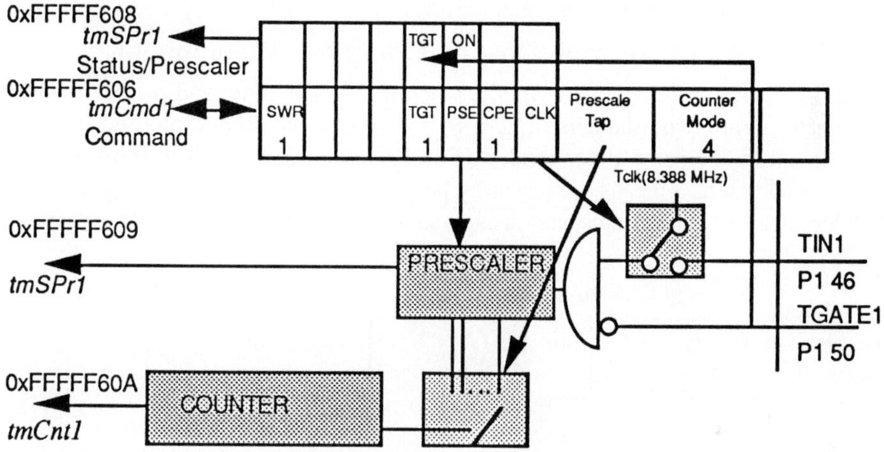

Figure 8-12. Period Timer.

The pulse width can be measured using an object of the class *PulseIn* shown below.

```
PulseIn:direct{ unsigned *pt; void Init(long,unsigned);long Input(void); }*P;
void PulseIn::Init(p,m) long p; unsigned m;{ pt=(unsigned*)0xffff600+((m-1)<<6);}
long PulseIn::Input() { register *status=(int*)&pt[4];
    pt[3]=0; while(!(*status&TGT)); while(*status&TGT);
    pt[3]=SWR+TGT+CPE+Div256+Pw; while(pt[4]&ON);
    return (((((-(long)pt[5])<<8)&0xffff00)/((~pt[4])&0xff))+18;
}
```

We would like to measure a period on a TGATE pin using the period measurement mode, whose procedure is like that of pulse width above but has value 5 put in the command register's Counter Mode field. However, that did not work for revision B silicon chips. Instead, we used the input capture mode discussed in the next section.

You may question why we might want to measure pulse width when we can already measure period, or vice versa. Usually the signal being measured is an analog signal, and this is converted to a digital signal by an analog comparator. Normally, the period is independent of the comparator's threshold, so it should be measured. The pulse width can depend on the comparator's threshold because the comparator outputs a high signal when the input is above the threshold; so the pulse width depends on the shape of the input and the threshold. The pulse width has to be measured if the waveform is not repetitive; in such a case, period could not be measured.

Initializing the SM is an illustration of the use of pulse width measurement. In Chapter 9, we will study the SM, which is used to communicate over a serial link. It requires a baud rate that matches the rate at which bits arrive on the serial link. A TM timer, configured to measure period, is suited to automatic determination of the bit rate and setting of the clock rate, using pulse width measurement. The sender should send the capital U character − ASCII code 0x55 − repetitively. Each time it is sent, it generates five pulses (or six pulses if the parity is set even). The pulse rate can be measured using the TM to establish the SM's baud rate.

8-3.4 Input Capture and Output Compare Mechanisms

The input capture output compare mode, when 0 is in the command register's counter mode field, permits simultaneous interrupt and frequency generation, and frequency measurement in the same timer module. See Figure 8-13. We will discuss the input capture mode first as a means of measuring period, then the output compare mode as yet and other means of generating square waves, and finally, we discuss the capture interrupt.

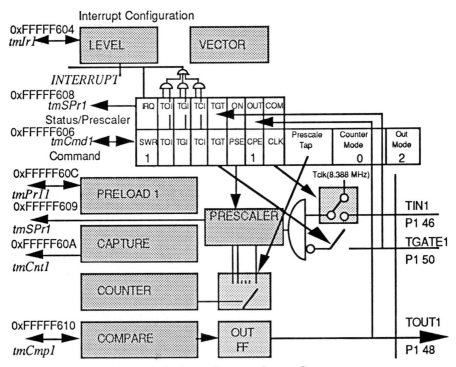

Figure 8-13. Input Capture, Output Compare.

The counter is read through a capture register in this mode only (actually it is always read through this register, being copied there from the counter every clock cycle). The count value is only copied into the capture register while the status register's gate interrupt flag TGI is F; thus the value is frozen in the capture register when the TGATE1 input rises until the TGI bit is cleared. In this mode, the counter continues to decrement whether or not the TGT command bit is set, which in all other modes would stop the counter.

The input capture mechanism can be used to measure the period of a signal on TGATE1 as shown in the procedure *Period*, by obtaining the time that it rises, the next time it rises, and then subtracting the second from the first (because the counter decrements).

```
long Period() { long n;
    tmCmd1=0;  tmCmd1=SWR+TGT+CPE+Div1+IcOc;
    tmSPr1=TGI; while(!(tmSPr1&TGI));n=tmCnt1;
    tmSPr1=TGI; while(!(tmSPr1&TGI));n-=tmCnt1; return n;
}
```

This technique can be implemented in an interrupt handler to evaluate the period every cycle, as shown in the class *PeriodIn*. The capture register value is saved in *value*, and the previous value of it in *lastValue*; Whenever the user wishes to get the most recent value of the period he or she merely subtracts the latter from the former.

```
struct PeriodIn:direct
    {unsigned value, lastValue, *pt; void Init(long,unsigned);long Input(void); };

void PeriodIn::Init(p,m) long p; unsigned m;{ register int *hndlr;
    lastValue=value=0; pt=(unsigned*)0xffffff600+((m-1)<<6);asm{move.l a4,saveA4}
    *pt=0x8d; pt[2]=0x640; pt[4]=TGI; pt[3]=SWR+TGI+TGT+CPE+Div1+IcOc; pt[8]=0;
    asm{ lea @0,hndlr } *((int **)0x100)= hndlr; asm{ and #0xfdff,sr } return;
asm{@0 movem.l a0/a4/d0/d1,-(a7)} asm {move.l saveA4,a4}
    lastValue=value; value=-pt[5]; pt[4]=TGI;
    asm{ movem.l (a7)+,a0/a4/d0/d1} asm {rte}
}

long PeriodIn::Input() { return value-lastValue;}
```

The output compare mechanism uses the compare register. If the command registers Output Mode is 2 *(Zero)*, when the compare register times out, the value of TOUT1 is L and when the compare register matches the count, the value of TOUT1 is H; this produces an asymmetric square wave with period *tmPr11*+1 and with high time *tmCmp1*. If the command registers Output Mode is 3 *(One)*, when the compare register times out, the value of TOUT1 is H and when the compare register matches the count, the value of TOUT1 is L; this produces an asymmetric square wave with period *tmPr11*+1 and with low time *tmCmp1*. This is used in the procedure *Wave* below to produce a waveform with period n+1 and 25% duty cycle (output H 25% of the time).

```
Wave(n) int n;{
    tmCmd2=0; tmCmd2=CPE+Div1+IcOc+One; tmPr11=n; tmCmp1=n>>2;
    tmCmd2+=SWR;
}
```

If the command register's Output Mode is 1 *(Tgl)* then the compare register is essentially ignored, and TOUT1 is a symmetric waveform with half-period *tmPr12*.

The output compare module can be used in the class *CompareOut* to generate an asymmetric square wave output from the high and low words of a long word, as in *SquWv* (Section 8-2.2). However, its advantage over the earlier technique is that the period can be fixed, in *tmPr11* and the duty cycle can be controlled simply by putting a value (< *tmPr11*) in *tmCmp1*.

struct CompareOut:direct

 *{unsigned value, lastValue, *pt; void Init(long,unsigned),Output(long); };*

void CompareOut::Init(p,m) long p; unsigned m;{ pt=(unsigned)0xffff600+((m-1)<<6);}*

void CompareOut::Output(n) long n; { unsigned m;

 m-=0x10001;pt[3]=0;pt[3]=CPE+IcOc+One;m=n>>16;pt[6]=n+m;pt[8]=m;pt[3]+=SWR;

}

Finally, we discuss the use of the compare interrupt and status bits COM and TCI. When the compare register matches the counter, the COM bit is set, but is cleared when the counter times out. The TCI status bit is set when the compare register matches the counter, and remains set until cleared by writing a T into it. If the TCI command bit is set, when the TCI status bit is set, and interrupt is generated. This interrupt can be used in any mode. It can be used with the TOI time out interrupt to provide two different timing interrupts from the same timer module, which are synchronized.

8-4 Conclusions

Frequency or phase analog signals are often generated naturally – by an AC tachometer, for instance – and may be used directly, in firing a TRIAC, for instance. Even when the signal is first an amplitude analog signal, conversion to frequency analog or phase analog signal simplifies the noise isolation and voltage level isolation between transducer and microcomputer. Moreover, several hardware and software techniques, including those that use a module like the TM, can be used to measure or generate frequency analog signals.

The TM is a very useful and attractive I/O device for measuring or generating frequency or phase analog signals. It is useful in generating square waves, pulses, and timing interrupts; it can measure events, frequency, period, and pulse width; and it can monitor period or pulse width to interrupt the computer if too long a value is noticed. It is very attractive because a single wire sends the signal to or from the TM. To the chip designer, it means that an I/O device can be put on a chip or inside a microcomputer chip without using a lot of pins. While counters take up a nontrivial amount of area on the chip, that area is comparatively cheap, while pins are in much shorter supply. Moreover, to the system designer, a single wire is easy to isolate with an optical isolator, to prevent the voltages of the system under test from getting to the microcomputer and the user, as well as to isolate noise generated in that system, to prevent it from getting into the microcomputer.

The TM was introduced to illustrate the discussion of the TM module. (There are counter/timers with quite different architectures, useful in different applications, but space limitations restrict what can be covered in one chapter.) The TM also illustrated how a single chip can be made more flexible when the devices in it are configured by setting the control word. This chapter prepares us for similar techniques in communication modules covered in Chapter 9 and display and secondary storage chips, covered in Chapter 10. You should now be familiar with the TM in general and with the TM in particular. Connecting their pins and writing software to initialize and use them should be well within your grasp.

Further information on the TM is available in the *MC68340 Integrated Processor User's Manual (MC68340UM/AD)*. As noted earlier, we have not attempted to duplicate the diagrams and discussions in that book because we assume you will refer to it while reading this book; and, because we present an alternative view of the subject, you can use either or both views.

Do You Know These Terms?

See the End of Chapter 1 for Instructions.

time out, square-wave, touch-tone signal, Johnson counter, asymmetric square wave, variable width single-shot, periodic interrupt, time delay interrupt, Strowger system, frequency, period, pulse width, input capture, output compare.

Communication Systems

The microcomputer has many uses in communication systems, and a communication system is often a significant part of a microcomputer. This chapter examines techniques for digital communication of computer data.

Attention is focused on a microcomputer's communication subsystem – the part that interfaces slower I/O devices like typewriters and printers to the microcomputer. This is often a universal asynchronous receiver transmitter (UART). Because of their popularity in this application, UARTs have been used for a variety of communications functions, including remote control and multiple computer intercommunications. However, their use is limited to communicating short (1-byte) messages at slow rates (less than 1000 bytes per second). The synchronous data link control (SDLC) is suitable for sending longer messages (about 1000 bytes) at faster rates (about 1,000,000 bits per second) – for sending data between computers or between computers and fast I/O devices. The IEEE-488 bus, for microcomputer control of instruments like digital voltmeters and frequency generators, and the SCSI bus, for communication to and from intelligent peripherals, send a byte at a time rather than a bit at a time.

The overall principles of communication systems, including the ideas of levels and protocols, are introduced in the first section. The signal transmission medium is discussed next, covering some typical problems and techniques communications engineers encounter in moving data. The UART and related devices that use the same communications mechanisms are fundamental to I/O interface design. So, we spend quite a bit of time on these devices, imparting basic information about their hardware and software. They will probably find use in most of your designs for communicating with teletypes or teletype-like terminals, keyboards, and CRTs, as well as for simple remote control. Finally, we look at the more complex communications interfaces used between large mainframe computers to control test and measurement equipment in the laboratory and to connect intelligent I/O.

Communications terminology is rather involved, with roots in the (comparatively ancient) telephone industry and in the computer industry, and some uniquely from digital communications. Communications design is almost a completely different discipline from microcomputer design. Moreover, one kind of system, such as one using UARTs, uses quite different terminology than that used to describe another, similar system, such as one using SDLC links. While it is important to be able to talk to communication system designers and learn their terminology, we are limited in what we can do in one short chapter. We will as much as possible use terminology associated with the so-called X.25 protocol, even for discussing UARTs, because we want to economize on the number of terms that we must introduce, and the X.25 protocol appears to be the most promising protocol likely to be used with minicomputers and microprocessors. However, you should be prepared to do some translating when you converse with a communications engineer.

On completing this chapter, you should have a working knowledge of UART communications links. You should be able to connect a UART, an M6850, or an M68681, to a microcomputer, and connect a UART or an M14469 to a remote control station so it can be controlled through the M6850 or similar chip. You should be able to use the M68332 Serial Communication Interface (SCI) or M68340 Serial Module (SM). You should understand the basic general strategies of communication systems, and the UART, SDLC, IEEE-488, and SCSI bus protocols in particular, knowing when and where they should be used.

9-1 Communications Principles

In looking at the overall picture, we will first consider the ideas of peer-to-peer interfaces, progressing from the lowest level to the higher level interfaces, examining the kinds of problems faced at each level.

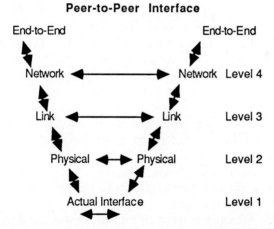

Figure 9-1. Peer-to-Peer Communication in Different Levels.

Data movement is *coordinated* in different senses at different *levels* of abstraction, and by different kinds of mechanisms. At each level, communication appears to take place between *peers* which are identifiable entities at that level; even though the communication is defined between these peers as if they did indeed communicate to each other, they actually communicate indirectly through peers at the next lower level. (See Figure 9-1.)

Consider this analogy. The president of company X wants to talk to the president of company Y. This is called *end-to-end* communication. The job is delegated to the president's secretary, who calls up the secretary of the other president. This is referred to as *network control*. The secretary doesn't try to yell to the other secretary but dials the other secretary on the telephone. The telephone is analogous to the *link control* level. But even the telephone "delegates" the communication process to the electronics and the electrical circuits that make the connection at the telephone exchange. This is the *physical control* level. End-to-end communication is done between user (high-level) programs. User programs send information to each other like the presidents in the analogy. Network control is done at the operating system level. Like the secretary, this software must know where the communications object is and how to reach this object. Link control is done by I/O interface software and is responsible for setting up and disconnecting the link so the message can be sent. Physical control actually moves the data. In the design of I/O systems, we are primarily concerned with link control and secondarily with physical control.

The peer-to-peer interfaces are defined without specifying the interface to the next lower level. This is done for the same reasons that computer architecture is separated from computer organization and realization, as we explained in Chapter 1. It permits the next lower level to be replaced by another version at that level without affecting the higher level. This is like one of the presidents getting a new secretary: The presidents can still talk to each other in the same way, even though communication at the next lower level may be substantially changed.

We now discuss some of the issues at each of the levels. At the lowest level, the main issue is the medium, and a secondary issue is the multiplexing of several channels on one link. The technique used to synchronize the transmission of bits may be partly in the physical interface level and partly in the link control level.

The *medium* that carries a bit of information is of great concern to the communications engineer. Most systems would probably use voltage level to distinguish between true and false signals. In other systems, mechanical motion carries information, or radio or light beams in free space or in optical fibers carry information. Even when the carrier is electric, the signal can be carried by current rather than voltage, or by presence or absence of a particular frequency component. The signal can be conveyed on two frequencies: A true is sent as one frequency while a false is sent as another frequency (*frequency shift keying*). More than one signal can be sent over the same medium. In *frequency multiplexing,* n messages are sent, each by the presence or absence of one of n different frequency components (or keying between n different pairs of frequencies). In *time multiplexing*, n messages can be sent, each one in a time slot every n*th* time slot. A frequency band or a time slot that carries a complete signal, enabling communication between two entities at the link control level, is called a *channel*. Each channel, considered by itself, may be *simplex* if data can move in one direction only, *half duplex* if data can move in either direction but only one direction at a time, or *full duplex* if data can move in both directions simultaneously.

Usually, a bit of information is sent on a channel over a time period, the *bit time period*, and this is the same time for each bit. The *baud rate* is the inverse of this bit time period (or the shortest period if different periods are used). The *bit rate*, in contrast, is the rate of transfer of information, as defined in information theory. For simplicity in this discussion, the bit rate is the number of user information bits sent per time unit, while the baud rate is the total number of bits – including user information, synchronization, and error-checking bits – per time unit.

In general, a clock is a regular occurrence of a pulse, or even of a code word, used to control the movement of bits. If such a (regular) clock appears in the channel in some direct way, the system is *synchronous*, otherwise it is *asynchronous*. In a synchronous system, the clock can be sent on a separate line, as the clock is sent inside a computer to synchronize the transmission of data. The clock can also be sent on the same wire as the data – every other bit being a clock pulse and the other bits being data – in the so-called *Manchester code*. Circuitry such as a phase-locked loop detects the clock and further circuitry uses this reconstructed clock to extract the data. Finally, in an asynchronous link, the clock can be generated by the receiver, in hopes that it matches the clock used by the sender.

Link control is concerned with how data are moved as bits, as groups of bits, and as complete messages that are sent by the next higher level peer-to-peer interface.

At the *bit level*, individual bits are transmitted; at the *frame level*, a group of bits called a frame or packet is transmitted; and at the *message level*, sequences of frames, called messages, are exchanged. Generally, at the frame level, means are provided for detection and correction of errors in the data being sent, since the communication channel is often noisy. Also, because the frame is sent as a single entity, it can have means for synchronization. A frame, then, is some data packaged or framed and sent as a unit under control of a communications hardware-software system. The end-to-end user often wishes to send more data – a sequence of frames – as a single unit of data. The user's unit of data are known as the message.

At each level, a *protocol* coordination mechanism is used. A protocol is a set of conventions that coordinates the transmission and receipt of bits, frames, and messages. Its primary functions in the link control level are the synchronization of messages and the detection or correction of errors. This term protocol suggests a strict code of etiquette and precedence countries agree to follow in diplomatic exchange, so the term aptly describes a communication mechanism whereby sender and receiver operate under some mutually acceptable assumptions but do not need to be managed by some greater authority like a central program. Extra bits are needed to maintain the protocol. Since these bits must be sent for a given data rate in bits per second, the baud rate must increase as more extra bits are sent. The protocol should keep efficiency high by using as few as possible of these extra bits. Note that a clock is a particularly simple protocol: a regularly occurring pulse or code word. An important special case, the *handshake protocol*, is an agreement whereby when information is sent to the receiver, it sends back an acknowledgment that the data are received either in good condition or has some error. Note, however, that a clock or a protocol applies to a level, so a given system can have a bit clock and two different protocols – a frame protocol and a message protocol.

The third level of peer-to-peer interface is the network level. It is concerned about relationships between a large community of computers and the requirements necessary so that they can communicate to each other without getting into trouble.

The *structure* of a communication system includes the physical interconnections among stations, as well as the flow of information. Usually modeled as a graph whose nodes are stations and whose links are communications paths, the structure may be a loop, tree graph, or a rectangular grid (or sophisticated graph like a banyan network or its homomorphic reduction).

A path taken by some data through several nodes is called *store and forward* if each node stores the data for a brief time, then transmits it to the next node as new data may be coming into that node; otherwise if data pass through intermediate nodes instantaneously (being delayed only by gate and line propagation), the path is called a *circuit* from telephone terminology. If such a path is half duplex, it is sometimes called a bus because it looks like a bus in a computer system.

Finally, the communication system is *governed* by different techniques. This aspect relates to the operating system of the system of computers, which indirectly controls the generation and transmission of data much as a government establishes policies that regulate trade between countries. A simple aspect of governance is whether the decision to transmit data are centralized or distributed. A system is *centralized* if a special station makes all decisions about which stations may transmit data; it is decentralized or *distributed* if each station determines whether to send data, based on information in its locale. A centralized system is often called a *master-slave* system, with the special station the master and the other stations its "slaves." Other aspects of governance concern the degree to which one station knows what another station is doing, or whether and how one station can share the computational load of another. These aspects of a system are very important, but are still the subject of considerable research and debate.

9-2 Signal Transmission

The signal is transmitted through wires or light pipes at the physical level. This section discusses the characteristics of three of the most important linkages. Voltage or current amplitude logical signals, discussed first, are used to interconnect terminals and computers that are close to each other. The digital signal can be sent by transmitting it at different frequencies for a true and for a false signal (frequency shift keying). This is discussed in the next subsection. Finally, the optical link provides an unprecedented capability to send data at very high rates. It will likely radically change our approach to communication systems, although, at the time of writing, it is still new and expensive. Some observations are offered on the optical link in the last subsection.

9-2.1 Voltage and Current Linkages

In this section, we discuss the line driver and line receiver pair, the 20-milliampere current loop, and the RS232 standard.

Standard high current TTL or LSTTL drivers can be used over relatively short distances, as the IEEE-488 standard uses them for a bus to instruments located in a laboratory. However, slight changes in the ground voltage reference or a volt or so of noise on the link can cause a lot of noise in such links. A *differential line* is a pair of wires in which the variable in positive logic is on one wire and in negative logic on the other wire. If one is high, the other is low. The receiver uses an analog comparator to determine which of the two wires has the higher voltage, and outputs a standard TTL signal appropriately. If a noise voltage is induced, both wires should pick up the same noise so the differential is not affected and the receiver gets the correct signal. Similarly, imperfect grounding and signal ringing affect the signal on both wires and their effect is cancelled by the voltage comparator. A number of driver and receiver integrated circuits are designed for differential lines, but some require voltages other than +5, which may not be used elsewhere in the system. An integrated circuit suitable for driving and receiving signals on a half duplex line, using a single 5-volt supply, is the SN75119, shown in Figure 9-2a. If driver enable DE (pin 7) is high, then the signal on IN (pin 1) is put on line LA (pin 3) and its complement is put on line LB (pin 2); otherwise the pins LA and LB appear to be (essentially) open circuits. If receiver enable RE (pin 5) is high, then the output OUT (pin 6) is low if the voltage on LA is less than that on LB, or high if the voltage on LA is greater than that on LB; if RE is low, OUT is (essentially) an open circuit. The *RS442 standard* (RS means recommended standard) uses basically this differential line, but a driver such as the Am26LS30 has means to control the slew rate of the output signal.

The 20-milliampere current loop is often used to interface to teletypes or teletype-like terminals. A pair of wires connects driver and receiver so as to implement an electrical loop through both. A true corresponds to about 20 milliamperes flowing through the loop, and a false corresponds to no current or to negative 20 milliamperes in the loop (for "neutral working" or "polar working" loops, respectively). A current, rather than a voltage, is used because it can be interrupted by a switch in a keyboard and can be sensed anywhere in the loop. A current is also used in older equipment because the 20-milliampere current loop was used to drive a solenoid, and a solenoid is better controlled by a current than a voltage to get faster rise times. The current is set at 20 milliamperes because the arc caused by this current will keep the switch contacts clean.

A 20-milliampere current loop has some problems. A loop consists of a current source in series with a switch to break the circuit, which in turn is in series with a sensor to sense the current. Whereas the switch and sensor are obviously in two different stations in the circuit, the current source can be in either station. A station with a current source is called *active*, while one without is *passive*. If two passive stations, one with a switch and the other with a sensor, are connected, nothing will be communicated. If two active stations are connected, the current sources might cancel each other or destroy each other. Therefore, one station must be active while the other is passive, and one must be a switch and the other must be a sensor. While this is all very straightforward, it is an invitation to trouble. Also, note that the voltage levels are undefined. Most 20-milliampere current loops work with voltages like +5 or -12 or both, which are available in most communication systems; but some, designed for long distance communication, utilize "telegraph hardware" with voltages upwards of 80 volts. Therefore, one does not connect two 20-milliampere current loop stations together without checking the voltage levels and capabilities. Finally, these circuits generate a fair amount of electrical noise which gets into other signals, especially lower level signals, and the switch in such a circuit generates noise that is often filtered by the sensor. This noise is at frequencies used by 1200-baud lines, so this filter can't be used in other places in a communication subsystem. The circuitry for a 20-milliampere current loop can be built with an opto-isolator, as shown in Figures 6-3a and 9-2b. If the current through the LED is about 20 milliamperes, the phototransistor appears to be a short-circuit; if the current is about 0 milliamperes, it is an open circuit and the output is high. The diode across the LED is there to prevent an incorrect current from destroying the LED.

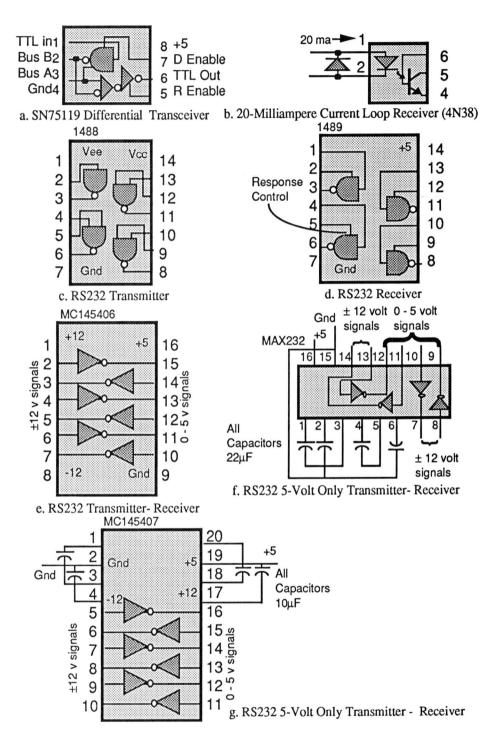

a. SN75119 Differential Transceiver

b. 20-Milliampere Current Loop Receiver (4N38)

c. RS232 Transmitter

d. RS232 Receiver

e. RS232 Transmitter- Receiver

f. RS232 5-Volt Only Transmitter- Receiver

g. RS232 5-Volt Only Transmitter - Receiver

Figure 9-2. Drivers and Receivers.

Table 9-1. RS232 Pin Connections for D25P and D25S Connectors.

Pin	Name	Function
1	Protective Ground	Connects machine or equipment frames together and to "earth"
2	Transmitted Data	Data sent from microcomputer to terminal
3	Receive Data	Data sent from terminal to microcomputer
4	Request to Send	(Full Duplex) enables transmission circuits (Half Duplex) puts link in transmit mode and disables receive circuitry
5	Clear to Send	Responds to Request to Send; when high, it indicates the transmission circuitry is working
6	Data Set Ready	(telephone links) The circuitry is not in test, talk, or dial modes of operation so it can be used to transmit and receive
7	Signal Ground	Common reference potential for all lines. Should be connected to "earth" at just one point, to be disconnected for testing
8	Data Carrier Detect	A good signal is being received
9	+P	+12 volts (for testing only)
10	-P	-12 volts (for testing only)
11		
		Used for more elaborate options
25		

An interface standard developed by the Electronic Industries Association (EIA) and other interested parties has evolved into the RS232-C (recommended standard 232, version C). A similar standard is available in Europe, developed by the Comite Consultatif Internationale de Telegraphie et Telephonie (CCITT), and is called the CCITT V.24 standard. These standards are supposed to be simple and effective, so that any driver conforming to it can be connected to any receiver conforming to it, covering the voltage levels used for the signals as well as the pin assignments and dimensions of the plugs. Basically, a false variable is represented by any voltage from +15 to +5 volts, and a true by any voltage from -5 to -15 volts (negative logic is used.) A number of specifications concerning driver and receiver currents and impedances can be met by simply using integrated circuit drivers and receivers that are designed for this interface – RS232 drivers and RS232 receivers. The MC1488 is a popular quad RS232 line driver, and the MC1489 is a popular receiver. (See Figures 9-2c and 9-2d.) The driver requires +12 volts on pin 14 and -12 volts on pin 1. Otherwise, it looks like a standard quad TTL NAND gate whose outputs are RS232 levels. The four receiver gates have a pin called response control (pins 2, 5, 9, and 12). Consider one of the gates, where pin 1 is the input and pin 3 is the output. Pin 2 can be left unconnected. It can be connected through a (33K) resistor to the negative supply voltage (pin 1) to raise the threshold voltage a bit. Or it can be connected through a capacitor to ground, thus filtering the incoming signal. This controls the behavior of that gate. The other gates can be similarly controlled. The MC145406 is a chip that combines three transmitter and three receiver gates in one chip (Figure 9-2e); and the MAX232 (Figure 9-2f) has two transmitters and two receivers, and a charge pump circuit that generates ±10 volts needed for the transmitter, from the 5-volt supply used by the microcomputer. (This marvelous circuit is just what is needed in many applications, but the currently available chips have a small problem: If the 5-volt supply turns on too fast, the charge pump fails to start; put a small – 10Ω – resistor in series with the 5-volt pin and put a large – 100µF – capacitor from that pin to ground.) Motorola also introduced the MC145407 (Figure 9-2f), a 5-volt only RS232 chip having a charge pump, like the MAX232, but with three input receivers and three output drivers, like the MC146406.

The RS232 interface standard also specifies the sockets and pin assignments. The DB25P is a 25-pin subminiature plug, and the DB25S is the corresponding socket – both of which conform to the standard. The pin assignments are shown in Table 9-1. For simple applications, only pins 2 (transmit data), 3 (receive data), and 7 (signal ground) need be connected; but a remote station may need to make pins 5 (clear to send), 6 (data set ready), and 8 (data carrier detect) 12 volts to indicate that the link is in working order, if these signals are tested by the microcomputer. These can be wired to -12 volts in a terminal when they are not carrying status signals back to the microcomputer.

9-2.2 Frequency Shift Keyed Links Using Modems

To send data over the telephone, a *modem* converts the signals to frequencies that can be transmitted in the audio frequency range. The most common modem, the Bell 103, permits full duplex transmission at 300 baud. Transmission is originated by one of the modems, referred to as the *originate modem,* and is sent to the other modem, referred to as the *answer modem.* The originate modem sends true (mark) signals as a 1270-Hertz sine wave and false (space) signals as a 1070-Hertz sine wave. Of course, the answer modem receives a true as a 1270-Hertz sine wave and a false as a 1070-Hertz sine wave. The answer modem sends a true (mark) as a 2225-Hertz sine wave and a false (space) as a 2025-Hertz sine wave. Note that the true signal is higher in frequency than the false signal, and the answer modem sends the higher pair of frequencies.

Some modems are originate only. They can only originate a call and can only send 1070- or 1270-Hertz signals and receive only 2025- or 2225-Hertz signals. Most inexpensive modems intended for use in terminals are originate only. The computer may have an answer-only modem, having the opposite characteristics. If you want to be able to send data between two computers, one of them has to be an originate modem. So an answer/originate modem might be used on a computer if it is expected to receive and also send calls. Whether the modem is originate-only, answer-only, or answer/originate, it is fully capable of sending and receiving data simultaneously in full duplex mode. The originate and answer modes determine only which pair of frequencies can be sent and received, and therefore whether the modem is capable of actually initiating the call.

Modems have filters to reject the signal they are sending and pass the signals they are receiving. Usually, bessel filters are used because the phase shift must be kept uniform for all components or the wave will become distorted. Sixth order and higher filters are common to pass the received and reject the transmitted signal and the noise, because the transmitted signal is usually quite a bit stronger than the received signal, and because reliability of the channel is greatly enhanced by filtering out most of the noise. The need for two filters substantially increases the cost of answer/originate modems. However, inexpensive chips incorporating these filters are now commonly available.

The module that connects the telephone line to the computer is called a *data coupler,* and there is one that connects to the originator of a call and another that connects to the answerer. The data coupler isolates the modem from the telephone line to prevent lightning from going to the modem, and to control the signal level, using an automatic gain control; but the data coupler does not convert the signal or filter it. The data coupler has three control/status signals. *Answer phone* ANS is a control command that has the same effect on the telephone line as when a person picks up the handset to start a call or answer the phone. *Switch hook* SH is a status signal that indicates that the telephone handset is on a hook, if you will, so it will receive and transmit signals to the modem. Switch hook may also be controlled by the microcomputer. Finally, *ring indicator* RI is a status signal that indicates the phone is ringing.

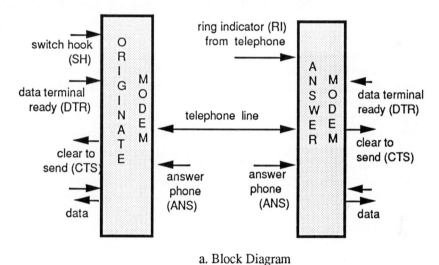

a. Block Diagram

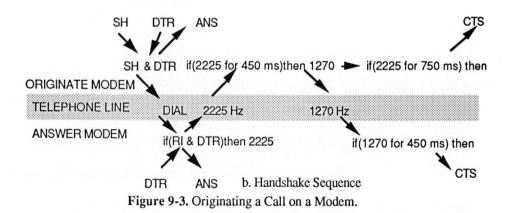

b. Handshake Sequence

Figure 9-3. Originating a Call on a Modem.

Aside from the fact that data are sent using frequency analog signals over a telephone, there is not much to say about the channel. However, the way an originate modem establishes a channel to an answer modem and the way the call is terminated is interesting. We now discuss how the Motorola M6860 modem originates and answers a call. Calling a modem from another, maintaining the connection, and terminating the connection involve handshaking signals *data terminal ready* DTR and *clear to send* CTS in both originate and answer modems. (See Figure 9-3a for a diagram showing these handshaking signals.) If a modem is connected to an RS232C line, as it often is, data terminal ready can be connected to request to send (pin 4) and clear to send can be connected to the clear to send (pin 5) or the data set ready (pin 6), whichever is used by the computer. Figure 9-3b shows the sequence of operations in the modems and on the telephone line, showing how a call is originated and answered by the Motorola M6860 modem chip.

The top line of Figure 9-3b shows the handshaking signals seen by the originator, the next line shows signals seen by the originator modem, the center line shows the telephone line signals, the next line shows signals seen by the answer modem, and the bottom line shows the handshaking signals seen by the answerer. As indicated, the originator asserts the switch hook signal. This might be asserted by putting the telephone handset on the modem hook or by an output device that asserts this signal. This causes the command ANS (answer phone) to become asserted, which normally enables the data coupler electronics to transmit signals. The telephone is now used to dial up the answerer. (Seventeen seconds are allowed for dialing up the answerer.) The answering modem receives a command RI (ring indicator) from the telephone, indicating the phone is ringing. It then asserts the ANS signal to answer the phone, enabling the data coupler to amplify the signal. The answerer puts a true signal, 2225 Hertz, on the line. The originator watches for that signal. When it is present for 450 milliseconds, the originator will send its true signal, a 1270-Hertz sine wave. The answerer is watching for this signal. When it is present for 450 milliseconds, the answerer asserts the CTS command and is able to begin sending data. The originator meanwhile asserts CTS after the 2225-Hertz signal has been present for 750 milliseconds. When both modems have asserted CTS, full duplex communication can be carried out.

Some answer modems will automatically terminate the call. To terminate the call, send more than 300 milliseconds of false (space) 1070 Hertz. This is called a *break* and is done by your terminal when you press the "break" key. The answer modem will then hang up the phone (negate ANS) and wait for another call. Other modems do not have this automatic space disconnect; they terminate the call whenever neither a high nor a low frequency is received in 17 seconds. This occurs when the telephone line goes dead or the other modem stops sending any signal. In such systems, the "break" key and low frequency sent when it is pressed can be used as an "attention" signal rather than a disconnect signal.

9-2.3 Optical Data Transmission

Transmission of data using light is no longer science fiction. A light transmitter, such as a LED or LASER, modulates the signal on the light. This is usually sent on a *light fiber* to a receiver, commonly a photodiode. Data can be sent at 20 megabaud or even higher – a gigabaud is feasible. The product of the data rate and the distance traveled is a constant for any given light fiber, however, so that data sent over long distances must be received and retransmitted every couple of miles.

Optical transmission will replace telephone lines in cities because one fiber can replace a few hundred pairs of copper wires. Bell Telephone can recover enough copper from under New York City to make that the largest copper mine in the world. Profits from the recovered copper may make installation of optical links quite attractive.

You may have noticed that some of the problems with I/O LSI chips are due to the fact that we are always short of pins. These problems will get worse as more and more logic can be put on the chip but the number of pins is not increased proportionally. Optical links between integrated circuits may someday replace most of an integrated circuit's pins and most of the printed circuit board's traces. Without the high capacity of optical links, we cannot satisfactorily get data into and out of those chips. We are currently studying this problem.

Optical links in communication systems are a bit of an embarrassment because of their unprecedented capacity. What can you do with a gigabaud line? (This is bottom-up design.) They clearly have use for communication between large computers and might be useful in microcomputer systems that are used to handling large amounts of data traffic in communication systems. The extraordinary capacity can be used to further distribute the components of a computer. The primary memory may be in another room. The organization of computing systems may be revolutionized.

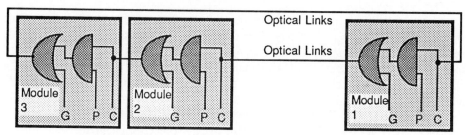

Figure 9-4. A GPC Linkage for Optical Communication.

While the technology is in its infancy, it is so important that we would like to mention a few of the exciting possibilities. One of these is called *ethernet*. The high-capacity electronic (or possibly optical) line is treated like a radio ether, and different transmitters send to different receivers at frequencies or time slices rather as ham radio operators do. We are studying the *general propagating communication* (GPC) link. (See Figure 9-4.) Each computer – or module or integrated circuit – has a generate (G) input for data, a propagate (P) for control, and an output named C. The P control is normally asserted to cause the data to propagate through the module, but can be negated to inhibit the data. By inhibiting the data at different modules, we cut the communication link into segments that act independently of each other. In each segment, the OR of the G inputs is sent leftward, or clockwise. The rightmost module can broadcast data to all modules to its left on the same segment, if all the other modules do not assert their G inputs. The leftmost module can collect the data from each of the G inputs in the same manner as a wire-OR bus collects data. Moreover, and this is very important, the segment can be made into a priority circuit, so that modules to the right in a segment have higher priority. If a module wants to compete for priority, it asserts the G signal. If the C signal is asserted, it means that some other module of higher priority is requesting a grant, so the module that receives such a signal should not be granted its request. The module that asserts G and receives a negated C is granted the request. Finally, perhaps you have recognized it, this is the carry circuit of a ripple adder. The optical link can be used to link parts of an adder together. (We refer to the connections as G, P, and C, and to this link as GPC, because these are the names of the signals on a carry-lookahead generator, which is a faster implementation of the ripple carry logic of Figure 9-4.)

The GPC is intuitively a good communication linkage because the P signal ANDed into the link can be used to cut the link at any desired point, while the G signal can be used to insert data just as is done on a wire-OR bus. Moreover, the ability to implement priority logic right on the communication linkage has profound effects. It is possible to establish the right to use a resource, including some time on the communication link, using a simple and efficient protocol, because the priority link does most of the work in hardware. By comparison, protocols to use the ethernet require more effort. The ability to break up the GPC into separate segments to get more data moved, and especially the ability to establish priorities, makes the GPC link attractive for optical communication systems.

9-3 UART Link Protocol

By far the most common technique for transmitting data are that used by the simple *Universal Asynchronous Receiver Transmitter* (UART) protocol discussed in this section. Software generation of UART signals, discussed first, is quite simple and helps to show how they are sent. The UART chip is then discussed. The UART-like chips, a special remote control chip, the M14469, the M6850 – designed for the 6800 family and the M68681 – designed for the 68000 family – are covered next. The M68340 Serial Module (SM), similar to the M68681, and the M68332 Serial Communication Interface (SCI) are discussed last. We also discuss object-oriented software for the M6850, SM and SCI to introduce serial communication interrupt handlers.

9-3.1 UART Transmission and Reception by Software

As noted earlier, the Universal Asynchronous Receiver Transmitter (UART) is a module (integrated circuit) that supports a frame protocol to send up to eight bit frames (characters). We call this the *UART protocol*. However, the UART protocol can be supported entirely under software control, without the use of a UART chip or its equivalent. A study of this software is not only a good exercise in hardware-software tradeoffs, but is also an easy way to teach the protocol; the software approach also is a practical way to implement communication in a minimum cost microcomputer. However, we do warn the reader that most communication is done with UART chips or their equivalent, and low-cost microprocessors such as the M68332 and M68340 already have a built-in UART on the microprocessor chip itself.

The UART frame format is shown in Figure 9-5. (The UART protocol is contained within the UART frame format.) When a frame is not being sent, the signal is high.

When a signal is to be sent, a *start bit*, a low, is sent for one bit time. The frame, from 5 to 8 bits long, is then sent 1 bit per bit time, least significant bit first. A parity bit may then be sent and may be generated so that the parity of the whole frame is always even (or always odd). To generate even parity, if the frame itself had an even number of ones already, a low parity bit is sent, otherwise a high bit is sent. Finally, one or more *stop bits* are sent. A stop bit is high and is indistinguishable from the high signal that is sent when no frame is being transmitted. In other words, if the frame has n stop bits (n = 1, 1 1/2, or 2) this means the next frame must wait that long after the last frame bit or parity bit of the previous message has been sent before it can begin sending its start bit. However, it can wait longer than that.

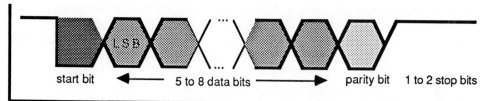

start bit ◄────── 5 to 8 data bits ──────► parity bit   1 to 2 stop bits

Figure 9-5. Frame Format for UART Signals.

In addition to the preceding format, the protocol has some rules for sampling data and for error correction. A clock, used in the receiver, is 16 times the bit rate, and a counter, incremented each clock time, is used to sample the incoming data. (The same clock is used in the transmitter to generate the outgoing data.) The counter is started when the input signal falls, at the beginning of a frame. After eight clock periods, presumably in the middle of the start bit, the input is sampled. It should be low. If it is high, the falling edge that started the counter must be due to some noise pulse, so the receiver returns to examine the input for the leading edge of a start bit. If this test passes, the input is sampled after every 16 clock periods, presumably in the middle of each bit time. The data bits sampled are reassembled in parallel. The parity bit, if one is used, is then sampled and checked. Then the stop bit(s) are checked.

The following are definitions of error conditions. If the parity bit is supposed to be even, but a frame with odd parity is received, a *parity error* is indicated. This indicates that one of the frame bits or the parity bit was changed due to noise. Note that two errors will make the parity appear correct – but two wrongs don't make a right. Parity detection can't detect all errors. Even so, most errors are single-bit errors, so most errors are detected. If a stop bit is expected, but a low signal is received, the frame has a *framing error*. This usually indicates that the receiver is using the wrong clock rate, either because the user selected the wrong rate or because the receiver oscillator is out of calibration. However, this condition can arise if the transmitter is faulty, sending frames before the stop bits have been timed out, or if more than one transmitter is on a link and one sends before the other's stop bits are completely sent. Finally, most UART devices use a buffer to store the incoming word, so the computer can pick up this word at leisure rather than at the precise time that it has been shifted in. This technique, called double buffering, was used in the parallel ports of the M68230 as discussed in Section 4-3.3. If the buffer is not read before another frame arrives needing to fill the same buffer, the first frame is destroyed; this error condition is called an *overrun error*. It usually indicates that the computer is not paying attention to the UART receiver, since if it were, it would empty the buffer before the next message arrives.

The UART communication technique is based on the following principle. If the frame is short enough, a receiver clock can be quite a bit out of synchronization with the transmitter clock and still sample the data somewhere within the bit time when the data are correct. For example, if a frame has 10 bits and the counter is reset at the leading edge of the frame's start bit, the receiver clock could be five percent faster or five percent slower than the transmitter clock and still, without error, pick up all the bits up to the last bit of the frame. It will sample the first bit five percent early or five percent late, the second ten percent, the third fifteen percent, and the last fifty percent. This means the clock does not have to be sent with the data. The receiver can generate a clock to within five percent of the transmitter clock without much difficulty. However, this technique would not work for long frames, because the accumulated error due to incorrectly matching the clocks of the transmitter and receiver would eventually cause a bit to be missampled. To prevent this, the clocks would have to be matched too precisely. Other techniques become more economical for longer frames.

A C procedure *SUart* to generate a signal compatible with the UART protocol is quite simple. The procedure is shown below and its description follows it.

```
SUart(c) char c;{
     int i,parity; char *out=0x10000;
     *out=0; delay(N); parity = 0;
     for(i=8;i>0;i- - ) { *out = c; parity ^= c; c = c >> 1; delay(N); }
     *out=parity; delay(N); *out=1; delay(N); delay(N);
}
```

In the above procedure we use the following delay procedure, whose argument is the time delay. Let N be the parameter that delays the time for a bit.

```
delay (t) int t;{ for (;t>0;t- -);}
```

The start bit is output from the least significant bit of the byte at 0x10000, and a delay subroutine is called to delay one bit time. Then the bits are written to the output port so the least significant bit is sent out the serial channel, and parity is updated with the exclusive-OR of parity and data so the least significant bit is the parity of the data sent. This is repeated for 8 data bits. Then the parity bit is output, and the stop bit is output. Appropriate delays are inserted between each bit that is sent serially.

A C procedure *RUart* to receive a UART frame is also quite simple. Again, the subroutine is shown below and its description follows it.

```
char RUart(){
     int i,parity,c; char *in=0x10000;
     do {while(*in & 0x80); delay(N/2);} while (*in & 0x80);
     parity = c = 0; delay(N);
     for(i=8;i>0;i- - ) { c| = (*in) & 0x80; parity ^ = c; c = c >> 1; delay(N); }
     parity ^= ((*in) & 0x80); if (parity & 0x80) { /* report parity error */;}
     delay(N); if (!((*in) & 0x80)) { /* report framing error */;}
     delay(N); if (!((*in) & 0x80)) { /* report framing error */;}
     return(c)
}
```

The while loop waits for the input to go low, and the do while loop confirms that it is still low after a half a bit time (using the procedure delay to delay a half bit time). Then, after a delay of a bit time, the least significant bit is picked up, and is exclusive-ORed with the computed parity bit. For eight steps, another bit is picked up, the parity is updated, and a bit delay is wasted. Then the transmitted parity bit is combined with the computed parity bit to determine if a parity error occurred, and the stop bits are checked.

Both the preceding C procedures are simple enough to follow. They can be done in software without much penalty, because the microprocessor is usually doing nothing while frames are being input or output. In an equivalent hardware alternative, essentially the same algorithms are executed inside the UART chip or an equivalent chip like the M6850. The hardware alternative is especially valuable where the microcomputer can do something else as the hardware tends to transmitting and receiving the frames, or when it might be sending a frame at the same time it might be receiving another frame (in a full duplex link or in a ring of simplex links). In other cases, the advantages of the hardware and software approaches are about equal: the availability of cheap, simple UART chips favors the hardware approach, while the simplicity of the program favors the software approach. The best design must be picked with care and depends very much on the application's characteristics.

9-3.2 The UART

The UART chip is designed to transmit and/or receive signals that comply with the UART protocol (by definition). This protocol allows several variations (in baud rate, parity bit, and stop bit selection). The particular variation is selected by strapping different pins on the chip to high or to low. The UART can be used inside a microcomputer to communicate with a teletype or a typewriter, which was its original use, or with the typewriter's electronic equivalent, such as a CRT display. It can also be used in other remote stations in security systems, stereo systems controlled from a microcomputer, and so on. Several integrated circuit companies make UARTs, which are all very similar. We will study one that has a single-supply voltage and a self-contained oscillator to generate the clock for the UART, the Intersil IM6403. (See Figure 9-6.)

The UART contains a transmitter and a receiver that run independently, for the most part, but share a common control that selects the baud rate and other variations for both transmitter and receiver. We discuss the common control first, then the transmitter, and then the receiver. The baud rate is selected by the crystal connected to pins 17 and 40 and by the divide control DIV on pin 2. If DIV is high, the oscillator frequency is divided by 16; if low, by 2^{11}. If the crystal is a cheap TV crystal (3.5795 MHz) and DIV is low, the baud rate is close to 110, which is commonly used for teletypes. When master reset MR, on pin 21, is high, it resets the chip; it is normally grounded. The other control bits are input on pins 39 to 35 and are stored in a latch inside the chip. The latch stores the inputs when pin 34 is high. This pin can be held high to defeat the storage mechanism, so the pin levels control the chip directly. Pin 36 selects the number of stop bits: low selects 1 stop bit, high selects 2 (except for an anomaly of little interest). If pin 35 is high, no parity bit is generated or checked, otherwise pin 39 selects even parity if high, odd if low. Pins 37 and 38 select the number of data bits per frame; the number is five plus the binary number on these pins. The user generally determines the values needed on these pins from the protocol he or she is using, and connects them to high or low. However, these inputs can be tied to the data bus of a computer, and pin 34 can be asserted to load the control latch to effect an output device. When the computer executes the reset handler, it can then set the control values under software control.

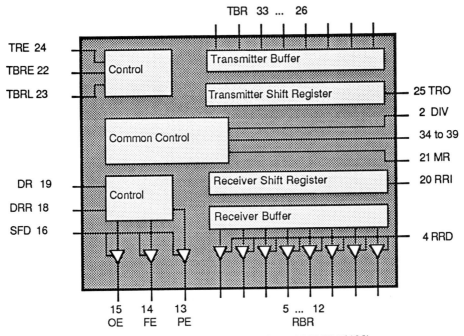

Figure 9-6. Block Diagram of a UART (IM6403).

The operation of the transmitter and receiver is compactly and simply explained in the data sheets of the 6403 and is paraphrased here. The transmitter has a buffer register, which is loaded from the signals on pins 33 (msb) to 26 (lsb) when transmitter buffer register load TBRL (pin 23) rises. If n < 8 bits are sent, the rightmost n bits on these pins are sent. Normally, these pins are tied to the data bus to make the buffer look like an output port, and TBRL is asserted when the port is to be loaded. When this buffer is empty and can be loaded, transmitter buffer register empty TBRE (pin 22) is high; when full, it is low. (SFD, pin 16, must be low to read out TBRE.) The computer may check this pin to determine if it is safe to load the buffer register. It behaves as a BUSY bit in the classical I/O mechanism. The data in the buffer are automatically loaded into the transmitter shift register to be sent out as transmitter register output TRO (pin 25) with associated start, parity, and stop bits as selected by the control inputs. As long as the shift register is shifting out part of a frame, transmitter register empty TRE (pin 24) is low. Figure 9-7 shows a typical transmission, in which two frames are sent out. The second word is put into the buffer even as the first frame is being shifted out in this double buffered system. It is automatically loaded into the shift register as soon as the first frame has been sent.

The receiver shifts data into a receiver shift register. When a frame has been shifted in, the data are put in the receiver buffer. If fewer than 8 bits are transmitted in a frame,

Chapter 9 – Communication Systems

the data are right justified. This data can be read from pins 5 to 12, when receive register disable RRD (pin 4) is asserted low. Normally these pins are attached to a data bus, and RRD is used to enable the tristate drivers when the read buffer register is to be read as an input port. If RRD is strapped low, then the data in the read buffer are continuously available on pins 5 to 12. When the read buffer contains valid data, the data ready DR signal (pin 19) is high, and the error indicators are set. (DR can only be read when SFD on pin 16 is high.) The DR signal is an indication that the receiver is DONE, in the classical I/O mechanism, and requests the program to read the data from the receive buffer and read the error indicators if appropriate. The error indicators are reloaded after each frame is received, so they always indicate the status of the last frame that was received. The error indicators, TBRE, and DR can be read from pins 15 to 13 and 22 and 19 when SFD (pin 16) is asserted low, and indicate an overrun error, a framing error, and a parity error, that the transmit buffer is empty, and that the receive buffer is full, respectively, if high. The error indicators and buffer status indicators can be read as another input port by connecting pins 22 and 19, and 15 to 13 to the data bus, and asserting SFD when this port is selected; or, if SFD is strapped low, the error and buffer status indicators can be read directly from those pins. When the data are read, the user is expected to reset the DR indicator by asserting data ready reset DRR (pin 18) high. If this is not done, when the next frame arrives and is loaded into the buffer register, an overrun error is indicated.

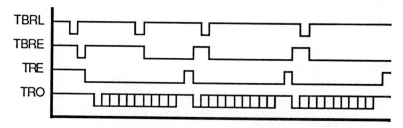

Figure 9-7. Transmitter Signals.

The UART can be used in a microcomputer system as follows. The control bits (pins 35 to 39) and the transmit buffer inputs (pins 26 to 33) can be inputs, and the buffer status and error indicators (pins 22 and 19, and 15 to 13) and receive data buffer outputs (pins 5 to 12) can be outputs. All the inputs and outputs can be attached to the data bus. TBRL, SBS, SFD, and RRD (pins 23, 36, 16, and 4) are connected to an address decoder so that the program can write in the control port or transmit buffer register, or read from the error indicators or the read buffer register. The TBRE signal (pin 22) is used as a BUSY bit for the transmitter; and the DR signal (pin 19) is used as a DONE bit for the receiver. When the UART is used in a gadfly technique, which can be extended to interrupt or even DMA techniques, the program initializes the UART by writing the appropriate control bits into the control port. To send data using the gadfly approach, the program checks to see if TBRE is high and waits for it to go high if it is not. When it is high, the program can load data into the transmitter buffer. Loading data into the buffer will automatically cause the data to be sent out. If the program is expecting data from the receiver in the gadfly technique, it waits for DR to become high. When it is, the program reads data from the receive buffer register and asserts DRR to tell the UART that the buffer is now empty. This makes DR low until the next frame arrives.

The UART can be used without a computer in a remote station that is implemented with hardware. Control bits can be strapped high or low, and CRL (pin 34) can be strapped high to constantly load these values into the control port. Data to be collected can be put on pins 33 to 27. Whenever the hardware wants to send the data, it asserts TBRL (pin 23) low for a short time, and the data get sent. The hardware can examine TBRE (pin 22) to be sure that the transmitter buffer is empty before loading it; but if the timing works out so that the buffer will always be empty there is no need to check this value. It is pretty easy to send data in that case. Data, input serially, are made available and are stable on pins 5 to 12. Each time a new frame is completely shifted in, the data are transferred in parallel into the buffer. RRD (pin 4) would be strapped low to constantly output this data in a hardware system. When DR becomes high, new data have arrived, which might signal the hardware to do something with the data. The hardware should then assert DRR high to clear DR. (DR can feed a delay into DRR to reset itself.) The buffer status and error indicators can be constantly output if SFD (pin 16) is strapped low, and the outputs can feed LEDs, for instance, to indicate an error. However, in a simple system when the hardware does not have to do anything special with the data except output them, it can ignore DR and ignore resetting it via asserting DRR. In this case, the receiver is very simple to use in a remote station.

9-3.3 The M14469

The M14469 is a "UART" specially designed for a remote station. We give a short description here and a full description in the Motorola data sheet for the chip. A CMOS chip, it can use an unregulated supply whose voltage can vary between 4.5 and 18 volts, and it uses very little current. It features a self-contained oscillator and an address comparator that permits the selection of a station when multiple stations are on the same link. A UART protocol is supported, in which the frame has even parity and 1 stop bit. The baud rate is determined by the crystal (or ceramic resonator) connected between pins 1 and 2, or by an external oscillator that can drive pin 1. The crystal (oscillator) frequency is divided by 64 to set the baud rate. A diagram of the M14469 is shown in Figure 9-8.

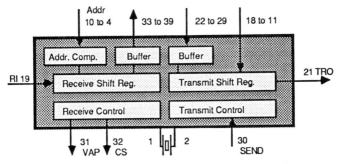

Figure 9-8. The M14469.

The receiver is a standard UART receiver with an address comparator. A 7-bit address is sent as the low-order 7 bits of an 8-bit word, the most significant bit being true. The station has a 7-bit address, which is selected by strapping pins 10 to 4 low if a 0 bit is needed, or leaving them open if a 1 bit is needed in the address (these pins have an internal pull-up resistor to make them high if they are not connected). If the incoming address is equal to the station address, the valid address pulse VAP (pin 31) is made high momentarily, and the station is said to be *selected*. A 7-bit data word is sent as the low-order 7 bits of a word, the most significant bit being false. A station that has been selected will put any data word into its receive buffer when the word is completely shifted in, and make a command strobe CS (pin 32) high momentarily just after this happens. Error status is not available on a pin, but if a parity or framing error is detected, an address will not select a station, data will not be transferred to the receive buffer, and VAP or CS will not be pulsed.

Note that a typical message will consist of a frame with an address (most significant bit true) followed by zero or more frames with data (most significant bit false). A single address frame can be used to trigger a remote station to do something, by asserting VAP in it when the address is recognized; or a message with an address frame followed by a number of data frames will cause the data to be stored in the receive buffer each time a data frame arrives, and will pulse CS to command something to be done with the data.

The transmitter is a conventional UART transmitter modified to send out 16 bits of data in two consecutive frames if SEND is made high when VAL or CS is asserted (or within eight data bit time units after that) and if it is not currently transmitting a pair of frames. Sixteen bits are sent from the signals on pins 11 to 18 and 29 to 22 by transferring the data on pins 11 to 18 directly into the transmitter shift register, and simultaneously transferring the data on pins 29 to 22 into the transmitter buffer. The data in the shift register are sent out (pin 11 data first) in the first UART frame, and the data in the buffer (pin 29 data first) are sent out immediately after that in the next frame. The data appear on the transmitter output TRO (pin 21) in negative logic. This output is in negative logic so that it can drive a transistor, which inverts the signal to power the link out of the station.

The chip is designed for full and half duplex, with some special provisions for the latter application. In full duplex applications, a master (likely an M6850 in a microcomputer) sends to all the slave stations (several M14469s) on one line (M6850 TxD output to RI input of each slave), while all the slave stations send to the master on another line (slave TRO output into transistor base, transistor collectors in each slave tied together in a wire AND bus line to RxD input of M6850), so that the master can be sending to a slave at the same time that a slave is sending to the master. In this case, VAP can be connected to SEND to send back the two frames as quickly as possible after a station is selected. The master should take care it does not send two address frames, one right after another, so that two slaves will send overlapping frames back. In the half duplex mode, a single bus line is used between master and all slaves so that the master can send data to the slaves or the slaves can send data to the master, but not at the same time. TxD and RxD in the master, and RI and the transistor collector in each slave, would be connected to this single line. In this application, SEND should be connected to CS so the slave that was selected will wait for an address frame and a data frame to be sent over the line from the master, before the slave returns its two frames. The master should wait for both frames to be returned before it sends more data on the same line.

To ensure the data have been received, handshaking is often used; and to permit handshaking, the M14469 is designed to prevent difficulties in the half duplex mode. The slave can be implemented so that the first frame it returns has its own station address. When the master sends a message, it can wait for the slave to respond with a frame having the address of the slave. If that frame is returned, the message must have been received without error and the slave must be active (as opposed to being shut off). This is a simple handshake protocol. However, if it is used in the half duplex mode, we don't want the return frame to be received by the same slave and for it to recognize its own address again to trigger itself nor do we want the return message stored in the receive buffer. Therefore, this chip is designed so that it deselects the receiver as soon as it begins transmitting a frame. And the frame being transmitted should be a data frame (most significant bit false) to prevent the address decoder from matching it, even though the frame really contains an address. This provision makes handshaking in a half duplex mode possible. However, the chip is designed that way, and these peculiarities are also apparent in the full duplex mode.

In the next section, we present a short program that shows how the M6850 can communicate to several M14469s over a full duplex line. The object of the program is to select station 3, send a word of data to it, and receive a word of data from it. An M14469 is configured as station 3 by wiring pins 10 to 4 and pins 17 to 11 to represent the number 3. The data to be sent back from this station are connected to pins 23 to 29. Handshaking is used, so the transmission on the link will look as follows: The master will send the slave's address, then 7 bits of data to the slave on the line from master to slave, then the slave will return its address and 7 bits of data on the other line.

9-3.4 The M6850

The M6850 is a "UART" that has been specially tailored to be used as an external chip for the 6800 microcomputer. It is called an *asynchronous communications interface adapter* (ACIA) by Motorola. As noted before, we don't use terms like PIA and ACIA because they are less specific than part numbers like M6821 or M6850, but we don't object to your using these terms. This section covers the M6850's highlights. The M6850 can be used with the Motorola M68332 microcomputer. It can also be used in other microcomputers, and other microcomputer manufacturers have special chips like the M6850 for their systems, which can also be used on the M68332.

A complete description is available in the M6850 data sheet. The M6850 is different from a UART like the IM6403 in the following ways. To save pins, a bit of the transmitter buffer input, a bit of the receive buffer output, a bit of the control port, and a bit of the buffer/error status port output are internally connected and then connected to a single pin on this chip. Thus, only eight pins are used to connect to the data bus. An external clock is needed to set the baud rate, and the transmitter can have a different clock than the receiver. Also, because this chip is designed to connect to a modem, discussed in the next section, it has three pins to control the modem so that the program can control it. Finally, it has a status port with interrupt request logic so that the M68332 can easily examine it in its interrupt handler. (A diagram of the M6850 is shown in Figure 9-9, assuming this chip is at locations 0x10000 and 0x10001.)

An M68B50 is connected to the M68332 system in the standard way. (See Figure 9-9 for the pin connections.) Pins 15 to 22 are connected to the data bus D[7 TO 0], pin 7 to IRQ6 if LEVEL 6 interrupts are used, pin 14 to the E clock, and pin 13 to the RW line. To select the chip, pins 8, 9, and 10 must be high, low, and high, respectively.

Pins 8 and 10 can be wired to +5 and pin 7 to a chip select line such as CS6. Pin 11 is normally connected to address bit 0, so it can select control/status if this bit is false or a data buffer if true. An external clock, such as a square wave produced by the TPU, is connected to pins 3 and 4 to set the baud rate for the receiver and transmitter, respectively. While these two clocks can be different, they are usually the same. Finally, pins 5, 23, and 24 are available to connect to a modem, as discussed in Section 10-2.2. If not used, pins 23 and 24 should be grounded to prevent false interrupts. Chip select CS6 and CS7 are initialized to select the chip and recognize level 6 autovector interrupts:

pinAssign(cs6,byte); pinAssign(cs7,byte); baseAssign(6,0x10000,k2);
baseAssign(7,0xffffff,k2); optionAssign(6,read+upper+as,synchronous,user+super,0);
optionAssign(7,read+upper+ds fast,0,6+avec);

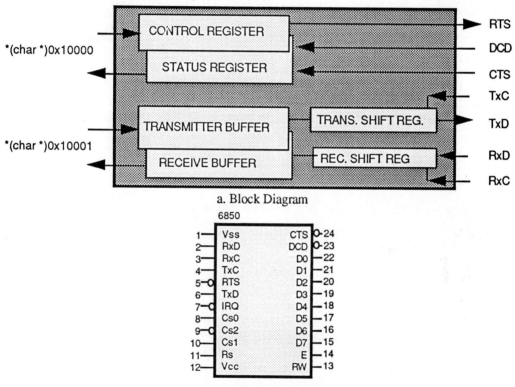

a. Block Diagram

b. Pinouts
Figure 9-9. The M6850.

The transmitter, with its buffer and shift register, and the receiver and its shift register operate just as in the UART. They are addressed in the same location because the transmit buffer is write-only, while the receive buffer is read-only. Once the control port is set up, a word is transmitted simply by writing it in location 0x10001, and an incoming word is picked up by reading it from location 0x10001.

The control port, written into at location 0x10000, sets up the baud rate (it is also set by the frequency of the external clocks), the frame format, and the interrupt mechanism. The transmitter interrupt control also controls a signal called request to send

RTS on an output pin, which can be used to control a modem. (These control values are shown in Table 9-2a.) The user determines the bit pattern from the protocol and sets this port up in a ritual. An example will be given shortly that uses this table.

Table 9-2. M6850 Control and Status Bits.

Bits	Function
1,0	Clock frequency
0 0	divide by 1
0 1	divide by 16
1 0	divide by 64
1 1	master reset

Bits	Function	RTS
6,5	Trans. int	RTS
0 0	disable	low
0 1	enable	low
1 0	disable	high
1 1	disable	low *

* Transmit data output is low

Bits	Function
4,3,2	Frame format
0 0 0	7 bits, even parity, 2 stop bits
0 0 1	7 data, odd parity, 2 stop bits
0 1 0	7 data, even parity, 1 stop bit
0 1 1	7 data, odd parity, 1 stop bit
1 0 0	8 data, 2 stop bits
1 0 1	8 data, 1 stop bit
1 1 0	8 data, even parity, 1 stop bit
1 1 1	8 data, odd parity, 1 stop bit

Bits	Function
7	receiver interrupt
0	disable
1	enable

a. Control Port

IRQ	PE	OVRN	FE	CTS	DCD	TDRE	RDRF

b. Status Port

The frame format is controlled by bits 4 to 2 in an obvious way. Note that the UART has more combinations, but the most popular combinations of data, parity, and stop bits are available in the M6850. The clock frequency is divided to get the baud rate under control of bits 1 and 0. If division is by 1, the baud rate is the same as the frequency of the clock input, which is set by an external oscillator. Each clock cycle shifts out 1 bit of data. This is useful for high baud rates, such as would be used to communicate between two microcomputers that are a short distance apart. Normally, division is by 16, as discussed in earlier sections. However, division by 64 is useful if a slow baud rate is desired and if the external clock would have to be divided by 4 in another (counter) chip to get the desired frequency. The last code for this field is the master reset. Unfortunately, this chip does not have a reset pin, unlike most of the other I/O chips in the 6800 family. Before it can be used, the M6850 must be reset by putting 11 into bits 1 and 0. The other bits can be 0. So the first thing to do with this chip is store 0x03 into the control port. This is usually done just before the control port is set up with the bits that determine the modes of operation. Be warned, moreover, that if this is not done, the chip will appear to be bad. The author spent a frustrating week and several chips finding this out. The transmitter is controlled by bits 6 and 5. If interrupts are enabled, each time the transmit buffer is empty an interrupt will be generated so the software can refill it. Interrupts should be enabled and an appropriate device handler should be used when a sequence of words is to be output as to a typewriter, if the microcomputer can do some useful work while the M6850 tends to transmitting the message. Interrupts should be disabled when the microcomputer uses the gadfly

Chapter 9 – Communication Systems

technique. The RTS signal is often used to control a modem. This (negative logic) signal is set by bits 6 and 5. If these control bits are 11, the transmitter outputs a low signal. This is used to test and to control a modem. Finally, bit 7 controls the receiver interrupt. If true, an interrupt is requested whenever the receive buffer is full (data are available) – so the software can move the word – or whenever there is an error in the receiver such as parity, framing, or overrun, or a problem with the modem indicated by a low signal on the data carrier detect DCD pin. Bit 7 should be true if interrupts are used to service the reader and false if the gadfly technique is used.

Suppose that a simple program is to be written to test the M6850's transmitter, using an oscilloscope to view the output. The word 0xC5 has an instructive pattern, so it will be continuously transmitted. The transmitter clock input is 1600 Hz, and the data are to be sent at 100 baud, with 8 data bits, even parity, and 1 stop bit. Neither the transmitter nor the receiver should generate interrupts, and RTS should be low. Consulting Table 9-2, the control bits should be as follows: bit 7 should be 0 to disable the receiver interrupt; bits 6 and 5 should be 00 to disable the transmitter interrupt and set RTS low; bits 4, 3, and 2 should be 110 to select 8 data bits, even parity, and 1 stop bit; bits 1 and 0 should be 01 to divide the clock rate, 1600 Hz, by 16, so they can deliver bits at 100 baud. The control word should be 0x19. The following program initializes the M6850 by first resetting it, then putting in the control word. Then a constant, 0xC5, is put into 0x10001 in a program loop so that every time the buffer is empty it is immediately refilled with the constant. (If the buffer is already full, writing another word into it does not cause an error but does cause it to lose the word that was in it. Normally the program checks a status bit to be sure this buffer is empty before filling it. But in this case, there is no harm in constantly writing the same word into it.) The output of the shift register would appear on an oscilloscope, as shown in Figure 9-10.

```
main(){
    *((char *)0x10000)=0x03; /*11 to bits 1,0 of M6850 cntrl to reset it*/
    *((char *)0x10000)=0x19; /* M6850 cntrl.: 8 data, even par., 1 stop */
    while (1) *((char *)0x10001)=0xC5; /*data to M6850 transmitter buffer reg.*/
}
```

The M6850's status bits can be read from location 0x10000. (See Table 9-2b.) RDRF (bit 0) is true if the receive buffer is full. TDRE (bit 1) is true if the transmit buffer is empty. Bits 2 and 3 indicate the signals from a modem, DCD and CTS, that normally indicate the data carrier is present and the channel is clear to send. FE, OVRN, and PE, (bits 4, 5, and 6) are the framing, overrun, and parity error indicators. IRQ (bit 7) is a composite interrupt request bit, which is true if the interrupt enable, control bit 7, is true and any one or several of the status bits 0, 2, 4, 5, or 6 are true or if control bits 6 and 5 are 01 and status bit 1 is true.

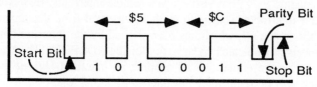

Figure 9-10. Output of a Test Program.

At the end of the previous section, we indicated that we would use an M6850 to communicate to the M14469s. The C program *Remote* sets up an M6850 to send 8 bits of data, even parity, and one stop bit per frame, and to divide the clock by 64. This is accomplished by putting 3 and then 0x1A into the control port. The address (0x83) is sent first, then the data. Then the receiver is checked for an incoming frame. Meanwhile, a counter is decremented to check if there is no response; the counter is initialized to a suitably large number to wait for any reasonable response. The contents of this frame is compared with the address that was sent out. If too much time elapses before the frame returns, or if it contains the wrong address, the program exits to report the error. Otherwise, the data picked up from the M6850 that was sent in the next frame after the address are left in D0, and this routine is left.

```
int Remote(c,acia) char c,int *acia; { int i,parity;
    *acia = 3; *acia = 0x1a; *(acia+1) = 0x83;
    while((*acia & 2)==0); *(acia+1) = c; i=33000;
    while((*acia & 1)==0) if((i - -) = = 0) {/* report error */};
    if(*(acia+1) != 0x83) {/* report error */};
    while((*acia & 1)==0); return(*(acia+1));
}
```

We now study an interrupt-based class *ACIA* for the M6850. Following sections have several similar classes, so we will create a general serial class *Serial*, of which *ACIA* is a subclass (*Serial* is an *abstract class*; it has no objects but only subclasses).

The class *Serial* has two queues, *QI* for input and *QO* for output, and corresponding pointers and sizes. The *Init* method initializes both queues. The *Input* method pops a character from the queue *QI*, which has been pushed by the interrupt handler when a character was received (indicated by assertion of the RDRF bit). The *Output* method pushes a character to the queue *QO*, which will be popped by the interrupt handler when there is room in the transmit data register (indicated by assertion of the TDRE bit).

```
struct Serial:IoDevice
    {Queue *QI,*QO; long Input(void); void Init(long, unsigned),Output(long);};
void Serial::Init(p,m) long p; unsigned m;{    inherited::Init(p,m); asm{or #0x70,sr}
    (QI=blessA(sizeof(Queue),Queue))->InitQ(10);(QO=blessA(sizeof(Queue),Queue))->InitQ(10);
}
long Serial::Input() { while(QI->Qlen==0); return QI->Pull(); }
void Serial::Output(d) long d; {while(QO->Qlen==QO->Qsize); QO->Push(d); }
```

The class *ACIA* is a subclass of *Serial*. Its *Init* method initializes both queues by sending an inherited *Init* message to its superclass, and then resets the ACIA as in the previous procedure *main*, but also enables receive interrupts. However, it does not enable transmitter interrupts. The *Input* method, inherited from the superclass, pops a character from the queue *QI*, which has been pushed by the interrupt handler when a character was received (indicated by assertion of the RDRF bit). The *Output* method pushes a character to the queue *QO* by sending an inherited *Output* message to its superclass, which will be popped by the interrupt handler when there is room in the transmit data register (indicated by assertion of the TDRE bit). However, since transmit interrupts are not initially enabled, to cause an interrupt with TDRE asserted to cause a character to be popped, the transmit interrupt must be enabled. This is done in *ACIA's Output* method only if *QO* had been empty (*SizeO* is 0 and becomes 1), and the transmitter is enabled after the character has been pushed onto the output queue. In the interrupt handler, if an item is popped from *QO*, making it empty (*SizeO* becomes 0), the transmit interrupt is disabled. Then transmit interrupts only occur when they are needed, when *QO* is not empty; otherwise, they do not occur to waste processor time.

struct ACIA: Serial { void Init(long, unsigned),Output(long),Terminate(void); };

*void ACIA::Init(p,m) long p; unsigned m;{ register char i; register int *hndlr;*
  *inherited::Init(p,m); *(char*)chip=0x03; *(char*)chip=0x99; i=*((char*)chip+1);*
  *asm{ move.l a4,saveA4} asm{lea @0,hndlr} *(int **)0x78=hndlr; asm{and #0xfdff,sr} return;*

▷ *asm{@0 movem.l d0-d1/d7/a0-a2/a4,-(a7) } asm{ movea.l saveA4,a4}*
  if ((i=(char*)chip) & 0x70) error |=(i>>4)&7;*
  if(i & 1) {QI->Push(((char*)chip+1)); error |= QI->Error()<<1;}*
  if((i & 2)&&(QO>Qlen)){
  * *((char*)chip+1)=QO->Pull(); /* pop a byte, put in output register */*
  * if(QO->Qlen==0)*(char*)chip=0x99; /* disable trans. interrupt */*
  }
  asm{movem.l (a7)+,d0-d1/d7/a0-a2/a4 } asm{ rte}

}

void ACIA::Output(d) long d;
  *{inherited::Output(d); if(QO->Qlen==1) *(char*)chip=0xb9; /* en. trns int if Q size was 0 */ }*

void ACIA::Terminate(){ while(QO->Qlen);(char*)chip=0; /* disable all interrupts */ }*

The *Input* method's queue's gadfly loop *while (Qlen);* could be better implemented in a multi-thread (Section 5-1.6) or multi-task (Section 5-3.3) environment by having an instance variable *Thread *sleepT;* in the *ACIA*, putting the thread or process to sleep indefinitely (*(sleepT = curThread) -> sleepTime = 0xffffffff;)* , and letting the interrupt handler wake it up when a word has been received and has been pushed on the input queue: (*sleepT -> sleepTime = 0;)* (See the Centronix printer object in Section 5-2.1). Similarly, the *Output* method's queue's gadfly loop *while (Qlen==Qsize);* could be better implemented in a multi-thread or multi-task environment by putting the thread or process to sleep indefinitely, letting the transmit interrupt handler awaken it when the handler has popped a word from the queue to make room.

9-3.5 The M68681 DUART

The *Dual Asynchronous Receiver Transmitter (DUART)* M68681, whose pin connections are shown in Figure 9-11a, is an I/O chip that includes two serial communication channels A and B, where channel A is shown in Figure 9-11b, as well as a parallel device and counter/timer subsystem of limited power, which are not discussed in this text. This chip will be used in Chapter 11 to show how device drivers are written. The communication channel is a bit more general than the M6850 ACIA, having its own clock generation submodule. We now discuss the pins, port bits, and an example of initialization of input and of output using this chip.

The data bus D[7 to 0], port selects RS[4 to 1], CLK, RW, DTACK, and RESET are connected to the M68332 or M68340 as described previously (e.g., Section 4-3.3 for the M68230). IRQ can be connected to one or more IrqX lines to request an interrupt, and an M68340 IackX can be connected to use external vectored interrupts. A 6-bit input device IP[5 to 0] can be used for parallel input, and an 8-bit output device OP[7 to 0] can be used for output, but some of the pins are used for other signals (e.g., receive clock, clear to send, and so on) connected to the communication channels. A crystal may be connected between X1 and X2; 3.686-MHz is used to get the baud rates discussed soon but the readily available 3.59-MHz crystal is suitable for projects, giving only a 2.6% error in the baud rates, well within the tolerance of the UART protocol. Alternatively, a clock can be applied to the X1 pin to get the transmit and receive clocks. Channel A has an input RXDA and output TXDA; and channel B, RXDB and TXDB for serial data.

In the port organization shown in Figure 9-11b, the registers in the area with the lighter background are shared between the channels, while those with the darker background from 0x10000 to 0x10003 are for channel A only; a similar set of registers from 0x10008 to 0x1000b are used for channel B only. There are also registers for the counter/timer and the parallel input and output ports, not shown in this figure. Data to be output are written into the data A port, and input data are read from the data A port. The receiver input is triple-buffered; up to three words can be held inside the chip while a fourth word is being shifted in, without loss of data. The baud rate is selected by the clock A port and some of the transmit and receive rates are specified by the SLS bit of the auxiliary control port. Clock A[7 to 4] determines the receive clock and A[3 to 0] determines the transmit clock frequencies. If A[7 to 4] and A[3 to 0] are 0xb, the serial data are transmitted at 9600 baud, regardless of SLS. A command is given by writing a byte in the command port; bits 6 to 4 reset the channel controller in different ways (0 does nothing, 1 resets the mode A pointer as discussed next, 2 resets the receiver, 3 resets the transmitter, 4 resets the error status), bits 3 and 2 control the transmitter, and bits 1 and 0 control the receiver (0 does nothing, 1 enables and 2 disables the transmitter or receiver). To just enable the transmitter, bits 6 to 4 and bits 3 and 2 are F to do nothing, and bits 1 and 0 are T, so the byte 0x01 is written into the control port. Note that it is possible to simultaneously reset the mode A pointer, enable the transmitter, and enable the receiver by putting 0x15 into the command port.

The control values are written into the mode A port, but the first byte written there or read from there just after a mode A pointer reset command is given is the top register (RRTS, and so on) and the later bytes read or written are the bottom register (LOOPBACK and so on). The top register has receiver RTS control (RRTS), interrupt select (IRQC), and error control (ERRC) bits, which should be 0 for operation analogous to the M6850. Parity is selected by the next three bits – 4 chooses no parity, and the number of data bits in a frame is selected by the last two bits – 3 selects 8 data bits. The lower register has LOOPBACK, which is used for looping the data through the receiver and transmitter in different ways and should be 0 for simple use; transmitter RTS control (TRTS); and clear to send control (CTSC), which should be 0 for simple operation of the channel. The last four bits select the number of stop bits, and should be 0xf for two stop bits. To select 8 data bits, no parity bits and two stop bits, we give the mode A pointer reset command and write 0x23 and then 0x0f to the mode A port.

The status A port has bits to indicate that a break is received (RBK), and a framing error (FE), a parity error (PE), or an overrun error (OE) has been detected. The transmitter has two status bits: one to indicate that the transmit buffer is totally empty (TE) and the other to indicate the transmit buffer has at least one free location so the transmitter is ready (TR). Similarly, the receiver has a receive buffer full (RF) and a receiver ready (RR) status bit. The interrupt status and interrupt mask registers can generate interrupts for the beginning or ending of a break (BKA), receiver buffer full (RFA) and transmitter ready (TRA). An interrupt vector port can be used for externally vectored interrupts.

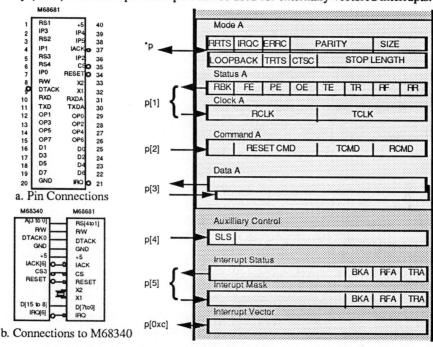

a. Pin Connections

b. Connections to M68340

c. Channel A Ports

Figure 9-11. The M68681 DUART.

The *#define* statements given below are in a file SM.h, which can be used to simplify programming of the M68681, as well as the M68340 SM discussed later. We define some values for initialization of the mode registers. For *mode register 1*:

```
#define rxRts 0x80        #define fifoStatus 0x40        #define blockError 0x20
enum{evenP,oddP=4,lowP=8,hiP=0xc,noP=0x10,dataP=0x18,addrP=0x1c};
enum{fiveBits,sixBits,sevenBits,eightBits};
```

For *mode register 2*:

```
enum{normal,echo=0x40,localLoop=0x80,remoteLoop=0xc0};
#define txRts 0x20        #define txCts 0x10        #define stop2 0xf
```

For the *baud rate register*:

```
enum{b50,b110,b134,b200,b300,b600,b1200,b1050,b2400,b4800,b7200,b9600,b38k
    ,b78k,sClk16,sClk};
```

For the *command register*:

```
enum{ resetP=0x10,resetR=0x20,resetT=0x30,resetE=0x40,resetB=0x50,startB=0x60,
    sTopB=0x70, astRts=0x80,ngtRts=0x90}; /* some are for the M68340 SM */
enum{enable=1,disable};        #define transmt 2        #define recevr 0
```

For the *status register:*

```
#define rBreak 0x80        #define fE 0x40           #define pE 0x20
#define oE 0x10            #define txEmpty 8         #define txRdy 4
#define fFull 2            #define rxRdy 1           #define chnlB 4
```

For the *interrupt status register:*

```
#define itxEmpty 8         #define ibrDlt 4          define irxRdy 2
#define itxRdy 1           #define ichnlB 4
```

Initialization of channel A for gadfly synchronization and the frame structure discussed above is accomplished by writing the baud rate in the clock A port, issuing the reset mode A to reset the receiver and transmitter, error status, and then the mode register pointer, then setting the frame structure in the mode port and enabling the transmitter and receiver in the command A port. We then repeatedly send the byte 0x55 and then receive it, using gadfly synchronization. This procedure *main* is:

```
main(){ register char i,*p;
    p[1]=(b9600<<4)+b9600; /*set baud rate*/
    p[2]=resetR+(disable<<recevr); p[2]=resetT+(disable<<transmt);
    p[2]=resetE; p[2]= resetP; /*reset all parts of the chip*/
    *p=noP+eightBits; *p=normal+stop2; /* set frame structure */
    p[2]=(enable<<transmt)+(enable<<recevr); /*enable transmitter and receiver */
    while(1) { while(!(p[1]&txRdy)); p[3]=0x55; while(!(p[1]&rxRdy)); i=p[3];} /*out-in*/
}
```

A interrupt-based class *Duart* discussed below is a subclass of *Serial* described in the previous subsection, and has two objects *D1* and *D2* for Duart channels A and B. Following *main* above, we initialize the command register, but registers that are common to both serial channels are initialized using the pointer *p*, while those that are different for channel A and channel B use the value *chip* as a pointer, which is initialized using the *inherited::Init(p+(m<<3),0);* message. The interrupt handler in *Init()* polls by sending messages to *Handler()* for each channel's device handler: *if((D1&&D1->Handler()) || (D2&&D2->Handler()));* as described in Section 5-1.4. If the object is initialized (its pointer is non-zero), the *Handler* method is executed to see if that channel requested an interrupt (verified using precomputed instance variable *myInt*); if it did not, it returns 0 to poll the other initialized channel. Also since we enable or disable transmitter interrupts by setting or clearing interrupt mask register bits (using precomputed instance variable pattern *trnsMsk*), but the chip's register is write-only, we save a copy of it in *IregValue* and modify and then output it; also since two different classes can access it, it is a global, rather than an object instance, variable.

```
struct Duart : Serial {
    char trnsMsk,myInt,*Ireg;
    void Init(long, unsigned),Output(long),Terminate(void); int Handler(void);
}*D1,*D2;
char IregValue;
```

void Duart::Init(p,m) long p; unsigned m;{ /* p is base address, m is 0 or 1 (channel)*/
   register int i; register int *hndlr;
   inherited::Init(p+(m<<3),0); Ireg=(char*)p+5; *((char*)chip+1)=(b9600<<4)+b9600;
   ((char)chip+2)=resetR+(disable<<recevr); *((char*)chip+2)=resetT+(disable<<transmt);
   ((char)chip+2)=resetE; *((char*)chip+2)= resetP; /*reset all parts of the chip*/
   (char)chip=noP+eightBits; *(char*)chip=normal+stop2; /* set frame structure */
   myInt=itxRdy|irxRdy; trnsMsk=itxRdy; if(m==0) {IregValue |=irxRdy; }
   else {IregValue |=irxRdy<<4; trnsMsk<<=4; myInt<<=4;}
   *Ireg = IregValue; *((char*)chip+2)=(enable<<transmt)+(enable<<recevr);
   p]0xc]=0x40; asm{lea @0,hndlr} *(int **)0x100=hndlr; asm{and #0xfdff,sr} return;

   ▶ *asm{@0 movem.l d0-d1/d7/a0-a2/a4/a5,-(a7)}*
       if((D1&&D1->Handler()) || (D2&&D2->Handler()));
       asm{movem.l (a7)+,d0-d1/d7/a0-a2/a4/a5 } asm{ rte}

}

   void Duart::Handler(){ int i;
       if ((i=(*Ireg& myInt))==0) return 0;
       if(i & (irxRdy | (irxRdy<<4))) {
           error |= ((*((char*)(chip+1))>>4)&0xf) | QI->Error();
           QI->Push(*((char*)chip+3));
       }
       if((i & (itxRdy | (itxRdy<<4))) && QO->Qlen) { *((char*)chip+3)=QO->Pull();
                                        if(QO-
>Qlen==0){*Ireg=(IregValue &=~trnsMsk);myInt&=~trnsMsk;}
       }
      return 1;
   }
   void Duart::Output(d) long d;
   inherited::Output(d); if(QO->Qlen==1){*Ireg = (IregValue|=trnsMsk);myInt|=trnsMsk;}}
   void Duart::Terminate()
      {while(QO->Qlen);*((char*)chip+2)=(disable<<transmt)+(disable<<recevr); }

9-3.6 The M68340 Serial Module

The two-channel *Serial Module (SM)* of the M68340 is that microcontroller's UART device; it is almost identical to the M68681 DUART, except that the interrupt vector is moved to be near the module configuration vector as is standard in M683xx devices, and MR2A and MR2B are put at higher addresses rather than being hidden behind MR1A and MR1B, and the M68681 timer and some I/O pins are not implemented. See Figure 9-12.

    The #*define* statements given below are in the file SM.h which was used for the M68681 in the previous section. The 16-bit 683xx-style registers are defined in 8-bit halves because registers in the serial module can only be read or written as bytes. The following 8-bit registers are separate for both channels; they are shown on the left for channel A and on the right for channel B. We also use the #*define* statements given in the last section for the fields in the SM registers, since they are the same as those of the M68681.

```
#define sMcrh *((int*)0xffff700)        #define sMcrl *((int*)0xffff701)
#define sIcrh *((int*)0xffff704)        #define sIcrl *((int*)0xffff705)
#define sMr1a *((char*)0xffff710)       #define sMr1b *((char*)0xffff718)
#define sMr2a *((char*)0xffff720)       #define sMr2b *((char*)0xffff721)
#define sSra *((char*)0xffff711)        #define sSrb *((char*)0xffff719)
#define sCsa *((char*)0xffff711)        #define sCsb *((char*)0xffff719)
#define sCra *((char*)0xffff712)        #define sCrb *((char*)0xffff71a)
#define sIpcr *((char*)0xffff714)       #define sAcr *((char*)0xffff714)
#define sIr *((char*)0xffff715)         #define sIp *((char*)0xffff71d)
#define sOpc *((char*)0xffff71d)        #define sOpst *((char*)0xffff71e)
#define sOpcl *((char*)0xffff71f)
```

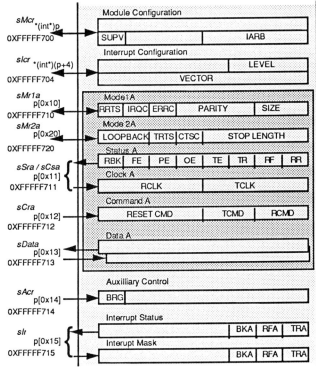

Figure 9-12. The M68340 Serial Module Channel A.

We illustrate the use of these constants to initialize and use channel A's transmitter and receiver, which are externally tied together so TXDA is wired to RXDA; any character sent from the transmitter is immediately received by the receiver for the same channel A. (This can be connected internally by changing *normal* to *localLoop*.)

```
main(){ register char i;
    sCra=resetR+(disable<<recevr);sCra=resetT+(disable<<transmt);sCra=resetE;
    sMr1a=noP+eightBits;sMr2a=normal+stop2;sCsa=(b9600<<4)+b9600;sAcr=0;
    sCra=(enable<<transmt)+(enable<<recevr);
    while(1) {while(!(sSra&txRdy));sData=0x55; while(!(sSrb&rxRdy)); i=sDatb;}
}
```

The initialization ritual is essentially identical to DUART's ritual described in the previous subsection, but with changes suggested at the beginning of this subsection.

A class *SerialModule* inputs and outputs serial data through a channel, A or B, of the SM. As we did in the class *ACIA* we have two queues. As in *Duart* we use global variable *IregValue* and instance variable *trnsMsk*. This *Init* method follows the *Duart Init* method, but it first initializes the interrupt registers as in any 683xx module, except that we cannot write 16-bit words in any SM register, as in *sIcr1=0x640;* so we write *sIcr1h=6; sIcr1l=0x40;* Then we follow the initialization shown in the procedure *main* above, or in *Duart*'s *Init* method.

```
struct SerialModule:Serial { char myInt,trnsMsk;
    void Init(long, unsigned), Output(long), Terminate(void); int Handler(void);
}*S1,*S2;

char IregValue;

void SerialModule::Init(p,m) long p; unsigned m;{ register int i; register int *hndlr;
    inherited::Init(0xffffff710+(m<<3),0); sMcr1l=0x8d; sIcr1h=6;sIcr1l=0x40;
    *((char*)chip+2)=resetR+(disable<<recevr); *((char*)chip+2)=resetT+(disable<<transmt);
    *((char*)chip+2)=resetE; *(char*)chip=noP+eightBits;
    myInt=itxRdy|irxRdy;trnsMsk=itxRdy; if(m==0) {IregValue |=irxRdy; }
    else {IregValue |=irxRdy<<4; trnsMsk<<=4; myInt<<=4;}
    sIr = IregValue; *((char*)chip+1)=(b9600<<4)+b9600; sAcr=0;
    *((char*)chip+2)=(enable<<transmt)+(enable<<recevr);
    asm{lea @0,hndlr}*(int **)0x100=hndlr; asm{and #0xfdff,sr} return;
    asm{@0 movem.l d0-d1/d7/a0-a2/a3/a4,-(a7) }
    if((S1&&S1->Handler()) || (S2 && S2->Handler()));
    asm{movem.l (a7)+,d0-d1/d7/a0-a2/a3/a4 } asm{ rte}
}

int SerialModule::Handler(){ int i;
    if ((i=(sIr & myInt))==0) return 0;
    if(i & (irxRdy | (irxRdy<<4)))
        {error |= ((*((char*)(chip+1))>>4)&0xf ) | QI->Error(); QI->Push(*((char*)chip+3)); }
    if((i & (itxRdy | (itxRdy<<4))) && QO->Qlen)
        {*((char*)chip+3)=QO->Pull(); if(QO->Qlen==0 ) sIr=(IregValue&=~trnsMsk);}
    return 1;
}

void SerialModule::Output(d) long d;
    {inherited::Output(d); if(QO->Qlen==1) sIr=(IregValue |=trnsMsk); }

void SerialModule::Terminate()
    {while(QO->Qlen); *((char*)chip+2)=(disable<<transmt)+(disable<<recevr); }
```

9-3.7 The M68332 Serial Communication Interface

The *Serial Communication Interface (SCI)* of the M68332, is part of its QSPI module that is able to move serial data asynchronously using an extension of the UART protocol, as the SM is in the M68340. We discuss the pins, port bits, and an example of initialization of input and of output using this chip.

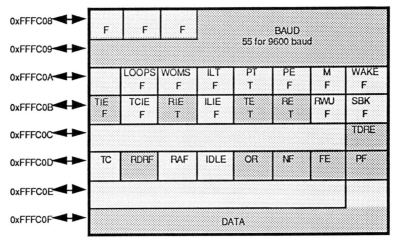

Figure 9-13. The M68332 Serial Communications Subsytem.

The SCI, a sub-module of the QSM, shares QSM's interrupt registers with the QSPI. The Config field IARB and VECTOR register are the same for the QSPI and SCI, however, the SCI interrupt vector is the value of VECTOR, which must be even, and the QSPI is the value plus 1. IF VECTOR is 0x40, the SCI interrupt address is 0x100 while the QSPI interrupt address is 0x104.

The commonly used SCI registers and fields are shown in Figure 9-13 in darker gray. Values to be used in the example below are shown in each field. The BAUD register sets the baud rate, from a half megabaud to 64 baud. A value of 55 sets the baud rate to 9600 baud. The control register TIE field enables transmitter interrupts when there is room in the transmit data register DATA (which is write-only), and RIE enables receiver interrupts when there is data in the receive data register DATA (which is read-only). The control register TE field enables the transmitter, and RE enables the receiver. These must be asserted to run the respective parts of the SCI, and that also configures the pins for SCI use rather than for parallel port D use. The status register TDRE field indicates there is room in the transmit data register, and RDRF indicates there is data in the receive data register DATA. The status register OR field indicates an overrun error, the NF field indicates noise has occurred, FE field indicates a framing error, and PF field indicates an overrun error has occurred in the receiver. These error bits are cleared when the status register and then the data register are read.

We illustrate a class *SCI* which is a subclass of *Serial*. It is similar to the *ACIA*, *Duart*, and *SerialModule* classes. The *Init* method initializes two queues, by calling its inherited *Init* method, and sets up the standard M68332 interrupt and the SCI control registers.

struct SCI: Serial { void Init(long, unsigned), Output(long),Terminate(void); };

void SCI::Init(p,m) long p; unsigned m;{ register int i; register int *hndlr;
    inherited::Init(0xfffc08,m); asm{ move.l a4,saveA4}
    *((int *)0xfffc00)=0xd; *((int *)0xfffc04)=0x640; /* QSM interrupt registers */
    *(int *)chip=55 /*9600 baud*/; *(int *)(chip+2)=0x2c; /* enable Xmt, Rcv, Rcv Int */
    asm{lea @0,hndlr}*(int **)0x100=hndlr; asm{and #0xfcff,sr} return;

Chapter 9 – Communication Systems

```
▶  asm{@0 movem.l d0-d1/d7/a0-a2/a4,-(a7) } asm{ movea.l saveA4,a4}
   if ((i=*((int *)((char*)chip+4))) & 0xf) error  |=i&0xf;
   if(i & 0x40) {QI->Push(*((char*)chip+7)); error  |= QI->Error()<<3;}
   if((i & 0x100) && QO->Qlen)
     { *((char*)chip+7)=QO->Pull(); if(QO->Qlen==0 ) *(chip+3)&=~0x80; }
   asm{movem.l (a7)+,d0-d1/d7/a0-a2/a4 } asm{ rte}
}
```

void SCI::Output(d) long d;
  *{inherited::Output(d); if(QO->Qlen==0) *((char*)chip+3) |=0x80;}*

void SCI::Terminate(){ while(QO->Qlen);((char*)chip+3)=0; /* disable all interrupts */ }*

The SCI has many additional features. Asserting control register's SBK sends a break (low signal). The LOOPS bit connects the transmitter output to the receive input to test the SCI; we set it to verify that the example above worked. WOMS enables open-drain transmitter output, so many of them can feed the same wire-OR line. An idle detect feature permits the SCI to determine if such a line is idle or is in use; the control register's ILT bit determines which of two types of idle line detection will be used; ILIE, whether an idle line will cause an interrupt, and IDLE indicates that the line is idle. The control register's PT, PE, and M bits determine what kind of structure a frame will have, allowing up to 9 bits of data, and allowing even or odd parity. The most significant data bit can be used as an address mark, as in the 14469; RWU enables wakeup to occur, and WAKE determines if an idle line or an address mark wakes up the SCI. Alternate transmit status TC indicates completion of transmission, and TCIE enables that to cause an interrupt, and RAF indicates if the receiver is active (i.e. receiving something).

9-4 Other Protocols

Besides the UART protocol, the two most important protocols are the synchronous bit-oriented protocols that include the SDLC, HDLC, and ADCCP, the X-25, the IEEE-488 bus protocol, and the Smart Computer System Interface (SCSI) protocol.

These are important protocols. We fully expect that many if not most of your interfaces will be designed around these protocols. If you are designing an I/O device to be used with a large mainframe computer, you will probably have to interface to it using a synchronous bit-oriented protocol. If you are designing a laboratory instrument, you will probably interface to a minicomputer using the IEEE-488 protocol, so the minicomputer can remotely control your instrument. Motorola has two integrated circuits: the M6854 for the synchronous bit-oriented protocol and the M68488 for the IEEE-488 bus protocol.

These are complex protocols. The chips are correspondingly complex. The M6854 has four control registers – 32 control bits – to be initialized in a ritual to configure the device. It has two status registers – 16 bits – to be analyzed in an interrupt handler. The M68488 has six command/address/polling registers with a lot of rituals to control the bus, and seven status/address/polling registers to analyze. While a full discussion of these chips and the communications protocols is not in the scope of this book on I/O interfaces, this book gives you thorough basic information on the UART protocol and on the fairly challenging initialization rituals needed to configure the M6840, which should prepare you to handle more complex chips and protocols. We will survey the key ideas of these protocols in this section. The first subsection describes the bit-oriented protocols. The second subsection will discuss the 488 bus. The final subsection covers the SCSI interface.

9-4.1 Synchronous Bit-Oriented Protocols

Synchronous protocols are able to move a lot of data at a high rate. They are primarily used to communicate between *remote job entry* terminals (which have facilities to handle line printers, card readers, and plotters) and computers, and between computers and computers. The basic idea of a synchronous protocol is that a clock is sent either on a separate wire or along with the data in the Manchester coding scheme. Since a clock is sent with the data, there is little cause to fear that the receiver clock will eventually get out of sync after a lot of bits have been sent, so we are not restricted to short frames as we are in the UART. Once the receiver is synchronized, we will try to keep it in synchronism with the transmitter, and we can send long frames without sending extra control pulses, which are needed to resynchronize the receiver and which reduce the efficiency of the channel.

Asynchronous protocols, like the UART protocol discussed in the last section, are more useful if small amounts of data are generated at random times, such as by a computer terminal. Synchronous protocols would anyway have to get all receivers into synchronism with the transmitter when a new transmitter gets control of the channel, so their efficiency would be poor for short random messages. Synchronous protocols are more useful when a lot of data are sent at once because they do not require the overhead every few bits, such as start and stop bits, that asynchronous protocols need. Bit-oriented synchronous protocols were developed as a result of weaknesses in byte- or character-oriented synchronous protocols when they were used in sending a lot of data at once.

The precursor to the bit-oriented protocol is the binary synchronous *Bisync* protocol, which is primarily character-oriented and is extended to handle arbitrary binary data. This protocol can be used with the ASCII character set. The 32 nonprinting ASCII characters include some that are used with the Bisync protocol to send sequences of characters. SYN - ASCII 0x16 is sent whenever nothing else is to be sent. It is a null character used to keep the receiver(s) synchronized to the transmitter. This character can be used to establish which bit in a stream of bits is the beginning of a character. Two Bisync protocols are used: one for sending character text and the other for sending binary data, such as machine code programs, binary numbers, and bit data.

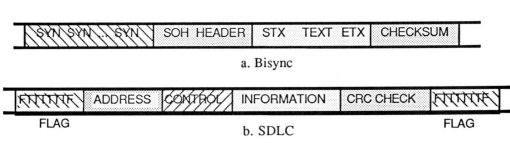

a. Bisync

b. SDLC

Figure 9-14. Synchronous Formats.

Character text is sent as follows: A header can be sent; its purpose and format are user defined. It begins with the character SOH – ASCII 0x01. An arbitrary number of characters of text is sent after the character STX – ASCII 0x02, and is terminated by the character ETX – ASCII 0x03. After the ETX character, a kind of checksum is sent. (See Figure 9-14a.)

To allow any data – such as a machine code program – including characters that happen to be identical to the character ETX, to be sent, a character DLE - ASCII 0x10 is sent before the characters STX and ETX. A byte count is established in some fashion. It may be fixed, so that all frames contain the same number of words, it may be sent in the header, or it may be sent in the first word or two words of the text itself. Whatever scheme is used to establish this byte count, it is used to disable the recognition of DLE-ETX characters that terminate the frame, so such patterns can be sent without confusing the receiver. This is called the *transparent mode* because the bits sent as text are transparent to the receiver controller and can be any pattern.

Bisync uses error correction or error detection and retry. The end of text is followed by a kind of checksum, which differs in differing Bisync protocols. One good error detection technique is to exclusive-OR the bytes that were sent, byte by byte. If characters have a parity bit, that bit can identify which byte is incorrect. The checksum is a parity byte that is computed "at 90 degrees" from the parity bits and can identify the column that has an error. If you know the column and the row, you know which bit is wrong, so you can correct it. Another Bisync protocol uses a *cyclic redundancy check* (CRC) that is based on the mathematical theory of error correcting codes. The error detecting "polynomial" $X**16 + x**15 + X**2 + 1$, called the CRC-16 polynomial, is one of several good polynomials for detecting errors. The CRC check feeds the data sent out of the transmitter through a shift register that shifts bits from the 15th stage towards the 0th stage. The shift register is cleared, and the data bits to be transmitted are exclusive-ORed with the bit being shifted out of the 0th stage, which then is exclusive-ORed into some of the bits being shifted in the register at the inputs to the 15th, 13th, and 0th stages. The original data and the contents of the shift register (called the CRC check bits) are transmitted to the receiver. The receiver puts the received data, including the CRC check bits, through the same hardware at its end. When done, the hardware should produce a 0 in the shift register. If it doesn't, an error (CRC error) has occurred. The Bisync protocol has means to request that the frame be sent over again if a CRC error is detected. If the frame is good, an ACK - ASCII 0x06 is sent, but if an error is detected, a NAK - ASCII 0x15 is sent from the receiver back to the sender. If the sender gets an ACK, it can send the next frame, but if it gets a NAK, it should resend the current frame.

Though developed for communication between a computer and a single RJE station, Bisync has been expanded to include *multi-drop*. Several RJE stations are connected to a host computer on a half duplex line (bus). The host is a master. It controls all transfers between it and the RJE stations. The master *polls* the stations periodically, just as we polled I/O devices after an interrupt, to see if any of them want service. In polling, the master sends a short packet to each station, so that each station can send back a short message as the master waits for the returned messages.

Bisync protocols have some serious shortcomings. They are set up for and are therefore limited to half duplex transmission. After each frame is sent, you have to wait for the receiver to send back an acknowledge or a negative acknowledge. This causes the computer to stutter, as it waits for a message to be acknowledged. These shortcomings are improved in bit-oriented protocols. Features used for polling and multi-drop connections are improved. And the information is bit-oriented to efficiently handle characters, machine code programs, or variable width data.

The first significant synchronous bit-oriented protocol was the *Synchronous Data Link Control* (SDLC) protocol developed by IBM. The American National Standards Institute, ANSI, developed a similar protocol, ADCCP, and the CCITT developed another protocol, HDLC. They are all quite similar at the link control and physical levels, which we are studying. We will take a look at the SDLC link, the oldest and simplest of the bit-oriented protocols.

The basic SDLC frame is shown in Figure 9-14b. If no data are sent, either a true bit is continually sent (idle condition) or a *flag* pattern, 0x7E (FTTTTTTF), is sent. The frame itself begins with a flag pattern and ends with a flag pattern, with no flag patterns inside. The flag pattern ending one frame can be the same flag that starts the next frame.

The frame can be guaranteed free of flag patterns by a five T's detector and F inserter. If the transmitter sees that five T's have been sent, it sends a F regardless of whether the next bit is going to be a T or a F. That way, the data FFTFFTTTTTTF are sent as FFTFFTTTTTFTTF, and the data FFTFFTTTTTFTF are sent as FFTFFTTTTTFFTF, free of a flag pattern. The receiver looks for five T's. If the next bit is F, it is simply discarded. If the received bit pattern were FFTFFTTTTTFTTF, the F after the five T's is discarded to give FFTFFTTTTTTF, and if FFTFFTTTTTFFTF is received, we get FFTFFTTTTTFTF. But if the received bit pattern were FTTTTTTF, the receiver would recognize the flag pattern and end the frame.

The frame consists of an 8-bit station number address, for which the frame is sent, followed by 8 control bits. Any number of information bits are sent next, from 0 to as many as can be expected to be received comparatively free of errors or as many as can fit in the buffers in the transmitter and receiver. The CRC check bits are sent next. The address, control, information, and CRC check bits are free of flag patterns as a result of five T's detection and F insertion just discussed.

The control bits identify the frame as an *information frame*, or *supervisory* or *nonsequenced* frame. The information frame is the normal frame for sending a lot of data in the information field. The control field of an information frame has a 3-bit number N. The transmitter can send up to eight frames, with different values of N, before handshaking is necessary to verify that the frames have arrived in the receiver. Like the ACK and NAK characters in Bisync, supervisory frames are used for retry after error. The receiver can send back the number N of a frame that has an error, requesting that it be resent, or it can send another kind of supervisory frame with N to indicate that all frames up to N have been received correctly. If the receiver happens to be sending other data back to the transmitter, it can send this number N in another field in the information frame it sends back to the transmitter of the original message to confirm receipt of all frames up to the N*th* frame, rather than sending an acknowledge supervisory frame. This feature improves efficiency, since most frames will be correctly received.

The SDLC link can be used with multi-drop (bus) networks, as well as with a ring network of the same structure as the GPC optical link (Figure 9-4). The ring network permits a single main, *primary*, station to communicate with up to 255 other *secondary* stations. Communication is full duplex, since the primary can send to the secondary over part of the loop, while the secondary sends other data to the primary on the remainder of the loop. The SDLC has features for the primary to poll the secondary stations and for the transmitting station to abort a frame if something goes wrong.

The SDLC link and the other bit-oriented protocols provide significant improvements over the character-oriented Bisync protocols. Full duplex communication, allowing up to eight frames to be sent before they are acknowledged, permits more efficient communication. The communication is inherently transparent, because of the five T's detection feature, and can handle variable length bit data efficiently. It is an excellent protocol for moving large frames of data at a high rate of speed.

The *X.25* protocol is a three-level protocol established by the CCITT for high-volume data transmission. The physical and link levels are set up for the HDLC protocol, a variation of the SDLC bit-oriented protocol; but synchronous character-oriented protocols can be used so that the industry can grow into the X.25 protocol without scrapping everything. This protocol, moreover, specifies the network level as well. It is oriented to packet switching. Packet switching permits frames of a message to wander through a network on different paths. This dynamic allocation of links to messages permits more efficient use of the links, increases security (since a thief would have to watch the whole network to get the entire message) and enhances reliability. It looks like the communication protocol of the future. While we do not cover it in our discussion of I/O device design, we have been using its terminology throughout this chapter as much as possible.

9-4.2 IEEE-488 Bus Standard

The need to control instruments like voltmeters and signal generators in the laboratory or factory from a computer has led to another kind of protocol, an asynchronous byte-oriented protocol. One of the earliest such protocol was the CAMAC protocol developed by French nuclear scientists for their instruments. Hewlett-Packard, a major instrument manufacturer, developed a similar standard which was adopted by the IEEE and called the IEEE-488 standard. Although Hewlett-Packard owns patents on the handshake methods of this protocol, it has made the rights available on request to most instrument manufacturers, and the IEEE-488 is becoming available on most sophisticated instruments and minicomputers and microcomputers.

Communications to test equipment has some challenging problems. The communications link may be strung out in a different way each time a different experiment is run or a different test is performed. The lengths of the lines can vary. The instruments themselves do not have as much computational power as a large mainframe machine, or even a terminal, so the communications link has to do some work for them such as waiting to be sure that they have picked up the data. A number of instruments may have to be told to do something together, such as simultaneously generating and measuring signals, so they can't be told one at a time when to execute their operation. These characteristics lead to a different protocol for instrumentation buses.

The IEEE-488 bus is fully specified at the physical and link levels. A 16-pin connector, somewhat like the RS232 connector, is prescribed by the standard, as are the functions of the 16 signals and eight ground pins. The 16 signal lines include an 8-bit parallel data bus, three handshaking lines, and five control lines. The control lines include one that behaves like the system reset line in the M68332 microcomputer. Others are used to get attention and perform other bus management functions. But the heart of the bus standard is the asynchronous protocol used to transmit data on the bus.

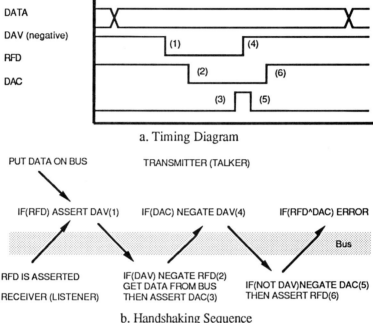

a. Timing Diagram

b. Handshaking Sequence
Figure 9-15. IEEE-488 Bus Handshaking Cycle.

An asynchronous bus protocol uses a kind of expandable clock signal, which can be automatically stretched when the bus is longer or shortened if the bus is shorter. The way this happens is the "clock" is sent from the station transmitting the data to the station that receives the data on one line, then back to the transmitter on another line. The transmitter waits for the return signal before it begins another transmission. If the bus is lengthened, so are the delays of this "clock" signal. The IEEE-488 bus uses this principle a couple of times to reliably move a word on an 8-bit bus from a transmitter to a receiver. (See Figure 9-15.)

The handshake cycle is like a clock cycle. Each time a word is to be moved, the bus goes through a handshake cycle to move the word, as shown in Figure 9-15. The cycle involves (negative logic) *data available* (DAV), sent by the transmitter of the data, and (positive logic) *ready for data* (RFD) and (positive logic) *data accepted* (DAC), sent by the receiver of the data.

If the receiver is able to take data, it has already asserted RFD (high). When the transmitter wants to send a data word, it first puts the word on the bus and then begins the handshake cycle. It checks for the RFD signal. If it is asserted at the transmitter, the transmitter asserts DAV (low) to indicate the data are available. This is step 1 in Figures 9-15a and 9-15b. When the receiver sees DAV asserted, it negates RFD (low) in step 2 because it is no longer ready for data. When the processor picks up the data from the interface, the receiver asserts DAC (high) to indicate data are accepted. This is step 3. When the transmitter sees DAC asserted, it negates DAV (high) in step 4 because it will soon stop sending data on the data bus. When the receiver sees DAV negated, it negates DAC in step 5. The data are removed sometime after the DAV has become negated. When it is ready to accept new data, it asserts RFD (high) in step 6 to begin a new handshake cycle.

The IEEE-488 bus is designed for some special problems in busing data to and from instruments. First, the bus is asynchronous. If the receiver is far away and the data will take a long time to get to it, the DAV signal will also take a long time, and the other handshake signals will be similarly delayed. So, long cables are automatically accounted for by the handshake mechanism. Second, the instrument at the receiver may be slow or just busy when the data arrive. DAC is asserted as soon as the data get into the interface, to inform the transmitter that they got there; but RFD is asserted as soon as the instrument gets the data from the interface, so the interface won't get an overrun error that a UART can get. Third, although only one station transmits a word in any handshake cycle, a number of stations can be transmitters at one time or another. Fourth, the same word can be sent to more than one receiver, and the handshaking should be able to make sure all receivers get the word. These last two problems are solved using open collector bus lines for DAV, RFD, and DAC. DAC, sent by the transmitter, is negative logic so the line is wire-OR. That way , if any transmitter wants to send data, it can short the line low to assert DAV. RFD and DAC, on the other hand, are positive logic signals so the line is a wire-AND bus. RFD is high only if all receivers are ready for data, and DAC is high only when all receivers have accepted data.

The IEEE-488 bus is well suited to remote control of instrumentation and is becoming available on many of the instruments being designed at this time. You will probably see a lot of the IEEE-488 bus in your design experiences.

9-4.3 The Smart Computer System Interface (SCSI)

The microcomputer has made the intelligent I/O device economical. In a lot of systems today, a personal computer communicates with a printer that has a microcomputer to control it, or a disk that has its own microcomputer. Communications between a personal computer and the intelligent I/O device can be improved with an interface protocol specially designed for this application. The *Smart Computer System Interface (SCSI)* is designed for communications between personal computers and intelligent I/O devices.

The asynchronous protocol is quite similar to the IEEE-488 bus, having a 9-bit (8 data plus parity) parallel bus, a handshake protocol involving a direction signal (I/O), a request (REQ), and an acknowledge (ACK). (See Figure 9-16.) (There are also six other control signals, and the interface uses a 50-pin connector.) Up to eight bus controllers can be on an SCSI bus, and they may be *initiators* (processors) or *targets* (disk drives). A priority circuit assures that two initiators will not try to use the SCSI bus at the same time. After an initiator acquires the bus, a command stage is entered. The 10-byte command packet selects a target controller and is capable of specifying the reading or writing of up to 256 bytes of data on up to a 1024-gigabyte disk. After the command packet is sent, data are transferred between the initiator and target.

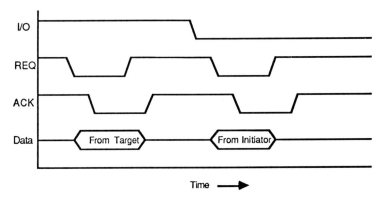

Time ⟶

Figure 9-16. SCSI Timing.

Each command or data byte is transferred using the direction, request, and acknowledge signals. The direction (I/O) signal is low when the requester wishes to write a command or data into the target, and high when it wants data. Whether the requester is sending data or a command, or receiving data, it drops the request line (REQ) low; and puts the data or command on the nine-bit parallel bus if sending them. If the target is to receive the data, it picks up the data and drops the acknowledge signal (ACK) low. If the target is to send the data, it puts the data on the bus and drops the acknowledge signal (ACK) low. When the initiator sees the ACK line low, it raises REQ, and if it is receiving data, it picks up the data from the data bus. When the target sees REQ high, it raises ACK high so the next transfer can take place. Up to 1.5 megabytes per second can be transferred on an SCSI bus this way.

The SCSI bus is specially designed for communication between a small but powerful computer like a personal computer, and an intelligent I/O device. Many systems that you build may fit this specification and thus may use an SCSI interface.

9-5 Conclusions

Communication systems are among the most important I/O systems in a microcomputer. The microcomputer communicates with keyboards, displays, and typewriters, as well as with remote control stations and other microcomputers, using the UART protocol. The microcomputer can be in a large computer system and have to communicate with other parts of the system using the SDLC protocol. It may be in a laboratory and have to communicate with instrumentation on an IEEE-488 bus. It may have to talk with other systems in a different protocol.

If you would like additional reading, we recommend the excellent *Technical Aspects of Data Communication,* by John McNamara, Digital Equipment Corporation (DEC). It embodies an exceptional amount of practical information, especially at the physical level, and also covers many of the widely used protocols. Motorola offers some fine applications notes on the SDLC protocol and its M6854 chip, such as *MC6854 ADLC, An Introduction to Data Communication,* by M. Neumann. For the IEEE-488 protocol using the M68488 chip, the applications note *Getting Aboard the 488-1975 Bus,* is very informative. These applications notes are well written and take you from where this book leaves off to where you can design systems using these protocols.

Further details on the MC68332 can be obtained from the *MC68332 SIM System Integration Module User's Manual (SIM32UM/AD)* Motorola Inc., 1989. As noted earlier, we have not attempted to duplicate the diagrams and discussions in that book because we assume you will refer to it while reading this book, and since we present an alternative view of the subject, you can use either or both views.

This chapter covered the main concepts of communication systems at the physical and link control levels. You should be aware of these concepts so you can understand the problems and capabilities of specialists in this field. You should be able to handle the UART protocol – the simplest and most widely used protocol – and its variations, and you should be able to use the M6850 and M68681, as well as the UART, in hardware designs. You should be able to write classes for the M6850 and SCI that utilize interrupts and sleep functions of multi-thread or multi-tasking environments. You should be able to write initialization rituals, interrupt handlers, and gadfly routines to input or output data using such hardware. Hardware and software tools like these should serve most of your design needs and prepare you for designing with the SDLC, IEEE-488, or SCSI interface protocol systems.

Do You Know These Terms?

See the End of Chapter 1 for Instructions.

coordinated movement, levels of abstraction, peer, end-to-end communication, network control, link control, physical control, medium, frequency shift keying, frequency multiplexing, time multiplexing, channel, simplex, half duplex, full duplex, bit time period, baud rate, bit rate, synchronous system, asynchronous system, Manchester code, bit level, frame level, message level, protocol, handshake protocol, communication system structure, store and forward, circuit, centralized, distributed, master-slave, differential line, RS442 standard, active station, passive station, RS232 standard, modem, originate, answer, data coupler, Answer phone, Switch hook, ring indicator, data terminal ready, clear to send, break, light fiber, ethernet, general propagating communication link, Universal Asynchronous Receiver Transmitter, UART protocol, start bit, stop bit, parity error, framing error, overrun error, selected station, Asynchronous Communications Interface Adapter, Dual Asynchronous Receiver Transmitter, Serial Module, Serial Communication Interface, remote job entry terminal, Bisync protocol, transparent mode, cyclic redundancy check, multi-drop, Synchronous Data Link Control, flag pattern, information frame, supervisory frame, nonsequenced frame, primary station, secondary station, X.25 protocol, IEEE-488 Bus, Handshaking Cycle, data available, ready for data, data accepted, Smart Computer System Interface, initiators, targets.

10

Storage and Display Systems

The previous chapter discussed the techniques by which microcomputers can communicate with other computers. A microcomputer may have to store data on a magnetic tape or disk. This stored data can be used by the microcomputer later, or it may be moved to another computer. Thus, on an abstract level, a magnetic storage medium can be an alternative to an electronic communication link. They may also have to communicate with humans, using LED or LCD displays covered in Chapter 6 or using more complex CRT displays. We now cover CRT display technology.

This chapter covers both the magnetic storage device and the CRT display. In each case, we will first describe the basic format of a storage or display device. Special purpose chips are quite easy to use and are likely to be designed into real systems. We show how such chips can be used with an M68332 or M68340.

In this chapter, we spend quite a bit of time on the details of video and disk formats. We also present some rather larger system designs and refer to earlier discussions for many concepts. We have somewhat less space for the important notion of top-down design than in previous chapters because the design alternatives for CRT and disk systems are a bit too unwieldy to include in this short chapter.

Upon completing this chapter, you should be able to implement a floppy disk interface. You should have gained enough information to understand the 3 1/2" double density floppy disk and you should be able to use a floppy disk controller chip to record and play back data for a microcomputer, or use it to move data to or form it from or to another computer. You should have gained enough information to understand the format of the black-and-white NTSC television signal and implement a realistic "dumb" terminal with the M68332 or M68340. Moreover, you will see some fairly complete designs similar to those you can build.

10-1 Storage Systems

Most microcomputers require either a communications system to move data into and out of them or a storage system to get data from or to save data in. The latter, called secondary storage, generally uses some form of magnetic medium. There are four useful alternatives for secondary storage. Audio cassette tape is the least costly storage system. It might be usable in storing some data in low cost systems, such as a weather monitor. Paper tape is generally more suitable for industrial monitoring and control systems, especially in environments hostile to computers. Floppy disk systems have become so cheap that they are more likely to be used in most small systems and inexpensive personal computers. Finally, hard disks provide larger and better storage for professional personal computers and word processors.

The first subsection describes techniques for data storage on a floppy disk format. In the next subsection, we will use a Western Digital WD37C65C chip, which is particularly easy to interface to personal computers and the M68332 or M68340 microcontroller, to show a real implementation of a floppy disk interface.

10-1.1 The 3 1/2" Floppy Disk Format

We now describe the 3 1/2" double density floppy disk format. Data can be stored on the disk using either of two popular formats. Figure 10-1 shows how a bit and a byte of data can be stored on a disk, using FM (single density) and MFM (double density) formats. The FM format is just Manchester coding, as introduced in Section 9-1. Figure 10-1a shows a bit cell, and Figure 10-1c shows a byte of data, in the FM format. Every 8 μseconds there is a clock pulse. If a 1 is sent, a pulse is put in between the clock pulses, and if a 0 is sent, no pulse is put between the clock pulses. MFM format provides half the bit cell size as FM format; it does this by using minimal spacing between pulses in the disk medium: MFM format has at most one pulse per bit cell. It is thus called "double density" storage. The idea is that a 1 cell, which has a pulse in it, doesn't need a clock pulse, and a 0 cell only needs a clock pulse if the previous cell is also a 0 cell. Figure 10-1b shows a byte of data in the MFM format. Every 4 μseconds there is a data bit. If a 1 is sent, a pulse is put near the end of the bit time; if a 0 is sent after a 1, no pulse is put between the clock pulses; and if a 0 is sent after a 0, a pulse appears early in the bit time. Note that data must be read or written at the rate of 1 byte per 32 μseconds, which is able to be implemented using indirect I/O in a 16-MHz M68332 or M68340 system. For the remainder of this section, we discuss the "double density" MFM format. The FM format is basically identical to the MFM format.

In addition to double density, *high density* also doubles the data storage capacity and the rate at which data is recorded and read. High density merely uses disks and drive heads that can store, read, and write data at twice the density and data rate of regular disks; every parameter, except the disk rotational speed, is merely doubled. 1.4 Mbyte floppies use high density. Further doubling implements a 2.8 Mbyte floppy storage capacity.

Data read from the disk are separated by a phase-locked loop (PLL) of the kind described in Section 6-5.3. The PLL synchronizes to the bit cell like a fly-wheel. Once the bit cell is locked on to, the data bits can be extracted from the input analog signal. The PLL must be designed to lock into the bit cells within 48 bit cell times.

A disk drive may have one or more disks, stacked pancake-style, and each disk may have one or two *surfaces*. Figure 10-2a shows a surface of a disk; a *track* is shown, and tracks are numbered – track 0 on the extreme outside, and track i+1 next towards the center to track i. Floppy disks have diameters of 8", 5 1/4", or 3 1/2", and these typically have at least 77, 35, and 35 tracks, respectively. The track spacing density is the number of tracks per inch and is generally 135 tracks per inch on 3 1/2" floppies.

Although disks exist which have a head on each track, generally disks have a single head per surface – used to both read and write the data on that surface – which is moved by a stepper motor to a track that is to be read or written. In a multiple surface disk, the same tracks are accessed on each surface by a comb-like mechanism holding the read-write head for each surface; the collection of tracks accessed at the same time is called a *cylinder*. We soon describe an example of an MFM 3 1/2" disk's track format. The formats for other types of disks are similar.

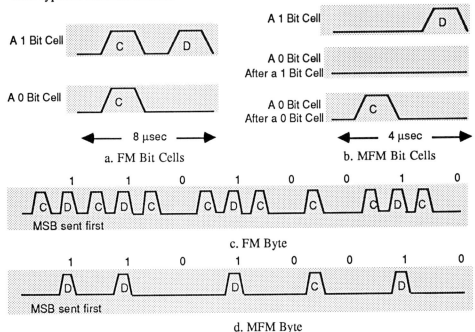

Figure 10-1. Bit and Byte Storage for FM and MFM Encoding of 3 1/2" Floppy Disks.

Relative to later discussions of the operation of the floppy disk controller, timing of head movements significantly affects the disk system's performance. The *step rate* is the rate at which the stepping motor can be pulsed to move the head from track i to track i+1 (step in) or to track i-1 (step out). There is also a *settling time*, which is the time needed to allow the mechanical parts to stop bouncing (see contact bounce in Chapter 6). Floppy disk drives have stepping rates from 2 to 30 milliseconds and settling times of about 30 milliseconds; we used a TEAC FD235HF-217 disk drive which had a stepping rate of 3 milliseconds and a settling time of 15 milliseconds. On such a drive, the time to move from track i to track j is $3*|\ i\text{-}j\ | + 15$ milliseconds. The average time to position from track 0 to a random track is the time to move over half of the (77) tracks of the disk. There is some additional time needed to get to the data on the track, as discussed soon. Thus, on the average, about 130 milliseconds would be used to move the head, and no data are transferred during that time.

The problem with a magnetic disk is that, to record data, a head must be energized before and deenergized after writing, and the process of energizing or deenergizing a head erases the data below the head. The track is thus organized with *fill* areas where data are not stored and where the head may be energized to begin, or deenergized to end, writing, and the data between these fill areas, called *sectors*, are written in their entirety if they are written at all. A disk's indivisible storage objects thus are sectors. Figure 10-2b shows the breakdown of a typical track in terms of sectors and the breakdown of a sector in terms of its ID pattern and data. There is an *index hole* on the disk (Figure 10-2a) that defines a track's beginning; it is sensed by an optical switch that provides an *index pulse* when the hole passes by the switch. The track first contains a 80-byte fill pattern. (Each fill pattern is 0xff.) There are then 15 sectors in one track of a double-sided double density MFM disk, as described soon. The remaining part of the track, after all sectors are written, is filled with the 0xff pattern.

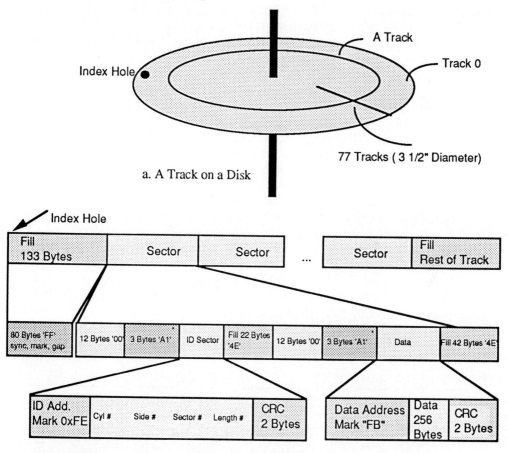

a. A Track on a Disk

b. Sectors In a Track

Figure 10-2. Organization of Sectors and Tracks on a Disk Surface.

Regarding the timing of disk accesses, after the head moves to the right track, it may have to wait half a revolution of the disk, on the average, before it finds a track it would like to read or write. Since a floppy disk rotates at ten revolutions per second, the average wait would be 50 milliseconds. If several sectors are to be read together, the time needed to move from one track to another can be eliminated if the data are on the same track, and the time needed to get to the right sector can be eliminated if the sectors are located one after another. We will think of sectors as if they were consecutively numbered from 0 (the *logical sector number*), and we will position consecutively numbered sectors on the same track, so consecutively numbered sectors can be read as fast as possible. (Actually, two consecutively read sectors should have some other sectors between them because the computer has to process the data read and determine what to do next before it is ready to read another sector. The number of sectors actually physically between two "consecutively numbered" sectors is called the *interleave factor*, and is generally about four.)

We need to know which sector is passing under the head as the disk rotates, since sectors may be put in some different order, as just described, and we would also like to be able to verify that we are on the right cylinder (track) after the head has been moved. When the read head begins to read data (it may begin reading anywhere on a track), it will examine this address in an ID pattern to find out where it is.

There is a small problem identifying the beginning of an ID pattern or a data field when the head makes contact with the surface and begins to read the data on a track. To solve this, there is a special pattern whose presence is indicated by the deletion of some of the clock pulses that would have been there when data are recorded in MFM format, and there are identifying patterns called the ID address mark and data address mark. The special pattern, shown in Figure 10-3, is said to have a data pattern of 0xA1 and a missing clock pulse between bits 4 and 5. Following it, the ID address mark 0xFE is used to locate the beginning of an ID pattern on a track. The data address mark similarly identifies the beginning of data in the sector, but is 0xFB rather than 0xFE.

The ID pattern consists of a 1-byte ID address mark (0xFE), a track number, side number, sector number and sector length (each is 1 byte and is coded in binary), and a 2-byte CRC check. The cylinder (track) number, beginning with cylinder 0 (outermost), and the sector number, beginning with either sector 0 (zero-origin indexing) or 1 (one-origin indexing), is stored in two of the bytes. A simple method of mapping the logical sector number into a cylinder and zero-origin indexing sector number is to divide the logical sector number by the number of sectors per track: The quotient is the cylinder number, and the remainder is the sector number. The double-sided disk's side number for the "top" is 0 and for the "bottom" is 1, and the sector length for a 256-byte sector is 1.

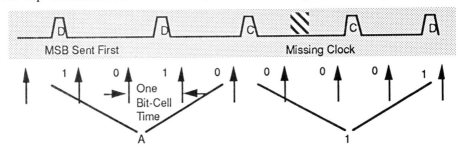

Figure 10-3. A Special Byte (Data=0xA1, Clock Pulse Missing between Bits 4,5).

A sector is composed of a pattern of 12 0s followed by 3 bytes of 0xA1 (in which a clock pulse is missing). There is then an ID pattern as just described, a 22-byte fill, and another pattern of 12 0s, followed by 3 bytes of 0xA1 (in which a clock pulse is missing). The 256 bytes of data are then stored. The ID pattern and the data in a sector have some error detection information called a CRC, discussed in Section 9-4.1, to ensure reliable reading of the data. The track may have a total capacity of about 6500 bytes, called the *unformatted capacity* of the track, but because so much of the disk is needed for fill, ID, and CRC, the *formatted capacity* of a track (the available data) may be reduced to 4600 bytes.

The *format* of a disk is the structure just described, disregarding the content of the data field. To *format* a disk is to write this structure. After a disk is formatted, when data are written, only the data part of the sector, together with its data address mark and CRC check, are written. The ID pattern is not rewritten. If it is altered, you will be unable to read or write the data in the sectors because the controller will be unable to find the sector, and you will have to reformat the disk, destroying all the data in it.

10-1.2. The Western Digital 37C65C Floppy Disk Controller

We now examine a hardware-software system for reading a double-sided double-density high-density 3 1/2" floppy disk using the Western Digital WD37C65C chip. We first catalog registers, and ports in the organization of the chip and all the chip's connections. Then we list the functions that the controller executes. Finally, we will present and describe the software used to control the chip.

The chip's organization has five registers, of which three are used in this section. The control register has a bit that is F for high and T for low density. The master status register has a request bit (Req) a data direction bit (Out) an execution phase bit (Exec) and five busy bits indicating the busy status of up to four drives and the controller. Finally, the data port is used to transfer data into and out of the device, and also to send commands into the device (as listed in Figure 10-4f) and get more detailed status from the chip (by reading the status bytes St0, St1, St2 and St3 as shown in Figure 10-4e). These registers and ports will be referenced in either the M68332 or M68340 using: *#define mStat *(unsigned char*)0x10000 #define data *(unsigned char*) 0x10001 #define conReg *(unsigned char*)0x10800.*

An output bit (M68332 port C bit 6 or M68340 port B bit 6) is used to reset the chip and an input bit (M68332 port F bit 7 or M68340 port B bit 7) is used to sense an "interrupt" that signals when an operation is completed. The data bus D permits the M68332 to read or write a byte in the WD37C65C. Four M68332 chip selects (Figure 10-4a) control transfers on the data bus: read (Rd) is asserted to read the master status register or data port; write (Wr), to write the control register or data port; chip select (Cs), to read or write the data port (if address A is 1) or read master status (if A is 0); and load control (Ldcr), to write the control register. The M68340 uses external logic with CS2 and CS3 to get these same signals using the same addresses (Figure 10-4b).

The 34-conductor cable connects the controller chip to the drive (Figure 10-4c). All odd numbered pins are grounded to reduce noise pick-up, and all signals are in negative logic. Motor control MOT is asserted true (grounded) to make the motor run continuously in this example, although the WD37C65C has means to control the motor. Output Step causes the drive's stepper motor to move to another cylinder, and Dirc specifies which direction to move the head. DS1 selects drive 1 and Hs selects the head used. Wd is the write data, and We is the write enable. Input Rdd is the read data, write protect Wp is asserted if a disk tab is positioned to prevent writing in the disk, Tr00 is the track 0 signal, and Ix is the index pulse signal; inputs use a pull-up resistor.

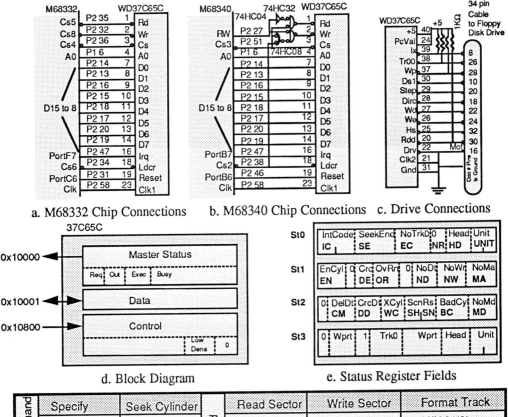

a. M68332 Chip Connections   b. M68340 Chip Connections   c. Drive Connections

d. Block Diagram   e. Status Register Fields

f. Command Summary

Figure 10-4. The Western Digital WD37C65C.

The user may wish to read one or more bytes from the disk. Since it is only possible to read whole sectors, the sector or sectors that the data are at are read, and the data are extracted once the sectors are read. To read a sector, the user must *seek* the track first, then *read* the desired *sector*. The two commands, seek and read sector, are given to the floppy disk controller. The seek command puts the read/write head in the disk drive over the desired cylinder, and the read sector command causes the data from a sector on the track to be read into primary memory. If the read/write head is definitely over the right cylinder, the seek command may be omitted. Also, in some floppy disk controllers having intelligence in them, the user only gives a read command regardless of where the read/write head is and an *implied seek* may be automatically generated as a result, without the user giving it, if the head is in the wrong place. The user may wish to write one or more bytes into the disk. To write a sector, the commands to *seek* and *write sector* are given as for the read operations above. Good programs often read a sector each time right after it is written to be sure there are no errors in writing the sector. A disk can be formatted by executing the *format* command on each track. Finally, when a disk is initialized, the position of the read/write head must be zeroed to later establish how to move it to a desired track. This operation is called *restoring* or *recalibrating* the drive.

The WD37C65C has the fundamental commands given above and additional assorted functions described below. (See Figure 10-4f.) *Specify* writes the step rate, head load, and head unload times to initialize the WD37C65C, *read id* will read the first valid id sector found on the track, *sense drive* will indicate the drive's status, and *sense status*, often used after an interrupt or a gadfly loop, will indicate the cause of the interrupt or termination of the loop. We will develop an object-oriented class to handle these operations in methods, as we did for other I/O devices.

The class *Floppy* declares user-oriented methods *InF* and *OutF* to input (read) a sector and output (write) a sector, *InitDisk* to initialize a disk, *SeekF* to seek a cylinder (track), and *FormatF* to format a disk. Methods *CheckF*, *TryDns*, and *SetupF* are used in these methods to "factor out" some common code from them. In addition, C procedures *wC*, *rC* ,and *InitDrive* are used with these methods where object instance variables are not referenced in them.

These methods use instance variables to prepare data to be sent as operands of commands, and save results of operations. Instance variables used for command operands (Figure 10-4f) indicate C the cylinder, H head, R sector, N data size which will be matched against a sector's id fields (Figure 10-2b). There are $2^{(N+7)}$ bytes of data in a sector, except when N is 0; then DTL indicates the data length. Also, EOT indicates the maximum number of sectors on a track, GPL indicates the length of the gap at the end of each sector. Instance variables get the status bits $St0$ to $St2$ that are read from the controller after many of the operations (Figure 10-4f): IC is an interrupt code that is 0 if there are no errors, seek end SE is 1 if a seek is completed, equipment check EC is 1 if, after a recalibrate command, track 0 is not sensed, head HD is the head and $UNIT$ is the drive number that was used in the command for which this status information is being read. End of cylinder EN is 1 if the sector being read is beyond the sector specified by EOT. Data error DE is 1 if a CRC error is detected in the id or data fields, overrun OR is set if data are lost when reading or writing a sector, no data ND is set if the command's requested id is not found in an id field on the track being read. Not writeable NW is set if a write request is made to a disk with pin Wp asserted (because the write protect tab is positioned to prevent writing on the disk), missing address *MA* and missing data *MD* are set if the address mark (0xFE or 0xFB) is not read. Wrong cylinder *WC* or bad cylinder *BC* are set if the command's requested id cylinder differs from that being read, *SH* and *SN* are set by scan commands we do not discuss here.

```
struct Floppy:direct {
    unsigned char C,H,R,N,EOT,GPL,DTL; /* Cyl Hd Sec Size End Gap DatLen */
    unsigned IC:2,SE:1,EC:1,NR:1, /* IntCode (2) SeekEnd(1) EqmtChk(1) NotRdy(1)*/
    HD:1,UNIT:2, /* HeadSelect(1) UnitSelect(2) */
    EN:1,:1,DE:1,OR:1,:1,ND:1,NW:1,MA:1, /* endCyl datEr ovRn nDat nWrt nAdr */
    :1,CM:1,DD:1,WC:1,SH:1,SN:1,BC:1,MD:1, /* cMk crc xCl scEq scNt xCl nAmk */
    Mt:1,Mf:1,Sk:1,WP:1,Hd:1,Ds:1,:2; /* Mtk,Mfm,SkDlt,wtPrt, HDns, dbleSided */
    unsigned surface,path,n,error,sectorsPerTrack,sectorsPerDisk,verify;
    int InitDisk(unsigned), SeekF(long),InF(long,char*),OutF(long,char*),
       FormatF(unsigned,unsigned),CheckF(void),TryDns(int,int); void SetupF(void);
}*f;
```

We use #*define* statements to simplify copying the status bytes into the object's bit fields: #*define ST0 *(&DTL+1)* #*define ST1 *(&DTL+2)* #*define ST2 *(&DTL+3)*.

The methods will be written to report errors that might help in debugging a system and to control up to four floppy drives. The *enum* statement below lists error numbers used. We use paths, much as OS-9 uses them, to distinguish among a multiplicity of disks that might be used at the same time, for instance to copy from one to another disk. Global variable *Path* is used in the *InitDisk* method to assign a unique path number to each disk as it is initialized, and global variable *curPath[i]* indicates which disk is currently in drive *i*. The *SeekF* method will indicate an error if the wrong disk is inserted, to prompt the user to change disks.

```
enum{drvErr=1,diskErr,addrErr,seekErr,sectorError,writeProtectErr,
    badFormat,readErr,writeErr,illOpErr, wrongDisk};
unsigned curPath[4],Path;
```

The M68332's class can be used after executing macros to set up its chip select control registers and initializing the drive using the *InitDrive* procedure. The latter returns 0 if initialization is successful; it is executed twice because the drive has 80 tracks, but the procedure restores only 77 tracks each time it is executed. The object is blessed and the disk is initialized. The disk can then be read, written or formatted, as is shown below:

```
main(){ char *p=(char*)0xc000; int i,j,showErr; /* for the M68332 */
    free=(char*)0x10000; *(char*)0xfffa04=0x7c; /*CLK=15.991Mhz */
    *(long*)0xfffa44=0x28ff0022; /* chipSelects all assigned together */
    baseAssign(4,0x10000,k2); optionAssign(4,rd+wr+upper+as,external,user+super,0);
    baseAssign(5,0x10000,k8); optionAssign(5,rd+upper+as,1,user+super,0);
    baseAssign(6,0x10800,k2); optionAssign(6,rd+wr+upper+as,external,user+super,0);
    baseAssign(8,0x10000,k8); optionAssign(8,wr+upper+as,1,user+super,0);
    if(InitDrive(0,3,16,15)){if(InitDrive(0,3,16,15)) return;}
    (f=blessA(sizeof(Floppy),Floppy))->InitDisk(0);
    f->InF(5,p); /* read sector 5, put it at 0xc000 for dumping using MacDi */
}
```

The M68340's *main* procedure is similar:

```
main(){ char *p=(char*)0xc000; int i,j,showErr; /* for the M68340 */
 free=(char*)0x10000; *(char*)0xffffff004=0x7c; /*CLK=15.991Mhz */
 CsAssign(2,0x10000,8,wait1+byte,rdWr);CsAssign(3,0x10800,8,wait1+byte,rdWr);
 if(InitDrive(0,3,16,15)){if(InitDrive(0,3,16,15)) return;}
 (f=blessA(sizeof(Floppy),Floppy))->InitDisk(0);
 f->InF(5,p); /* read sector 5, put it at 0xc000 for dumping using MacDi */
}
```

We begin by presenting a simplified sector input method *InF*, which will be replaced by a full version later, to introduce the *SeekF*, *CheckF*, and *SetupF* methods and *wC* and *rC* procedures, WD37C65C's command, execution and result phases, and its use of gadfly loops to synchronize data input and output. The *InF* method sends a *SeekF* message, which computes C, H, and R, and executes a seek command if the head is not already on the desired cylinder. The read sector command (Figure 10-4f) is then given. First, during a *command phase*, nine bytes are written to the data port using the *WC* procedure, which before each byte is written, gadflies until the two most significant bits of the master status register (Req and Out) become TF, signifying that the WD37C65C is ready for an input. The Mt, Mf, Sk bits, signifying options multitrack, MFM, and skip deleted sector, and the remaining *0x06* representing the read sector command, are sent in the first byte. Then the surface, which is the head and drive number, is sent. The cylinder, head, sector, and size bytes are sent exactly as they should appear in the sector's id (Figure 10-2b), and the last sector, format gap size and data length are sent to complete the command phase. The bytes from surface to gap size must be sent in both *InF* and *OutF*, so their *wC* calls are efficiently factored into the method *SetupF*. The *execution phase* reads the sector's data, gadflying on the Req bit of the master status register for each byte read. Finally, the *result phase* uses the *rC* procedure to read each byte of the result, gadflying until Req and Out become TT, signifying that the WD37C65C has an output byte ready to be read. The status registers St0 to St2 are read, then the sector's cylinder, head, sector, and size bytes are read back exactly as they appeared in the sector's id (Figure 10-2b), to permit the software to verify that the right sector was read. Because the *InF* and *OutF* methods require reading these same inputs, we factor the *rC* procedure calls into the method *CheckF*.

```
Floppy::InF(a,p) long a; register char *p; { register int i;
  SeekF(a); wC(6+(Mf<<6)); SetupF(); wC(DTL);/* read sect */
  for( i=(1<<(n+7)); i>0; i- -){ while(mStat>=0); *p++=data;} CheckF();
}
wC(c) char c;{ while((mStat&0xc0)!=0x80); data=c;}
rC(){ char c; while((mStat&0xc0)!=0xc0); c=data; return c; }
void Floppy::SetupF(){wC(surface);wC(C);wC(H);wC(R);wC(N);wC(EOT);wC(GPL);}
Floppy::CheckF(){ unsigned char c=C,h=H,r=R,n=N;
  if((ST0=rC())&0x80) { error=illOpErr; return 1;}
  ST1=rC();ST2=rC();C=rC();H=rC();R=rC();N=rC();
  return (ST1&0x7f) || (ST2&0x33) ;
}
```

From this example, the reader should see that movement of data to or from the WD37C65C always uses handshaking, such as gadflying on some master status bits. The read sector (also read id, write sector, and format) commands go through three phases: command where control values are sent to the chip, execution where data are read or written, and result where status is read from the chip. Other operations (sense drive, sense status) have only a command and a result phase, and the remainder (specify, recalibrate, and seek) have only a command phase.

The *InitDrive* procedure initializes the WD37C65C by supplying the step rate, head load time and unload time, each given as a procedure parameter in milliseconds. This procedure must be executed just once before any other commands are given to the chip because it resets the chip, sets up some parameters, and recallibrates (restores) the drive. A disk need not be in the drive when it is executed. The procedure's parameters are shifted and inverted where necessary, and used in the specify command (Figure 10-4f). Then the sense drive command reads the status of the chip and reports an error if it fails to return expected results. A command to restore the drive is given, and a gadfly on the interrupt pin (M68332 port F bit 7 or M68340 port B bit 7) waits for the head to be restored. The command to sense status checks status register 0, where bit 5 has been set if the drive is restored correctly. We show the M68332 procedure. The M68340 procedure uses port B for ports F and C.

```
InitDrive(drive,step,unload,load) unsigned drive,step,unload,load; { int d;long l;
    /* step rate (1-16) head unload time <240 head load <254 - all msec.*/
    assgF=0x7f;/* port F bit 7 irq, end of op */
    portC=0x40;portC=0; /* apply reset pulse to the 37C65 */
    wC(3); wC(((-step)<<4)|(unload>>4));wC((load+1)|1); /* specify command */
    wC(4); wC(drive&=3); d=rC(); /* sense drive status */
    if((d&0xa0)!=0x20) return drvErr; /* chip or drive not working */
    wC(7);wC(drive); /* restore head (recalibrate) */
    while(portF>=0); /* gadfly on drive being in execution mode */
    wC(8); d=rC()&0xf8; rC(); /* sense interrupt status */
    if(d!=0x20) return drvErr; /* chip or drive not working */
    return 0;
}
```

The *InitDisk* method must be used before we read or write sectors in each disk. The path number is uniquely assigned to the object and the drive being used. The sense drive command is used to check to see if the disk is write protected. Instance variables are initialized to require verifying each write sector operation, to inhibit multi-track reads, but skip deleted sectors. A method *TryDns*, discussed later, is tried with different arguments to test whether the disk uses MFM or high density, and the test result is recorded in the instance variables *Mf* and *Hd*. *TryDns* tests the opposite side of the disk to see if it is double-sided; if so *Ds* is set too. Finally, the gap length and number of sectors per track are determined from these results, and left in instance variables.

The *InitDisk* and *FormatF* methods use an array *scGpl* to get the number of sectors per track and the gap length for reading and writing data, and formatting the disk:

```
unsigned char scGpl[8][3]={{0xf,7,0x1b},{9,0xe,0x2a},{5,0x1b,0x3a},{0,0,0},{0,0,0},
    {0xf,0xe,0x36},{9,0x1b,0x54},{5,0x35,0x74}};
```

```
Floppy::InitDisk(Drive) unsigned Drive; { int d;char s[14];
    curPath[surface=Drive&3]=path=Path++;/* keep track of which disk is in drive */
    wC(4);wC(surface); d=rC(); /* sense drive status */
    if((d&0xa0)!=0x20) return error=drvErr; /* check drive not initialized error */
    WP=(d&0x40)>>6; /* write protect */ verify=1; /* initially, request verification */
    Mt=0;Sk=1; /*single sector skip deleted sectors */
    if(TryDns(0,0)&&TryDns(0,1)&&TryDns(1,0)&&TryDns(1,1)) return error=diskErr;
    if(n=N) DTL=0xff; else DTL=0x80; /* if N=0 use 128 bytes per sector */
    Ds=1; surface=(Drive&3)|4;if(TryDns(Mf,Hd)) Ds=0;/* check if double sided */
    if(!(sectorsPerTrack=scGpl[d=n+(Mf<<2)][0])) return diskErr;
    GPL=scGpl[d][1]; if(Hd) { sectorsPerTrack<<=1;}
    sectorsPerDisk=sectorsPerTrack*80*(Ds+1); return error=0;
}
```

The method *TryDns* tries to read any sector id on the disk with a specified value for MFM and high density. It uses the read id command (Figure 10-4f) which gadflies on the interrupt request pin's value and has a result phase that is the same as the read sector command, but only reads the id, and not the data, of a sector. It executes without error if the density on the disk matches the requested density. *InitDisk* uses *TryDns* up to four times on side 0 to establish the density of the disk, and then with the established density on side 1 to see if that side is also formatted the same way. We show the M68332 procedure; the M68340 procedure uses port B for ports F and C.

```
Floppy::TryDns(mfm,high) int mfm,high;{
    if(Hd=high) conReg=0; else conReg=2;Mf=mfm;
    wC(0xa|(Mf<<6));wC(surface); /* read id */ while(portF>=0); /* gadfly */
    CheckF(); return ((ST0&0xf8)!=0)|| ST1|| (ST2&0x33); /* check applicable errors */
}
```

The M68332 *SeekF* method moves the head to the cylinder having the sector that is to be read or written. (The M68340 procedure uses port B for ports F and C.) Its parameter is the logical sector; we divide that by the number of sectors per track, as established by the *InitDisk* method, using the remainder as the sector number in a subsequent read or write sector command and the quotient as the cylinder number. We divide in assembler language to avoid using THINK C's divide subroutine, which is not downloaded into the M68332 or M68340, and to simultaneously extract both the quotient and remainder. However, if the disk is double-sided, the least significant bit of that cylinder number is the head (side) number and the former number is halved. A seek command is given only if the disk head is not already on the desired cylinder.

```
Floppy::SeekF(a) long a; { unsigned i;
    if(curPath[i=(surface&3)]!=path) return error=wrongDisk;
    if(a>=sectorsPerDisk) return error = addrErr; /* address not in disk, exit */
asm{ move.l a,d0 /* divide the address a */
    divu.w sectorsPerTrack,d0 /* by the sectorsPerTrack */
    move.w d0,i /* quotient is track number,side */
    swap d0 /* remainder is */
    move.b d0,R /* sector number */
}
```

```
EOT=R; N=n; /* endOfTrack = current cylinder to read/write 1 track, get sector size */
if(Hd) conReg=0; else conReg=2;
surface&=~4; if(Ds) { surface|=(H=i&1)<<2; i>>=1;} /* double sided */
if(C==i) return 0; C=i; /* if current cylinder then do not seek */
wC(0xf);wC(surface);wC(C); /* seek cylinder C on surface SURFACE */
while(portF>=0); /* gadfly on drive being in execution mode */
wC(8); ST0=rC(); if((rC()!=C)||((ST0&0xf8)!=0x20)) return error=seekErr; return 0;
}
```

The actual *InF* method we use is similar to the simplified method described earlier, but attempts to read sector a into a buffer at address p until that is done without error or up to six attempts have resulted in errors, and it uses assembler language to read the data. The error handling strategy attempts to move the head in one cylinder after the second try, and out one track after the fourth try, to read a sector that might be written slightly off track. The embedded assembler language is used to read high density MFM disks; the earlier C statements are just a bit too slow for this fast mode. Writing the last command byte (*DTL*) immediately begins the execution phase of the read sector operation; *DTL* is written directly in *InF* rather than in a subroutine to avoid executing RTS instructions, to avoid overrun errors when reading high density disks. This routine also detects abnormal termination, when the master status register's execution bit is cleared, to prevent hanging up if the controller fails to read the expected number of bytes.

```
Floppy::InF(a,p) long a; register char *p; {
    register int i; unsigned errorCount;
    if(error) return error; /* if an error has occurred earlier, do not read a sector after all */
    for(errorCount=0;errorCount<6;errorCount++){/* try 6 times, return when no error */
        if(errorCount==2)SeekF(a-sectorsPerTrack*(Ds+1));/* on 3rd try, step in */
        if(errorCount==4)SeekF(a+sectorsPerTrack*(Ds+1));/* on 5rd try, step in */
        error=0; if(SeekF(a)) continue; i=(1<<(n+7))-1;
        wC(6+(Mf<<6)); SetupF(); while((mStat&0xc0)!=0x80); data=DTL; /* read sect */
asm{@0
    move.b mStat,d0 /* gadfly on drive request for data */
    bpl.s @0
    and.b #0x20,d0 /* if no longer in execution phase, exit */
    beq.s @1
    move.b data,(p)+ /* input a byte of data */
    dbra i,@0
@1 }
        if(!CheckF()) return 0;
    }
    return error=readErr;
}
```

The *OutF* method, like the *InF* method, attempts to write sector a taking data from a buffer at address p, until no error is detected or six attempts have resulted in errors. The method returns a nonzero value if the write operation fails. If the write sector command appears to have succeeded, and the *verify* instance variable is nonzero, the sector that was just written is read again using the *InF* method to verify that it is properly stored and can likely be read later without errors. This extra *verify* step slows down the writing of sectors by a factor of about 10 because a sector is written and a whole disk revolution later the same sector is read. Verification is indispensable when the data being written might be lost forever if it is not written correctly. By clearing the *verify* instance variable, this verify step will be omitted to speed up the writing of sectors, but the user should attempt to check the writing of data by reading them later. This can be done when copying a whole disk. The destination disk is first fully written, without verifying each sector, and then each sector on the disk is read just to verify it.

```
Floppy::OutF(a,p) long a; register char *p; {
    register int i; unsigned errorCount; char verifyBuffer[1024];
    if(error) return error; if(WP) return error=writeProtectErr;
    for(errorCount=0;errorCount<6;errorCount++){/* try 6 times, return when no error */
        if(errorCount==2)SeekF(a-sectorsPerTrack*(Ds+1));/* on 3rd try, step in */
        if(errorCount==4)SeekF(a+sectorsPerTrack*(Ds+1));/* on 5rd try, step in */
        error=0; if(SeekF(a)) continue; i=(1<<(n+7))-1;
        wC(5+(Mf<<6)); SetupF(); while((mStat&0xc0)!=0x80); data=DTL; /* write sec */
asm{@0
    move.b mStat,d0 /* gadfly on drive request for data */
    bpl.s @0
    and.b #0x20,d0 /* if no longer in execution phase, exit */
    beq.s @1
    move.b (p)+,data /* output a byte of data */
    dbra i,@0
@1 }
    if(!CheckF()) { if(verify)InF(a,verifyBuffer); return 0;}
    }
    return error=writeErr;
}
```

The *FormatF* method will format an entire disk according to the *mode* parameter. A double-sided double-density (MFM) high-density disk will be formatted with 256-byte sectors if *mode* is 29. The method establishes the density and side information from the *mode,* and checks the drive's functionality and the disk's write protection. It then obtains the gap length and number of sectors per track from the array *scGpl* and returns an error if the requested format is illegal. The format command (Figure 10-4f) is given for each track. Before each format command is given, a seek command is given to move the head to the desired track, but the *SeekF* method is not used because the track is not formatted, it probably returns errors. For each track for the format command, four bytes are supplied for each sector, which are the cylinder, head, sector and size that will be written in the sector's id fields. These are prepared in the local variable array *d* before the format command is given. The command then appears to write these id values much as the *OutF* method writes data into a sector. For double-sided disks, after one seek command moves the heads, both the top and bottom tracks in that cylinder are formatted. The sector numbers are written into the array *d* and thus put into the id fields of consecutive sectors, with all the even-numbered sectors being written first and then all the odd-numbered sectors written later, where each is written in increasing order of sector numbers. This provides an interleave factor of *sectorsPerTrack*/2 which gives slightly better performance than an interleave factor of 0. For an interleave factor of 0, if consecutively numbered logical sectors are read or written, each takes one full disk revolution because after logical sector i is read or written, the head will have just passed logical sector i+1 before the command is given to read logical sector i+1, and that sector will be read the next time it is met after a full disk revolution has passed. For an interleave factor of *sectorsPerTrack/2*, logical sector i+1 will be read after sector i, after half a disk revolution has passed. After the whole disk is formatted, each sector is read to check for errors. If no errors are detected, the format operation is verified. We show the M68332 procedure; the M68340 procedure uses port B for ports F and C.

```
Floppy::FormatF(drive,mode) unsigned drive,mode;{
    /* mode 0=128, 1=256, 2=512, 3=1024, add 4 for MFM, add 8 for Ds, add 16 for Hd */
    unsigned char d[256][4]; unsigned i,j,k,l; long a; register unsigned char *end,*dp;
    error=0; Hd=mode>>4; Ds=mode>>3; Mf=mode>>2; N=mode&3;
    wC(4); wC(surface=drive&3); j=rC(); /* get drive status */
    if((j&0xa0)!=0x20) return error=drvErr; if(j&0x40) return error=writeProtectErr;
    if(!(j=sectorsPerTrack=scGpl[i=(mode&=7)][0])) return error=diskErr; GPL=scGpl[i][2];
    if(Hd) {sectorsPerTrack<<=1; conReg=0;}
    else conReg=2; end=(unsigned char*)d+(sectorsPerTrack<<2);
    for(i=0;i<30;i++) {d[i][3]=N; d[i][2]=((i<<1)+(i>=j))%sectorsPerTrack;}
    for(l=0;l<80;l++){ /* 80 cylinder */
        for(i=0;i<30;i++) d[i][0]=l; /* track, sector (interleaved)*/
        wC(0xf);wC(surface);wC(l); /* seek cylinder C on surface SURFACE */
        while(portF>=0); /* gadfly on drive being in execution mode */
        wC(8); ST0=rC(); rC();
        for(k=0;k<=Ds;k++) { /* for each head */
            for(i=0;i<30;i++) d[i][1]=k;
            dp=(unsigned char*)d; wC(0xd+(Mf<<6));wC(surface+(k<<2));
            wC(mode&3);wC(sectorsPerTrack);wC(GPL); wC(0); /* format */
            while((unsigned char*)dp<end){ while((mStat&0x80)==0); data=*dp++;}
            CheckF(); if(IC||EC||ST1||(ST2&0x33)||error)return error=badFormat;
        }
    }
    InitDisk(drive); /* note: FormatF can be executed without first executing InitDisk */
    for(a=0;a<sectorsPerDisk;a++){ /* verify all sectors can be read without error */
        if(InF(a,(char *)(dp=(unsigned char*)d))) return error;
    }
}
```

There are many possible improvements to the example above. A curious anomaly of the technique used in *InitDisk* to automatically determine a disk's format: if the disk had been formatted as double-sided, and then formatted again as single-sided with the same density, this procedure decides the new format is also double-sided. A better way would be to try to read sector *sectorsPerTrack* from side 0 cylinder 1. If that succeeds, the disk is single-sided. The interleave factor can be set to about 4 to significantly improve performance. The methods used gadfly synchronization; by inverting WD37C65C's interrupt request and using that as IRQ6 rather than the M68332's port F (or the M68340's port B) bit 6, interrupt synchronization could be used. Moreover, if the M68340 were used, DMA could be used to transfer the data.

Each operating system organizes its disks differently; we briefly describe OS-9's file organization. The disk is formatted with 256 bytes per sector, using MF or MFM, low or high density and single or double sides. Data are organized in *files,* where a file is a collection of one or more segments, and a *segment* is a sequence of consecutive logical sectors on the disk. For instance, if there is room on the disk at logical sector 0x503 for just eight sectors (a first segment can be fit there) and there is room starting at logical sector 0x7F3 for the remaining sectors, a 0x903 byte file named MYDATA might be stored in two segments; the first 0x800 bytes might be stored in eight sectors in the first segment starting at logical sector 0x503, while the last 0x103 bytes would be stored in two sectors in the second segment starting at logical sector 0x7F3. (A file needing more than one segment is *fragmented.*) A file is described by a sector called a *file descriptor* (say at logical sector 0x12E). Its contents give the current file size and a segment list whose entries are the logical sector of the beginning and length of each of the segments of the file. A *directory* is used to find the files: In it, an ASCII string file name and the logical sector of its file descriptor are stored for each file. The directory is itself just a file, with its own file descriptor. To find a file with a given name, the operating system searches the directory for a matching name and gets the logical sector of its file descriptor. For our example, the string "MYDATA" and the logical sector number 0x12E are in the directory file. From there, it can find any sector in it.

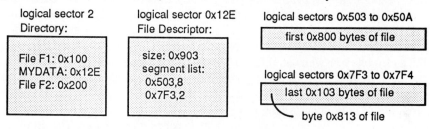

Figure 10-5. OS-9 File Format.

File sectors are perceived by the end user as if they were consecutively numbered, even though they may be in different segments. To read a given byte, OS-9 measures out the sizes of each segment from the file descriptor to find the segment and the sector in it containing the desired byte, and then gets the logical sector the given sector is in. For instance, to read the sector containing MYDATA's byte 0x813 which must be in file sector 0x8, the directory is searched for the string "MYDATA", to get the logical sector 0x12E. The first sector in the second segment has the desired sector. So it reads logical sector 0x7F3 of the disk; byte 0x813 is that sector's byte 0x13. The operating system does not have to go through all this each time a sector is read, but it keeps the computed locations used in the last access and tries to use them in the next access where possible.

To write a new file or expand an existing file, we avoid writing over existing files' sectors. A group of k contiguously numbered logical sectors are called a *cluster,* which is the basic unit of allocation on a disk (k may be 1). In a *bit map,* which is stored in one or more sectors on the disk, unused clusters are represented by 0s and used clusters by 1s. Unused clusters are chosen from this bit map and marked as being used, when a new file is created or an old file is expanded.

When a disk's files become fragmented, disk access times are increased because, while we often read or write consecutive file sectors, they correspond to logical sectors which tend to be located in different cylinders, requiring multiple seek operations. We can *collect garbage* by rewriting the files so they use one segment per file. Then consecutive sectors can often be read with fewer seek operations.

This rather long example shows almost all the key routines needed to handle a WD37C65C floppy controller chip, to read and write data on a 3 $^1/_2$ " floppy disk. With this example, you now have enough information to build a practical disk interface.

10-2 Display Systems

A microcomputer may be used in an intelligent terminal or in a personal computer. Such systems require a display. Any microcomputer requiring the display of more than the few digits an LED or LCD display can handle may have to use a CRT display.

This section describes the concepts of CRT display systems. We present the format of the NTSC black-and-white signal. We generate a video signal using video RAM, and timing signals using the M68332 TPU or M68340 TM, to implement a realistic CRT display system. It can be used as the display part of a useful terminal.

10-2.1 Raster Display Format

A *National Television System Committee (NTSC)* signal is used in the United States and Canada for all commercial television. A computer display system consists of the CRT and its drive electronics – essentially a specialized TV set – and hardware and software able to send pulses to time the electron beam, which is a stream of bits to make the TV screen black or white at different points. Figure 10-6 diagrams the front of a TV screen. An electron beam, generated by a hot cathode and controlled by a grid, is deflected by electromagnets in the back of the CRT and made to move from left side to right side and from top to bottom across the face of the CRT. More electrons produce a whiter spot. The traversal of the beam across the face is called a *raster line*. The set of raster lines that "paint" the screen from top to bottom is a field. NTSC signals use two fields, one slightly offset from the other, as shown in Figure 10-8a, to completely paint a picture *frame*.

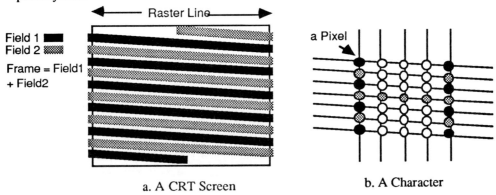

a. A CRT Screen   b. A Character

Figure 10-6. The Raster Scan Display Used in Television.

In NTSC signals, a frame takes 1/30th second and a field takes 1/60th second. The raster line takes 1/15,750th second, a field has 262 1/2 raster lines and a frame has 525 raster lines. As the beam moves from side to side and from top to bottom, the electron beam is controlled to light up the screen in a pattern. Figure 10-6b shows how a letter H is written in both fields of a frame. A *pixel* is the (smallest controllable) dot on the screen; a clear circle represents a pixel having no light, and a dark circle (black for field 1 and gray for field 2) shows a pixel where there is light on the screen.

The *NTSC composite video signal* is an analog signal, diagrammed in Figure 10-7. The displayed signal is an analog signal where a maximum voltage (about $1/2$ volt) produces a white dot, a lower voltage ($3/8$ volt) produces gray, and an even lower voltage ($1/4$ volt) produces a black dot. The part of the signal corresponding to the time when the electron beam is moved to the left side (*horizontal retrace*) or to the top (*vertical retrace*) occurs between the displayed parts. At these times, *horizontal sync* and *vertical sync* pulses appear as lower voltage (0 volts) or "blacker-than-black" pulses. The CRT system uses a *sync separator* circuit to extract these pulses so it can derive the horizontal and vertical sync pulses, which are used to time the beam deflections on the screen. This signal is called the composite video signal because it has the video signal and the sync signals composed onto one signal. If this signal is to be sent over the air, it is modulated onto a radio frequency (r.f.) carrier (such as channel 2). Alternatively, the separate video, horizontal, and vertical sync signals can be sent over different wires to the CRT system, so they do not need to be separated; this gives the best resolution, such as is needed in 1024-by-1024 pixel CRT displays in "engineering workstations." The composite video is used in character displays that have 80 characters per line. The r.f. modulated signals are used in games and home computers intended to be connected to unmodified home TV sets, but are capable of only about 50 characters per line.

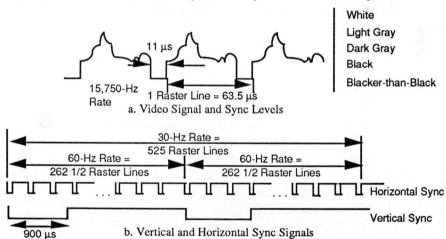

Figure 10-7. The Composite Video Signal.

The frequency of the vertical sync pulses, which corresponds to the time of a field, is generally fixed to 60 Hz to prevent AC hum from making the screen image have bars run across it, as in cheap TVs. It is also about the lowest frequency at which the human eye does not detect flicker. American computer CRTs almost universally use this vertical sync frequency. The horizontal sync frequency in computer CRTs is usually about 15,750 Hz, as specified by the NTSC standard, but may be a bit faster to permit more lines on the screen yet keep the vertical sync frequency at 60 Hz. The magnetic beam deflection on the CRT is tuned to a specific frequency, and the electronics must provide horizontal sync pulses at this frequency, or the picture will be nonlinear. The pulse widths of these horizontal and vertical pulses are specified by the electronics that drive the CRT. Thus, the CRT controller must be set up to give a specific horizontal and vertical frequency and pulse width, as specified by the CRT electronics.

10-2.2 A Video DRAM CRT Controller

Data can be displayed on a TV screen using a *bit-mapped CRT controller*. Recently, for instance in the Macintosh Classic II, *video RAMs* have been used to supply a CRT display signal; they are DRAMs that appear to be primary memory to the processor (see Section 3-3.5) which also have an independent serial port that can provide a stream of bits to the screen, so that a bit in DRAM memory is displayed as a pixel on the screen.

Figure 10-8 gives the logic diagram of a video DRAM and other components to make a bit-mapped M68332 CRT display. The TMS44C250, a (256K,4) DRAM, requires timing signals RAS and CAS, derived from the M68332's chip select Cs6 by the 21199 delay line and 74HC32 OR gate. The M68340 uses CS3 in place of CS6. Multiplexers 74HC157 provide M68332 address lines A[17 to 9] when RAS falls, and A[8 to 0] when CAS falls, to chip address lines a[8 to 0]. (Some peculiarities of this diagram are discussed later in this section).

We can use the M68332 program *main* below to verify that the DRAM works before we attempt to use the video RAM functions, checking the DRAM for bad address or data lines, using checkerboard test patterns. If a data line is bad, the procedure *checker* returns a value with a T bit where any wrong data bit is found, and if an address line is bad, *main*'s *i* index identifies the address line that is not functional.

```
main(){ int i; long loc; unsigned char v; /* for the M68332 */
    pinAssign(cs6,byte);baseAssign(6,0x100000,k512);
    optionAssign(6,rd+wr+upper+as,1,user+super,0); refresh(); asm{and #0xf8ff,sr}
    for(i=0;i<18;i++) {if(checker(0x140000,1L<<i,0x40000>>i)) break; }
}
```

The M68340 program *main* uses CS3 in place of CS6.

```
main(){ int i; long loc; unsigned char v; /* for the M68340 */
    CsAssign(3,0x100000,wait1+byte,rdWr); refresh(); asm{and #0xf8ff,sr}
    for(i=0;i<18;i++) {if(checker(0x140000,1L<<i,0x40000>>i)) break; }
}
```

Both use the *checker* procedure as a subroutine.

```
unsigned char checker(Base,Range,Size) long Base; register long Range,Size;{
    register long i,j; register char *p,v,k;
    p=(char*)Base; for (i = k = 0; i < Size; i++)
        { for ( j = 0; j < Range; j++ ) *p++ = k; k = ~ k; }
    p=(char*)Base; for (i = k = 0; i < Size; i++)
        { for ( j = 0; j < Range; j++ ) if( v=(*p++) ^ k) return v; k = ~ k; }
    return 0;
}
```

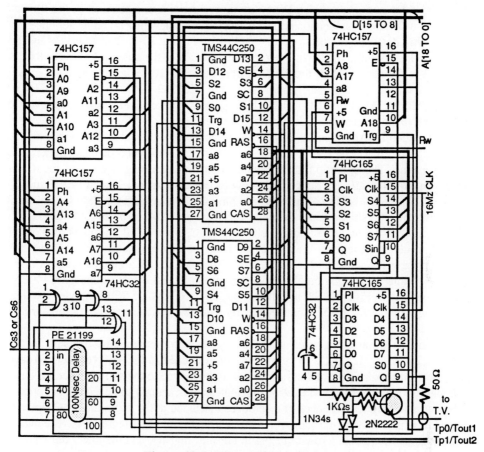

Figure 10-8. Video DRAM display.

This memory must be refreshed at least every 8 milliseconds. A simple refresh mechanism uses the SIM's periodic interrupt; its handler in *refresh*, executed every 8 milliseconds, reads a byte at each of 512 consecutive row addresses to refresh memory.

```
void refresh(){ register int *iPtr;
  *(char*)0xfffa01=0xe; *(long*)0xfffa22=0x6420042;
  asm{lea @0,iPtr} *(int **)0x108=iPtr; return;
    asm{@0 move.l a0,-(a7)
    movea.l #0x140000,a0
    @1  tst.b (a0)
    adda.l #0x200,a0
    cmpa.l #0x180000,a0
    blo @1
    move.l (a7)+,a0
    rte
    }
}
```

The video port of the video DRAM outputs a serial byte stream on S[7 to 0] from consecutive DRAM byte locations (to be discussed below), which is further serialized by shifting this data out of the upper 74HC165 of Figure 10-8. The lower 74HC165 provides a load pulse to the upper 74HC165 and a clock to the video RAM every 8 CLK cycles. Bits are sent through the 2N2222 transistor at a 16 MHz rate, where they are combined with a sync pulse, generated by the M68332 TPU on TP0 and TP1 or M68340 TM on TOUT1 and TOUT2, which gives a "blacker-than-black" sync level, to directly drive the composite video input of a TV set.

The video DRAM supplies a stream of bytes which will generate the video signal. The TMS44C250 accesses 4 bit words and Figure 10-8 uses two of these to access a byte at a time. The operation is best understood by examining one bit of the 4 bits inside the TMS44C250. To read a bit, a row of DRAM memory is read (see Figure 3-18b) as if to select a bit to be output to the M68332, but instead the TMS44C250 puts this entire row in a shift register (actually it is a static RAM) to be shifted out of a pin S7, S6, ... S0 on the rising edge of the shift clock SC. Once a 512 bit row is read out of DRAM into the shift register, 512 SC clock cycles can independently shift 512 bits out without interfering with the M68332's use of the DRAM as a conventional primary memory. While the discussion above applies to one bit, all 4 bits in one TMS44C250 and thus a byte in Figure 10-8, are shifted out on each edge of SC. 512 bytes are thus shifted out while the DRAM is independently available for use as primary memory by the M68332.

In order to shift out more than 512 bytes, a command must be sent to the TMS44C250 every 512 bytes to copy a row from DRAM to the shift register. To save pins, the command and the address of the row to be moved to the shift register are time-multiplexed on normal DRAM control and address pins; though these techniques appear to be unusual, they are instances of techniques discussed at the beginning of Chapter 4. The address is sent using the address register output technique (Figure 4-3c). The high 9 bits of this address select a row to be put in the shift register, and the low 9 bits select a byte in it which is shifted out first. Observing that the output enable OE on a normal DRAM is only used in the later part of a memory cycle, the chip designers apply the the command to this same pin in negative logic (now called the transfer register select TRG pin) when RAS falls; however, later in the cycle it is used as the DRAM output enable. The upper left 74HC157 of Figure 10-8 supplies TRG; the command to transfer to the shift register, on pin 10, is sent when RAS falls, and later it is asserted low (pin 11 is grounded) to enable outputs when we read a byte from the DRAM. (The write enable W similarly carries a command signal, but we do not use this command, so we negate W (H) when RAS falls.) We derive this transfer command from an address bit, using an address line output technique (Figure 4-3d). The (256K,8) video RAM is enabled for a 512K range of memory from 0x100000 to 0x180000. When reading a byte from the range 0x100000 to 0x13ffff, address A[23 to 19] = 0x01 selects the video RAM and address bit A18 is L, asserting the command; the DRAM row A[17 to 9] is transfered to the shift register and shifting begins at byte A[8 to 0] in it. When reading or writing a byte from the range 0x140000 to 0x17ffff, address A[23 to 19] = 0x01 selects the video RAM and address bit A18 is H, negating the command, which effects normal reading or writing the byte in memory; the byte is read or written into DRAM memory. We show the M68332 procedures first, then the M68340 procedures.

```
#define hTime 34      /* for the M68332 */
#define vTime (262*hTime+hTime/2)
void startSync() { register int *p1; /* start sync, handle sync and refresh */
  asm{ or #0x700,sr } displayP=(char*)0x100000; refreshP=(char*)0x140000; Field=0;
  p1=(int *)0xfffe00; p1[0]= 0xb; p1[4]=0x640; /* set IARB, VECTOR, LEVEL */
  asm{ lea @0,p1 } *((int **)0x100)= p1; /* set up interrupt addr. */
  asm{ lea @2,p1 } *((int **)0x104)= p1; /* set up interrupt addr. */
  *(int *)0xffff00=0x93; /* set up channel control */
  *(long *)0xffff04=hTime+((hTime-6L)<<16); /* set up horiz. period, high time */
  *(int *)0xffff10=0x93; /* set up channel control */
  *(long *)0xffff14=vTime+((vTime-(hTime*25L))<<16); /* vert period, highTm */
  Cfs =0x99; Hsr =0xa; Cpr =0x7; /* prepare chan 0,1 */
  IntEn =3; asm{ and #0xf8ff,sr }; /* enable interrupts */
  return;
```

▷
```
  asm 68020{@0 move.l a0,-(a7)
  movea.l displayP,a0
  tst.b (a0) /* transfer page to video output */
  adda.l #0x100,a0 /* next page address to displayP */
  move.l a0,displayP

  movea.l refreshP,a0
  cmpa.l #0x150000,a0 /* if at end of quarter of DRAM */
  blo @1
  movea.l #0x140000,a0 /* start at beginning */
  @1 tst.b (a0) /* refresh low quarter of DRAM */
  tst.b 0x10000(a0) /* refresh next quarter of DRAM */
  tst.b 0x20000(a0) /* refresh mid quarter of DRAM */
  tst.b 0x30000(a0) /* refresh high quarter of DRAM */
  adda.l #0x200,a0 /* next page address to refreshP */
  move.l a0,refreshP
  tst.w 0xfffe20
  move.w #0xfffe,0xfffe20 /* remove interrupt */
  move.l (a7)+,a0
  rte
```

▷
```
  @2 move.l #0x100000,displayP
  not.w Field
  beq.s @3
  move.l #0x100080,displayP
  @3 tst.w 0xfffe20
  move.w #0xfffd,0xfffe20 /* remove interrupt */
  rte
  }
}
```

The M68332 procedure *startSync* above sets up the M68332 TPU channel 0 to generate horizontal sync pulses using PWM output (Section 7-2.2) and interrupts (Section 7-2.4) every horizontal scan period as needed by the NTSC standard (Figure 10-7). TP0 is low 11 μsec. and has a period of 63.5 μsec. (actually the period is 64.2 μsec.). Channel 1 similarly generates 16.666 millisec. vertical sync pulses which are low for 900 μsec., and interrupts every vertical scan period. *startSync* initializes pointers *displayP* and *refreshP* for the interrupt handlers. The M68340 procedure is very similar, substituting the TM for the TPU.

```
#define hTime 531     /* for the M68340 */
#define vTime (262L*hTime+hTime/2)/4
void startSync() { register int *p1; /* start sync, handle sync and refresh */
    asm{or #0x700,sr} displayP=(char*)0x100000; refreshP=(char*)0x140000; Field=0;
    tmMcr1=0x8d; tmIr1=0x640; tmCmd1=0; tmCmd1=CPE+TOI+Div1+VdSqu+Tgl;
    tmMcr2=0x8d; tmIr2=0x641; tmCmd2=0; tmCmd2=CPE+TOI+Div4+VdSqu+Tgl;
    tmPr11=94; tmPr21=hTime-94; tmPr12=4*hTime; tmPr22=vTime-4*hTime;
    tmCmd1+=SWR; tmCmd2+=SWR; tmSPr1=TOI; tmSPr2=TOI;
    asm{ lea @0,p1 } *((int **)0x100)= p1; asm{ lea @2,p1 } *((int **)0x104)= p1;
    asm{ and #0xfdff,sr }; /* enable interrupts */
    return;
    asm 68020{@0 move.l a0,-(a7)
    movea.l displayP,a0
    tst.b (a0) /* transfer page to video output */
    adda.l #0x100,a0 /* next page address to displayP */
    move.l a0,displayP
    move #TOI,0xffffff608 ; tmSPr1
    movea.l refreshP,a0
    cmpa.l #0x150000,a0 /* if at end of quarter of DRAM */
    blo @1
    movea.l #0x140000,a0 /* start at beginning */
    @1 tst.b (a0) /* refresh low quarter of DRAM */
    tst.b 0x10000(a0) /* refresh next quarter of DRAM */
    tst.b 0x20000(a0) /* refresh mid quarter of DRAM */
    tst.b 0x30000(a0) /* refresh high quarter of DRAM */
    adda.l #0x200,a0 /* next page address to refreshP */
    move.l a0,refreshP
    move.l (a7)+,a0
    rte
    @2 move.l #0x100000,displayP
    not.w Field
    beq.s @3
    move.l #0x100080,displayP
    @3 move #TOI,0xffffff648 ; tmSPr1
    rte
}}
```

The procedures *main* below display vertical bars on the screen.

char *refreshP,*displayP; int Field,Line; /* global pointers, counters */

```
main(){ int i=0;  /* for the M68332 */
  pinAssign(cs6,byte);
  baseAssign(6,0x100000,k512); optionAssign(6,rd+wr+upper+as,1,user+super,0);
  for(refreshP=(char*)0x140000;refreshP<(char*)(0x140000+264*0x100L);)
    *(refreshP++)=(i^=0xff);
  startSync(); while(1) asm{ STOP #0}; /* stop, wait for interrupts, repeat forever */
}

main(){ int i=0;  /* for the M68340 */
  CsAssign(3,0x100000,wait1+byte,rdWr);
  for(refreshP=(char*)0x140000;refreshP<(char*)(0x140000+264*0x100L);)
    *(refreshP++)=(i^=0xff);
  startSync(); while(1) asm{ STOP #0}; /* stop, wait for interrupts, repeat forever */
}
```

Note that a screen line displays for 63.5-11 = 52.5 µsec, and one byte displays for 482 nsec; a screen line uses 109 bytes (872 bits or pixels). A DRAM row outputs 512 bytes, so the same DRAM row can store four screen lines. The horizontal handler after label *@0* sends *displayP* to the video RAM and updates *displayP*. This transfers a DRAM row to shift register to display a quarter of the row during the next vertical trace. The vertical handler after *@2* reinitializes *displayP* to the top of the display buffer. The horizontal handler also refreshes memory four words at a time, effectively accomplishing what the handler in the procedure *refresh* did within each 8 millisecond refresh period, so another PI or TPU interrupt is not needed to refresh DRAM.

To effect interleaving of fields in a frame (Figure 10-6a), the last vertical scan of a field must be half as long as a normal scan; this is implemented by setting the vertical period to 262 1/2 times the horizontal period in the *#define vTime (262 * hTime + hTime / 2)* statement. Also, the vertical handler will alternatively set up the address of the beginning of the buffer, or the address of the 128th byte in it, as the initial address used in the horizontal handler to transfer a DRAM row to the shift register, but the horizontal handler increments the address by 256. This effectively displays every other line in each field of the frame. The pixel in screen row i column j thus essentially corresponds to bit $j\%8$ of byte $0x140000 + i*128 + j/8$.

The procedure *main* above can be modified to display other patters than vertical bars. To clear the display, we execute the loop: *for(refreshP = (char*)0x140000; refreshP< (char*)(0x140000 +264 * 0x100L);) *(refreshP++)=0;* To display a line, essentially from top left to bottom right on the screen, we then execute the loop:

```
for(i=0,refreshP=(char*)0x140000;refreshP<(char*)0x150000;){
    switch (i){
    case 0: *(refreshP+=0x80)=0xc0;i=1;break;
    case 1: *(refreshP+=0x80)=0x30;i=2;break;
    case 2: *(refreshP+=0x80)=0xc;i=3;break;
    case 3: *(refreshP+=0x80)=3;refreshP++;i=0;break;
}};
```

Characters can be displayed on the screen by the procedure *drawChar* below. Simple eight line by sixteen column characters are stored in an array, as the five-character array *tbl* illustrates. The array row *tbl[2]* illustrates a slash character '/' where each row has two white pixels, corresponding to T bits. These are moved by *drawChar* to the video RAM where they are automatically displayed. A backslash character '\' is stored in *tbl[1]* and a solid square in *tbl[0]*. The reason the solid square has alternating T and F bits is that our cheap display, a TV with a 5 MHz bandwidth, behaves as a low pass filter, emphasizing horizontal lines because they have lower frequency components than vertical lines. We compensate by chopping up horizontal lines. A character 'A' is stored in *tbl[3]* and a 'B' is stored in *tbl[4]*. Note the chopping of horizontal lines.

```
unsigned tbl[5][8]={
    {0xaaaa,0xaaaa,0xaaaa,0xaaaa,0xaaaa,0xaaaa,0xaaaa,0xaaaa},/* tbl[0] block white */
    {0xc000,0x3000,0xc00,0x300,0xc0,0x30,0xc,3},/* tbl[1] backslash */
    {3,0xc,0x30,0xc0,0x300,0xc00,0x3000,0xc000},/* tbl[2] slash */
    {0x300,0xCC0,0x3030,0xC0C0,0xC0C0,0xaaa8,0x8080,0x8080},/* letter A */
    {0xaa80,0x8020,0x8020,0xaa80,0x8020,0x8020,0x8020,0xaa80}/* letter B */
};
```

The procedure *drawChar(c,x,y)* draws a character, whose pattern is stored in array row *tbl[c]* with its upper left corner at display row *x* and column *y*. Register pointers *letter* and *screen* are set up in C, and used in assembler language to copy the array row onto the video RAM area for the character's display.

```
void drawChar(c,x,y) char c; unsigned x,y;{
    register int bit; register long *screen; register unsigned *letter;
    letter=tbl[c];  screen=(long*)(0x140000+((x>>3)&0xfe)+(y<<7));bit=x&0xf;
asm{
    moveq #7,d1
@0 clr.l d0
    move.w (letter)+,d0
    lsl.l  bit,d0
    or.l d0,(screen)
    add #128,screen
    dbra d1,@0
}}
```

The procedures above are the basis for the Macintosh's QuickDraw routines. A set of these routines can be used to draw lines, rectangles, ellipses, arcs, and letters using different fonts. A class can be created whose methods do these things for the M68332. Some other improvements are needed to make this section's techniques useful. We really display on the screen only while the main program is executing the *STOP #0* instruction. This instruction responds to interrupts with small and constant delay. If a general program were running, the interrupt latency time would be variable, being long when a long instruction like *divu.l* is interrupted at its initiation and this would result in jagged edges as the handler transfers data from DRAM to shift register at different times. One way to compensate is to let another TPU channel interrupt the processor just before the horizontal interrupt occurs, whose handler just executes the *STOP #0* instruction, so the horizontal handler always executes with small and constant latency.

This section introduced a realistic bit-mapped display for a terminal. The system shown in Figure 10-8 is suitably flexible so you can further experiment with it to get a comprehensive understanding of displays. We encourage you to study it.

10-3 Conclusions

This chapter introduced two common interfaces: the secondary storage and the CRT display. These rather complete case studies give a reasonably full example of common interface designs. They also embody the techniques you have studied in earlier chapters. Besides presenting these important interfaces, this chapter serves to show how the techniques in the other chapters will find extensive application in almost any interface design.

For further reading on floppy disks, we strongly recommend the data sheets for the 37C65C from Western Digital. Harold Stone's "Microcomputer Interfacing" has additional general information on the analog aspects of storage devices.

Do You Know These Terms?

See the End of Chapter 1 for Instructions.

high density, surface, track, cylinder, step rate, settling time, fill area, sector, index hole, index pulse, logical sector number, interleave factor, unformatted capacity, formatted capacity, format, seek, read sector, implied seek, write sector, restore, recalibrate, command phase, execution phase, result phase, fragmented disk, file descriptor, directory, file sector, cluster, bit map, garbage collection, National Television System Committee (NTSC), raster line, frame, pixel, NTSC composite video signal, horizontal retrace, vertical retrace, horizontal sync, vertical sync, sync separator, bit-mapped CRT controller, video RAM.

11

Operating Systems and Device Drivers

Earlier chapters have shown how an I/O device can be controlled by software and time can be managed by procedures and methods, written in C. This final chapter shows how such a device can be controlled through an operating system device driver. The user will call the device driver by an operating system service call (as introduced in Section 5-3.3), so that to him or her, all devices appear to be simple to use and interchangeable with each other (as introduced in Section 4-5). It contains all the code needed to control the I/O device.

The main topic of this chapter will show device drivers for the M6821 PIA (Section 4-3.2) and M68681 DUART (Section 9-3.5). These drivers will be shown for the Microware operating system OS-9, which is a derivative of the UNIX operating system.

We first introduce the operating system to understand what a device driver is and what an operating system is supposed to do, because without that background, the complexity of a device driver seems unwarranted. You probably already know much of the material in this section, but if you do not, you have to understand the environment of a device driver rather thoroughly before you study it.

We then study a device driver. This section can be scanned over at a high level, in order to understand the idea of a device driver and appreciate its complexity and its power. This section can also be read in detail, to learn a great deal about programming in general and the writing of device drivers for OS-9 in particular.

Upon completing this chapter, the reader should understand what an operating system device driver is and how it controls an I/O device. He or she should be able to use operating system I/O system calls and should be prepared to study an operating system technical manual in order to write a device driver for a UNIX-like operating system.

11-1 What Is an Operating System?

In this section we discuss what an operating system is. We identify the main functions and features of an operating system, then the features of this state-of-the-art operating system OS-9. We show why we use OS-9 in this chapter. We then survey the component parts of such a system. This example serves to introduce the nature of multitasking operating systems in general, sufficient for the understanding of how a device driver works.

11-1.1 Three Views of an Operating System

In this introductory section, we present three different views of the operating system. It can be thought of as a main program, for which all user's main programs are subroutines, as a collection of frequently used subroutines, and as an extension of the hardware.

The notion of an operating system began with the need to assist users to more efficiently use large machines. Well before operating systems became common, users signed on, and sat at, the computer while it ran, just as you may have run I/O experiments on a computer in the laboratory for earlier sections of this book. After many users began using these machines, the large machines were run by human operators who fed the machine with data on punch cards and thus controlled it. Later, a program called the *operating system* replaced the human operator and scheduled the loading of punched cards and the use of the machine. Later still, remote CRT terminals were used, and the operating system quickly sequenced the programs in the computer, controlling computer time and resources for most efficient use of the machine. One large machine appeared to be many small machines, one for each user. In this sense, the operating system was the main program, and each user's program was a subroutine of that program.

The phenomenon we called factoring (Section 2-3.3) began to be useful in operating systems. If a large number of users use the same program segment, such a segment would be reproduced in each program. It would be more efficient to put such a program in one place, where all the user's programs would be able to use it. The omnipresent operating system was selected for most of these program segments that were originally in most user's programs, and the operating system became essentially a collection of commonly used program segments.

A third view of the operating system is as an extension to the hardware. A computer includes I/O chips which are quite difficult for the typical programmer to control. You have to read a book like this to know what they are doing. If they were controlled by subroutines, written by someone who read this book, the subroutines' users would be isolated from needing to know all that detail. They would only need to know the conventions for calling the subroutine. The subroutine call instruction would appear rather like a machine instruction, except that it would execute more slowly. The subroutine call is thought of as atomic and indivisible; the programmer learns to use it without knowing how it works, much as he or she learns about a machine instruction. In this sense, I/O subroutines augment the instruction set of the computer, especially to handle I/O.

The program segments should be used in the same way whenever possible. Rather than calling them with a JSR instruction and ending them with an RTS instruction (a subroutine convention), they are often called by some kind of TRAP instruction which behaves like a vectored interrupt. The OS-9 operating system uses an 683xx TRAP #0 instruction, followed by a word that specifies the particular program segment number to be executed, as in

```
        TRAP    #0
        DC I$WRITE
```

where I$WRITE is a 16-bit constant defined elsewhere to correspond to the program segment used to write data to I/O devices. This *system call* will act as a virtual instruction to write an I/O device's data. All such program segments are called by a system call this way, which in OS-9 is a TRAP #0 with a word following it that indicates which segment to execute.

High-level languages were then designed to use these system calls. It is difficult to find a widely used high-level language that does not depend on these system calls. For instance, C generally utilizes the UNIX operating system calls. The operating system can become essential to the environment for the running of programs written in such high-level languages. It is more a support for high-level languages, whether or not it is used, as originally used, to efficiently schedule many users on an expensive computer.

The personal computer generally uses operating systems to support high-level languages. Generally, the operating system must be run when the computer is started, and will call the user's application, and the user's application will call various program segments in the operating system using a system call. The user's application can handle I/O, including I/O to a special-purpose I/O device, using such system calls. The application can also access an I/O device directly, such as was done in the C programs shown in earlier chapters, or an assembly language program segment can be embedded in a high-level language to access I/O devices. However, if a program segment called a *device driver* is part of the operating system to access the device, then any program and all programs can use the same system call to use this device driver. The I/O device is available to any and all high-level languages with equal ease. A programmer that hacks away in BASIC to get an understanding of a process, and then rewrites the process in a C program, can use the same driver without modification, to make it easier to switch from one language to another.

Before we leave this motivational discussion, we observe that the environment created for the high-level languages includes the architecture, which is essentially the instruction set of the computer, together with the system calls. This creates a *virtual architecture*, which is the appearance of the machine as seen by the programmer. A virtual architecture is a view seen by some programmer other than the system programmer (who sees the real architecture), and there may be a hierarchy of virtual architectures. The virtual architecture seen by the compiler and compiler writer is the set of machine language instructions in the machine and the system calls to the operating system. The virtual architecture seen by the applications programmer is the high-level language supported by the compiler. Ultimately, the application has some capabilities and procedures for its use, and this is the final "architecture" of the system, as it appears to the user of that application.

11-1.2 Functions and Features of an Operating System (OS-9)

In this short section, we will discuss these features as they are available in OS-9. We first discuss why we use OS-9 and then describe the characteristics of OS-9. In an overview, we discuss memory management, time management, communication, and high-level I/O. Later we will focus on the last component, high-level I/O, and features of such a system. The user should then be able to adapt the ideas to any operating system; and this is especially easy for UNIX and UNIX-like operating systems that include OS-9.

UNIX is widely used in larger microcomputer systems. However, it is large and sophisticated, and having been developed over many years, it has some anomalous features that are difficult to teach in one chapter. By comparison, OS-9 has a number of advantages. OS-9 was written for the Motorola M6809 microprocessor and later adapted to the M68000, M68020 and M683xx microprocessors. As it was originally developed for a small but powerful 8-bit computer, it was carefully designed and economically implemented. It was written by a small company which exercised tight control over its development and it is therefore rather clean and free of "features." Further, OS-9 was developed as a *multitasking* operating system, in which a number of different essentially independent user programs or parts of them, called *processes,* are run at the same time, each taking different turns using the machine in *time-sharing* mode. OS-9 is perhaps the most compact and simple operating system in which the student can "poke around" in a multitasking operating system. The requirements of a multitasking operating system make the device driver somewhat more complex. Studying OS-9 device drivers prepares you for other multitasking operating system device drivers.

The 6809 being very similar to the 68000, and it to the 683xx, OS-9 was fairly easily ported to the 68000 and then the M683xx and the design was very well suited to this machine. OS-9 is capable of running on smaller 683xx-based microcomputers, which may use a modest sized disk or may be designed using ROMs without a disk at all. An operating system that does not use floppy or hard disks, but uses ROMs to store it, is called *ROM-based.* In fact, it is being used in the Compact Disk Interactive (CD-I) development by Phillips Corp. of the Netherlands and Sony in Japan, which has been joined by Matsushta and Thompson. The CD-I is a compact disk storage system, using compact disks like you may be using in your stereo system, but is more than just a raw storage of digital data on a compact disk (as is a CD-ROM), because it includes rather powerful object-oriented search capabilities that require sophisticated software to implement them. In order to economically develop the processing required by CD-I, high-level languages are useful, and an operating system is needed to support them. Such an operating system, where an operating system and applications programs are permanently built into the hardware and the whole is considered as a single indivisible system, is called *embedded.* OS-9 is used for that project because the CD-I unit will be an 683xx-based system with ROM and no hard or floppy disks to support the operating system. Future complex real-time systems similar to that used in CD-I, perhaps one that you may design, may need an embedded ROM-based operating system. OS-9 may well be chosen for that design for the same reasons that it was chosen for the CD-I project. Thus, OS-9 is a good operating system in which to demonstrate a real I/O device driver.

The operating system provides program segments and data structures to handle the functions of memory management, time management, communication, and high-level I/O. These functions of the operating system are discussed next.

Memory management refers to the assignment of memory to users as they request memory. Both primary memory and disk memory are initially "owned" by the operating system and are "rented" to applications programs as they are stored on the disk or loaded into memory, or as they request disk or primary memory for data.

Primary memory is organized around a *memory map* (see Figure 11-1). In OS-9, as in most operating systems using an 683xx, RAM is assumed at lowest memory addresses, and ROM are at higher, and I/O devices are at highest memory addresses, with any unused addresses between RAM and ROM and I/O devices. Because the 683xx puts its exception handler addresses in low memory, low memory is used for the operating system that requires the use of these addresses. However, phantoming (Section 5-3.2) is used to provide ROM at locations 0 to 7 for correctly starting the reset handler. The rest of the data needed by the operating system are placed in low memory too. In OS-9, the lowest 8K bytes of memory are used by the operating system for its data, including the addresses it uses for handling exceptions.

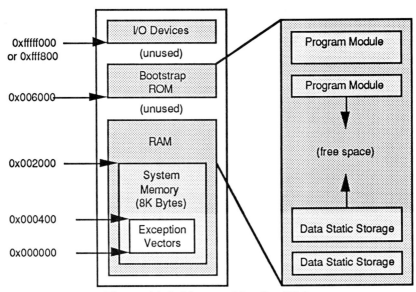

Figure 11-1. Memory Map for OS-9.

As applications programs are run by the operating system, the operating system needs to store their code and their data in primary memory. Code and data are stored separately for two reasons. One reason is that only data should be modified; code should not be modified. Note that the 683xx addressing modes that use the program counter do not permit writing to memory for that reason. Data can be constant data, which behave like code and are stored together with code, and variable data, which are stored separately. A second reason is that two processes might be running that use the same code. The code and constant data will be stored just once for the sake of efficient use of memory, and two different copies of the variable data will be stored: one copy being used by one process and the other copy being used by the other process. The code for a process is stored in a contiguous block of memory which we will soon call a module, in the highest addressed memory where such a module can be put. Generally, a process creates a second process (we say it *forks* the *child* process and is its *parent* process); the child stops running (we say it *dies*) before the parent dies. In this simple case, allocation and deallocation of modules is similar to pushing them onto and popping them from a stack (see Section 2-1.3); the operating system "pushes" the whole code for a process onto the "program stack" when it starts the process, and "pops" it off when the process is completed. Child processes have their code pushed later, and popped sooner, than their parent, so a stack is naturally suited to the storage of code. However, when many processes fork new processes and these processes die in a disorganized pattern, modules are put in the highest memory where they will fit, rather than at the top of the stack. Constant data used by a process are similar to the code of a child created by its parent. Constant data are stored on the same "stack" as is code. The same argument applies to the storage of variable data so they are also allocated on a "stack." Further, as noted in Section 2-1.3, the two "stacks" can be made to grow in opposite directions – the code "stack" building from the highest address in RAM towards lower addresses, and the data "stack" building from the lowest address in RAM towards higher addresses, so the unused space between the "stacks" serves to expand either "stack," and so that the operating system data are in low memory as noted in the previous paragraph. This scheme is used in OS-9. The operating system, considered the parent of all user application processes, has its code at the highest address, and its data at the lowest address, and as processes are created, their code is "pushed" at lower addresses than the operating system code and their data are "pushed" at higher addresses than the operating system data.

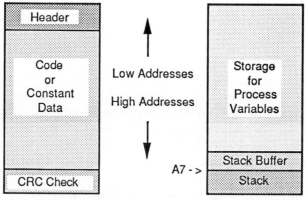

a. Program or Data Module   b. Data Static Storage

Figure 11-2. Data Storage for OS-9.

Code and constant data are stored in *memory modules*. (See Figure 11-2a.) Each inseparable piece of code or inseparable piece of constant data will be stored in a module; the code may be a "subroutine" or a collection of related "subroutines" or the data may be a "table" of some constant data. (However, a code module might not be a true subroutine; it might be called by some means other than a JSR instruction.) A module contains an ASCII character string – its *module name* – by which it is known to the operating system. If a process is to fork another process or needs to find data in a module, it must supply the name of the module; the operating system will search all the modules to locate one that has a matching name, and it will start to execute the code in that module or provide the address of data in the module. A module is packaged with a module header and a CRC checksum, at the beginning and end of the code or data, respectively. The *header* contains information about the module, the module size and type (whether it is code or data, for instance, so we will not attempt to execute a data module as if it were code), a pointer to its module name, which is used to identify it, and other information useful to the operating system. The *CRC check* at the end of the module is the "checksum" computed on all the bytes in the module, as if they were sent over a communication channel (see Section 9-4.1); it is used to verify that the module is correctly loaded into memory before it is used. Data may or may not be stored as a *descriptor*. A descriptor is a data structure with *fields* that store various constants and "describes" something. It is vaguely like a table, in an informal sense. Constant descriptors are stored in modules. Finally, modules can be in ROM, in the area above the RAM and I/O devices, as well as in the high end of RAM. (See Figure 11-1.) RAM-located modules can be loaded from disk only when they are needed. ROM-located modules need not be loaded from disk, so they seem to be "loaded instantaneously" when they are needed. In a ROM-based system, all modules might be in ROM. In a disk-based operating system, as a minimum, a program used to read in the operating system from the disk, the *bootstrap*, is usually in ROM.

Two mechanisms are used to store variable data. *Static storage* is used to hold most variable data. (See Figure 11-2b.) As noted earlier, the static storage for a process is allocated on a stack that builds from low toward high memory. It is called "static" storage because it remains unaltered when a process is stopped and is left exactly as it was when the process is stopped until it is restarted. By comparison, "dynamic" storage is deallocated when the process is stopped and reallocated when it is restarted. Static storage has most of the data needed by a process. It also has the stack buffer in it, and in it the stack pointed to by user stack pointer register A7. Each different process has a different static storage, which is "pushed" on the "data stack" as the process is forked and "popped" when the process dies. In each static storage there are variable data for the process and a stack buffer for the stack referenced by the stack pointer A7. Of course, the stack referenced by A7 is used to store return addresses for subroutines, and may be used for subroutines to pass arguments and store local variables, as discussed in Chapters 1 and 2.

In addition to the static storage generally used for variable data, OS-9 uses descriptors to store variable data, but they are not stored in modules as constant data descriptors are stored. Nor are they stored in static storage. The operating system uses a different system call to get room for a variable descriptor than the call to get room for static storage, and these descriptors are stored in high RAM memory rather than low memory. Such variable descriptors are used to describe a process (process descriptor) and to describe an I/O "path" (path descriptor) as we discuss later.

The header is automatically generated for you if you use Microware's assemblers or compilers. Using THINK C's compiler, we generate a header by embedding assembler language *dc*s in the Macintosh memory and downloading it with the program. A header, shown below for an executable program module, provides information about the module to OS-9, such as the module's size (word 3), (pointer to) its name (word 7), permissions (word 8), entry point (word 21), static storage and stack sizes (words 23, 24).

```
    dc.w 0x4afc,1,0,AboutProg+0xa,0,0,0  /* id, sysrev, size, owner */      Module
    dc.w @1+0xe,0x555          /* offset to name. access permission */      header
    dc.b 1,1,0xc0,0            /* type, lang, attr, revs */
    dc.w 0                     /* edition */
    dc.l 0,0,0,0,0,0           /* useage,symbol,dummy[4] */
    dc.w 0,@3+0x32             /* offset to where execution begins */
    dc.l 0,sizeof(staticStorage),0x100  /* trap address, memory size stack size, */
    dc.w 0,@7+0x42,0,@8+0x46   /* init data, init ref */
@1  dc.b "Prog",0             /* the module's name is put somewhere in it */
    /* assembler language "glue" code is put here, and starts with label @3 */
@7 dc.l 0,0                    /* initialization data: put 0s if not used */
@8 dc.l 0,0                    /* init reference data : put 0s if not used */
```

Finally, we briefly mention disk storage. We have outlined the general structure of an OS-9 disk in Section 10-1.2. The allocation of files on the disk is done in a manner similar to the allocation of primary memory for modules; in fact the same system calls are used to allocate both disk and primary memory. A module, loaded into memory as an indivisible unit, can be stored in a file. The name of the file, accessed through the disk directory, can be the same as the module name and usually is the same, to avoid confusion, but the file name can be different, to permit multiple versions of a module to be stored on a disk. Finally, a file can have more than one module in it, and it can store raw ASCII or binary data to be used by an application.

Recall that in a multitasking operating system, a number of different processes are run at the same time, each taking different turns using the machine (as detailed in Section 5-1.6). We review that discussion and extend it a little here. *Time management* is the function of the operating system that schedules the processes so that each process gets a fair share of the processor and machine. A *multi-thread* scheduling technique permits some other work to be done while this routine waits for real-time interrupts, but all threads are compiled together and can share global variables (Section 5-1.6). A *multi-tasking* scheduling technique further permits separately compiled programs, that cannot share global variables, to share the machine (Section 5-3.3). Time-sharing provided by OS-9 further permits separate users to use a single computer. Mechanisms are provided so that users can be prevented from interfering with each other. Generally, processes waiting for I/O sleep. In this mode, time-sharing really steals from a process time that it cannot use because it is waiting for I/O, and gives this time to other processes. However, since some processes have no I/O, a real-time clock is used so that other processes can use the machine (Section 5-1.6). In this mode, time-sharing slows the machine's response time proportional to the number of processes, but a priority mechanism permits some processes to run more often. Higher-priority processes get use of the processor after more ticks, so they appear to be executed faster than low-priority processes.

Time-sharing affects the synchronization mechanisms used in a system. In the mode where a process waits for an I/O device, the interrupt synchronization technique (Section 5-1.3) is used; when the device enters the done state it generates an interrupt; the interrupt handler eventually restarts the process. If an I/O chip is not capable of generating interrupts, each time a tick is handled, the I/O devices can be checked as if in a gadfly loop (Section 5-1.2), just one check per device per tick, to see if the device is in the done state. The program segment that is executed if a device is found to be in the done state is essentially the same as an interrupt handler. Even devices that do not actually generate interrupts can appear to have interrupts, as long as there is a real-time clock to generate interrupts (ticks). Incidentally, the applications programmer should not use conventional real-time synchronization (Section 5-1.1) because he or she has very little control over the time slices of the processor, and if control is attempted, the effectiveness of time management is seriously degraded. But real-time interrupt synchronization (Section 5-1.6) can be used. That effectively delays that process for that number of ticks. However, the delay is accurate to within only one tick interval (often about 10 msec.) and is a minimum delay rather than an exact delay, since other processes may actually gain control of the machine at the time when the prescribed number of ticks has occurred.

While communication between processors can be accomplished by means of global variables in multi-threaded environments, or by I/O devices in any system, the operating system provides a means of communicating among multi-tasking or time-sharing processes in a single processor, using *signals*. Recall from the previous discussion that processes are restarted after an interrupt has occurred in a device they are waiting on. The interrupt can occur, and in fact will occur, when the process is sleeping, so some other process will be running on the computer when that interrupt occurs. The interrupt handler has to communicate with the process to restart it, and may also send some message to the process to do something unusual, such as to abort a process when a control-C is typed on a terminal. Note that the interrupt is not for the process that is currently running and that is interrupted, but for one of several processes that are sleeping. The message is sent by means of a signal. A signal is sent from the interrupt handler to the process that is waiting for the device to become done. This signal appears to be a software emulation of the interrupt request line that sends messages from I/O chips to the computer. However, it is implemented by putting some number (the message) into a field of the process's process descriptor, and changing another field in the process descriptor so the process will compete for time slices, and eventually start running. When the process begins to run, it should check the number (message) in its process descriptor to see what, if anything, is requested by the message. Interrupt handlers send signals to the process that is waiting for the completion of an activity that generated the interrupt. These same signals can be sent from one process to another, even though neither is an interrupt handler, and they can be sent to a process that is not sleeping if that process has set up a program to receive and interpret the message (a *signal intercept handler*).

High-level I/O is effected by operating system calls. An I/O device will be accessed by an *I/O path*, which is maintained by means of a *path descriptor*. A *path number* is assigned to the path as an index into a vector of (pointers to) objects (see the example at the end of Section 5-1.3). The system calls parallel the methods we developed for object-oriented I/O (Section 4-5). An *open* call will generally initialize the I/O device in the manner of the initialization rituals discussed earlier, and will allocate and initialize the path descriptor, and finally, will assign a path number to this path. A *read* call will request the reading of data from the device, and a *write* call will request the writing of data to the device. A *close* call will turn off the device and will deallocate the path descriptor. There are other system calls to a device for special needs. To specify what device is to be used in read, write, close, and other calls, the programmer supplies the path number as a parameter to these calls. The path number, an integer, serves to identify the path after it is opened. Rather than dealing with all the details of how a chip is initialized and how it is controlled, the programmer using high-level I/O merely has to learn how arguments are passed to and from the system calls that effect high-level I/O.

We now consider some of the features of this operating system that are consistent with the functions just described. These include modular software, reentrancy, position independence, single entry and exit points, device independence, and path redirection.

Modular software is a feature of the memory module technique. Each inseparable unit of code is put in a module. The module can be shared among several processes that execute code in it. This feature requires that the code be reentrant (see Section 1-1.1) because one process must be able to use the same code module when another is using it; the first process must be able to "re - enter" the code after it is stopped and the second process started. Moreover, the module can be placed anywhere in memory, wherever the operating system finds room for it. This requires that the code be position independent (see Section 1-2.1). Finally, the module can and should have a single entry point and a single exit point (see Section 2-2.2) to simplify debugging. OS-9 even attempts to exit from a code module from the same exit point whether or not an error has occurred. If no error occurs, the carry bit C and data register D1 are left cleared; but if an error occurs, the carry bit is set and an identifying error number is left in register D1.

OS-9's high-level I/O manages I/O devices to achieve *device independence*. The high-level I/O system calls are made the same way for all I/O devices, as much as possible, so that a program that is written to output characters, say to the terminal display, can output them to a printer, put them in a disk file, or send them to some other I/O device, without changing the program at all. Only the open call will open a different device or file, and from there on, the I/O system calls will be identical regardless of which device the data are sent to. If all output devices are identical to each other, in the sense just given, and all input devices are similarly identical to each other, in that sense, then the system exhibits device independence. A similar concept is *path redirection*. A path can be opened by the operating system. The user can substitute a device different than the one intended by the programmer.

11-1.3 Components of an Operating System (OS-9)

In this section, we discuss several key modules used in OS-9; namely, the kernel, shell, utilities, managers, drivers, and descriptors. These modules are described in the context of their relationships to the device driver we study in the next section. Although about thirty modules are in a typical OS-9 operating system, only those listed in this section are important to the discussion of the driver for the PIA or DUART.

Figure 11-3 shows the key modules that relate to the terminal device driver using the DUART. We use it to show a general description of modules used in OS-9.

The *kernel* is one or several modules that must be run before any other modules under control of the operating system are run. The kernel is responsible for all the basic functions (memory management, time management, and communication by means of signals) provided by the operating system – essentially all the basic functions except I/O. The kernel is responsible for initialization. It is started first and initializes the operating system's global variables. The kernel is entered whenever an operating system call is made. In the 683xx, all system calls, which are TRAP #0 instructions, are immediately vectored to a program segment in the kernel. The word following the TRAP #0 instruction is read by this program segment in the kernel, to determine which function is to be executed. The particular operation requested by the system call is executed as a subroutine of this program segment. Many of these subroutines, such as for memory and time management functions, are also in the kernel modules.

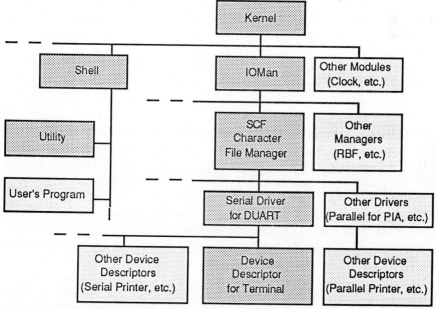

Figure 11-3. Module Relationships for a Terminal in OS-9.

I/O system calls are executed by a collection of modules called managers and drivers. Factoring, discussed in Sections 2-3.3 and 11-1.1, is used to compact the code and make it easy to introduce new I/O devices into the system. There will be tens of I/O devices in a typical personal computer. If a function, such as the outputting of individual characters from a stream of characters, is required in all or many I/O system calls, it is factored out of each of the individual program segments that control different devices and put into a higher level routine, of which the original program segments are subroutines.

I/O system calls are processed, just after they are initially processed by the kernel, by an *I/O manager* called IOMAN. IOMAN handles all the functions that are common to all the devices. In particular, since we wish to have device independence, all I/O system calls are forced to look alike to the programmer using the system calls, so there is a lot of code that is common to all devices, and code is needed to make all the I/O devices look alike. IOMAN, in short, is a result of and is responsible for implementing device independence. It provides a standard interface to the programmer using the system calls.

There are two significant groups of I/O devices: those that are similar to terminals and those that are similar to disks. There are other groups as well, but in most simple systems, these two groups are present. All I/O devices that resemble terminals are processed by an intermediate *Sequential Character File manager* called SCF. System calls to devices such as the serial I/O chip, the DUART, and parallel output for printers using the M68230, are processed in part by SCF. SCF takes care of all the functions that are required for a device of this type, such as the recognition and processing of carriage return and backspace characters. All I/O devices that resemble disks are processed by an intermediate *Random Block File manager* called RBF. System calls to devices such as the floppy or hard disks, or compact disks, would be processed in part by RBF. RBF takes care of all the functions that are required for a device of this type, such as creating and reading directories, to find files on a disk.

Modules that actually move data to and from I/O chips are *device drivers*. There is a driver to control the M6821 chip, as we will discuss in the next section. There is a different driver for the DUART. One device driver is put into the system for each different type of I/O chip to be controlled by the operating system. If a system has two separate M6821 chips, only one driver will usually control both of them. They will be a little different, though, and their differences will be described in *device descriptors*. There is exactly one device descriptor for each I/O device. Some I/O chips have more than one device in them, such as the M6821, and some chips can control more than one hardware device as the floppy disk controller can control two or more disk drives; each separate device in a chip or separate hardware device controlled by a chip will have its own device descriptor. In effect, the device driver has the code that is common to all the devices that use a particular chip type, but a device descriptor has all one device's special constants.

Note that factoring is used to compact the code needed to control I/O devices, and factoring also makes the writing of device drivers considerably easier than it would be without factoring. If you add a new device to your system, you may not even need to write any new code; if the system already contains a chip of the kind you are adding, all you write is a new device descriptor; if the system does not contain such a chip but someone else has written a driver for that chip, you add his or her driver and all you write is a new device descriptor. If you write a device driver, you do not have to write all the code it actually uses; code that is factored out, say into SCF and IOMAN, is written for you. You only write the code needed to put data into and take data from your chip. That is encouraging. However, this notion of factoring does make the writing of device drivers more difficult too. You have to follow many more rules to make it work with more than one chip, using device descriptors for each chip added to the system, and you have to satisfy the interface to SCF, and other modules in the operating system.

A module called the *shell* is responsible for requesting information from the user. It provides a "command line interpreter" to request a line of text from the user and execute what the user requests. After the computer is started and the kernel is executed, the shell is executed in order to request a command from the user. In OS-9, it puts the character "$" on the terminal. The user can write a line to load and run a program; we will illustrate this shortly. The user will write his or her own or buy other's *application programs*. Some programs are commonly provided with the operating system. A *utility* is a program that does some operation that is often needed by users in any system. A utility DIR is a program that outputs the directory of a disk to a terminal. Utilities LIST, COPY, and DEL list an ASCII disk file to the terminal, copy one file onto another, and delete a file. In the philosophy of factoring, if a program is expected to be needed in all or most systems, it is written as a utility and provided with the operating system. Utilities are often very simple programs that merely use a few operating system calls, as LIST calls on the operating system to read characters from the disk and write those characters to the terminal. Some rather complex utilities are specialized and have their own names. An *editor* is a utility that lets a user write text into and modify text in a file. A *compiler* is a utility that parses text written according to the rules of a high-level language and ultimately generates a disk file containing machine language instructions that can be executed later. We call the editor and compiler utilities in this discussion. However, that is not really precise. If an editor or compiler is provided with an operating system, we would say it is a utility; but if obtained separately, they are application programs.

We illustrate the use of the shell to run utilities. To list a file called FILE1 to the terminal, the user responds to the $ prompt by writing

$ LIST FILE1 (carriage return)

This line tells the shell to find a module called LIST, if it is in memory, or read in a module from a disk file called LIST, and execute that module. The module is written to obtain the rest of the command line after the program module/file name LIST, which in this example is "FILE1", and use it for *parameters*. Different programs use the characters like "FILE1" on the command line in different ways, depending on the parameters to be specified by the user. LIST is written so it will use the parameter, "FILE1", as the path name of the file to be opened, using an open system call. As LIST reads characters from the disk file using read system calls from the disk, it outputs them to the terminal using write system calls to the terminal. When all the characters on the file have been read, LIST will close the path using close system calls and terminate.

11-1.4 Environment of a Process

We now consider a C program that outputs the line "Hello World" on the terminal. This simple program illustrates the ideas of a module header and assembler language code that links the operating system to the code compiled from a C procedure.

Although the C procedures will be written as usual, some "glue code" techniques are needed to link THINK C with OS-9. Assembler language "glue code" executed when a process begins, calls THINK C's procedure *main* from OS-9, and a procedure *write* written in assembler language calls OS-9's system call I$WRITE from THINK C.

When OS-9 forks to a process using this module, the C procedure *main* is executed. It generally needs to use static storage for variables and it may need to access the parameters entered on the shell command line as just discussed. We utilize C's declaration of register pointer variables, knowing that (if objects are not used in the procedure) register A4 is the first register assigned, and register A3 is assigned next, to register pointer variables. The procedure main, shown below, is described further below it.

```
main(){
        register staticStorage *ss; register char *parameter;
        ss->errno=0;
        write(1,"HI THERE",8); /* write 8 characters to standard output path */
        return ss->errno;
}
```

The parameter characters can be read into a *char c* by *c=(*parameter++);* but static storage variables require some more general mechanism; *structs* are found to be useful:

```
        typedef struct staticStorage {
            int errno;
        } staticStorage;
```

All static storage variables like *errno* used in the module are declared to be elements of this *struct* and are accessed using expressions like *ss->errno* as shown in main above.

Code put after the module header (Section 11.1-2) following the entry point label @3 adjusts OS-9's values, as they are initialized when the process is forked to, to be used by THINK C as pointers in register variables, and calls the module's C procedure *main*. (A non-OS-9 technique sets up A5 to point to global variables stored in the module.)

```
@3 exg a5,a3              /* move OS-9's parameter pointer to a reg. ptr. */
    move.l a6,a4          /* move static storage ptr. to another reg. ptr. */
    move.l 0x20(a5),a6    /* we put an adjustment to global pointer in hdr */
    add.l a6,a5           /* add to the add. of hdr, put where C uses it */
    bsr main             /* call the main program in the module */
    move.l d0,d1          /* after returning, put error code in d1 */
    trap #0              /* system call to */
    dc.w 6              /* exit to OS-9 */
```

A C procedure *write* is used to call the I$WRITE system call. Later in the chapter we show how macros can be used to call the system in place of a procedure like *write*. It moves the procedure's arguments to the registers that the system call requires they be in.

```
static write(path, buffer, count) int path; char *buffer; long count;{
        register staticStorage *ss;register int i;
    asm { move.b path,d0      /* the system call requires the path number */
            movea.l buffer,a0  /* the location of the buffer, and the buffer size */
            move.l count,d1    /* these procedure parameters are moved as req'd */
            trap #0           /* this is the actual OS-9 system call */
            dc 0x8a           /* 0x8a indicates the call is an I$WRITE call */
            bcs.s @0          /* if an error, carry is set when the call is over */
            clr.l d0          /* if no error, clear the procedure's return value */
            return
    @0    move.l d1,ss->errno   /* otherwise return error signal as func. result */
}}
```

The C procedure *main* can call C procedures, it and its subprocedures can have local variables, and they can have global variables. However, since these global variables are stored in the (read-only) module, they should be used only as constants. (Note that character strings like *"HI THERE"* are stored and accessed as if globals, using register A5.) Any variables shared by procedures must be put in the *struct staticStorage* and accessed using expressions like *return ss->errno;* or *move.l d1,ss->errno* in assembler language. These static storage variables are not initialized by OS-9 or THINK C; your program should initialize them before using them. If a procedure uses objects, then A4 is used to access objects and is not used for the first declared register pointer variable, but A3 is used for it. Such procedures using objects will require a little more care, but can also be written for OS-9 modules.

The reader should review how "glue" code gets between THINK C and OS-9. These techniques will be extensively utilized in the writing of C device drivers.

11-2 A PIA Driver

We now look inside the rather simple parallel printer driver to see how a system call is executed. If *Prog* described above has its output redirected to the printer as in:

$ Prog >/P(carriage return)

the file can be printed instead of displayed on the screen. We need to have a descriptor P and a driver PIA in memory. These modules are described in later subsections.

11-2.1 Environment of an I/O Write System Call

We now focus on the execution of the sequence of operating system and subroutine calls and interrupts, and data that are stored, in order to execute an operating system call to print the message "Hello World". Figure 11-4 illustrates the calls and interrupts for the I$WRITE system call, using a path through the PIA driver, the M6821 chip and the printer.

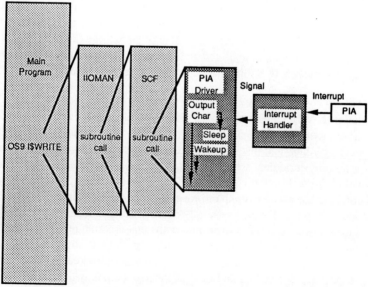

Figure 11-4. I$WRITE Call to a Parallel Printer in OS-9.

As we saw in Section 11-1.4, *main* executes an I$WRITE systems call. Note for later discussion that a process with a process descriptor and a process number is executing *main*. As we saw, parameters to I$WRITE are the path number (in data register D0), designating which open path is to be written to, the number of characters to be written (in D1), and an address of a buffer where input characters will be written (in A0). The user specifies a number of characters to be written in one I$WRITE system call, but the device driver writes one character at a time. IOMAN passes one character at a time to SCF and the driver PIA. SCF takes care of supplying a line feed after each carriage return (auto-line feed), putting nulls (0) after carriage returns for slow mechanical devices that need time to move the carriage (null padding) and so on. The driver has several procedures in it; one of these is responsible for writing characters. It puts one character into the M6821 data register (see Section 4-3.2) which causes it to be printed, as in the Centronics example in Section 5-2.1. The printer's ACK signal may be asserted immediately if the character is accepted. However, the printer's queue can be full, because programs may generate long lines of characters to be output, whose length could be greater than the size of the queue. So rather than gadflying on the ACK signal, the driver puts the process to sleep, and when the character is printed, the M6821 will generate a vectored interrupt. This process will not request time slices to execute it, because it has nothing to do until the printer's queue empties somewhat, but all other processes will be executed more frequently because this process does not request time slices.

When the printer's ACK signal is asserted, an interrupt occurs. The interrupt is actually processed by a handler in IOMAN, which calls a subroutine kept in the PIA device driver module. An autovectored or vectored interrupt in general may be shared by several devices; IOMAN will set up pointer registers for and then call on the subroutine in each device driver using the interrupt. PIA's interrupt subroutine is set up to handle an interrupt from the M6821 when the device driver is initialized. Executing the device driver's interrupt subroutine clears the interrupt and sends a signal "wakeup" to the process that is asleep. However, it sends a signal if and only if the process is asleep; otherwise sending would be unnecessary and in fact will kill the process, causing a fatal error. That process wakes up sometime later and gets a turn to use the processor. When the PIA device driver write subroutine receives the "wakeup" signal, it exits to SCF and IOMAN. IOMAN continues to output the requested amount of characters in the buffer, specified by the system call parameters, by calling the driver's write subroutine as discussed above.

11-2.2 Storage Areas for a Driver

We now describe the different storage areas, their meaning, and the access methods used by the device driver. (See Figure 11-5.) Recall from previous discussions that a descriptor is really just a table of data, and that constant descriptors such as the device descriptor may be kept in read-only modules, while descriptors of variable data such as the process descriptor and the path descriptor are kept in RAM for the user by the operating system, and are identified to the user by a path or process number and a pointer to them.

Each user has paths that are essentially consecutively numbered as they are opened, and the operating system translates them into paths that are unique for each path for each user. It is generally possible for one user to have two paths to the same device, and for two users to have paths to the same device. The path descriptor keeps all the variable data that is unique to a path, for each path. For example, one path may use the escape character as an end-of-file marker, while another may use control-Z for the same purpose. The end-of-file character is kept in the path descriptor. Each path can have a different end-of-file character. The user can change his or her end-of-file character for a path without changing the end-of-file characters for other users or other paths, even if the paths all use the same device. When the PIA device driver is entered to write characters to the M6821, it accesses the path descriptor for the path that is currently writing data in the M6821.

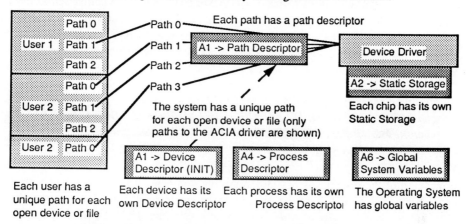

Figure 11-5. Data Used in the PIA Driver.

The device descriptor (Figure 11-3) for the parallel printer is given below:

```
dc.w 0x4afc,1,0,AboutDescriptor+8,0,0,0 /* id, sysrev, size, owner */
dc.w @3+0xe,0x555              /* offset to module name, access permission */
dc.b 0xf,0,0x80,0             /* type, lang, attr, revs */
dc.w 1                        /* edition */
dc.l 0,0,0,0,0,0             /* useage,symbol,dummy[4] */
dc.l 0x10002                  /* 0xfffc00 port <<<<< */
dc.b 25,1,5,3                 /* vector, irqlvl, prior, mode <<<<< */
dc.w @1+0x38,@2+0x3a,0,0,0,0,0 /*fmgr,pdev,devcon */
dc.w @1-2                     /* 0x1c option count */
dc.b 0                        /* type <<<<< */
dc.b 0,0,0                    /* upc, bsp, delLine */
dc.b 0,1,0,0                  /* echo, autolinefd, eoLine null, eoPagePause */
dc.b 66,0,0,'M'-0x40          /* pageLen, bsp del eorec */
dc.b 0x1b,0,0,0              /* oef, reprt dupLine pause */
dc.b 0,0,0,0                  /* kbdInt, kbdAbt bspOut bell */
dc.b 1,0                      /* parity code, baud */
dc.w @3+0x5e                  /* output device offset */
/* dc.b 0x11,0x13,9,4        /* xon, xoff, tab, tab width */
@1   dc.b "Scf",0;           /* name of manager <<<<< */
@2   dc.b "PIA",0;           /* name of driver <<<<< */
@3   dc.b "P",0              /* name of descriptor module <<<<< */
```

There is exactly one such device descriptor (module) for each device in any chip that is in the system. The ASCII character string name *P* of the device descriptor is used as the path name /P for the device, since the device descriptor is unique for each device. ASCII strings in the device descriptor enable the operating system to find the device driver"*PIA*"and manager *"Scf"* and a binary address enables it to find the chip *dc.l*

0x10002. In addition to the aforementioned pointers, the device descriptor contains the initial values of variables associated with a path, as implied by Figure 11-5: special characters like end-of-record, Booleans that permit or deny various features such as whether input characters are *echoed,* that is, immediately output by the driver, and numbers, such as the number of lines on a printer's page. These will be copied to the path descriptor.

The device descriptor will be defined in C using a *struct* and accessed using a register pointer variable much as we accessed static storage in a main program in Section 11-1.5. A *struct* that corresponds to the device descriptor *P* shown above is:

typedef struct deviceDescriptor {

> *long dummy1[12]/* module header */,Port; char Vector,IRQLvl,Prior,Mode;*
> *unsigned FMgr,PDev,DevCon,dummy2[4],Opt;*
> *char DTP,UPC,BSO,DLO,EKO,ALF,NUL,PAU,PAG,BSP,DEL,EOR,EOF;*
> *char RPR,DUP,PSC,INT,QUT,BSE,OVF,PAR,BAU; unsigned D2P;*
> *char XON,XOF,TAB,TABS;*

} deviceDescriptor;

The meaning of these values is not important, but you can compare the *struct* with the assembler language definition of the device driver to understand them. For instance, *PAR* is the value of *dc.b 1 /* parity code */.* It usually indicates a UART frame's structure including the parity. For the parallel printer, it will indicate whether (1) an M6821 port A is used, or (0) its port B is used, to send data to the printer. IOMAN copies these device descriptor's special characters, Booleans and numbers into the path descriptor to be used and possibly modified by the driver's procedures. The path descriptor will similarly be defined in C using a *struct* and accessed using a register pointer variable. Note that many variables in it (e.g. *DTP* to *TABS*) have the same name as variables in the device descriptor; they are just copies of the former variables. It also has some variables (e.g. *PD* to *SysGlob*) used by IOMAN and SCF, which must be maintained for each path.

typedef struct pathDescriptor {

> *int PD; char MOD,CNT; long DEV; unsigned CPR;*
> *long RGS,BUF,USER,PATHS;*
> *unsigned COUNT; long LProc,ErrNo,SysGlob; char dummy1[0x80-0x28];*
> *char DTP,UPC,BSO,DLO,EKO,ALF,NUL,PAU,PAG,BSP,DEL,EOR,EOF;*
> *char RPR,DUP,PSC,INT,QUT,BSE,OVF,PAR,BAU;*
> *unsigned D2P; char XON,XOF,TAB,TABS;*
> *long TBL; unsigned Col; char Err;*

} pathDescriptor;

One area of static storage is associated with each chip that has been initialized, regardless of how many open paths there are to the chip. In a sense, a device driver is a software package that virtualizes the hardware chip – a software chip – and the static storage is used in this virtual chip the way internal registers are used in the hardware chip. (Parenthetically, we wish that hardware chips had the input-output specifications that the device driver has; the functions and parameters of the driver would be the commands and I/O registers of the chip. Then all chips would be identical to the software, removing one level of software from operating system I/O.) The *Init* routine in the device driver, is then executed. *Init* in the device driver can be written to take additional information from the device descriptor. For instance, other procedures in the PIA driver may need a *char *** pointer to the chip; the device descriptor will not be easily accessible when these routines are executed, but static storage is always accessible. To set up the pointer, the chip address from the device descriptor can be copied into static storage when Init is run. (The chip address is also put into static storage by IOMAN, but a second copy will be used to simplify the C procedures using vector indexing, which turns out to be messier using the variable put there by IOMAN.)

A *struct* is used to define the variables used for the driver's static storage:

typedef struct staticStorage {
   long PORT; unsigned LPRC,BUSY,WAKE,Paths,dummy1[17];
   struct staticStorage *DEV2; char TYPE,LINE,PAUS,INTR,QUIT,PCHR,ERR;
   char XON,XOFF,dummy2[0x46-0x3b], Hangup, dummy3[0x54-0x47];
   char *callerStack,*global,*processDescriptor;
   int saveSr,devIntLev; /* user-specified variables for THINK-C */

   char *PIA; /* this is (the only) special variable needed in PIA - other variables
      can be put here in static storage if they are needed */
}staticStorage;

The variables up to *callerStack* are required by OS-9 and are used in IOMAN and SCF. Beyond that, a driver programmer may append variables needed to run the driver's procedures. A pointer to the process descriptor is initially available to get to the system call caller's registers, to get data associated with the process (which is the process of the main program that executed the I$WRITE system call), and a pointer to the global variables of the operating system is also available. In order to implement THINK C's procedures without too many unwieldy conventions, we use the pointers *callerStack*, **global*, and **processDescriptor* in static storage to hold these pointers for drivers that may need them. The interrupt level needs to be manipulated in well-written drivers, and the variables *saveSr* and *devIntLev* are put in static storage to keep track of these levels. Most drivers will need additional variables; these, like *char *PIA* in this driver, can be appended to the end of the static storage, and are declared at the bottom of the *struct*.

11-2.3 Procedures in a Driver

The device driver consists of a number of C procedures, namely *Init*, *Read*, *Write*, *GetStat*, *PutStat*, *TrmNat*, and a procedure that handles interrupts. OS-9 finds their entry points by a vector of addresses, the address of this vector being in the header's execution offset. See Figure 11-6.

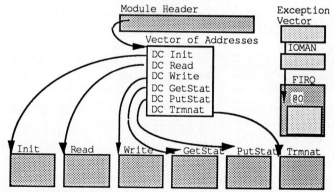

Figure 11-6. Procedures and Vector of Addresses in a Device Driver.

We enter *Init* and *Write* though assembler language "glue" code that sets up the register pointer variables used to access the device or path descriptor and static storage. The "glue" code for *Init* and *Write* is put after the module header. The vector of addresses is after the label @0, and for instance the address of the init subroutine is at @2.

```
@1 dc.w @2+base,@3+base+2,@4+base+4,@5+base+6,@6+base+8,@7+base+0xa,0
@2 exg.l a2,a4                      /* init: put static storage pointer into a4 */
   move.w sr,V->saveSr /* save for init's setup */
   bsr.s @12
   bsr Init
   bra.s @8
@3 bsr.s @11                        /* read */
   bsr Read
   bra.s @8
@4 bsr.s @11                        /* write */
   bsr Write
   bra.s @8
@5 bsr.s @11                        /* getstat */
   bsr Getstat
   bra.s @8
@6 bsr.s @11                        /* putstat */
   bsr Putstat
   bra.s @8
@7 bsr.s @11                        /* terminate */
   bsr Trmnat
@8 move.w V->saveSr,sr              /* Re-enable Interrupts, Clear Carry */
   move.l d0,d1                     /* exit: THINK-C's return value as an error */
   beq.s @9                         /* if error code not zero */
   or #0x1,ccr                      /* set carry also */
@9 move.l d7,d0                     /* return character from read(), in data (d7); */
   rts                              /* return to SCF */
@10 dc.b "Driver",0                 /* module name */
@11 exg.l a2,a4                     /* put static str ptr into a4, 1st register variable */
   move.w sr,V->saveSr              /* save for exit, F_Sleep */
   move.w V->devIntLev,sr           /* inhibit interrupts */
@12 move.l a1,a3                    /* common entry: re-arranges regs for THINK-C */
   move.l a5,V->callerStack         /* save seldom used variables CallerStack, */
   move.l a6,V->global              /* OS9 system global, procDes in static storage */
   move.l a2,V->processDescriptor   /* put path descr/device desc in a3, 2nd reg var */
   move.l V->PORT,a2                /* pointer to chip */
   lea @0,a5                        /* ponter to module */
   add.l 0x20(a5),a5                /* add reg 5 offset, to get to THINKC's globals */
   move.l d0,d7                     /* put data or function code into "data" variable */
   rts
```

Each entry first executes the common subroutine beginning at @12. This subroutine sets up static storage variables *callerStack*, *CallerStack*, and *processDescriptor*, and moves the register values supplied by OS-9 when the driver is called to where THINK C will be able to use them as register pointer variables. The *Init* procedure is then called, and finally the common exit subroutine beginning at @8 is executed. That subroutine takes care of reporting errors and returning data, as needed by OS-9 and as convenient for THINK C, for any procedure in the driver.

11-2.4 Initialization

In Section 4-3.1, we introduced the initialization ritual for I/O devices. In this subsection, we study the initialization of a path to a device.

The *Init* procedure in the device driver is called the first time a program executes an I$OPEN system call to a chip controlled by the device driver, but is not called if a device on the chip has been opened before. It is responsible for (1) initializing the device static storage, (2) initializing the device control registers, then if interrupts are used, (3) executing an operating systems call F$IRQ which configures IOMAN to handle this driver's interrupts, and (4) enabling interrupts if necessary. Step (3) must be done before step (4) or the operating system may be unable to handle an interrupt that occurs when the device is being initialized. The code is shown next, and a discussion follows it.

```
Init(){
    register staticStorage *V;register deviceDescriptor *M;register char data;
    V->TYPE=M->PAR; V->PIA=(char*)M->Port; /* init Static Storage */
    pinAssign(cs3,byte); baseAssign(3,V->PORT,k2);/* init Device Control Registers */
    optionAssign(3,rd+wr+upper+as,synch,user+super,0);
    pinAssign(cs4,byte);baseAssign(4,0xffffff,k2);
    optionAssign(4,rd+upper+ds,fast,0,avec)|(M->Prior<<1);
    *(char*)0xfffa05|=0x80;/* 1 MHz E clock */  V->PIA[1]=0; V->PIA[0]=0xff;
    if(V->TYPE==1) V->PIA[1]=0x3f; else V->PIA[1]=0x2f;
    data=V->PIA[0]; /* "read" the data reg to remove int.*/
    F_Irq((M->IRQLvl)+24,M->Prior,V->PORT); /* insert int. handler in IOMAN */
}
```

The first line declares the register pointer variables that were set up in the "glue" code to access the device descriptor and static storage. The device descriptor variable *PAR*, which designates whether M6821's port A or port B is to be used, is copied from its device descriptor location *M->PAR* to static storage *V->TYPE* where it can be available in *Write* and possibly other procedures to differentiate the code need to access port A from port B (the device descriptor is no longer available in them). Similarly, the device descriptor *Port* is copied into static storage's *PIA. In* general, all static storage variables are initialized (however, IOMAN clears static storage, so no variables initialized to 0 need be initialized in *Init,* and IOMAN puts the device descriptor *Port* into static storage's *PORT*). That was part of responsibility (1) introduced in the preceding. The next seven lines initialize the SIM and M6821 control registers, as part of responsibility (2). We set up chip select CS3 to select the M6821 at the address given by the static storage variable *PORT* and chip select CS4 to handle autovector interrupts at a level designated by the device descriptor's *Prior* variable. We also set up the M68332 E clock to be 1 MHz to handle an MC6821; an MC68B21 can run at 2 MHz which will be provided by the M68332 if this change is not made. The M6821's control register is then initialized. The control port of port A devices, indicated by *TYPE* being 1, is set to 0x3f to use 1-bit output; port B devices, indicated by *TYPE* being 0, initialize the control port to 0x2f to use handshake synchronization. We then read the M6821 data register before enabling its interrupts, so if IRQA1 or IRQB1 happened to be set when interrupts are enabled, a false interrupt is not requested. Finally, we set up PIA's interrupt handler as part of responsibility (3) using the F$IRQ system call in the *F_Irq* procedure described below, which also contains the interrupt handler itself. The handler subroutine is after label @2 in *F_Irq* because its address is needed in A0 for the system call and is locally available in the procedure. Finally, interrupts will be enabled when the C procedure *Init* exits to the "glue" logic common exit subroutine at label @8. In *F_Irq* the registers are set up for the system call as required by OS-9 from the parameters supplied to the procedure, which are taken from the device descriptor. Note that static storage, normally kept in register A4, needs to be in A2 for OS-9's conventions, and needs to be restored for THINK C's conventions.

```
F_Irq(vector, priority, port) char vector, priority; long port;{
    register staticStorage *V; register char *global; register int data;
asm{lea @2,a0
    move.b vector,d0                /* vector */
    bne @0                          /* if vector is 0, clear addr to remove interrupt */
    sub.l a0,a0                     /* A0 is cleared to remove an int. in Term */
@0 move.b priority,d1               /* priority */
    move.l port,a3                  /* port address */
    exg.l a4,a2                     /* static storage */
    trap #0                         /* F_IRQ system call */
    dc.w 0x2a
    exg.l a4,a2                     /* static storage */
    bcc.s @1
    move.l d1,d0                    /* return error signal as procedure result */
    return
@1 clr.l d0
    return
@2 move.l a2,a4  /* handler: move static storage pointer */
}
    data=V->PIA[0]; if(V->WAKE){ F_Send(V->WAKE,1); V->WAKE=0;} asm{ rts }
}
```

The interrupt handler, a subroutine ending in RTS and not RTE as we ended handlers in Chapter 5, has a short assembler language "glue" code to set up static storage's pointer so the rest of the procedure, in C, can use static storage variables. The F$SEND system call, used to send signals to wake up a sleeping process, is put in the *F_Send* procedure:

```
F_Send(id,signal) int id,signal;{ asm{
    move.w id,d0                    /* process id */
    move.w signal,d1                /* signal */
    trap #0                         /* system call */
    dc.w 8                          /* F_Send sends signal */
    bcc.s @0                        /* if error was returned */
    move.l d1,d0                    /* return error signal as procedure result */
    return
@0 clr.l d0
}}
```

The interrupt handler, the procedure it calls, and the use of signals, will be explained in the following subsection describing the outputting of characters to the printer.

To summarize, *Init* is responsible for initializing the device static storage, initializing the device control registers, and if interrupts are used, for executing an operating systems call F$IRQ which configures IOMAN to handle this driver's interrupts, and enabling interrupts if necessary. That is not really terribly complicated. It is more complex than a simple device initialization ritual, but it all makes sense, even if you study it in greater detail than we described it here.

11-2.5 Write Procedure

The Write procedure is called whenever the I$WRITE system call is executed, and is called each time a character is to be written. If I$WRITE has a count of five in D1, this procedure should be called five times by SCF. This procedure's job is to output a character each time it is called.

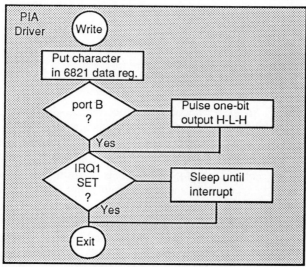

Figure 11-7. Flow Chart for PIA's Write Procedure.

Write (Figure 11-7) writes one character, which OS-9 put in D0 and "glue" code moved to *data* (D7). Its main function is to write a character and exit. However, whereas M6821's port B automatically pulses CB2 when the data register is written into if handshake mode is selected, port A must use a one-bit output mode and CA2 must be pulsed. The printer should return an ACK, setting IRQ1, but if IRQ1 is not promptly set, the driver should put the process to sleep and arrange for a wakeup signal.

```
Write() {
    register staticStorage *V;register pathDescriptor *PD;register char data;
    V->PIA[0]=data; /* output data; for b-sided pias this puts a pulse on CA2 */
    if(V->TYPE==1){V->PIA[1]=0x37;V->PIA[1]=0x3f;}/* one-bit out for port A */
    for (data=0;data<10;data++); /* insert delay */
    if(V->PIA[1]&0x80) return 0; /* if ACK quickly returns, just exit */
    V->WAKE=V->BUSY;F_Sleep(); /* else sleep; wake up when interrupted */
}
```

Write uses *F_Sleep* to set up parameters for and to call on the F$Sleep system call, when the process has to wait.

```
F_Sleep(){register staticStorage *V;asm{
    clr.l d0 /* sleep forever - until interrupt awakens */
    move.w V->devIntLev,sr /* enable interrupts */
    trap #0 /* F_Sleep: sleep indefinitely */
    dc.w 0xa
    bcs.s @1
    move.l V->processDescriptor,a0
    move.w 0x26(a0),d1 /* get signal */
    beq @0 /* if 0, it is wakeup signal, exit normally */
    cmp #3,d0 /* if 2 or 3, is deadly signal, return signal as error */
    bls @1
    moveq #1,d1 /* an unused error code */
    btst #1,0x1c(a0) /* if process state comdemn bit set */
    bne @1 /* then error exit */
@0 clr.l d0
    return
@1 move.l d1,d0 /* return error signal as procedure result */
}}
```

Before calling *F_Sleep*, *Write* copies the process ID, which was put in the static storage variable *BUSY* by IOMAN, into the static storage variable *WAKE*. The value in *WAKE* is used in the interrupt handler embedded in *F_Irq* in the last section. OS-9 has no process 0, so a 0 in *WAKE* indicates no process is asleep, waiting for a signal, and no signal need be sent. If the value of *WAKE* is nonzero, it is the ID of a process waiting for a signal, and the interrupt handler must send a signal to awaken that process.

The interrupt handler subroutine embedded in *F_Irq* in the last section is called by the interrupt handler in IOMAN whenever any interrupt is caused, on the autovector or vector specified by the call to F$IRQ in the *Init* procedure. This subroutine exits with carry set if the M6821 did not request an interrupt. If it did request an interrupt, it sends a signal using *F_Send* at the end of the last section. That system call will put the signal value in a byte, location 0x26 of the process descriptor. When the sleeping process awakens, at the bottom of *F_Sleep* shown above, it gets the location of the process descriptor from static storage's variable *processDescriptor* and gets the stored signal from it. If the stored signal is a 0, the signal, wakeup, causes the process to resume without error. However, if the signal is 2 or 3, which can be sent from a keyboard when control C or control Q is pressed, causes the process to resume with an error code 2 or 3, which will normally cause it to die. *F_Sleep* returns the error code as the function result in D0, which *Write* also returns, which the "glue" logic returns as an error result in D1.

Trmnat is called when I$CLOSE is used to remove the printer from use. It merely turns off M6821's interrupts by clearing its control register, and removes the interrupt from IOMAN's poling table, using an F$IRQ system call with a 0 value for an address.

```
Trmnat(){
    register staticStorage *V;register deviceDescriptor *M;
    V->PIA[1]=0;F_Irq(0,0,0);/* remove interrupt, return error form F_Irq */
}
```

Besides the *Init, Write, Trmnat* and the interrupt handler subroutine that we discussed, other procedures have to be put in the device driver for other functions. *Read,* analogous to *Write,* is responsible for inputting data by putting them in an output queue. *GetStat* and *PutStat* are used by I$GETSTAT and I$PUTSTAT system calls. They are "wildcard" system calls used to obtain the status or modify the "status" of the driver. They are called "wildcard" because the writer of a driver can use them for any operation that is not handled by I$READ and I$WRITE. The user specifies a parameter that selects one function among the wildcard functions available for a driver. In a sense, whereas I$READ reads data from an input data register and I$WRITE writes data to an output data register, I$GETSTAT reads control bits from a "status register" of the virtual I/O device, and I$PUTSTAT writes control bits into a "control register" of the virtual I/O device. There are some fairly standard I$GETSTAT and I$PUTSTAT system calls. For example, for a disk drive, an I$PUTSTAT system call is used to "rewind" a file, to reposition to the beginning of a file. Standard calls are taken care of in IOMAN or SCF if possible, so that the driver need only execute code for the nonstandard calls, or calls that use static storage data that are available only in the driver and are implemented differently in different drivers. These procedures *Read, GetStat,* and *PutStat,* are not used in the PIA driver, but they must be put into the driver because other drivers need them. They are just empty procedures.

Read () {} GetStat () {} PutStat () {}

The driver above is fully practical and is used to drive a parallel printer. It illustrates the basic ideas of the flow of control between a user's program, IOMAN, SCF, the driver's procedures and the interrupt handler. This simple example also illustrates the use of "glue" code used between THINK C and the OS-9 operating system, and the use of *structs* to access the device and path descriptors and the driver's static storage. However, this rather complex environment does not appear to be much more useful than an object-oriented interface as we illustrated in Section 5-2.1. A more complex driver for the DUART device in the next section will illustrate a number of additional concepts that make drivers and therefore operating systems useful in an embedded controller like the M68332 or M68340.

11-3 A DUART Driver

We now examine a more complex driver, for the DUART to illustrate the capabilities of an operating system and device driver.

11-3.1 DUART System Calls

The main program will open a path to the DUART, for reading input data and for writing output, and will then read and output characters until a error occurs or the letter 'Q' is typed. While this can be more or less accomplished by setting the Boolean descriptor variable *EKO,* which automatically echoes the input character, we clear that variable and echo characters in *main* itself in order to illustrate most system calls needed to handle I/O. We write the main procedure to need some static storage. A mixture of *int* and *char* variables can be declared in a struct as needed to allocate all variables needed in the module. The variable *isError* is used by macros to indicate the presence of an error.

typedef struct staticStorage { int errno;char isError,b[3];} staticStorage;

The procedure *main* requires a number of system calls, I$OPEN, I$READ, I$WRITE, and I$CLOSE. Each is implemented in a macro, rather than a procedure with embedded assembly language, to make it even more easily accessible in a C procedure. Though written on several lines below, each macro must be written entirely on one line in the compiler's source code. Generally, each merely puts arguments into registers where OS-9 expects them, calls the system, and puts the error result to static storage variable *errno* and sets static storage variable *isError* if an error occurred, otherwise they return a path number, the number of bytes read or written, or getstat information. The macro arguments must correspond to legal operands for the instructions that use them when the macro is expanded. Unused operands (e.g. *data2* for *getstat*) must be filled in with dummy variables. These macros are usually declared in a header file, from which they can be called when they are needed.

```
#define open(path,name,mode) asm{move.b mode,d0} asm{movea.l name,a0}
    asm{trap #0} asm{dc 0x84} asm{scs ss->isError} asm{move d1, ss->errno}
    asm{move d0,path} asm{move.l a0,name}
#define read(path,buffer,size) asm{move path,d0} asm{move.l buffer,a0} asm{
    move.l size,d1} asm{trap #0} asm{dc 0x89} asm{scs ss->isError} asm{move d1,
    ss->errno} asm{ move.l d1,size}
#define write(path,buffer,size) asm{move path,d0} asm{move.l buffer, a0} asm{
    move.l size,d1} asm{trap #0} asm{dc 0x8a} asm{scs ss->isError} asm{move d1,
    ss->errno} asm{ move.l d1,size}
#define readln(path,buffer,size) asm{move path,d0} asm{move.l buffer, a0} asm{
    move.l size,d1} asm{trap #0} asm{dc 0x8b} asm{scs ss->isError} asm{move d1,
    ss->errno} asm{ move.l d1,size}
#define writeln(path,buffer,size) asm{move path,d0} asm{move.l buffer, a0} asm{
    move.l size,d1} asm{trap #0} asm{dc 0x8c} asm{scs ss->isError} asm{move d1,
    ss->errno} asm{ move.l d1,size}
#define getstat(path,code,buffer,data2,data3) asm{move path,d0} asm{move code,d1}
    asm{ move data2,d2} asm{ move data3,d3} asm{ move.l buffer,a0} asm{trap #0}
    asm{dc 0x8d} asm{scs ss->isError} asm{move d1, ss->errno} asm{move.l d2,data2}
#define setstat(path,code,buffer,data2,data3) asm{move path,d0} asm{move.l buffer,a0}
    asm{ move code,d1} asm{ move data2,d2} asm{ move data3,d3} asm{trap #0}
    asm{dc 0x8e} asm{scs ss->isError} asm{move d1,ss->errno}
#define close(path) move.l mode,d0} asm{trap #0} asm{dc 0x8f} asm{scs ss->isError}
    asm{move d1, ss->errno}
```

The main program declares a local variable to store the path number, opens, reads from and writes in and then closes the path. Note that after each system call, *ss->isError* is checked; if it is set then *ss->errno* is returned to the calling glue code as an error.

```
main(){ register staticStorage *ss; register char *parameter; int path;
    open(path,"/T",3); if(ss->isError) return ss->errno; /*open T in read-write mode:*/
    while(! ss-> isError) { /* read a line, if first character is 'Q' stop, else write line */
        read(path,ss->b,3); if(ss->isError) return ss->errno; /* the shell closes opened paths */
        if(ss->b[0]&0x5f)=='Q') write(path,ss->b,3); if(ss->isError) return ss->errno;
    }
    close(path); if(ss->isError) return ss->errno;
    return 0; /* signal error condition to process that forked this process */
}
```

11-3.2 DUART Descriptor and Static Storage

Each device needs its own descriptor that points to its chip, driver and manager, and that specifies its unique characteristics. A quick examination of the DUART descriptor *T* illustrates that it is very similar to the descriptor *P* for the M6821. Note that this DUART port is 0x10004 (to use the chip's channel B), the driver's module name is *DUART*, and the manager's module name is *Scf*. In this descriptor, Booleans such as those enabling upper case conversion, echo, and auto line feed, are turned off, and appropriate numeric counts, such as the number of nulls after a carriage return (0) and the number of lines on a page (0x18 = 24), and special characters such as end-of-record ('M'-0x40 is control M, which is 0xd), keyboard abort ('E'-0x40), and keyboard interrupt ('C'-0x40) are provided for this device. The parity code and baud are used to initialize control registers in the device, using some standard code values.

```
    dc.w 0x4afc,1,0,AboutDescriptor+8,0,0,0 /* id, sysrev, size, owner */
    dc.w @3+0xe,0x555           /* offset to name, access permission*/
    dc.b 0xf,0,0x80,0           /* type, lang, attr, revs */
    dc.w 1                      /* edition */
    dc.l 0,0,0,0,0,0,0,0x10004  /* useage,symbol,dummy[4] port <<<<<*/
    dc.b 25,1,5,3               /* vector, irqlvl, prior, mode <<<<< */
    dc.w @1+0x38,@2+0x3a,0,0,0,0,0 /*fmgr,pdev,devcon */
    dc.w @1-2                   /* 0x1c option count */
    dc.b 0,0,0,0,0,0,0          /* type,upc,bsp,delLn,echo,autollf,eoLn,null */
    dc.b 0,0x18,8,0x18,'M'-0x40 /* Pause, pageLen, bsp del eorec */
    dc.b 0x1b,'D'-0x40,'A'-0x40,0x17 /* oef, reprt dupLn pause */
    dc.b 'C'-0x40,'E'-0x40,'H'-0x40,'G'-0x40 /* kbdInt, kbdAbt bspOut bell */
    dc.b 0,0xe                  /* parity code, baud */
    dc.w @3+0x5e                /* output device offset */
    /* dc.b 0x11,0x13,9,4       /* xon, xoff, tab, tab width */
@1  dc.b "Scf",0               /* name of manager <<<<< */
@2  dc.b "DUART ",0            /* name of driver <<<<< */
@3  dc.b "T",0                 /* name of descriptor module <<<<< */
```

This driver has variables to handle two queues and two flags, put on the bottom of *staticStorage*. We show all of *staticStorage* and the new variables in it below the blank line. *QI[ISIZE]*, *SizeI*, **inPI*, and **outPI* are used for the input queue, *QO[OSIZE]*, *SizeO*, **inPO*, **outPO*,**endI*,**endO* are used for the output queue, *TrnsDis* signifies the transmitter is disabled, *remoteOff* signifies the remote transmitter is turned off, *myInt* is the interrupt enables for the device controlled by this driver, and *trnsMsk*is this device's transmit interrupt enable bit pattern.

```
typedef struct staticStorage {
    long PORT; unsigned LPRC,BUSY,WAKE,Paths,dummy1[17];struct staticStorage *DEV2;
    char TYPE, LINE, PAUS, INTR, QUIT, PCHR, ERR,XON, XOFF;
    char dummy2[0x46-0x3b], Hangup, dummy3[0x54-0x47];
    char *callerStack,*global,*processDescriptor;int saveSr,devIntLev;/* to restore irq level */
    int ImmData,SigPrc[3]; /* variables following are specific to this device */
    char QI[ISIZE],SizeI,*inPI,*outPI,QO[OSIZE],SizeO,*inPO,*outPO,
        *endI,*endO,*Ireg,TrnsDis,remoteOff,myInt,trnsMsk;
}staticStorage;
```

11-3.3 DUART Initialization

The initialization of the DUART device includes initialization of its input and output queues, of the DUART registers, and of the interrupt mechanism. We show the M68340's initialization procedure; the M68332 will initialize CS6 to select the chip and CS7 to recognize the devices's interrupt level as an autointerrupt level. The queues are initialized first. To initialize the DUART registers, we use the *register char *chip* which is provided by the assembler language glue logic that precedes this C procedure. The device descriptor's chip address, 0x10004, is automatically put into register A2 (Section 11-2.3) which is used whenever *chip[i]* is used, and into *V->PORT*. We use the device descriptor's field *IRQLvl* to select the interrupt level. In order to prepare to handle interrupts, we have to disable interrupts. The descriptor's *IRQLvl* field is shifted to bits 11 to 8, combined with the value of the 683xx's status register picked up in the assembler language glue logic that precedes this C procedure, put into the descriptor variable *devIntLev* as it will be used in the status register, and moved to the status register in assembler language, to inhibit interrupts at level *IRQLvl*. The *F_IRQ* procedure is then called to call the operating system *F_IRQ* system call to insert *DUART's* interrupt handler address into OS9's interrupt handler. The *DUART's* interrupt handler subroutine is embedded in the *F_IRQ* procedure, as we saw it done with the PIA driver. We show the *F_IRQ* procedure here, including the assembler language glue to prepare to use C code in the handler routines, but we have extracted the body of these routines to be put near the procedures that interact with them. Just after this *Init* procedure is executed, a procedure *Putstat* (Section 11-3.6), with "open" (0x2a) option, is executed to initialize the DUART baud rate and frame structure. We will study this setup later.

The M68681's write-only interrupt mask register must be ORed and ANDed into; a copy of it is kept in location 0x100 so that two drivers can access its value. This use of a true global variable is not recommended in OS-9; a more involved linking of static storage from the first opened device to later opened devices is an alternative but that code is quite messy.

```
setMask(){register staticStorage *V;
  *(char*)((V->PORT&~0xf)+5)= (*(char*)0x100 |=V->trnsMsk);V->myIntl=V->trnsMsk;}


clearMask(){register staticStorage *V;
  *(char*)((V->PORT&~0xf)+5)= (*(char*)0x100 &=~V->trnsMsk);V->myInt&=~V->trnsMsk;}


static Init(){
  register staticStorage *V;register deviceDescriptor *M;register char *chip; register char data;
  V->endI=(V->inPI=V->outPI=V->QI)+ISIZE;V->endO=(V->inPO=V->outPO=V->QO)+OSIZE;
  CsAssign(3,V->PORT&~0xf,8,noDsack,rdWr);*(char*)0xffffff006 |=(1<<(M->IRQLvl));
  chip[2]=resetR+(disable<<recevr); chip[2]=resetT+(disable<<transmt); chip[2]=resetE;
  V->myInt=itxRdy|irxRdy;V->trnsMsk=itxRdy;if((V->PORT&4)==0){*(char*)0x100 |=irxRdy; }
  else {*(char*)0x100 |=irxRdy<<4; V->trnsMsk<<=4; V->myInt<<=4;}
  clearMask(); chip[2]=(enable<<transmt)+(enable<<recevr);
  V->devIntLev=((M->IRQLvl)<<8|(V->saveSr&0xf8ff));asm{move.w V->devIntLev,sr}
    F_Irq(M->Vector=(M->IRQLvl)*4+0x60,M->Prior,((V->PORT)&~0xf)+5); /* insert interrupt */
}
```

```
static F_Irq(vector, priority, port) char vector, priority; long port;{
    register staticStorage *V; register char *global; register char *chip; register int
data,status;
asm{lea @2,a0
    move.b vector,d0   /* vector */
    bne @0             /* if vector is 0, clear address to remove interrupt */
    sub.l a0,a0
@0   move.b priority,d1 /* priority */
    move.l port,a3     /* port address */
    exg.l a4,a2        /* static storage */
    trap #0            /* F_IRQ system call */
    dc.w 0x2a
    exg.l a4,a2        /* static storage */
    bcc.s @1
    move.l d1,d0       /* return error signal as procedure result */
    return
@1   clr.l d0
    return
@2 movem.l a3/a4/d6/d7,-(a7)
    move.l a2,a4 /* move static storage pointer */
    /* move.l a3,port move.l a6,global ; not needed in this eaxample */
    }
    if((status=(*chip)&V->myInt)==0) {asm{movem.l (a7)+,a3/a4/d6/d7} asm{or #1,sr} asm{ rts }}
    if(status&(irxRdy|(irxRdy<<4))) { /* receive interrupt */    See Section 11-3.5 }
    if((status&(itxRdy|(itxRdy<<4))) && (V->SizeO || V->ImmData)
    { /* xmit interrupt */   See Section 11-3.4 }
    asm{movem.l (a7)+,a3/a4/d6/d7} asm {and #~1,sr} asm {rts}
}
```

11-3.4 DUART Write

The *Write* procedure, called by SCF when I$WRITE is called, outputs one character, taken by IOMAN from the system call's buffer. Compare it, shown below and diagrammed in Figure 11-8, to the PIA *Write* procedure, Section 11-2.5. *Write* essentially pushes a byte into the output queue, which is popped by the interrupt handler when a byte can be put in the DUART. However, if the queue is full, the process sleeps until an interrupt pops a byte from it. Some subtleties regarding this program and the interrupt handler are explained following the discussion of the later program segment.

```
static Write() {
    register staticStorage *V;register pathDescriptor *PD;register char *chip;register char data;
    while(!V->SizeO) {V->WAKE=V->BUSY;if(F_Sleep()) return;}
    V->WAKE=V->BUSY;F_Sleep(); /* note return error code from F_Sleep */
    if(V->inPO > V->endO) V->inPO = V->QO;  *(V->outPI++)=data;
    if((V->SizeO==0) && ! V->TrnsDis) setMask(); /* enable trns int */
    V->SizeO++; return 0;
}
```

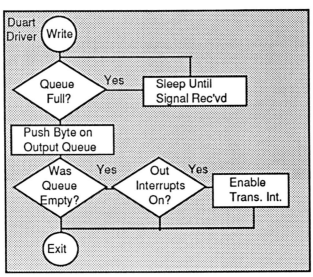

Figure 11-8. Flow Chart for DUART's Write Procedure.

The interrupt handler routine, shown below, is part of *F_IRQ* procedure described in the previous section, and is entered, as shown on the first line below (duplicated in the previous procedure), when the DUART has an empty output buffer *(chip-> STATUS & 0x100)* and the output queue has some data *(V->SizeO)* or some immediate data held *in V->ImmData* must be sent. The latter can be an XON or an XOFF character that is to be sent to a remote device to enable or disable its transmission. The first line of the handler sends immediate data if there is any. If *V->TrnsDis* was set (upon receiving an XOFF signal from a remote device), then the transmit interrupt is disabled and the procedure is left. A byte is then popped from the output queue into the DUART data register *chip->RT*. The handler and *Write* interact to enable transmit interrupts only if the output queue has some data (there is no reason to continuously interrupt if no data are to be sent). A signal is sent to a sleeping *Write* procedure when the queue length has decreased below a threshold value where there is room for several more characters on it.

```
if((status&(itxRdy|(itxRdy<<4))) && (V->SizeO || V->ImmData)){
    if(V->ImmData) { *(char*)((V->PORT)+3)=V->ImmData; return V->ImmData=0; }
        if(V->TrnsDis) { clearMask(); return 0;}
        V->SizeO--;if(V->outPO>V->endO)V->outPO=V->QO;*(char*)((V->PORT)+3) =
            *(V->outPO++);
        if(V->SizeO == 0) {clearMask();} /* if queue empties, disable trans int */
        if((V->WAKE)&&(V->SizeO< (OSIZE-THRESHOLD))){ F_Send(V->WAKE,1);
            V->WAKE=0;}
```

11-3.5 DUART Read

The *Read* procedure, called by SCF when I$READ is called, inputs one character, to be put by IOMAN into the system call's buffer. The procedure, shown below, and diagrammed in Figure 11-9, is, like DUART's *Write* procedure, basically pops a byte from the input queue, returning it to SCF. However, if that queue is empty, it sleeps, to be awakened when an interrupt pushes a byte into the queue. Using an I$PUTSTAT system call, a user can request a signal be sent when a character arrives. *Read* first checks if such a request is pending and a character is then requested; if so it returns with an error as this illogical combination will later result in an error. It also sends XON to a remote device if its queue empties sufficiently, and records and returns any errors.

```
static Read() {
    register staticStorage *V;register pathDescriptor *PD;register char *chip;register char data;
    if(V->SigPrc[0]) return 0xf6;
    while(!V->SizeI) {V->WAKE=V->BUSY;if(F_Sleep()) return;}
    V->SizeI--; if(V->outPI > V->endI) V->outPI = V->QI; data = *(V->outPI++);
    if(((V->SizeI < THRESHOLD) && V->XON) && V->remoteOff)
        {V->ImmData=V->XON; setMask(); V->remoteOff=0;}
    if(V->ERR){PD->Err=V->ERR; V->ERR=0; return 0xf4; /* return read error */}
    return 0;
}
```

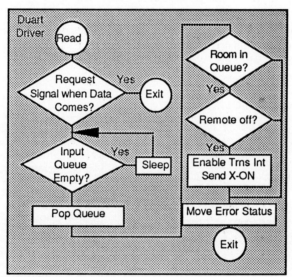

Figure 11-9. Flow chart for the DUART Read Procedure.

The DUART interrupt handler at the end of Section 11-3.3 includes a section to handle received characters, as shown below and diagrammed in Figure 11-10. The first line (duplicated in the earlier procedure) indicates that the program segment is executed if the receive buffer is full *(status&(irxRdy|(irxRdy<<4))* where *status* is the DUART status register value that was read earlier to check if this device requested an interrupt. The I$READ system call inputs raw data without checking it for special control characters, but the I$READLN system call, which is almost identical to I$READ, checks for special control characters such as abort (control-E). We use I$READ to read *raw data* and I$READLN to read *"cooked data"* such as ASCII text with control characters. In the latter case, *V->PCHR, V->INTR, V->QUIT, V->XON,* and *V->XOFF* are copies of similarly named variables in the path descriptor, which are initialized from similarly named variables in the device descriptor. In the former case, they are cleared to 0. (Note that a null character 0x00 is not used to send information in ASCII, so setting these special codes to 0 prevents them from matching received information characters). These special characters are checked in the interrupt handler because they must be responded to promptly, before a program executes a system call that calls the *Read* procedure and even if it does not call *Read*. The middle of the handler below checks for such control keys. If a pause character control key (control-W) is received, output from the (echo) device is stopped. If a interrupt character control key (control-C) is received, a signal is sent to the process which can be used to invoke a debugger program. If a quit character control key (control-E) is received, a signal is sent to kill the process. If an XON control key (control-S) is received, the transmitter is enabled to send more data (*V->TrnsDis = 0*), and if there are data in the output queue, transmitter buffer empty interrupts are immediately enabled. Finally, if an XOFF (control-Q) is received, the transmitter is prevented from sending more data (*V->TrnsDis = 1*), and if there are data in the output queue, transmitter buffer empty interrupts are immediately disabled. Finally, the character is pushed on the input queue to be popped by the *Read* procedure (except for XON and XOFF which are not needed after they are recognized). A queue overflow is noted as the same error which is returned from the DUART when its hardware queue overflows. If a signal is to be sent when data are received, it is sent now, and if the input queue grows too large, XOFF is set to be sent by the output handler, and a wakeup signal is sent to a sleeping *Read* procedure. Observe that this driver's interrupt handler, like *PIA*'s handler, sends a wakeup signal if *Read* set *V->WAKE* just before going to sleep. *Read's F_Sleep* resumes without error when this occurs.

Receiver Interrupt Handler

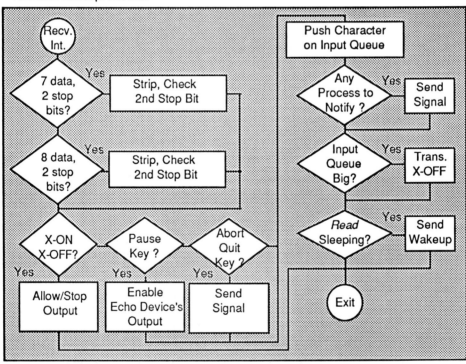

Figure 11-10. Flow Chart for the DUART Receive Interrupt Handler Procedure.

```
if(status&(irxRdy|(irxRdy<<4))){ data=*(char*)((V->PORT)+3); /* get data */
    V->ERR |= ((*((char*)(V->PORT+1))>>4)&0xf); /* get error status */
    if(data){ /* if non-null character, handle special characters */
        if(data==V->PCHR) if (V->DEV2) V->DEV2->PAUS=1;
        if(data==V->INTR) F_Send(V->LPRC,3); if(data==V->QUIT) F_Send(V->LPRC,2);
        if(data==V->XON ) {V->TrnsDis = 0; if(V->SizeO) setMask(); return 0;}
        if(data==V->XOFF) {V->TrnsDis = 1; if(V->SizeO) clearMask(); return 0;}
    }
    if((V->SizeI++)>ISIZE) V->ERR |= 0x10; /* overrun error */
    else { if( V->inPI > V->endI) V->inPI= V->QI; *(V->inPI++)=data;}
    if(V->SigPrc[0]){F_Send(V->SigPrc[0],V->SigPrc[1]);V->SigPrc[0]=0;}
    if(V->SizeI==(ISIZE-THRESHOLD)){V->ImmData=V->XOFF;V->remoteOff=1;}
    if(V->WAKE){ F_Send(V->WAKE,1); V->WAKE=0;}}
```

11-3.6 DUART Getstat, Setstat and Trmnat Procedures

The *DUART* driver has more substantial *Getstat* and *Setstat* procedures than the
dummy procedures used in the *PIA* driver. The *Getstat* procedure, shown first, handles
all I$GETSTAT system calls that are not handled in IOMAN or SCF. The particular case
of the I$GETSTAT system call, passed in its argument D1, is put in variable *data* by the
drivers assembler language glue code. Cases 0 (used to read the path descriptor options), 1
(to check if any input is available, as used in the BASIC IN$KEY subroutine), and 6
(used to see if input is terminated) are passed to this *Getstat* driver routine, although
cases 0 and 6 do not need anything in this particular driver. Case 1 returns with an error
code $0xf6$, which signifies the device is not ready, if the input queue is empty, with no
error if the queue is nonempty, and with another error code if a "real" error occurs.

```
static Getstat() {
    register staticStorage *V;register pathDescriptor *PD;register char *chip;register char data;
    switch (data){
        case 0: return 0; /* get register baud, parity */
        case 1: if(*(long*)(V->callerStack+4)=V->SizeI) return 0; /* get size of input */
                                return 0xf6; /* return errorNotReady */
        case 6: return 0; /* SS_EOF always is o.k. */
        default: return 0xd0; /* unknown service request */
    }
}
```

The *Putstat* procedure, like *Getstat*, gets its case in the variable *data*. Case 0,
used to modify the driver's path descriptor variables, is executed in the driver's *Putstat*
procedure in order to modify the DUART Baud and control registers to be consistent with
any changes that are made in that data. Case 0x2a is used right after a path is opened, after
the *Init* procedure has been executed, to finish initializing the chip; it used exactly the
same code as does case 0. The user-supplied value for the baud rate is in *PD->BAU* and
the user-supplied value for the frame structure is in *PD->PAR*. These are translated into
the DUART's control register values using vectors *BaudTbl* and *ParTbl*, shown below
the procedure. We check that the user-supplied values are in the range of the vectors, and
we check the requested frame structure for values that the DUART can handle, by putting
-1 in *ParTbl* if the DUART is not capable of the requested frame structure.

Case 0x1d sends a break, which is a low signal for longer than a frame time, and case 0x1a requests that a signal be sent when a character arrives. If there are data in the input queue the signal is sent immediately, otherwise the destination of the signal which is the current process ID, and the value of the signal to be sent, are saved in a vector *SigPrc* and sent by the receive interrupt handler when data are received in the DUART. Note that the *Read* procedure returns an error if such a request is pending, to avoid sending a signal to a process that is not waiting for it, which will kill the process. Cases 0x24 to 0x27 can be used to control a modem's RTS signal, and respond to its DCD signal; since the DUART doesn't have these signals, this driver returns I$GETSTAT of these cases with an unknown service request error.

```
static Putstat() { register staticStorage *V;register pathDescriptor *PD;
    register char *chip;register int data; register char *ptr;
    switch (data&0xff){
        case 0: case 0x2a:  /* opt, open */
            if(PD->BAU>16) return 0xcb; data=BaudTbl[PD->BAU];
                if(data<0)return 0xcb;/* illegal values */ chip[1]=(data<<4)+data;
            chip[2]= resetP; /*reset mode reg. pointer */
            chip[0]=(ParTbl[PD->PAR&3]<<2)+3-((PD->PAR>>2)&3);/*put in mode reg. 1 */
            chip[0]=StopTbl[(PD->PAR>>4)&3]; /* put in mode reg. 2: set frame */ return 0;
        case 0x1d: chip[2]= startB; chip[2]= stopB; return 0; /* send break */
        case 0x1a: /* send signal when data is ready */
            if(V->SigPrc[0]) return 0xf6; /* notReadyError if signal waiting */
            if(V->SizeI) {F_Send(PD->CPR,*(int*)(V->callerStack+10));return 0;}
            V->SigPrc[0]=PD->CPR;V->SigPrc[1]=*(int*)(V->callerStack+10);setMask();
            return 0;
        /* case 0x24: return 0;  request to send on;  case 0x25: return 0;  request to send off */
        /* case 0x26: return 0;  sleep until data carrier detect on */
        /* case 0x27: return 0;  sleep until data carrier detect off */
        case 0x42: /* remove any pending signals */
            if((PD->CPR==V->SigPrc[0])&&(PD->PD==V->SigPrc[1]))V->SigPrc[0]=0; return 0;
        default: return 0xd0; /* unknown service request */
    }
}

char BaudTbl[16]={0,-1,1,2,-1,4,5,6,-1,-1,8,-1,9,0xa,0xb,-1};
char ParTbl[3]={4,1,0},        StopTbl[3]={7,8,0xf},
```

The *Trmnat* procedure, called when an I$CLOSE system call is executed, essentially disables all interrupts, removes this driver's interrupt from the polling table, and turns off the device. However, there may be data in the output queue which has not been sent out when the I$CLOSE system call is executed. If there are data in it, the procedure sleeps, being awakened each time data are popped from the queue, until the queue is empty. When it is empty, the driver terminates.

```
static Trmnat(){ register staticStorage *V;register deviceDescriptor *M;register char *chip;
    V->BUSY=V->LPRC=*(int*)V->processDescriptor+50; /* copy process ID */
    while (!V->SizeO){V->WAKE=V->BUSY; if(F_Sleep()) return;}
    chip[2]=(disable<<transmt)+(disable<<recevr); F_Irq((M->IRQLvl)+24,M->Prior,0);
}
```

This driver contains many features of a practical driver for a terminal. However, we have not covered all the features of a good operating system's device driver. An important point to be observed, though, is that device drivers are more suitable than objects when handling I/O devices that require considerable checking and a wide range of features. Not only is a great deal of the code factored out of the driver into IOMAN and SCF, but also the code in the driver can handle these features. There are standard error codes and I$SETSTAT and I$GETSTAT cases that the user has defined in the operating system's documentation, so that these do not have to be documented, as they would be for an object-oriented device. Consider the size and complexity of writing an object for the DUART, as we did in Section 8-3.6, with all the features of this device driver. Clearly, device drivers are more suited to complex devices than objects are, and objects are more suited to simple devices like A-to-D converters and square-wave generators. Clearly, both are useful in embedded computer microcontrollers, and both are available in the M68332 and M68340, as we have shown in this book.

11-4 Conclusion

A device driver is generally used to control an I/O device in a larger microcomputer that uses an operating system. Having a device driver for an I/O device enables the device to be used by many utilities and applications programs, even if they are written in different languages. However, device drivers have several levels of overhead, so they are slow compared to applications programs and objects that directly control I/O devices. You still may find it better to control a device in C, or in assembler language embedded in C, in object methods or in a C subroutine (or similar methods in other high-level languages). Further, although the knowledge of how a device works and how to control it, taught in the first nine chapters of this book, is essential to writing device drivers, the code that actually reads from or writes in the device is a very small part of the driver's code. The main part of the code has to implement the conventions of the operating system: setting up and using static storage and descriptors with the correct offsets, sending and receiving signals, and so on. It appears that device drivers are fundamentally a part of the operating system, and only incidentally related to I/O hardware (although we restate that a knowledge of hardware is essential); in fact, writing a device driver is an excellent way to gain an understanding of how an operating system works. We find it more useful for that purpose than the traditional operating system course, although that course is valuable for other reasons. See *Operating System Design and Implementations,* by A. S. Tanenbaulm, Prentice Hall, 1987 for a more traditional coverage of operating systems.

A driver, in OS-9, is a collection of six subroutines called from a manager, and one called to handle interrupts. Each of these subroutines is reasonably simple. We described the *Init, Read* and other procedures of two drivers. Once the concept of device, path, and process descriptors and static storage are understood, the driver is very sensible. The reader should attempt to apply the ideas presented in this chapter to other operating systems, and to other devices.

This text has been fun for us. Microcomputers like the M683xx are such powerful tools that it challenges the mind to dream up ways to use them well. We sincerely hope you have enjoyed reading about and experimenting with the M683xx microcomputer.

Do You Know These Terms?

See the End of Chapter 1 for Instructions.

operating system, system call, device driver, virtual architecture, multitasking process, time-sharing, rom-based operating system, embedded operating system, memory map, fork, child process, parent process, process dies, memory modules, module name, header, crc check, descriptor, data structure field, bootstrap, static storage, time management, multi-thread, multi-tasking, signal, signal intercept handler, i/o path, path descriptor, path number, open call, read call, write call, close call, device independence, path redirection, kernel, i/o manager (IOMAN), sequential character file manager (scf), random block file manager (rbf), device drivers, device descriptor, shell, application program, utility, editor, compiler, getstat, setstat, trmnat.

Index